The Transmission of Well-Being

Margarida Durães, Antoinette Fauve-Chamoux,
Llorenç Ferrer & Jan Kok (Eds)

The Transmission of Well-Being

Gendered Marriage Strategies and Inheritance Systems in Europe (17th–20th Centuries)

PETER LANG
Bern · Berlin · Bruxelles · Frankfurt am Main · New York · Oxford · Wien

Bibliographic information published by Die Deutsche Bibliothek
Die Deutsche Bibliothek lists this publication in the Deutsche Nationalbibliografie; detailed bibliographic data is available on the Internet at ‹http://dnb.ddb.de›.

A catalogue record for this book is available from The British Library, Great Britain.

Library of Congress Cataloging-in-Publication Data

The transmission of well-being : gendered marriage strategies and inheritance systems in Europe (17th-20th centuries) / Margarida Durães ... [et al.].
p. cm.
Includes bibliographical references and index.
ISBN 978-3-0343-0056-8 (alk. paper)
1. Marriage--Economic aspects--Europe--History. 2. Inheritance and succession--Social aspects--Europe--History. 3. Domestic relations--Europe--History.
4. Married women--Europe--Social conditions. I. Durães, Margarida.
HQ611.T73 2009
306.85094'0903--dc22

2009030260

This publication is supported by COST and the European Social Science Foundation:

ESF provides the COST Office through an EC contract.
COST is supported by the EU RTD Framework programme.

Text design: Daniel Freitas, University of Minho (Portugal).
Illustrations: L'Artiere di Carlo Dottor – Montalcino (Italy).

Cover illustration: Wilhelm Maria Hubertus Leibl, *Der Spargroschen,* 1877.

Cover design: Thomas Jaberg, Peter Lang AG

ISBN 978-3-0343-0056-8

Hochfeldstrasse 32, CH-3012 Bern
info@peterlang.com, www.peterlang.com, www.peterlang.net

Preface

The present publication is the result of international research activities realized in the frame of an Action sponsored by COST, and supported by the EU framework programme. The four editors are deeply grateful to Professor Cristina Borderias, University of Barcelona (Spain), Chair of the COST Action A34 on *Gender and Well-Being. Interactions between Work, Family and Public Policies.*[1] They acknowledge permanent help from the European Science Foundation which provided the scientific and technical secretariat for COST and encouragements from David Gronbaek. All COST representatives from the Individuals, Societies, Cultures and Health (ISCH), particularly Dr Julia Stamm and Dr Laura Alipranti deserve our gratitude.

This book entitled *The Transmission of Well-Being. Gendered Marriage Strategies and Inheritance Systems in Europe (17th–20th Centuries)* is a selection of papers presented during the Second COST Symposium held at University of Minho, campus of Azurem, Guimarães, Portugal, 25–28 April 2007. The meeting was dedicated to "The transmission of well-being: marriage strategies and inheritance systems in Europe, 17th-20th centuries" and attracted more than eighty participants from twenty-two different countries who worked in eight panels. Thirty-eight papers were presented.

The editors wish to express their appreciation of the encouragements and daily help they received from the Centre de Recherches Historiques of the Ecole des Hautes Etudes en Sciences Sociales/Centre National de la Recherche Scientifique (France), the University of Minho (Portugal), the International Institute of Social History, Amsterdam (The Netherlands), the University of Barcelona (Spain) and from the International Commission for Historical Demography (ICHD/CIDH). They are very grateful to Marco van Leeuwen, Professor at University of Utrecht (The Netherlands) and to Isabel dos Guimarães Sá, Professor at University of Minho, Research Centre for Social Sciences/ICS, Department of History (Portugal) who assumed the coordination between the Nucleo de Estudos de População e Sociedade/Neps (University of Minho), the Secretariat of the COST project in Barcelona (Ms Conchi Villar and Mireia Singleton) and the Netherlands ESTER office (Ms A. van der Veen-Mooij, N.W. Posthumus Instituut, University of Groningen, Faculty of Economics and Business, The Nether-

1 Website: http://www.ub.edu/tig/GWBNet.

lands), so that the Symposium was held in conjunction with a successful ESTER (European graduate School for Training in Economic and social historical Research) PhD seminar on "Intergenerational transfer of inequalities (marriage patterns, social mobility, inheritance systems)", gathering 15 students as part of the event.

They thank the active discussants of the Minho conference, particularly Professors Marie-Pierre Arrizabalaga (France), Béatrice Craig (Canada), Anne-Lise Head-König (Switzerland), Mary Louise Nagata (France/USA), Michel Oris (Switzerland), Alastair Owens (United Kingdom), Isabel dos Guimarães Sá (Portugal), Carmen Sarasúa (Spain), Sølvi Sogner (Norway), Richard Wall (United Kingdom) and two anonymous referees for their insightful comments on earlier versions of the papers. They also acknowledge wise suggestions by Jacques Fauve and Janet Marcus. Warm gratitude is addressed to Daniel Freitas (University of Minho, Portugal) and Carlo Dottor (Montalcino, Italy) for their assistance in preparing the manuscript and to Katherine Tschopp and Thierry Waser of Peter Lang AG for their patience and advice during the publication process.

DURÃES, Margarida (Portugal)
FAUVE-CHAMOUX, Antoinette (France)
FERRER ALÒS, Llorenç (Spain)
KOK, Jan (The Netherlands)

May, 2009

The Organisation COST

COST – the acronym for European Cooperation in Science and Technology[2] – is the oldest and widest European intergovernmental network for cooperation in research. Established by the Ministerial Conference in November 1971, COST is presently used by the scientific communities of 35 European countries to cooperate in common research projects supported by national funds.

The funds provided by COST – less than 1 percent of the total value of the projects – support the COST cooperation networks (COST Actions) through which, with EUR 30 million per year, more than 30 000 European scientists are involved in research having a total value which exceeds EUR 2 billion per year. This is the financial worth of the European added value which COST achieves.

A "bottom up approach" (the initiative of launching a COST Action comes from the European scientists themselves), à la carte participation (only countries interested in the Action participate), "equality of access" (participation is open also to the scientific communities of countries not belonging to the European Union) and "flexible structure" (easy implementation and light management of the research initiatives) are the main characteristics of COST.

As precursor of advanced multidisciplinary research, COST has a very important role for the realisation of the European Research Area (ERA) anticipating and complementing the activities of the Framework Programmes, constituting a "bridge" towards the scientific communities of emerging countries, increasing the mobility of researchers across Europe and fostering the establishment of "Networks of Excellence" in many key scientific domains such as: Biomedicine and Molecular Biosciences; Food and Agriculture; Forests, their Products and Services; Materials, Physical and Nanosciences; Chemistry and Molecular Sciences and Technologies; Earth System Science and Environmental Management; Information and Communication Technologies; Transport and Urban Development; Individuals, Societies, Cultures and Health. It covers basic and more applied research and also addresses issues of pre-normative nature or of societal importance.

2 Web: http://www.cost.esf.org.

Table of Contents

Part II

WELL-BEING AND PROPERTY TRANSMISSION

Part III

FEMALE LIFE COURSE AND WELL-BEING OUTSIDE MARRIAGE

List of Contributors

AMORIM, Norberta, University of Minho, Transdisciplinary Research Centre Culture, Space and Memory/CITCEM (Portugal)

ARRIZABALAGA, Marie-Pierre, University of Cergy-Pontoise (France)

CRAIG, Béatrice, University of Ottawa, Department of History (Canada)

DURÃES, Margarida, University of Minho, Research Centre for Social Sciences/ICS, Department of History (Portugal)

FAUVE-CHAMOUX, Antoinette, Centre de Recherches Historiques, Ecole des Hautes Etudes en Sciences Sociales/CNRS, Paris (France)

FERRER ALÒS, Llorenç, University of Barcelona, Faculty of Geography and History (Spain)

KOK, Jan, Virtual Knowledge Studio and International Institute of Social History (The Netherlands) & Catholic University of Leuven (Belgium)

LAGIDO, Emília, doctoral student, University of Santiago de Compostela & University of Minho (Portugal)

MACHADO, Helena, University of Minho, Research Centre for Social Sciences/ICS, Department of Sociology (Portugal)

MATOS, Paulo Lopes, New University of Lisbon, Centre for Overseas History (Portugal)

MORING, Beatrice, University of Cambridge (United Kingdom)

NAGATA, Mary Louise, Centre de Recherches Historiques, EHESS/CNRS, Paris (France) and Francis Marion University (United States)

REY CASTELAO, Ofelia, University of Santiago de Compostela, Facultade de Xeografía e Historia (Spain)

PAPING, Richard, University of Groningen, Faculty of Arts (The Netherlands)

SÁ, Isabel dos Guimarães, University of Minho, Research Centre for Social Sciences/ICS, Department of History (Portugal)

SANTOS, Carlota, University of Minho, Research Centre for Social Sciences/ICS, Department of History (Portugal)

SZOŁTYSEK, Mikołaj, Max-Planck-Institute for Demographic Research, Rostock (Germany)

SOGNER, Sølvi, University of Oslo, Department of History (Norway)

TELSTE, Kari, Norwegian Museum of Cultural History, Oslo (Norway)

VINTILĂ-GHIŢULESCU, Constanţa, Institut Nicolae Iorga, Bucarest (Romania)

Introduction

Historicizing Well-Being from a Gender Perspective

Margarida DURÃES, Antoinette FAUVE-CHAMOUX,
Llorenç FERRER ALÒS and Jan KOK

This volume is part of a collective effort to rethink the history and current situation of "well-being" in Europe. The COST Action on *Gender and Well-Being: Interactions between work, family and public policies*[1] brought together scholars from various disciplines to reflect on better indicators for well-being and to work towards a better understanding of processes that lead to a more equal distribution of well-being. In particular, the Action focused on gender inequality in well-being. Many economic indicators, such as household budget surveys, fail to bring to the fore gender differentials, which may be caused by differences in power between men and women. Measuring and understanding gender differentials in well-being requires a systematic effort. The Cost Action represented such an effort, by organizing a series of five conferences on, subsequently, (1) well-being indicators (Harris, Gálvez and Machado forthcoming), (2) the role of the family in providing well-being in the past, (3) the gender division of paid and unpaid labour, (4) the role of institutions and (5) the role of collective action in promoting well-being.

In this book we present a selection of the papers presented during the conference "The Transmission of Well-Being: Marriage Strategies and Inheritance systems in Europe from 17th–20th Centuries", held in Guimarães, Portugal in April 2007. We explored how marriage and family affected the well-being of women in European societies of the past. Why the exclusive focus on the family? The reason is that in societies of mass poverty the distribution of resources between and within families is one, if not the key, element of well-being. The family not only offered material but also emotional resources, which fits the multidimensional character of

1 Website: http://www.ub.edu/tig/GWBNet.

well-being. How are we to understand regional variation in the position of women within families across Europe?

Currently, there is increasing recognition for the fact that the remarkable regional differences within Europe with respect to family aspects of well-being, e.g. housing and care for the elderly by children or other kin (Keck and Blome 2008), have long historical roots. As Saraceno (2008, 48) puts it "[…] family arrangements belong to the *longue durée* and involve some kind of cultural path dependence". In this respect, an important concept is *family system.* Family systems can be defined as the normative, preferred pattern of family practices (Skinner 1997). Although affected by social and economic changes and by family laws, the cultural norms central to family systems are highly persistent (Reher 1998; Therborn 2004; Bahle 2008). To what extent did family norms and rules effectively obstruct women in realizing their potential (their capabilities)? To what extent can their relatively inferior position be ascribed to a normative family hierarchy? What kind of changes in female position was visible over time? How did their position differ between social groups? By comparing evidence from many countries of Europe, over a relatively long time span, this book offers building blocks for a much-needed comparative, cross-national and historical perspective of well-being in Europe.

To enhance comparability, we have narrowed down the general questions to several topics, which we anticipated would be able to reveal the impact of family rules on female well-being. First, we want to compare the (relative) position of women in the widely varying practices of inheritance. What were their possibilities to (re)gain control of resources accumulated by their parents or their husband? What kind of anticipatory arrangements could they make during their lifetimes? Second, when judging the effect of family systems on well-being, the situation of vulnerable groups in societies is particularly interesting. Therefore, we study and compare the position of widows and of elderly women in various countries. Third, we focus on the role of marriage. Marriage was a transition of major importance, providing status and standing within communities and livelihood and protection for dependents. Depending on the regional rules of family formation, marriage could mean the start of an independent household. Moreover, marriage linked different families, forged enduring networks and brought together properties that sustained the couple. Social reproduction, that is, preserving status and wealth of families, could require elaborate marriage *strategies* to find and bind suitable marriage partners.

Fourth, if marriage offered status, respect and a bundle of rights (e.g. regarding inheritance), it also excluded single women, unmarried mothers and illegitimate children from these channels to well-being. Thus, the workings of family rules and rights are explored by looking at life courses of persons who remained celibate and those who were born out of wedlock. Before introducing these four topics in greater detail, a short introduction to European family systems is necessary.

Family Systems in Europe

Family systems can be classified in different ways, either focusing on household typologies, on inheritance rules, on (age at) family formation, on (regionally different) family norms or on a combination of these aspects (see Van Poppel and Oris 2004 for an overview). A rather influential typology, based on the combination of coresidence and inheritance practices, has been developed by Emmanuel Todd (1985; 1987; 1990). In his view, family systems stand for persistent elementary inter-personal relationships, which are transmitted from one generation to the next and form the roots of global variation in attitudes towards equality and authority. In Todd's perspective, cultural norms related to *equality* find their expression and are perpetuated by inheritance practices. Partible inheritance means equality among siblings, at least among brothers, whereas impartibility sets one favored child apart from the others. Likewise, norms related to *authority* are expressed in and reinforced by patterns of co-residence. Authoritarian systems prescribe co-residence of married children with their parents, whereas in non-authoritarian systems neo-local residence of married couples is the preferred pattern. By combining those two dimensions, Todd creates a matrix with four different family systems. In doing so, he builds on the pioneering work of Le Play (1879; see also Therborn 2004, 6–7).

The first system is characterized by both neolocal residence and egalitarian inheritance. Todd names this the "egalitarian nuclear family system". The second, the "absolute nuclear family system" also has neolocal residence, but allows for impartible inheritance. The third, the "authoritarian or stem-family system" is defined by coresidence of married couples in two generations and by impartible inheritance. In principle, this implies that the older generation co-resides only with the heir and his/her spouse and children. The fourth is the "incomplete stem-family system", where the formal rules prescribe egalitarian inheritance, but where impartible inheritance predominates. Finally, the "community family" combines partible inheritance with co-residence of more than two married couples in two generations or more. Todd refined the model further by adding another basic anthropological principle: the incest taboo. In most societies, the incest taboo results in rules prescribing exogamy. In some societies, however, these rules are relaxed to allow for marriage between cousins (Todd 1990).

In Europe, the main systems according to Todd's classification are the following (see also Kok, forthcoming):

> 1. The *egalitarian nuclear family* system is characterized by partible inheritance and neolocal residence upon marriage. The relations between parents and children are relatively strong, as complete division of parental property is delayed until the death of the parents (Duranton *et al* 2009). Division of plots may be counteracted by endogamous marriages (Augustins 2002; Oris 2003, 202). The choice of the marriage partner is free. Descent (and property transmission) is generally bilateral, that is through men and women alike. The latter factors provide for a relatively good position for women (Todd 1985; 1987). It exists in various European regions (northern and eastern France, north-western and southern Italy, central and southern Spain, central Portugal, Greece, Romania and Poland).
> 2. The *absolute nuclear family* system has the same characteristics as the former, but inheritance is not always equal. The father can make a will favouring only one child. It can be found in southern and eastern England, eastern Scotland, northwestern France, Holland and other coastal regions of the Netherlands, Denmark and Norway (Duranton *et al* 2009).
> 3. The *authoritarian family* system is commonly known as the stem family. Authoritarian families are characterized by impartible inheritance, with the male heir co-residing with the parents. However, female succession is not uncommon, thus descent is bilateral. Marriages are exogamous and generally arranged by the parents. In this system, married women hold a strong position. It is found in west of Great Britain, northern Spain, south western France, much of Germany and central Europe, as well as much of southern Sweden, northern Spain and northern Portugal.

4. The *incomplete stem family* (Todd 1990) is to be found in areas such as Belgium where lingering inegalitarian practices and formal egalitarian laws collide.
5. *Exogamous community family* systems exist in the Balkans *(zadruga)*, central Italy, Finland, Hungary, Bulgaria and Russia (Kaser 2002). The joint families' characteristic of this system may consist of parents and several married brothers with their wives and children. The household is generally split up after the death of the father. Thus, a new cycle begins with a nuclear, a stem and, finally, a joint phase. Marriages are arranged by the parents. Inheritance is equal among brothers but descent is strictly patrilineal, leaving women in a rather weak position in the household of their father-in-law.

According to Todd (1987), women's positions are strongest in those family systems that combine bilateral descent with co-residence of three generations, as in the stem-family systems. Nuclear family systems with bilateral descent take an intermediate position, whereas patrilineal and joint systems come last. Obviously, the status of women is not determined only by rules of inheritance and coresidence. Their inclusion/exclusion and hierarchical position is based very much on religious ideology, family laws and popular traditions. According to Therborn (2004), European patriarchy was relatively mild; women's position was relatively favourable due to bilaterality, free choice of spouse, adult marriage and neolocal residence (also Hartman 2004). However, superior rights of husbands and fathers were still firmly entrenched in civil laws. The rise of male breadwinner families prolonged European patriarchy into the 20th century (Therborn 2004, 24).

In our book, we focus on three questions. First, what did women's position within marriage and family systems imply for their (relative) well-being, that is, their capability to sustain themselves in widowhood, their capability to manage property, their capability to run a household et cetera? Second, how did women manage to "bend the rules" to their own advantage? What room was there to develop strategies to improve their position? A number of articles study wills or lawsuits precisely with this question in mind. Finally, how did the introduction of the *Code Civil* and various family laws in the 19th century change the "rules of the game"? Did people bend the rules to preserve the underlying family formation structures or do we perceive real shifts in the structures?

Marriage Strategies

Clearly, marriage is linked to well-being in various ways. Its importance in economic, emotional, symbolic and legal senses can hardly be underestimated. First of all, marriage can be seen as a contract ensuring the spouses of mutual material and emotional support. In societies without alternative systems of support, marriage was crucial to avoid a lifelong dependency on kin, army, convent or poor relief. It also formed an important symbolic *rite de passage* into adulthood. In many societies, the social status of spinsters and bachelors was ambiguous, at best. Marriage formed the only socially recognized access to sexuality and procreation. Finally, marriage offered security, by giving spouses legal rights to commonly acquire property. However, the institution of marriage also tended to reinforce inequalities, both between social groups and between genders. Explicit or not, the social norms prescribing who were appropriate partners tended to exclude people from other regions, other denominations, other races and other social classes. In particular when property was involved, the choice of a partner tended to be put under strict parental supervision and could even become subject of parental "strategies", as we shall see shortly. Marriage did not offer men and women equal positions. Marital laws underpinned male authority over women, in terms of decision-making regarding property or residence. Finally, in regulating descent, the institution of marriage created out-groups such as single mothers and illegitimate children. Their fate will be discussed in a subsequent section.

In this section, we will explore how different family systems gave rise to different sets of choices regarding marriage or celibacy of children and partner selection. These "sets of choices" can be called "strategies", but we will have to discern carefully between the strategies of parents and children, and between strategies of men and women. When were women benefiting from (marriage) strategies and when were they victimized by them? What was their own scope for planning and improving their well-being through marriage within the different family systems of Europe? We will first compare marriage patterns and "strategies" across family systems. Then, we will assess to what extent marriage offered women access to well-being through their own agency. Finally, we will evaluate what the chapters introduced in this section contribute to our thinking on marriage strategies and what kinds of further research is needed.

Family System and Marriage Strategies

In this section, various family systems are represented: the egalitarian nuclear family in Romania, Azores and Alto Minho, and the authoritarian or stem family system in Basque Country.

In Romania, an equal division of parental property existed. The sons claimed their share upon marriage, after which they would set up their own household. The youngest son would inherit the parental farm and care for his parents until their death (Kaser 2002, 384). Thus, we find in Romania an outpost of the nuclear family within a wider region of predominantly complex family systems. When property was tied to land, such a system was fraught with inherent tensions. Indeed, Vintilă-Ghițulescu describes on the one hand the elaborate system of patriarchal control, backed up by the Church, which ensured that children would not go against their father's strategies to retain the patrimony. Forging alliances through marriage was at the core of those strategies. Parents would continue to control their children even after their marriages. On the other hand, Vintilă-Ghițulescu shows how sons used the law to claim larger shares from their fathers or larger dowries from their father-in-law. Likewise, partibility threatened the viability of landholdings in the Portuguese region of Alto Minho and the Azores islands. Lagido shows how Alto Minho couples used dispensation from Church regulations against consanguineous marriages as a strategy to counteract fragmentation. In the Azores, the specific ecosystem made farming even more vulnerable to fragmentation. Amorim and Santos emphasize local and social homogamy as a means to counteract this.

Finally, impartible inheritance coupled with stem families was found in the Basque provinces of Southern France and Northern Spain. Around 1800, the continuity of traditional inheritance custom became problematic as the Napoleonic civil code prescribed partibility. Arrizabalaga describes how Basque parents and heirs ingenuously worked within the constraints set by the new law in order to keep the family "House" intact. In their elaborate strategy, timing was crucial. Property division was delayed until the death of the last remaining spouse. In this way, the designated heir was given time to provide dowries and compensate his siblings. By providing these compensations relatively early, that is, at a time when the siblings were in need of additional resources (e.g. at marriage), the heir managed to strike a favorable bargain. That is, the compensations were less valuable than the shares the siblings would have received after the death of the parents. Thus the heir could eventually reassemble the siblings' shares into his (or her) own hands.

Strategy and Well-Being

Most of the strategies described in these chapters are deployed by parents (or often only the male heads of households) to make sure that a) their children had a relatively good start in life, and b) that their endowments did not threaten the family patrimony. This patrimony was not just a bundle of assets belonging to the parents. In the case of the Basques, the House was an integral and inalienable part of the family as it united subsequent generations. In Romania, parents had to deal with collective "property" of their clan. Depending on the nature of the patrimony and the size of the family, marriage strategies meant deciding for children whether they would marry or remain celibate as well as whom they would marry. Marriage partners had to bring in dowries or shares that could compensate other children.

The "agency" of the children themselves seems to have been limited. This was particularly the case in 18th century Romania, where church and state backed up the patriarchal authority of the father. On the other hand, in several chapters we find evidence of (female) agency in devising strategies to improve their well-being. As mere pieces in dynastic chess games, Portuguese princesses were not utterly devoid of means to counter the loneliness and alienation at foreign courts. Sá describes in her chapter how they brought their own staff and used their trousseau to limit homesickness, corresponded widely with kin, and used their allowances and dowers to increase their autonomy, as far as possible. In Lagido's chapter we gain the impression that rural women in northern Portugal actively used the dispensation opportunities to improve their chance on the marriage market.

The chapters disclose a great deal of gender inequality, not only in terms of inheritance but also in strategic opportunities to improve their situation. For instance, Basque women could not use their dowry to claim a share of their in-law's property, whereas marrying-in sons-in-law could do so. Also, women did not have the same opportunity as their brothers to emigrate, work and enlarge their dowry, in order to be able to achieve upward social mobility through marriage. Thus, even though the Basque Country gave women a remarkable even chance to become heiresses, the social position of the non-inheriting daughters was generally lower than the position of non-inheriting sons. Arrizabalaga concludes that women "lost out" in this system in particular when they had many siblings and when they were lower in the sibling order.

In principle, in past societies, well-being can be described and measured in terms of individual shares inherited, social status gained through marriage etc. Likewise, we can determine the difference between individual heirs and non-heirs, between older and younger born siblings, and between sons and daughters. In the interpretation of well-being, however, we risk projecting our current ideals onto the past. In her article, Sá emphasizes that for the princesses she studied the sense of fulfilling duties to God and to their royal families contributed to their well-being. In more ordinary settings as well, we should not underestimate the important "capability" of contributing to collective well-being. Arrizabalaga provides many examples of Basque women who renounced their legitimate share to preserve the House for the heir. Was this indeed important for their (psychological) well-being? Or were they merely victims of a socialization process that stressed the self-denial of women and the assertiveness of men?

Marriage Strategies Revisited

How can our chapters contribute to the theory and methodology of the study of strategies in general and of marriage strategies in particular? In the 1960s, the introduction of the concept of "strategy" formed a healthy antidote to the dominant structuralist approach, bringing individual agency back to anthropology and history. In this respect, the work of Pierre Bourdieu (1972) on marriage strategies has been highly influential. Bourdieu emphasized collective strategies of kin groups, which, however, were not necessarily conscious. In his view, family strategies originated in customs *(habitus)*, transmitted through socialization, which informed the choices peasants made regarding inheritance and marriage. These deeply-ingrained customs ensured that, for instance, Pyrenean families maintained their "House" or patrimony over many generations by carefully timing and arranging the marriages of their children. In their important essay on the strategy concept, Viazzo and Lynch (2002) criticized Bourdieu and his followers in history for a rather "structuralist" view on family strategies. In their view, the notion of customary, unconscious strategies of entire groups does not clarify the role of individual agency in the past. We will discuss their critique in more detail and evaluate to what extent our approach brings the discussion on strategies forward.

A first point of criticism is the scope of (marriage) strategies. Bourdieu and some of his followers explored patterns of marriage and property concentration in (a large number of) subsequent generations, deducing strategic principles behind these patterns. Viazzo and Lynch (2002) question whether people could really plan for the long term given the uncertainty, unpredictability and incompleteness of information that characterized the past. Also, inferring strategies from patterns of property concentration entails the risk of teleology, in particular when "unsuccesful" families are not (or no longer) visible in the sources (see also Engelen 2002; Kok 2002). In our selection of papers, long-term strategies are not the issue as the focus is mainly on first and second generations. In most of the papers, a statistical analysis of (demographic) behaviour is augmented with detailed life stories and material from wills and court records. The combination of qualitative and quantitative material allows the authors to combine motives (of parents and others) and actual plans with their impact on lives. Moreover, a truly prospective life course analysis has been followed by Arrizabalaga, in her chapter on Basque families, which allows for the comparison of "successful" and "unsuccessful" strategies in terms of individual life chances.

The second critique of Bourdieu's approach is that is does not take into account the reality of multiple and sometimes incompatible strategies (Viazzo and Lynch 2002, 442). For instance, the possibility of migration brought an entirely new factor in the equation, as is testified by Arrizabalaga. In fact, designated Basque heirs opted frequently for migration to the Americas, in order to save money and acquire a wealthier farm than the one they could inherit from their parents. In some regions with outmigration, parents had to ensure that at least one child would stay to continue the farm and take care of them in old age. Thus, deals had to be made with the heirs, such as early succession of headship and retirement contracts that stipulated how the heirs were to provide for the parents

(Verdon 1979). Viazzo and Lynch also noted that in areas with a lively land-market, the strategies described by Bourdieu become obsolete. Indeed, as has been shown by Segalen (1991), Damsma and Kok (2005) and Paping in this volume, farmers who could monetarize their assets were much more flexible in arranging early marriages for their children and providing them with farms or shops to set up independent households. By focusing mainly on specific strategies, our chapters do not disclose the full "repertoire" of strategies (Van der Linden 2002) at the disposal of households. Ideally, we should like to know how inheritance and marriage strategies interacted with opportunities to migrate, to find employment outside agriculture, and to use financial tactics.

A third problem with an approach of strategies embedded in traditions and customs is that is does not clarify how innovation and adaptation come about. A good example of such innovativeness is Arrizabalaga's chapter which describes how Basque parents faced the challenge to remain within the changed laws of succession and yet provide for the intact transmission of the property to a single heir.

A final problem lies in the model of collective strategies, suggesting family harmony. This "harmonic" model has been criticized for neglecting the unequal positions of the sexes and generations within families, leading to exploitation of some members for the benefit of others. In our chapters, several authors have "deconstructed" the harmony model by looking closely at the different interests of parents and sexes. Thus, in Vintilă-Ghițulescu's chapter we see patriarchy at work in eighteenth-century Romanian society. Marriages were arranged by the parents whereas individual choices of the children came at the risk of disinheritance. In the Basque lands, sons had in general more strategic leverage within the system than daughters. Future research on marriage strategies will have to pursue this line by looking more rigorously at the different actors involved in marriage strategies.

Well-Being and Property Transmission

Family and the Inheritance of Property

In Western Europe the majority of the families were production units, meaning that they had sufficient capacity to produce for self-subsistence or for the market. With regard to families that lived on only one skill, they had the knowledge and tools for the development of the specific activity. With regards to peasant families, they held property of land or leased it in a short or long time span and in quantities sufficient or insufficient. Even families who were living as tenants had sufficient rights that guaranteed their own survival. Families whose income came totally from salaried work were few in number.

Families had to seek the most efficient way to exploit the resources they had in hand, since the well-being of their members depended on this, but there was a contradiction in this: they were subject to biological laws, meaning, they were born, raised, reproduced, grew old and died. Moreover, reproduction implies having various children – the means of production might not be sufficient to sustain all of them – and looking for alliances with other families to find men or women to reproduce. Therefore, the family cycle was based on safe-guarding the means of production for all of its members and the most delicate task was to prepare how those means were to be distributed on the death of the preceding generation. In this context, the transmission of assets was fundamental to ensure that an adequate standard of welfare was maintained. Previously we introduced the problems concerning marriage strategies and how to achieve advantageous bonds. Now we need to talk about the transmission systems.

These decisions affected social reproduction of individuals and their present and future well-being; and it was conditioned by social, political and economic structures which the historical process had developed. The situation was not the same for eastern peasants (Kaser 2002), who could not decide their hereditary strategy, as for a small vine-grower from the south of France who had his lands leased to a local land owner. The context was defined by local particularities, and conditioned all types of practices developed to maintain capabilities and maximum well-being.

Systems of Transmission of Property and Well-Being

In this process of transmitting property that was organized alongside the vital cycle, families had to face different options. Firstly, family heads needed to have a clear notion of the possibilities of management of their possessions (if owner, tenant, artisan...) and how far they could go. Secondly, they faced the dilemma of how the production means that assured the social and economic level of the family could be maintained with a high number of children. If shared, all would have less capacity of production; if they did not share, one benefited and the rest were afflicted. Thirdly, it had to be ensured that, when sharing its assets, the older generation which pass them on was looked after and not abandoned by the new generation who inherited the property. Fourthly, how would it be ensured that in the transmission of assets no one was left out in the process (widows, step-children...)? To resolve these issues it was fundamental to ensure the future well-being of all those involved in the process and there were many answers.

In general terms, we can point out two "philosophies" in the organization of the transmission of assets, each of them with its advantages and inconveniences and with variable solutions to the problems we have previously discussed. Over time, History has configured legal frameworks, everyday practices have validated solutions and turned them into tradition, and at the same time they have been changed when experience proved they did not work. The differentiated access to resources – which in essence defines social groups – generated different hereditary responses. The diversity found in Europe is the result of the different legal, cultural, economic and livelihood experiences. Each system, with its variables, answers the same problems and each answer in itself has its own contradictions. Individuals resolved some aspects well, but others not so well. The multiple answers to taking care of the parents, of widowed persons, of the future of sons, mean that the system of transmission of assets is rich in institutions and solutions. These solutions have to be thought of as ways that are adapted to achieve the well-being of all family members. In his model, E. Todd (1990) did not take into account the institutions and practices that were developing in each region to counter the negative effects of determined hereditary options.

The Egalitarian System

The first grand philosophy is the egalitarian. All descendants are equal; hence it is necessary that property is equally distributed amongst all. As the practice becomes more egalitarian, women's position is reinforced since the woman is considered an equal to her siblings and has the same bargaining power. The principal contradiction is that if children were to equally share out the inheritance, it would be impossible to dispose of sufficient production means to reproduce the social and economic capacity of the previous generation. Where this option is carried out, the families must develop strategies to evade a general social downfall: wed cousins or neighbours to compensate land loss; buy back land from some brothers; temporary migrations in search of resources outside the community; numerous single men and women who distribute their plots amongst married siblings etc. Without these strategies, the general well-being would be menaced.

Precisely due to the difficulties that continual land fragmentation posed, the distribution of property takes diverse forms: only males receive a share in the distribution; the sharing includes personal and real property in equal terms; the distribution takes into account primogeniture and the youngest children are also rewarded.

Moreover egalitarian philosophy involves many problems which need to be solved. Who will look after the parents? When is the property to be inherited? At the death of the parents? What will the sons do while they have not yet inherited? Depending on what one seeks, the answer or practice differs. Concerning provisioning for the parents, for example, one can decide to have them spend some time in each of the sibling's household, or one can compensate one of the children in the sharing of property and in exchange he or she will take care of the elderly parents... Each solution that is applied generates arguments to justify it and opens door for the appearance of problems and institutions to sort them out. The well-being of the family members will depend on the efficiency of these institutions and their practices. Their discovery is fundamental in the analysis of well-being from the point of view of inheritance of assets.

Margarita Durães examines the inheritance of property in North Eastern Portugal where the predominant legal framework is based on egalitarianism, similar to the system which existed in the Kingdom of Castile. Despite this, the legal practice does not necessarily coincide with the actual practice carried out by peasants. Through the analysis of their wills; one sees that they developed means of non-egalitarian transmission of land; under these practices daughters were often favoured. In the region of Braga, access to land was through a tenancy agreement and land could not be divided; therefore it had to be inherited as a whole by only one child. Thus, we witness non-egalitarian practices within a legal framework where an egalitarian model prevailed but where one child was nonetheless chosen to inherit main family property. One of the daughters was often selected to be the privileged inheriting successor ("heiress"), and the parents' argument supporting this decision was that they would be better taken care of in their old age or in illness. In this case, sons received monetary compensations that were thought to serve them better if they emigrated, joined the church or chose to purchase land. In this area of Portugal, the family's search for welfare was conditioned by the way in which the elderly were taken care of within an egalitarian environment. In this case, daughters were favoured over sons because they were better at taking care of their parents.

The Non-Egalitarian System

A totally different option in the process of property transmission is the non-egalitarian system. The family chooses a child, the eldest, youngest or any, male or female, who will receive the integral patrimony, with the idea that resources thus generated serve to position the rest of the kin in a better-off position. These resources, generated in a generation's life-span, could not match what the heir or heiress had inherited: social downfall was also a characteristic of the system for non inheriting children and families elaborated different strategies to evade it. A daughter, if not an heiress, was not well off since she usually had to abandon her native house and enter her husband's house, the value of her dowry being the main element of the marriage arrangement. In few cases did she become part of a better off society.

Despite this reasoning there were many options and aspects to resolve: who would be designated heir among the children? When would the heir inherit? How were the parents to protect themselves once they had given away their property? What happened when the heir or heiress widowed?

How was the heir's widow protected? What did the heir's spouse receive for his or her work? What was the destiny of children second in line? Was there gender equality in their fate? Who would inherit if the heir had no descendants? Who would take care of him or her in his or her old age? Each question could be answered in many ways, and each answer had its own contradictions and resulted in new problems. The system tried to institutionalize the decisions and justify the negative effects, precisely to avoid conflicts which came from the contradictory answers but at the same time it tried inventing practices and institutions to face them.

Llorenç Ferrer's contribution to this volume is an analysis of the diverse institutionalized practices that developed in Northern Spain in areas where a non-egalitarian system prevailed; it is precisely these contradictions which will be analysed. In Catalonia, for instance, the heir was always chosen according to male primogeniture (first born son), which helped clarifying any doubt amongst children and gave way to an easier socialization, whilst in areas, such as the Spanish Basque country, parents were to chose the child whom they thought should inherit, which was to increase conflicts amongst siblings. In Catalonia, the hereditary chain was defined to clearly foresee what would happen if male primogeniture rule failed for lack of children; in some areas any other sibling could be picked; but even so, there had to be a Family Council solving emergency situations. When there was no household heir, this council searched for a nephew or suggested some "marriage at home" that would help solve this situation (a convenient marriage arrangement within the family, largely speaking). When a woman was widowed, she was protected through the *usufructo* or other similar alternatives, since she was the weakest link in the succession process. When a woman was in a position of daughter-in-law and found widowed without children, she returned to her parent's house. There are a few examples of these practices that were carried out in order to avoid incidents that could occur in any given circumstances and to also clarify the rules of the game in moments of crisis. By institutionalizing solutions, families who lived in a non-egalitarian system minimized problems and conflicts, so that these rules, altogether, were nothing else than a mechanism to preserve the well-being of the family unit as a whole.

Beatrice Craig ponders on the role of women in their access to resources taking as a case study the French middle class families employed in the textile industry, in Lille and Tourcoing. Usually men managed the businesses. But what happened when women became widows? Answers to this question were not homogenous. Throughout Western Europe, in some places widows were favoured as in Norway and The Netherlands whilst in others such as Germany they were not. A widowed person was always put in a difficult situation: the family couple was broken and there was need to evolve into a new family equilibrium; widowers and widows had to deal with arising problems. Legal rights protected widows. In Lille and Tourcoing in 19th century Northern France, merchant families and enterprises were organized in partnership systems or "societies" in which the financial input of all parties was recognized. The question of gender was not raised in itself. According to the marriage contract, after a husband had died, a widow held her own part of the enterprise and the *usufruct* of her husband's portion and, given this strong position, she took charge of the business. Her children would have to wait until her death to take possession of the enterprise. Family resources were therefore in the hands of a family widow.

Hereditary Systems and Resources

Various specificities of access to resources in each family context determined many outcomes and options. In a non-egalitarian system, for example, second born children can remain unmarried and stay all their lifelong in their natal family home if there were no opportunities of making a living outside. If there were, there was the option of investing by sending them away to become apprentices or to engage in commercial activities. In this case, the pressure in the transmission of property could also be affected. By contrast, when a strict equal distribution of assets was the norm, there was no particular pressure in the family: there were possibilities of employment in other activities, and since the inherited share was less important to new households, individuals had access to resources allowing them to purchase and rebuild a patrimony. The economic context and the available resources were important so that families could safeguard the well-being of their members. We could say that the economic (and political) opportunities in this context were a variable that conditioned strategies of inheritance.

Beatrice Moring positioned herself alongside this line of analysis. For three different regions of Northern Europe (South-Eastern Finland, South-

Western Finland and Northern Sweden), she examined family formation models and the strategies families adopted when facing different economic realities. Important changes occurred during the eighteenth century. The predominant model was the nuclear family, and it was characterized by the choice of one heir who would provide for the parents well-being in old age. The norm was to maintain undivided the family property at each generation. Age at marriage was late. These mechanisms were used to give individuals security within each generation. With the economic and demographic changes that occurred in these areas during the 18th century, family strategies were modified in different ways. In Western Finland and Northern Sweden, where by law the partition of land was banned, the tendency was to a later marriage. In Eastern Finland where legislation permitted partition of land and cohabitation of family members, early marriage was common and pressure on resources increased, resulting in serious proletarianization. The work carried out by Beatrice Moring illustrates how family practices that used to provide well-being and security to families were altered and had to be rethought when main changes occurred in local economic conditions and affected access to resources.

Richard Paping followed a similar path. He focused for his part on the region of Groningen (The Netherlands), a capitalist agricultural area completed with proto-industrial activities. In this case the interest revolves around the study of social mobility of individuals since this is a good indicator to know if families were capable or not of providing welfare to all household members. Welfare does not depend solely on patrimony, but from a social point of view, on the chosen spouse's capabilities and on what one makes for a living. In that sense, the level of education plays an important role. From these elements, one can consider that the level of well-being, which could be provided to the children who were not eligible to succeed on the family farm, depended in good measure on resources acquired outside the family patrimony. Lucrative job opportunities and business were offered outside agriculture. The provision of welfare in this system consisted precisely in the provision of material resources and non material mechanisms in order to access them. Therefore, capitalist economy provided more opportunities for both men and women who were not successors.

From our point of view, the development of the capabilities and well-being of individuals (men and women) cannot be comprehended solely from the traditional perspective of the historiography of family; it must be set in relation to the transmission of property system or to definite celibacy or also related to late marriage or agrarian systems. In fact, all variables were part of a single main family strategy: how to reproduce socially in the framework of the economic and political situation, and how to provide individuals capabilities and well-being to achieve this.

Finding a suitable marriage partner often required elaborated family strategies in the past. Whether "arranged" of not by parents or kin, marriage offered rights, constraints and a specific *status* to women. Single women were excluded from the "married" status but could also be mothers. In the third part of this book, we explore what family rules applied in past Europe to single mothers and to children born out of wedlock, searching for socio-cultural continuities or discontinuities when comparing which the present state of the European society.

Female Life Course and Well-Being outside Marriage

Massive "illegitimate behavior" is one of the problems of our time: as it happens, in many cultures, patterns of family life apparently develop independently from formal marriage, with little care for old legal frameworks, while – or, maybe, because – it is expected that social security and welfare would provide the same services as they did before, particularly to single mothers and their children. Trying to apprehend and explain births out of wedlock and the unmarried cohabitation phenomenon means being confronted with strongly intertwined political, economic and religious factors, which all are at stake in this issue.

To analyze how, how much and why societies of the past did more or less tolerate bastardy,[2] single motherhood and marital-type cohabitation of one type or another was one of our concerns in the *Gender and Well-*

2 The common law of England, like all European legal systems, distinguished between *legitimate* children, full members of the family, and *illegitimate* children or *bastards*. This was considered more severe than other civil laws or canon law which recognized that a child born illegitimate could become legitimate by the marriage of his parents, while, for the common law, to be legitimate, a child had to be born after his parents' wedding (Cretney 2003, 544).

Being project during the Second Symposium at University of Minho,[3] Portugal, a region precisely where illegitimacy is known to have been an important phenomenon during the 18th and 19th centuries. Such an inquiry in history ought to help understanding the reasons behind so different treatments as attested in past European countries together with understanding and solving questions of the present.

Definitions of Unmarried Cohabitation

Some societies of the past saw in cohabitation only a preparation for marriage, a trial marriage, or *mariage à l'essai*. For other groups, cohabitation was plainly an alternative to marriage, as it was the case in Latin America, where consensual or visiting unions were always common (Hammel 1981). It could be said that only conflicts between cohabiting partners reveal differences between marriage and cohabitation. At the present international and European level, the questions concerning private international law and aspects of cohabitation outside marriage and registered or not partnerships were debated in the frame of the permanent *Hague Conference on Private International Law* (HccH).[4] In a document dated May 2000, we read that the law applicable to unmarried couples was drawn up in December 1987 and that "the problem of the law applicable to unmarried couples should not be ignored by the Conference, even though it does not require urgent consideration at this time" (Hague Conference on Private International Law 2000). This subject was adopted for study, but without any particular priority.

In the same document, it was mentioned that a previous report, dated 1992 "surveyed the status of the unmarried couple in comparative law, and possible approaches to resolve the private international law problems surrounding *free unions*. The Note summarised the findings of the study as follows:

3 See final Programme of the Minho conference, 25–28 April 2007 on: http://www.ub.edu/tig/GWBNet.

4 Since 1893, the *Hague Conference on Private International Law* (HccH), a melting pot of different legal traditions has developed and serviced conventions which respond to global needs in the area of international protection of children, family and property relations.

> It shows, through a comparison of internal legal systems, that a wide range of solutions has evolved. Some systems regulate all the relationships arising from cohabitation; others focus on certain aspects only; still others leave the whole subject outside the law. As far as private international law is concerned, legal writers have so far offered few solutions, and the positive law elements are few and far between. (Hague Conference on Private International Law 2000, article 2, p. 2)

The report concluded, nevertheless, that the phenomenon of "international cohabiting couples" was an established one in Western Europe, that it was likely to gather momentum now that the frontiers of Eastern Europe have largely opened up, and that the same situation is to be found in Latin America where free unions are extremely common, as was noticed above.

The question of adoption was intensely studied by international lawyers but problems concerning paternity recognition – even when cohabitation of some kind between unmarried parents may be evidenced – need further study at the European Union level by policy makers. Since family historians have been aware of national and regional variations of proportions of births out of wedlock, their knowledge on such a present phenomenon should not be neglected, and the studies selected in the present volume demonstrate the usefulness of historical background so that legal provisions may be constructed with some respect to traditional customs and identity of the people.

The birth rate outside wedlock gives some indication of the extent of cohabitation outside marriage, although not precisely measuring it. In today's Europe, these rates vary widely, even within different regions: they range from five percent to more than 60 percent (Eurostat 2008a). The distinction between a "registered partnership" and "marriage" raises very serious juridical problems. In the current literature, the term "registered partnership" is used in a wide meaning, covering all forms of cohabitation outside marriage, that, in order to be valid, need to be officially registered. The exact conditions and effects of the institution differ from country to country. "Unmarried cohabitation", as used in a HccH document dated March 2008, should be understood as referring to *concubinage* or *de facto* unregistered unions (Harnois and Hirsch 2008). This note highlighted the fact that in many legal systems the term "unmarried cohabitation" is not defined:

> As a general principle one can state that legal systems that attribute legal consequences to unmarried cohabitation are more likely to establish a definition of the

> term or elaborate general conditions to distinguish unmarried cohabitation from other relationships. (Harnois and Hirsch 2008, article 4, p. 20, p. 9)

Further sections of the same report consider aspects of family rights relating to children born from these unions, pointing out main problems which are not new for family historians and historical demographers:

> Establishment of the parent-child relationship (filiation) between a child and the mother's cohabitant is more difficult than where the parents are married to one another. This is because a presumption of paternity, provided for by many jurisdictions where parents are married, is not applicable to cohabiting couples. (Harnois and Hirsch 2008, article 65, p. 19)

Specific legislations like PACS in France *(Pacte Civil de Solidarité)*[5] concern both heterosexual and homosexual stable couples and some other residential arrangements of two adults (brother and sister, two brothers, two sisters may arrange a PACS). In 2008, 94 per cent of registered PACS in France were between heterosexuals partners: when ten marriages are contracted, four Pacs are registered and one out of two children currently born has non married parents (Rault 2009). From the juridical point of view, *pacsed* partners are considered as single (or widowed or divorced) and the children born during their unions, if any, even recognized by their parents, are born out of wedlock. Dissolution of a PACS partnership is easier to register than a divorce. But for ten PACS concluded, one only dissolves, while the proportion of divorces is much higher when compared to marriages concluded (about one out of three marriages ends by divorce). For insurance or fiscal reasons, end of *pacsed* common life (when partners are both alive) is not systematically followed by formal dissolution, since the registered private contract provides a protection to each partner (males and/or females, whatever the gender kind of PACS), in case of hardship. PACS guarantees some well-being in old age for the surviving partner (particularly women who still have no right to get a reversion pension, thanks to common properties, protection of lodging, reciprocal donations and other advantages). Some homosexual *pacsed* partners may try adopting a child or have his/her own child adopted by his partner to secure generational transmission. But in France, most *pacsed*

5 PACS/ Pacte Civil de Solidarité (civil pact of solidarity) was enforced in 1999 in France. It is a contract between two adults of same or different sex, defining rights and obligations. It brings some protection to partners concerning property rights, succession and taxation. A similar legislation is found for example in the Netherlands.

partners, as was noticed above, belong to the heterosexual group and quite a few raise their own children, officially born out of wedlock.

Births Out of Wedlock: A Massive Phenomenon in Present Europe

In today's Europe, births out of wedlock account for an increasing share of total births, reflecting the growing popularity of marital cohabitation: in 2005, almost 33 percent of all births in the European Union (27 countries) were of this kind. A majority of the children born in Sweden and Estonia were born to unmarried parents, and around 40 percent of those born in Denmark, France, Latvia, Slovenia, Finland and the United Kingdom were also born outside of marriage in 2005 (Eurostat 2008a, 40). Most of the parents probably lived in a stable union.

The growing proportion of illegitimate births partly corresponds to the number of these unmarried couples, but only partly since social permissiveness concerning this type of birth, more or less comprehensive, also interferes. Proportion of births out of wedlock varies considerably from one country to another: about 2 percent for Israel or Japan, more than 60 percent for Iceland. Such a noteworthy scattering attests how variable is the significance of illegitimate births in the different cultures (Sardon 2006). For eight West- and North-European countries, the proportion of illegitimate births is more than 40 percent – that is Scandinavian countries, Iceland, France and the United Kingdom. But in these countries we observe stabilisation of the statistical figures. Since the end of the Soviet Empire, Baltic countries – especially Estonia and Latvia – register a number of births out of wedlock very similar to one of their Scandinavian neighbours. Also noteworthy is the variation in the former parts of contemporary Germany: 20.6 percent illegitimate births in the old RFA against 55.4 percent in the ex RDA. History plays a major factor in differentiated reproductive behaviour.

Variations in figures of illegitimacy cannot be understood without considering cultural, social and religious norms and customs. To what extent births out of wedlock are and were resulting from individual or family strategies was one of the main concerns in the Gender and Well-Being project debates.

Beyond Morals: Illegitimacy as a Gender Strategy of Survival

In his introduction to *Bastardy and its Comparative History*, in 1980, Peter Laslett referred to Kingley Davis, and to his essay dated 1939 as the real beginning of the sociological study of bastardy (Laslett 1980; Davis 1939). This pioneer study was called "Illegitimacy and the social structure". Until then, said Laslett, the frequency of illegitimate babies was taken only, more or less, "as an index of the moral state of the community". In England bastardy has been studied for a considerable time: for example, in 1892, Albert Leffingwell attempted to analyse the geographical and social distribution of illegitimacy (Leffingwell 1892). During the 19th century, an increasing proportion of those children born out of wedlock obtained a legitimate status when their parents married: in France, at the national level, this legitimation concerned 18 percent of them in 1801 and 32 percent in 1900, which notes a tendency to integrate children born out of marriage to the family of their parents, so improving their well-being and securing the standard of living of their mothers.[6] In Iceland, a high proportion of bastard children were also legitimated when their parents later married. They were born to stable or stabilised couples living in *concubinage* (Gardarsdottir 2000; 2002). It is difficult to know for the other children born out of wedlock (who were not legitimated at some point of their life course) if they were the result of some parental cohabitation, consensual union, or were just born to a single mother, by accident. All chapters gathered in the third section of this volume enlighten this question.

For the 19th century, Paolo Matos studied the high levels of illegitimacy in the Azores Islands, a very catholic Portuguese society in the middle of the Atlantic, where he was able to distinguish three different non marital behaviours:1) having bastards with a known father, 2) having bastards without a known father and 3) having bastards later legitimized (Matos 2007). In his contribution to the present volume, the author puts in practice this classification (see his Table 8) and develops it, focusing on the island of St Jorge, choosing as a field study the parish of Rebeira Seca, trying to understand in which state of well-being the mothers of bastard children lived along their life and if they experienced some kind of social

6 In France, at a national level, illegitimacy figures increased from 4.7 percent in 1801 to 7.2 in 1851, and 8.8 percent in 1900 (van de Walle 1980).

mobility, from birth to death. To trace male and female life courses, he relied on historical sources as state population statistics, life events from parish registers, confession and communion listings. To life histories Matos added socio-economic information from tax lists (particularly the *predial contribution*[7] of 1881 which allows linking professional activities and annual collectable income of each head of household, male or female), family inventories and wills. In Rebeira Seca, 22.8 per cent of household heads were females. The author was therefore able to reconstruct household income, particularly to evaluate family standards of living, tracing the evolution of socio-economic status over time, distinguishing between land owners, rural workers and fishermen families. He reconstructed life histories of their children, sons and daughters. In 1860, according to parish registers, one fourth of the children born was out of wedlock. With such a high rate, illegitimacy was not only a social or economic phenomenon, but also a cultural phenomenon of reproduction.

These illegitimate children were not abandoned and were integrated to the daily social or religious life of their mother and maternal family group, whatever their social class. Illegitimacy, although contrary to religious precepts, was in fact socially admitted: single mothers were not excluded, be it from their native house or from their parents' inheritance. This is a main difference with many European rural and urban contexts of the time where so many illegitimate babies fell in charge of local communities, religious institutions or ended in foundling hospitals where their mortality was very high (Sá 1996; Fauve-Chamoux 2002).

Local patterns of family transmission gave material and financial advantages to single females living with their aging parents, as soon as they provided help in old age and contributed to family and individual well-being. Having bastards was a way to provide continuity of the house when a legitimate marriage was not accessible for family reproduction. Children born out of wedlock corresponded to some long-term strategies of lineage survival and constituted a family insurance. Multi-generational residential arrangements favoured single mothers who could work while children were taken care of by older members of the households, in absence of a husband, when most male adults used to quit the country for work away. This was also the case in Iceland (Gardarsdottir 2000; 2006). Some regions of Northern Minho knew similar family strategies and illegitimate

7 The *predial contribution* was a tax to be paid on properties. It was taken both on farm land and urban estates.

children were welcomed. Some Pyrenean mountainous communities presented similar features as Norway (Fauve-Chamoux 1995; 2006), Alpine regions (Mitterauer 1983), or Scotland (Blaikie 2005).

Matos' classification of children born out of wedlock could be used in some further studies, in a comparative perspective. A first step would be to classify Portuguese illegitimate children according to the *General Law of the Portuguese Kingdom.*[8] In Ribeira Seca, it is interesting to note numerous cases where single mothers finally could marry their children's father later in life and so sort out their "marital" situation, which was out of the question for legal reasons in case of adultery or of relations with a priest. Transition to marriage was not open to all of them in a catholic society where divorce did not exist before 1910.[9] Male partners could be married, gone or dead. As for inheritance, it is noticeable that many unmarried women coresiding with their old parents, when inheriting, benefited from a *preciput* taken on the *third* free portion of the family assets to be transmitted, or some other advantage settled by the parent's will. Assisting parents in their old age was a moral, and also a financial, duty supported by daughters in this society of male emigration. Many females accepted the burden of raising children out of wedlock, working and caring for aging parents. In exchange they received help and escaped social marginalisation. These women managed to keep a decent standard of living along their life course and acceded to some family inheritance, without going through the marriage status and without a dowry.

To summarize, in the Portuguese society of the Island of St Jorge, marriage was not open to all women given the scarcity of men, impediments

8 Until 1867, when the first Portuguese *Civil Code* was published, the family law was part of the Edits of the Kingdom; the last ordinances were taken by Philip the Second, King of Spain and Portugal from 1580 to 1598 *(Ordenações Filipinas).*

9 The insolubility of Catholic marriages was respected in Portugal until the Divorce Law of November 1910 which remained in force until the celebration of the Concordat between the Vatican and the Portuguese Republic of 7 May 1940. This Concordat established that Catholic marriages could not be dissolved by divorce. Concerning civil marriages the previous system was retained. The new Portuguese *Civil Code* of 1966 maintained the system established by the Concordat regarding Catholic marriages. However, this legislation hindered the dissolution of civil marriages by divorce: it eliminated the objective grounds for divorce, it required that divorce by mutual consent should be preceded by a judicial process of separation between the spouses and property, and it enabled the judge to deny the divorce request and to order a separation although divorce had actually been requested, when the circumstances of the case would so require.

for kinship and the local system of *post mortem* transmission of properties. With a high celibacy regime, late marriage and male emigration, births out of wedlock must be considered as a strategy of survival: these illegitimate children were integrated into the maternal line. When they were recognized by their biological father, children born out of wedlock could get some more support from their paternal lineage and their mothers more advantages and well-being. This is why determining paternity was considered of major importance for the well-being and future of these children.

Determination of Paternity for Securing Individual Well-Being

In her study of paternity investigations in Northern Portugal (Vale Court), Helena Machado explains the complexity of legal systems, particularly when they are based on ownership and inheritance of assets through the male line. She explores the social relationships as they appear in the proceedings of the Portuguese courts of Law between the first Portuguese *Civil Code* enforced in 1867 and the new Portuguese *Civil Code* of 1966 which made judicial investigation of paternity mandatory.[10] The author argues that, during this period, single mothers and their children aspired to the material and symbolical resources of the putative father and tried to have their inheritance rights recognized. Inspired by the French Napoleonic *Civil Code* (1804), the Portuguese family law (1867) restricted investigations about paternity. Actually most Western European legal systems stemmed from Roman Law which included the automatic presumption of paternity of husband within marriage: "the father is the one attested by marriage".[11] An illegitimate child had to be legally affiliated in order to take part in inheritance. According to the 1867 *Civil Code*, only legitimate and legitimated heirs on the day of the wedding ceremony could inherit a *legitime* share. Children who were legitimated later (even by a judicial verdict) could only get a part of the free third of the total inheritance. They had no right to a *legitime* share. After the 1910 Portuguese Revolu-

10 Presently, inquiries of paternity are compulsory in Portugal, Germany and most Scandinavian countries, when the birth certificate of a child does not show the identity of the father (Cretney 2003).

11 *Pater est, quem nuptiae demonstrant.*

tion, a reform of the *Civil Code* enlarged possibilities of paternity investigations: it included cases of seduction of the bastard's mother by promise of marriage or other cases performed with abuse of authority or trust. For Machado, cases of this later kind illustrate the patriarchal nature of gender relations of the time. Classical examples were masters seducing their young innocent maid servant. More reforms were introduced in the revised Portuguese *Civil Code* in 1977. Up to that date, wife and children were under the husband's and father's authority, following Roman law principles.

In most cases, during the period under study by Machado, paternity recognition suits were started by adult illegitimate children after the death of the presumed father, so it appears that the major aim of their claim was to gain some access to paternal inheritance. Some biological fathers used to give presents to the infant child, to cover some of his/her mother's expenses and provide better chances of well-being to both of them. Some rich fathers contributed to food, lodging and education of the child. But these were rare cases. Protection of children without a legitimate father was a main concern for all European communities, legislators and policy makers of the past, because most children born out of wedlock were at heavy risk of death or misery.

Providing Welfare to Children Born out of Wedlock and their Mothers

In England, Sir William Blackstone, one of the Justices of the Court of Common Pleas, explained, around 1750, that bastards had nearly no rights:

> The rights which appertain to a bastard are very few, being only such as he can *acquire*; for he can *inherit* nothing, being looked upon as the son of nobody, and sometimes called *filius nullius*, sometimes *filius populi*[12] [...] The capacity of the bastard consist principally in this, that he cannot be heir to any one, neither can he have heirs, but of his own body; for being *nullius filius*, he is therefore of kin to nobody, and has no ancestor from whom any inheritance blood can be derived. (Blackstone 1756)

12 "Nobody's child" or "the child of the people".

From this statement, we see how belonging to a maternal line was not a concept for an 18th century English noble man impregnated by patrilineal cultural norms. Before Frédéric Le Play, advocates of family transmission through female line and heiresses – but still within an authoritarian stem-family system – were rare (Fauve-Chamoux 2003). In any case, the life and welfare of children born out of wedlock were heavily dependent on the ability of their mother and putative father, if any, to provide them with every day care and other support in infancy. It was consequently common in Europe that most illegitimate children born out of wedlock were socially disadvantaged and suffered poverty, if they survived, because it is well known that illegitimate babies, because they were so often neglected and not breastfed by their mothers and could be abandoned to charity, had a high mortality (Fauve-Chamoux 2002). Many state laws followed dominant religious principles in family and marriage matters, even when customs and practices differed from one community to another.

Kari Telste strongly outlines that, for long, premarital sexual relations were prohibited by law in Norway. By the 1589 *Marriage Act*, non-marital cohabitation was defined as "illegal". So was the law until 1972! Anyway, the study of popular customs in this Scandinavian country shows that many couples had children before getting married and that this was not at all considered as "immoral" by common people. So the author stresses the gap between the law and popular opinion and practice. A wedding was a very expensive social event. Besides customs, court cases helped define what marriage meant. Husband and wife were supposed to help each other in everyday life and domestic economy. By the end of the 18th century, marriage had lost in Norway its reformed religious content, although the wedding ceremony was associated with religious rituals.

In her chapter, Telste retraces the legal changes of the rights of children born out of wedlock in Norway from the 17th century to the present; she focuses on the relationship between children and their fathers and shows how social benefits were introduced, also how they positively affected the living conditions of bastards. Among unwed mothers, many were maids. In the 1730s a system of poor relief was introduced to help them. In 1763, an *Ordinance of Maintenance* was proclaimed so that putative fathers would contribute to the upbringing of their illegitimate children. This was reinforced in 1794 and again in 1821, but many absent fathers escaped their financial responsibilities and bastard children suffered neglect. In 1915 important reforms founded the Norwegian welfare state, but single mothers were still under pressure to find jobs to support themselves and their child. Today, cohabiting fathers assume their responsibilities to a higher degree.

The social and cultural acceptance of bastardy varied enormously in Europe. There were societies where illegitimacy carried little stigma. In some European communities of the past, particularly in mountainous areas where house systems were attested, there may have been "some matrilineal system of child rearing that could, if necessary, omit the mothers themselves" (Blaikie 2005), particularly when they were working as domestic servants or outside the natal home. This remark stresses the extraordinary connexion between the European illegitimacy map – still to be properly traced – and the stem-family map as was traced by Le Play for the late 19th century (Fauve-Chamoux and Ochiai 2009, 44–46), cartography to be put in parallel with the negative relationship between hospitals for foundlings and the stem family.[13]

Where males were fewer and/or often absent, females had a large access to inheritance and gender division of work was not strict in practice. This was mentioned above for the Portuguese Island of St Jorge. This feature is again particularly clear in Northwestern Spain. In her contribution, Ofelia Rey shows that women made up the majority of the population of working age in Galicia. As legal norms were flexible, daughters benefited from privileged treatment in the division of their parents' inheritance and the transmission of patrimony. Besides their legitimate portion, they had full control over their personal belongings, their dowry and were allowed an usufruct over their husbands assets (if married). On the Atlantic costal areas, 25 percent of the households had a female head. As in the Azores Islands mentioned previously, due to high male emigration, possibilities to marry were scarce. A large proportion of adult women remained single: they worked in agriculture, fishing or textile production. They might have had illegitimate children; they ran their own households and at the same time looked after their aging parents. Because their high capacity as care givers was recognized, they inherited land and a large part of family assets (Rial García 2001). By contrast, in interior Galicia, women who could not find a suitable partner lived in the family farm under their older

13 The conjugal family form was preponderant where there were more institutions for foundlings and for aging parents, while the stem family was to be found where less institutions and supports were created and available. In a way, this confirms Peter Laslett's "nuclear-hardship hypothesis" (Laslett 1988).

brother's headship and were not independent. For the poorest women, domestic service provided labour and secured everyday well-being. Going to Madrid to be a maid was a common experience for young women.

Bastard Bearers, Domestic Service and House Systems

Historical statistics from European capital cities show that the great majority of urban mothers of illegitimate children were domestic servants (Ward 2005). Others occurred among factory employees. In the countryside, servants and agricultural labourers had "natural" children. Among these categories, certain modes of living connected with occupation are immediately responsible. It is not so much due to poverty. Commentators insisted on "promiscuity" and loose morals as factors of *libertinage*. Addressing this point, Peter Laslett had argued that some groups had a possible predisposition to sexual non-conformism and he explored, as a sociologist, what he called the "bastardy prone sub-society" and social attitudes to bastard-bearing (Laslett 1980b). Proletarianization, he thought, could lead to bastardy or prostitution. In England, many monographic studies gathered an astonishing amount of knowledge on the repetitive phenomenon of illegitimate births (Levene, Nutt and Williams 2005).

Laslett insisted on the repetitive bastard-bearing phenomenon, and on the genealogical connection between bastard bearers, a fact that historical demographers meet in field studies.[14] The fact that this repetition may be linked – even due – to migration is a topic previously discussed by Richard Smith and Andrew Blaikie, who both connected the phenomenon with temporary migration and domestic service (Smith 1980; Blaikie 1993; 1998; 2005). This link is also explored in recent research on 19th century Geneva, where it seems – and this is an exception – that the servant subgroup, a high population as in all large European towns, was not more at risk of illegitimacy than the other low class groups of migrant and working unwed females (Schumacher, Ryczkowska and Perroux 2007).

In other 19th century cities, notably in Paris, a considerable number of couples, who had never been united by a marriage ceremony, lived to-

14 This was the case for Fauve-Chamoux when studying the 18th century city of Rheims and the 19th c. rural village of Esparros in Central Pyrenees (Fauve-Chamoux 1995; 2002a; 2002b).

gether, and reared children. Probably the great majority of these were impelled to this by poverty or because they did not care so much about opinion. Dechristianisation and secularisation of everyday life took place. Nevertheless, divorce was not possible in France before 1884 (Fauve-Chamoux 2001).[15] Furthermore, to explain *concubinage*, the influence of legislation is to be considered: every legal condition and impediment restricting marriage inevitably tended to increase the number of illegal unions and illegitimate offspring.

If a "house" or "Hof" system of transmission was the norm as it was the case in Alpine or Pyrenean valleys, marriage was open to family "heirs" or "heiresses" and their chosen partners, while most non-succeeding children could have more sexual freedom but less access to marriage. This is the case in the central Pyrenees (Fauve-Chamoux 1995). If having legitimate children was, for each generation, only important and necessary for the unique reproductive couple in charge of the reproduction of the "House", then other children – non-heirs, sons and daughters, *cadets* and *cadettes*[16] – could circulate in the community, being apprentices or servants in a house or family other than their native one, work to amass a nest egg to become independently established (or branch out), and enjoy sexual experiences. They could have children, without the burden of running the family house and managing family patrimony. This "marginal" behavior might have concerned large categories of the population. In other words, we tend to think that stem-family systems may have played a major role in high regional illegitimacy figures in parts of Europe where inegalitarian systems are practiced.

John Hajnal, along with Peter Laslett, outlined clearly what he saw as the chief elements of marriage and household patterns in Northwestern Europe. He argued that it was service (whether domestic, farm or industrial) by young men and women that ensured high ages at first marriage and the formation at marriage of a new household (Hajnal 1965; 1983; Laslett 1965; 1977; 1988). However, it was also evident that service

15 There were no really permissive divorce laws and policies in early modern Europe, and divorcing was still usually expensive, except in the short period of the French Revolution, when divorce was made accessible to ordinary people. It meant that remarriage was only open to widows or widowers: separated individuals were not eligible for remarriage.

16 The French word *cadet* is now synonymous of "youngest" child; it originated from Gascony where *capdet* was meaning "captain". Youngest sons often went to serve in the army.

played a key role in radically different household systems. For example, it rendered stem families viable by removing surplus labor forces, both seasonal and non seasonal, from these households. Labor migrants went where they could generate the necessary income to maintain the family system through the marriage of the heir, or through helping some of those who were not to inherit the family land (Duroux 2004). In Western Europe, the circulation of young men and women greatly helped to equalize the supply and demand of labour. Regional differentiation may be striking, but reasons for going into service may differ fundamentally (Fauve-Chamoux 2004). Life-cycle service, as defined by Laslett, was not a reality for all servants in early modern times: it was not always just a temporary stage of life course. It could become a permanent occupation up to old age, for men and women alike, when marriage was not achieved. Female servants could experience downward social mobility, with phases of unemployment, occasional prostitution and even experience jail for various crimes. Others managed to specialize in their jobs and reached better status.

Anyhow, be they Spanish, Norwegian or Portuguese, it appears that single mothers always put their hope in a marriage in proper form. And secular laws mirrored Western church laws in this respect, maintaining that marriage so powerfully sanctifies a relationship that even retroactively it can "undo" illegitimacy. For a woman, being married was equivalent to being under her husband's authority and having her old age secured, but at the cost of not heading her own household, even if she could be "at home" a respected "mistress" and administrator of her house (rarely in Europe her native "house").

Female Headship, Widowhood and Old Age

Recent European research on single women and widows covered different aspects. Some authors studied the type of work and living conditions open to women "alone" (meaning without a spouse, or, for Sølvi Sogner in Norway, without a life companion), their income, types of residence (alone or together with someone), mobility and life course; they noted how relative and often difficult was their independence from any conjugal framework (Wall 2002). Others recorded how influential were the family structures and networks; they also observed the slow building, in the various Western societies, of mutual aid and assistance systems, of retirement and social security benefits, particularly in Northern Europe (Lynch 2003; Moring and Wall forthcoming).

Historians of old age have been very active in this field and outlined many aspects of widowhood (Henderson and Wall 1994; Kertzer and Laslett 1995), linking historical research with present problems raised by population aging and the emergence of a socio-economically important *Third Age* (Laslett 1989). Frouke Veenstra and Kirsten van der Ploeg edited a useful selected bibliography on *Widows in Western History* (Veenstra and van der Ploeg 1995) and noted that few studies dealt seriously with the household conditions of widows during the early modern period. Olwen Hufton developed her work on eighteenth century Britain and France (Hufton 1995) and considered also spinsters and other women alone. The fate of widows in the past aroused renewed interest when statistical corpus appeared and gave quantitative information about widowhood and potential remarriage.

Gender Inequality Facing Remarriage

Remarriage was recognized as widespread in times when death affected marriage as much as divorce does today. Gender affected chances to remarry according to place, time and type of community considered, with a permanent feature: widows remarried less than widowers (Dupâquier *et al.* 1981). The fate of Western European women living "alone", be they widows or unmarried, childless or not, due to their important proportion in the population, especially urban population, did attract at last historical attention (Fauve-Chamoux 1983). In France, it was particularly clear, as shown by Fauve-Chamoux in her contribution, that, legally as well as customarily, marriage settlements and types of inheritance could be different according to the regional long history, cultural traditions and family transmission systems, with a necessary impact on potential female remarriage. The presence or absence of dependent children appeared as playing an important role in remarriage decisions. Two other factors were also considered: the duration of the matrimonial union which the spouse's death interrupted and the age of the surviving spouse when widowhood occurred.

A better gender approach of main remarriage factors such as age at widowhood, proportion remarrying, interval between death of spouse and remarriage, rural versus urban marriage market, dependent children and living standards, allows to evaluate how specific urban societies were in preindustrial Europe. For a non well-off widow, remarrying was probably one of the best ways to maintain a satisfactory standard of living. But statistical figures do not bring such a simple picture of the past. Urban women probably had other priorities than rural women, and their mentality, culture, aspiration for independence and concepts of well-being may have been different.

Remarriage of Widows: Difficult or Avoided?

Various analyses of remarriage models in pre-industrial European societies attest a general decline of remarriage frequency during the 18th century. Most investigations of nuptiality in early-modern Western Europe focused on the relatively late entry into first marriage for both men and women and high levels of celibacy, comforting pioneering studies by John Hajnal and Peter Laslett who pointed out the specific European marriage patterns of the past (Hajnal 1965; 1983; Laslett 1977). Philippe Ariès considered that the effects of remarriage were

> the reverse of those of late marriage. Late marriage and high mortality act as a brake on reproduction and may lead to a dangerous situation for the community. Remarriage on the other hand compensates for high mortality and is an incentive for fertility (Ariès 1981, 31).

Remarriage constituted one element of the traditional demographic pattern of Europe. However, in its traditional form, remarriage disappeared in Europe mostly during the demographic transition of the 19th century, but we know now that a substantial decline in the proportion of marriages involving people remarrying occurred at a much earlier period. For instance, Wrigley and Schofield showed, for rural England, that, while 25 or 30 percent of those marrying in the 16th c. were remarrying later, this proportion declined to around 10 percent by the 19th century (Wrigley and Schofield 1981, 212). For female remarriage, this decline was clearly confirmed by Jeremy Boulton for 17th and early 18th c. London (Boulton 1990). But Boulton showed also that lack of wealth did not always prevent widows from remarrying. By these findings, he was challenging some of Vivien Brodsky's previous conclusions concerning the privileged position of craftsmen and tradesmen widows towards remarriage, in late Elizabethan London (Brodsky 1986).

Household Position in Old Age

Study of remarriage may integrate some useful knowledge about demographic and socio-economic parameters. It would also be a way to reconstruct whether or not widows had some interest in remarrying. Widows could work, support themselves, become household heads after their husband's death, live alone or with their children if they had some resources, and remain independent. If they had enough available, in terms of income and enough assurance of care from children, family network, maids or neighbours to face old age, why would they voluntarily decide to accept a new husband's authority? What is the relationship between remarriage and poverty or well-being? How are we to interpret the notable mistrust of female remarriage by European clergymen or the hostility against some remarriages that we can read in local events like *charivaris*? (Segalen 1981). Sogner's chapter, based on the well-being of the elderly people without a life-companion *(enslig)*, in the rural Norwegian parish of Rendalen in 1910, helps understand changing widowhood models with time.

As noted above with Kari Telste's contribution, before the modern welfare state was put in practice after the Second World War in Norway, according to law, parents and children, and couples had obligations of mutual support. Widowhood and childlessness therefore made aging people vulnerable, particularly women. Among women aged 60 and over, 23 percent were heading their own household, 46 percent lived with kin, 8 percent were servants, another 8 percent were lodgers and the remaining 15 percent depended, as registered "paupers", on local assistance. On the male side, 40 percent were heads of their households, be they farm owners or "cottars". Women outnumbered men as servants and paupers. At the time the 1910 census was taken, local assistance provided to paupers was organized according to the Norwegian *Poor Law* which was put in force in 1900. It put an end to traditional systems of municipal support which used to organise a turning duty (of two weeks) between local farms for giving food and lodging to parish paupers. A Poverty Commission was, in preindustrial times, responsible for this rotation system of sharing care-giving to “deserving poor”.

One third of senior men lived with the benefit of a “retirement contract”. The same proportion is true for women, but with various positions in their own household. The principle of a retirement contract was the transfer of rights to a successor in exchange of specified goods and services during the remaining life time. In this farming and dairy land context, the contract holder could move to some separate dwelling close by. The household approach of living conditions proposed by Sogner, with a comparative view on the situation during the 19th century, shows that most senior women who could not enjoy the presence of a living companion often earned their living and at the same time benefited from family help in the form of a retirement contract, even when single. The poorest one received enough poor relief to survive. But three out of four elderly women without a husband or life companion were not heading their own household.

Female Headed Households

“Husbandless” households were usually small-sized: lack of money compelled single women not to support other individuals, or widows not to keep all their children at home, putting some of them in apprenticeship, leaving them to the care of some institution, or even abandoning them, as did so many unmarried mothers in the 18th century. Mikołaj Szołtysek studies female well-being within the large limits of the historical 18th century Kingdom of Poland, taking as an indicator the proportion of female headship and relying on a very large population sample (84 parishes). As expected, females rarely headed their own household in such a rural preindustrial context (4.2 percent), and their households were, as elsewhere in Europe, smaller, less viable than male headed ones and, for the more affluent ones, included fewer servants. At the aggregate level, family and household dependency ratios were almost the same for male- and female-headed households.[17] The study of sex ratios reveals that most young women left home earlier than young men and spent some time on the labour market, even if a majority of life-cycle servants were males. Although eligible to inherit immovable properties in traditional Poland, both from a father and from a deceased spouse (Guzowski 2007), women's capabilities to manage real property and their own life were reduced. In an urban context, females headed households much more often, and the proportions presented by Szołtysek for 1791 – 19 percent for Wieluń, 22.7 for Kraków and 24.8 percent for Warsaw – were very close to the ones attested in Western European cities (Fauve-Chamoux 1983; 1993). The importance of males and females living as "inmates" in rural households is discussed. Nearly a quarter of the families included some individuals which apparently had no kin relation with the head of the household and who were not domestic servants. They could be lone mothers with children or solitary persons.

In forced absence of longitudinal data, this analysis remains of great interest, as the author is led to put into question some normative well-known socio-economic relationship models between Polish landlords and peasant families of the time. Widows could take headship and resign in favour of their son; they could buy and sell land, a fact which supposes in practice some autonomy of serf communities under the conditions of "the second serfdom", when manorialism relied on compulsory male and female labour. Therefore applying a basic "capability approach" to such populations would be somewhat problematic. Under their specific socio-economic regime, provisions for care concerning orphans, women alone, widows and aging individuals may have taken in Poland other forms than those traditionally present in Western European communities of the time.

17 *Family dependency* is defined as the number of people in the family aged 0–13 and 55 and older ("consumers") to the number aged 14–54. *Household dependency* refers to the corresponding ratio for the household (that is, including servants, but not inmates).

Provisions for Care

European societies do differ from others, for instance Asian societies, where traditionally marriage for women is early and universal, and remarriage a matter of family or custom and not an individual decision (Fauve-Chamoux 2005; Fauve-Chamoux and Ochiai 2009). But Nagata's chapter in the present volume reveals that efficient forms of public assistance also existed in Japan during the Tokugawa period (1600–1868), when family help was not available to needy persons. In the town of Kyoto, this care was provided in the form of rice or cash by neighbourhood funds in case of major emergencies as floods, famine or other disasters. Other help was regularly provided by Buddhist temples and by professional trade associations. Local laws regulated civil society and local taxes were administered by a council of heads of households for each neighbourhood. These officials were in charge of registering family headship succession, adoption, and retirement. They dealt with the future of abandoned children, looked for wet nurses and adoptive parents. They were also able to provide a proper dowry to some needy orphan girls, as some specific funds did in Europe (Lynch 2003).

In Japan, anyway, the best way to ensure good care in old age was to marry and rely on family members for regular support. Having children and a successor was fundamental, hence the current adoption of an heir in the absence of a suitable son. This chosen heir could be a son-in law or any other person chosen for his abilities to run the house and manage the family incomes, be it business, farming or fishing activities. Taking charge of older family members' well-being and of all needs for life was the responsibility of the head and successor. It included providing dowries to brides, administrating servants and apprentices, giving protection, food, all care and lodging to close kin, illegitimate children and second wives, if any. It covered also proper ancestor worship, expensive regular memorial ceremonies and family cemetery arrangements.

In the Japanese stem-family system, the best way to provide assistance was coresidence. There was some reluctance for coresidence with non-stem kin (like uncles, cousins, in-laws) and non-kin, and Nagata notes some gender differences in residential patterns observed from mid-nineteenth population registers *(Shūmon ninbetsu aratame chō),* easy to compare with similar documents in European countries, like Belgium or the Netherlands. Elderly widows preferred to live with a married child and grandchildren than to live alone.

Conclusion

The papers in this volume address the role of the family for providing well-being in the past from four perspectives: marriage strategies, transmission of property, well-being outside of marriage, and the questions of female headship, widowhood and old age.

In the rural societies of historical Europe, the well-being, even survival, of many families depended on their access to viable landholding. Preserving this access for future generations was a prime concern. For craft families that produced market commodities, the skills and tools of their craft were an equally important patrimony to develop and pass on to provide for the well-being of future generations. Few families survived on wage work which was considered an unstable basis to provide for the well-being of a family and all its members. The methods for preserving this patrimony and passing it on to the next generation, or not, were shaped by ecological, political, social and legal constraints and economic opportunity as the family balanced the individual ambitions of its members with the need to provide adequate well-being to the whole.

Depending upon these constraints and the phase of commercialization, the transmission of the family property to the next generation could be relatively equal or unequal. Egalitarian inheritance had the potential of dividing the patrimony to the point that the individual units would not be sufficient to support the well-being of each heir. Non-egalitarian inheritance also meant non-inheriting children were potentially dependent upon the heir for their well-being and had less freedom or support for their own ambitions. Whether equal or unequal, the challenge was to find the best way to provide well-being for all.

In this setting, marriage performed a specific function. Parental strategies surrounding the marriage of children were designed to counteract the division of property. For this reason, marriage between kin or "exchange marriages" were common in several parts of Europe. Sometimes children were kept from marrying at all. However, children could also use their share of the family patrimony to exploit opportunities elsewhere, marry someone of higher status and gain more "well-being" than successors to management of the family property who were often burdened with the care of parents and unmarried siblings.

Some societies saw marriage as a process that began with a period of cohabitation. When this process was interrupted by mortality or migration, cohabitation could result in illegitimate births. In others, cohabitation was plainly an alternative to marriage. In the Western past, illegitimacy was often a gender strategy for the survival and continued well-being of family and community rather than sexual anti-conformism. In the context of proletarianization and in the absence of strong family support for single mothers, determination of paternity was a key issue for securing the well-being of mothers and children.

In the past, one of the concerns of inheritance systems had been whether and how to provide for the well-being of unmarried mothers and their illegitimate children as well as determining who had the responsibility to care for them. Presently, in Europe, new inquiries such as those of the Hague Conference on Private International Law or new legislations like, in France, *Pacte Civil de Solidarité/PACS* open new alternatives, offering more protection to non married couples (90 percent heterosexual). But, even recognized by their unmarried – often "pacsed" – parents, children are still legally considered as illegitimate. In 2007, this situation concerned half of the births in France and, in today's Europe, extra-marital births account for an increasing share of total births (globally a third), reflecting the growing frequency of extra-marital cohabitation. The "Gender and Well-Being" project results enlighten a massive and specific phenomenon of our time.

Well-being can be defined as the ability to be secure against poverty. The studies in this volume provide many examples of marriage strategies that limit the risk of property fragmentation that would endanger entire communities. These strategies serve the well-being of the collectivity. However, well-being can also be seen as the ability of adults to make autonomous decisions regarding their own lives. Then, of course, position in the sibling order or illegitimacy could severely limit individual strategies. Conflicts about the choice of partner or the dowry were rampant. So, one could try to change the path laid out by the parents. Several authors describe flexibility within marriage and inheritance systems, but also suggest that men had more opportunity to bend the rules and lower negative consequences from doing so than women.

For working women who could not find a suitable partner, perhaps because they were too poor or most males of their generation were migrating, having a child was a way to secure their old age. In this book some authors studied the type of work and living conditions open to single women who had no spouse or life companion. Others recorded the influence of family structures and networks as well as the slow building of mutual aid and assistance systems, of retirement and social security benefits, particularly in Northern Europe. Comparative views with historical Japan were also presented: in general, the best way for men and women to ensure good care in old age was to marry and rely on family members for regular support. Having children was fundamental. When care of the older generation and sick and disabled family members was the responsibility of a single heir, strategies for replacing a missing heir were a key question of both inheritance and marriage. Gender inequalities facing remarriage were stressed and it was clear that urban societies in preindustrial Europe were places where people living alone were numerous and in need, particularly women and migrants.

In the past, the predominance of the family economy, whether in agriculture, commercial activities or wage work, meant that the family was the main provider of resources, through its internal mechanisms of redistribution as well as through its intergenerational transfers. In this book, family rules and flexible departures from them regarding inclusion and exclusion, family mechanisms of redistribution and transfers of resources, and family care arrangements for children, singles and elderly have been analyzed and compared in their regional variations. In the end, the family was the first source for gaining well-being and the final safety net for maintaining the security and well-being of all its members. Any study of gender and well-being in the past must consider both how families provided for the well-being of their members and how this security was passed to the next generation to provide the basis for their security in the future.

We have used the concept of family systems as a heuristic device for comparative research into gender differences in access to and control of resources, into the relative security offered by marriage, and into systems of old age care. Family systems differ in the strength of parental control over adult children and thus, to a certain extent, in the opportunity of individuals to pursue their own goals and strategies to attain well-being. Finally, they differ strongly in the ways illegitimacy was accepted, notwithstanding prohibitive religious rules and legal systems. Thus, they constitute an underlying mentality that can still account for the remarkable variation in cohabitation and births outside marriage in contemporary Europe.

Although the concept of family systems has proven fruitful, more work is needed to explore whether and how they also affect relations between the sexes and the generations in urban contexts, in propertyless families, and in the emerging middle classes. From this perspective, the period between the late nineteenth century and the middle of the twentieth century needs further exploration. In particular in the Eastern European context, it remains to be seen to what extent family patterns reflect continuation with the past (Therborn 2004; Kera and Kessler 2008).

References

ARIES, Philippe, 1981, "Introduction", in Jacques DUPÂQUIER, Etienne HÉLIN, Peter LASLETT, Massimo LIVI-BACCI and Sølvi SOGNER (eds), *Marriage and Remarriage in Populations of the Past*, London, Academic Press, pp. 27–40

AUGUSTINS, Georges, 2002, "The perpetuation of families and the molding of personal destinies", in David I. KERTZER and Maurizio BARBAGLI (eds), *Family Life in the long nineteenth century, 1789–1912*, New Haven, Yale University Press, pp. 322–348.

BAHLE, Thomas, 2008, "Family policy patterns in the enlarged EU", in Jens ALBER, Tony FAHEY and Chiara SARACENO, *Handbook of Quality of Life in the Enlarged European Union*, London and New York, Routledge, pp. 100–125.

BLACKSTONE, William, 1756, *An Analysis of the Laws of England. To which is prefixed an Introductory Discourse on the Study of the Law*, Oxford, Clarendon Press.

BLAIKIE, Andrew, 1993, *Of Illegitimacy, Sex and Society: Northeast Scotland, 1750–1900*, Oxford, Clarendon Press.

–, 1998, "Scottish Illegitimacy: Social Adjustment or Moral Economy?", *Journal of Interdisciplinary History*, 29, 2, pp. 221–241.

–, 2005, "The household economics of illegitimacy: some preliminary interpretations", paper presented at Social Sciences History association/SSHA, Portland, session on "Economic and household response to illegitimacy".

BOURDIEU, Pierre, 1972, "Les stratégies matrimoniales dans le système de reproduction", *Annales E.S.C.*, 27, 4–5, pp. 1105–1127.

BRODSKY, Vivien, 1986, "Widows in late Elizabethan London: remarriage, economic opportunity and family orientations", in Lloyd BONFIELD, Richard M. SMITH and Keith WRIGHTSON (eds), *The World we have Gained. Histories of Population and Social Structure*, Blackwell, Oxford, pp. 122–154.

CRETNEY, Steve, 2003, *Family Law in the twentieth century: a History*, Oxford, Oxford University Press.

DAMSMA, Dirk and KOK, Jan, 2005, "*Ingedroogde harten*? Partnerkeuze en sociale reproductie van de Noord-Hollandse boerenstand in de negentiende en vroeg-twintigste eeuw", in Jan KOK and Marco H. D. VAN LEEUWEN (eds), *Genegenheid en gelegenheid. Twee eeuwen partnerkeuze en huwelijk*, Amsterdam, Aksant Academic Publishers, pp. 285–307.

DAVIS, Kingsley, 1939, "Illegitimacy and the social structure", *The American Journal of Sociology*, 45, 2, pp. 215–233.

DUPÂQUIER, Jacques, HÉLIN, Etienne, LASLETT, Peter, LIVI-BACCI, Massimo and SOGNER, Sølvi (eds), 1981, *Marriage and Remarriage in Populations of the Past*, London, Academic Press.

DURÃES, Margarida, 1998, "Nécessités économiques et pratiques juridiques: problèmes de la transmission des exploitations agricoles. L'exemple portugais (XVIIIe–XXe siècles)", *Mélanges de l'École Française de Rome. Italie et Méditerranée*, tome 110, pp. 373–388.

DURANTON, Gilles, RODRÍGUEZ-POSE, Andrés and SANDALL, Richard, 2009, "Family types and the persistence of regional disparities in Europe", *Economic Geography, 85,1, pp.23-47.*

DUROUX, Rose, 2004, "Emigration, gender, and inheritance: A case study of the High Auvergne, 1700–1900", in David R. GREEN and Alastair OWENS (eds), *Family Welfare. Gender, Property and Inheritance since the Seventeenth Century*, Westport CT, Praeger, pp. 47–72.

ENGELEN, Theo, 2002, "Labour Strategies of Families: A Critical Assessment of an Appealing Concept", *International Review of Social History*, 47, 3, pp. 453–464.

EUROSTAT, 2008a, "In the spotlight. Demographic change: challenge or opportunity?", Europe in figures, *Eurostat Yearbook 2008*, Eurostat on line, Luxembourg. http://epp.eurostat.ec.europa.eu/portal/page/portal/publications/eurostat_yearbook

–, 2008b, "Living conditions and Welfare", *Europe in Figures, Eurostat Yearbook 2008*, Eurostat on line, Luxembourg.
http://epp.eurostat.ec.europa.eu/portal/page/portal/publications/eurostat_yearbook

FAUVE-CHAMOUX, Antoinette, 1983, "The importance of women in an urban environment: the example of the Rheims household at the beginning of the industrial revolution", in Richard WALL, Jean ROBIN and Peter LASLETT (eds), *Family Forms in Historic Europe*, Cambridge, Cambridge University Press, pp. 475–492.

–, 1993, "Households forms and living standards in preindustrial France: from models to realities", *Journal of Family History*, 18, 2, pp. 135–156.

–, 1995, "The Stem family, demography and inheritance", in Richard L. RUDOLF (ed.), *The European Peasant Family and Society*, Liverpool, Liverpool University Press, pp. 86–113.

–, 2001, "Marriage, widowhood and divorce", in David I. KERTZER and Marzio BARBAGLI (eds), *Family Life in Early Modern Times, 1500–1789, The History of the European Family*, vol. 1, Yale, Yale University Press, pp. 221–256.

–, 2002a, "Changes in policy towards abandoned children and differential mortality: the case of 18th century Rheims", in Hilde SANDVIK, Kari TELSTE and Gunnar THORVALDSEN (eds), *Pathways of the Past, Essays in Honour of Solvi Sogner on her 70th Anniversary,* Tig og Tanke, University of Oslo, Oslo, pp. 39–58.

–, 2002b, "Widows and their living arrangements in preindustrial France", *The History of the Family, an International Quarterly,* 7, 1, pp. 101–116.

–, 2003, "Female transmission in comparative perspective", in Emiko OCHIAI (ed.), *The Logic of Female Succession: Rethinking Patriarchy and Patrilinearity in Global and Historical Perspective*, Kyoto, Nichibunken, pp. 11–29.

–, 2004 (ed.), *Domestic Service and the Formation of European Identity*, Bern, Peter Lang.

–, 2006, "Family reproduction and stem-family system: from Pyrenean valleys to Norwegian farms", *The History of the Family: an International Quarterly,* Special issue dedicated to the memory of Tamara Hareven (1937–2002), 11, 3, pp. 171–184.

FAUVE-CHAMOUX, Antoinette and OCHIAI, Emiko (eds), 2009, *The Stem Family in Eurasian Perspective. Revisiting House Societies*, Bern, Peter Lang.

GARDARSDOTTIR, Olof, 2000, "The implication of illegitimacy in late-nineteenth-century Iceland: the relationship between infant mortality and the household position of mothers giving birth to illegitimate children", *Continuity and Change*, 15, 3, pp. 435–461.

–, 2002, *Saving the Child. Regional, Cultural and Social Aspects of the Infant Mortality Decline in Iceland, 1770–1920*, Umeå, Umeå University.

–, 2006, "Extramarital births and marriage patterns in Iceland in a long time perspective", paper presented at Social Sciences History association/SSHA, Minneapolis, session on "Single mothers and bastardy revisited".

GUZOWSKI, Piotr, 2007, "Marriage strategies and inheritance system in Polish peasant families in the 15th–17th centuries". Paper presented at the COST ACTION A34 Second Symposium "The Transmission of Well-Being: Marriage Strategies and Inheritance Systems in Europe (17th-20th Centuries)", University of Minho, Guimarães-Portugal, 25–28 April, 2007.

HAJNAL, John, 1965, "European Marriage Patterns in Perspective", in David V. GLASS and David E.C. EVERSLEY (eds), *Population in History,* London, Arnold, pp. 101–140.

–, 1983, "Two kinds of pre-industrial household formation system", in Richard WALL, Jean ROBIN and Peter LASLETT (eds), *Family Forms in Historic Europe,* Cambridge, Cambridge University Press, pp. 65–104.

HAMMEL, Eugene A., 1981, "Introduction to part 2: Laws and customs relating to remarriage", in Jacques DUPÂQUIER, Etienne HÉLIN, Peter LASLETT, Massimo LIVI-BACCI and Sølvi SOGNER (eds), *Marriage and Remarriage in Populations of the Past*, London, Academic Press, pp. 81–93.

HARNOIS, Caroline and HIRSCH, Juliane, 2008, *Note on development in internal law and private international law concerning cohabitation outside marriage, including registered partnerships, for the attention the Council of April 2008 on General Affairs and Policy of the Conference*, Preliminary Document No 11, March, The Hague, Permanent Bureau of Hague Conference on Private International Law (HccH). http://www.hcch.net

HARRIS, Bernard, GÁLVEZ, Lina and MACHADO, Helena (eds), forthcoming, *Gender and Wellbeing in Europe: Historical and Contemporary Perspectives,* London, Ashgate.

HARTMAN, Mary S., 2004, *The Household and the Making of History. A Subversive View of the Western Past*, Cambridge, Cambridge University Press.

HENDERSON, John and WALL, Richard (eds), 1994, *Poor Women and Children in the European Past*, Routledge, London.

HUFTON, Olwen, 1995, *The Prospect Before Her. A History of Women in Western Europe*. Volume One. *1500–1800*, London, Harper Collins Publishers.

KASER, Karl, 2002, "Power and inheritance. Male domination, property, and family in Eastern Europe, 1500–1900", *History of the Family. An International Quarterly*, 7, 3, pp. 375–395.

KECK, Wolfgang and BLOME, Agnes, 2008, "Is there a generational cleavage in Europe? Age-specific perceptions of elderly care and of the pension system", in Jens ALBER, Tony FAHEY and Chiara SARACENO, *Handbook of Quality of Life in the Enlarged European Union*, London and New York, Routledge, pp. 72–99

KERA, Gentiana and KESSLER, Gijs (eds), 2008, "Urban household and family in twentieth century East and South-East Europe", special issue, *The History of the Family. An International Quarterly*, 13, 2, pp. 119–125.

KERTZER, David and LASLETT, Peter (eds), 1995, *Aging in the Past: Demography, Society, and Old Age*, Berkeley and Los Angeles, University of California Press.

KOK, Jan, 2002, "The Challenge of Strategy: A Comment", *International Review of Social History,* 47, 3, pp. 465–485.

–, Forthcoming, "The Family Factor in Migration Decisions", in Jan LUCASSEN, Leo LUCASSEN and Patrick MANNING (eds), *Migration History. Multidisciplinary Approaches*, Leiden, Brill.

LASLETT, Peter, 1965, *The World we have Lost*, London, Methuen.

–, 1977, "Characteristics of the Western Family Considered Over Time", *Journal of Family History*, 2, 1, pp. 89–115.

–, 1980a, "Introduction: comparing illegitimacy over time and between cultures", in Peter LASLETT, Karla OOSTERVEEN and Richard M. SMITH (eds), *Bastardy and its Comparative History: Studies in the History of Illegitimacy and Marital Nonconformism in Britain, France, Germany, Sweden, North America, Jamaica and Japan*, London, Edward Arnold, pp. 1–64.

–, 1980b, "The bastardy prone sub-society", in Peter LASLETT, Karla OOSTERVEEN and Richard M. SMITH (eds), *Bastardy and its Comparative History: Studies in the History of Illegitimacy and Marital Nonconformism in Britain, France, Germany, Sweden, North America, Jamaica and Japan*, London, Edward Arnold, pp. 217–240.

–, 1988, "Family, kinship and collectivity as systems of support in pre-industrial Europe: a considerations of the 'nuclear-hardship' hypothesis", *Continuity and Change*, 3, 2, pp. 153–175.

–, 1989, *A Fresh Map of Life. The Emergence of the Third Age*, Cambridge (Mass), Harvard University Press.

LEE, James Z. and CAMPBELL, Cameron D., 1997, *Fate and Fortune in Rural China: Social Organization and Population Behaviour in Liaoning, 1774–1883*, Cambridge, Cambridge University Press.

LEFFINGWELL, Albert, (1892) 1976, *Illegitimacy and the Influence of Seasons upon Conduct*, New York, Arno Press.

LE PLAY, Frédéric, 1877–79, *Les ouvriers européens. Étude sur les travaux, la vie domestique et la condition morale des populations ouvrières de l'Europe*, Tours, A. Mame et fils, 6 vols.

LEVENE, Alysa, NUTT, Thomas and WILLIAMS, Samantha (eds), 2005, *Illegitimacy in Britain, 1700–1920*, Basingstoke, Palgrave Macmillan.

LYNCH, Katherine A., 2003, *Individuals, Families and Communities in Europe, 1200–1800. The Urban Foundations of Western Societies*, Cambridge, Cambridge University Press.

MATOS, Paulo Lopes, 2007, *O Nascimento fora do Matrimónio na freguesia da Ribeira Seca da Ilha de São Jorge (Açores): 1800–1910*, Guimarães, Núcleo de Estudos da População e Sociedade.

MITTERAUER, Michael, 1983, *Ledige Mütter. Zur Geschichte illegitimer Geburten in Europa*, München, Beck.

MITTERAUER, Michael and SIEDER, Reinhard, 1982, *The European Family*, Oxford, Basil Blackwell.

MORING, Beatrice and WALL, Richard, forthcoming, *The Welfare of Widows in Northern Europe*, London, Boydell and Brewer.

OLIVEIRA, Guilherme de, 2002, "Grounds for divorce and maintenance between former spouses", Portugal, on line paper, University of Coimbra.
http://www2.law.uu.nl/priv/cefl/Reports/pdf/Portugal02.pdf

ORIS, Michel, 2003, "The history of migration as a chapter in the history of the European rural family: An overview", *History of the Family. An International Quarterly*, 8, 2, pp. 187–215.

Permanent Bureau of Hague Conference on Private International Law (HccH), 2000, *Private international law and aspects of cohabitation outside marriage and registered partnerships, Note drawn up by the permanent Bureau, for the attention of the Special Commission of May 2000 on general affairs and policy of the Conference*, Preliminary Document No 9, May, The Hague, Permanent Bureau of Hague Conference on Private International Law.
http://www.hcch.net

RAULT, Wilfried, 2009, *L'invention du Pacs. Pratiques et symboliques d'une nouvelle forme d'union*, Paris, Presses de Sciences Po.

REHER, David S., 1998, "Family Ties in Western Europe: Persistent Contrasts", *Population and Development Review*, 24, 2, pp. 203–234.

REY CASTELAO, Ofelia, 2006, "Les femmes seules du Nord-Ouest de l'Espagne: trajectoires féminines dans un territoire d'émigration, 1700–1860", *Annales de Démographie Historique*, 2, pp. 105–133.

RIAL GARCIA, Serrana, 2001, "Las mujeres y el patrimonio en dos comunidades costeras de las Rías Bajas", *Obradorio de Historia Moderna*, 10, pp. 89–120.

SÁ, Isabel dos Guimarães, 1996, "Abandono de crianças, ilegitimidade e concepçoes pré-nupciais em Portugal," in Vicente PÉREZ MOREDA (ed.), *Expostos e ilegítimos na realidade ibérica do século XVI ao presente, Actas do III Congresso da ADEH*, vol. 3, Porto, Edições Afrontamento, pp. 37–58.

SARACENO, Chiara, 2008, "Patterns of family living in the enlarged EU", in Jens ALBER, Tony FAHEY and Chiara SARACENO, *Handbook of Quality of Life in the Enlarged European Union,* London and New York, Routledge, pp. 47–72.

SARDON, Jean-Paul, 2006, "Évolution démographique récente des pays développés", *Population*, 61, 3, pp. 225–300.

SCHUMACHER, Reto, RYCZKOWSKA, Grazyna and PERROUX, Olivier, 2007, "Unwed mothers in the city. Illegitimate fertility in 19th century Geneva", *The History of the Family: an International Quarterly,* 12, 3, pp. 189–202.

SEGALEN, Martine, 1981, "Mentalité populaire et remarriage en Europe occidentale", in Jacques DUPÂQUIER, Etienne HÉLIN, Peter LASLETT, Massimo LIVI-BACCI and Sølvi SOGNER (eds), *Marriage and Remarriage in Populations of the Past*, London, Academic Press, pp. 67–80.

–, 1991, "Mean age at marriage and kinship networks in a town under the influence of the metropolis: Nanterre, 1800–1850", *Journal of Family History*, 16, 1, pp. 65–78.

SMITH, Richard, M, 1980, "Family reconstitution and the study of bastardy: evidence from certain English parishes", in Peter LASLETT, Karla OOSTERVEEN and Richard M. SMITH (eds), *Bastardy and its Comparative History: Studies in the History of Illegitimacy and Marital Nonconformism in Britain, France, Germany, Sweden, North America, Jamaica and Japan*, London, Edward Arnold, pp. 86–93.

SKINNER, G. William, 1997, "Family systems and demographic processes", in David I. KERTZER and Tom FRICKE (eds), *Anthropological Demography: Toward a New Synthesis,* Chicago, University of Chicago Press, pp. 53–95.

THERBORN, Göran, 2004, *Between Sex and Power. Family in the World, 1900–2000*, London and New York, Routledge.

TODD, Emmanuel, 1985, *The Explanation of Ideology. Family Structures and Social System,* Oxford, Basil Blackwell.

–, 1987, *The causes of Progress: Culture, Authority and Change*, Oxford, Basil Blackwell.

–, 1990, *L'invention de l'Europe*, Paris, Seuil.

VAN DER LINDEN, Marcel, 2002, "Introduction", in Jan KOK (ed.), *Rebellious Families. Household Strategies and Collective Action in the Nineteenth and Twentieth Centuries*, Oxford/New York, Berghahn Books, pp. 1–23.

VAN DE WALLE, Etienne, 1980, "Illegitimacy in France during the nineteenth century", in Peter LASLETT, Karla OOSTERVEEN and Richard M. SMITH (eds), *Bastardy and its Comparative History: Studies in the History of Illegitimacy and Marital Nonconformism in Britain, France, Germany, Sweden, North America, Jamaica and Japan*, London, Edward Arnold, pp. 264–277.

VAN POPPEL, Frans and ORIS, Michel, 2004, "Introduction", in Frans VAN POPPEL, Michel ORIS and James Z. LEE (eds), *The Road to Independence. Leaving home in Western and Eastern Societies 16th–20th centuries*, Bern, Peter Lang, pp. 1–29.

VEENSTRA, Frouke and VAN DER PLOEG, Kirsten, 1995, "Widows in Western History", in Jan BREMMER and Lourens VAN DEN BOSCH (eds), *Between Poverty and the Pyre. Moments in the History of Widowhood*, London, Routledge, pp. 247–251.

VERDON, Michel, 1979, "The Stem Family: Toward a General Theory", *Journal of Interdisciplinary History* 10, 1, pp. 87–105.

VIAZZO, Pier Paolo and LYNCH, Katherine A., 2002, "Anthropology, Family History, and the Concept of Strategy", *International Review of Social History*, 47, 3, pp. 423–452.

WALL, Richard, 2002, "Introduction. Widows: perceptions, demography, residence patterns, and standard of living", *The History of the Family: an International Quarterly*, Special issue, 7, 1, pp. 3–12.

WARD, Peter W., 2005, "The welfare of female servants. Five case studies (Bologna, Boston, Edinburgh, Utrecht, Vienna)", in Suzanne PASLEAU, Isabelle SCHOPP with Raffaella SARTI (eds), *Proceedings of the Servant Project/Actes du Servant Project*, vol. 5: *The Modelization of Domestic Service*, Liège, Editions de l'Université de Liège, pp. 91–106.

WRIGLEY, Edward A. and SCHOFIELD, Roger S. with LEE, Ronald and OEPPEN, Jim, 1981, *The Population History of England, 1541–1871*, London, Edward Arnold.

PART I

MARRIAGE STRATEGIES

Marriage Strategies and Well-Being among 19th Century Basque Family Property Owners

Marie-Pierre ARRIZABALAGA

What does the study of inheritance and marriage strategies tell us about gender differentiated treatment of well-being within Pyrenean family property owners in the nineteenth century? Under the Civil Code of 1804, families had the obligation to secure equal well-being to their children and to partition their patrimony equally between them, male or female. Yet succession and land data analysis show differently. Families continued to perpetuate aspects of ancient unequal inheritance practices so that in the end sons (especially older ones) enjoyed better destinies and social mobility than daughters (especially younger ones).

These practices originated in the ancient regime when all Pyrenean provinces imposed impartible inheritance and the exclusion of the heir's siblings. The system did secure well-being to most children but unequally (Yver 1966; Le Roy Ladurie 1972; Poumarède 1972; Zink 1993; Béaur 2004). Codified in the fifteenth and sixteenth centuries, these customs sustained different types of impartible inheritance practices, from strict male or female primogeniture in Lavedan, Barèges and the Basque Country (Lafourcade 1989; Fougères 1938; Cordier 1859),[1] to male primogeniture in Bearn and the Baronies (Zink 1993; Poumarède 1972) to strict male inheritance regardless of birth order in French Catalogne (in the Eastern Pyrenees) (Assier-Andrieu 1981). In other parts of France except Brittany (the land of equal inheritance; Segalen 1985), unequal inheritance through male primogeniture prevailed to maintain family land undivided, or almost undivided (Assier-Andrieu 1990).

When the Civil Code was implemented, Pyrenean families naturally feared for the house system because the law forced the equal partition of the family patrimony between all the children, thus forbidding impartible

1 The system is known as *aînesse intégrale*. Eugène Cordier argued that, influenced by Roman law in the eighteenth century, Barèges and Lavedan slowly abandoned these practices in favor of strict male primogeniture.

inheritance to a single heir and the unequal distribution of assets. According to the law, strict equality guaranteed the equal well-being of all the children. Its implementation however endangered the economic viability of Pyrenean communities. Frédéric Le Play argued further that the law threatened the eco-equilibrium of Pyrenean families, communities, provinces as well as the prosperity and progress of the nation (Le Play 1871, 9–10; 1878, Ch. 30; Chenu 1994). Families for their part were concerned about their continued presence within the community as well as about the family house and line. The law was indeed egalitarian in its objectives but it had economic and human side effects for small and medium-sized properties and risked to threaten many with bankruptcy.

Using Basque family reconstitutions, property transmission data, and land registers, this paper will demonstrate that ancient Pyrenean practices survived the Revolution: families perpetuated impartible inheritance to a single heir and therefore the unequal distribution of patrimony. Pyrenean families however struggled to maintain their assets intact while compensating all children to secure them "decent" destinies and status. Though unequal, the system could only survive with children's concessions. In the end, older children were often guaranteed a better well-being than younger children and sons a better one than daughters. Thus the new system treated the heirs differently depending on gender and birth order.

Sources and Methodology

Information from civil registers, inheritance records and land registers in the Basque Country after the implementation of the Civil Code of 1804 will be used as sources to study inheritance practices and the way Pyrenean women were secured well-being within the family in the nineteenth century. As in other Pyrenean regions, Basque women benefited from the Civil Code because, in principle, they were secured equal access to family assets and therefore equal treatment under the law. They could indeed demand their legal, equal share of inheritance. Yet could they truly be secured equal treatment when impartible inheritance prevailed? Nineteenth and twentieth century data from most sources will show that in some cases women enjoyed the advantages of the Code and were treated like men. In other cases, however, they still received traditional unequal shares of the inheritance, which was detrimental to their well-being. Anyway, they were inclined to self-sacrifice and self-abnegation for the survival of the family house, the lineage, and the name in the community.

For the purpose of this demonstration, we will use 120 genealogies from six different villages scattered through the three French Basque provinces: four located in the highlands and two in the lowlands.[2] After selecting 120 couples married in the early 1800s (20 in each of the six villages constituting the first-generation cohort), we searched for their children and spouses (the second-generation cohort) and their grandchildren and spouses (the third-generation cohort) in the births, deaths, and marriages records of their village of birth and in all surrounding villages within a twenty-mile radius, as well as in those of Basque towns, surrounding Bearnais villages and towns, and the cities of Bayonne and Pau. This three-generational family reconstitution work has involved the tracing of the individual life experiences of about 3000 people in the rural Basque Country, in towns, in cities, and overseas between 1800 (for the 120 couples) and the 1990s (for the third-generation descendants).[3] We thus searched through the civil records of about 150 villages for two centuries (Arrizabalaga 1998, 323–328).

Next, the research involved the consultation of all public land registers available on the six villages of the sample and all neighboring villages (a total of 38 villages). We focused our attention on the official land registers *(Cadastre),*[4] where we traced the 120 couples' and their descendants' property and their value. In addition, we consulted their local inheritance

2 Family reconstitution involved the selection of 20 couples in each of the six villages in the three French Basque provinces: 20 couples in Sare (a mountain village in the province of Labourd), 20 couples in Aldudes and 20 couples in Mendive (two mountain villages in the province of Basse Navarre), 20 couples in Alçay (a mountain village in the province of Soule), 20 couples in Isturits, and 20 couples in Amendeuix (two lowland villages in the province of Basse Navarre). All these villages were distant and isolated from Bayonne, the provincial capital.

3 The third-generation children were born in the late nineteenth century or early twentieth century. Some of them died in the 1980s and 1990s. It was therefore necessary to consult archives until the late twentieth century.

4 *Cadastre. Matrice des propriétés foncières*, serie 3P3, Archives Départementales des Pyrénées-Atlantiques (ADPA). *Cadastre. Matrice des propriétés bâties*, serie 3P2, ADPA.

records (the *Enregistrement*),[5] which provide the official transcriptions of property settlements (with details on marriage contracts, dowries, testaments, deeds of gifts or *donations*), indicating families' assets, their value, and their distribution prior to and at death. Those records help to identify the single heir and to outline family strategies to benefit one child over the others and to keep the property undivided *(indivis)*. The data also show how the other children were compensated and to what they were entitled. The conclusions below which derive from the cross analysis of the above mentioned data, indicate the existence of gender differentiated treatment leading to unequal destinies.

Women and Impartible Inheritance within the Civil Code

Individual well-being was indeed a priority for Pyrenean families but the well-being of the house was perhaps more important, hence the impartibility of real estate, and unequal gender treatment. Though the law prevented families from transmitting patrimony unequally, Pyrenean families elaborated various complex strategies with the help of *notaires* in order to evade the law. Together they found legal means to perpetuate ancient unequal practices, transmitting the house and land to one child and compensating more or less equally the other children (less rather than more equally though).[6] The new strategies however imposed constraints. Children had to be self-effacing and accept concessions so that compensations appeared legal, equal and final. These strategies to avoid impoverishment after successive partitions and the sale of patrimony evolved into four

5 *Enregistrement. Mutation après décès*. Records from seven cantonal seats: Labastide-Clairence, Hasparren, Saint-Jean-de-Luz, Ustaritz, Saint-Etienne-de-Baïgorry, Saint-Jean-Pied-de-Port, Saint-Palais, Mauléon-Licharre. Serie Q, ADPA, 269 volumes. This research also involved the consultation of the notary records of four cantonal seats: Espelette, Saint-Etienne-de-Baïgorry, Saint-Jean-Pied-de-Port and Tardets, serie III E, ADPA. Yet, the notary records were often defective or incomplete.

6 Christine Lacanette-Pommel also shows how Bearnais families used the law to achieve impartible inheritance of real property. When disadvantaged, children sued the single heir for full equal compensation, especially daughters (2003).

stages. What were they and how did they affect women and their well-being?

The first stage to families' post-Civil Code succession strategies was to delay inheritance until the two spouses died. Parents needed time to both find the money to compensate their other children, secure each child's well-being, and avoid land partition. For that matter, parents postponed devolution and included reciprocal gifts in their marriage contracts. Each spouse owned the assets he or she brought into marriage, and both shared the ones acquired afterwards.[7] In addition, each spouse granted the survivor some rights over his or her own assets; the survivor received the ownership of all of them; or the ownership of half and the usufruct of half; or the usufruct of the whole. The couple thus ensured that control over all their assets would last until the death of the second spouse. Family property owners also worked with the *notaire* to legally transmit assets to one child and compensate the other children, more or less equally before the surviving parent's death. Other strategies were adopted to both acquire all the siblings' shares and to secure their well-being. The second stage consisted in selecting a single heir for the real estate assets and allowing him or her to marry into the house. Basque parents no longer limited their choice of heir to the first-born son or daughter (as in the past) but selected any of their children, irrespective of sex or birth order, to the point that more than half of the single heirs were daughters (Arrizabalaga 2002a; 2002b; 2004) (Table 1). At first glance, women did not seem to be discriminated against, as in other regions in the Pyrenees – Bearn,[8] the Baronies[9] – and even in Cantal.[10]

7 The 1804 Civil Code identified this as "régime de la communauté réduite aux acquêts". Each spouse owned his or her personal assets (property for the heir or heiress and the dowry for his or her spouse) and the two spouses together owned the assets (land or other assets) acquired during marriage.

8 In Bearn where male primogeniture had earlier prevailed, families also selected women as heiresses in the nineteenth century. According to Christine Lacanette-Pommel, one third of all single heirs were women in the early nineteenth century, and half in the mid nineteenth century, as a result of emigration (2003, 65, 119).

9 Rolande Bonnain argues that one third of the heirs in the Baronies in the nineteenth century were women in a region where male primogeniture had earlier prevailed (Bonnain 1996; Fauve-Chamoux 2003).

10 The same phenomenon seems to have taken place in Cantal. Rose Duroux argues that, due to emigration, more women in Cantal inherited the family assets over their broth-

Table 1. Heirs and heiresses among family property owners' children (second generation) and grand-children (third generation) in the nineteenth century. Percentages

	Second generation	*Third generation*
Heiresses	53.6	55.9
Heirs	46.4	44.1
Total	100	100
	(N=69)	(N=111)

Sources: From family reconstitutions, and the cross analysis of civil registers, land and succession registers as earlier described.

Contrary to the past, however, the heir or heiress did not inherit all family assets at marriage but only in steps. At marriage, the heir or heiress could only be granted an extra share *(préciput)* equal to one third when there were two children, and one quarter when there were three children or more (article 913 of the Civil Code). The value of this share was noted in the marriage contract. Thus the strategy consisted in selecting the single heir or heiress, allowing him or her to marry and stay into the house (Arrizabalaga 1997a) and securing him or her a greater share of family resources upon marriage. As families were usually large,[11] the heir or heiress received a *préciput* worth one quarter of the assets, not to be divided between the siblings. Subsequently, he or she found solutions to acquire the rest of the assets before the two parents died. For their part, the parents elaborated various strategies to compensate the other siblings or have them relinquish their shares of inheritance. In any case, upon marriage, the heir or heiress legally owned one quarter of the family patrimony and later he or she could anticipate acquiring his or her legal share of the assets (his or her share over the other three quarters which should be divided between all siblings). Thus, children were given unequal access to well-being, the preferred child being granted a greater share of the assets. Yet, as potential heirs, all received the same education or training, which they could then use to settle comfortably even when they did not inherit or marry an heir

ers who instead emigrated to Spain. Indeed, there were more than 60 percent heiresses (Duroux 2004).

11 In the first half of the century, there were four children in each family on average and three and a half in the second half of the century, hence the obligation to partition assets between at least three but often four children.

or heiress. What is certain is that these strategies were implemented exactly in the same way no matter the sex of the heir.[12]

In order to secure decent well-being to the other children, families had to elaborate additional strategies for both men and women, in the third stage of their inheritance strategies. They strove to acquire money to compensate the other children and allow them to marry into their social group (endogamous strategies) in the community or nearby. For that matter, families collected a dowry in cash upon marriage from the heir's or heiress' spouse, equal to the *préciput* (usually 25 percent of the assets) which they used to purchase 25 percent of the assets from the heir's or heiress' siblings. Thanks to this dowry, at least one sibling received assets to marry into a family of property owner within the same social group, which secured him or her equal well-being. In the process, the heir and the spouse were ensured to own more than half of the assets: a quarter share as *préciput*, another quarter share with the spouse's dowry, and the heir's or heiress' legal share (depending on the number of siblings). Yet children who were not privileged had to be compensated so that the heir or heiress could acquire the rest of the family assets (Arrizabalaga 2005b).[13]

The fourth stage consisted in elaborating yet other strategies to collect the remaining shares of the assets. Consequently, families either saved money or even borrowed money to provide the other siblings with compensation. They did so before the parents' death. By law, they were not obliged to compensate the excluded children before the parents' death. Yet, they often did so, providing them with assets when they were young and needed it the most. By doing so, they regained control of the other children's share early, and for less than their real value. As siblings needed help to settle down, they often accepted a lower compensation, especially women, as we will argue. In any case, siblings used their education as potential heirs and therefore their training as property managers as well as their early compensation to either marry into a family of equal status in the community or nearby. Otherwise women usually could mi-

12 Similar strategies were elaborated in other areas in France (Bonnain *et al.* 1992; Bouchard *et al.* 1998; Augustin 1989). In this manner, the stem family system survived the Revolution in the Pyrenees (Comas d'Argemir and Soulet 1993; Chiva and Goy 1981; 1986; Fauve-Chamoux 1984; 1987; 1993a; 1995; 2002; Fine-Souriac 1987; Fauve-Chamoux and Ochiai 1998).

13 Single inheritance was systematic. Only 10 percent of the family houses approximately were sold on the market, and only in cases of emigration, celibacy, death or indebtedness.

grate to cities while men usually could emigrate to America. In exchange for this early, yet lower, compensation, siblings signed deeds of gifts (*donation* acts), accepting parents' deals as a final compensation and promising never to demand additional compensation later. The heir and heiress thus collected most, if not all, the shares of the inheritance at a cheap price. In this process, families managed to get around the law to impose impartible inheritance of real property to the benefit of one child while compensating the other children more or less equally. It appears that these strategies secured equal treatment and well-being to the two oldest children, male and female alike (as heirs/heiresses or as heirs'/heiresses' spouses) but not to the younger ones, especially women (Arrizabalaga 2005a).

Family, Gender Specific Treatment of Heirs and Heiresses

Family reconstitutions indicate that, contrary to the Alps where only men inherited (Collomp 1983), in the Pyrenees, both men and women could be single heirs in the nineteenth and twentieth centuries. Similarly, others married heiresses or heirs (Fauve-Chamoux 2003; Fauve-Chamoux and Ochiai 1998), emigrated or married away (Bouchard *et al.* 1998; Segalen and Ravis-Giordani 1994; Lorenzetti *et al.* 2005). Yet, men and women were not treated equally. Women did not have the same access to property as men and they were not secured equal well-being. Furthermore, family reconstitutions, succession records, marriage contracts, *préciputs*, dowries, deeds of gifts (*donation* acts), and testaments indicate that women in the same position as men did not receive equal treatment, rights, and status. This was due to their sex and birth rank, and to specific marriage strategies, economic conditions, and family size.

Heirs, especially first-born heirs, seemed to be granted earlier and greater well-being than heiresses (even first-born ones) though both heirs and heiresses were apparently treated equally, receiving the same *préciput* or extra share of inheritance. The data show that women were not granted the power they hoped for in the family house as heiresses and had to wait until their father's death to acquire decision-making powers in the house.

Women's powers as heiresses were therefore probably not so strong as male heirs' during the parents' life time. Considering the number of first-born sons (about 20 percent) who relinquished headship, it seems that heirs also had difficulty enjoying the power position they hoped for within the house while fathers were alive but not so much as heiresses.

Heirs indeed enjoyed a higher status than heiresses (Arrizabalaga 2006b). They married within their social group or better: their marriage contracts indicate that their wives brought a dowry amounting to one quarter of the value of the family assets (equal to the *préciput*). These women sometimes came from large, wealthier families, but some other families could not find the money to provide their many children with a dowry to marry within their social group. They therefore had to marry lower-class heirs. Thus heirs' wives had greater chances to experience downward social mobility (Arrizabalaga 2005a). In the same way, heiresses sometimes married men of lower-status. As a result of massive male emigration within their social group or men's marriage into a wealthier family, heiresses, especially those of lower birth rank, married hard-working, thrifty lower-class laborers, even sharecroppers who had managed to save enough to collect a sizable cash dowry which allowed them to marry into a better-off propertied family. Marriages with sharecroppers were not looked at favorably in the community but families needed the money to compensate the departing siblings and therefore accepted them (Bourdieu 1962; 1972; 2002). The advantage was that parents were secured full authority in the house through life, having obedient, submissive heiresses and sons-in-law working for them.

Heiresses' husbands therefore had better marriage opportunities than heirs' wives. They had greater resources and therefore had greater chances of experiencing better destinies and upward social mobility. They received an adequate dowry from their parents and increased it through savings (in America perhaps) so that they could gather a larger dowry than their sisters and marry a wealthier heiress. Besides, they used the Civil Code to demand rights which heirs' wives at first did not obtain. They demanded co-ownership rights of their wives' inherited assets allowing their dowry to be incorporated into the family assets to compensate their wives' siblings (something heirs' wives and lower-class sons-in-laws could not obtain). That explains why so many first-born sons relinquished headship. They used their dowry and savings to marry into a wealthier family, forcing their parents-in-law to grant them co-ownership and therefore power in the house. Families accepted these deals, particularly in the second half of the nineteenth century, because they needed the sizable cash money which sons-in-law brought into the marriage as well as their full involvement and implication in the well-being of the family house.

The data clearly show that women did not enjoy such rights and powers for several reasons. Women could not save as men could and therefore were unable to collect a larger dowry than what their parents could give them. Besides they were not in a power position to demand co-ownership probably because of their "smaller" contribution to farm work.[14] When they received a dowry worth one quarter of the family assets (in families of three or more), women married an heir of equal status. But, contrary to men in the same position, they married and died owning their dowry only, though it had been invested into the family assets and used to purchase the heirs' siblings' shares of the inheritance. When women received a dowry worth less than the quarter share of the family assets (in families of four or more), they could only marry an heir of lower status. Thus unable to save money in the way their brothers could, they often experienced downward social mobility as they married beneath them. To make things worse, they did not obtain the right of co-ownership. Consequently, male heirs and heiresses' husbands remained in the same social strata or experienced upward social mobility, whereas heiresses and heirs' wives remained in the same strata or else knew downward social mobility. Women, therefore, no matter their position, were not secured equal treatment and equal well-being through marriage as men in equal positions. Among the remaining children, younger women were the ones who experienced the lower well-being because families often had difficulty collecting the money to compensate them, especially in large families (Arrizabalaga 2005a). What were the other children's destinies and well-being?

14 Men's and women's division of labor within the Basque house was such that men were responsible for land tasks and women for home tasks, which probably led parents to consider men's contribution in the house to be greater and more important than women's, though women did contribute to land tasks as well.

Children's Differentiated Treatment by Sex and Birth Order

Older sons and daughters were indeed settled rather comfortably as heirs or heiresses or as heirs' or heiresses' spouses,[15] yet these older sons sometimes envisioned other options. Rather than wait for the younger siblings' departure before marrying, they received their equal share of the inheritance and emigrated. They often had better destinies and social mobility in America. But younger children, especially women, had greater difficulty to do so well. Men used their dowry to marry into a family of property owner, while others accepted more respectable urban jobs (as civil servants, artisans or priests) or emigrated to America. They were given money to finance their voyages across the Atlantic Ocean and their settlement in America.[16] Once in America they generally fared well and encouraged their siblings, nieces and nephews to follow them, even paying for their transatlantic fares. Once in America, men often had a business (artisans, farmers or ranchers) and women married well-established immigrants (Arrizabalaga 2006c). Younger women in the family however were rarely given compensation before their parents' death. Even after the death of the parents, few were given compensations because the heir or heiress could not collect the money. Some refused to force the heir or heiress to get indebted and accepted to relinquish their rights to inheritance for the sake of the family house and line. In any case, by the time they were entitled to inheritance (after parents' death), they were often older women and already established more or less comfortably. As younger siblings, these women therefore did not have equal destinies and social mobility (Arrizabalaga 2003; 2005c). Their self-abnegation served the purpose of the family house and lineage. Contrary to some families in Bearn, they refused to force the sale of the family assets, especially when the value of their shares was less than 15 percent of the family assets (in families with five children or more). They were so devoted to the family that they accepted to give up their shares of the inheritance, signing a deed

15 Except when first-born sons or daughters had been conceived out of wedlock, had acted against parents' will, or had given birth to an illegitimate child.

16 They first settled in Argentina and Uruguay in the mid-nineteenth century, then in Chili and Mexico in the second half of the century, and finally in the United States and Canada around the turn of the century (Arrizabalaga 1996; 1997b; 2000).

of gifts (a *donation* act) or a last will *(testament)* in favor of the heir or heiress of the family house (or the one of the next generation).[17]

While men received a compensation (even at lower value) to emigrate to cities or more commonly to America, women sometimes received nothing. These women experienced downward social mobility whether it be in villages or cities. While some married down, with very modest property owners or landless farmers or artisans in the village, others remained single in the family house or in their village throughout their lives. Many however settled in cities where their education as potential heiresses and their capacity to make decisions were appreciated. They however only found low-paid unskilled jobs such as shop keepers or maids or skilled jobs as seamstresses or cooks and received wages that allowed them to live a decent, but not comfortable life (Arrizabalaga 2006d). In such circumstances, one may wonder why these single women did not marry in cities or join their successful brothers in America. It seems that, when they could not marry into their social group, they preferred celibacy and rarely America (Arrizabalaga 2007). Half of the women who settled in French cities remained single and experienced downward social mobility while the other half opted for exogamous marriage with rather well-off artisan property owners or civil servants who secured them upward social mobility (Arrizabalaga 2006b). Consequently, unmarried men and women were those who showed self-sacrifice and self-abnegation for the sake of the family house and lineage. Among them, men however did better than women (Arrizabalaga 2005d).

As the case studies below will show, families tried to treat sons and daughters rather equally but that was possible only when families were small, with only two or three children. Larger families had difficulty treating their children equally. The eldest, especially sons, enjoyed better well-being than the youngest, especially younger women.

17 Succession registers *(Enregistrement)* indicate that some single men and women were "indigent", owning nothing, not even their share of the inheritance. Actually they had earlier signed donation acts or testaments in favor of the heir or heiress of the house.

Case Studies of Inheritance and Marriage Strategies

Small-sized families were generally successful in treating their male and female children equally. Jean A. and Marie A. acquired 5 hectares of land in Alçay in the early nineteenth century. They had three children, Alexis (first-born), Pierre (second-born), and Marie (third-born). Pierre died a single man in 1847 before his parents' death. As only two children were left, inheritance was easy and smooth. Alexis received the larger share *(préciput)*, one third of the family assets when he married Elizabeth Q. who in turn brought a dowry of 2,375 francs. This money was then used to compensate Marie (second born) who married Jean A., the heir of a property of 16 hectares. Alexis thus inherited two thirds of the family assets, the *préciput* share and his legal share of the inheritance. He then bought back his sister's share with his wife's dowry. When he died, he owned all the family assets while his wife died owning her dowry only, though Alexis used his wife's money to compensate his sister for her share of the inheritance. Similarly, Marie, his sister, died owning her dowry only, though it had been used to compensate her husband's siblings. The only compensation that women received was the reciprocal deed of gifts *(donation mutuelle)* which was part of the marriage contract. As widows, they were secured the control of their husbands' assets until the next generation heir or heiress took over. Despite these concessions, women did not have complete equal access to property, never being guaranteed co-ownership of the husbands' assets, as the law required.

Families sometimes treated men and women unequally especially younger ones. Pierre H. and Marie E. owned a house and 12 hectares of land in Sare. They had four children, three of whom reached adulthood: Jeanne-Marie, their first-born daughter, Baptiste their second-born son, and Jean-Martin their third-born son. As a first-born child, Jeanne-Marie was selected as the heiress when she married Pierre Joseph E., the heir of a house and 22 hectares of land. It was unusual that two heirs married each other because neither of the two brought a dowry into the house. That might explain why Jeanne-Marie's two brothers never married and lived all their lives with her. When they died, the two brothers abandoned their shares of the inheritance to their sister. The couple maintained its status and did not merge the two inherited properties; Jeanne-Marie's two brothers taking care of her family's assets and her husband his family assets. In the next generation, however, the two properties were divided again. Jeanne-Marie and Pierre-Joseph had five children. Gracieuse, their first-born daughter, was excluded from inheritance because she had an illegitimate child and married a landless farmer in the community. Though she was later given a small property, she experienced downward social mobility. Pierre, the second-born son, inherited his mother's assets and Jeanne, the third-born daughter, inherited her father's assets, both maintaining their status. Jean-Martin, the fourth-born son, was given the money to emigrate to America where he fared well as a sheep owner and Jean-Léon, the fifth-born son, remained single at her sister's. None of the unmarried brothers demanded their legal shares of the inheritance. While Jean-Martin fared well, Jean-Léon experienced downward social mobility, as did his older sister, the one who had married without parental approval. In any case, what this case and others below indicate was that single inheritance and unequal well-being continued to prevail despite the law.

First-born children sometimes relinquished headship because they refused late marriages, having to wait until younger siblings departed from the house before marriage. Dominique and Marie H., the heiress of a property of eight hectares, had four children in Alçay in the early nineteenth century. While waiting for her siblings' departure, Marie, the first-born daughter, started her life as a servant in the nearby town of Tardets. There she married Pierre M., a professional driver and a civil servant who successively moved to the towns of Saint-Jean-Pied-de-Port and Saint-Palais. She therefore had to renounce headship and probably received a dowry, a sum in exchange for her share of the inheritance. She then lived a decent life in town. Her second-born brother, Pierre, also refused headship, preferring a life of subordination and service as a celibate in the house. He later left his share of the inheritance to the heiress. Catherine, the third-born daughter, established herself in Pau where she was employed as a maid. There she met a civil servant (a postman) and lived a quite decent life. Engrace, the fourth-born daughter, was the one who inherited the family assets when she married Philippe A., the son of a local family property owner. The latter brought a dowry of 1,500 francs into the marriage while Engrace received the *préciput* share worth one fourth of the family assets. Philippe's dowry was used to compensate the two sisters or to pay back the debts due to their compensations. Together Engrace and Philippe controlled half of the assets (the *préciput* and the quarter share acquired with the dowry), to which was added Engrace's legal share (19 percent of the shares). As Pierre later donated his 19 percent share, the couple controlled 88 percent of the assets. They then had time to get the rest of the shares. Upon marriage, Engrace and Philippe signed reciprocal deeds of gifts to keep the assets together over time. In the next generation, inheritance decisions were easy as Engrace and Philippe had three children. Marie, the first-born daughter, and Pierre, the third-born son, emigrated to America. Pierre, the second-born son, inherited all the family assets. Before departing to America, the siblings received compensations and signed deeds of gifts in Pierre's favor.

Heiresses' husbands' legal rights were indeed more respected than heirs' wives'. Dominique I. married an heiress, Marie H., and used the Civil Code to enforce his rights. Upon marriage, he brought a dowry of 399 francs which was later used to buy some of his wife's shares of the inheritance. As a compensation for his dowry, he demanded the management and the co-ownership in the family farm. In addition, the couple acquired more land throughout their life (which doubled the size of the family assets), making Dominique and Marie co-owners of most of the assets. In the next generation, Engrace, the heiress, inherited the extra quarter share of the family assets *(préciput)* upon marriage and her husband, Philippe A., brought a dowry worth 1,500 francs. In addition, he bought most of Engrace's siblings' shares of the inheritance, worth 3,550 francs. When he died, he declared himself co-owner of the assets which came from his wife's parents. Women did not enjoy such rights when they married heirs however. Indeed, Marie B. married Raimond E., an heir from Alçay. Marie brought 3,550 francs as a dowry into her marriage, to be invested into the property. The dowry however brought her nothing. When she died in 1842, she only owned her dowry, not an unusual case, it seems.

Inequalities indeed prevailed between heirs and their spouses, but they also prevailed between older and younger siblings. Dominique J. inherited his parents' property (eight hectares) when he married Marie N. in the early nineteenth century. The latter brought a dowry of 750 francs which was then used to pay back Dominique's debts (due to earlier compensations). As debt payments were made in the presence of a notary, Dominique was forced to make Marie co-owner of the inherited assets. This was a rare case. The couple had four children, who were not treated equally. Brigitte, the first-born daughter, was the single heiress as she received an extra *préciput* share worth one quarter of the assets upon her marriage with Pierre B. who in turn brought a dowry worth 1,620 francs. The dowry was probably not used to compensate Marie, the second-born daughter, when she married and emigrated to Montevideo (Uruguay), but it certainly allowed Brigitte to constitute Raimond's dowry (1,400 francs) to marry Marguerite E., an heiress. With this dowry, Raymond, the third-born son, later purchased Marguerite's siblings' shares of the inheritance and became co-owner of his wife's inherited property. The first three children were socially stable, marrying into their social group and maintaining their social status. Simone, the forth-born daughter, however, did not do so well. She worked as a weaver throughout her life and married a landless farmer. She therefore experienced downward social mobility. She was unable or unwilling to get her share of the inheritance and therefore died "indigent" (owning no assets).

Among the few very wealthy families, equal compensation was impossible without partition. In these rare occasions, the older children received better treatment than the younger children, especially women. Dominique and Jeanne acquired several houses and 100 hectares of land through their life in Isturits. Jeanne was the heiress of several houses and land worth 199,700 francs. Dominique brought a dowry of 15,000 francs into the marriage. In addition, he possessed 78,000 francs which he used to acquire his wife's siblings' shares of the inheritance in his name. He bought two of his wife's sisters' shares of the inheritance, worth 20,000 francs each, and later acquired additional land. Before marriage, they signed a contract which stated that each owned their personal assets and inherited property and co-owned the assets acquired during their married life. By the time Dominique died, one child had received a quarter share (the *préciput*) and his wife a quarter of the assets in usufruct. Together they controlled the assets and blocked partition. The problem was that there were ten children to establish, all of whom survived adulthood. Partition became inevitable in this case. Each of the three oldest children inherited a house and 30 hectares of land. The younger children received a compensation which was smaller than their legal share, yet the compensation was decent enough. However they could not marry into their social group. Actually, six of them remained single. In the end, Joannes, the first-born son, received 4,000 francs as a dowry to marry an heiress who eventually inherited her family's property of 23 hectares. Gracieuse, the second-born daughter, never married but received a dowry which was large enough to allow her to live in the town of Hasparren as a self-supported retired person. When she died, she left her property to the family's heir. Jean-Baptiste, the third-born son, received a dowry (6,000 francs) which he used to marry the heiress of 33 hectares. Pierre, the fourth-born son, used his compensation to emigrate to Cuba where he became a merchant and died unmarried. Pierre, the fifth-born son, is the one who inherited his parents' house with 28 hectares of land. His wife brought 6,200 francs as a dowry. The five next children, Baptiste, Jean, Jeanne, Dominica, and Gratianne received a compensation for their share of the inheritance, the men emigrated to America where they became merchants and the women entered convents. Celibacy among seven out of the ten children thus allowed the three oldest children to settle comfortably while their younger siblings sacrificed marriage for the sake of traditions and of the family. While the men enjoyed great freedom of movement and upward social mobility in America, the women entered convents to avoid down marriages. More than the men, the women were the ones who sacrificed their life for single inheritance, for the house, for the family and therefore experienced downward social mobility, even in well-to-do families.

Conclusion

As inheritance and marriage practices in the Pyrenees – and in the Basque Country in particular – show, women were probably treated more favorably than in other places in France because, contrary to other areas, women could become heiresses even when they had older and younger brothers. Furthermore, when families were small, men and women were treated equally and parents had the money and willingness to do so. A closer analysis of the data however indicates that women were actually treated unequally in the same position as men and especially in large-sized families. In such families, inequalities also prevailed between older and younger children and between men and women. Though all men and women in propertied families received an education as potential heirs or heiresses, men had greater access to ownership than women, often receiving a larger dowry than their sisters. Even when men and women were given equal opportunity and ownership, they did not enjoy the same rights or powers and therefore had different destinies. Contrary to heirs, heiresses had to obey parents until they died and later share decision-making powers with their husbands. Besides, some occasionally married lower-status men but never wealthier heirs. Consequently, older sons experienced upward social mobility more often than older daughters in the same position. Younger daughters had to do with their dowries, which, when the family was large, amounted only to a small portion of the assets, only enough to marry smaller farmers or sharecroppers. Those younger daughters consequently experienced downward social mobility more often than younger sons.

When men and women neither inherited nor married heirs, their destiny and social mobility were sometimes unfavorable, especially for women. Rather than accept downwardly mobile marriages, some remained single, whether in the native village or in cities. Others finally improved their status by marrying out of their social group (exogamous marriage practices), with civil servants or artisan property owners in towns or cities. They could have gone to America where their brothers fared well but few did. They instead remained single as unskilled employees capable of supporting themselves as self-sustained independent women. Men who did not inherit or marry an heiress generally emigrated to America where they often fared well, some remaining single rather than marrying outside their cultural group, with the hope perhaps to return home. Others married before settling in America permanently. In any case, for these men and women, status was maintained or improved through marriage and emigration to America and through exogamous marriage with civil servants or male property owners in cities. It is clear that, despite parents' efforts, some forms of inequalities prevailed. Children seemed to accept these inequalities, willingly or unwillingly, never forcing land partition. Their self-abnegation has secured the survival of the Pyrenean house system until today.

References

ARRIZABALAGA, Marie-Pierre, 1996, "Réseaux et choix migratoires au Pays Basque. L'exemple de Sare au XIXe siècle", *Annales de démographie historique*, pp. 423–446.

–, 1997a, "The stem family in the French Basque Country: Sare in the nineteenth century", *Journal of Family History*, 22, 1, pp. 50–69.
–, 1997b, "Structures familiales et destins migratoires à Sare au XIXe siècle", *Lapurdum*, II, pp. 237–255.
–, 2000, "Les Basques dans l'Ouest américain, 1900–1910", *Lapurdum*, V, pp. 335–350.
–, 2002a, "Female primogeniture in the French Basque Country", in Emiko OCHIAI (ed.), *The Logic of Female Succession: Rethinking Patriarchy and Patrilineality in Global and Historical Perspective*, Kyoto, International Research Center of Japanese Studies, pp. 31–52.
–, 2002b, "Les héritières de la maison au Pays Basque au XIXe siècle", *Lapurdum*, VII, pp. 35–55.
–, 2003, "Comment le marché de l'emploi national et international a-t-il influencé les destins individuels au sein de familles basques et les modalités de transmission du patrimoine au XIXe siècle?", in Christian DESSUREAULT, John DICKINSON and Joseph GOY (eds), *Famille et marché (XVIe–XXe siècles)*, Sillery (Québec), Septentrion, pp. 183–198.
–, 2004, "Stratégies de l'indivision et rapport à la terre après le Code civil: le cas basque au XIXe siècle", in Gérard BEAUR, Christian DESSUREAULT and Joseph GOY (eds), *Familles, terre, marchés. Logiques économiques et stratégies dans les milieux ruraux (XVIIe–XXe siècles)*, Rennes, Presses Universitaires de Rennes, pp. 171–183.
–, 2005a, "Pyrenean marriage strategies in the nineteenth century: the Basque case", *IRSH*, 50, pp. 93–122.
–, 2005b, "Succession strategies in the Pyrenees in the 19th century. The Basque case", *The History of the Family: an International Quarterly*, 10, 3, pp. 271–292.
–, 2005c, "Migrations féminines – migrations masculines: des comportements différenciés au sein des familles basques au XIXe siècle", in Luigi LORENZETTI, Anne-Lise HEAD-KONIG and Joseph GOY (eds), *Marchés, migrations et logiques familiales dans les espaces français, canadien et suisse, 18e-20e siècles*, Bern, Peter Lang, pp. 183–195.
–, 2005d, "Basque women and migration in the nineteenth century", *The History of th Family. An International Quarterly*, 10, 2, pp. 99–117.
–, 2006a, "Destins de femmes dans les Pyrénées au XIXe siècle: le cas basque", *Annales de Démographie Historique. Itinéraires féminins*, 2, pp. 135–170.
–, 2006b, "Droits, pouvoirs et devoirs dans la maison: la place des hommes et des femmes au sein des familles basques depuis le XIXe siècle", *Vasconia*, 35, pp. 155–183.
–, 2006c, "Urban Migrants and Domesticity in the 19th Century: the Basque Case", in Suzy PASLEAU, Isabelle SCHOPP with Raffaella SARTI (eds), *Proceedings of the Servant Project*, Vol. IV, Liège, Editions de l'Université de Liège, pp. 303–327.
–, 2007a, "Les femmes pyrénéennes et l'émigration transatlantique aux XIXe et XXe siècles: une réalité mal connue", in Natacha LILLO and Philippe RYGIEL (eds), *Rapports sociaux de sexe et immigration. Mondes atlantiques, XIXe–XXe siècles*, Paris, Publibook, pp. 59–70.
–, 2007b, "L'émigration des Pyrénéennes en Amérique du Nord aux XIXe–XXe siècles", in Marie-Pierre ARRIZABALAGA (ed.), "Les femmes et l'émigration en Amérique

Nord/Women and Emigration to North America", *Histoire sociale/Social History*, special issue, 40, 80, pp. 269–295.

ASSIER-ANDRIEU, Louis, 1981, *Coutume et rapports sociaux. Etude anthropologique des communautés paysannes du Capcir*, Paris, Editions du CNRS.

–, (ed.), 1990, *Une France coutumière. Enquête sur les "usages locaux" et leur codification (XIXe–XXe siècles)*, Paris, Editions du CNRS.

AUGUSTINS, Georges, 1989, *Comment se perpétuer? Devenir des lignées et destins des patrimoines dans les paysanneries européennes*, Nanterre, Société d'ethnologie française.

BEAUR, Gérard, 2004, "Land transmission and inheritance practices in France during the Ancien Régime: differences of degree and kind?", in David R. GREEN and Alastair OWENS (eds), *Family Welfare. Gender, Property, and Inheritance since the Seventeenth century*, London, Praeger, pp. 31–46.

BEAUR, Gérard, DESSUREAULT, Christian and GOY, Joseph (eds), 2004, *Familles, terre, marchés. Logiques économiques et stratégies dans les milieux ruraux (XVIIe–XXe siècles)*, Rennes, Presses Universitaires de Rennes.

BONNAIN, Rolande, 1996, "Houses, heirs and non-heirs in the Adour Valley. Social and geographic mobility in the nineteenth century", *The History of the Family: an International Quarterly*, 1, 3, pp. 273–296.

BONNAIN, Rolande, BOUCHARD, Gérard and GOY, Joseph (eds), 1992, *Transmettre, hériter, succéder. La reproduction familiale en milieu rural: France – Québec, XVIIIe–XXe siècles*, Lyon, Presses Universitaires de Lyon.

BOUCHARD, Gérard, DICKINSON, John and GOY, Joseph (eds), 1998, *Les Exclus de la terre en France et au Québec (XVIIe–XXe siècles). La reproduction familiale dans la différence*, Sillery (Québec), Septentrion.

BOUCHARD, Gérard, GOY, Joseph and HEAD-KONIG, Anne-Lise (eds), 1998, *Problèmes de la transmission des exploitations agricoles (XVIIIe–XXe siècles)*, Rome, Editions de l'Ecole Française de Rome.

BOURDIEU, Pierre, 1962, "Célibat et condition paysanne", *Etudes rurales*, 5–6, pp. 32–135.

–, 1972, "Les stratégies matrimoniales dans le système de reproduction", *Annales E.S.C.*, 27, 4–5, pp. 1105–1127.

–, 2002, *Le Bal des célibataires. Crise de la société paysanne en Béarn*, Paris, Seuil.

CHENU, Alain (ed.), 1994, *Les Mélouga, une famille pyrénéenne au XIXe siècle* (textes choisis de F. Le Play *et al.*), Paris, Nathan.

CHIVA, Isaac and GOY, Joseph (eds), 1981, *Les Baronnies des Pyrénées. Maisons, mode de vie, société*, Tome I, Paris, Editions de l'EHESS.

–, 1986, *Les Baronnies des Pyrénées. Maisons, espace, famille*, Tome II, Paris, Editions de l'EHESS.

COLLOMP, Alain, 1983, *La Maison du père. Famille et village en Haute-Provence aux XVIIe et XVIIIe siècles*, Paris, Presses Universitaires de France.

CORDIER, Eugène, 1859, *Droit aux Pyrénées. Barèges, Lavedan, Béarn et Pays Basque*, Paris, A. Durand.

COMAS D'ARGEMIR, Dolors and SOULET, Jean-François (eds), 1993, *La familía als Pirineus*, Andorre, Impremta Solber.

De CHARNISAY, Henry, 1996, *L'émigration basco-béarnaise en Amérique*, ré-édition, Biarritz, J. and D. Editions.

DUROUX, Rose, 2004, "Emigration, gender, and inheritance: a case study of the High Auvergne, 1700–1900", in David R. GREEN and Alastair OWENS (eds), *Family Welfare. Gender, Property, and Inheritance since the Seventeenth century*, London, Praeger, pp. 47–71.

FAUVE-CHAMOUX, Antoinette, 1984, "Les structures familiales au royaume des familles-souches: Esparros", *Annales E.S.C.*, 39, 3, pp. 513–528.

–, 1987, "Le fonctionnement de la famille-souche dans les Baronnies des Pyrénées avant 1914", *Annales de démographie historique*, pp. 241–262.

–, 1993a, "Les frontières de l'autorégulation paysanne: croissance et famille-souche", *Revue de la Bibliothèque Nationale*, 50, pp. 38–47.

–, 1993b, "Household forms and living standards in preindustrial France: from models to realities", *Journal of Family History*, 18, 2, pp. 135–156.

–, 1995, "The stem family, demography and inheritance: the social frontiers of auto-regulation", in Richard L. RUDOLF (ed.), *The European Peasant Family and Society*, Liverpool, Liverpool University Press, pp. 86–113.

–, 1998, "La reproduction familiale en milieu paysan: le destin des exclus", in Gérard BOUCHARD, John DICKINSON and Joseph GOY (eds), *Les Exclus de la terre en France et au Québec (XVIIe–XXe siècles). La reproduction familiale dans la différence*, Sillery (Québec), Septentrion, pp. 73–91.

–, 2002, "Strategies of household continuity in a stem-family society: from heirship to headship", in Renzo DEROSAS and Michel ORIS (eds), *When Dad Died – Individuals and Families Coping with Distress in Past Societies*, Bern, Peter Lang, pp. 121–139.

–, 2003, "Le rôle des femmes dans la transmission des biens en France", in Christian DESSUREAULT, John DICKINSON and Joseph GOY (eds), *Famille et marché (XVIe–XXe siècles)*, Sillery (Québec), Septentrion, pp. 245–260.

FAUVE-CHAMOUX, Antoinette and OCHIAI, Emiko (eds), 1998, *House and the Stem Family in EurAsian Perspective*, Kyoto, Nichibunken/ International Research Center for Japanese Studies.

FAUVE-CHAMOUX, Antoinette and OCHIAI, Emiko (eds), 2009, *The Stem Family in Eurasian Perspective. Revisiting House Societies, 17th–20th centuries*, Bern, Peter Lang.

FINE-SOURIAC, Agnès, 1987, "La famille-souche pyrénéenne au XIXe siècle. Quelques réflexions de méthode", *Annales E.S.C.*, 42, 3, pp. 478–487.

FOUGERES, Alain, 1938, *Les droits de famille et les successions au Pays Basque et en Béarn d'après les anciens textes*, Bergerac, H. Trillaud.

GREEN, David R. and OWENS, Alastair (eds), 2004, *Family Welfare. Gender, Property, and Inheritance since the Seventeenth century*, London, Praeger.

LACANETTE-POMMEL, Christine, 2003, *La famille dans les Pyrénées. De la coutume au code Napoléon*, Estadens, PyréGraph.

LAFOURCADE, Maïté, 1989, *Mariages en Labourd sous l'Ancien Régime. Les contrats de mariage du pays de Labourd sous le règne de Louis XVI*, Bilbao, Universitad del País Vasco.

LE PLAY, Frédéric, 1871, *L'Organisation de la famille selon le vrai modèle signalé par l'histoire de toutes les races et de tous les temps*, Paris, Tequi.

–, 1878, *La Réforme sociale en France déduite de l'observation comparée des peuples européens*, 3 volumes, Paris, Dentu.

LE ROY LADURIE, Emmanuel, 1972, "Système de la coutume. Structures familiales et coutumes d'héritage en France au XVIe siècle", *Annales E.S.C.*, 27, 4–5, pp. 825–846.

LORENZETTI, Luigi, HEAD-KONIG, Anne-Lise and GOY, Joseph (eds), 2005, *Marchés, migrations et logiques familiales dans les espaces français, canadien et suisse, 18e–20e siècles,* Bern, Peter Lang.

MEHATS, Claude, 2005, *Organisation et aspects de l'émigration des Basques de France en Amérique: 1832–1976*, Vitoria-Gasteiz, Gobierno Vasco.

POUMAREDE, Jacques, 1972, *Les Successions dans le Sud-Ouest de la France au Moyen Age*, Paris, Presses Universitaires de France.

SEGALEN, Martine, 1985, *Quinze générations de Bas-Bretons. Parenté et société dans le Pays Bigouden Sud, 1720–1980*, Paris, Presses Universitaires de France.

SEGALEN, Martine and RAVIS-GIORDANI, Georges (eds), 1994, *Les Cadets*, Paris, CNRS Editions.

YVER, Jean, 1966, *Egalité entre héritiers et exclusion des enfants dotés: essai de géographie coutumière*, Paris, Editions Sirey.

ZINK, Anne, 1993, *L'héritier de la maison. Géographie coutumière du Sud-Ouest de la France sous l'Ancien Régime*, Paris, EHESS.

Consanguineous Marriages as a Strategy of Well-Being

An Example from 19th Century Alto Minho

Emília LAGIDO

Over the last few decades, the family has been the focus of several studies that, in a diversified, anthropological, sociological and, above all, historical perspective, have led to a general and, at the same time, particular view, of the domestic group. This range of studies has been motivated by the fact that within the family – the basic operating cell of social organisation –, a series of phenomena converge, including demographic, economic, cultural, consuetudinary and those of power structure, while the system is reproduced and continued (Chacon 1992, 14). It is in this sense that relations between marriage, family structure and the rules for forming distinct domestic units seem so important.

Demographic and social factors are conditional for the constitution of marriage alliances that are very often consanguineous, in the past as well as in the present. However, in the case of Portugal, there are few studies on matrimonial consanguinity. This theme, common for anthropologists (Lévi-Strauss 1967), is rarer for historians, who incline more towards the perpetuation of aristocratic lineage rather than the consanguinity in rural households (Monteiro 2007; Cunha 2000). In Portugal, references to this kind of marital alliance appear in some demographic studies.[1] In this study, we aim to determine the importance of cross-cousin marriage in two rural locations of Alto Minho, Santa Maria de Âncora and Santa Maria da Vinha de Areosa, where, in the 19th century, land was a scarce and dispersed resource that had to be preserved.

1 See studies published by the *Núcleo de Estudos de População e Sociedade* (NEPS), *Instituto de Ciências Sociais* of University of Minho. A deep analysis of consanguineous marriages is rarely possible in the past.

These two localities are examples of a society where the men have a principal role, but when they are absent for long periods, the women, even though defined as the weaker sex, often deal with family succession and pursue marriage strategies which made possible the maintenance of most unbroken property (Bretell 1991). Land is, in Alto Minho, a desirable target, being based on the familial economy of domestic production. Given the pressure on this source of wealth and the impossibility of social mobility, the solution for many *minhotos* (inhabitants of rural Minho) was to depart to other localities to relieve the pressure on the land in order to prevent its dispersal. Noted in innumerable sources since remote times, this emigration prevented one problem, but caused others, for example the lack of men to contract marriages and the channelling of decision-making power to females.

Taking these aspects into consideration, we intend with the present study to analyse the factors that led to consanguineous marriages. We shall measure the frequency of this form of marriage and evaluate to what extent it may be interpreted as a strategy for maintaining family wealth and well-being.

Normative Context and Marriage Prohibitions for Kinship and Affinity

Obviously, marriage is an individual act, but it is also conditional on the economic situation of the family, the dynamics of the social group in which the family is embedded, and the cultural norms surrounding marriage. With respect to these norms, we need to distinguish between the agricultural and the religious world. Since the Council of Trent, the Church was responsible for standardizing the procedures regulating the obtaining of marriage dispensation. "Marrying when and whom and delegating certain things to certain individuals were issues in which the State and the Church played an important role as standardizers of procedures" (Scott 1999, 167).

Since the fourth century, the Catholic Church promulgated a set of prohibitions for marriage between relatives. However, with the relaxation that occurred in the tenth century, reforms became necessary that established the refusal of marriage between relatives until the seventh degree of kinship. In the eleventh century, the ecclesiastical reforms of the Gregorian movement increased the jurisdiction of the Church on marriage, and defined the forbidden degrees of alliance, which among others insisted on the consent of the contractors (Gouesse 1986).

After the Council of Lateran of 1215, this situation was changed, and the degree of kinship was reduced to the fourth level[2] at the same time that it increased the severity of the evidence necessary to establish the legalities of these alliances. Apart from the aforementioned kinship between blood relatives, spiritual kinship or affinity was also forbidden: an impediment to marriage existed between the godfather or the godmother (at baptism or confirmation) on the one hand, the godchild or his/her father and mother on the other, as well as the godchild and the children of the godfather or godmother (Goody 1983). Affinity and kinship through marriage were evaluated and counted by degrees, like natural kinship, and marriage was impeded up to the fourth degree. Nevertheless, reconciling the "rigour of the law" with the "mercy that is due to people", the Pope reserved the possibility of conceding dispensations allowing in particular marriages between relatives and in-laws in the third and fourth degree. In this way, the Holy See or its delegates could dispense from the impediments of ecclesiastical or Canon law.

In the meeting of the prelates during the Council of Trent (1545–1563), marriage was again subject to regulations. However, the new resolutions inferred clearly that it was sufficiently easy to get dismissal for the marriage in third degree if "enough cause" existed. The release was a form admitted to profile the prohibitions and also provided to the Church the control (and the attainment of incomes) of the marriage that was in disagreement with its formal norms, norms that, in their extreme formularization, promulgated in the eleventh century, seemed to have deliberately been done to be transgressed (Goody 1983, 132). In the following centuries, the situation evolved and the number of dispensations increased, though, in the case of the aristocracy, they were considered "almost" normal. That is why there are a greater number of studies on this question for the aristocracy.

2 If we match the canon degree to a generation, prohibition in the fourth degree takes into account individuals that share a great-great-grandparent.

In Portugal, the legislation that actually regulated the procedure to obtain marriage dispensation was the synodal constitutions, a product of the Diocesan Synods, or rather the Diocesan Synods of Braga. For the 19th century, the set of religious precepts that governed Minhotan marriages were the *Synodal Constitutions of the Archbishopric of Braga,* of D. Sebastião de Matos e Noronha published by D. João de Sousa in 1697, which were in force until the year 1919.

Within this normative set – which is not specific to Portugal – there are "diriment impediments" and "prohibitory impediments". Diriment impediments, which can be overcome by means of a dispensation, are, for kinship and affinities and for "public honesty". According to this last impediment, a *fiancé* could not, after breaking an engagement, contract marriage with a relative of his former *fiancée.*

In their Chapter 9, *The Synodal Constitutions of the Archbishopric of Braga* regulated dispensations concerning *the Sacrament of Matrimony.* This included Constitution II, dealing with *The impediments that prohibit and annul matrimony and those that only impede,* where marriage dispensations were included in the group of diriment impediments. These are: having kinship up to the 4th degree and having kinship up to the 4th degree of lawful affinity. If the affinity is unlawful, it does not go beyond the 2d degree; having legal kinship comes from any kind of adoption. Constitution XI, subordinate to the Chapter *Of those that marry or become betrothed knowing that there is an impediment,* is a chapter that deals with the penalties for those who, knowing that they were related, contracted marriage and those who, having requested dispensation, had sexual relations before being dispensed.

Historical Sources

To discover the importance of consanguinity in the aforementioned two parishes of Alto Minho – Santa Maria de Âncora and Santa Maria da Vinha de Areosa –, we used as main source the marriage dispensations, a documentation that belongs to the ecclesiastical records of the District Archives of Braga. The records were started in 1660. Before 1820 the documentation is extremely scarce but it greatly increased as the 19th century progressed. Therefore, the present study was carried out only for the nineteenth century.

Various problems arise from the analysis of this documentation. First, the lack of cataloguing makes consultation difficult. Second, we note a difficulty of quantification: we suspect that part of the documentation was sold to pay the Mitra expenses[3] that, in a period of monetary shortage, were aided by the sale of documents to pay for current expenses. Lastly, we need to use the source with some precaution due to both the stereotypical answers given by future brides and grooms to facilitate obtaining the dispensation and to the brevity of the writers. This is particularly clear in Âncora compared to other parishes such as Areosa, obliging us to consult also the parish registers which recorded local marriages.

Still, even though we have only access to thirty-seven request files for dispensation of the community of Santa Maria de Âncora and sixty-four of Areosa, we consider that this documentation contains valuable information. The marriage dismissals are precious pieces of documentation, that allow us to understand the nature of the consanguineous impediments as well as the motivations of the future wives to request such dismissals to the archbishopric of Braga although incurring a long and expensive period of waiting.

This source material allows a social study of consanguinity; we are able to explain and understand the reasons for choosing a partner to whom one was already related – these reasons can be economic, spatial and social. At the same time, the process of requesting dismissal of the degrees of kindred of consanguinity and affinity revealed the role played by the Church. The set of prohibitions demonstrated the Churches' desire to hinder or to reduce endogamy. In agricultural families, endogamy was high, and there were scarce offers of marriage.

How did the process of requesting for matrimonial dispensation work? According to Isidro Dubert, "once the theoretical possibilities of finding a spouse without family ties have run out, the request for dispensation is used" (Dubert 1989, 169). In this way, in some request files, the names were listed of the single and/or widowed males from the place where the betrothed lived, persons who had no kinship with the future bride and the reason why they did not serve as a matrimonial partner. These justifications range from age difference to social position and include physical defects.

3 Paying ceremonies when a new bishop was appointed.

In order to ask for a marriage dispensation, the following documents needed to be gathered before going to Braga: Front page; Petition; Apostolic Brief; Justifications of the brief; Commission; Letter of excommunication; Matrimonial Justifications and Declaration of the parish priest.

The following step of the process consisted of sending to the parish, by the synodal examiner and provisor in the entire archbishopric, a Commission that was responsible for ascertaining the truth of the declarations made by the petitioning betrothed couple from the neighbours. This procedure is outlined in the *Synodal Constitutions of the Archbishopric of Braga,* in Chapter XVI, *That our provisor, general vicar and those of the districts in matrimonial issues question the parties and examine the witnesses for themselves.* This constitution regulated the process of inquiry of the supplicants and the witnesses and could be systematized in the following way:

- The provisor, general vicar or marriage judge or those of the district, at the beginning of any matrimonial process, asked successive questions to the plaintiff and the defendant, to ascertain the truth;
- The witnesses gave statements;
- It was possible that this procedure be handed to some of the district vicars;
- The causes for the dispensation would have to be legitimate and urgent.

Five adequate witnesses were convened for the purpose, generally of an advanced age. After being sworn in, they had to answer questions and to reconstruct the family genealogies of the supplicants, from the branch to which they belong. The next step consisted of questioning the petitioning betrothed and, finally, of analysing the different reasons that lead to the petition, with the parish priest summarily testifying to the truth of the claims that there is no family interference. This process for obtaining matrimonial dispensation was similar to the one observed in Galicia, as Isidro Dubert described it.

> This inquiry apparatus has a dual objective: to avoid the falsification of witnesses and to dissuade other couples, thus seeking to maintain the prominence of the Christian matrimonial model. For this reason, the Church does not neglect the warning, taking advantage of any occasion, about the spiritual and moral risk that this kind of bond supposes, and its concern becomes clear from later dates through

literature of a preventive nature originating from the celebration of the different ecclesiastical Synods (Dubert 1989, 170).

We shall consider now how often parishioners of the two villages under study decided to engage themselves in this procedure.

Understanding Endogamous Marriages in Alto Minho

The first village, Santa Maria de Âncora is an agricultural community situated in the North of Alto Minho that, after the municipality redefinition in 1836, passed from the council of Viana to the council of Caminha. It is delimited by the river Âncora, the mount of Tarrugem and the sea (Figure 1).

In this northern Portugal community, during the 19th century, nuptiality was restricted by a series of constraints of social and economic nature, including the constant imbalance in the matrimonial market, originating mainly from the considerable mobility of males, high ratio of celibacy and delayed marriage. To these characteristics, scarcity of land should be added. Land availability and land owning affected the social and economic rank of a new family *nucleus*. All over Minho, land was extremely divided in small plots – a characteristic of the *minhota* landscape – therefore owning land was a condition for any social upward mobility and a guaranty of family well-being. With the objective to acquire land, an important number of men left their parish to obtain enough savings. Interestingly, in Alto Minho, mobile men specialised in stone masonry, "exporting" this knowledge to other regions of the Portuguese kingdom and foreign countries, particularly to Spain (Castile, Andalusia) and Brazil. While men were absent, women took the rein of "their home" and substituted men in the power to decide and in the work on the properties they were acquiring (Bretell 1991).

Figure 1. Location of the two localities under study in Alto Minho: Santa Maria de Âncora, in the North, and Santa Maria da Vinha de Areosa, closer to Viana do Castelo

Beyond male migration, other strategies have been adopted by families because it was necessary to acquire and to keep landed property. Among these strategies we stress geographic endogamy, consanguineous marriages, delay in the age of first marriage, the limitation of second marriages and high levels of celibacy. These behaviours influenced human reproduction levels and also economic and social reproduction.

Gérard Delille (1994, 323–340) considered marriage between relatives a general phenomenon in Europe during the Early Modern Period, mainly in three zones: South of Italy and Sicily, South of Iberian Peninsula and Northwest France. Alto Minho could probably be added to this group. Indeed, Areosa is closer to Viana do Castelo than the previous community under study, but Areosa presented similar demographic characteristics, while the social structure was rather different: there was a larger proportion of farmers and servants, and less land owners than in Santa Maria de Âncora. Men were frequently absent, which led to power being often in female's hands. This situation is noticeable in testamentary wills, where we found a great number of wills of "common hand"[4] registered by married couples at that time. Besides, it was common that couples decided to leave the free "third" part *(terço)* of their inheritance to their children.[5]

Between the cases that mark the preference for the children in order to secure the continuity of their "house", we noticed some strange decisions. For example, João Gonçalves, in 1741, sick and dying, asked for a parish priest to write a will. Then he declared that he had a daughter and that his wife, to whom he decided to leave the full usufruct of the "third" part, was pregnant. After the father's death, if the posthumous child was a male, the daughter would get the full property of the third part, but, from her inherited property she should give 30,000 *reis* to her younger brother. On the contrary, if the posthumous child happened to be a female, then the older daughter would only inherit half of the third part *(terco)*, the other half part becoming the full property of the younger daughter (Durães 2006, 11). This gender difference used to play a great role in Alto Minho when family transmission was at stake.

Although the nineteenth century was a time of demographic growth (without major demographic crises), we notice that, in the localities under study, this population growth occurred in a very weak way, a situation that can be explained by permanent strong out-migration movements (Durães and Lagido 2007, 17). Âncora counted 579 inhabitants in 1801 and Areosa up to 1,249 inhabitants. At the end of the century, in 1884, the population reached 775 and 1,567, respectively.

4 The will of "common hand" was written by the spouses before the death of one of the members; each of the spouses, in case he/she would die before the other, would give all his assets to his surviving partner.

5 A testator could freely dispose of one third of his personal assets to advantage one or several descendants, or unrelated person or persons. This part was called *terço* (a third).

Figure 2. Consanguineous marriages subject to matrimonial dispensation and total number of marriages celebrated in Âncora, Alto Minho (1800–1889)

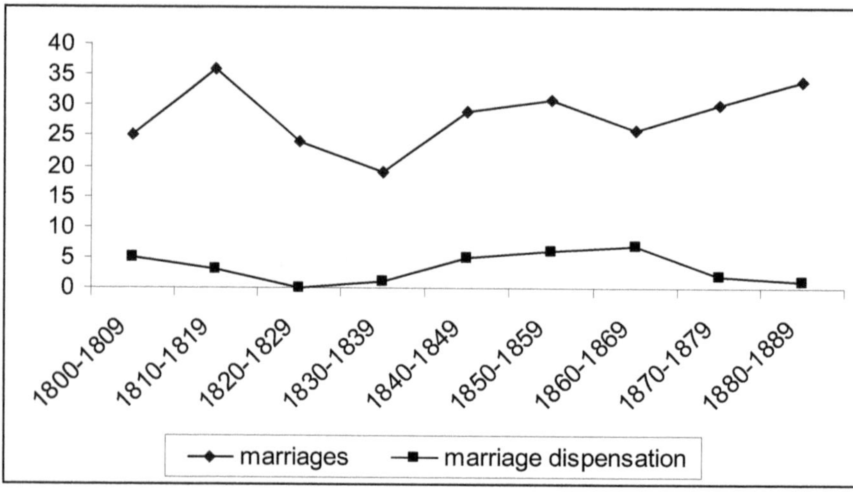

Sources: Parish registers. Marriages celebrated with dispensation, compared to all marriages celebrated and registered in Santa Maria de Âncora.

Figure 3. Consanguineous marriages subject to matrimonial dispensation and total number of marriages celebrated in Areosa, Alto Minho (1800–1889)

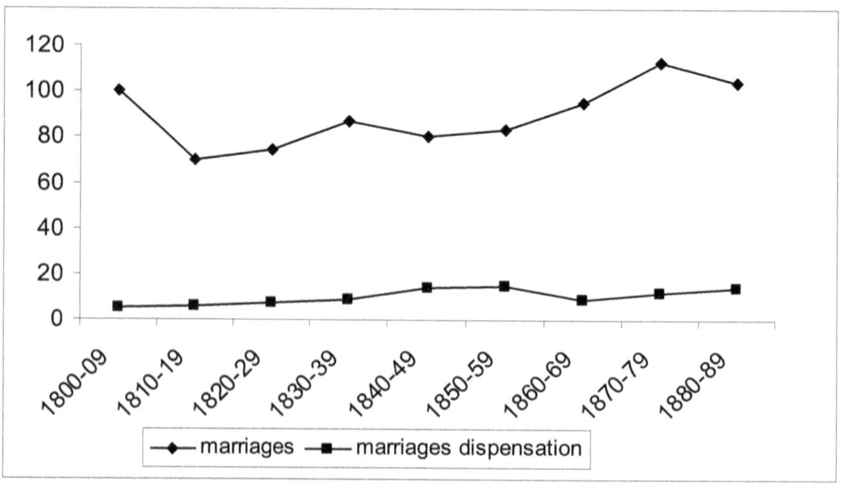

Sources: Parish registers. Marriages celebrated with dispensation, compared to all marriages celebrated and registered in Santa Maria da Vinha de Areosa.

Did the proportion of consanguineous marriages follow the same trend as population during this period? The analysis of the parish documentation concerning Santa Maria de Âncora[6] shows that consanguineous marriages subject to matrimonial dispensation were not exceptional occurrences throughout the 19th century. In the 1850s and 1860s, this type of marriage between cousins was rather more frequent than in previous decades (Figure 2).

However, this situation was nothing new in as much as the movement of marriages in this community increased in the 1850s, to enter into decline in the following decade, which proves to us that consanguinity mostly followed nuptiality trends, up to 1870. In the last period of the 19th century, the proportion of marriages between relatives decreased.[7]

At the same time, geographical endogamy was high. This can be seen from the preference for choosing a spouse in the same parish, between 1840 and 1910, in a proportion of 58.2 percent of the men and 83.2 percent of the women. In a borough with a small population, such as Santa Maria de Âncora, this preference invites us to consider the relationship between geographic endogamy and matrimonial consanguinity. This relation is cited by authors such as Ofelia Rey Castelao (1990, 249), for the near Spanish region of Galicia. The connection between social space and values, uses and customs leading to greater endogamy is considered of major importance. For his part, Hortensio Sobrado Correa (1998, 201), studying the lands of Lugo, in interior Galicia, argued that acquaintance between future spouses prior to marriage was frequent in such communities, which would facilitate family and work relations in the event of coresidence of the new couple with the older generation.

This latter situation comes to the fore in the request for dispensation presented by José Gomes and Alexandrina Paz, related in the 3d degree, in which the witnesses stated that the bride:

> is over 24 years old, has never been married and until now there has been no man to her liking with whom she could marry and only with the supplicant she gave her

6 In the parish registers, priests noted total number of marriages and those celebrated with matrimonial dispensation, so that religious inspectors would be precisely informed.

7 This behaviour was also detected by for Zeeland, in Holland, at the end of the nineteenth century and beginning of the twentieth century, when the proportion of consanguineous marriages diminished (Bras and van Poppel 2007).

> word for pleasure and domestic comfort. (District Archives of Braga. Marriage celebrated with dispensation)

Another example is the case of José Fernandes Gonçalves and Maria Teresa Ramos, farmers, related in the 4th degree, who indicated that:

> they are from honest families of the borough; they wish to marry to conserve the friendship and harmony that there has always been between the families; they are poor and live off the trade of farming, she cultivates her parents' lands and he his own and leased lands. (District Archives of Braga. Marriage celebrated with dispensation)

Such difficulties were manifest in Areosa, where the number of marriages fluctuated while consanguineous union reached a peak in the 1850s (Figure 3).

In Santa Maria da Vinha de Areosa, as we have seen for Âncora, the trend in the proportion of marriages with dispensation followed, more or less, the general nuptiality trend of the locality. However, in the 1880s, the last decade under observation, we note a different tendency than previously. Anyway, the marriage market remained clearly unfavourable to women as masculinity figures (or sex ratio) declined further from 76 men per hundred women in 1801 to 66 men per hundred women in 1884.

Concerning this situation of scarcity of male partners, the requests for dispensations give us much information, as, for example, the case allowing Domingos Enes Capeio, bachelor, and Inácia Martins Loureiro, widow in Areosa to get married. In her petition, it is related that in the place where she lived she did not have "men with whom she could marry unless different in ages". Likewise, Rosa Rodrigues Lomba, 37 years, asked for the dismissal of the second consanguinity degree to marry Daniel Fernandes Reis, relating that in Povoença,[8] where she lives, there are "86 houses with twenty men, some very poor, others of advanced age and some relatives".

We also studied the matrimonial dispensations of the 19th century in the District Archive of Braga from 1800 and up to 1889 and the resulting figures, for the two localities of Alto Minho under study, is presented below and compared to data from the corresponding parish registers (Table 1).

8 Povoença, belonging to Areosa, is very close to Viana do Castelo.

Table 1. General marriage trend and consanguineous marriages subject to matrimonial dispensation registered in the parish registers and requests of matrimonial dispensation in the archiepiscopacy of Braga, for Âncora and Areosa (1800–1889)

	Âncora			*Areosa*		
	All	Consan-guineous marriages in RP	Requests in Braga	All	Consan-guineous marriages in RP	Requests in Braga
1800–1809	25	5	0	100	5	0
1810–1819	36	3	0	70	6	2
1820–1829	24	0	0	74	7	2
1830–1839	19	1	4	87	9	3
1840–1849	29	5	5	80	14	10
1850–1859	31	6	6	83	15	16
1860–1869	26	7	9	95	9	9
1870–1879	30	2	6	113	12	11
1880–1889	34	1	5	104	14	11

Sources: Parish registers, marriage registrations for Santa Maria de Âncora and Santa Maria da Vinha de Areosa. Requests of matrimonial dispensation in District Archives of Braga.
Note: "RP" means parish registers.

The analysis of detailed figures (Table 1) allows us to see that, in Âncora, parish priests were not that careful when registering the couples who had asked for matrimonial dispensation. This becomes clear when we compare the number of licenses requested in this parish and in the district archives of Braga, mainly in the last three decades. In Areosa, however, registration of engaged people who asked for matrimonial license was much more accurate. Nevertheless, in a general way, there were no big differences, neither in the number nor in the distribution in time. If we look at the three first decades in Âncora and at the first decade in Areosa, we do not find any corresponding requests of matrimonial license in the district archives of Braga while some cousins were said to have obtained permission to marry. Probably some files disappeared in the archiepiscopacy.

In the parish of Âncora, when compared with the global number of marriages celebrated, the percentage of consanguineous marriages (34.6 percent) is more important than that of Areosa (11.3 percent). The proportion of consanguineous marriages in Âncora was the highest in the 1860s, while in Areosa the highest figure is found in the 1850s, with 19.3 percent of all marriages celebrated.

Our detailed analysis of the requests of matrimonial license kept in the archiepiscopacy Archives of Braga leads us to conclude that the forbidden matrimonial consanguinity between bride and groom was concentrated in the distant relations, mainly in the 4th degree of kinship (35.5 percent in Âncora and 26.4 percent in Areosa) and that there were no significant alterations of this model through the period under study, which had already been observed above when looking at the parish registers data. We see that the frequency of matrimonial consanguinity in the 3d degree (19.4 percent for Âncora and 20.8 percent for Areosa) were second in importance and that the matrimonial consanguinity in the 2d and 1st degrees – those marriages that supposed a deliberate intention of alliance – actually concerned very few couples (Âncora presented a percentage of 6.5 percent and Areosa, 7.5 percent). Besides, there was also a significant percentage, in both parishes, of marriages that accumulate double degrees. The percentage of engaged people who accumulated more than one consanguineous degree was 38.7 percent in Âncora, mainly in the 3d and 4th degrees. In Areosa, 45.3 percent of those who asked for matrimonial license were kin to more than one degree, this situation being, as in Âncora, more frequent in the third and fourth degrees. When analysing the region of Tierra de Montes, in Spanish Galicia, Camilo Fernandez Cortizo (2004, 95) suggested that this kind of kinship aimed at reinforcing the cohesion and identity of consanguinity (blood).

Marital Status and Age and Characteristics of Related Partners

Considering now the marital status of those who asked for matrimonial license, we see that, in general, most brides and grooms were contracting marriage for the first time. However, while in Âncora there were two widowers and two widows who choose a partner marrying for the first time, in Areosa remarriage was more common, since 20.3 percent of the *fiancés* were widowers marrying single females and 10.9 percent of the *fiancées* were widows marrying single males. Widowed persons needed to replace the dead spouse by someone he/she was acquainted with and who would take care of the children (in case there were any). The new spouse would help with the household chores and even with the farm management. Although there were more widowers than widows who asked for matrimonial license, it is curious that there were a significant number of women who did the same.

Let us consider the case of a country woman, Inácia Martins Loureiro, widowed to Manuel Afonso Barreiros, who needed to marry again, two years after her husband's death, and choose her cousin in the third degree, Domingos Enes Capeio. The main motivation for this choice was clear for the witnesses who declared:

> she needs to marry because she has no man at home to take care of the farmstead and of the farmland she pays for, due to the fact that she is a widow and does not want to take a farm servant, not to be exposed to gossip. (Requests of matrimonial dispensation in District Archives of Braga)

This example shows us the responsibility a woman had to face as landowner and as breadwinner. Remarriage allowed this widow to get the male help she needed for keeping her agricultural exploitation running, without employing a male servant and putting her reputation at risk.

Matrimonial licenses were requested mostly by single people looking for a first union. In this process, marriage between relatives resulted from a well defined strategy and not from some simple search for a marriage partner. This was an opinion already expressed by Isidro Dubert, concerning marriage formation in Galicia (1989, 172).

Thanks to the references that appear in the dispensation processes or within parish data, we learn about brides' and grooms' ages at marriage. Age was considered to be an important factor in the license allowance, mainly for women. It was assumed that single women who were over 24 would have more difficulties in finding a husband and would be more exposed to the "world's dangers". Thus, this age factor was used as an argument in the license request, implying that the woman, until then, had not yet met a man she could marry, except a relative or a man that was not her peer. However, a more accurate analysis lets us see that this is not a valid argument; the average age at first marriage was rather advanced and, as in other communities of Minho, women married even later than men.

Age at first marriage was very important as it regulated fertility (Hajnal 1965), mainly in parishes where people respected the religious principles. In the Portuguese case, Robert Rowland (1988, 113) observed that the average age for first marriage varied from south to north. In the north, mainly in the northwest region, the age for the first marriage was more advanced especially for females, which was seen as an impediment to population growth. This was certainly the case in the parishes we studied. In Santa Maria de Âncora, we calculated that the mean age at first marriage for men, between 1800 and 1849, was 26.2 years and for women, 27.1 years (Lagido 2004). In the following period, between 1850 and 1899, age at marriage was even higher with 28.8 for men and 28.1 for women. By comparison, in Areosa between 1800 and 1819 the overall average age at marriage was 24.8 for women and 24.4 for men. Between 1820 and 1836, mean age increased to 26.9 for women and 25.5 for men.

Concerning those who requested a matrimonial license, their average age was 31.5 for men and 28.6 for women in Âncora, and 31.9 for men and 27.6 for women in Areosa (Table 2). Therefore, in the 1830s, in the parish of Areosa, the age was advanced mainly for males, who got married in their late 30s (39 years old) while women were then aged 24.3 but got married later with the following decade (aged 29.1 years). In Âncora, there is a tendency for male age at marriage to increase with time and for the female age at marriage to decrease.

Table 2. Mean age of engaged males and females who asked before marriage for matrimonial dispensation in the archiepiscopacy of Braga, in Âncora and Areosa (1800–1889)

	MALES		*FEMALES*	
Years	Âncora	Areosa	Âncora	Areosa
1810-19		25.5		24.0
1820-29		25.0		24.5
1830-39	38.3	39.0	34.8	24.3
1840-49	29.5	29.5	30.8	29.1
1850-59	28.6	33.3	28.8	28.9
1860-69	30.4	36.6	28.0	26.3
1870-79	30.8	29.1	25.6	28.7
1880-89	34.7	30.6	26.0	27.1
Mean	31.5	31.9	28.6	27.6

Sources: Requests of matrimonial dispensation in District Archives of Braga. Santa Maria de Âncora and Santa Maria da Vinha de Areosa.
Notes: Ages are not available in Ancora before 1830.

We also notice a difference in ages between partners: in most cases, men were older than women. This difference of ages between bride and groom reached a maximum of eleven years in Âncora and thirty four years in Areosa. Nevertheless, in most cases engaged people were almost the same age. There were also some very young *fiancés*, as was the case with Manuel Afonso Barreiros and Custódia Fernandes de Carvalho, from Areosa, both farmers, cousins in third and fourth degrees, who asked for matrimonial license in 1856. They were 18 and 19 years old, respectively, and as a reason to get the license they alleged that the place they lived in (Povoença, very close to Viana do Castelo) had:

> 85 inhabited houses and although in those houses there were men older than 14, among singles and widowers, most of them were away and from those who lived there, some were very poor, others did not have or hope to have anything, some were too close, others in a very advanced age or even old and many were crippled. (Requests of matrimonial dispensation in District Archives of Braga)

However, among those who asked for license, the younger ones were the exception. The age range in Âncora was between 21 and 55 for men and 18 and 50 for women and in Areosa, 18 and 60 for men and 19 and 41 for women. This situation makes it possible to allege an advanced age as an important factor when asking for matrimonial license.

The age difference between engaged people should be pointed out, especially when the woman was older than the man. This was the case of Severino Franco, 29 years old, single, stonemason, who requested authorisation to marry his cousin in the third degree, Maria Rosa de Azevedo, widow, 37 years old, occupied in farming and sewing, stating that "the father-in-law and aunts need to fix their house as they are at an advanced age" and also that in "Aspra there are no more than six single lads relatives or mismatched".[9]

The engaged people's jobs show characteristics of these rural communities of Alto Minho. Thus, in Areosa, the prevalence of farmers – 62.3 percent of the declared jobs for men – points to the importance of consanguineous marriage as a way of maintaining family property during the 19th century. In the case of women, this percentage increased to 86.5 percent, an important factor for understanding the valorisation of land as a source of wealth and social advancement. Other male jobs were related to building construction – whitewasher, mason, woodworker and plasterer – although they were not so significant in a general way.

9 Requests of matrimonial dispensation in District Archives of Braga, Santa Maria de Âncora.

In Âncora, there were more male jobs related to building and construction, characteristics of the locality: there were 33.3 percent masons and only 29.6 percent farmers. However, female occupations show us the relevance of women in working the land: 77 percent of the brides who asked for matrimonial licence were active in agriculture.

Reasons for Contracting a Consanguineous Marriage

Finding the real causes that determined the request for dispensation was not an easy task since stereotypical assertions allowed by ecclesiastical law were systematically used, such as the lack of suitable people with whom to wed, poverty, lack of a dowry, the fact that the woman was over 24 years old, and the potential harm to the morality of those cited and of the parish. The parish priests were providing very little information, especially if we compare this community to others where requested files were much richer both in terms of justification and the greater variety of reasons that led to the arguments for dispensation.

Our sample allows us to determine that the most frequent reason given for requesting dispensation was that the *fiancée* was over 24 years old without having contracted marriage. Overall, 50 percent gave this as a legitimate and urgent reason for the dispensation. It is the allegation used by Manuel Afonso Gomes and Maria Rosa Afonso, aged 25 and 24 respectively, who pointed out the fact that she:

> has found no man until now of equal status, with whom she could contract marriage; request from Your Excellency Matrimonial dispensation in the said relationship with the cause 24 et ultra, *forma pauperum*,[10] since they cannot appeal to Rome because of the delay; they are both poor. (Requests of matrimonial dispensation in District Archives of Braga)

However, upon more careful analysis, we see that the bride is going to be benefited by her mother in her will with a third portion *(terço)*[11] "in re-

10 Attested as being poor, the couple had not to pay to obtain the necessary matrimonial dispensation.

11 As see above, note 5.

payment of good services", which may lead us to infer that marriage would have, in this family, more pressing economic motives than those presented.

As in the aforementioned example, this is not the only motive presented for obtaining the dispensation. Normally, apart from the fact that the *fiancée* was older than 24, there was also the fact that she was poor and had not, until then with the supplicant, any other pretender.

Poverty, as mentioned above, was another reason mentioned in almost all the processes we accessed. However, how was it possible that "poor and miserable" people who said they had nothing could pay the high costs of the marriage dispensation process?

In the examples analysed, the costs ranged from 1,368 *reis* up to 2,092 *reis*, which leads us to suppose that only those who had some wealth could actually apply for this petition, with the amount often being provided by the progenitors as legal inheritance, which once again suggests a family strategy. Nevertheless, in some cases, the high cost of the process would lead to the failure of the strategy of some families with fewer resources who sought to block the entries of new relatives, restricting the family nucleus and leaving, in this way, the possibility for the wealthier farming families.

The predisposition for consanguineous marriage was considered, by some authors, to be motivated by a restricted matrimonial market (Fernandez Cortizo 2004, 96–100), a situation mentioned previously as one of the conditions found in the parishes under study. This situation was indicated by most persons who requested dispensation: the scarcity of men. This is the case of Domingos Francisco da Carreira and Mariana Fernandes, relatives in double degree, 3d and 4th, who pointed out that "where they live are small places and there is no man with whom she can marry that is not a relative or mismatched and even moving to another place" the problem would persist. To justify this situation there was a list of single young people in the place where the two betrothed lived, given as one of the components of the process.

Another example was that of José Rodrigues, painter, 24 years old and Maria Teresa Rodrigues, a weaver aged 31, who were relatives in double degree, 2d and 4th.

> [She] is much older than 24 and has not found a man of equal status so this marriage is extremely urgent so that the orator does not remain insulted and exposed to the dangers of the century and as they cannot appeal to Rome… they are poor and

> miserable; she has never been married and almost all the lads of her age are relatives or of a different status; the father is absent, living by the trade of carver; she lives alone with her mother who is paralysed, the house has few neighbours and evildoers have already attempted an insult. (Requests of matrimonial dispensation in District Archives of Braga)

In this case the fragility of the female condition is given as a fundamental motive for the celebration of nuptials. Other reasons arise to justify the need for marriage, even incurring the sin of incest. These include reputation, and prior and/or repeated copulation provided that it is affirmed that they occur as a result of:

> fragility and not with the intention of being easily dispensed; and they want to marry otherwise there will be a scandal and she will remain of ill repute and unmarried; marrying ends the scandal; she was not forced or constrained. (Requests of matrimonial dispensation in District Archives of Braga)

These motivations were not rare in Âncora, where there seems to have been more parochial monitoring than in Areosa. In this respect, the case of Custodio Manuel and Teresa Enrique, cousins in the first degree, is enlightening. They requested marriage dismissal in 1824 alleging *copula in forma pauperum.*[12]

The transgressions of the religious norm of chastity prior to marriage, although condemned by the Church, could lead to the correction of the error through matrimony. This permission surpassed the incestuous relationship by reintegrating the transgressors into the Christian social body, in this way managing to lessen the damage of the social order caused by the breach in religious principles (Dubert 1989, 174). As this was considered a serious and harmful behavioural deviation from the parochial morality, this situation called for the intervention of the community involved in this scandal, who then became the target of public pardon and penitence. We found an example of this deviant behaviour in the community of Âncora.

This is the case of João Francisco dos Barreiros, aged 55, widower, and Cipriana Fernandes, aged 50, widow, farmers, brother and sister-in-law who lived in the same house and whose sin was divulged by their children. As a penalty, they were forced to pay 10,000 *reis* to the orphaned and abandoned children. Apart from the joint pecuniary penalty,

12 See above, note 10.

they were individually to pray, on their knees, twenty rosaries to Our Lady, to listen to eighteen masses, in addition to the precept mass, to visit the way of the cross sixteen times, to fast for two days, to confess and take communion twice with their parish priest and, finally, to perform a public penitence, both of them being present at a mass, standing up, he without a cape or capote and she without a mantle or mantilla so that they could be seen by everyone on two Sundays or holy days. At the mass, each of them had to carry a lighted half-pound white wax torch in their hands, asking out loud for forgiveness from God and the people, for the scandal and ill treatment. Once the mass would end, they were to go and prostrate themselves before the altar and give the rest of the torches to the Holiness and Our Lady. This case proved the parochial vigilance on behavioural deviations during this period.

Temporary male migration, an important characteristic of these communities, could be another reason to justify the need for a consanguineous marriage. In the case of Antonio Afonso do Cruzeiro and Maria Teresa Gonçalves, relatives in double degree, 2d and 4th, migration constituted a strong argument to underline the urgency to celebrate their marriage:

> because of the brevity with which he has to make a distant journey: he usually goes to make his living in Extremadura where he usually remains some time; the widowhood of her mother needing to establish her house. (Requests of matrimonial dispensation in District Archives of Braga)

In Areosa this kind of situation was frequently expressed. In the case of Daniel Fernandes Reis, 46 years, who requested dismissal to contract matrimony with Rose Rodrigues Lomba, 37 years, his cousin in 2d degree, migration of the groom was of a longer distance, towards Brazil. He explained that:

> he came back from Rio de Janeiro almost with the main intention to deal with this marriage and [...] return back to the same empire, Brazil, to deal with some life businesses. (Requests of matrimonial dispensation in District Archives of Braga)

José Afonso Viana, aged 53, provided another example, arguing that:

> he was enough time in the empire of Brazil, where he got enough goods that allows him to have a decent life, and now has arrived to have honest and precious sustentation without having any need in the farming work. (Requests of matrimonial dispensation in District Archives of Braga)

However, finding himself ill, he felt the necessity to have someone caring for his well-being, who would treat him well and he therefore contracted the marriage with his cousin, Maria Alfonso Bamba, 19 years, for

> the best affection that he has been treated and [...] mainly in the times where he more suffers.

The heard witnesses related that this marriage was definitely advantageous for the bride because she was "very poor".

All the reasons expressed in the Requests of matrimonial dispensation that we consulted in District Archives of Braga intended to improve access to marriage, even if it was between relatives. This strategy to obtain kinship dispensation was increasing the number of married couples in parishes in which permanent celibacy was high. In Âncora, between 1740 and 1799, 9.7 percent of the men and 32.6 percent of the women remained unmarried. In consequence, the number of legitimate births also improved.

Conclusions

Our analysis of a sample of requests for consanguineous marriage dispensations in two rural communities of Alto Minho allows us to argue that such unions did not result only from individual strategy and reactions to strict impediments imposed by Canon Law. When analysing the contents of wills we saw that most of the consanguineous marriage partners benefited from the goods of their own parents and would inherit the *terço*, the third part of their parents' personal assets, which means that they were sure to get some advantage for their new family, so that the well-being of their house would be better secured. Marrying a close relative must be seen within the framework of a much more complex family strategy that involved a series of motives aimed at avoiding the division of patrimony by continuing the family line, re-establishing links between family branches and preventing the formation of separate households or isolated groups.

In this way, family doctrine was oriented towards making matrimony a patrimonial issue. The strategy of the domestic groups was geared towards obtaining land and extending the size of family operations, restricting economic decisions as well as rationalising issues such as matrimonial unions that would serve as a basis for the gender division of work, making the rural household an economically viable cell.

Consanguineous marriages intended to reunite divided patrimony and avoid splitting it. Although this reason was not expressed in the requests for dispensation kept in the archiepiscopacy of Braga, it did appear in a concealed manner, particularly when it was declared that marriage served to preserve "friendship and harmony" between families and that there was "pleasure and domestic comfort" in its celebration. In the same way, the fact that only one couple argued that they had no previous knowledge of the family relationship between them shows us that transgression against the norm was intentional.

Alto Minho was a region in which land was excessively divided. The family strategy of maintenance of the patrimony was hampered by an egalitarian right of succession that imposed equality between all legitimate heirs, which meant that only one child could contract marriage at home and the others would have either to marry outside, remain celibate or emigrate.

Migrations transformed women into active and powerful actors, able to take decisions and manage the family farm. In the two *minhotas* parishes under study, Santa Maria de Âncora and Santa Maria da Vinha de Areosa, a specific image of the 19th century Portuguese woman can be discerned. Females did not belong there to a "weak sex", but were responsible persons in farmers' families, running the farm in absence of migrant males and caring for children as well as for old, aging or disabled members of their family. Matrimonial consanguinity proved to be a constant feature throughout the 19th century. In any case, we stress that this conclusion is only a limited contribution to the wider issue of gender roles and family reproduction in historical rural Minho, of which only general lines were pointed out.

Keeping a decent level of well-being and preserving family continuity was a major concern for relatives, future brides and grooms requesting a matrimonial dispensation to be allowed to marry kin in one's parish.

References

AUGUSTINS, Georges, 1989, *Comment se perpétuer. Devenir des lignées et destins des patrimoines dans les paysanneries européens*, Nanterre, Société d'ethnologie française.

BARRERA GONZALEZ, Andrés, 1990, *Casa, herencia y familia en la Cataluña rural*, Madrid, Alianza.

BERTRAND, Annie and RODRIGUEZ JIMÉNEZ, Pablo (eds), 2000, *A través del tiempo. Diccionario de fuentes para la historia de la familia*, Murcia, Universidad de Murcia.

BESTARD, Joan, 1998, *Parentesco y modernidad*, Barcelona, Paidós.

BLANCO CARRASCO, José Pablo, 1999, *Demografía, familia y sociedad en la Extremadura moderna, 1500–1860*, Universidad de Extremadura.

BONTE, Pierre (ed.), 1994, *Épouser au plus proche. Inceste, prohibitions et stratégies matrimoniales autour de la Méditerranée*, Paris, EHESS.

BRAS, Hilde, VAN POPPEL, Frans, and MANDEMAKERS, Kees, 2007, "Kin marriage in The Netherlands: Law and practice in the 19th century", paper presented at *Second Symposium of Cost Action A34*, Guimarães.

BRETTELL, Caroline, 1991, *Homens que Partem Mulheres que Esperam. Consequências da Emigração numa Freguesia Minhota*, Lisboa, D. Quixote.

CHACON, Francisco (ed.), 1990, *Historia Social de la Familia en España*, Alicante, Instituto de Cultura Juan Gil-Albert.

CHACON, Francisco and HURTADO, Juan, 1992, "Matrimonio y consanguinidad en Lorca y su comarca, 1723–1850", in Francisco CHACON JIMENEZ and Juan HERNANDEZ FRANCO (eds), *Poder, familia y consanguinidad en la España del Antiguo Régimen*, Barcelona, Anthopos, pp. 177–250.

CUNHA, Mafalda Soares, 2000, *Casa de Bragança 1560–1640. Práticas Senhoriais e Redes Clientelares*, Lisboa, Estampa.

DEROUET, Bernard, 2001, "Parenté et marché foncier à l'époque moderne: une réinterprétation", *Annales Histoire, Sciences Sociales*, 56, 2, pp. 337–368.

–, 1996, "Les pratiques de l'alliance en milieu de communautés familiales (Bourbonnais, 1600–1750)", in Guy BRUNET, Antoinette FAUVE-CHAMOUX and Michel ORIS (eds), *Le choix du conjoint*, Paris, CNRS, pp. 227–251.

DELILLE, Gérard, 2001, "Réflexions sur le 'système' européen de parenté et d'alliance (note critique)", *Annales Histoire, Sciences Sociales*, 56, 2, pp. 369–380.

–, 1994, "Consanguinité proche en Italie du XVIe au XIXe siècle", in Pierre BONTE (ed.), *Épouser au plus proche. Inceste, prohibitions et stratégies matrimoniales autour de la Méditerranée*, Paris, EHESS, pp. 323–340.

DUBERT, Isidro, 1989, "Estudio histórico del parentesco a través de las dispensas de matrimonio y de los archivos parroquiales en la Galicia del Antiguo Régimen. Primera aproximación", in José Carlos BERMEJO BARRERA (ed.), *Parentesco, familia y matrimonio en la Historia de Galicia*, Santiago de Compostela, Tórculo Edicións, pp. 167–191.

DUBY, Georges, 1991, *Amor e Sexualidade no Ocidente*, Lisboa, Terramar.

DURÃES, Margarida, 2000, *Herança e Sucessão. Leis, práticas e costumes no termo de Braga. Séculos XVIII–XIX*, PhD, Universidade do Minho, Braga.
–, 2006, "Migrations internes et stratégies héréditaires", Paper presented at *XIV International Economic History Congress,* Helsinki.
DURÃES, Margarida and LAGIDO, Emília, 2007, "Migrações. Trajectórias e impactos na reprodução e organização da família e sociedade camponesa minhota (séc. XVIII–XIX)", Paper presented at *XXIV Congresso Nacional de História da ANPUH*, Unisinos, S. Leopoldo - RS.
FERNANDEZ CORTIZO, Camilo, 2004, "Espacios matrimoniales y reproducción social en la Galicia occidental en el siglo XVIII", *Revista de Demografía Histórica*, XXII, I, pp. 77–119.
GOODY, Jack, 1983, *The Development of the Family and Marriage in Europe*, Cambridge, Cambridge University Press.
GOUESSE, Jean-Marie, 1986, "Mariages des proches parents (XVIe–XXe siècle). Esquisses d'une conjoncture", *Le modèle familial européen. Normes, déviances, contrôle du pouvoir*, Rome, École Française de Rome, pp. 31–61.
HAJNAL, John, 1965, "European Marriage Patterns in Perspective", in David V. GLASS and David E. EVERSLEY (eds), *Population in History. Essays in Historical Demography*, London, Arnold, pp. 101–143.
LAGIDO, Emília, 2004, *Santa Maria de Âncora (1624–1910). População e Sociedade*, Dissertation in History of Population, Universidade do Minho, Braga.
LEBRUN, François, 1983, *A vida conjugal no Antigo Regime*, Lisboa, Rolim.
LEVI-STRAUSS, Claude, 1967, *Les structures élémentaires de la parenté*, Paris, PUF [first edition 1949].
MONTEIRO, Nuno, 2007, *Elites e Poder: entre o Antigo Regime e o Liberalismo*, Lisboa, Imp. Ciências Sociais.
REY CASTELAO, Ofelia, 1990, "Mecanismos reguladores de la nupcialidad en la Galicia atlántica. El matrimonio a trueque", *Obradoiro de Historia Moderna*, Santiago de Compostela, pp. 247–268.
ROWLAND, Robert, 1988, "Sistemas matrimoniales en la Península Ibérica (siglos XVI–XIX)", in Vicente PEREZ MOREDA and David REHER (eds), *Demografia Histórica en España*, Madrid, El Arquero, pp. 72–137.
SCOTT, Ana Sílvia, 1999, *Famílias, formas de união e reprodução social no noroeste português (séculos XVIII e XIX)*, Guimarães, NEPS/Universidade do Minho.
SOBRADO CORREA, Hortensio, 2001, *Las tierras de Lugo en la Edad Moderna. Economia campesina, familia y herencia, 1550–1860*, A Coruña, Fundación Pedro Barrié de la Maza.
SOUSA, Fernando and ALVES, Jorge, 1997, *Alto Minho. População e Economia nos finais de setecentos*, Lisboa, Ed. Presença.
SOUSA, João de (ed.), 1697, *Synodal Constitutions of the Archbishopric of Braga by D. Sebastião de Matos e Noronha*, Braga.
SUTTER, Jean, 1968, "Fréquence de l'endogamie et ses facteurs au XIXe siècle", *Population*, 23, 2, pp. 303–324.

Cousin Marriage and Well-Being among the Portuguese Royal Family during the 15th and 16th Centuries

Isabel dos Guimarães SÁ

This study deals with two separate issues: in the first part, royal marriages will be set in historical context, and I shall argue that cousin marriage was often among the causes for bitter conflict and violence among branches of the same family. Those situations became particularly explosive when such alliances took place among branches of the same family competing within the kingdom itself, because the dangers of internal war arose.

The second part will deal with the ways in which princesses and queens could adapt to their difficult situation of sequential child bearers in foreign courts. My purpose is to demonstrate how property, especially in what concerns domestic goods, contributed to the well-being of these women, who, in spite of their royal status, enjoyed subaltern positions in relation to their husbands. I shall argue that the control women exerted over their dowries was limited, and that they lived mainly on annual rents paid by their husbands; on the other hand, the trousseau constituted their full property and played a crucial role in the construction of their identity.

Cousin Marriage among the Portuguese Royals in Historical Context

During the fifteenth and sixteenth centuries cousin marriage became a constant among royals. Motives for marrying within the same family were various, but they rested mostly on dynastic interests. Within the Portuguese royal family, these marriages started to take place within several branches of the same family, all of them within the Portuguese kingdom.

From 1490 onwards, these inbreeding marriages would take an international character, as marriage partners were increasingly chosen outside the kingdom, especially in the Spanish Habsburg monarchy. Cousin marriage did not disappear; neither did conflicts among kin, but the dangers of internal armed conflict ceased.

These alliances began with João I, the founder of the new dynasty of Avis, who married Philippa of Lancaster in 1387. Some of his grandsons and granddaughters married between themselves (see family tree Figure 1), mainly because he endowed his children with vast seigniorial estates that created the need for alliance, or at least required reciprocal neutralization, so that the royal family would not be out-shaded by their relative's households. Let us give some examples: João I and Duarte I, the first two kings of Avis, married foreign princesses. João I married Philippa of Lancaster, and several of his sons survived until adulthood, each having his own duchy. João's heir, Duarte, married Leonor, the daughter of king Ferdinand of Aragon (died 1416), but already in his generation a marriage between cousins took place. His younger brother João (1400–1442) married in 1424 Isabel (1402–1465), the daughter of the duke of Braganza, Afonso. Such marriages became systematic in the following generation. The next king Afonso V, married his uncle Pedro's daughter, Isabel, whilst his brother Fernando, second in line to the throne, in 1447, married Beatriz, daughter of infante João (died 1442) and Isabel of Braganza (died 1465).

Let me start by referring, although briefly, the reasons why the king of Portugal, Afonso V married infante Pedro's daughter. The latter was regent during Afonso's minority (who was left orphan at six years old), but he was reluctant to give up his regency, as he had created a pool of enemies. Two "factions" had appeared, and Pedro's opponents were led by the duke of Braganza, Afonso, who felt defrauded by the fact that his own daughter, Isabel, had not been appointed to marry the heir to the throne, Afonso V. By the time Afonso V's heir, prince João (future João II) married, in 1471, marriages were celebrated within the king's family and the two existing ducal houses, the Braganza and the Beja-Viseu, offered a pool of brides to choose from.

The Braganza family originated from an illegitimate son of king João I, Afonso, who had married Beatriz, the daughter of the constable Nuno Álvares Pereira, whilst the Viseu-Beja family corresponded to the second son of Duarte, Fernando (1433–1470), who had married Beatriz, the daughter of his uncle João and Isabel of Braganza. The fact that Fernando was designated as the adoptive child and heir to Henry the Navigator (died 1460), and became the only heir to João, his father-in-law, plus his own ability to generate assets, transformed the house of Viseu into one of the powers competing for the throne in the following years.

Enmeshed family interests motivated bitter rivalries, often leading to violence. This social and political turbulence has been one of the favorite subjects of Portuguese historiography, especially among medievalists, and it will not be further explored in this paper. Many historians have explored these dynastic wars and upheavals thoroughly.[1] Dynastic marriages were appeasing in so many ways, as they deflected danger of internal wars through alliances between potential enemies, but they often had the opposite effect of actually promoting uneasiness and bitter conflict. When negotiated in international arenas, they were strategically arranged in order to achieve the absorption of kingdoms into composite monarchies, especially as a result of Habsburg dynastic policies. These incorporations, as it is known, were at the root of revolts and wars, where the goals of the conspirers and rebels were invariably the independence of their nations. As examples, we could refer to Catalonia, Naples or Portugal, not to mention the Lower Countries and Holland, if we limit ourselves to the example of the Spanish composite monarchy. These marriages could thus be the cause for collective dissatisfaction, but they also gave origin to individual malaise, namely in what concerns the quality of life that princesses and queens had to endure. Although several devices were set in order to create well-being for queens and princesses, we must note that their subaltern condition as wives to kings and princes, as well as their role in dynastic biological reproduction, often meant harsh living conditions and personal unhappiness. As their main purpose in life was pregnancy and childbirth, their health could be devastated as a result. Bartolomé Bennassar has well illustrated this issue in a recent book (Bennassar 2006).

1 The recent biography of João II includes accounts of these conflicts, and a vast bibliography on the subject (Fonseca 2005).

Figure 1. The Avis Dynasty, the Ducal Houses of Braganza and Beja-Viseu of Portugal, and the Trastamaras of Spain (1385–1490)

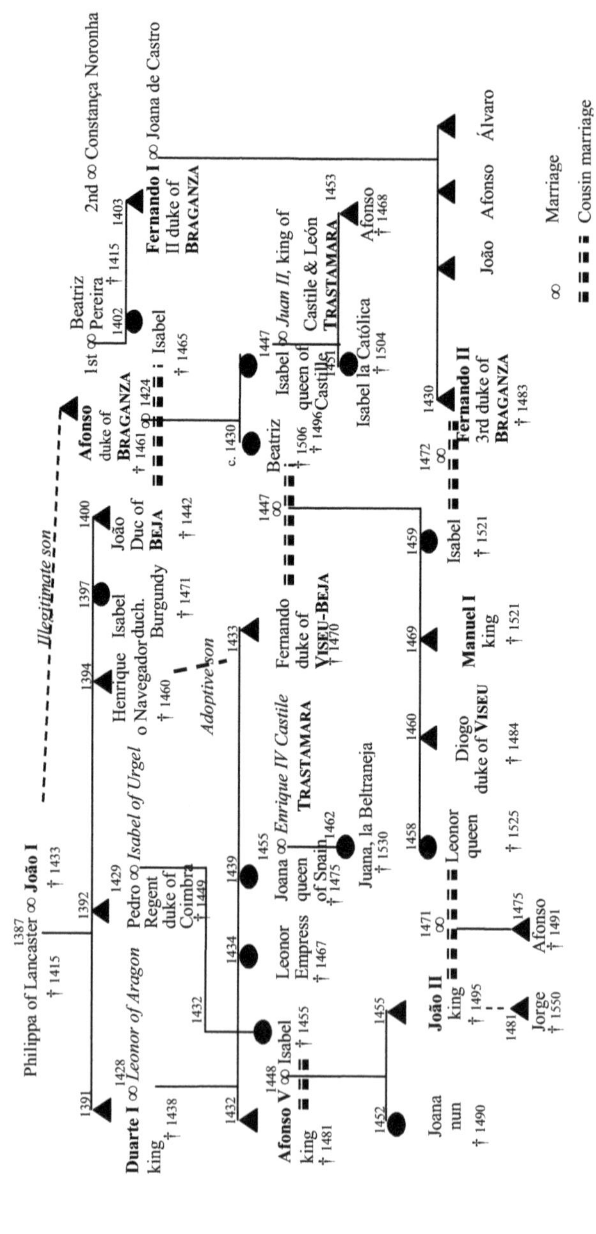

Let us go back to the initial marriage of the Avis dynasty,[2] that of João I with Philippa of Lancaster. Ten children would be born to the couple; the youngest, João, would marry Isabel, the daughter of his father's only illegitimate son Afonso. In 1401, Afonso had married Nuno Álvares Pereira's daughter, Beatriz; Pereira was then the kingdom's hero as the war commander who had led the Portuguese to victory against Castile in the previous war of independence (1383–1385). The marriage of his daughter Beatriz with the illegitimate son of the king is at the root of the creation of a lineage second in importance after the king's, as Afonso would become the first duke of Braganza.

In this first Avis generation of the new Portuguese dynasty, this 1424 alliance between João, duke of Beja and Isabel de Braganza would be the only consanguineous marriage. But among king João I's grandchildren, there were two marriages between first cousins: in 1448, the successor to the throne, Afonso V (1432–1481), married Isabel de Coimbra (1432–1455), the daughter of his older uncle, who had been regent of the Portuguese kingdom during his minority, Pedro, duke of Coimbra. In 1447, Afonso's brother, Fernando, duke of Viseu (born 1433), had married his cousin Beatriz (c. 1430–1506), daughter of his uncle João, duke of Beja, referred to above, thus joining this branch of the family once again to the Braganzas. At next generation, in 1471, the only son of Afonso V, prince João (1455–1495), future João II, would in turn marry Leonor (1458–1525), one of the daughters of Fernando, duke of Viseu-Beja, and Beatriz.

Married within the Portuguese royal family, two of the entirely Portuguese queens lived during the period under our analysis: Isabel (1432–1455), wife of Afonso V, and Leonor (1458–1525).[3] As we shall see, both lived through bitter family feuds.

A first wave of family violence took place during the late 1440s when two factions collided, one reuniting Afonso V's supporters, and those of his uncle and father-in-law, Pedro (1392–1449). The two armed forces clashed at the battle of Alfarrobeira (20 May 1449), where Pedro was killed and his small army defeated.[4] This battle had a negative effect on

2 João was the natural son of king of Portugal Pedro I (1320–1367). He was Grand Master of the Order of Avis and was declared king of Portugal by the Portuguese *Cortes* in 1385, after his brother Fernando 1, unique legitimate male heir, died in 1383 without a male descendance.

3 The other queen, from the 14th century, is Leonor Teles (1350–1386), second wife of Fernando I (1345–1383) (see Barbosa 1727, p. 364 onwards).

4 For the most comprehensive study of the battle of Alfarrobeira, see Moreno 1979.

the image of the king, raised and devoted to the ideals of chivalry, because he had allowed his uncle's corpse to remain unburied in the field during several days.[5] His daughter, Queen Isabel, made her best efforts to grant her father a decent burial place but she died in 1455, at the age of 23, soon after having given birth to their son João.[6] Chroniclers state that there was suspicion of poisoning: whether this is true or not is neither relevant, nor possible to verify, but it informs us about the bitter scars that followed civil war. Alfarrobeira was to have an international resonance, as one of Pedro's sisters, Isabel (1397–1471), had married the duke of Burgundy, Philip the Good (1396–1467), and she assumed the task of protecting her brother's allies, as well as hosting some of his orphaned children in Burgundy's court, and thus Bruges became a place of refuge for his supporters (Sousa Viterbo 1905; Apfelstadt 2000, 183–184). By then, the Braganzas were already major actors in the political scene, as the young king Afonso V had relied on the duke of Braganza's substantial military help against the regent (Gomes 2006, 65–67).

Family problems would continue during the next generation. In the 1480s more cousin blood would be shed. As mentioned above, Prince João married into his uncle Fernando's family, having wed Leonor in 1471. Fernando, duke of Viseu, was also duke of Beja after marrying Beatriz in 1447, and he had inherited Henry the Navigator's estate after his death in 1460. At the time of his own death in 1470, not only his assets had notably increased (Lopes 2003, 24–106), but also his political influence through marriage. In 1447, Isabel, his wife's sister, had married Juan II of Castile and would be the mother of Isabel la Católica. Later, in 1472, his own daughter, Isabel, would marry the 3d duke of Braganza, Fernando II. The scene was set again for conflict: the Viseu-Beja were united to the Braganzas and developed in the meantime strong affinities with the Castilian court. Three main contenders were in place: the Braganzas, the duke of Viseu and the king. The Braganzas were the most politically and socially influential, while the household of the duke of Viseu was the wealthiest (Cunha 1988, 269–290). With the two ducal households united, and linked to the Castilian monarchy, trouble awaited João II when he became king in 1481.

Fernando II, third duke of Braganza, and Diogo, duke of Viseu, both brothers-in-law to king João II, were accused of conspiring against the

5 On this chivalric "stain", see Gomes 2006, 78–79.

6 João II will reign from 1481 to his death, in 1495.

king on two occasions (1483 and 1484). Both died, Fernando being tried and executed, and Diogo being killed at the hands of the king himself without formal legal formalities. Their allies also suffered the consequences of treason: more than 50 persons were executed, escaped from the kingdom, or faced harsh imprisonment leading to death. Both conspiracies bear the suspicion that the queen of Castile Isabel la Católica gave support to the rebels. The involvement of the Catholic kings, as far as sources go, if they actually gave their support to any conspiracy, was marked by prudence. There are no sources that actually prove that Isabel and Fernando acted with the conspirators, but they might have joined them if they had been successful.

Friction between the two kingdoms, Portugal and Spain, has again to be set in context: they were still enjoying a fragile peace after a disastrous attempt of João II's father, Afonso V, to take part in the succession war that divided supporters of Isabel's rights to the throne against the supporters of Juana the Beltraneja (1462–1530), daughter of Afonso's sister Joana and Enrique IV of Castile. After the battle of Toro in March 1476, a peace treaty followed, but mutual fear would end only with the marriage, in 1490, of Afonso, João's only son and heir, to Isabel, the eldest of the Catholic kings' four daughters. This wedding had been a part of the peace negotiations, and it was preceded by a long period of waiting because they were small children at the time of the peace treaty. While they were too young to marry, a solution had to be found in order to prevent the re-start of war. In fact, between November 1480 and May 1483, both royal families held each other's heirs as hostages in the town of Moura, under the responsibility of the widowed duchess of Viseu-Beja, Beatriz, in what became known as the *terçarias* agreement. A few days after they were terminated, and king João II had regained possession of his only child, he ordered the imprisonment of the duke of Braganza, Fernando II, under the accusation of conspiracy.

The duke was sentenced by a grand jury who demonstrated his treacherous contacts with the Castilian courts with the purpose of dethroning João II. It is not known whether Isabel la Católica ever dreamt seriously of incorporating the kingdom of Portugal; although it is a fact that the conspirers were members of her family. Duchess Beatriz, mother-in-law both to Fernando II duke of Braganza and to João II, was her mother's sister; no wonder Queen Isabel took care of the exiled Braganzas in her court after the brutal suppressing of the duchy of Braganza by João II in 1483

(Córdova Miralles 2002, 138). The fact that both women were in good terms is shown by the fact that the initial peace negotiations after Toro took place between them in Alcantara, a modest town just outside the Portuguese frontier with Castile (Costa 2005, 46–47).

Both conspiracies were actually accompanied by king João II's measures against eventual military reactions against himself either after he imprisoned the duke of Braganza or when he killed Diogo duke of Viseu. Such conspiracies could not, at any cost, be transformed into rebellions. In the first case, the towns and castles held by the duke of Braganza were summoned to confirm his allegiance to the king. In the following months, João II traveled up north, to the domains of the duke, in order to make his authority effective as their new lord, as the duchy was suppressed in consequence of the conspiracy (Pina 1977, 918–919, 926; Resende 1973, 60, 73–74). During the night of the murder of the duke of Viseu, in Setúbal, he ordered the city walls to be closed and the streets patrolled (Resende 1973, 80). During the next weeks, the king departed on a military venture to the castle of Sabugal, where the alcaide's wife had refused to surrender the fortress (Pina 1977, 932; Resende 1973, 85–86). It is the case of Diogo's mother, who ordered the immediate surrender of the town of Moura, which used to be one of her son's towns (Chaves 1983, 182–183).

Endogamous Alliances: Family Problems but Collective Security

Most historians have stressed the political meanings of these conflicts, but I would like to call attention to the fact that these were family matters. Most contenders were relatives before marrying into one another's families; consanguinity would enmesh conflicts further. Furthermore, these episodes bear little resemblance with justice: even if there was a trial in the case of the duke Fernando II of Braganza, apparently abiding to the existing laws and juridical procedures, what happened to most suspects was pure revenge, the latter being perceived by contemporaries as a right of the offended (Moreno 1970, 47–103; Liss 2004, 79). Instead of insisting on political issues, I would like to stress the emotional character of these conflicts. As we know, the word "family" had an extended meaning, embracing not only blood relatives, but also the members of the household, especially *criados*, that is, those who had been entrusted as children to another household in order to be raised and educated (Gomes 2003, 205–208). King João II is said to have expressed his sadness for having been betrayed by his relatives on the occasion of both conspiracies, especially in what concerns the duke of Viseu, Diogo. Chroniclers mentioned that he had been brought up as a son, and was his first cousin, and his wife's brother.[7] Anger and thirst for revenge were not only derived from offended pride, but could also mean a genuine sense of loss at being betrayed by a close relative. A Polish traveler, Nicolaus von Popplau wrote, after having been at the Portuguese court at the time Diogo was killed, it was rare that the devil did not interfere in marriages arranged between close kin and as such he could not approve of papal dispensations (Liske 1878, 37).[8]

Cousin marriage thus, being incorporated in such endogamous alliances, was one of the sources of constant internal trouble, and could stir up conflicts, instead of creating balanced power relationships between households. During the sixteenth century, the number of marriages arranged among Portuguese households would diminish, at least in what concerns the most probable heirs to the throne, but first-cousin marriages would continue between Portugal and Spain. The fact that internal cousin marriages tended to be less frequent is significant, as it means that monarchs had consolidated their position of superiority vis-à-vis their internal rivals and dispensed with the need to incorporate them further in their blood.

The most important royal marriages in Portugal during the sixteenth century would be negotiated exclusively with the Spanish royal family. Eight such marriages followed until 1580: King Manuel I was to marry Isabel of Aragon on her second marriage (her former husband Afonso had died tragically in a horse accident in 1491), and later her sister Maria. His third marriage would be to Charles V's sister Leonor. As to his son and heir João III (1502–1557), he would marry another one of Charles's sisters, Catherine of Austria (1507–1578), whilst his own sister Isabel

7 On the expression of such emotions in João II's chronicles, see Resende 1973, 48–49, 75 and Pina 1977, 909–912, 922, 928–933.

8 Travels of Nicolás de Popielovo (1484), Joannes Dantiscus (1519–31), Enrich Lassota de Steblovo (1580–1584) and Jacobo Sobieski (1611).

(1503–1539) would acquire the title of empress through her marriage with Charles himself. By 1543, his daughter Maria (1527–1545) would marry the prince of Castile, Philip (later Philip II), whilst his son would marry Juana. By 1565 the last alliance between the Avis-Beja family and the Habsburgs would take place, when Maria, daughter of prince Duarte and granddaughter of Manuel I, married the prince of Parma, Alessandro Farnese, grandson of Carlos V's illegitimate daughter Margarida de Austria (Bertini 2000, 45).

The dynastic game was similar to a Russian roulette: the first branch of the family that did not have an heir to succeed would be taken over by the other. In fact, this was similar to what happened after João II's death in October 1495: his only son Afonso having died in 1491, the crown passed on to the brother of the duke of Viseu, the duke of Beja, who became Manuel I (1495–1521).[9] Again, it happened in 1580 when Philip II became king of Portugal using his legitimate right to inherit the Portuguese throne. If his use of force through the invasion of Portugal in the course of that year can be questioned, he was no doubt the best positioned contender according to the existing rules of succession. These were in fact inheritance rules, and kingdoms simply passed on to their heirs. The dynastic demographic roulette set the destiny of Portugal for the next sixty years, as it did with several other political units of early modern Europe.

Gender, Transmission of Property and Well-Being

So far, we have dealt with collective expectations provided by cousin marriage, such as peace prospects, alliance against enemies, and dynastic prosperity. In short, such marriages were supposed to provide collective security for entire kingdoms and their peoples. Failure of reaching these goals often meant war, conquest or incorporation. Let us consider now the individual level, mainly what concerned the well-being of brides by way of what was exchanged in marriage deals. As we know, their reproductive capabilities were at the core of the success of the system. How could their

9 As a result of this dynastic shift, the dynasty of Avis is designated as Avis-Beja after 1495.

situation as child bearers be eased? How did they cope with the disadvantages of expatriation to foreign courts? How were they to escape the misfortunes of rejection, widowhood or infertility?

If these marriages were devised to ensure political security, they implied all the misfortunes that are well know to historians, and that French historian Bartolomé Bennassar has recently studied (Bennassar 2006, 71–158). Having babies was the queens' purpose in life, often at the risk of death. In times of heavy child mortality, the future of their offspring was worsened by the fact that consanguinity carried out increased danger of disease, either mental or physical, to their children. Catherine of Austria, married to her first cousin João III, was not herself the daughter of a consanguineous marriage. Her mother was Juana the Mad who had married Philip the Fair, duke of Burgundy. But João III's consanguineous relatives went way up to his great grandparents. In any case, of the nine children of the couple, only two of them would survive until adolescence, but they would be dead aged less than twenty by the time their own father died in 1557. A single grandson would survive, Sebastião (1554–1578), the posthumous son of prince João and Juana de Austria. Even if queens succeeded in having children who lived until adulthood, many died during child labor or its sequels. It was the case of Isabel, first wife of Manuel in 1496, of her sister Maria in 1517, following the birth of her tenth child, and again Maria (1527–1545), first wife of Philip II, giving birth to Don Carlos.

Besides their life-consuming task of bearing children, most royal marriages meant queens consort would live as expatriates. In the Portuguese case, most marriage contracts stated that they would acquire the groom's nationality upon marriage. Travel to the court of the groom would rarely be followed by a return trip: most would not see either father or mother again, nor their brothers and sisters. Neither would most marriages provide the comfort of conjugal affection, as they were arranged to pursue the interests of the families. If Empress Isabel (1503–1539) seems to have enjoyed the respect and love of her husband Charles V, neglect and contempt were more likely than otherwise. In such circumstances, how were princesses to create security devices that would lead them to live through all those misfortunes in strange places?

It is difficult to give a single answer to this question. Many factors might provide them with a sense of security and well-being. We shall name only just a few:

1) A sense of fulfilling their duty conforming to God's will. Religion was a key feature in the way these princesses lived through their frequently unhappy lives. No wonder that attendance to mass in court chapels, private prayers in their oratories, the assistance of confessor priests, and the staging of elaborate religious rituals never ceased to increase during the sixteenth century. Spiritual comfort, Crowley tell us, was more important than physical well-being before the 18th century; it certainly helped them to face adversity (Crowley 2001, 3–4).
2) A sense of fulfilling duty as daughters of kings and kings' consorts. Obeying the authority of patria potestas, as well as God's will, prevented them from bearing the weight of the consequences of their own decisions.
3) Contact with family through frequent correspondence, often accompanied by gift exchange. Among the latter, the importance of foodstuffs that could not be found locally must be stressed. To exchange delicacies became a sign of mutual affection and letters often refer to it. For instance, even if Catherine of Austria, wife of John III had grown up apart from her brothers and sisters, she took part in a gift and counter-gift practice together with her siblings Maria of Hungary, Charles V and Ferdinand (Viaud 1994, 73).[10]
   In what concerns the use of letters, some could be foundational, such as the instructions for their daughters' married lives as princesses and queens that parents often wrote before they left home. One of such examples is the letter Manuel I gave his daughter before leaving to Piedmont. Very significantly, the letter ended by advising Beatriz to live by the examples of her two grandmothers: Beatriz, duchess of Beja-Viseu, and queen Isabel of Castile.[11]
4) The fact that princesses lived in foreign countries should be eased by the company of ladies-in-waiting also originating in the same court, as well as the male staff of their households. The latter often traveled to and from home, bringing fresh news. Also, they shared the same language, the same memories, identical manners, and sometimes the same

10 See also Instituto dos Arquivos Nacionais/Torre do Tombo (henceforth IAN/TT), *Corpo Cronológico*, parte I, maço 88, doc. 77 [1552.08.02, Lisbon], whereby Catarina of Áustria sent bird game to her sister Maria.

11 Biblioteca da Ajuda, Cód. Ms. 51–VIII–1, "Istruzione del Re di Portogallo Emanuele a Beatrice Duchezza di Savoya sua figlia in lingua portoghese e dal medesimo sottoscritta", fls. 1–7.

"national" dress codes. This tradition can be found since the Middle Ages; Isabel, duchess of Burgundy (1397–1471), not only took her wet-nurse to Bruges, but also men and women who would perform duties in her chamber (Sousa Viterbo 1905). The Portuguese women who became queens of Castile, Isabel (married in 1447) and Joana (married in1455) also kept a Portuguese entourage with them; Catherine of Austria (1507–1578) lived with the household she brought from Tordesilhas during most of her married life in Portugal.

5) The princess' trousseau was also formed by elaborate groups of objects that were carried from home to her new court. Jewelry, clothing, tableware, and liturgical apparatus, often passing on from mother to daughter or from aunt to niece formed a very significant element in providing the princess or queen with a sense of identity. They were not only symbols of power and magnificence, representing the dynastic importance of their family, but also were meant to make the princess/queen feel at home, or at least keep a sense of her identity through memorabilia.
6) The increasing importance of bodily care, materialized either in objects connected with well-being, or in the attendance of barbers, surgeons and doctors. Trousseaus were increasingly composed of utensils used for the care of the body; professionals in health care constantly supervised the princesses' well-being, often through the monitorization of every bodily function.
7) Marriage contracts provided queens with assets that allowed them to live according to their status, and dowers prevented them from being either rejected or widowed without financial compensation. King João I organized and institutionalized the "Casa da Rainha", a group of rents, lands and towns granted to the queens consort (Rodrigues 2007a, 5). Queens could also receive money allowances in rents perceived by royal financial institutions.

Most of these devices that provided comfort in alien lands were included in the marriage contract. Besides making arrangements concerning the political well-being of the countries concerned, such contracts tried to further the bride's interest. The property exchanged through these marriages could be formed by several elements: the dowry, a sum the bride's family should pay to the groom; the trousseau, that is, the list of equipment that the household of the princess would need; the dower, a sum that the husband should pay in case the marriage was off through annulment or childless widowhood; the lands, rents and towns belonging to royal property that the queen would possess during her lifetime; and the amount of the annual allowance available to the wife's expenses and maintenance of her household[12]. The control that women could exert over these different elements of property varied. If it was virtually inexistent in what concerns the dowry, it could be almost total when it came to exerting seigniorial rights over their lands, administering its rents, spending the allowance or disposing of the trousseau (Rodrigues 2007b, 143–145).

Dowry and Trousseau: Material and Symbolic Values

The dowry, always the most significant sum, was entirely due to the husband and would be returned to the bride's family only if the wife did not bear children. Most royal husbands considered it as their own: the case of Charles V is well known, using dowry money in order to finance his war enterprises (Lozano 2005, 157). Very significantly, the most valuable part of the *trousseau*, that is, jewelry and objects made of precious metal or stones were also part of the dowry and not entirely available to the woman. Proof is that a committee formed by representatives of the two contractors was due to assess their value and agree on the amount of money they were worth. This procedure was to take place after the wedding and upon arrival of the princess to her court of destiny.[13] Again, Charles V is known to have disposed of Isabel's jewelry on behalf of the economic needs of his army. Being so, we must suggest the ambiguous nature of precious valuables within the bride's property, since they were half between the dowry and the trousseau.

After the husband's withdrawal of the dowry's money and jewelry, everything included in the trousseau was considered as being the wife's property. She could bequeath it, give it away or dispose of it in any other

12 On the complexity of the denominations of matrimonial assets, as well as their variance over time, see Debris 2005, 395–468.

13 IAN/TT, gaveta XVII, 9-16. "Quitação das jóias do dote da princesa D. Maria. 1544.07.06"

way she wanted. These were in fact the queens' private possessions: they included her books of prayer and devotion, the liturgical apparatus needed for their chapel and sometimes also their private oratory, bed linen, table cloths, clothing, kitchenware and objects concerned with personal hygiene and bodily care. Another significant feature of the trousseaus is that they were elaborated as collective equipment, that is, they should serve the queen's entourage, formed mainly by women but also by some men, normally devoted to writing and account activities or to the religious cult. If some of these objects were to be exhibited at public ceremonies as testimonies to the wealth of the original courts of the princesses, others were exclusively concerned with domestic private use. It is not impossible that expatriated princesses and queens relied on them to create a friendly environment in often hostile and harsh foreign courts.

We can think that queens enjoyed a similar independence in what concerns administrating the annual allowances they were given in order to support their household. These monies originated mostly in land revenues, but there were cases in which the royal treasury was so strained by expenses that other arrangements had to be made, or even marriages avoided. In Portugal, there was a period in the sixteenth century when the lands traditionally allocated to ensure the queen's revenues were held by the widowed queen Leonor, who lived until the end of 1525 (Braga 1992, 74).[14] As a result, allowances for the successive queens of Portugal had to be paid by the Spanish monarch or compensated by other provisional arrangements: it was the case of Isabel, Maria, Leonor and Catherine. There was also a difference between the allowances a royal wife was given according to her status, the sum increasing the moment her husband became king. This was no doubt caused by increased expenses due to heavier pressures in what concerns conspicuous displays of wealth.

Marriage contracts were explicit on all these issues in order to prevent these women from being deprived of means of support, as it was unthinkable that they would ever return to their countries or live in foreign ones in dire straits. Nevertheless, such situations might happen episodically: Catalina of Aragon is known to have lived in poverty in England, and princess

14 On the arrangements made to compensate the three Manuel I's successive wives, see Rodrigues 2007a, pp. 9–10.

Maria of Portugal faced delays in her allowance that motivated panicked letters to her father king João III (Ferrandiz 2005, 225–292).[15]

To marry a daughter, however, might be unaffordable altogether for royal families in times of financial difficulties. During the late fifteenth century, expenses could be somewhat cut if these princesses entered convent, but even so they could be expensive to the royal treasury. In fact, they held small courts in convent, having to provide for their household members such as servants and slaves in all life's needs (clothing, food, marriage and old age) as well as keeping a train of life in accordance with princely status, even if the observant mendicant rules they often entered denied them the right to luxury.[16]

Also, we must keep in mind that marrying a bride meant other significant expenses related to lavish weddings or travel to another court. Princesses not only carried numerous trunks with their trousseaus, but were also accompanied by an extended entourage. In pre-fiscal states, meeting those expenses often meant assembling parliaments and obtaining permission from the representatives of the third estate to raise money to finance the wedding.[17] Needless to say, the cost of such marriages was much higher on the bride's family than on the groom's. Families had to compensate for the heavy costs of marrying their daughters through forms of capital other than economic profit. These compensations were thus mainly political: either reassurance of peace between the two contractors, alliance against common enemies, or just the satisfaction of marrying daughters to prestigious dynasties. In any case, the wedding festivities, often lasting weeks, became prized moments for parents' families to boast their prosperity, even if sometimes artificially or with ruinous consequences.

Dowries could be worth many years of royal annual revenues: when Manuel I married his daughter Beatriz to Charles III, duke of Savoy in 1521, he spent 60 million *réis* in her dowry, and 60 million in her wedding and travel expenses to the city of Nice (Resende 1973, 319–334). This was more than the total of the royal revenues in 1518 – 114 *contos de*

15 On the difficulties of providing financially for Maria of Portugal's household in Spain, see IAN/TT, *Corpo* Cronológico, part I, maço 73, doc. 23 [1544.06.25, Valhadolid], and part I, maço 75, doc. 80 [1544.10.26, Valhadolid].

16 Concerning the case of infanta D. Joana (1452–1490), sister to king João II, see Gomes 2006, pp. 97–101.

17 João II had to assemble a hundred thousand *cruzados* reuniting the parliament and asking the people for a monetary contribution (Resende 1973, 144–145; Pina 1977, 961).

réis –, and only the fact that the king exacted high profits from Asian commerce allowed for such expenses.[18] By the end of that year, when Manuel I died leaving his third wife Leonor as a widow with a baby daughter, Maria (1521–1577), the people of Lisbon demanded that she did not return to France with her child in order to avoid her dowry money from leaving the country (Góis 1955, 180).

João III's policies concerning marriage and dowry were even more expensive, as he insisted on making repeated ruinous deals with Charles V in what concerns the well-being of the royal treasury. The dowry he received in 1525 for having married Charles V's sister, Catherine, was 4.5 times inferior to the sum he was to give his sister, Isabel, to wed the emperor at the same time.[19] Both affairs became difficult on the account of the Moluccas' problem. Magellan and Elcano circumnavigation trip had raised the problem of Portugal's right to the Moluccas, where the Portuguese were already trading. We know today that the archipelago was within the limits of the Portuguese territory according to the treaty of Tordesilhas (1494), but since there was no way of calculating longitude at the time, the problem was not solved even with the astronomic sum paid by João to marry his sister to Charles V. Four years later, a payment of 350 thousand ducats to the latter would finally settle the dispute.[20] Well-being between monarchs came at a price, and it is well known that dynastic interests took the lead. Obviously, no discounts for family were available in such marriage deals. The two monarchs negotiated the next wave of marriages during the 1540s, having agreed on a double affair: João's daughter Maria would marry Charles's heir, Philip and the latter's sister, Juana, would wed João, the heir to the Portuguese throne. Bartolomé Bennassar has counted nine double cross marriages in Early Modern European monarchies, most of them being actively promoted by the Spanish branch of the Habsburg kings.[21]

18 More information concerning the revenues of the Crown can be obtained in Godinho 1978, pp. 33–74.

19 See marriage contracts in As *Gavetas da Torre do Tombo*, 12 vols., Lisboa, Centro de Estudos Históricos Ultramarinos, 1960–1977, vol. VII, pp. 433–455.

20 On the disturbance that the Mollucas caused in marriage negotiations see Buescu 2005, pp. 141–142 and Buescu 2007, pp. 121–125. About the settlement of the dispute over the Moluccas archipelago see Albuquerque 1994, pp. 755–758.

21 They corresponded to eighteen weddings which took place between 1497 and 1615 (Bennassar 2006, 53).

Body-Care, Well-Being and Female Identity

The proportion of jewelry and trousseau in the dowries varied, but it rarely exceeded 30 percent of the total value. There is an evolution concerning the number and type of objects that composed the trousseau. By 1447, the inventory of the trousseau of Manuel I's mother, Beatriz the duchess of Beja-Viseu, married in 1447, was composed of circa 34 boxes (trunks and coffers) and included few pieces of furniture; personal objects included some mirrors and combs, as well as a wash basin for hair. There were many saltcellars but few pieces of cutlery, and only knives and spoons. Textiles made the bulk of the objects included in her trousseau, which also included a chessboard, a typical luxury item feature in this period. Her books of devotion were only two, a missal and a breviary. The trousseau also included equipment to dress mules and horses. At the end of the inventory there was a statement concerning the total weight of silver and gold included in the objects listed (Sousa 1947, 289–296).

Her homonymous granddaughter Beatriz (1504–1538) would take a more diversified array of objects to Piedmont when she married the duke of Savoy in 1521: three books of hours of gold and silver, a psalter, and six non-specified books in parchment also decorated with gold and silver. Her trousseau included the entire furnishings and liturgical apparatus needed for a private chapel, the usual jewelry and textiles for bed and table, and the usual chessboard. Novelties concerned tableware that included numerous forks and knives and all sorts of silverware to serve food and drink. Furniture included several portable tables and writing desks. Objects concerned with body care and physical well-being boomed, in accordance with what is known of objects in the Renaissance household (Cavallo 2006, 174–187). Beatriz's possessions even included a sixteenth century novelty, the fan, whose use had been recently imported from Asia. Body care was entrusted to a variety of wash basins with diversified purposes (feet, hair, hand, etc.). There was also a beauty case *(estojo de toilete)*, perfuming pans, several chamber pots and a toilet box. Altogether, her bridal assets required an amount of 53 boxes and trunks as containers.

By the time princess Maria married Philip (later Philip II), the 1544 inventory of her trousseau listed only objects containing silver, gold or precious stones. Less valuable objects such as textiles meant for daily use or kitchenware disappeared from the lists. It is probable that a separate inventory was elaborated to include those; in any case, only the list of the most precious objects has survived until today. By the 1540s, a new distinction took shape: the liturgical equipment of such a trousseau was divided between the objects dedicated to the bride's chapel and those that would furnish her private oratory. The latter already existed during the fifteenth century and was generally placed near beds in princely chambers, but this inventory points to a specific room dedicated to Maria's personal use.

Many sources are lacking concerning inventories of trousseaus, as these three were the only ones found for this period, and the third, as we have seen, is little more than a section of the dowry, as it listed exclusively the objects with high market value. Nevertheless, their contents suggest the increasing importance of the care and the well-being of the body, as well as the emergence of the need for a place which the princesses could use as refuges from the indiscretions of court life, even if it was only for the purpose of praying.

Conclusions

During most of the fifteenth century, the absence of the principle of primogeniture in what concerns distribution of property among the kings' siblings, created a need to re-establish equilibrium through rather unpredictable rearrangements, one of them being cousin marriage. Although not all marriages were consanguineous and the Crown continued to marry its brides with European allies, members of legitimate and illegitimate branches of the Portuguese royal family inter-married, creating tensions that often could lead to danger of internal armed conflict. However, from the 1490s onwards, marriage alliances tended to be systematically deflected abroad, although the Portuguese crown tended to concentrate marriage deals within the Spanish court, thus transferring endogamy to an Iberian setting. It soon became a dynastic game whose predictable consequence would be incorporation in a composite monarchy. Marriages within close family would prove to stir conflicts and violence that could be deflected abroad, even at the risk of a demographic lottery that would leave one of the dynasties without heirs and force it to be incorporated into another.

Princesses and queens were thus often dislocated to foreign courts and harsh environments, where kin relations were of little comfort. They had little control of their dowries, which was their husbands' property, living out of their rents, allocated by husbands or parents. On the other hand, these women were in full control of their trousseaus that, besides testifying to their high rank and status, must have played an important role in securing well-being and a sense of identity to their lives. Together with the company of their entourage, mainly formed by ladies-in-waiting and other staff that accompanied them, the importance of material possessions must be taken into account in what concerns the adaptation of these women to their new environments. As the sixteenth century went on, the number and variety of items in the trousseaus increased, namely in what concerns objects related to bodily hygiene and devotion. Care of the body and of soul represented islands of privacy in rather public court lives.

References

ALBUQUERQUE, Luís de, 1994, "Molucas", in Luís de ALBUQUERQUE (ed.), *Dicionário de História dos Descobrimentos Portugueses*, vol. II, Lisbon, Caminho, pp. 755–758.

APFELSTADT, Eric C., 2000, "Bishop and Pawn: New Documents for the Chapel of the Cardinal of Portugal at S. Miniato al Monte, Florence", in Kate J. P. LOWE (ed.), *Cultural Links between Portugal and Italy in the Renaissance*, Oxford, Oxford University Press, pp. 183–205.

REGO, António da Silva (ed.), 1960–1977, As *Gavetas da Torre do Tombo*, 12 vols., Lisboa, Centro de Estudos Históricos Ultramarinos, vol. VII, pp. 433-455.

BARBOSA, José, 1727, *Cataloguo chronologico, histórico, genealógico, e critico, das Rainhas de Portugal, e seus filhos, ordenado por D. José Barbosa, clérigo regular, académico real da história portugueza, e chronista da Sereníssima Casa de Bragança*, Lisboa Occidental, Officina de Joseph Antonio da Sylva, impressor da Academia Real.

BENNASSAR, Bartolomé, 2006, *Le Lit, le Pouvoir et la Mort. Reines et Princesses d'Europe de la Renaissance aux Lumières*, Paris, Éditions de Fallois.

BERTINI, Giuseppe, 2000, "The Marriage of Alessandro Farnese and D. Maria of Portugal in 1565: Court Life in Lisbon and Parma", in Kate J. P. LOWE (ed.), *Cultural Links between Portugal and Italy in the Renaissance*, Oxford, Oxford University Press.

BRAGA, Paulo Drummond, 1992, "Da gestão de um património. Análise da Chancelaria da rainha D. Maria, mulher de D. Manuel I", *Beira Alta*, 51, 1–2, p. 74.

BUESCU, Ana Isabel, 2005, *D. João III*, Lisboa, Círculo de Leitores, pp. 141–142.

–, 2007, *Catarina de Áustria Infanta de Tordesilhas Rainha de Portugal*, Lisboa, Esfera dos Livros.

CAVALLO, Sandra, 2006, "Health, beauty and hygiene", in Marta AJMAR-WOLLHEIM and Flora DENNIS (eds), *At Home in Renaissance Italy*, London, Victoria and Albert Museum Publications, pp. 174–187.

CHAVES, Álvaro Lopes de, 1983, *Livro de Apontamentos (1438-1489). Códice 443 da Colecção Pombalina da B.N.L.*, introdução e transcrição de Anastácia Mestrinho SALGADO e de Abílio José SALGADO, Lisboa, Imprensa Nacional/Casa da Moeda.

CORDOVA MIRALLES, Álvaro Fernández de, 2002, *La Corte de Isabel I. Ritos y ceremonias de una reina (1474–1504)*, Madrid, Dykinson.

COSTA, João Paulo Oliveira e, 2005, *D. Manuel I*, Lisboa, Círculo de Leitores.

CROWLEY, John, 2001, *The Invention of Comfort*, Baltimore, Johns Hopkins University Press.

CUNHA, Mafalda Soares da, 1988, *Estratégias Senhoriais na Regência do Infante D. Pedro*, offprint of "Estudos Medievais", Porto.

–, 2000, *A Casa de Bragança, 1560–1640. Práticas senhoriais e redes Clientelares*, Lisboa, Estampa.

DEBRIS, Cyrille, 2005, *"Tu, félix Áustria, nube". La Dynastie de Habsburg et sa politique matrimoniale à la fin du Moyen Age (XIIIe-XVIe siècles)*, Turnhout, Brepols.

FERRANDIZ, Vicenta Ma Marquez de la Plata y, 2005, "Catalina de Aragón (1485–1536). Una soberana renacentista para Inglaterra", in Vicenta Mª Marquez de la Plata y FERRANDIZ (ed.), *Mujeres Renacentistas en la Corte de Isabel La Católica*, Madrid, Editorial Castalia, pp. 225–292.

FONSECA, Luís Adão de, 2005, *D. João II*, Lisboa, Círculo de Leitores.

GODINHO, Vitorino Magalhães, 1978, "Finanças públicas e estrutura do Estado", in *Ensaios II, Sobre História de Portugal*, 2d ed., Lisboa, Sá da Costa, pp. 33–74.

GÓIS, Damião de, 1955, *Crónica do Felicíssimo Rei D. Manuel*, Coimbra, por ordem da Universidade.

GOMES, Rita Costa, 2003, *The Making of a Court Society. Kings and Nobles in Late Medieval Portugal*, Cambridge, Cambridge University Press.

GOMES, Saul António, 2006, *D. Afonso V*, Lisboa, Círculo de Leitores.

LISKE, Javier (ed.), 1878, "Viaje de Nicolas de Popielovo por España y Portugal", in *Viaje de extranjeros por España y Portugal en los siglos XV, XVI, y XVII*, traducidos del original y anotados por F. R., Madrid, Casa Editorial de Medina (1996 reprint, Valencia, Librerías París-Valencia).

LISS, Peggy K., 2004, *Isabel the Queen. Life and Times*, revised edition, Philadelphia, University of Pennsylvania Press (first edition, 1992, Oxford, Oxford University Press).

LOPES, Sebastiana, 2003, *O Infante D. Fernando e a Nobreza Fundiária de Serpa e Moura (1453–1470)*, Beja, Câmara Municipal.

LOWE, Kate J. P. (ed.), *Cultural Links between Portugal and Italy in the Renaissance*, Oxford, Oxford University Press.

LOZANO, J. Sebastián, 2005, "Choices and Consequences: The Construction of Isabel de Portugal's Image", in Theresa EARENFIGHT (ed.), *Queenship and Political Power in Medieval and Early Modern Spain,* Aldershot, Ashgate, pp. 145–162.

MORENO, Humberto Baquero, 1970, "A Conspiração contra D. João II: o julgamento do duque de Bragança", *Arquivos do Centro Cultural Português*, Paris, vol. II.

–, 1979, *A Batalha de Alfarrobeira. Antecedentes e Significado Histórico*, 2 vols., Coimbra, Biblioteca Geral da Universidade de Coimbra.

PINA, Rui de, 1977, "Chronica d'el rey D. João II", in Manuel Lopes de ALMEIDA (ed.), *Crónicas de Rui de Pina*, Porto, Lello & Irmão, pp. 909–933.

RESENDE, Garcia de, 1973, *Crónica de D. João II e Miscelânea* [with an Introduction by Joaquim Veríssimo SERRÃO], Lisboa, Imprensa Nacional/Casa da Moeda.

RODRIGUES, Ana Maria S. A., 2007a, "For the Honor of Lineage and Body: the Dowers and Dowries of Some Late Medieval Queens of Portugal", *e-Journal of Portuguese History*, 5, 1, Summer. See:
http://www.brown.edu/Departments/Portuguese_Brazilian_Studies/ejph/html/issue9/html/arodrigues_main.html

–, 2007b, "The Queen Consort in Late-Medieval Portugal", in Brenda BOLTON and Christine MEEK (eds), *Aspects of Power and Authority in the Middle Ages*, Turnhout, Brepols, pp. 141–145.

SOUSA, António Caetano de, 1947, "Enxoval da Infante D. Brites, quando casou com o Infante D. Fernando", *Provas da História Genealógica da Casa Real Portuguesa,* tomo I, livro III, Coimbra, Atlântida, pp. 289–296 [first edition between 1739 and 1748].

SOUSA VITERBO, Francisco Marques de, 1905, "D. Isabel de Portugal, duqueza de Borgonha. Notas documentaes para a sua biographia e para a historia das relações entre Portugal e a Côrte de Borgonha", *Archivo Histórico Portugês*, vol. III, Lisboa, pp. 81–106.

VIAUD, Aude (ed.), 1994, *Lettres des Souverains Portugais à Charles Quint et à l'Impératrice (1528–1532) conservées aux archives de Simancas*, Paris, Fondation Calouste Gulbenkian.

Marriage Strategies, Women's Dowries and Conflicts between Relatives in Romanian Society (18th century)

Constanța VINTILĂ-GHIȚULESCU

Marriage as a fundamental social practice encompassed all social groups, while it was structured and defined by practices and patrimonial strategies as well as by customs and ecclesiastical law. Moreover, peasants and boyars,[1] merchants and burghers tried to enhance their social standing, wealth or business by contracting good marriages. An abundant secondary literature deals with this connection between marriage arrangements and social or economic advantages, or between marriages and inheritance systems (Laslett 1965; Goody *et al.* 1976; Claverie and Lamaison 1982; Collomp 1983; Stone 1984; Erikson 1990; Klapisch-Zuber 1990; Rogers 1999; Viazzo and Lynch 2002). Eighteenth century Romanian marriage is of particular interest because of special traits, such as the high marriage rate, the legal obligation to marry and endow all children and the low marriage age (age 14–15 for girls, 19–20 for boys). Furthermore, although monastic vocation was a matter of personal choice, the church found other ways to impose a series of legal impediments, which subsequently put limitations on the matrimonial market. Considering all these factors, the present investigation will examine matrimonial strategies and their effects on household economies in the Wallachian/Romanian context.

1 Until the eighteenth century, there was no legislation concerning the status of this social category, called the "boyars"; land ownership was generally regarded as the distinctive class criterion. The constitution of 1740 decreed by Prince Constantin Mavrocordat set the principles to classify the Wallachian nobility, where "boyars" were only individuals holding a high office. Furthermore, they were divided into classes: the elite, comprising boyars of the high offices from the "great ban" to court fodder master *(clucer de arie)*, also members of the princely council *(Divan)* and the *underlings*, who were boyars with lesser offices. First class boyar families were exempted from taxes, while the boyars of second rank only partially. However, owning large estates and an illustrious ancestry were the key elements for acquiring power, despite authority's attempts at defining high office holders more as "civil servants" closely attached to the central power (Cernovodeanu 1986, 249–257).

The present research is based on the analysis of largely unpublished archival material, judicial archives, last wills and testaments, dowry lists or ownership documents.[2] Along with these primary sources, I shall also use legal codes and some narrative documents from eighteenth century Wallachia. Lack of parish registers, population censuses and historical investigations makes it necessary to use a large number of case-studies to support my own arguments.

"As Master over all his Property": the Father and his Authority

The church organized its strategies of control to secure social order within the parish through direct control over families. On the lowest rung were the children, who owed respect and had to obey their parents even after they came of age and sometimes even after they left their family and moved into another one. A young man became "independent" after reaching his age of majority, legally set at 25 years old by the "Law projects" of Mihail Fotino (1765, 1766)[3] and the "Caragea Code of law" in 1818 (Zepos and Georgescu 1982, 487–488; *Legiuirea Caragea* 1953, 8). Once they reached legal age, sons and daughters became "masters" over their own possessions and were free to administer it and to behave "as they wished" as long as they obeyed the law.

The legal power granted by adulthood theoretically provided offspring of either gender with the right to choose a spouse according to their own wishes. Fotino however stipulated that only a son "who has attained majority can marry without his parent's consent", and thus the legislator ignored similar situations when a daughter officially came of age (Zepos

2 Manuscript Sources are mainly the following: at Biblioteca Academiei Române [Romanian Library of Academy], Bucharest (BAR), Registers of Romanian Church about dowry, testaments, divorce and mores, 1700–1800; at Direcția Arhivelor Nationale Istorice Centrale [Department of National Archives], Bucharest (DANIC), Registers of Romanian Church about dowry, testaments, divorce and mores, 1700–1800. File Episcopia Buzău [Diocese of Buzău], File Achiziții Noi [New Documents Acquired].

3 Mihail Fotino was a law-maker, judge, prefect and councilor to the throne between 1756 and 1782, and author of several law books and legislative projects (Georgescu and Popescu-Mihuț 1989, 58–61).

and Georgescu 1982, 456). Later on, in 1818, an article of law stated that "men and women of 25 years old are considered of age", and that "they can dispose of their wealth as they want according to the law" (*Legiuirea Caragea* 1953, 8). The discrepancy between Fotino's proposal and the adopted piece of legislation is not to be overlooked: Fotino referred to "daughter/girl", while the new code of law used the term "woman". In my opinion, the shift in terminology underscores the fact that the legislation regulated the status of adult women – married, divorced or widowed – rather than that of unmarried daughters who had no possessions or dowries of their own. Contemporary debates concerning majority, as reflected in the archives, rarely dwelled on the age (of men) as a determining factor for emancipation. Criteria for reaching adulthood revolved mostly around behavior: marriage meant leaving the family and obtaining the right to manage one's wealth or share of inheritance, the right to hold offices and the duty to pay taxes, all of which indicated a different social status. Parents and parents-in-law could demand temporary custody over their son or son-in-law only when the above listed rights and duties were badly exercised (squandering money on alcohol or on playing cards, neglect of office and family). Such cases were not numerous and show that the court mostly agreed to custodies over very young men, in their early years of marriage; the argument was that youth were reckless. The age of majority for daughters is never an issue in the documents. Once married, they came under the authority of their husband and his family; divorce and widowhood implied a certain degree of independence, but relatives and the community were always keeping a vigilant eye on them.

Since in practice most marriages were concluded before the age of majority, children were kept under the economic and social control of their families. Marriage strategies were determined by the head of the household, and did not require the consent of the young bride or groom – this is different from western European practices, as the Council of Trent had imposed consent as "the prime matter of sacrament", while also trying to force people to marry in churches as opposed to clandestinely. Although parental consent was theoretically not necessary, it could not be avoided due to the requirements for banns, the presence of the priest and of two or three witnesses and the recording of the marriage in the parish register. In England these issues were not regulated until the 1753 Marriage Act (debates starting a lot earlier, in the seventeenth century) which imposed the publication of banns or obtainment of a marriage license, the consent of parents in the case of minors and a church ceremony (Bologne 1995, 223–228; Stone 1977; Menchi and Quaglioni 2001). K. Ritzer states that the Ortodox Church did not require a "formal manifestation of consent", adding:

> such written or verbal declaration of consent were formulated before the spouses-to-be went to Church; or the Church would have considered the fact that both bride and groom observed the religious ritual was in itself enough manifestation of consent (Ritzer 1970, 212).

In theory, a son or a daughter could reject the partner chosen by his or her parents at a high cost: they stood to be disinherited, banished from the family or confined to a monastery. There are cases when children appealed to the ecclesiastical court to annul the paternal decision, bringing forth consent, love or social and economic status as arguments. The courts rarely granted an annulment except when illegitimate children were involved.

Women were on the second rung of this legal construct. Customary law and church canons strictly prescribed the status of a wife: faithfulness and obedience were the two crucial elements for the conjugal bond.

At the top, we find the head of the family, holding responsibilities towards each member of the household. He in fact controlled the domestic order; therefore, church and central authority endowed the *pater familias* with full power over his wife and daughters, full authority over his sons until their marriage; this could be extended in cases of misbehavior or of breaking the unwritten social code that regulated daily life. The cohesion of the social system could be secured, at least temporarily, by imposing strict social rules on individuals. Fathers and heads of families did exert extended power and control over their families but at the same time, they were immediately penalized when they were considered "weak", unable to control their households. The ecclesiastical court took an active interest in investigating complaints brought to their attention by a family member or by the parish priest. The father was punished publicly; for instance he was forbidden to attend church services (but could still stand on the church's doorstep), and the priest could not visit his house. The range of punishments could go as far as a fine, imprisonment, or anathema (formal cursing from the Church). What was worse for an eighteenth century Christian than a break, even if temporary, of the ties to the community he belonged to?

The head of the family played the leading role in the household economy; he had to work for the benefit of all. This position of main provider granted him first of all power of control over his wife: the husband had the right to punish her, with punishments ranging from slaps to killing if she was adulterous. This right was sanctioned in the codes of law, approved of and supported by the church and accepted by the women (Ghițulescu 2004, 252–320). However, a father's authority over his children was most obvious before and after they married. A father's main duty consisted of raising and feeding his children, of endowing and marrying them, a responsibility which was part of the collective mentality and was restated by the central power when deviations occurred. Thus, when Metropolitan Cozma discovered in 1792 that there was an alarming raise in premarital relationships and births out of wedlock, he scolded the parents and primarily the fathers. He advised them to make sure that they followed the right steps towards marrying the children, that girls were provided with dowries and married to "suitable" men (Urechia 1896, 101–105).[4] Domestic authority was justified by the father's ownership of the patrimony. Documents speak of the father who decided the fate of his children "as master over all his belongings" (Urechia 1896, 55–56). He chose the spouses, accepted proposals, negotiated dowry or inheritance, and signed the nuptial agreements. Under these circumstances, financial and economic interests dominated marriages, and sons and daughters had no other choice but to obey. Otherwise, they stood to lose their dowries or their share of the inheritance.[5] State authorities did not condone attempts to break away from paternal domination. Thus, when Stan from Măgurele village in Ilfov county brought a claim against Petre because he would not agree to Stan's marriage to his daughter Ilinca (who had already consented to the marriage and had entered into a sexual relationship with her suitor), the judge issued a sentence according to the Code of law, chapter 254, namely that

4 Ordinance reissued consistently until 1829. See Urechia, 1896, 428–429, 4 July 1792, 24 August 1805. DANIC, mss. 139, ff. 194r–195v, f.l. f.z. 1793; BAR, mss. 3935, ff. 65r-v, ff. 227v–228r, ff. 230r-v; mss. 4027, ff. 95r-v, 15 October 1819, 16 April 1822, 10 December 1822, 12 February 1829.

5 See the case of Costandin from Vălenii de Munte, Prahova county, banished by his father, Moise Vătaful, for being engaged without his consent and to a person who was not part of the father's plans. After only a short resistance, the son obeyed his father and broke the engagement, arguing that "he has nothing, but his father was feeding and providing for him" (BAR, mss. 642, ff. 67r-70v, 14 June, 5 July, 16 September, 5 October, 9 October 1795).

"the marriage of a girl against her parents' wish is to be stopped".[6] While the father had his way, he was obliged to marry his daughter "to whom he would please" within the following four months. Naturally, the behavior prescribed by legal or ecclesiastical ordinances or in local customs differed from comportments in real life. Preventing social practices from becoming norms was a main goal of the central authority. The unsuitable, outdated legislation[7] compelled judges to create such practices themselves, because "the maintenance of social order demands compromise" (Kuehn 1991). The differences between legal prescription and practices are obvious and other studies have already emphasized them (Stahl 1965; Wall 1983; Cuisenier 1994; Cerutti 2003).

The implicit blessing of the parents is closely related to the economic principles that surround marriages. In cases of widowhood or divorce, the dowry, the wedding present and the third of the husband's fortune to which the wife is entitled to could only be recovered if such public support and consent of the families had been given. Dowry could be seized only after a divorce granted for adultery. For all other separation reasons, the wife could theoretically retain her dowry regardless of the existence of children. Thus, the dowry was rightfully hers as a means of support, and it also increased her chances of remarrying. All decisions in divorce cases took into account this legal stipulation, and the judges were extremely scrupulous in establishing the exact value of the dowry. Goods that had been damaged during the marriage had to be replaced. In practice, this was not a straightforward process, and women often had to go back to court to recover their dowries. Widows always kept their dowry, although the absence of children could lead to conflict with the former husband's family (Ghițulescu 2004, 236–245, 390–397).

6 BAR, mss. 4024, f. 190v, 11 February 1799.

7 *Îndreptarea legii* [The Correction of the Law], first printed in 1652, was a mix of civil law, penal law and canon law and bears the imprint of old Byzantine legislation. Throughout the 18th century a number of other code books were published, but *Îndreptarea legii* continued to be used until 1864 when the ecclesiastic court was abolished.

Women and their Work

Marriage strategies as well as conflicts surrounding dowries were closely connected to the status of women and their role in the household economy. The place of women in the Romanian economy has yet to be investigated. Our hypothesis is derived from our archival research and aims only at providing the outlines of this role. A woman's work consisted mostly in running her own household. "The man brings in, the woman administers" is an expression often found in the judicial archives. Thus, a husband's duty was to provide, while the wife ran the household. Her work revolved around the members of the family, feeding and dressing them properly. Daily chores included cooking, spinning, weaving, washing and looking after the family garden and the poultry. Often women lent a hand in the field or in the shop. This work almost never had a monetary value (Hufton 1991, 42) but was an essential "economic activity" (Wiesner 1993, 83) for the smooth running of the household.

In Wallachia, a largely feminine economic sector did not develop as in other European countries (Maza 1983; Meldrum 2000; Dubert 2001; Fauve-Chamoux 2004). One cause could be the extended serfdom of gypsies in noble or rich merchant households as well as in well-to-do families. This assured an efficient domestic service and reduced any demand for labor outside the household. The situation changed only with demographic growth and urban development in the second half of the eighteenth century, when domestic service expanded in urban areas. Many young women, wives and widows streamed into the towns of Wallachia searching for a dowry, a husband or for mere survival. But communities and families alike were reluctant to accept the employment of married women. This reluctance was more obvious in the countryside; a married woman who went to search for a job in the city was suspect, her honour in doubt, as mentioned elsewhere (Wiesner 1993, 89).

Married women did not, however, leave their families to seek employment unless forced by circumstances, such as extreme poverty, alcoholic or abusive husbands or inability to feed their children. Neaga from Vlăiculeşti (district of Ialomiţa) accused her husband of failing to provide for her and bring money home, and furthermore, of having left her without food and protection during an uprising. In these circumstances she was forced to leave her village and seek employment in town. For five years, she waited patiently "for him to show some compassion for her", but, as the husband declared, "having come to dislike each other", there were no prospects for reconciliation. In this case, the couple's economic situation deteriorated gradually, while the man, who had the obligation to provide, failed to do so, and even consented to his wife leaving the home to earn her own keep.[8]

If abandoned, hungry and cold, a woman tried to look after herself and her children by doing odd paid jobs: weaving and sewing, knitting socks, washing shirts and linen. Such menial work did not embarrass husbands, some profited from their wives' activities. Most, however, found it totally unacceptable for her to "have her own way" and take up a job. When she stayed at home, he could keep an eye on her, and everything happened in the restricted domestic space or within the local community. When a woman went into service, she worked in a space inaccessible to the husband. Apart from arousing suspicions, a woman's taking up a job had other disadvantages from a man's point of view: as head of the household who failed to provide economically, he found his authority challenged; secondly, being away all the time, she could no longer look after her own home. Consequently, the man claimed his wife back and demanded the cancellation of any work contract that was signed without his knowledge. The court usually upheld his demand, but demanded from him an assurance that in the future he would fulfil his duties.[9]

For example, facing such difficulties, Licsandra explained: "She hired herself out because he didn't ensure that she had a home and he doesn't bring any good". And there is the husband's scowling discourse: "As my wife, Licsandra, took on a job without my knowledge, I lodged a complaint to His Holiness". When the investigation started among the neighbours, the court learned that the man was an alcoholic, "he spends whatever he earns on drink". The ecclesiastical judge offered a compromise, signed by both of the spouses: "She can keep her job only a while; in the meantime he must find a job and pledge to build a house";[10] Voica, from Ploieşti (Prahova district), left her small town to work as a nurse in Bucharest. She placed her children under her mother's care; this decision stirred up her husband's discontent and rage. The court, solicited by the

8 DANIC, mss. 140, ff. 156v–157r, 15 March 1794.

9 BAR, mss. 3932, ff. 33r–34r, 2 August 1799. See also BAR, mss. 634, f. 46v–47r, 27 August 1769, mss. 636, ff. 23v–25r, 31 January 1781.

10 BAR, mss. 638, f. 178r, 23 February 1784.

husband, required that the wife return home, because "she took on a job without her husband's knowledge and will. A woman has to obey her man; so, she must be forced to follow her husband and to give up her job. Of course, she could keep her job only if her husband wants it".

According to the law, the wife was not allowed to leave the house without the husband's permission; except for visiting relatives (*Îndreptarea legii* 1962, 221). Theoretically she was supposed to ask for permission even for calling on neighbors. In law and in custom, this provision clearly created an inferior standing for married woman. Cases I have looked at in the archives show a variety of situations, some in which women obeyed their spouses and others where they were strong enough to stand up for themselves and defy male authority. The absence of certain legal institutions such as the notary public or the solicitor enabled a woman to plead her case in front of the court, to bring forward her own complaint and make her voice heard (Vintilă-Ghițulescu 2004/2005, 188–210). She could dispose of her dowry and fortune, and she often received support from the men in her own family, who were interested in protecting their patrimony. This discrepancy between written law which included women in inheritance and customary law which excluded female members who had received their dowry served as a means to juggle between the two legal options. Boyars especially never agreed to put down in writing the customary law (which would have mirrored the judicial practice of the country) but preferred the ambiguity of the legal system. The ecclesiastical court resorted to the same attitude, by constructing an entire legal norm from the social practices it aimed at enforcing. Women, too, tried to make use of this social and legal ambiguity.

"Because he was not of my Kind": Marriage Strategies and Familial Interests

From my own research into this field, I conclude that a variety of matrimonial strategies can be identified, as strong testimonials for each family's interest to conclude "a good marriage", but especially to "maximize economic and symbolic profits associated with the establishment of a new relationship" (Bourdieu 1980, 250). Criteria in choosing a spouse are many, dictated by the long-term interest of each *pater familias* but also by custom and society.

Firstly, these strategies unfolded within communities, social categories, business partnerships, neighborhoods and friendships. Peasants preferred not to leave their village, and even when they did, they chose a community close to their home. Priests tended to build "dynasties" by serial alliances, which often involved sending their daughters to marry in a remote village or having a daughter-in-law from a different community.[11] Town dwellers had a wider choice, because the city (i.e. Bucharest and Iași) gathered a mixed population, rural and urban, drawn from all over, even as far as the Balkans. Even here however, a successful artisan or shopkeeper set his eyes on the children of a fellow tradesman, who could be a possible future partner, as spouses for his own children. Boyars built more complex marriage strategies, as for them the social stakes were higher: they wanted to become connected to a certain network and to rise another step on the social ladder (Nicoară 2001, 155–157; Ghițulescu 2004, 106–117; Ungureanu 2004, 59–123; Vintilă-Ghițulescu 2006, 18–59). Rich merchants were in a similar position, their goal however was to enter into a different social class. They imitated the aristocratic lifestyle and acquired offices in order to reach the status of high nobility. The strongest strategy for entry into the ranks of the boyars, and acceptance by them remained marital alliances with the nobility (Lazăr 2007, 233–293).

Secondly, social differences were strongly marked; therefore, the social position of each person placed him/her in a rigid social hierarchy. Any straying from this place was visible and immediately penalized, first through gossip, then through the intervention of the community or even in the court of justice. It is the bitter truth that Dina from Bucharest learned from her own experience, well aware of the social differences that made her marriage impossible:

> I was neighbour with the abovementioned, and many times he impudently came over to me, lured me by all sorts of means and with promises that he would marry me, but I always pushed him away, knowing that he is the son of a merchant and I am poor, unfit for him. But he kept saying that even though he is the son of a merchant he wanted

11 Orthodox priests had to be married when they were ordained, under strict conditions: they could marry only once in a lifetime and the bride had to be a virgin. Widowed priests were not allowed to remarry, and divorce theoretically led to defrocking.

> to take me. I never accepted his requests, knowing, as many others do, that he is a bad sort (November 1802).[12]

Similarly, Voichiţa Cireşeanca Văleanca, petty noblewoman from an ancient and respected family in her market town, refused a *mésalliance* for her daughter, whose hand was sought by Costandin, the son of Moise the steward, recently ennobled "by the back door" thanks to his job.[13] The community was quick in showing contempt when boyar Răducan Topliceanu kidnapped the daughter of Tudorache the furrier from Râmnicu Sărat. Răducanu's brothers reminded the girl's father, aggressively, of his social position, inferior to that of the young man. In this story, there was no place for the feelings of the lovers for one another or those of the family.[14] Sanda, a peasant from Poiana Lungă, Dâmboviţa county, was told by the Metropolitan that love and hopes were not nearly enough for marrying Hadji Ioniţă, son of the merchant Hadji Tănasc. She acknowledges her own inferior standing:

> and after the advice his Holiness has given me, coming to my senses and seeing that I could not marry him, because he was not of my kind, we reached an agreement (February 1795).[15]

The woman was an important piece in plays of matrimonial strategies. From the primary sources, it is evident how she moved along social hierarchies upwards or, more often, downwards, by obeying a decision already made, fulfilling someone else's interest or ambition. Marrying persons of inferior social positions occurred more frequently within the social and political elite. The royal ordinance of Ştefan Racoviţă from 30 July 1764 tried to regulate marriages between local noble families and *Greek* merchants on one side, and alliances between locals and foreigners who came with or without a "trade" to Wallachia (Ghiţulescu 2004, 127–129). Later this rule was incorporated into the *Pravilniceasca Condică* (1780) code of law, which stipulated punishment for those who marry their daughters or sisters "to bad or ill famed" persons, "without regard to the honor of their family". This policy was however beneficial to both parties: the father or the brother could keep the dowry, the groom accepted a

12 BAR, mss. 3934, ff. 27r–28r, 25 November 1802.
13 BAR, mss. 642, ff. 66v–67r, 5 July 1795.
14 BAR, mss. 653, ff. 41v–42r.
15 BAR, mss. 641, ff. 122v, 23 February 1795–26 February 1795.

smaller dowry in exchange for alliance to a prestigious family, and the marriage eased his way into society (*Pravilniceasca Condică* 1957, 95–96). Knowing that norm and practice did not mirror one another, boyars, rich merchants, wealthy artisans and peasants included *mésalliances* in their marriage strategies. These arranged marriages however could not entirely stifle social pride: women more often than men were constantly reminded of their inferior rank. A young girl entering a *mésalliance* only became aware this was socially degrading after the wedding. Tensions and dissensions led to insults and verbal attacks, namely that "he is low born", "she is of better family than him", "she is a daughter's noble", "she is a petty noblewoman, while he is a peasant who works other people's land".[16]

"Unwilling to give his Sister's Dowry": Patrimony as Apple of Discord

In eighteenth century Romanian society, the marriage of a daughter could not happen without a proper dowry whose value depended on social rank. The economic sacrifices of each family were high, especially when daughters outnumbered the male descendants. In popular sayings and in collective thought, girls were called "millstones", difficult to get off the shoulders of the family, difficult to settle down and a burden to the household. Written norms, marriage customs and ecclesiastical rules sketch the paths followed by peasants and boyars in carrying out their duty.

Customary inheritance law prescribed equal division of the patrimony between all sons; girls were only entitled to their dowry, and the youngest son had the right to remain in the family home. The endowment of sons and daughters took place at two crucial moments: at their marriage and on the death of their parents. The privileged moment when each child received a share of the paternal wealth was nevertheless marriage.

16 BAR, mss. 3932, ff. 68r–69r, mss. 638, ff. 155v–157v, DANIC, mss. 140, ff. 16r–17v, Urechia, 425–426.

As Bourdieu has argued, "marriage is not the product of an ideal rule but the result of a strategy" (Bourdieu 1972, 1107); the system of inheritance described above was not static and allowed many alterations. When marrying girls was a pressing necessity, the rule that prohibited endowing girls with immovable property or providing them with a lesser share than their brothers was often broken.[17] In such cases, fathers had to face opposition from the other members of the family, who considered that their rights were not respected. So long as the father was alive, sons and daughters who had already left the household often had recourse to lawsuits to voice their discontent about their shares. Children still living under father's roof were in a lesser position to show their discontent; moreover, the father took them as witnesses for instance when writing a dowry act (a recurrent expression being "and my son was present at this agreement"). This strategy should pay off after the death of their father, when they could protest and change paternal decisions.

Boyar Mareş negotiated the marriage of his first daughter, Catrina, to Eftimie Ghezdoveţ, a captain of mercenaries, and promised to give a generous dowry. His investment was worth his while, because the future son-in-law belonged to a wide network of alliances, which would serve Mareş to marry off his other children. They signed an agreement, but the father died before the wedding took place. In his will, the boyar gave his entire estates to his wife on condition that this marriage was fulfilled and that the remaining eight children were married as well. These paternal decisions were immediately challenged by three sons, who disagreed with the size of the promised dowry and with their stepmother becoming the executor. They asserted their "right over the patrimony" and "the necessity to marry the other three sisters suitably".[18]

The death of the father put his sons in charge of the endowment and of marrying the girls in the family. Despite written contracts with the groom's family and the testament, the brothers avoided carrying out the promises made by their father. Ştefan Bărbătescu, a noble man, asked his

17 A daughter can inherit the entire patrimony when there are no male heirs. The son-in-law is made into "son", thus becoming an heir and carrying on the family name (Stahl 1956, II, 117).

18 Urechia 1896, 440–445, 24 May 1794. The sons did not win their case in the court, because the last will has legal power. The ecclesiastical tribunal decided that since the father had gathered his fortune with his own labour and effort, he had the right to dispose of it as he wished. The last wills and testaments were a powerful instrument for the strategies of the fathers, because they had full authority.

brother-in-law for an extension before he initiated a formal lawsuit, pledging to pay the balance of the dowry even though it was his brother who was in debt. The siblings were in court, because none of them wanted to take responsibility for endowing their sisters. When their father suddenly passed away intestate, they took advantage of the situation: they refused to deliver the dowry promised to the first-born daughter and to marry the second daughter of the family.[19] This situation was not unique; even in cases when fathers did leave behind a last will with strict instructions to their heirs, problems occurred. Thus, although Hera received (along with the entire family fortune) the obligation to endow his sister, he denied responsibility and pushed the mother to give up her dowry. Ilinca Brezoianu, the mother, refused, too, arguing that since the son was in possession of the entire patrimony, he was the one responsible for the dowry as well. Although the mother eventually gave in, she still was adamant about reminding everyone that according to the customary law, the son who held the patrimony also had to look after his younger siblings:

> when the time came for my daughter to be married, I told my son Hera to give her a dowry from his father's house (i.e. fortune), as ban Mareș (the father) ordered. Because he did not want to give the dowry to his sister Ancuța, I had great quarrels with my son Hera, because he took all that belonged to his father (December 1714).[20]

Conflicts over dowries were quite numerous. They opposed fathers-in-law and sons-in-law, the latter being joined by their new brides who thus became enemies of their original families. Let us see the steps taken in the ritual of marriage. In order to marry off his daughter, the father offered a dowry. The payment though took place in various stages. On the day of the formal engagement, the groom was offered the dowry list as a sign of entering the agreement, an official inventory written in front of many witnesses: the parish priest, the bride's father and brothers, blood relatives, neighbours and friends. Their signatures validated the document, but their presence was also a guarantee for the finalization of the marriage agreement.[21] Dowry payment began the day after the wedding celebrations, but according to the law, the father or the head of household had two years at

19 DANIC, Achiziții Noi, MMDCCLXXXIII/69, 5 December 1795.

20 DANIC, Achiziții Noi, CLXXVIII/2, 20 December 1714.

21 During this period, neither notaries nor parish registers exist in Romanian society. The presence of the priest was therefore strongly required, he was considered to have the authority of legal guarantee for authenticity.

his disposal to fulfill the dotal agreement.[22] Disputes often started even on the following day. Going to court was also preceded by negotiations and renegotiations over the dowry list; fathers found themselves forced to give away land (part of a vineyard or half an orchard) to make good on their part of the agreement. When the parties could not reach a mutually satisfactory arrangement, they went to court. Sons-in-law were favored by the legal provisions and by social practice. Deacon Gheorghe from Căpşuna Village, in Vlaşca county, was summoned to court by his son-in-law Ion, who claimed that parts of the dowry had been overdue for six years. The court decided that he was entitled to receive from his father-in-law "a horse, a pig, a fur coat, some plum trees and one row of vines" as soon as they returned to their home village; the local rector was called to be a guarantor for the sentence.[23] In other cases, sons-in-law faced complaints that they abused the confidence of their in-laws and took over goods that were not promised or written down in the dotal agreement. Pârvan accused his son-in-law, priest Tudor from the village of Negrei, Olt county, of deceiving him. When the dotal inventory was drafted twelve years previously, the groom had written down 100 parcels of land instead of 60 as he had been told.[24] Priest Lupu found himself at odds with both his sons-in-law, whose sides were taken by his daughters too. In this particular instance, the conflict was stirred by the fact that the father wanted to leave his entire estate to his only son. The malcontent sons-in-law started rumors that the father-in-law was in debt towards them, and the daughters tried to forge ownership papers on different parts of the estate. In his last will, the father described the situation of each child, when and how he endowed them, the repeated threats and extortion attempts and the false claim of his daughters:

> and if my daughters, Mihalcea and Vişa, produce letters alleging that I gave them land Pârşcovu, it should not be believed, because I testify on my very soul that I have not given them a single piece of land (January 1716).[25]

Prosperity did not depend solely on the wife's dowry and the husband's wealth. It also needed harmony and agreement between partners about the division of labor and the role of each gender in the household economy.

22 DANIC, mss. 143, ff. 211v–213v, 27 May 1793.
23 BAR, mss. 637, ff. 222r-v, 29 June 1785.
24 DANIC, Achiziţii Noi/ MMDCCLXXXIII, 28 September 1792.
25 DANIC, Episcopia Buzău, XLVIII/168, 8 January 1716.

Moral support and emotional connections to the other members of the family groups was also crucial. However, parental meddling in the life of a married couple was a reality that struck William Wilkinson, the English consul to Bucharest.[26]

> It is customary in Wallachia for parents to interfere in their married children's family concerns, and to exercise nearly the same authority over them after marriage as before. They are often seen as busy in intriguing to bring on a separation, as they had been active in seeking husbands or wives for them (Wilkinson 1821, 150–151).

This daily interference had negative effects on the partners and inevitably influenced the couple's prosperity. Alongside economically motivated complaints, the judicial archives contain a large amount of court material, lawsuits caused by the interference of parents-in-law, brothers-in-law, sisters-in-law, uncles and aunts in the decisions of the married couple. While the woman kept strong ties with her own family, she also let herself be influenced by their opinions, eventually refusing to integrate into the husband's kin. Some husbands even drew a visiting schedule between wife and relatives,[27] others were granted court orders to diminish the interference of in-laws (Ghițulescu 2004, 262–268).

Patrimony sparked conflict between blood relatives but also between relatives by marriage (Durães 2000). Eighteenth century Wallachian judicial archives show that court cases concerning patrimony were the most widespread. Almost all noble families were involved in litigation over properties, estates, dowries or inheritance; peasants were confronted with a similar situation.

Explanations for these tensions lie in the marriage strategies, devised to satisfy the interests of a limited number of people. In an economy where cash was scarce, dowries were almost always converted into immovable goods (land, orchards, and vineyards); this practice in turn created discontent among the male members of the group, who were the privileged beneficiaries of the inheritance system. In a society where there was a high marriage rate and endowing each child was an obligation, the

26 William Wilkinson was English consul in Bucharest and Iassy between 1814 and 1818. During this time he traveled extensively through the country, collecting information on the economic potential of the Romanian Principalities for the British government. His testimonials confirm my findings in the judicial archives concerning particular cases, even though he does not offer names or other such details.

27 BAR, mss. 4024, ff. 149r-v, 21 July 1798.

patrimony was not sufficient for everyone. Thus families faced situations in which promises could not be honored by the appointed term, or brothers refused to give over shares of the inherited wealth for the dowry of their sisters. Eventually the patrimony was disintegrating with each generation.

When faced with a high number of legitimate heirs and the permanent shortage of ready cash, the head of the family devised compensation aimed at pleasing everyone. He offered his heirs social and symbolic capital, which became more important than material capital for the sons' social ascent. A family's prosperity was based therefore on several pillars: economic capital, social capital, symbolic capital and harmony within the domestic group. Conflicts between relatives were not caused exclusively by economic troubles but also had a strong emotional component. These emotional discords were a strong factor in undermining the wealth and material prosperity of a family.

References

BOLOGNE, Jean-Claude, 1995, *Histoire du mariage en Occident*, Paris, Hachette.

BOURDIEU, Pierre, 1972, "Les stratégies matrimoniales dans le système de reproduction", *Annales E.S.C.*, 27, 4–5, pp. 1105–1125.

–, 1980, *Le sens pratique*, Paris, Edition de Minuit/MSH.

CERNOVODEANU, Paul, 1986, "Mobility and Traditionalism: the evolution of the boyar class in Romanian Principalities in the 18th century", *Revue des Etudes Sud-Est Européennes*, XXIV, 3, pp. 249–25.

CERUTTI, Simona, 2003, *Giustizia Sommaria: pratiche e ideali di giustizia in una società di Ancien Regime (Torino, XVIII secolo)*, Milano, Feltrinelli.

CLAVERIE, Elisabeth and LAMAISON, Pierre, 1982, *L'impossible mariage. Violence et parenté en Gévaudan XVIIe, XVIIIe et XIXe siècles*, Paris, Hachette.

COLLOMP, Alain, 1983, *La maison du père. Famille et village en Haute-Provence aux XVIIe et XVIIIe siècles*, Paris, PUF.

CUISENIER, Jean, 1994, *Le feu vivant: la parenté et ses rituels dans les Carpates*, Paris, PUF.

DUBERT, Isidro, 2001, "Attraction urbaine et dynamiques migratoires du service domestiques en Galice, 1752–1924", *Annales de Démographie Historique*, 1, pp. 155–176.

DURAES, Margarida, 2000, "Heranças: solidariedades e conflictos na casa camponesa minhota (sécs. XVIII-XIX)", *Biblos*, LXXVI, pp. 155–186.

ERIKSON, Amy Louise, 1990, "Common Law versus Common Practice: the Use of Marriage Settlements in Early Modern England", *The Economic History Review*, 43, 1, pp. 21–39.

FAUVE-CHAMOUX, Antoinette, 2004, *Domestic Service and the Formation of European Identity. Understanding the Globalization of Domestic Work, 16th–21th centuries*, Bern, Peter Lang.

GEORGESCU, Al. Valentin and POPESCU-MIHUT, Emanuela, 1989, *L'organisation d'Etat de la Valachie (1765–1782)*, Bucharest, Editura Academiei Române.

GHIȚULESCU, Constanța, 2004, *În salvari si cu islic. Biserică, sexualitate, căsătorie si divort în Tara Românească a secolului al XVIII-lea* [*Shalvar and Ishlık. Church, Sexuality, Marriage and Divorce in Eighteenth-Century Walachia*], Bucharest, Humanitas.

GOODY, Jack, THIRSK, Joan and THOMSON, E. P. (eds), 1976, *Family and Inheritance: Rural Society in Western Europe, 1200–1800*, Cambridge, Cambridge University Press.

HUFTON, Olwen, 1991, "Le travail et la famille", in Arlette FARGE and Natalie ZEMON DAVIS (eds), *Histoire des femmes en Occident*, vol. III, Paris, Plon, pp. 27–57.

ÎNDREPTAREA LEGII (1652), 1962, Bucharest, Editura Academiei Române.

KLAPISCH-ZUBER, Christiane, 1990, *La maison et le nom. Stratégies et rituels dans l'Italie de la Renaissance*, Paris, EHESS.

LASLETT, Peter, 1965, *The World we have Lost*, London, Methuen.

LEGIUIREA CARAGEA (1818), 1953, Bucharest, Editura Academiei Române.

KUEHN, Thomas, 1991, *Law, Family and Women. Toward a Legal Anthropology of Renaissance Italy*, Chicago, University of Chicago Press.

LAZAR, Gheorghe, 2007, *Les marchands en Valachie, XVIIe–XVIIIe siècles*, Bucharest, Institutul Cultural Român.

MAZA, Sarah, 1983, *Servants and Masters in Eighteenth-Century France*, Princeton, Princeton University.

MENCHI SEIDEL, Silvana and QUAGLIONI, Diego (eds), 2001, *Matrimoni in dubbio. Unioni controverse e nozze clandestine in Italia dal XIV al XVIII secolo*, Bologna, il Mulino.

MELDRUM, Tim, 2000, *Domestic Service and Gender 1660–1750. Life and Work in the London Household*, Harlow, Pearson Education.

NICOARĂ, Toader, 2001, *Transilvania la începuturile timpurilor moderne (1680–1800). Societate rurală și mentalități collective* [Transylvania in the early modern age. Rural Society and Collective Mentalities], Cluj-Napoca, Dacia.

PRAVILNICEASCA CONDICĂ (1780), 1957, Bucharest, Editura Academiei Române.

RITZER, Korbinian, 1970, *Le mariage dans les Eglises chrétiennes du Ier au XIe siècle*, Paris, Ed. du Cerf.

ROGERS, Nicholas, 1999, "Money, Marriage, Mobility: The Big Bourgeoisie of Hanoverian London", *Journal of Family History*, 24, 1, pp. 19–34.

STAHL, Henri, 1998 (first edition 1965), *Contribuții la studiul satelor devălmașe românești*, Bucharest, Cartea Românească.

STONE, Lawrence, 1977, *The Family, Sex and Marriage in England 1500–1800*, Oxford, Oxford University Press.

STONE, Lawrence and FAWTIER STONE, Jeanne C., 1984, *An Open Elite? England, 1500–1880*, Oxford, Oxford University Press.

UNGUREANU, Mihai-Răzvan, 2004, *Convertire şi integrare religioasă în Moldova la începutul epocii moderne* [Conversion and Religious Integration in Moldavia in the Early Modern Age], Iaşi, Editura Universităţii "Alexandru Ioan Cuza".

URECHIA, Vasile Alexandru, 1896, *Istoria românilor*, Bucharest.

VIAZZO, Pier Paolo and LYNCH, Katherine A., 2002, "Anthropology, Family History, and the Concept of Strategy", *International Review of Social History*, 47, 3, pp. 423–452.

VINTILĂ-GHIŢULESCU, Constanţa, 2004–2005, "Divorce and Divortiality in Eighteenth-Century Romanian Society", *Südost-Forschungen*, 63–64, pp. 188–210.

–, 2006, *Focul amorului: despre dragoste şi sexualitate în societatea românească, 1750–1830* [Fire of love: about love and sexuality in Romanian Society], Bucharest, Humanitas.

WALL, Richard, 1983, "The Household: Demographic and Economic Change in England 1650–1970", in Richard WALL, Jean ROBIN and Peter LASLETT (eds), *Family Forms in Historic Europe*, Cambridge, Cambridge University Press, pp. 1–63.

WIESNER, Merry, 1993, *Women and Gender in Early Modern Europe*, Cambridge, Cambridge University Press.

WILKINSON, William, 1820, *An Account of the Principalities of Wallachia and Moldavia: Including Various Political Observations, Relating to Them*, London, Longman *et al.*

ZEPOS, Pan and GEORGESCU, Valentin Al. (eds), 1982, "Nomicon Procheiron, by Michel Fhoteinopoulous à Bucarest (1765–1777)", *Annuaire du Centre de Recherche de l'Histoire du Droit Grec, 1977–1979*, Athènes, Académie d'Athènes, pp. 24–26.

Marriage Strategies in Azorean Communities of Pico Island (19th Century)

Differentiated Female Behaviour in Choosing a Lifelong Partner

Norberta AMORIM and Carlota SANTOS

It is our opinion that through historical demography we cannot only reach a better knowledge of living conditions of females in the past, from the early-modern to the contemporary period, but also dig deeper into the history of the family. Databases prepared originally for demographical analysis, are open to systematic improvement by following individual life courses in the genealogical chain, and by combining sources containing sociological or cultural information. Good quality sources are available regarding the nineteenth century, allowing us a thorough analysis of family reproduction, conditions of female well-being and access to marriage, sexual life and reproduction.

Pico Island, in the Azores archipelago, is where we have created rich digitalised databases and accomplished a systematic linkage of different nominative sources, completed with a collection of orally transmitted memories. Our first results revealed high levels of child survival on the island and high longevity of the population (Amorim 1992; Mesquita 1998; Santos 2004; Amorim 2005). This phenomenon of low mortality, that we assume to be a major well-being indicator, clearly reveals the women's important role in the familial economy. Indeed, within these mainly rural communities, the parting of women from agricultural work allowed a greater dedication to the members of the domestic household and, frequently, the development of small craft industries which added to the families' income.

The aim of the present study is to analyse differential strategies for biological and social reproduction in different communities of Pico Island, addressing the incidence of geographical endogamy – in relation to female well-being –, models of spouse selection and the evolution of the mean age at first marriage, considering the different social strata and the particular context of male emigration and socio-economic changes during the nineteenth century. Regional differences will be stressed.

Ecological Characteristics of Pico Island

The Azores islands (Figure 1), uninhabited when discovered by Portuguese navigators in the fifteenth century, occupy a total area of 2,344 km^2. The archipelago, formed by nine islands of volcanic origin, is situated in the Atlantic Ocean some 1,500 km from the European mainland, with an orientation SE–NW with a spread of 600 km.[1] Pico is part of the central group of islands (Terceira, Graciosa, S. Jorge, Pico and Faial), where Pico and Faial are only 6 km apart from each other.

The Pico Island, with a surface area of 433 Km^2 and 14,806 inhabitants nowadays (Instituto Nacional de Estatística 2001), had more than 30,000 inhabitants in the beginning of the nineteenth century. Pico is a recent island, dominated by a mountain elevated 2,351 metres above sea level. The population, conditioned by the complex orography, was established in the lower parts of the littoral where the best lands for fruit and vegetable cultivation are situated. The highlands were occupied by pastures of over 800 metres in altitude, and by woods where some native botanic species of Azores proliferate. The need to overcome the agricultural limitations has favoured maritime activities, by stimulating the fishing and, from the 19th century on, the whale industry.

The soil is poor for cereal crops, especially in the western region, which is basically occupied by the municipality of Madalena. The mild climate and the soil characteristics create favourable conditions for the development of viticulture assuring the exportation of a high quality wine to Northern Europe, Russia, the United States of America and Brazil.

1 The spread of 600 km has the following coordinates: Santa Maria, (36° 55' 43'' N; 24° 46' 15'' WG); Corvo (39° 43' 23'' N; 31° 16' 24'' WG).

Figure 1. Map of the Azores archipelago

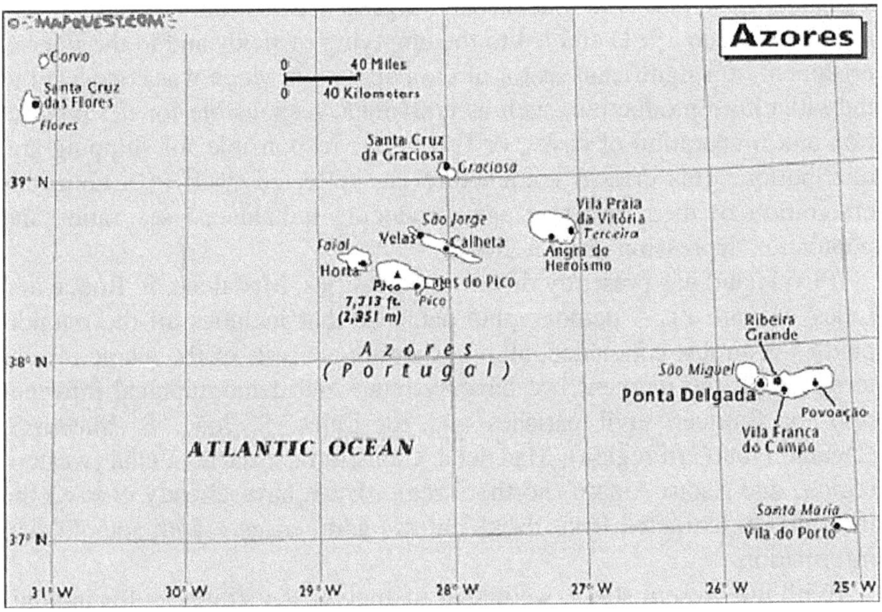

Notes: The Azores archipelago is defined in three geographical groups of islands: the Eastern group (S. Miguel and Santa Maria); the Central group (Terceira, Graciosa, S. Jorge, Pico and Faial); the Western group (Flores and Corvo).

Figure 2. Map of Pico Island, Azores. Localization of parishes, distributed nowadays by three municipalities: Madalena, S. Roque and Lajes

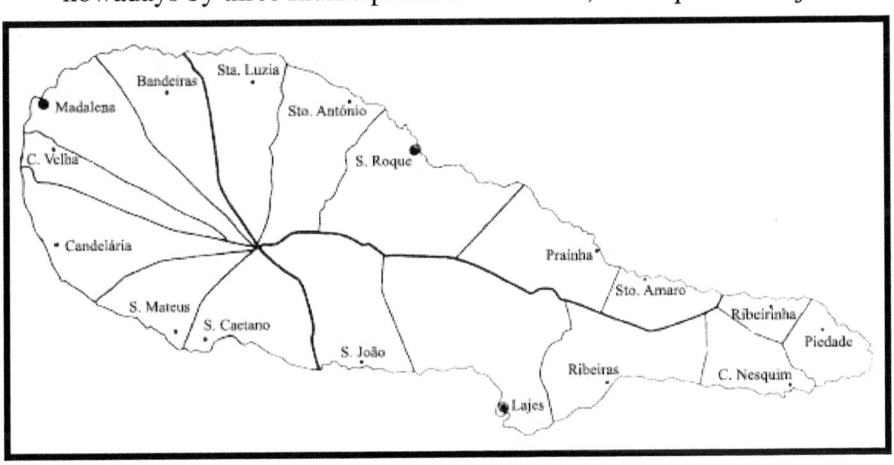

From 1853 on, the wine production of Pico was drastically reduced by a plague of *oidium* which devastated a great part of the vineyards in the region (Macedo 1981) and led to the emptying of fields and to the impoverishment of a significant sector of the population which was connected to the viticulture production, such as craftsmen, responsible for the production and preparation of casks, or fishermen, responsible for shipping and distribution. This critical conjuncture has reflected itself in a notorious emigration of men in active age, producing unbalanced sex ratios and population depression (Santos 2004).

Pico Island has presently three municipalities, Madalena, S. Roque and Lajes[2] (Figure 2). A demographic database that includes all the municipalities is almost concluded, allowing future analysis of the whole insular territory. At the moment, we have systematized demographical information for fourteen civil parishes and for Lajes, S. João, S. Mateus/S. Caetano (southern region), Madalena, Candelária, Criação Velha (western region) and Santo Amaro (northern region); we have already crossed the information extracted from fiscal sources and censuses with sociological information.

With the present study, we intend to analyse the strategies for biological and social reproduction of different communities during the 19th century. Adopting a micro-analytical perspective, we address the incidence of geographical endogamy and the evolution of the mean age at first marriage, considering the different social strata. Indeed, in these societies where a subsistence economy predominated, the selection process of the spouse was strongly conditioned by the need to ensure the enlargement of the means of subsistence that the system of egalitarian inheritance tended to fragment over the generations. Besides, the mean age at marriage reflects personal strategies of temporary emigration, intended to assemble economical conditions for the construction of a new household that could enable continuation of the social status.

In a more complex community, Lajes, with a defined urban nucleus corresponding to one third of the parish population, we proceeded to a statistical analysis of biological and social reproduction in the majority

2 Nowadays, the municipality of Madalena comprises the parishes of Madalena, Bandeiras, Criação Velha, Candelária, S. Mateus and S. Caetano. The municipality of S. Roque comprises the parishes of S. Roque, Prainha, Santo Amaro, Santo António and Santa Luzia. The municipality of Lajes comprises the parishes of Lajes, S. João, Ribeiras, Calheta de Nesquim, Piedade and Ribeirinha

groups (farmers, rural workers, fishermen and craftsmen). We reserved for case studies the minority groups (property owners and the urban nobles) evidencing the adopted strategies not only for the preservation of the economic level or social status, but also for its valorisation.

Individual and Family Sources for Longitudinal Analysis

The basic sources used in this study were the births, marriages and deaths recorded in parish registers, organised and analysed by applying the methodology of "parish reconstitution" (Amorim 1991). For further nominative linkage of information we were lucky to also collect the following available sources.

a) *Róis de confessados (status animarum)* were annual gatherings of information about the population that was obliged to respect some parish precepts. Made by the parish priest, these lists aimed to supervise the abidance of the ecclesiastical rules. Since the end of the 1860s or in the beginning of the next decade, all the inhabitants of each parish were noted, including minors, turning this source into a proper population census.

b) Passport records were kept since 1859 with reference to the parish of origin, name, age, profession, as well as height, eye or hair colour and other particular characteristics.

c) In the early years of the 1880s, the property records of several parishes of the island were registered. For each of them, the following aspects were identified: property owner's name, rustic or urban property parcels, its area (measured in *ares* and *braças*), crop type, collectable income (in *réis*) for the calculation of the predial contribution.

For our research project, all individual and family information from these sources was systematically gathered and linked to a map of each plot and house.[3] All registered property owners were identified by name, ad-

3 Project "Espaços Urbanos e Rurais. Micro-análise dos comportamentos demográficos, mobilidades geográfica e social e dinâmicas culturais (séculos XVI a XX)", Fundação para a Ciência ea Tecnologia, Lisbon. See research programs of the Núcleo de Estudos de População e Sociedade/Neps, I.C.S., Universidade do Minho.

dress, size and number of property they owned, as mentioned, making it possible to establish connection between families and land property owned, as well as to evaluate their economical resources.

d) Population rolls were organized by households. They referred to 1836 (for the Lajes municipality) and to 1838 (for the municipalities of Madalena and S. Roque). They were elaborated for civil administrative reasons, specifying professions of male household heads, while the female work was generally omitted. In the case of the 1836 census, households were classified according to two categories, property owners and non property owners. We learn how these householders made a living: whether they lived exclusively out of their property income or from any kind of wage paid by the State (except military salary). It is mentioned if they made their living exclusively out of their work, or if they added to their work some other income or salary. The beggars, which could be fixed or ambulant beggars, were also identified.

Data Linkage and Research Method for Reconstructing Marriage Strategies

The specificity of the available sources to be linked with demographic data conditioned the type of possible analysis for each one of the communities under study. We decided to maximize the exploitation of the respective sources.

For the parishes of Madalena, Criação Velha and Candelária, we crossed the information from the 1838 population rolls with the respective demographic databases, in order to proceed to the analysis of differential behaviours within those populations. In the absence of specific references to female work as a source of family income, family behaviours were analysed according to the profession of the household head. Given that it was difficult to know exactly the standard of living of a family, the mentioned profession was taken mainly as an indicator of social status and its belonging to some structural group with distinctive characteristics.

For S. João, Santo Amaro and Lajes we created databases, as systematic as possible, including all reconstructed life courses of inhabitants up to 1883, when property records were gathered in those villages, so that all property owners were well identified, be it of rural or urban real estate.

By studying *róis de confessados* and property records, each house was located in the proper place, site or street. All members of each family were identified and, in the case of a procreating family, we included the children who were later born in the parish. We tried to find the affiliation of each individual, his date of birth, eventually his date of marriage or death and, if that was the case, the exact or approximate date of exit from the island. We also tried, for the heads of each residential unit, to find the residence of first degree relatives, parents or siblings, if still living. For each property owner, we created a file with the respective properties, rural or urban, referring to site, area, crop type, type of house and collectable income.

In the case of S. Caetano (that integrated the parish of S. Mateus until 1886), inhabitants were listed in 1861, but the fact that the property records were not from the same year did not allow us to establish a systematic connection between each family and property.

The complex orography of Pico Island and its isolation – until very recent times (Rocha 1991) – strongly limited spouse selection not only to the parish's area but even to the place of residence. Economic and socio-cultural factors contributed simultaneously to the intensification of this tendency. In fact, the structure of small property owning itself stimulated social proximity and created solidarity ties between rural workers that owned small parcels of land they cultivated to guarantee the living of the family, advising the concentration of property via marriage and avoiding its excessive division, induced by a system of egalitarian inheritance.

Thanks to rich information resulting from the linkage process between nominative demographic databases and lists of the inhabitants and property records, we proceeded to the analysis of the levels of geographical endogamy and average age at first marriage observed throughout the 19th century in the western, northern and southern regions, noting existing variations between different occupational groups.

Western Pico's Model of Spouse Selection

We found rather high rates of exogamous marriages in Criação Velha, where one groom out of five was an outsider (Table 1). By contrast, Candelária stands out with the highest percentage of endogamous marriages in any of the analysed periods (79.5 percent for the period 1800–1849 and 83.2 percent for 1850–1899). This difference reflects geographical proximity and kinship relationships that were established by the families of Madalena throughout the nineteenth century with families of another parish (Santos 2004), explaining 21 percent of mixed marriages involving mainly men from Madalena and women from Criação Velha. But in all parishes belonging to the western region of Pico Island, some family relationships were also established with nearby Faial Island: these relationships were easy to entertain and they enlarged their horizons.

Table 1. Endogamous and exogamous unions, western parishes of Pico Island, Azores, all marriages, by periods (1800–1899). Percentages

Periods of marriage	Total Number of marriages	Endogamous unions both from the parish %	All exogamous Unions %	Exogamous unions female outsider %	male outsider %	both outsiders %
Madalena						
1800–1849	783	75.4	24.6	9.1	13.8	1.7
1850–1899	569	71.0	29.0	9.0	14.9	5.1
Criação Velha						
1801–1849	331	70.4	29.6	6.6	20.9	2.1
1850–1899	256	69.5	30.5	6.3	21.9	2.3
Candelária						
1800–1849	737	79.5	20.5	4.2	13.9	2.4
1850–1899	446	83.2	16.8	5.8	9.0	2.0

Sources: Madalena, Criação Velha and Candelária data sets (3122 marriages).

Although the marriage market of the individuals living in the first half of the 19th century can be globally defined by a strong endogamy and by the reduced marital mobility of females, we see a clear difference between the surrounding area of the Madalena port, easily connected to the city of Horta in Faial and other islands, contacts which stimulated marriage projects with individuals that were born outside, and the geographically more distant rural areas of Pico.

Table 2. Origin of outsider spouses in exogamous unions, western parishes of Pico Island, Azores (1800–1899). Percentages

Origin of outsider spouse	Madalena %	Criação Velha %	Candelária %
Pico (S.Roque and Lajes)	54.9	64.7	37.3
Faial	26.5	21.6	49.1
Other Azorean islands	11.9	9.8	10.2
Other countries	6.7	3.9	3.4
	100	100	100
Pico and Faial	81.4	86.3	86.4

Sources: Madalena, Criação Velha and Candelária, data sets.

However, analysing in detail all exogamous unions during the 19th century (when one of the spouses was not born in the parish or municipality) that have been celebrated in each of the three western parishes, we notice that the relationship with Faial Island was anyway relatively intense in Candelária, in 49.1 percent of the cases, whereas Madalena was preferentially oriented towards other islands of the Azores archipelago or towards more distant localities of the continent, Brazil or the USA (Table 2). Throughout the nineteenth century, the variety of occupations was quite narrow, with a vast majority of farmers, rural workers and fishermen declared in the population roles of 1838. Big property owners and public workers were concentrated at the administrative centre.

Endogamy rates were higher and more stable among the farmers and rural workers, reaching already 88.8 percent in the first half of the century, than among property owners. The fishermen group approached those rates during the first period, falling significantly behind during the second part of the 19th century (Table 3).

Table 3. Endogamous and exogamous unions, western parishes of Pico Island, Azores, marriages by socio-professional groups and periods (1800–1899). Percentages

Periods of marriage	Total Number of marriages	Endogamous unions both from the parish %	All exogamous Unions %	Exogamous unions female outsider %	Exogamous unions male outsider %	Exogamous unions both outsiders %
Farmers+ Rural workers						
1800–1849	429	88.8	11.2	5.4	5.4	0.4
1850–1899	700	88.0	12.0	4.5	6.7	0.6
Fishermen						
1800–1849	90	87.8	12.2	6.7	5.5	0.0
1850–1899	170	81.2	18.8	5.9	10.6	2.3
Craftsmen						
1800–1849	70	72.8	27.2	2.9	21.4	2.9
1850–1899	116	69.0	31.0	6.0	23.3	1.7
Property owners						
1800–1849	56	64.3	35.7	10.7	19.6	5.4
1850–1899	86	65.1	34.9	8.1	14.0	12.8

Sources: Madalena, Criação Velha and Candelária data sets (1717 marriages).
Notes: Marriages where occupation is known.

Whereas the craftsmen's sector occupied an intermediate position, the property owner's group presented a maximum incidence of exogamous marriages, especially those involving outsider women. The difference from other groups was remarkable in the case of marriages between brides and grooms who were both outsiders to the parish, going up to 5.4 percent (in the period 1800–1849) and 12.8 percent in the following period.

Central Pico's Model of Spouse Selection

Not surprisingly, in the parishes of S. Caetano, S. João and Santo Amaro, which are more distant from a direct connection to Faial Island, parish endogamy was more intense. This self-enclosure was not only centred on the parish, but also applied to the place of residence and neighbourhood or quarter attachments. In fact, for the inhabitants of Pico, it did not make much sense to speak of S. Caetano, S. João or Santo Amaro as undivided spaces (Amorim 2004; 2005; 2006)). In each of these parishes, we can clearly distinguish two communities with different spaces, strong identities and sense-of-belonging symbols.[4] In S. Caetano, there is the Prainha quarter and the Terra do Pão quarter; in S. João, Companhia de Cima and Companhia de Baixo; in Santo Amaro, Terra Alta and Fajã.

To evaluate how frequently individuals chose a spouse from the same site, we adopted specific criteria to be applied to these three parishes. For each inventoried individual, married or widowed, the place of residence of the first degree consanguine kin (parents or brothers, if residents) was considered. If the parents, or at least one of them, were still alive, their place of residence was taken as the individual's origin.

In the cases where we identified three or more siblings of an individual with deceased parents, the place where most of them lived was considered to be the origin of the family. In cases where two siblings residing in a different place from the individual were identified, the place where those siblings lived was considered to be the origin of the family. In the case of two siblings residing each in a different place, the place of residence of the observed individual was considered as the origin place of the family. All the other cases of individuals born in the parish were considered as omitting place information, locating them in the parish. When it was not possible to clarify the residence of first degree relatives, but their dates of birth were known, we located the individual in the parish.

According to these criteria, S. Caetano had a very strong parish endogamy in the mid-nineteenth century (Table 4), with 95 percent of the men and 93 percent of the women – married or widowed and deceased spouses – born in the same space. Few outsider men were found: ten we suppose to be from S. Mateus, one from S. João, two from Candelária, one from Madalena, one from Bandeiras and one from S. Jorge, adding one of unknown origin. However, it is worth noticing that S. Caetano was declared as an autonomous parish from S. Mateus only in 1886. Concerning women, there are fourteen that we suppose to be from S. Mateus, six from S. João, one from Lajes and two of unknown origin.

4 Some of the sense-of-belonging landmark symbols are the S. Caetano Church, located in Prainha quarter, and Santa Margarida Church in Terra do Pão quarter, both in S. Caetano parish, as well as the Espírito Santo chapels that were constructed near those churches. In what concerns S. João, both Companhia de Cima and Companhia de Baixo have their own Espírito Santo chapels.

Table 4. Endogamous and exogamous unions in S. Caetano, a central/southern parish of Pico Island, Azores, spouse origin by local quarters and residence criteria (1861), by gender. Percentages

Residence of first degree Consanguine kin*	Place of residence*					
	Terra do Pão quarter		Prainha quarter		S. Caetano parish	
	Men	*Women*	*Men*	*Women*	*Men*	*Women*
S. Caetano Same place	63	71	61	61	62	65
S. Caetano Different place	6	4	4	5	5	5
S. Caetano Unidentified place	26	21	29	25	28	23
S. Caetano: Total	95	96	94	91	95	93
S. Mateus	3	1	3	6	3	4
S. João	1	2	0	2	0	2
Other parish of Pico	1	1	1	0	2	0
Other Azorean islands	0	0	1	0	0	0
Unidentified parish	0	0	1	1	0	1
Other parishes	5	4	6	9	5	7
Total	100	100	100	100	100	100

Sources: S. Caetano listing for 1861 and reconstructed population data sets.
Notes: *Residence criteria: for each inventoried individual, married or widowed, the place of residence of the first degree consanguine individuals (parents or brothers, if residents) was considered. If the parents, or at least one of them, were still alive, their place of residence was taken as the individual's origin.
Terra do Pão and Prainha are different quarters of S. Caetano parish.

Analysing same-place behaviour, and subtracting the cases of unidentified place, we see that, of the 96 men we know to have been born in Terra do Pão, only 8 went to Prainha to marry. Of the 118 men we know to have been born in Prainha, only 8 sought Terra do Pão for marriage, a smaller proportion than the first one. Among the 104 women born in Terra do Pão, 6 married in Prainha. From the 121 born in Prainha, only 9 married in Terra de Pão.

The difference of attraction between each place does not appear to be very significant. Men from Terra do Pão who married in Prainha constitute about 8 percent of the total, whereas 7 percent of the men from Prainha married in Terra do Pão. Female percentages were respectively 6 percent and 7 percent. Through our observation, we can also state that spouse selection in S. Caetano was mostly occurring within the place of residence, street or dirt road, which is only possible due to the relative concentration of the urban spaces and the connections created between small property owners that searched viability for the exploitation of their small farms.

From the figures we found for Santo Amaro in 1883, a strong parish endogamy is also evidenced, though not as accentuated as in S. Caetano. In fact, 78.9 percent of the men living in Santo Amaro – or deceased spouses of the residing women – were born in the parish. In the case of women, this percentage reached 82.5 percent (Table 5).

Table 5. Endogamous and exogamous unions in Santo Amaro, a central/northern parish of Pico Island, Azores, spouse origin by local quarters and residence criteria (1883), by gender. Percentages

Residence of first degree consanguine kin*	Place of residence*					
	Terra Alta quarter		Fajã quarter		Santo Amaro parish	
	Men	*Women*	*Men*	*Women*	*Men*	*Women*
Santo Amaro Same place	42.9	46.3	54.2	63.9	50.0	56.8
Santo Amaro Other place	10.0	5.0	0.8	3.4	4.2	4.1
Santo Amaro Unidentified place	22.9	27;5	25.8	17.6	24.7	21.6
Santo Amaro: Total	75.8	78.8	80.8	84.9	78.9	82.5
Prainha	4.3	3.8	4.1	3.4	4.2	3.5
Piedade	1.4	8.7	1.7	2.5	1.6	5.0
Ribeiras	5.7	3.7	5.0	2.5	5.3	3.0
Other parish of Pico	2.8	2.5	1.7	2.5	2.1	2.5
Other Azorean islands	5.7	0	4.2	1.7	4.7	1.0
Unidentified parish	4.3	2.5	2.5	2.5	3.2	2.5
Total	100	100	100	100	100	100

Sources: Santo Amaro listing for 1883 and reconstructed population data sets.
Notes: * Residence criteria: for each inventoried individual, married or widowed, the place of residence of the first degree consanguine individuals (parents or brothers, if residents) was considered. If the parents, or at least one of them, were still alive, their place of residence was taken as the individual's origin. Terra Alta and Fajã are different quarters of Santo Amaro parish.

Contrary to what we expected, the parish of Pico which offered more grooms to Santo Amaro's women was Ribeiras, and not the neighbouring parishes of Prainha or Piedade. This is the result of the lack, at the time, of a connection road surrounding the island, which made contacts easier through the woods. The pastures of Santo Amaro were connected to Ribeiras, and their maritime communities also shared preferential connections. Outsider women mostly came from Piedade. Of the outsider men that married in Santo Amaro and resided in the parish by 1883, nine were born in other Azorean islands, mainly S. Jorge and Terceira. In the case of outsider women, only two were not born in Pico. Thus in 1883 Santo Amaro, no one married a person born outside of the archipelago.

If we analyse the situation by place, we verify that, in Terra Alta, marriage with outsider men was more frequent than in the previous example, going up to 24.2 percent against Fajã's 19.3 percent. As in most of the other parishes, most men marrying Terra Alta's women came from Ribeiras and other Azorean islands. In the case of women, there was more variation between each place. Terra Alta attracted mostly women from Piedade (Ribeirinha was, at the time, part of the Piedade parish) than from any other parish of Pico, and there were no women from outside the island. In Fajã, most women came from Prainha, but without significant differences from the parishes mentioned in Table 5.

For those born in Santo Amaro, the results found for local endogamy, without considering the unidentified individuals, are very interesting. Of the men born inside the parish and residing in Terra Alta by 1883, or deceased husbands of resident women, 81 percent were born in the place. The corresponding percentage of native-born among women residents, or deceased wives of resident men, was 90.2 percent. In Fajã, the percentage of men is of 98.5 percent, and of women, 95 percent. It appears to be clear that both places of the parish of Santo Amaro, Terra Alta and Fajã, were communities with few endogamous relationships. We have to verify that, in any given case, marriages in other places of the parish were in lesser number than those outside of it. However, men from the smaller place, Terra Alta, were more attracted to Fajã than the contrary. We admit that the greater attraction for Fajã could come as a result not only of its higher richness in terms of productive soil, but also of the existence of more diverse occupational activities.

In the case of S. João we still find high levels of geographical local endogamy, though inferior to those of Santo Amaro and close to those registered in S. Caetano (Table 6).

Table 6. Endogamous and exogamous unions in S. João, a central/southern parish of Pico Island, Azores, spouse origin by local quarters and residence criteria (1883), by gender. Percentages

Residence of first degree consanguine kin*	Place of residence* Companhia de Cima quarter		Companhia de Baixo quarter		S. João parish	
	Men	*Women*	*Men*	*Women*	*Men*	*Women*
S. João Same place	76	82	71	76	73	78
S. João Different place	9	6	4	7	6	7
S. Mateus	8	6	11	7	10	7
Lajes	5	2	5	5	5	4
Other parish of Pico	1	4	4	5	3	4
Faial parish	1	0	2	0	1	0
Other Azorean islands	0	0	3	0	2	0
Total	100	100	100	100	100	100

Sources: S. João listing for 1883 and reconstructed population data sets.
Notes: * Residence criteria: for each inventoried individual, married or widowed, the place of residence of the first degree consanguine individuals (parents or brothers, if residents) was considered. If the parents, or at least one of them, were still alive, their place of residence was taken as the individual's origin.
Companhia de Cima and Companhia de Baixo are different quarters of S. João parish.

Oddly enough, it was in the smaller place, Companhia de Cima, that the percentage of spouses of both sexes born in the same place was higher: 76 percent of the men and 82 percent of the women with access to marriage had the same geographical origin. In the case of Companhia de Baixo, these percentages were 71 percent and 76 percent, respectively.

Companhia de Baixo showed a larger receptivity towards other parishes. Of the neighbouring parishes, S. Mateus and Lajes, marital relationships were established the most in S. Mateus. Marriages with individuals from other Pico parishes or Azorean islands rarely happened. However, we found men born in Terceira, Graciosa and S. Miguel who married women from Companhia de Baixo who had emigrated to Brazil or to the USA, and who later returned with their families. No individual from Madeira Island or from the continent was identified.

Age at First Marriage as an Indicator of Well-Being

In Pico Island, the mean age at first marriage increased during the 19th century for both men and women. This was a direct consequence of a depressed economic conjuncture which intensified differential migratory movements. Furthermore, well-known demographic auto-regulating mechanisms were at work (Hajnal 1965), with female reproductive capacity being reduced as women began their sexual life late.[5]

Our study of the age at first marriage focuses on the Western region of Pico, for which, as explained above, we gathered a considerable set of data on marriages and individual female and male life courses from 1800 to 1899. It was a chance to compute not only ages of marriage partners which were recorded when the marriage ceremony was performed, but to calculate the exact age of bride and grooms from their local birth registration. In this way, in a transversal perspective, we observed, for the 19th century, all marriages which appeared to be potentially "useful" from a female reproductive capacity point of view.

The western region of Pico Island that was extremely dependent on viticulture was particularly affected by the *oidium* plague from 1853 onwards. Given this context of economic crisis, emigration toward medium and long distance destinations intensified, especially for men, and first marriage for both sexes was delayed while sex ratios became more and more unbalanced, leaving many females without a possible spouse and putting their future well-being in danger (Santos 2004).

Delaying First Marriage in Western Pico

The detailed study of three western parishes of Madalena, Criação Velha and Candelária shows clear population depletion, an increased lack of

5 Theoretically, female biological reproductive capacity starts around age 12 and rarely lasts after age 49.

men and first marriage seriously delayed after 1850, affecting timing and probability of access to first marriage, particularly for women (Table 7).

Table 7. Mean age at fist marriages, in three western parishes of Pico Island, Azores, by gender and periods (1800–1899). Percentages and figures

Periods of Marriage	Men		Women	
	N	Age	N	Age
Madalena				
1800–1849	578	28.9	635	25.6
1850–1899	405	30.8	473	27.8
Criação Velha				
1801–1849	266	27.8	288	25.0
1850–1899	207	29.9	240	27.3
Candelária				
1800–1849	561	26.6	590	24.2
1850–1899	355	28.3	379	27.0
Together (western region)				
1800–1849	1,405	27.8	1,513	24.9
1850–1899	967	29.7	1,092	27.4

Sources: Madalena, Criação Velha and Candelária data sets
Notes: Partners marrying for the first time and aged less than 50 years old.

Considering the three different parishes under study, we notice, in a context of advanced ages at first marriage when compared to other European regions for the same period (Henry and Houdaille 1979; Flinn 1981), a serious delay in Madalena during the early 19th century, whereas women of Candelária delayed their marriage later in time.

Proceeding to a comparative analysis of marriage behaviours observed within the different occupational groups, we notice significant variations of the mean age at marriage that point to a considerable influence of socio-cultural aspects associated with land property, also verified in other regions of continental and insular Portuguese territories (Brettell 1986; Amorim 1987; Mesquita 1998; Scott 1999) (Table 8).

Table 8. Mean age at fist marriages, in three western parishes of Pico Island, Azores, by gender, by occupational groups and periods (1800–1899). Percentages and figures

Periods of marriage	Men		Women	
	N	Age	N	Age
Farmers + Rural workers				
1800–1849	358	28.2	363	24.8
1850–1899	576	29.7	610	27.6
Fishermen				
1801–1849	77	24.9	79	23.3
1850–1899	130	26.8	155	25.7
Craftsmen				
1800–1849	49	27.9	62	25.2
1850–1899	80	28.5	103	25.4
Property owners				
1800–1849	40	28.7	44	24.6
1850–1899	49	39.2	63	27.8

Sources: Madalena, Criação Velha and Candelária data sets.
Notes: Marriages where occupation is known. Partners marrying for the first time and aged less than 50 years old.

As a matter of fact, in any of the analysed periods, the wives of fishermen always married at the youngest ages, in spite of the advanced age registered among women who married between 1850 and 1899, and compared to the mean age of the craftsmen's wives of the same period. Craftsmen present intermediate and stable figures, for both sexes.

The mean ages at marriage of farmers, rural workers and property owners were always the highest ones, mainly for men presenting similar values during the first half of the century. However, after 1850, the mean age at first marriage for male property owners rose extremely. This phenomenon suggests new constraints regarding the passing on of big property during their lifetime or through succession, and also difficulties in activating homogamous matrimonial alliances with the objectives of preserving or concentrating assets.

We now raise the question of whether rural communities of central Pico Island experienced similar changes concerning mean age at first marriages during the 19th century.

Regional Differences in Age at First Marriage

The average ages at first marriage in S. Mateus,[6] S. João and Santo Amaro were also very high, with time variations of some significance in each parish.

Table 9. Mean age at fist marriages, in three central parishes of Pico Island, Azores, by gender, and periods (1800–1899). Percentages and figures

Periods of marriage	Men		Women	
	N	Age	N	Age
*S. Mateus**				
1800–1849	779	27.8	878	25.0
1850–1899	533	30.3	627	28.5
S. João				
1800–1849	267	29.2	325	26.1
1850–1899	198	29.2	252	27.5
Together (central/southern region)				
1800–1849	1,046	28.1	1,203	25.5
1850–1899	731	30.0	879	27.9
Santo Amaro (central/northern region)				
1800–1849	146	28.3	200	27.0
1850–1899	156	29.5	182	26.1

Sources: S. João, S. Mateus/S. Caetano (central/southern region) and Santo Amaro (central/northern region) data sets.
Notes: Partners marrying for the first time and aged less than 50 years old.
* S. Caetano was a part of the large S. Mateus parish until 1886.

Considering two long periods of half a century, the high mean age at first marriage for women resulted from perturbations of the matrimonial market caused by increasing male emigration. This did not happen in Santo Amaro, in central/northern region, where only the male mean age at first marriage increased from the first to the second period of the 19th century. It was only there in the two last decades of the 19th century and the first two decades of the 20th century (Amorim 2005) that the female mean age was reduced, respectively, to 24.4 and 23.6 years of age, an unmatched result in other parishes. In S. Caetano and S. João, the reduction of the

6 S. Caetano was a part of the large S. Mateus parish until 1886.

mean age at first marriage is only more notorious in the first decades of the 20th century (Amorim 1992).

Figure 3. Evolution of the mean age at first marriage for men in the western and southern regions of Pico Island, Azores (1800–1899).

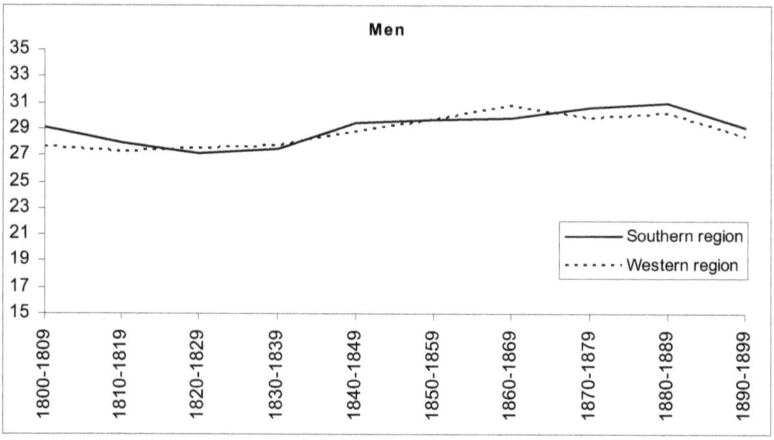

Figure 4. Evolution of the mean age at first marriage for women in the western and southern regions of Pico Island, Azores (1800–1899).

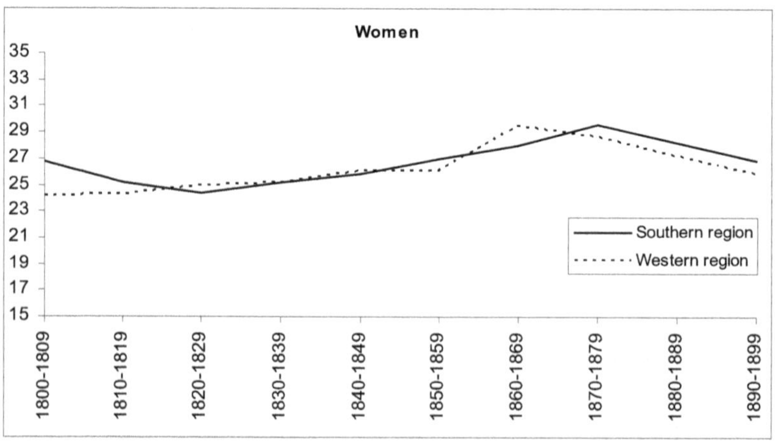

Sources: Madalena, Criação Velha and Candelária (western parishes) data sets; S. João, S. Mateus/S. Caetano (central/southern region) data sets.
See Amorim 1992; 2004; 2006 and Santos 2004.

On the other hand, if we compare the evolution of the mean ages by decade in the southern and western regions of the island (Figure 3 and Figure 4) we see that, for all women, age at first marriage was more sensitive to conjunctural changes and was particularly affected by the agricultural crisis that hit the islands from 1853 onwards.

Western Pico's Women Condemned to Celibacy

Using another indicator, definitive celibacy between 1860 and 1899, we see that, in the western region of Pico, women were more vulnerable to the effects of economic crisis than in other regions of the Island. However, the percentage of women who did not marry and who spent their life without a spouse is also very high in the southern region, a consequence of long distance male emigration which finally touched the whole island at the end of the 19th century (Table 10).

Table 10. Definitive celibacy, comparing western and southern regions of Pico Island, Azores, by gender (1860–1899). Percentages and figures

Pico Island	Men			Women		
	Deaths (total)	Single Aged 50+	Definitive Celibacy (%)	Deaths (total)	Single Aged 50+	Definitive Celibacy (%)
Western region	722	74	10.3	869	206	23.7
Southern region	695	72	10.4	872	200	22.9

Sources: Madalena, Criação Velha and Candelária (western parishes) data sets; S. João, S. Mateus/S. Caetano (central/southern region) data sets.
See Amorim 1992, 2004, 2006 and Santos 2004.
Notes: Definitive celibacy is calculated from the proportion of adults aged 50 and over at death.

Family Reproduction facing Pauperization in Southern Pico

The social reproduction of the family is necessarily combined with marriage strategies and biological reproduction, given social conditions, environmental challenges and individual responses to circumstances. The following analysis focuses upon a socially more complex community, the parish of Lajes, southern region of Pico Island, which presented an urban nucleus and a large rural area with four well-defined quarters.

In the list of the parish's residents in Lajes, for 1836, we can clearly distinguish, among householders, property owners who make a living exclusively out of the income from their property, those who add to their work some other income or pay and those who live exclusively off of their mechanic work or industry, besides those who live in some way out of State wages, except militaries, and fixed-place beggars (List of the parish's residents in Lajes, 1836).[7]

Considering the final counts in the list of inhabitants, we estimated that, out of a total of 822 householders (males and females) counted in 1836, only 13 percent were not property owners (107 heads households). We identified those who made a living exclusively out of their property income (52 individuals heading 6 percent of the families), those who added to their work some other income or salary (662 individuals or 81 percent) and those who lived exclusively out of their work (95, or 12 percent). Besides, 13 *state waged* clergymen were listed separately, as well as 10 beggars, these being counted as a part of the first and second categories. We find interesting results by establishing a relation between male occupation and property owning (Table 11).

If we do not consider clergymen, lawyers and clerks receiving wages, the male professional group with limited access to property was that of fishermen. Those accumulating some income constituted 73 percent, whereas the percentage of farmers or shepherds in an identical situation was over 90 percent. In an inferior position relatively to farmers or shepherds, craftsmen had a closer relationship with property than fishermen. The families who could make a living out of the income from their properties were predominantly those of farmers, most of them with shepherd

7 There is no reference to ambulant beggars

children or employees, and those of urban property owners, some with noble ranks, to whom no activity was connected.

Table 11. Male professional property owning and activity, Lajes, southern region of Pico Island, Azores, list of residents, 1836, by households. Percentages and figures

Professions/activities	Sufficient income from property	Income + work	Without income	Total
	%	%	%	%
Farmers	81	19	0	100
Shepherds	5	92	3	100
Rural workers	2	91	7	100
Fishermen	0	73	27	100
Craftsmen	2	87	11	100
Others*	4	48	48	100
Without activity	12	73	15	100

Sources: Lajes, list of residents, 1836, by households.
Notes: For 531 heads of households included in this table, we were able to establish a relationship between profession and property.
* Clergymen, lawyers and clerks

By also exploring the property record of 1883, we ranked male residents in Lajes, in four levels: two levels of property owners and two of workers. In the property owners' group we distinguished the landlords, whose collectable income was of more than 100,000 *réis,* from those whose collectable income surpassed 20,000 *réis,* but remained under 100,000 *réis*. These could be considered as well-to-do property owners, who did not need to work for someone else. Among the workers, we distinguished those with collectable incomes of between 1,000 and 19,000 *réis,* with householders oscillating between being comfortably off and rather poor, most of them owning their own house and some property, but needing to work for someone else in order to make a living for their family. Finally, we considered those who had less than 1,000 *réis* of collectable income who might own a small house and a vegetable garden, but were considered as poor.

If we compare the ranks of 1836 with those of 1883, by analysing property owners (making a living out of their property's income), comfortably off individuals (income and work), and poor individuals (work), we find the same 12 percent of men in the lower rank, but with some differences in the top rank. While, in 1836, 8 percent of families headed by men made a living from their income (according to the parish priest who made the list), in 1883 we found 5 percent of male property owners with 20,000 or more *réis*. However, this comparison presents some difficulties, because we did not consider, on the later date, those householders who, by total lack of property, are not mentioned in the property records, and we include some single men or widowers that did not appear as household heads in the list. On the other hand, the initial rank of the classification of property owners, medium or comfortably off, for those individuals with more than 20,000 *réis* might be restrictive. Moreover, we should not forget the fact that individuals with a collectable income of more than 18,000 *réis* might also be considered as belonging to that rank.[8]

By analysing the information in the roll of 1883, which specified the different socio-professional male categories, and by focusing on working heads of household, we might approach differential family behaviours and living conditions of farmers/rural workers, fishermen and craftsmen. In this document, individuals considered as property owners (with a collectable income over 20,000 *réis*) were excluded.

A first observation focuses on the evolution, from 1836 to 1883, of the percentages of workers from the three chosen groups. While on the first date, 16 percent of the workers were connected to the sea, on the second date the respective frequency was up 23 percent, an increase that points to a decrease of farmers/rural workers (from 71 percent to 65 percent) and craftsmen (13 percent to 11 percent). It is important, however, to verify to what extent this change within different groups was the same as the change concerning property. In spite of the relative increase of the number of fishermen, the percentage of those in the position of comfortably off to poor stays the same between the two documents, including the large group of householders receiving from 100 to 20,000 *réis*. At the same time, it appears that an impoverishment of farmers/rural workers and craftsmen took place, though the delicate nature of this observation would advise us to be cautious in our conclusions (Table 12).

8 In the list of 1883, the parish priest classified as property owners some household heads with collectable income below 20,000 *réis*, but not in every case.

Table 12. Position of male workers with respect to property, Lajes, southern region of Pico Island, Azores, comparing 1836 list of residents and 1883 property records, by households. Percentages

	Comfortably off to poor		Poor		Total	
	1836	*1883*	*1836*	*1883*	*1836*	*1883*
Farmers + Rural workers	93	88	7	12	100	100
Fishermen	73	73	27	27	100	100
Craftsmen	89	77	11	23	100	100

Sources: Lajes, list of residents, 1836, by households; 1883 property records.
Notes: Using 1836 list of residents, we identified those who made a living exclusively out of their property income, those who added to their work some other income or salary and those who lived exclusively out of their work
Using property record of 1883, we ranked male residents in Lajes, in four levels: two levels of property owners and two of workers (comfortably off to poor and poor).

We may, however, conclude that significant oscillations within the parish's social structure were non-existent in the mid 19th century, when there was a clear predominance of workers that, in their vast majority, had a house to live in and some land or garden for alimentary support. The relative increase of the number of fishermen may require an explanation of a sociological or even biological nature.

Intergenerational Models of Reproduction: Socio-differentiation in Southern Pico

For a differential analysis of the biological reproduction over three successive generations, we have chosen two indicators: the average age at first marriage and the reproductive success down to the third generation. For this purpose, we selected fertile couples that started their marital life between 1810 and 1829. Thus, we could benefit, in a large number of cases, from the identification of professions made in the population list from 1836, which is not always given in the parish records of that time. On the other hand, these chronological markers allowed us to identify, in the roll of 1883, the social situation of the third generation in adult age. For the same group of couples, we calculated the average age at first marriage, for men and women.

Table 13. Socio-differential intergenerational reproductive patterns, Lajes, southern region of Pico Island, Azores, fertile couples starting between 1810 and 1829. Mean age at first marriage by gender and mean number of children born

Occupational groups	Mean age at first marriage		Children (Mean number born)	Grandchildren (Mean number born)
	Men	*Women*		
Property owners	28.6	25.9	6.0	10.6
Shepherds	25.9	23.9	5.9	21.4
Farmers	27.2	25.5	4.9	9.8
Fishermen	24.0	23.1	7.3	13.8
Craftsmen	25.8	25.0	7.0	13.4
Whole population of Lajes	26.7	25.0	5.6	11.9

Sources: Lajes, database, including all couples formed after 1800.
Notes: This table includes fertile couples who had children and grandchildren locally.

Late marriage was more frequent among male property owners (aged 28.6), followed by farmers (27.2), shepherds and craftsmen (about 26), and finally, falling far behind, fishermen (aged 24) (Table 13). These extreme results were expected, knowing that fishermen, who start work at a very young age, would need minimum resources to start a family according to the social demands of the group, whereas property owners would have to find the conditions to do so, through inheritance, matrimonial connections or emigration at a young age, in order to maintain or improve their birth-given status. The most surprising result is the difference between the behaviour of shepherds and farmers, who were expected to present more similarities.

As for women of respective socio-professional groups, there was a parallel with male behaviour. Wives of fishermen and of shepherds married at a younger age (before they turned 24), followed by wives of craftsmen (25), of farmers (25.5) and those of property owners, whose first marriage took place when they were about 26 years of age. The predominance of farmers in the community influenced the mean age at first marriage which was estimated for the whole population of Lajes parish during that period: 26.7 for males and 25 for females.

We also noticed that the average number of descendants for these fertile couples of Lajes, southern region of Pico Island, is 5.6 children, whereas the average number of their grandchildren born in the same community was only twice the number of their children.

Considering the different occupational groups, clear differences can be observed. The difference of behaviours between shepherds and farmers is still surprising. In fact, shepherds seem to have established themselves more significantly in terms of progeny, followed by fishermen, craftsmen, property owners and, finally, farmers.

Keeping in mind the limited number of observed individuals, we are led to consider, in the case of shepherds, not only the importance of dairy products (milk, cheese and whey) in the daily maintenance of the family well-being, but also the possibility that the clearing of new extensions of woods may have contributed, at the time, to the fixation of the family's workforce. On the other hand, the obligation of going to the pastures, located hours away from the village, on a daily basis, as well as the need of clearing the pastures every year (which demanded a great human effort concentrated in the summer), may have caused a decrease in the desire for emigration.

In second position, fishermen stand out for their great reproductive success in the community. Apparently, marine activities corresponded well with family reproduction, which explains the increase of fishermen between 1836 and 1883.

Oddly, we found a higher number of grandchildren among property owners than among farmers. One could expect the latter to be more prone to migrate to the new world, but the fact that passport records do not distinguish shepherds from farmers stops us from reaching a definitive conclusion. Still, it is possible to analyse whether or not land-working individuals were more attracted towards emigration than individuals with a maritime activity.

A Gender Approach of Emigration in Southern Pico

Though legal emigration is only known from 1859 onwards, it is possible to proceed to the observation of differential behaviours in later periods, as passport records state the professions of emigrants, who, until the beginning of the 1870s, preferred Brazil and, later, the USA (Table 14).

Table 14. Legal emigration by gender and male occupational groups, Lajes, southern region of Pico Island, Azores, 5 years periods, 1860–1899

5 years periods	*Men*	*Women*	*Both*	Male occupational group				
				Farmer	*Fisher-man*	*Crafts-man*	*Property owner*	*Other*
1860–1864	47	20	67	34	2	1	2	8
1865–1869	76	35	111	52	5	2	4	13
1870–1874	119	50	169	82	10	6	10	11
1875–1879	70	30	100	53	4	7	2	4
1880–1884	87	62	149	62	9	7	7	2
1885–1889	37	75	112	22	1	1	8	5
1890–1894	62	76	138	45	3	3	3	8
1895–1899	16	49	65	8	2	1	4	1
1860–1899	514	397	911	358	36	28	40	52

Sources: Lajes, database. Passports records allowing emigration, from 1859.

The distribution of men by occupational groups indicates that farmers represented 70 percent of emigrants, fishermen 7 percent, craftsmen 5 percent, property owners 8 percent and others, where we included students, businessmen and individuals without occupation (most of them had 2 or 3 passports to the same destination), made a total of 10 percent (Table 14).

By isolating the working population in the total of residents counted in 1883, we estimated that 65 percent would be farmers, 23 percent fishermen and 11 percent craftsmen. Out of the 442 emigrants belonging to these three categories, 85 percent were farmers, 9 percent fishermen and 7 percent craftsmen. Thus, the modest migratory movement of fishermen might, at least partially, explain their greater local reproductive success.

For a reflection on the social reproduction throughout the 1800s, we started with the data provided by the roll of 1883, relating the situations of that period with those lived by the respective ancestors identified in the population listing of 1836. Bearing this in mind, we selected the two most socially different groups – fishermen and property owners – in order to compare the two and to compare them with the other groups.

The observation of reproduction and professional homogamy in the case of fishermen reveals a frequent articulation with the workers' and shepherds' groups, sometimes with the craftsmen, as if one's professional choice depended not as much on family tradition but on personal tendencies or on the evolution of the work market. However, fishermen living in the privileged fishing areas of Ribeira do Meio or Vila passed their profession on to their children more often, and married daughters of other fishermen more frequently (Table 15).

Table 15. Occupational group of fishermen' parents and parents-in-law by gender and male occupational groups, Lajes, southern region of Pico Island, Azores, for mid-19th century couples resident in the parish in 1883

	Fisherman	Shepherd	Rural worker	Craftsman	Other	Total
	%	%	%	%	%	%
Fisherman	49	4	39	4	4	100
Wife	38	11	39	10	2	100

Sources: Lajes, database; mid-19th century couples.
Notes: The municipality of Lajes comprises nowadays the parishes of Lajes, S. João, Ribeiras, Calheta de Nesquim, Piedade and Ribeirinha.

In fact, results presented here indicate that only 49 percent of the fishermen with known ancestors and residents in Lajes by 1883 were children of other fishermen, 39 percent were children of workers, and the rest were children of shepherds, craftsmen and others, and among the "others" we can count two farmers and two individuals of unknown profession (Table 15).

Fishermen searched for wives among daughters of fishermen and workers, 39 percent in both cases, then turning to the daughters of shepherds and craftsmen. We could not find any farmer's daughter marrying a fisherman. Among the two groups of property owners, we have, however, encountered an accentuated difference. Big property owners, most with noble ranks, residing in Lajes, Rua Direita da Vila, were to be distinguished clearly from farmers or shepherds distributed throughout the parish.

As the small number of property owners do not allow for statistical analysis, we shall study their respective behaviours by using two case studies, representative of the two levels of property owners defined above.[9]

A Case Study: Small Rural Property Owner

A property owner, living out of his income in Lajes, in the southern region of Pico Island, descended of an eight sibling family. His wife descended from a five sibling family. The couple registered four children in Lajes:

1. The eldest daughter, born 27th of July, 1829, married at the age of 23 a son of property owners from neighbouring S. João parish, where they lived.
2. The eldest son, born 11th of September, 1832, might have emigrated. We don't have any information since birth.
3. The second son, born 25th of October, 1834, married at the age of 34 the eldest of 6 children of a property owner's couple, from the same place of Silveira. In 1885, his collectable income was 26,756 *réis,* maintaining his position as rural property owner. This couple had 8 children, but only one of them had children in the parish. Four of them died during childhood, two emigrated and one of their daughters died as a single woman at the age of 69.
4. The second daughter, born 24th of August, 1838, married at 30 years of age with a property owner, 49 years old. In 1885, the collectable income of her husband was of 20,484 *réis.* They had 7 children, all surviving childhood. Three of them left the parish, a daughter died as a

9 In the property owners' group we distinguished the landlords, whose collectable income was of more than 100,000 *réis,* from those whose collectable income surpassed 20,000 *réis,* but remained under 100,000 *réis.*

single woman at the age of 84, and the other three left descendants in the parish.

As we can observe in this case, from 1836 to 1883, the situation of usage of property was repeated. Adequate matrimonial alliances, definitive celibacy and emigration were the adopted strategies in this family. Because of high mortality, only four out of the 15 grandchildren from the first generation couple would have access to marriage.

However, the reproduction of the property owner status wasn't always possible in other cases. The egalitarian property division practised in the region, as well as the low death rates, led to an impoverishment, especially as the exploitation of rocky and distant land only became profitable with the incorporation of great human effort which the family, in its different cycles, could or could not undertake.

Another Case Study: An Urban Big Property Owner

To exemplify the category of urban property owners, we selected the genealogy of a *sargento-mor* (sergeant major) from Lajes, married with a noble woman from S. Roque (central/northern region).

1. The eldest son of this couple inherited the family properties as a *morgado*[10] and his residence was located in Lajes, Rua Direita by 1836, the place where most urban property owners lived. His collectable income was 356,185 *réis*. He married on 6th November, 1823 an aristocrat woman, 22 years old, one of the children of a captain from Lajes and his spouse, born in the parish of Matriz, city of Horta, Faial Island. There were only four known legitimate children of this marriage:

   1.1 The eldest son, born 20th of September, 1824, died during childhood.

10 *Morgadio* is a non-egalitarian inheritance system of transmission to a privileged male heir, usually the older son *(morgado)*. It is similar to *majorat (fideicommis)* or Spanish *mayorazgo*.

1.2 The eldest daughter, born in 10th of August, 1825, also died during childhood.
1.3 The second son, born 5th of September, 1834, had an unknown destiny.
1.4 The third son, born in 1838, married at the age of 30 a woman of the same age, a comfortably off property owner's daughter. By 1885 his collectable income was of 356,185 *réis*.
  1.4.1. We only know of one daughter of the couple, found in the death records. It is supposed that this daughter, who died at the age of 17, had been born before her parents' marriage.

The big property owner also had another child of a single young woman, born 20th of December, 1812, daughter of a rural worker and a woman who died giving birth.

1.5. This illegitimate son, born 26th of July, 1837, was identified at birth by the names of his parents. As an adult, he used his father's complete name, as well as his mother's surname. By 1885 he had a collectable income of 218,536 réis, which, though lower than his half-brother's, still clearly included him in the big property owner's group.
Married on 27th of November, 1852, at the age of 15, with a woman aged 14, born in S. João, daughter of a captain, he had six legitimate children:
  1.5.1 The eldest daughter, born 3d of December, 1856, married at the age of 21 a noble man, son of another noble man from Piedade parish who had, by 1885, a collectable income of 175,500 réis.
  1.5.2. The eldest son, born 13th of December, 1860, died as a single man at the age of 56.
  1.5.3. The second son, born 20th of September, 1865, married at 42 years of age with a noble woman, aged 31, daughter of a man having a collectable income of 42,982 réis. However, his maternal grandmother had, at the time, a collectable income of 269,173 réis.
  1.5.4. The second daughter, born 17th of September, 1869, died at the age of 17.

1.5.5. The third daughter, born 18th of January, 1876, died at the age of 5 months.
1.5.6. The third son, born 9th of September, 1878, died at the age of 17.
1.5.7. An illegitimate son, born 6th of February, 1859, before his half brother was born, was also a single woman's son. This woman was daughter of a property owner with 48,801 *réis* collectable income, and also living in Lajes, Rua Direita. By 1883 he was a teacher in Lajes and he had a collectable income of 33,530 *réis*. He married at 21 years of age a captain's daughter. His mother-in-law had, by 1885, a collectable income of 139,541 *réis*.

Notice that both the *morgado* and his illegitimate son had illegitimate children when married, and established them as heirs. We shall now follow the life course and descendance, in Lajes parish, of the *morgado*'s sisters.

2. The eldest daughter of the *sargento-mor* from Lajes, was born in Lajes, 18th of March, 1792. She married at the age of 15 with a noble man born in Faial Island. The couple registered 3 children in Lajes, leaving it afterwards.
3. The youngest daughter, born 8th of February, 1800, married at 17 years of age a captain, son of the major captain from Lajes.[11] Still a resident by 1883, she was, as we could see, rated as having a big property owner's collectable income. The couple had 10 children baptised in Lajes:

   3.1. The eldest daughter, born 9th of June, 1819, married at the age of 29 a noble man from Piedade and left the parish.
   3.2. The second daughter born 2d of January, 1821, married at the age of 22 a noble man from S. Roque and also left Lajes.
   3.3. The eldest son, born 30th April, 1824, unknown destiny.
   3.4. The second son, knight of the order N. Sra. da Conceição, of Vila Viçosa, married an aristocrat woman from the parish of Castelo

11 She was referred previously with a collectable income of 139,541 *réis*, because her daughter married a cousin, born illegitimate on 6th of February, 1859, who was a teacher in Lajes and he had in 1883 a collectable income of 33,530 *réis*.

Branco, Faial Island. The couple registered 4 children in Lajes, none having descendants.

3.5. The third son, born 25th of July, 1830, had two children with a single woman, born 28th of October, 1836. They got married afterwards, at 42 and 35 years old, recognizing their children. They had two more children within marriage. By 1885, the householder had a collectable income of 72,056 *réis*.

3.6. The third daughter, born 26th of January, 1833, must have died as a child, considering that a sister was later baptized under the same name, though there is no record of her death in Lajes.

3.7. The fourth daughter, born 8th of October, 1834, married at age 22 with a noble man from Castelo Branco, Faial Island. She left Lajes.

3.8. The fifth daughter, born 20th of August, 1837, died after birth.

3.9. The sixth daughter, born 22d of January, 1839, died aged 8.

3.10. The youngest daughter, born 12th of September, 1843, married at age 23 a property owner, son of a man from Melgaço in the mainland and a woman born in Lajes. They registered 5 children, but only one daughter married in Lajes. The collectable income of the householder was of 42,982 *réis*, by 1885.

As verified in this last example, social homogamy has been systematically pursued in the group of big property owners of Lajes, frequently enlarging the marital market beyond the island. Known extra-marital connections occurred mainly with daughters of small property owners, and the resulting children were later recognized.

The non-egalitarian inheritance system of *morgadio* created in order to defend Portuguese landlords interests in a general frame of egalitarian inheritance, made it possible to maintain undivided a great amount of family property until 1834, when the system was abolished. The high reproductive behaviour of this aristocratic urban family of Lajes conduced, in the following generations, to the division of the family patrimony. In a period of monetary depreciation, some descendants of those landlords from Lajes looked for public employment in the urban nucleus or outside this area. Others embraced a religious career and a great number chose the way of emigration, selling their undivided property. Successful emigrants in Brazil or in the USA were the main buyers of these lands.

Conclusion

We argue that different regional models of spouse selection were found in communities on Pico Island. Parishes with a possibility of direct sea connection with nearby islands were more frequently engaged in marriage with outsider individuals, males and females, like in Madalena in relation to the Faial Island or, to a lesser degree, in Santo Amaro in relation to S. Jorge Island. In the rural western villages of Candelária, S. Caetano and S. João we observed very high levels of endogamy, sometimes influenced, as in the case of S. João, by the return of emigrants who married in the USA. The marriage exchange model of Central Pico, in S. Caetano, S. João and Santo Amaro, reveals also a very strong endogamy by place of residence and a sense of local identity, according to quarters and customs.

In the western region of Pico Island, the comparison of the percentages of endogamous marriages within the different occupational groups has shown that, throughout the entire 19th century, farmers, rural workers and fishermen selected their spouses mostly within the parish's space, whereas the marriage mobility of craftsmen, and property owners, was always remarkably more intense.

Age at first marriage may perfectly be used as a well-being indicator: the figures of the mean age at first marriage, for males and females, present different models in each community or occupational group. In the western region of Pico Island, in a context of higher male age, the population in general, and of both sexes, married late. Property owners always married late, whereas couples whose resources were based on maritime activities stand out for the precocity of their first wedding.

When the *oidium* plague devastated vineyards in mid-19th century (beginning in 1853) the old economic dependence of the region towards viticulture pushed young males to emigrate. This clearly disturbed sex ratios and the normal balance of the marriage market, contributing to a general delay of marriage throughout that period and strong difficulties for young women to find suitable marriage partners. Many women had to accept late marriage, and often permanent celibacy, with a risk to their future well-being and reproductive capacities. At the same time, illegitimacy increased, as it did in other Azores Islands. Differential emigration influenced the age at first marriage in Pico Island, especially within those rural communities which were particularly far from the outside world.

In Lajes, in the southern region of Pico, we have carried out a detailed intergenerational analysis of the social and biological family reproduction system over three generations. Considering the various occupational groups, we observed that fishermen used to engage in marriage at an early age, that their children (sons and daughters) married within the same group and that their grandchildren were preferentially kept within the community, creating a demographic growth throughout the 19th century.

Rural workers stand out as the largest group of the population. They were strongly subject to emigration, and they improved their social status by successfully returning home. Small property owners developed strategies for social reproduction at the same level, through late marriages, female celibacy and through sometimes unsuccessful migratory experiences. Social balance, in an egalitarian inheritance system, would become precarious if one of these preventive family strategies in spouse selection stopped being followed or lost its effectiveness.

Big urban property owners, a minority within the property owners' minority itself, chose homogamous unions of local character or searched outside the island for prestigious alliances lacking inside the community. The low incidence of matrimonial alliances with small local property owners must be considered, to a large extent, as connected with the existence of illegitimate children.

References

AMORIM, M. Norberta, 1987, *Guimarães 1518–1819. Estudo Demográfico*, Lisboa, I.N.I.C.

–, 1991, "Uma metodologia de Reconstituição de Paróquias desenvolvida sobre registos portugueses", *Boletín de la Asociación de Demografia Histórica*, IX, 1, pp. 7–25.

–, 1992, *Evolução Demográfica de três paróquias do Sul do Pico (1680–1980)*, Braga, University of Minho.

–, 2004, *O Pico. A abordagem de uma ilha. As Famílias. As famílias de S. João nos finais do século XIX*, Vol. 1, tome 1, Câmara Municipal das Lajes do Pico/NEPS.

–, 2005, *O Pico. A abordagem de uma ilha. As Famílias. As famílias de Santo Amaro nos finais do século XIX*, Vol. 1, tome 2, Câmara Municipal de S. Roque do Pico/NEPS.

–, 2006, *O Pico. A abordagem de uma ilha. As Famílias. As famílias do espaço de S. Caetano entre os séculos XIX e XX*, Vol. 1, tome 3, Câmara Municipal da Madalena/NEPS.

BRETTELL, Caroline, 1986, *Men who migrate, women who wait. Population and History in a Portuguese Parish*, Princeton, Princeton University Press.

FLINN, Michael W., 1981, *The European Demographic System, 1500–1820*, Suffolk, The Harvester Press.

HAJNAL, John, 1965, "European marriage patterns in perspective", in David V. GLASS and David S. C. EVERSLEY (eds), *Population in History*, London, Edward Arnold, pp. 101–143.

HENRY, Louis and HOUDAILLE, Jacques, 1979, "Célibat et âge au mariage aux XVIIIe et XIXe siècles en France, II. Âge au premier mariage", *Population*, 34, 2, pp. 403–442.

Instituto Nacional de Estatística/INE, 2001, *Recenseamento da População e da Habitação (R.A. dos Açores). Censos*, Lisbonne, Instituto Nacional de Estatística.

MACEDO, António Lourenço S., 1981, *História das quatro ilhas que formam o distrito da Horta*, fac-símile, vol. 3, Angra do Heroísmo, Direcção Regional dos Açores.

MESQUITA, Maria Hermínia Morais, 1998, *Evolução demográfica da Criação Velha, paróquia do Sul do Pico (1801–1993)*, Ponta Delgada, Direcção Regional da Cultura.

ROCHA, Gilberta Pavão Nunes, 1991, *Dinâmica Populacional dos Açores no Século XX. Unidade, Permanencia, Diversidade*, Ponta Delgada, University of Azores.

SANTOS, Carlota M., 2004, *Biodemografia do concelho da Madalena – estrutura demográfica e genética de uma população açoriana da ilha do Pico*, PhD dissertation, Braga, University of Minho.

SCOTT, Anna Volpi S., 1999, *Famílias, Formas de União e Reprodução Social no Noroeste portugués (Séculos XVIII e XIX)*, Guimarães, NEPS/ICS, University of Minho.

PART II

WELL-BEING AND PROPERTY TRANSMISSION

When Generation Trumped Sex

Widow's Well-Being and the Transmission of Family Business in 19th Century Northern France

Béatrice CRAIG

Well-being is an elusive concept because it is partly subjective. Nonetheless, scholars have favoured seemingly "objective" criteria which can be quantified, like wealth, income level or access to consumer goods, to measure degrees of well-being. As Robeyn argued, material resources are not important in their own right, but for what they make possible, "that is the capabilities that a person can generate" from them (Robeyn 2007). What really matters is the extent to which individuals can take advantage of those resources to fulfil their needs and aspirations. Access to material goods is not irrelevant: poverty is after all not very conducive to well-being, unless one belongs to a mendicant order. But it is not the entire story. Its importance is also time and place specific. Access to goods and resources loomed larger in the life of past populations for instance, because most of them lived in a state of constant penury. Even members of the "middling sort" could not take for granted that their basic physiological needs would always be met.

Material criteria nonetheless present difficulties when assessing the well-being of individuals in the past, as individuals were not necessarily the ones who had access or control over resources and material goods. In many cases, such access was collective or derivative. Married women, for instance, shared in the use of family property which was more often than not controlled by their husband. Similarly, when families were productive units, income was earned collectively, and also remained under the control of the father/husband. Furthermore, constraints like the law, or social norms could facilitate or impede individual capabilities from benefiting from existing resources. Gender was one such constraint. Feminist historians and social scientists have reminded us that various household or family members did not necessarily share equally, or fairly, in the common resources – and therefore did not necessarily enjoy similar levels of material well-being. Treating the household/family as an undifferentiated unit hides power relationships within it, especially as girls and women usually ranked low on the social hierarchy. Inequalities within the household or even community often worked at women's disadvantage.

Widowhood had the potential to bring these inequalities to light, and to precipitate conflicts. Widows and heirs competed for the resources left by the husband. Having legal rights to those resources, as well as effective means of defending them was therefore an important component of a widow's well-being. Gender norms directly or indirectly shaped those legal rights and reinforced or weakened women's means of defending them. Sandvik's study shows that access to such rights was not uniform through Western Europe (Sandvik 2007). In Germany, local authorities and the courts sided with the [male] guilds and with journeymen in their struggle against widows who tried to continue the family workshop. The courts also allowed sons to sell their mothers' property without her consent. Courts and local authorities preferred land and workshop to be in the hands of male household heads, a preference clearly shaped by the belief a person's position on the social and economic hierarchy was determined by his or her sex and marital status.

In Norway, on the other hand, the Courts took the side of the widows, as long as they were competent. According to Sandvick, "Norwegian widows benefited from a very clear law that admitted the widow's right to continue their husband's tenure." One could however add that the law was crystal clear because contemporary gender norms admitted to women's economic competency and agency. Competency mattered as much as sex in determining a person's access to resources, which was not the case among German farmers and craftsmen.[1]

Widow's agency could lead to conflicts between their interests and aspirations and that of their sons. In Norway, generation trumped sex, but Norwegian sons (at least among farmers) visibly chafed at their continued dependence and contested the subordination of sex to age. In some other parts of Europe, women's competency and the subordination of sex to age were naturalized and went unchallenged. This was particularly true of the

1 Beachy has shown that the opposite was true among Early Modern German merchant trading families, and the States ensured that widows could continue the family firms by relieving those widows from guardianship. Merchant traders believed widows were competent. Gender norms are therefore class bound as well (Beachy 2002).

Low Countries, including the area that became the French Flanders after 1668. The Customs of the French Flanders had systematically favoured the surviving spouse, irrespective of sex, over the children, adult sons included (Yver 1953; 1954). Pre-existing gender norms governing property transmission were not significantly modified by the introduction of the Napoleonic Civil Code in 1804. Industrialization did not lead to new practices either, neither did the progress of the "separate sphere ideology", which ascribed women to the domestic sphere, and coded the economy and politics male. The Napoleonic Code made it possible to subordinate the interests of widows to the ones of adult sons – but it did not require it either, and its provisions could easily be used to reach the opposite end. This is exactly what occurred among the middle class of the Lille region in the nineteenth century. There, gender was only one factor determining intra-household power hierarchies. Widows continued to enjoy broad economic rights combined with the means to defend them if need be. This in turn allowed them to have choices, such as taking over the family business, handing it over at a time of their own choosing, or even stopping business altogether if this suited them better.

Lille and Tourcoing in the Nineteenth Century

Both Lille and Tourcoing were fast growing industrial centers, and offered ample opportunities for going into, or staying in business. Tourcoing, on the Belgian border, is an old textile centre, which specialized in wool combing, spinning and weaving as early as the Middle Ages. Attempts at developing a cotton industry in the late eighteenth and early nineteenth century turned unsatisfactory, and the town's manufacturers largely reverted to wool and woollen production after 1820. Mechanization quickly followed: spinning in the 1830s, wool combing in the 1850s, and finally weaving in the 1860s. By the 1880s, hand weaving was a slowly dying trade. As mechanization progressed, mills became larger (Fohlen 1956; Toulemonde 1966; Delsalle 1985; Lottin 1986; Daumas 2004). Textile firms also began to integrate; usually, they combined some preparing activities with spinning, combining spinning and weaving, or adding a dye work to the factory. This did not spell the demise of the small producer. Even at the end of the century, auxiliary tasks continued being performed by small shops in town. At the beginning of the century, Tourcoing had been a city of relatively small businesses. By the end of the century, its economic landscape was dominated by a fair number of large firms, towering over an ever changing swarm of small ones (see Table 1).[2]

Table 1. Textile firms in Tourcoing, 1835–1911

Year	All firms	Number of firms headed by a woman	% of firm headed by a woman	Number of integrated businesses	N of integrated businesses headed by a woman
1835	154	15	9.7	15	2
1840	140	14	10.0	6	1
1852	136	8	5.9	15	2
1857	134	6	4.5	15	1
1862	149	12	8.1	15	3
1867	155	12	7.7	11	0
1872	151	15	9.9	16	0
1877	181	17	9.4	13	1
1882	178	20	11.2	17	3
1887	208	22	10.6	21	6
1892	195	21	10.8	24	1
1897	174	16	9.2	26	1
1901	174	16	9.2	33	2
1906	158	16	10.1	24	1
1911	155	16	10.3	41	4

Sources: 1835 – AMTg, Report of the *préfet* dated 27 February 1833; other years, AMTg, Matrices de patentes.

2 For main sources see: AMTg, Archives municipales de Tourcoing, Matrices de patentes, 1835–1901; AMTg, Archives municipales de Tourcoing, Tables de population 1820–1836; AMTg, Archives municipales de Tourcoing, Recensements, 1851, 1881, 1886; ADN, Archives départementales du Nord, 3Q538, Enregistrement des contrats de mariage; ADN, Archives départementales du Nord, 6U2 & 6U5, Tribunal de commerce, Actes de société, 1800–1905; ADN, Archives départementales du Nord, J1472 Greffes de Me Émile Lefebvre; ADN, Archives départementales du Nord, J1022 Greffes de Me Jules Lefebvre; ADN, Archives départementales du Nord, J1442 Greffes de Me Gruloy; Archives des Établissements Vrau, Rue du Faubourg de Roubaix, 59000 Lille, *Correspondances familiales*.

Women rarely headed the largest concerns, but were not over represented among small factory owners either. More accurately, they were under represented at both ends of the spectrum. Structural changes did not reduce the importance of family firms and sole proprietorships. Through the nineteenth century, Tourcoing was a city of family businesses. The families provided most of the capital and managerial skills.[3] Corporations were a rarity. Of the twenty five Tourcoing joint stock companies registered at the tribunal de commerce[4] (registration of all forms of partnerships was compulsory) between 1800 and 1899, nineteen were incorporated after 1890 and only two were textile manufacturing concerns (Table 2). One of the two, a wool combing firm had only seven share holders – five siblings, the manager and the accountant. The manager and the accountant held respectively forty nine and one of the 3,000 shares.

Table 2. Tourcoing partnerships registered at the Tribunal de Commerce. Textile manufacturing firms only

Year	SNC	SC	SCA	SA	Total
1800–1829	17				17
1830–1839	18				18
1840–1849	11	1	1		13
1850–1859	37	5	1		43
1860–1869	58	16		1	75
1870–1879	44	14	1		59
1880–1889	63	14	2		79
1890–1899	57	17	1	1	76
Total	305	67	6	2	380

Sources: AND, Tribunal de commerce, Actes de sociétés, 1800–1899.

Notes: SNC = *Société en nom collectif*; SC = *Société en commandite*; SCA = *Société en commandite par actions.* Silent partners may sell their share with permission of other partners; SA = *Société anonyme*: Joint stock company

3 The business tax rolls *(Matrice de patentes)* identify the owner(s) of each business. In the case of a partnership, the principal partner (who pays the bulk of the tax) is also identified. Sole proprietorship is therefore easy to identify.

4 AND, *Tribunal de commerce*, Actes de sociétés, 1800–1899.

The other joint stock companies were service providers (tramway companies for instance), and increasingly, consumer good cooperatives. Partnerships involving non family members were also not the norm. They often took the form of a *société en commandite*: one or more silent partners, forbidden by law to get involved in management, provided all or part of the firms' capital. In return for their non involvement in management, their liability was limited to their investment. Still, the majority of the *sociétés en commandite* involved people related to each other: individuals with no taste – or no skills – for business bankrolled other family members. Simple partnerships *(sociétés en nom collectif)* were also overwhelmingly partnerships between close relatives: fathers and sons or sons-in-law, or siblings.

Lille, chef Lieu of the *Département du Nord*, had also been a textile center since the Middle Ages (Lambert Dansette 1954; Fohlen 1956; Trenard 1977; Hirsch 1991; Pouchain 1998). Its economy was more diversified than the one of Tourcoing. In Tourcoing, almost everything revolved directly or indirectly around textile. Besides textile, Lille also processed agricultural commodities, and manufactured earthen ware and furniture, and later various modern household appliances. Lille was also a garrison town, an administrative center, the seat of a judicial district, and one of several State and Catholic faculties in the second half of the century. The middle class provided a growing market for the retail sector, which not only expanded, but diversified rapidly. Lille also acted as a redistribution center for the surrounding area, leading wholesalers, brokers, bankers and insurers to set up shop within its walls. As in Tourcoing, trading and manufacturing remained the preserve of family businesses-either sole proprietorship or partnerships between immediate family members. Joint stock companies were rare there as well, and limited to utilities, the financial and cooperative sectors, and the media. In the two towns then, business assets were family assets.

Widows of Means

The law made it possible for women to get a share of those assets, and the families made no effort to limit their rights, on the contrary. Marriage was usually the first opportunity for middle class women to receive assets. Some may have owned some real or personal estate in their own right during their singlehood, but more frequently, women did not have property to their name till they received a "dowry". Although this was the term used by the marriage contracts, "dowries" were really advances on inheritance, to be deducted from their share of the estate of the first parent to die. The nature of the assets transferred is rarely mentioned in the marriage contracts. Among merchant traders and manufacturers however, the dowry was often a debt against the parent's business – the young people only received the yearly interest on the amount, and the capital remained in parental hands.

Unless a woman married in separation of property (which almost never happened in those two towns), her assets were administered by her husband. He could dispose of her personal property, but not of her real estate, unless the couple was married under *communauté réduite aux acquêts* (community limited to increases), in which case all her assets at marriage were considered her *propres* (patrimonial property) and protected. In Lille and the surrounding area, the *communauté réduite aux acquêts* was the choice of a large majority by the middle of the century, although a fraction of the *propres* of the bride and groom were usually put in the community[5] (Hirsh 1991). Only people who owned very little property adopted the other types of community. Well-to-do women also received inheritances through their life: from their parents – and according to the Civil Code they were to share equally in these inheritance with their other siblings; not infrequently, they also inherited from uncles, aunts or siblings who had died childless, and occasionally from a more distant relative or friend; these legacies swelled their patrimony, their *propres,* and were therefore legally protected. There is no evidence that women inherited different assets than men – in fact, unless there was a compelling reason to do otherwise, the *notaires* (the layers who supervised the devolution of estates to

5 See ADN/Archives départementales du Nord, Enregistrement, contrats de mariage.

the heirs) strove to give each child a similar mix of assets.[6] Inheritance was not gendered. Women who were not married could do what they wanted with their property as soon as they came of age at 21.

Married women regained control of their *propres* at widowhood, and received half the value of the *communauté,* of the goods jointly owned by the couple during marriage. As a rule, marriage contracts in this region also gave the survivor the usufruct of the other half of the *communauté*, as well as of all the *propres* of the predeceased, unless there were children in which case the usufructs were reduced to a quarter of the community and half of the *propres*. Alternately, the marriage contract could stipulate that the survivor receives the ownership of his or her half of *communauté*, the usufruct of a quarter of the said *communauté*, and ownership of a quarter of the predeceased property *(propres)*. A *preciput* (which was a sum of money) equivalent to the value of furniture and wardrobe was also common. The *preciput* was paid before any distribution of the estate had taken place and was neither part of the share of community nor of the *propres.* Women from the middle and upper middle class therefore became widows of means. They normally walked away from the *notaire*'s office in control of more than half the couples' assets, and benefiting from the usufruct of a good part of the remainder. Two examples will show what this meant in practical terms.

Léandre Richebé, a merchant brewer and son of a former suburban mayor died in 1869. He left a wife, Sophie Angelique Delobel, and 8 under age children.[7] Sophie and Léandre had married in 1850 in *communauté réduite aux acquêts.* He had brought 40,000 francs into marriage, and she had brought 30,000 francs. Sophie got her dowry back and 5,000 francs in preciput. She also received half of the considerable amount of real estate held by the couple *en communauté*. The couple's real estate included a large house, a brewery, five pieces of farm land, and forty two public houses. Léandre was also to receive a share in the succession of a cousin who had been the largest real estate owner in town. Sophie was entitled to the usufruct of half her husband's *propres,* and of a quarter of the communauté. She was therefore a rich widow, and in a position to carry on the business without difficulties, if she so chose. She so chose.

6 In one example of departure from this norm, the brother was living in Paris, and the sister in Lille. Her share consisted mostly of real estate, and his, of moveable.

7 AND, J1472.

Widows did not always take over because their children were too young, as the following example shows.

François Philibert Vrau, a thread manufacturer in Lille died in 1870 at 78. He left a 61-year-old widow, Sophie, two married daughters and a 40-year-old son.[8] François Philibert had formed an informal association with his only son Philibert and one of his two sons-in-law, Camille Feron-Vrau. In his will François Philibert asked that his wife get control over all the goods that had been acquired since marriage *(la communauté)*. She could remain at the head of the firm, or go into partnership with Philibert and Camille. Should Camille die, his wife could replace him. If those arrangements were not doable, Sophie Aubineau-Vrau was to receive the factory, the equipment, the merchandises, the clientele and the dwelling house as her share of the post mortem settlement. Under the law, Sophie could not receive all of the couple's property. The Code civil did not allow parents to disinherit their children, even for the benefit of the surviving spouse. François Philibert's alternative settlement however is more or less what happened when the estate was settled six month later. The couple's real and personal estate (including the thread making factory) amounted to 1,027,547 francs. Mme Vrau was entitled to 130,830 francs (she owned 46,591 francs at marriage, and inheritances from her brother, sister, maternal grand mother and maternal grandfather). M. Vrau had brought considerable assets and even more considerable debts into marriage. In other words, his *propres* were negative. The debts were paid by the *communauté*, and consequently his estate owed the *communauté* 35,000 francs. Mme Vrau received the value of her *propres* (130,830 francs), half the *communauté* (448,359 francs), and a quarter of her husband's estate, 140,733 francs, for a total of 719,922 francs (70 percent of the family assets), plus the usufruct of another 140,733 francs. The three children received 93,822 francs (less their dowries, and in the case of the unmarried son, of a 60,000 francs loan) in full ownership, and 46,911 francs encumbered by their mother's usufruct. Mme Vrau took the factory, the equipment, most of the working capital and most of the goods in stock. The children shared the rest of the working capital and goods in stock.

Like most of the women from their social class, those two widows benefited from the decision taken by their parents to marry them in *com-*

8 ADN, J 1022–59.

munauté réduite aux acquêts, supplemented by as generous a usufruct as the law allowed. As a result, they received a considerable share of the family property, share which could not be challenged in court by other heirs. (Widowers, incidentally, benefited in the same way – marriage contract testamentary provisions were scrupulously symmetrical.) The children had to wait for their mother's death not only to inherit those assets, but even to benefit from most of their inheritance from their father, encumbered as it was by the mother's usufruct. Marriage contracts also almost always provided that the usufructs would end if the widow or widower remarried. This may explain why so few middle class people remarried in the nineteenth century.

The middle class of this region took full advantage of the options provided by the Code civil to favour the widow over the children, because this fitted their tradition. This is the way things had always been done. The Custom of Lille and the Custom of the Castellany (the latter applied to Tourcoing), abolished in 1804, had given widows extensive rights over the couple's property (Taillard 1849; 1908). Under customary law, a widow with children had received, in addition to her share of community, the use of the remainder of the common personal property till remarriage (and half afterwards). If she and her husband had had burgher rights in the city at the time of the birth of at least one live child, the survivor gained ownership of the deceased's personal property. This practice, called *ravestissement*, was particularly favourable to the survivor as within the city, real estate was considered personal property.[9]

Lille and the surrounding area had then been part of a legal system, and of a culture, which had given widows the means to succeed their husband. The 1804 Code civil made the perpetuation of this culture unproblematic. Women married in community could succeed their husbands because they owned most of the business in the first place. The children, especially if there were several, owned only a minority share.

Communauté and *ravestissement* reflected an understanding of women's role common in Early Modern England, France, and the Low Countries (and their colonies). Women were expected to marry, and when married to act as "deputy husband" to use Laurel Ulrich's apt phrase (Ulrich 1983). Their function was to support and assist him in his various endeavours and to replace him when incapacitated (Butel 1976; Clark

9 The *ravestissement* was not unique to Lille. Yver has noted its existence in the Custumals of French Flanders, Hainault, Brabant and parts of Artois (Yver 1953; 1954).

1981; Chassagne 1981; Prior 1985; Davidoff and Hall 1987; Collins 1989; Clark 1992; Rabuzzi 1995; Sharpe 2002; Beachy 2002a; 2002b). As Ulrich noted, the "deputy husband" was acceptable because she did not challenge existing gender hierarchies: the wife was the husband's agent, not an autonomous individual. In the Low Countries and the parts of France covered by customary laws, the deputy role extended to the widows. When the male head died, his deputy naturally continued his activities for the benefit of the lineage. The intra familial hierarchy ranked children below parents, irrespective of sex. This arrangement deprived sons of their autonomy, but was functional as far as the whole family was concerned. It prevented a premature division of assets which could have jeopardized the family's economic activities, and gave sons the time to gain experience and develop their own networks.

Females Successors and Partners

Through the century, many widows simply took over. The proportion of female headed business remained more or less constant through the century. According to the censuses, 10.7 percent of the Tourcoing manufacturers and merchants were female in 1796, and 10.4 percent in 1886 (7.8 percent in 1821 and 6.7 percent in 1851) but only 4.3 percent in 1911. Censuses are notorious for under reporting women's occupations. The more reliable business tax rolls[10] indicate that the proportion of textile firms headed by a woman went from 9.7 percent to 10.3 percent between 1835 and 1911, with a dip at mid century as well (Table 1). In Lille, according to the city directories, the proportion of manufacturers and merchants who were women went from 6.4 percent in 1830 to 6.0 percent in 1900.[11]

Ten per cent seems low, and may suggest that few women succeeded their husband. How common was it for women to take over? Precise fig-

10 All business owners had to pay this yearly tax.

11 The Lille city archives burned in 1916, consequently neither the census schedules nor the business tax rolls or *matrices de patente* are available. The city directories started in 1830.

ures would require a long range longitudinal study beyond the scope of this study. We may however derive rough estimates from the censuses and business tax rolls. The 1881 Tourcoing census lists a total of fifty manufacturers, merchant traders, and people who were living off their means *(propriétaires* or *rentiers)* who were widowers, and ninety two who were widows. Of the men, 50 percent were inactive (living off their means) and 56 percent of the women were inactive. Widows of textile businessmen therefore do not seem to have rushed into retirement at a faster rate than men from their class.[12] Neither were they inclined to move with their children: only two of the men and three of the women did not head their household.

Widows never exceeded 15 percent of the heads of households through the 19th century; a proportion of one business in ten headed by a woman (usually a widow) would suggest that probably more than half the widows who headed a household took over the family business. If taking over was not universal, it was frequent enough to appear a normal thing to do.[13]

Not all widows took over the business single handedly. Some formally went into partnership with children. In a region where banks were slow to develop and joint stock companies avoided, partnership was the commonest way to secure additional capital for one's business. Widows may or may not have needed the financial assets of their children to continue the family business. The children however often had no choice but pool their resources and rely on their mother's financial backing to do so (as in the case of the Vrau family above). Unmarried siblings also formed partnerships rather than divide the assets of a going concern. The commonest form of association was the simple or unlimited liability partnerships. Slightly less than a quarter of such partnerships in Tourcoing involved women and the articles of association deposited at the *Tribunal de Commerce* give a glimpse of the nature of the arrangements. One third of the women were widows; 14 percent were married and half were single – single women are over represented because, contrary to their mothers, they had no choice but to go into partnership with their siblings if they wanted to stay in business. Most widows were in partnership with one or

12 Unfortunately, one cannot do the same calculation for 1911 – the other year for which data on the middle class was systematically collected, as the census no longer gave marital status.

13 See AMTg – Census 1796–1886; Matrices de patentes 1835–1901; Almanach Vanackere 1830–1850; Annuaires Ravet Anceau 1860–1902.

several children. Widows were less likely to have the signature – that is the right to financially engage the firm – than single women. One none-theless should not assume widows who became partner automatically exchanged one patriarch for another. The articles of association suggest the relationship between mother and children ran the entire possible range.

On the one hand was Mme Vrau, whom we have already met. A month after the settlement of her husband's estate and the division of the community, Mme Vrau, listed as merchant trader, her 41-year-old son Philibert Vrau, merchant trader, and 39-year-old son-in-law Camille Feron, also merchant trader, entered into a partnership. All had signing rights. Son and son-in-law owed all their time and industry to the firm. Control and supervision belonged to Mme Vrau, who could take part in the management of the firm when she saw fit. In case of disagreement between the partners, Mme Vrau was to decide "in all sovereignty".[14] Mme Vrau was to get half the profits and her two partners one sixth each; the last sixth was for workers benefits.

Mme Vrau however was not as much of a martinet as the wording of the articles of association suggest. The family papers present us with the picture of a woman who spent a good part of her life keeping her family from falling apart.[15] Sophie Vrau had been involved in the running of the business in various capacities before her husband's death. She had also smoothed the path between a very practical husband and a son who took ten years to "find himself" only to decide he wanted to become a monk (father killed that idea on the spot: Philibert's duty was to succeed him). The ultra-sensitive, mercurial Camille worshiped his brother-in-law who could do no wrong in his eyes. Mme Vrau, and her husband, may have been convinced the "young" ones needed a tutelary figure, and should not be trusted too much with the family fortune. The men not only did not object, but could not imagine taking decisions without mother's approval. Sophie Vrau was provided with daily business reports which she read very carefully, and held "board" meetings in her bedroom, which she rarely left. She was, in other words, the chairwoman of the board, and her son and son-in-law were her directors. By and large however, she does not appear to have interfered with their decisions. The ferocious clause in the articles of association was more insurance than by-law.

14 ADN, 6U2653, 8/4/1871.
15 See Archives des Etablissements Vrau.

Widows may remain solely in charge even in circumstances which should have precluded their playing any active role. Marie Munroe, widow of William Drummond, one of a few English industrialists established in Lille was a case in point. In 1850, Marie Drummond, identified as a linen manufacturer, went into partnership with her son John William Drummond, foreman of her factory and Louis Leleu, building contractor. They created a society to spin flax and flax burr for 14 years under the name Veuve Drummond and Cie, in a village north of Lille, and in a plant leased since 1850. Each partner provided 10,000 francs of capital, and shared profits and losses equally.

Marie was the only administrator, had sole signing rights and could not delegate it. She was compensated for those duties by the exclusive use of a house and garden on the premises, in addition to free coal and lamp oil. John William "under the direction of the said lady, his mother [remained] in charge of the internal management of the factory and the supervision of the workers" for 50 francs a week. A final clause stipulated that the French language would be used to keep the books. Consequently Mme Drummond was authorized to hire a clerk at company's expenses for the purpose. The lady, in other words, did not master the French language adequately. One could presume that John, who dealt with workers on a daily basis, had a better command of the language. Nonetheless, he was shut off any part in the formal process of decision making. Mme Drummond could decide in all sovereignty as well.[16] Was she power hungry, or afflicted by a son who was good on the ground but had no business sense?

Other widows, although clearly not interested in merely cheering from the side line, showed no inclination to keep their sons on a tight leash. Some stayed long enough to ensure a smooth transition, and then retreated into the role of mentor. Fifty-two-year-old Denise Colette Liagre-Hauterive, brewer, for instance formed a partnership with her son Charles Tiburce, also brewer, in 1884. They both had signing and managing rights, and Mme could appoint another of her sons or a stranger to replace her as a co-manager. She was also allowed to transfer her share of the business to her sons Albert and Georges, who would not have signing rights. As long as she personally attended to the business, Charles would handle marketing *(les affaires du dehors)*. Eight years later though, she was the only one mentioned in the tax lists; the sons had disappeared.

16 See AND, Greffes de notaires, J 1442-33, Etude de Me Gruloy.

Mme Liagre-Hauterive's original intention may have been to gradually withdraw from the business, as had her colleague Adèle Francoise Dubois, veuve Brice in Lille. In 1867, the widow Brice and her son Charles Edouard had started a partnership to trade in iron, cast iron, and ironware. The partnership was to last ten years; in 1874, the two partners extended it for an additional six, and altered the articles of association. Both partners kept the signature, but Mrs Brice would henceforth devote to the affairs of the firm only the time she judged appropriate, without being under any obligation to do so. She could, if she saw fit, limit herself to giving advice concerning the operations of the business and its overall management, without having, as in the past, to play an active role in the firm.[17] Men did retire from the business, transferring their rights to their children. Women did the same.

The striking feature of the articles of association between widows and their children is their lack of uniformity. Any possible arrangement can be found. This suggests that widows stepping into the breach left by their deceased husband were part of the norm – how they would share power and responsibility with their children was something to negotiate with them. Age, experience, abilities, interests came into play. Widows were in a good position to negotiate. Their moral authority as mother was strengthened by their majority share of the assets – a share that the children could not contest, because the law did not allow them to do so. The family was a hierarchy, and the different members were not equal – but widows were not low on the hierarchy. They clearly had more room to make choice than their children.

Conclusion

Unsurprisingly, feminist historians have focused on the gender dimension of access to resources. Gender however is not the sole, not even necessarily the primary factor shaping power relationship within the household. The fact married women were almost universally placed under the author-

17 AND 6U2 656, 18 August 1874.

ity of their husband in historical societies should not hide the fact not all women were married, and that in many western societies, unmarried women above a given age, and widows, were their own mistresses. Widowhood could give women legal access to resources, which would provide for their support, and ensure their autonomy. This could pit them against sons (or even sons-in-law) thinking those resources should belong to them, and open the door to law suits. In and around Lille, the 1804 Civil Code *(Code Napoleon)* allowed, and local legal traditions encouraged, people to enlarge the rights of surviving spouses. This was done through testamentary clauses included in marriage contracts, clauses which could not be challenged in court, nor be modified by the spouses after marriage. Widows thus gained unchallengeable and extensive control over the assets of the family, which in turn guaranteed their autonomy, and the continuation of pre-revolutionary female economic roles.

References

Almanach du commerce, des arts et métiers des villes de Lille, Armentières, Roubaix et Tourcoing, Lille, Vanackère, 1829–55.

Annuaire de l'arrondissement de Lille, Lille, Ravet-Anceau, 1852–1902.

BEACHY, Robert, 2002a, "Business was a Family Affair: Women of Commerce in Central Europe, 1680–1870", *Histoire sociale–Social History*, 34, pp. 307–30.

–, 2002b, "Women without Gender: Commerce, Exchange Codes, and the Erosion of Female Guardianship in Germany, 1680–1830", in David GREEN and Alastair OWENS (eds), *Family Welfare: Gender, Property and Inheritance since the Seventeenth Century*, Westport, Praeger Press.

BRIET, Henri, 1908, *Le droit des gens mariés dans les coutumes de Lille*, Lille, Le Bigot frères.

BUTEL, Paul, 1976, "Comportements familiaux dans le négoce bordelais au 18e siècle", *Annales du Midi*, 28, pp. 139–157.

CHASSAGNE, Serge, 1981, *Une femme d'affaires au XVIIIe siècle*, Toulouse, Privat.

CLARK, Alice, 1992, *Working Life of Women in the Seventeenth century*, with an introduction by Amy Louise ERICKSON, London, Routledge (first edition London, 1919).

CLARK, John G., 1981, *La Rochelle and the Atlantic Economy during the Eighteenth Century*, Baltimore, Johns Hopkins.

CODACCIONI, Félix-Paul, 1976, *De l'inégalité sociale dans une grande ville industrielle, le drame de Lille de 1850 à 1914*, Lille, Presses universitaires de Lille.

COLLINS, James B., 1989, "The Economic Role of Women in Seventeenth Century France", *French Historical Studies*, 16, pp. 436–70.

DAUMAS, Jean-Claude, 2004, *Les territoires de la laine, histoire de l'industrie lainière en France au XIXe siècle*, Villeneuve D'Ascq, Septentrion.

DAVIDOFF, Leonor and Catherine HALL, 1987, *Family Fortunes, Men and Women of the English Middle Class, 1780–1850*, Chicago, University of Chicago Press.

DELSALLE, Paul, 1985, *La brouette et la navette, tisserands, paysans et fabricants dans la région de Roubaix et de Tourcoing*, Dunkerque, Editions des Beffrois.

FOHLEN, Claude, 1956, *L'industrie textile au temps du Second Empire*, Paris, Plon.

HIRSCH, Jean-Pierre, 1991, *Les deux rêves du commerce; entreprise et institution dans la région lilloise, 1780–1860*, Paris, EHESS.

LAMBERT-DANSETTE, Jean, 1954, *Quelques familles du patronat textile de Lille-Armentières, 1789–1914. Origines et évolution d'une bourgeoisie*, Lille, Raoust.

LOTTIN, Alain, 1986, *Histoire de Tourcoing*, Dunkerque, Edition des Beffrois.

POUCHAIN, Pierre, 1998, *Les maîtres du Nord du XIXe siècle à nos jours*, Paris, Librairie académique Perrin.

PRIOR, Mary (ed.), 1985, *Women in English Society 1500–1800*, London, Methuen.

RABUZZI, Daniel, 1995, "Women as merchants in Eighteenth Century Northern Germany: The Case of Stralsund, 1750–1830", *Central European History*, 28, pp. 435–456.

ROBEYNS, Ingrid, 2007, "Social justice and the gendered division of labour: Possibilities and limits of the capability approach", paper presented to the COST ACTION A 34 conference, Barcelona, 25th–27th June 2007.

SANDVIK, Hilde, 2007, "The security of widowhood and old age", paper presented to the COST ACTION A 34 conference, University of Minho, 25th–28th April 2007.

SHARPE, Pamela, 2002, "Gender in the economy: Female merchants and family business in the British Isles, 1600–1850", *Histoire sociale–Social History*, 38, pp. 283–306.

TAILLARD, 1849, *Recueil d'actes des XIIe et XIIIe siècles, en langue romano-wallonne du Nord de la France*, Douai.

TOULEMONDE, Jacques, 1966, Naissance *d'une métropole, Histoire économique de Roubaix-Tourcoing au XIXe siècle*, Tourcoing, G. Frère.

TRÉNARD, Louis (ed.), 1977, *Histoire d'une métropole, Lille, Roubaix, Tourcoing*, Toulouse, Privat.

ULRICH, Laurel Thatcher, 1983, *Good Wives. Images and Realities in the Lives of Women in Northern New England, 1650–1750*, New York, Oxford University Press (first ed. New York, Knopf, 1982).

YVER, Jean, 1953, "Les deux groupes de coutumes du Nord: le groupe picard-wallon", *Revue du Nord*, pp. 197–220.

–, 1954, "Les deux groupes de coutumes du Nord: le groupe flamingant", *Revue du Nord,* pp. 5–36.

Providing Well-Being to Women through Inheritance and Succession

Portugal in the 18th and 19th Centuries

Margarida DURÃES

Minho was a densely populated region where the possession of land was a symbol of power and social prestige and where all the peasants had a small plot of land – be it in private property or with a life-long lease[1] – which was cultivated to support the family. In this region, equality between all the heirs seemed to be the basis of the family, social and economic organization. Still today, this principle is respected by most families. Over the centuries before the welfare state, however, the principle of equality between legitimate heirs underwent adaptation in order to secure well-being to each in the family.

Thus, the main goal of this study, focusing on the Braga region (Figure 1), is to analyze inheritance practices as they were implemented in the eighteenth and nineteenth centuries with the intent to formulate an unequal property transmission model highlighting families' willingness to provide for all children while advantaging peasant widows and peasant unmarried women to guarantee them well-being. In the process, the model will show families' concern to secure health and retirement assistance to the family elderly in particular.

Well-being, as defined here, is a condition founded on the ownership of a minimum set of material wealth, such as material commodities (which secured minimal subsistence to the family) but also as emotional commodities (affection, emotions and feelings which are the result of intra-familial human, personal relations).

1 In the region of Braga under study here, life-long "emphyteotic" lease was very common *(amphiteosis),* because most of the land in the past belonged to religious communities (see below, *aforamento em vidas*).

As a consequence, well-being must not only be understood as a concept with material content to be measured and evaluated but also with psychological content which remains beyond measurement. Correspondingly, in past times, material well-being or this set of provisions necessary for survival such as food, lodging, wood for heating and cooking, and clothing was secured through devolution. Houses, agricultural property, and other everyday objects were some of the material possessions which also guaranteed well-being through devolution. Beyond this material wealth, however, old regime societies provided assistance through sickness and old age. Well-being depended on the nature and quality of life-long emotional ties which led to donations, rewards, and promises proportional to the services and assistance willingly provided. In order to enjoy vital well-being, therefore, Minho peasants in North-Western Portugal used to write wills, legal acts, which they meant to write to use the law as conveniently as possible to satisfy the interests and needs of the family.

The primary objective of this chapter is to define the two types of opposite laws imposed in Portugal through the General Law of the Portuguese Kingdom *(Ordenações Filipinas),*[2] one part of the law imposing equal partition between all legitimate heirs (male and female) upon privately-owned movable property *(bens móveis)* and the other part of the law affecting life-long, transmissible land-lease property *(bens imóveis vinculados*) under unequal single inheritance rules (involving the selection of a main heir who then was imposed specific conditions to enjoy preferential treatment). The demonstration will show that all the strategies highlighted testators' willingness to secure themselves well-being through life as well as that of the most vulnerable members of the family (the widowed spouse and unmarried children). The study of devolution strategies in rural Minho region, around Braga, will allow us to argue that preferential treatment was generally secured to the children living with parents through life, among which female family members were more numerous than male members. Yet, as the demonstration will show, non privileged children were not altogether excluded and preferred children did not always get the best deals.

2 Until 1867, when the first version of the Portuguese Civil Code was published, family laws were formulated in royal Ordinances written by Philip II, King of Spain and Portugal from 1580 to 1598, called *Ordenações Filipinas* (see Fac-simile edition, 1985).

Figure 1. Location of twelve rural localities under study in Minho within the council of Braga

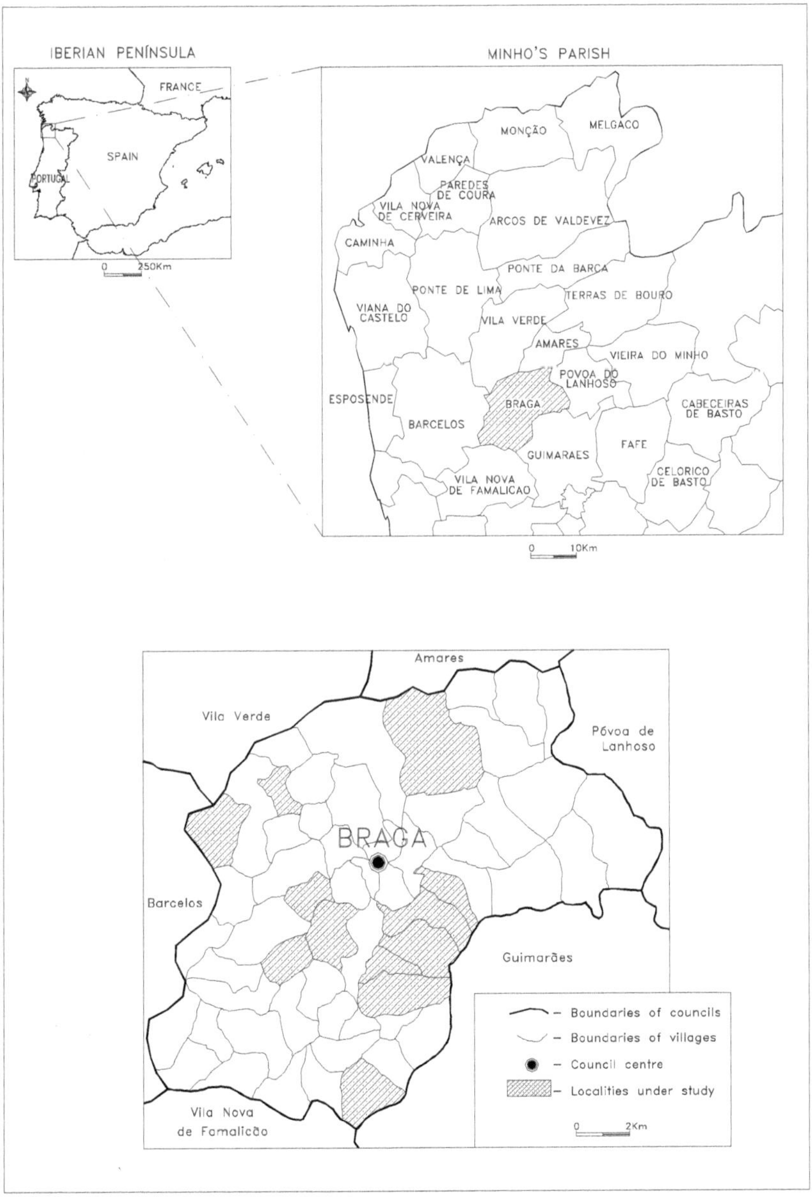

Sources: Wills

For this study, we made use of the wills written by the inhabitants of twelve rural communities of Braga, the majority of whom were small peasants under *aforamento em vidas* contracts,[3] which were life-long land contracts on aristocratic or religious property to be transmitted to a single heir. In this way we have established a sample of 1,372 wills that cover the period between 1720 and 1820. The complete documents include information on succession and inheritance indeed with religious references as well (Durães 2000, 52–57).

In the eighteenth century, wills had become more complex than previously. In general, they began with a prologue *(prólogo)* with Christian greetings (the sign of the cross),[4] the testator's identification (name, marital status, address) and a statement on the testator's health conditions (that he or she was indeed physically sick but in good mental spirit as the law required for will writing). Following these statements, there began the religious call *(preâmbulo religioso)* when the testator offered his or her soul to God, to the Virgin Mary, to her son Jesus Christ, and to all the saints, thus reflecting on life and death and justifying the writing of the will. In the same process, the testator made religious donations and demands to be satisfied for his or her redemption (as clothes, donations, funeral location, masses, and other religious ceremonies among other demands). It is only after expressing these religious concerns that the list of material dispositions and all other succession and inheritance declarations began.

All legitimate heirs were successively identified and other information as the testator saw fit were provided. At that very moment, the main heir was clearly identified, so were the reasons and the conditions for him or her to receive preferential treatment. A *terço*, a third portion of inheritance could be freely attributed.[5] Then the assets were partitioned, indicating

3 Contracts *aforamento em vidas* were life-long land-lease contracts which Minho peasants could sign with aristocratic land owners (lords, counts and others) but more importantly with religious land owners (monasteries, convents, bishops, and Braga's archbishop).

4 *Saudação* (or *sinal da cruz*).

5 *Terço* was the part of family or personal assets which a testator could freely dispose of to advantage one or several descendants, or unrelated person or persons.

debts, loans, usufructs, and donations. Finally, life-long individual and family accounting was made for the peace of the deceased person's soul. The act ended with the *escatocolo*, naming the witnesses, the writer of the act, and the place and date of the will.

Thus, during the 18th and 19th centuries, wills still indicated religious concerns, notably people's worry for their salvation. Despite this concern, wills assumed another important function: organizing the family's economic and social life after the death of the testator. From that moment onwards, it was clear that wills were used to express essential cultural concerns, those which linked salvation and proper property partition. By analysing this set of information, it is possible to give a picture of people's mental representations of death, to outline the behaviours that responded to family decisions as those derived from succession and inheritance, and to define testator's strategies to secure continuity in the management of his or her house after death (Rodriguez Jiménez and Molinié-Bertrand 2000). Thanks to all the information which wills provided it is possible to discern testators' strategies to secure survival to all the members of the family, particularly those living in the house together. A "proper death" was one which indeed provided for salvation through religious donations but it was also one which guaranteed well-being to all surviving family members.

A Gender Portrait of Testators

But who were the testators? The analysis of the sample wills written by people originating from the various social and professional groups, all representing Minho's rural society, indicates the prevalence of female peasant wills, which was not so common in Europe (Vovelle 1979). Indeed Minho's women wrote wills more often than men, as the data in Table 1 show (Durães 2000, 70–76). These wills were written in the late stage of an individual's life course first because it was required to be over fourteen years old and economically autonomous to write a will, second because testators waited after the selection of the single heir to write their will, and third because of their religious concern about salvation when death approached (Durães 2000, 81). In rural Minho, all women contributed for this over-representation of female wills (Table 1).

Table 1. Distribution of wills by sex and civil status of the testator, in rural Minho, council of Braga (1720–1820). Percentages

	Single	*Married*	*Widow(er)s*	*TOTAL*
Men	31.8	51.8	38.4	42.7
Women	68.2	48.2	61.6	57.3
TOTAL	100	100	100	100

Sources: Archive of Braga's District. Parish registers and Wills' Books of 12 parishes of Braga's rural area.
Note: Total number of wills under observation here: 1,372 cases.

Widows and single women without heirs were more numerous to write wills than men with the same marital status (respectively 61.6 percent to 38.4 percent and 68.2 percent to 31.8 percent). The proportion of married women writing wills was about the same as that of married men (among married individuals, 48.2 percent were females compared to 51.8 percent males). This situation was indeed not frequent in Europe, yet it was also commonplace in other regions of Portugal (Roque 1982, 20) as in Spanish Galicia. This is the result of demographic as well as economic, social and psychological factors.

Among the demographic factors to consider, three played a greater influence: mortality, migration and female celibacy. Although there were a higher number of male births, it appears that more boys died during childhood than girls. This created an imbalanced sex ratio in favour of women, a figure caused indeed by this higher male child mortality and aggravated by massive adult male emigration (Amorim 1987, 335–337). This phenomenon was particularly visible for adult and old age groups (Cruz 1970). Not only were men fewer but many indeed emigrated, leaving a number of women without scopes of marriage. Thus, women's representation was greater than men's and permanent celibacy was high (especially female celibacy). For single people, wills were important because they could plan to give their patrimony as they wished.

In the absence of legitimate heirs, these unmarried men and women used wills as a way to distribute their riches and also for the salvation of their soul, sometimes spending their entire fortune for it. The mentioned demographic factors indeed explain the female over-representation

(57.3 percent) or the high number of celibate people. However, they do not provide enough information to understand the behaviour of widows and married women. Many of these women signed wills as an expression of "cultural traditions" and of "the interiorisation of social roles, within and outside the family" (Araújo 1997, 98).

Widowers wrote wills mainly to set aright their house and to avoid any kind of conflicts between heirs. Widows for their part wrote wills in significant number as a result of their higher life expectancy. Besides, after the death of their husband, they used wills in order to reinforce their role within the family and to gain more power and social prestige. Since widows became the head of the house, they used the right to write their will to choose their successor (Guimarães 1986, 557–560).

Married women wrote wills about as often as married men for legal reasons indeed but above all for economic, social and emotional motives. Until the Portuguese Civil Code of 1867 it was common that husband and wife expressed their last spiritual wishes in the same document. They also appointed "each other" as the main heir and beneficiary of the patrimony. They also mutually attributed the "reserves and usufructs" of the totality or the main part of the agricultural incomes. The main aim of this act was to guarantee the subsistence and well-being of the surviving spouse.

In the rural area and especially in peasant families, the writing of a will was one of the moments that widowed or married women used to express their social identity, in the same way as men did in the same situation. In this way, women reflected attitudes in their peasant society, justifying the way they behaved through life and how they perceived life and death.

Portuguese Inheritance Laws before 1867 Civil Code

Whatever the content of the will was, it could not contradict the law or else it was null and void. Therefore it is necessary to outline more precisely the main clauses of the General Law of the Kingdom *(Ordenações Filipinas)*: those laws imposed equal partition upon privately-owned movable property *(bens móveis)* but allowed unequal inheritance upon lifelong, transmissible land-lease property *(bens imóveis vinculados)* which often advantaged women (the spouses and heiresses in particular) and secured them well-being. So, what were the judicial principles of the General Law of the Kingdom for our period of study (1720–1820)?

At the birth of the nation, customary law served as an auxiliary law to supplement the General Law on issues which the latter otherwise ignored. Yet this customary law was gradually abandoned and replaced by the General Law of the Kingdom in the eighteenth century to dictate state policies on all aspects of the political, social and economic life. The rules on inheritance were enforced after the publication of the first royal compilations.[6] This General Law of the Kingdom made a clear distinction between "inheritance" and "succession", two concepts that referred to different types of transmission mechanisms.

"Inheritance" referred to various privately-owned property *(bens partiveis),* a family concept which considered of primary value individual well-being within the family, each individual heir having an equal importance as a person and therefore deserving equal treatment with an equal share. This system as a consequence imposed the equal partition of all family assets between all heirs, all privately-owned property being equally distributed between all sons and daughters upon parents' death.

"Succession" by contrast referred to a concept that affected life-long, leased land *(bens imóveis vinculados)*, which considered land of primary value and imposed the impartibility of agricultural business or farms under land-lease contracts transmitted over generations. These contracts imposed the full transmission of this land-lease property to a single heir, to be advantaged over the other descendants and named in testators' wills.

Thus, in the General Law of the Kingdom or *Ordenações*, the rules regulating "inheritance" of privately-owned property were rules which imposed equal partition between all legitimate heirs,[7] the sacredness of the *legitime*,[8] the definition of the extra share or *terço*,[9] the indication of the three succession lines (descendants, ascendants, and collaterals). In this system, the spouse could only "inherit" the family assets if there were no

6 See note 2 above about the *Ordenações Filipinas.*

7 Legitimate heirs in the General Law of the Kingdom or *Ordenações* were first the children, second the direct ascendants (parents), and third direct collateral relatives (brothers and sisters) or other collateral relatives (nieces and nephews and others).

8 The *legitime* was the part of the family assets which was to be equally distributed between all legitimate heirs after paying all debts and expenses due to religious donations as well as after giving the third part or *terço* if the testator donated it to someone.

9 See note 5 above.

possible living heirs beyond the tenth degree. By contrast, the rules of the General Law regulating the "succession" of leased land property *(bens imóveis vinculados)* were very different because leased property could not be divided. The leased aristocratic or religious/ecclesiastic land was to be kept undivided. The rules imposed therefore single "transmission" of life-long lease land properties, the primacy of the surviving spouse over other successors, the primacy of male heirs over female heirs and the oldest children over the youngest ones. As a consequence, in this system of leased land contracts, inequality between children was established.

Minho's peasants had to adapt to these two sets of rules. On the one hand, the rule on owned property imposed the unbreakable *legitime* and the equal partition of family patrimony between all heirs (though the extra share or *terço* could be attributed to one or several persons) and on the other hand, the non egalitarian rule imposed the indivisibility of leased land and the selection of a single successor to be advantaged over all other heirs. We felt a need to distinguish these concepts of "inheritance" and "succession" to distinguish owned property law from leased property law. In this context, "succession" must be perceived as the transmission of statutes, duties, rights and roles to be carried out within the domestic and social community, for those peasants, while "inheritance" signified the equal transmission of rights over the goods that constituted the family patrimony. The family patrimony was a complex set of agrarian goods as well as all goods that were part of the family's material wealth. The agricultural exploitation comprised the whole agrarian patrimony – partible and impartible – part of which could actually constitute the material goods.[10]

10 It was important for their well-being that individuals, males and females, could have access (at least usufruct) to both types of property subjected to the two sets of laws: privately-owned property subject to equal partition and land from leased land subject to single inheritance regulations.

As Table 2 indicates, the testators of our sample chose mostly the single succession system, together with universal or beneficed "inheritance". From the 1,372 testators that designated the form of succession and division, 54.1 percent chose to name a single heir/successor, to whom they offered the totality of the partible and impartible estate, having to compensate other siblings. But, besides, 13.8 percent of testators decided to name a privileged/beneficed heir but they donated only the "third" (available share of the partible goods) to that advantaged heir. Finally, only 7.1 percent equally partitioned all the partible assets between all heirs, after paying the necessary expenses and some possible debts.

Table 2. Ways to succeed and divide the patrimony by sex and civil status of the testator, in rural Minho, council of Braga (1720–1820)

	Men			*Women*			*TOTAL*	*%*
	Single	Married	Widower	Single	Married	Widow		
Universal Inheritance	101	98	110	206	68	159	742	54.1
Beneficed Inheritance	2	46	27	1	63	50	189	13.8
Equalitarian Inheritance	3	19	20	9	12	34	97	7.1
Spouse/Husband and Heir/heiress	0	133	0	0	138	0	271*	19.8
Spouse/Husband Usufructuary	0	20	0	0	14	0	34	2.6
Legacy	5	1	1	22	0	10	39	2.6
TOTAL	111	317	158	238	295	253	1,372	100

Sources: Archive of Braga's District. Parish Registers. Wills' Books of 12 parishes of Braga's rural area.
Note: Category "Spouse/Husband Heir/heiress" will be later considered jointly with "Beneficed Inheritance" category.

Contrary to what we expected, these behaviours were not exclusively those of peasants' lessees and not only caused by the judicial rules. When we analyzed testators' wills and when we identified their social status, we realized that single heir and universal inheritance clearly had primacy not only among leasing peasants but also among propertied families (the latter using the extra share or *terço* and a compensation system in favour of the other siblings to go around the law and impose single inheritance).

To summarize, we may say that single or universal inheritance was a legal system among land-leasing families of rural Minho because the General Law of the Kingdom legally allowed them to favor one heir. This unequal system however was illegal among propertied families with private assets because for them the General Law imposed the equal distribution of all assets among all heirs. To go around the law and secure a unique successor, propertied peasant families compensated the excluded children paying them more for their share of the inheritance in order to keep the family assets intact from one generation to the next and avoid law suits, while preserving a viable farm and avoiding partition. The only propertied families who could successfully establish a single successor, however, were wealthy ones, those who could collect enough wealth to compensate excluded children. Otherwise, family private property was systematically divided up between heirs.

Keeping in mind that our present sample, situated in the Braga district, was socially characterized mainly by peasants' lessees, who had to satisfy two sets of judicial laws over material estates, partible and impartible ones, and that these rules made a clear distinction between equal part of assets inherited by each child and the rural farm transmitted to a unique successor, we tried to construct a systematised model with these concepts to be added to the previously mentioned models. This systematised model should enable us to perceive the logic behind the transmission of material goods to heirs, especially to women, determine peasant strategies to secure women's well-being, and evaluate the way these were provided for compared to men. Were women treated equally to men? Were they equally provided for in wills?

The Selected Heir: Male or Female?

In the council of Braga under study, the testator was only partly free to decide to whom he would donate his or her patrimony because the law imposed some restrictions in order to protect the closest members of the family from total exclusion. It was because of these legal restrictions that family ties guided the various ways material and symbolic patrimony was distributed in the Minho peasant society.

The analysis of Table 3 indicates that children were most often chosen by the testators (44.4 percent) followed by the surviving spouse (26.7 percent) and finally collateral relatives (22.6 percent). After taking a closer look at the data, however, we notice that the married testators actually preferred their surviving spouse first and second only their children. This preference was even more striking considering that spouses who were named universal or beneficed heirs, were also the usufructuary of the totality or main part of the family business. That is why wills were most commonly used by surviving female spouse in the peasant society. Nonetheless, behind the inheritance practices there were other reasons for these choices, among which female spouses' image and roles in the peasant society play an important role. It is necessary to analyse the different expressions and the content of the wills in order to get a picture of married women's roles and place in the peasant family.

Table 3. Choice of successors and family ties by sex and civil status of the testator, in rural Minho, council of Braga (1720–1820)

	Men			*Women*			TOTAL
	Single	Married	Widower	Single	Married	Widow	
Not mentioned	1	0	0	5	0	1	7
Direct descendants	7	125	145	22	97	213	609
Spouse	0	181	0	0	185	0	366
Ancestors	5	1	0	4	2	0	12
Collaterals	48	4	2	109	4	10	177
·Uncles/Aunts	0	0	0	1	0	0	1
Nephews/Nieces	37	4	6	59	6	20	132
Godsons	1	0	1	2	0	0	4
Other relatives	4	1	1	5	0	3	14
Without consanguinity	8	1	3	31	1	6	50
TOTAL	111	317	158	238	295	253	1,372

Sources: Archive of Braga's District. Parish Registers. Wills' Books of 12 parishes of Braga's rural area.

The content of the wills indicates that testators chose women as main heirs and successors because of their wisdom, their experience, and their ability to cultivate, rule and manage the agricultural exploitation, making them the most efficient administrators (Durães 2000, 376–385). In difficult moments when the survival and the well-being of the family were at risk, matrimonial confidence and solidarity were revealed in the testator's last will, probably prompted by an approaching early death, before his wife. To her the testators trusted the management of the house and assured that she could secure the economic survival and the well-being of the family. The married testatrix had a similar behavior. Married women – in case they would die first – mostly chose their surviving husband to run the agricultural exploitation. Different expectations were expressed: when men chose their wives (as future widows) as their main successor, they imposed that their widow would never remarry and show good moral and social conduct. When women chose their husbands (as future widowers) as their main successor, however, they expressed no condition. Widowers could very well remarry and this was actually encouraged, especially when children were young. Therefore, married men and women did not make a will only because they were married but more importantly because they had young children, with the intention to later name someone trustable who would inherit the rights and duties stated in the life-long lease contract for the farm. In this way, 36.2 percent of the testators who named direct descendants as successors were married testators, but 59.8 percent married testators named their spouse (Table 3).

All the descendants were present in the wills because the law forbade their exclusion at the time of succession and inheritance. They were considered as compulsory heirs as the Portuguese judicial system did not allow total exclusion, except in some rare cases. For this reason, testators were usually very careful when they indicated and named their descendants. In general, they named them by birth order, starting from the oldest one to the youngest one. They mentioned their marital status, their residence, and whether or not they had already left the parents' house. In the latter case, they mentioned the date of departure and the destination, the compensation the family had paid (if any), whether they were satisfied with their compensation or not, whether they had received a dowry or not, when they had received it, its value, and whether they had the right to receive additional compensation or not. All this was declared because it was necessary to reach some agreement and to see who had already been helped or not. In this way, they wished to avoid apparent inequalities and secure the well-being of those who remained in the house under the authority of the named successor. Yet, among all the descendants who was the chosen one to become the universal or main successor/heir in the peasant house?

A Privileged Male or Female Child with Responsibilities and Charges as Successor

As we can see in Table 4, the testators of our sample did not feel obliged to donate their patrimony to the first-born child nor to the male descendants. Among the descendants who were chosen as the main successor and heir (in 41.4 percent of the cases), the first-born son (in 38.7 percent of the cases) had a small edge over the first-born daughter (in 25.5 percent of the cases). However, if we consider only the sex of the descendants, ignoring birth order, female descendants (in 48.2 percent of the cases) had as great a chance to be advantaged as male descendants (in 51.8 percent of the cases).[11] This trend appeared throughout the period that we have analysed, and it allows us to reaffirm and to understand the important role that Minho's women played in the family and in the peasant economy. In Minho, the female descendants were not excluded from family succession, unlike in other regions where written laws had been influenced by Roman law (and therefore encouraged male succession, particularly first-born males). Indeed in Minho, daughters enjoyed the same rights to family succession and inheritance as sons.

While the state law indicated that men should be preferred over women in the succession, in reality the opposite happened and women were chosen over men because parents used testamentary prerogatives to name women as their successors. The testators, who chose a woman to be the main heir, justified their decision in the following way: to guarantee their protection through old age, to express gratitude for the affections and services given through sickness or to compensate for the salaries that should

11 Percentages here are calculated on direct descendants (499 children).

have been paid for earlier and for the work done in the house through the years. The chosen woman could be a daughter or a granddaughter of those that had direct descendants, and a sister or a niece of those without children.

Table 4. Choice of a successor, by sex and family position, in the universal and beneficed inheritance, in rural Minho, council of Braga (1720–1820)

	Testators with Children		*Testators without Children*		
	Universal Inheritance	Beneficed* Inheritance	Universal Inheritance	Beneficed* Inheritance	Total
Spouse/Husband	75	40	196	33	344
First-born male	172	21	0	0	193
First-born female	103	24	0	0	127
Male	47	7	0	0	54
Female	49	43	0	0	92
Youngest Child male	6	6	0	0	12
Youngest Child female	12	9	0	0	21
Grandchildren	7	2	5	0	14
Collaterals	0	0	153	1	154
Ancestors	0	0	12	0	12
Uncles/Aunts	0	0	1	0	1
Nephews/Nieces	0	0	117	1	118
Others	0	0	54	2	56
For the soul	0	0	4	0	4
TOTAL	471	152	542	37	1,202

Sources: Archive of Braga's District. Parish Registers. Wills'Books of 12 parishes of Braga's rural area.
Notes: *The category "Beneficed Inheritance" includes here "Spouse/Husband or Heir/heiress" category mentioned in Table 2 above.

The figures thus reveal the prevalence of an unequal hereditary system that privileged a universal heir and excluded all the others from succession. However, these figures deserve a closer analysis in order to discern the multiple conditions that were associated with this system and that reduced its effects. In this way, looking at inheritance conditions and at the way many heirs dealt with these succession practices, we can better understand the systems of land transmission. Indeed, despite inequality, heirs did try to be *fair* (Wall 1998), making the costs of transmission quite high and difficult to pay sometimes with only their incomes, especially when the property was small. Truly, the costs of single inheritance to favor the universal and beneficed heirs were sometimes high because money had to be collected and it was rather rare to find for the deceased person's salvation, dowries or legacies from the *legitime*, simple legacies, usufructs, pensions and debts.

Correspondingly, the expenses for the funeral or for salvation reached about 50 percent of the total costs for the universal heir, in our sample, and 62 percent for the beneficed heir (Table 5). These heirs were responsible for the payment of theses expenses except when the surviving spouse received all assets in usufruct. When this happened, the spouse became responsible for paying all the expenses due to succession and inheritance.

Table 5. Type of costs for the universal heir and the beneficed heir, in rural Minho, council of Braga (1720–1820)

Categories	*Universal Heir*	%	*Beneficed Heir*	%	*TOTAL*	%
For the soul	687	46.9	166	61.9	853	49.2
Legacies/*Legitime*	203	13.8	14	5.2	217	12.5
Legacies	246	16.8	43	16.1	289	16.7
Usufruct	153	10.4	6	2.2	159	9.2
Debts	177	12.1	39	14.6	216	12.4
Mentions in wills	1,466	100	268	100	1,734	100

Sources: Archive of Braga's District. Parish Registers. Wills' Books of 12 parishes of Braga's rural area.
Notes: The category "Beneficed Heir" includes here "Spouse/Husband and Heir/heiress" category mentioned in Table 2 above.
Percentages are calculated from wills mentioning a universal heir (1,013 wills), a beneficed heir (189 wills) and together (1,202 wills). Categories are non exclusive: each will may express one or several conditions. Pious legacies are numerous, followed by other legacies and payment of *legitime* to other children and other dispositions, particularly payment of debts.

First and foremost, the way salvation was secured was by constituting a set of goods and services that the heir had to arrange for the testator's burial: the shroud and exhibition of the corpse, the religious ceremonies, and the funeral meal (Araújo 1997, 98).

When the deceased person rested in peace, a new phase started with masses given in the intentions and the devotions of the deceased, and donations distributed to the institutions or people named in the will (priest, poor, shelters, convents). Adding all the costs of these acts, the universal or beneficed heirs of our sample ended up paying an expense that could reach from the 10,000 *reis* for a humble care to 30,000 *reis*, for a first-rate care, without ostentation though. In addition to all these obligations, the named heir also had to pay the testator's debts. The wills not only helped to reveal the reality about money shortages in these rural communities but also about how common these were in other Minho's regions. Everybody owed money to everybody. Parishioners, priests, merchants, craftsmen, lessees, farm managers, renters and day-labourers were some of the social groups that had run into debts or had lent money to others who in turn had run into debts or had lent money from others.

After the testators' death, most of the heirs had to make accounting for what they were entitled to receive and pay in order to collect the amount of money that was owed to them after paying the testators' debts. However, in our sample, very few testators (147) referred to the amount of debts and to the name of creditors. Despite the incomplete information, we may argue that mainly men declared the existence and the amount of their debts (Table 6). Women were less inclined to declare debts and when they did, these were mainly small debts (65 percent). Women were not the ones who contacted debts most often in the Minho rural society. On the contrary, they were the main creditors. Since these women possessed some savings, which they had received from the *legitime*, dowries and legacies or from their work, their family and neighbours borrowed some money from them. Besides women, landlords, renters, pharmacists, surgeons, masons, blacksmiths and carpenters were also creditors of small amounts of money. The creditors of large amounts of money were the descendants with no succession rights, brothers and relatives, clergymen, merchants and the *Misericórdia* (charitable institution). Information on debts and credits indicate that people in the rural communities were permanently indebted. Foremost, they revealed the difficulties these people had to face to pay their debts. Some of these debts were passed down to the next generations through wills.

Table 6. Distribution of the amount of debts for universal and beneficed heirs according to the sex of the testator, in rural Minho, council of Braga (1720–1820), in *reis*

Amount in reis	*Male testators*	*Female testators*	*Together*	*%*
< 5,000	9	6	15	10.2
5,000 – 10,000	8	4	12	8.2
10,000 – 30,000.	23	22	45	30.6
30.000 – 50,000	15	16	31	21.1
50,000 – 100,000	17	7	24	16.3
> 100,000	13	7	20	13.6
Total of cases	85	62	147	100
Total amount of debts	5,570,795	3,451,481	9,022,276	

Sources: Archive of Braga's District. Parish Registers. Wills' Books of 12 parishes of Braga's rural area.

The named heirs also had to pay the legacies from the *legitime* or the dowries given to the descendents excluded from succession and inheritance. However, only 13.8 percent of the named heirs were obliged to comply with these payments. Three reasons explain this non-compliance. Firstly, the legacies from the *legitime* were only for direct descendants, given that the children were considered compulsory heirs. Considering that many were unmarried or married and widowed testators without any descendants, the universal heirs were not obliged to pay the legacies from the *legitime* but they had to pay other expenses such as pensions and usufructs. Secondly, the heirs that did not receive the usufruct straight away, despite being named, were also not obliged to pay the above-mentioned costs. These costs were the responsibility of the usufructuaries. Thirdly, in this sample, there was a significant number of wills which indicated that dowries and legacies from the *legitime* had already been paid for by parents, when the children married, were ordained or emigrated. In these circumstances, the will was used to officially name the successor and heir and to declare the other descendants as "paid and satisfied of the possible *legitime*".

The desire to "help" the ones that had left the house, to give each one of the descendants "his or her part in money" or the obligation to "give the brothers their share after subtracting all expenses" were expressions repeatedly used in the studied wills. These expressions indicate that the choice and nomination of a universal successor/heir was not done for free. After his or her nomination, the main or universal heir had several obligations as paying the debts, giving the legacies, paying the pensions, distributing the usufructs, giving the *legitime* to the other descendants and taking the necessary care for the testator's salvation. Therefore, we can conclude by arguing that being chosen to succeed and inherit the family's agricultural business had more symbolic advantages than material ones. The heir/successor inherited the rights over the house and over the agricultural land, the animals and the agricultural tools, the saved and future crops as well as the personal estates. But the price to pay was usually much higher than the profits he or she received and made. What did men and women gain from succession or inheritance though? The heir inherited a name, a place in the community, the prestige and power and this inheritance could not be bought. That is why the named heir had symbolic advantages over the other descendants.

Securing Well-being to the Excluded Children

After paying the debts, the funeral expenses, and the religious donations and after the surviving spouse's well-being was secured with the certainty that he or she would be provided with a house to live, food, assistance through life, the testator had the obligation to secure the well-being of the children who still lived in the house and who were excluded from succession. These prerogatives were so important in the acts that many wills listed the items and sums of money to be distributed. Conflicts between siblings living together were a constant reality which forced testators to provide minimal survival to every one of them. Fearing conflicts between the single heir and the excluded children and about the future harmony in the house after their death, testators wished to secure a certain well-being especially to the excluded women residing in the house by reserving parts of the house and sufficient revenues for them to live independently from the main heir or heiress. These sums "when conveniently calculated [...] could really be favourable" to the interests of the excluded children.

In fact, as Maria de Fátima Brandão noted, the inheritance parts were only available after the death of the parents and demanded the participation of the debts and expenses. On the contrary, the monetary compensations were clear of debts and expenses and were usually paid for when the children left the house to marry (Brandão 1994, 246).

Table 7. Composition of the descendants' legacies from the *legitime* paid by the successors and universal heirs according to gender, in rural Minho, council of Braga (1720–1820)

	Male testators	*Female testators*	*Together*	*%*
Money	144	183	327	68.4
Clothes	4	24	28	5.9
Household linens	2	26	28	5.9
Jewelleries	0	18	18	3.8
Furniture	4	10	14	2.9
Safes	10	27	37	7.7
Beds	1	5	6	1.2
Animals	1	4	5	1.0
Lands	3	4	7	1.5
Tools	1	7	8	1.7
TOTAL	170	308	478	100

Sources: Archive of Braga's District. Parish Registers. Wills' Books of 12 parishes of Braga's rural area.

Table 7 shows that most part of the legacies from the *legitime* were in money, clothes, household linens, jewelleries and safes (precious material wealth indeed). By giving these objects in advance, it was possible for the peasants' daughters to marry someone with the same social status. Therefore, it was mainly for their single daughters that testators offered considerable sums of money as well as other goods of significant value, which all together made up their dowry. Minho's peasants invested more in the female members of the family than in the male ones, because daughters did not have other possibilities to settle down comfortably but through marriage. But this behaviour created other disparities between the heirs who were excluded from land access.

The main purposes of the legacies from the *legitime* in money were to finance marriage, priesthood, replacement in another employment and emigration (Table 8). Not all descendants could live in the house so as to keep the agricultural exploitation undivided. The logic of the whole system was to preserve the farm land undivided and help the members of the family excluded from succession when parents were still alive. When this happened, the peasant families tried to provide money for their descendants depending on their resources.

Table 8. Distribution of the legacies from the *legitime* in money paid by main successors and universal heirs to their siblings, by gender, in *reis*, in rural Minho, council of Braga (1720–1820). Percentages

Value in *reis*	*Excluded Sons*	*Excluded Daughters*	*Together*
< 10,000	14.7	8.9	11.4
10,000 – 20,000	17.5	15.6	16.4
20,000 – 60,000	38.5	36.7	3.5
60,000 – 100,000	4.8	6.0	5.6
> 100,000	24.5	32.8	29.1
TOTAL	100	100	100

Sources: Archive of Braga's District. Parish Registers. Wills for 12 parishes of Braga's rural area.
Note: In four cases the amount of money is unknown. Number of cases under observation here: 323 excluded children (143 sons and 180 daughters).

The main purposes of the legacies from the *legitime* in money were to finance marriage, priesthood, replacement in another employment and emigration (Table 8). Not all descendants could live in the house so as to keep the agricultural exploitation undivided. The logic of the whole system was to preserve the farm land undivided and help the members of the family excluded from succession when parents were still alive. When this happened, the peasant families tried to provide money for their descendants depending on their resources.

This helped to avoid future conflicts between the named successor/heir, who had to pay high expenses, and the excluded descendants who otherwise became economically dependent. About one hundred wills in our sample illustrated this situation when testators named their descendant to inherit the land, outlined what had been distributed to the other children, and stated whether they were happy or not. The descendants that had already left their father's house, with a financial help from the family, had three possibilities or options. Firstly, they were totally excluded from the parents' will and forbidden to claim additional compensation from the heir. Secondly, they were not "excluded" but the parents' will suggest that they had already been compensated and were satisfied. The will also mentioned a set of reasons to punish them in the case they did not accept their parents' decision. Thirdly, they could claim their share but all that they had previously received from the parents was deducted from their share of the *legitime*, which was calculated only from the partible goods[12] and after they had paid all the expenses and debts. To sum up, all strategies were meant to help daughters to marry within the social group and to discourage the claims of the descendants who had already left home and were established outside the parents' house.

The named heirs also had to pay the legacies. In general, legacies were used to pay services and to show testators' affection and friendship towards their families and friends, as well as to distribute some personal objects to those who deserved them. The testators without descendants or compulsory heirs were the ones who most often used this legal assistance to share their patrimony. Therefore, legacies were found in the wills of married testators as well as childless married or widowed testators. However, it appears that there were also and occasionally testators with children. They used legacies to increase the *legitime* of the non-successors, to help reduce the disparities between children, to express gratitude to the ones who had helped through sickness and old age or to protect the descendants with physical ailments.

But the main beneficiaries of these legacies were nephews and nieces, sisters, godsons, servants and neighbours. These donations were similar to the legacies from the *legitime* and included small amounts of money, clothes, household linens, jewelleries, safes, animals (bees, sheep, oxen), weapons, crops, agricultural and viticultural tools, weaver's looms, images of saints, land leases, salaries and some small properties (enclosures, hills, plots, gardens). It was not because of the above-listed legacies that the successors/heirs were overcharged, however. Usually legacies were paid for with goods from the house or with lent money. The heirs' inheritance could be somewhat reduced because of legacies yet the expenses were not as high as the legacies from the *legitime*, which really reduced the size of inheritance and could even force the heirs to debts.

Legitimes and legacies were sometimes followed by usufructs and pensions that aimed to help unmarried and widowed relatives. In the perspective of possible difficulties that could arise between the named heir and

12 As explained above, excluding land-lease property *(bens imóveis vinculados)*.

his close family, the testator usually tried to ensure that all had a house to live in and enough to survive. For this, he donated them several small secondary buildings or a room in the main house, land for kitchen-gardening or other purposes, as well as a part or the totality of the usufruct over the inherited property. Though the surviving spouses and descendants were the ones who most benefited from these advantages, especially before receiving the *legitime* and if they were still single, the childless testators also worried about the survival of the relatives or people they particularly cherished because they had lived together or they had been treated with kindness or been assisted through sickness and old age. This explains why usufructs and pensions were given to sisters and brothers, ascendants, nephews and nieces, maids and even to one slave.

Conclusion

To sum up, before the Portuguese Civil Code was published (1867), all succession and inheritance strategies for Minho peasants to transmit their houses followed two opposite sets of rules within the General Law of the Kingdom *(Ordenações Filipinas)*: the laws which imposed equal partition of privately-owned property and the laws which imposed impartible succession of land-lease property, the dominant system of family transmission in this region, particularly in the district of Braga under study here, as a result of the forms of land exploitation adopted by the landlords.

The General Law of the Kingdom has always proclaimed that the descendants of propertied families had equal rights to inheritance and reaffirmed the sacredness of the *legitime* equal share. Yet, the easy way to have access to land was by leasing contracts and these followed a set of rules that determined the succession and forbade the division of the land. Because of this, Minho peasants elaborated a set of family strategies that secured equality, indivisibility and protection through old age and sickness. The first two objectives, equality and indivisibility, were fulfilled using the rules of the law and testamentary succession. The guarantee of protection through old age was obtained as people had the freedom to write a will. This legal act has always been one of the major characteristics of the national inheritance law. Despite equality though, wills were used to transmit the extra share or *terço* (to be freely distributed) in order to protect the most vulnerable members of the family, namely widows and unmarried women.

Depending on the interests and the needs of each family or social group, the judicial system was modified by a set of practices where succession and inheritance were two different processes. It was possible to inherit the management of the house, its name, its status and its position within the community, its titles, the respect and the work that went with it, but also the debts and expenses for descendants' compensations. Besides, it was possible to inherit the real estate *(allodials)* or its value (lands with life-long contracts)[13] and the partible goods (furniture, clothes, jewelleries, money, working tools, and animals, among other things).

Even though the Laws of the Kingdom relegated the surviving spouse to the group of non-compulsory heirs, he or she was usually named the main successor or at least the usufructuary of the whole or a large part of the agricultural business. These laws also, in principle, privileged the male heirs and relegated women to a secondary position. Parents however always tried to place women at an equal footage with their brothers and in some circumstances, female descendants were even preferred to male descendants. Our demonstration though showed that because of testators' demands and other legal obligations, excluded children were somehow compensated and therefore not altogether excluded and single heiresses (in particular) were indeed preferred but this preferred position however could be burdensome.

Thus, the Laws of the Kingdom not only established equality between the compulsory heirs but they also forbade the division of rented properties. As a consequence, the peasants always found ways to conciliate these two rules, though they seemed incompatible at first sight. Thus, we can state that practices prevailed over the law. The latter was not forgotten or set aside but it was only avoided when specific family circumstances demanded and allowed it.

When the liberal reforms were imposed in the course of the nineteenth century, however, it became more difficult to continue these practices. With the confiscation of ecclesiastic property, peasants were given the

13 See above, about transmissible land-lease property *(bens imóveis vinculados)*, *amphiteosis* or *aforamento em vidas*, opposed to real estate hold in absolute independence *(allodials)*.

opportunity to regain their rights and unite the practical domain with the property real domain. As the foundations of the seigniorial regime were destroyed, the judicial regime of land exploitation was also transformed. Most of the agricultural farms that were leased became free properties upon which the egalitarian laws of the General Law of the Kingdom were applied. Minho's family farms experienced then a period of division and dispersion enhanced by the economic difficulties caused by the system of single succession/universal heir, by the rise of demographic pressure and mainly by the cultural system dominant in Minho, where the possession of land was the most important element of prestige, social and economic power. From this moment onwards it became more difficult to persuade heirs to accept money in exchange for their parcel of land.

In this manner, with the liberal reforms, the egalitarian practices soon prevailed despite single inheritance and universal heirship. This became rare and difficult to maintain. These practices however continue to exist in Portugal as publications in the various social science journals testify. Despite the mechanisms and forms of assistance that the contemporary society and the welfare state have elaborated and guaranteed in recent years, Minho peasants wish to die at home with their close relatives around them. Today, as well as in the past, testamentary inheritance and practices aim at securing the surviving spouse well-being guaranteeing him or her all necessaries until death. Today, as in the past, demographic conditions extending female life expectancy allow women to benefit the most from current transmission strategies.

References

AMARAL, António Caetano, 1945, *Para a História da legislação e costumes de Portugal*, Porto, Livraria Civilização.

AMORIM, Norberta, 1987, *Guimarães 1580–1819. Estudo Demográfico*, Lisboa, Inst. Nac. de Invest. Científica, pp. 335–337.

–, 1999, "O Minho: comportamentos demográficos através da informação paroquial", *Ler História*, 3, pp. 9–43.

ALVES, Jorge Fernandes, 1994, *Os Brasileiros. Emigração e retorno no Porto oitocentista*, Porto, Ed. Autor.

ARAÚJO, Ana Cristina, 1997, *A morte em Lisboa. Atitudes e representações (1700–1830)*, Lisboa, Editorial Notícias.

ARIÈS, Philippe, 1981, *História Social da Criança e da Família*, Rio de Janeiro, Guanabara.

AUGUSTINS, Georges, 1982, "Esquisse d'une comparaison des systèmes de perpétuation des groupes domestiques dans les sociétés paysannes européennes", *Archives Européennes de Sociologie*, 23, 1, pp. 39–69.

–, 1989, *Comment se perpétuer? Devenir des lignées et destins des patrimoines dans les paysanneries européennes*, Nanterre, Société d'ethnologie.

BRANDÃO, Maria de Fátima, 1994, *Terra, Herança e Família no Noroeste de Portugal. O caso do Mosteiro no séc. XIX*, Porto, Edições Afrontamento.

CABRAL, J. de Pina, 1989, *Filhos de Adão, filhas de Eva*, Lisboa, D. Quixote.

COLLOMP, Alain, 1981, "Conflits familiaux et groupes de résidence en Haute-Provence", *Annales E.S.C.*, 36, 3, pp. 408-425.

COSTA, Mário Júlio de Almeida, 1996, *História do Direito Português*, Coimbra, Almedina.

CRUZ, António, 1970, *Geografia e Economia da Província do Minho nos fins do século XVIII, por José Gomes de Vilas-Boas*, Porto, FLUP.

DESCAMPS, Philippe, 1935, *Le Portugal. La vie sociale actuelle*, Paris, Firmin Didot.

DURÃES, Margarida, 1992, "No fim, não somos iguais: estratégias familiares na transmissão da propriedade e estatuto social", *Boletin de la Asociación de Demografia Histórica*, 10, 3, pp. 125–141.

–, 1998, "Nécessités économiques et pratiques juridiques: problèmes de la transmission des exploitations agricoles. L'exemple portugais (XVIIIe–XXe siècles)", *Mélanges de l'École Française de Rome. Italie et Méditerranée*, tome 110, pp. 373–388.

–, 2000, *Herança e Sucessão. Leis, Práticas e Costumes no Termo de Braga (sécs. XVIII-XIX)*, PhD, Universidade do Minho, Braga.

FARIA, Ana Mouta, 1987, "Função da carreira eclesiástica na organização do tecido social do Antigo Regime", *Ler História*, 11, pp. 29-46.

FLANDRIN, Jean-Louis, 1979, *Orígenes de la familia moderna*, Barcelona, Critica.

GUIMARÃES, Elina, 1986, "A mulher portuguesa na legislação civil", *Análise Social*, 22, 92–93, pp. 557–560.

HESPANHA, António Manuel, 1978, *A História do Direito na História Social*, Lisboa, Livros Horizonte.

LEANDRO, Maria Engrácia, 1998, *Sociologia da Família. Metodologia e Programa.* Relatório apresentado à Univ. do Minho para provas de Agregação, Braga.

MACFARLANE, Alan, 1990, *História do Casamento e do Amor*, S. Paulo, Companhia das Letras.

MEDEIROS, Fernando, 1985, "Groupes domestiques et habitat rural dans le Nord du Portugal", *Les campagnes Portugaises de 1870 à 1930: Images et réalités, Actes du Colloque d'Aix en Provence*, Paris, Centre culturel Portugais.

NETO, Maria Margarida Sobral, 1984, "Uma Provisão sobre foros e baldios: problemas referentes a terras de 'logradouro comum' na região de Coimbra, no século XVIII", *Revista de História Económica e Social*, Lisboa, 14, pp. 91–101.

Ordenações Filipinas, 1985, Livro IV, Ed. Fac-simile, Lisboa, Fundação Calouste Gulbenkian.

RODRIGUEZ JIMÉNEZ, Pablo and MOLINIE–BERTRAND, Annie, 2000, "Testamentos" in Annie MOLINIÉ-BERTRAND and Pablo RODRIGUEZ (eds), *Através del tiempo. Diccionario de Fuentes para la historia de la familia*, Murcia, Universidade de Murcia, pp. 171–176.

ROQUE, João Lourenço, 1982, *Atitudes perante a Morte na região de Coimbra de meados do séc. XVIII a meados do séc. XIX. Notas para uma investigação*, Tese complementar, Coimbra, FLUC.

SCOTT, Ana Sílvia Volpi, 1999, *Famílias, Formas de União e Reprodução Social no Noroeste Português (séculos XVIII e XIX)*, Guimaraes, NEPS/University of Minho.

SEGALEN, Martine, 1981, *Sociologie de la famille*, Paris, Armand Colin.

SILVA, Rosa Fernandes, 1981, *Paisagem agrária das planícies e colinas minhotas. Contrastes e mutações*, PhD, University of Porto.

TELLES, Inocêncio Galvão, 1963, *Apontamentos para a História do Direito das Sucessões Português*, Revista da Faculdade de Direito da Universidade de Lisboa, vol. XV.

TELLES, José Homem Corrêa, 1851, *Questões e várias Resoluções de Direito Emphyteutico*, Coimbra.

VOVELLE, Michel, 1979, "Un préalable à toute histoire sérielle: la représentativité sociale du testament (XIVe–XIXe siècles)", in Bernard VOGLER, *Les actes notariés, sources de l'histoire sociale (XVIe–XIXe siècles)*, Strasbourg, ISTRA.

WALL, Karin, 1998, *Famílias no Campo. Passado e presente em duas freguesias do Baixo Minho*, Lisboa, D. Quixote.

Men, Women and Property in Finland and Sweden in the 18th and 19th Centuries

Beatrice MORING

The causal effect of economically difficult times or of an increase in economic opportunities on ages at marriage within populations depending on wage labour has been demonstrated by Wrigley and Levine (Levine 1977, 104–110; Wrigley 1983, 98, 121–125). As proletarians are sensitive to economic conditions, some assessment of the level of proletarianisation might have an explanatory value for the issue of family formation in the past. It is indeed interesting that, in Scandinavia, the country with the highest level of proletarians in the 18th century, Denmark, also had the highest ages at marriage. The increase in urbanisation and social stratification in the 19th century was followed by a general increase in age at marriage in all Nordic countries. Socioeconomic differences in marriage age were a feature of the 18th and 19th centuries. In Nordic society, apart from scrambling for a livelihood, the landless were at times barred from marriage unless they acquired access to land, a craft or employment (Moring 2003, 84–87).

In sociological research, the connection between marriage and a positive economic situation has been seen as self evident. The studies of Hareven and her colleagues of historical populations in the USA have also revealed the effect created by specific familial conditions (Ankarloo 1976, 132; Elder 1976, 28; Hareven 1978a; 1978b; 1994). One of the firm critics of static systems and the calculation of averages, Michael Anderson, has never relented in his emphasis on the need to understand families as existing in a particular social environment. Some historical anthropologists, however, did not only see the importance of the social, but also that of the physical environment, as a phenomenon with impact on economic organisation, and therefore the basic structures that influence the timing and nature of family formation (Anderson 1971; Lofgren 1974, 22–24, 27–31; Viazzo 1989, 7–8, 42–44).

In this study, the aim is to analyse family formation and strategies in local populations. The localities represent the far southwest and southeast of Finland and northern Sweden. Family strategies would have been tailored to fit the needs at a particular point in time. Therefore generalisations are sought through an examination and understanding of the conditions of life. These conditions include economic opportunities, ecology, legislation, social structure, and all factors connected with these issues. The people in the localities are believed to reflect the response on individual level to particular economic regimes and changes in these. The routes into marriage and out of the home taken by young people do not only reveal the different strategies of different socio-economic groups but also the variation in opportunities of children of the same family and of different gender and birth order. While actions when young are ruled by existing options their consequences are far reaching. The opportunities for well-being in old age, in the case of women, were governed by changes in society creating or closing niches for families.

Legislation and Custom

The family, as it emerges in Nordic legislation of the Middle Ages, was an institution for the maintaining of security based on a landholding over which the family had the control. The society generating these laws was one where the farming class had a strong input in the lawmaking process. The system was aimed at preserving the holding as a viable unit. The law guaranteed the right of the family to the land, of the old to have a safe old age and of the young to grow up without want. All members of the family had "birth right" to the family land.[1]

Inheritance of family land gave the right to hold and the right to use. Disposable objects, cattle, grain and money could be owned outright by an individual or held jointly. In a situation of departure of an individual from the household, these items could be divided. Money earned working outside the farm was also individual property. The right to inheritance in some form or another was calculated both on the male and the female line. Family land could only be divided between descendants of the family if

1 See King Kristoffer's Law 1442, regulations about land.

the units were economically viable. "New land" taken up for cultivation from bog-lands or woods could be used for augmenting the farm. Land could, however, be temporarily alienated in the form of a retirement settlement or, from the 1740s, as a croft, which after a specified number of years or lifetimes reverted back into the farm.[2]

The Nordic legal code prescribed that when the parents handed their land over to one of their children, the child was obliged to take care of the father and mother for the rest of their lives. The care in old age constituted the payment for the farm and made it possible to transfer the farm undivided to one heir. This transfer of rights and obligations laid the basis for inter-generational co-residence patterns. The right of the farmer to appoint his successor, often the eldest male or female, was a right conceived as central for the autonomy of the Nordic farming class. In situations of increasing population pressure, alternative strategies for securing the future of the children were to divide the farm or younger sons were allowed to establish crofts on the land. The land-population ratio of Sweden and Finland and parts of Norway made a development within the agricultural sector, based on these strategies, possible until the 19th century when the increase of the landless groups reached unsurpassed levels (Aarnio 1991, 58–61; Jutikkala 1958, 53, 328–329; Pylkkänen 1990, 174–181; Sogner 1979, 290–292).

The number of people needed for the effective running of a farm varied depending on geography and the structure of the economic activity. The units functioned through a balancing of the work of family members and servants. All household members were expected to work for the farm according to their capacity and ability. If the reward for the work did not take the form of upkeep for life, the departing individual had the right to compensation for the work input in addition to extracting his or her personal property. The transmission of farms between generations could be secured using retirement contracts, or adoption and wills, with an underlying philosophy that those who stayed and worked received preferential treatment. The heir brought his or her partner into the parental household and by her work input she became part of the unit with right to support in old age. Although primogeniture was the general practice, an absent eldest son was bypassed in the transfer.[3]

2 See 17th century court records mentioned in Jutikkala 1957; 1958; Pylkkänen 1990; Korpijaakko 1985.

3 See 17th century court records (Moring 2003).

The Household and the Environment

When standard systems of household classification are applied to regions with set-field systems, in pre-industrial Finland, the existence of cohabitation between parents and one married child can be established for large parts of the country. In 17th and 18th century central and western Finland, 20–30 percent of the households were of the so called "stem-family" type. However, comparison of taxation records with parish registration data and court records have revealed that the actual numbers were probably higher, as old women were not always well registered (Friberrg 1954; Jutikkala 1957, 191; Nallimaa-Luoto 1990, 68–69; Pylkkänen 1990, 370–424). During the 17th and 18th centuries, families with two or more married couples could be found in the Finnish archipelago of the Baltic. However, while married brothers did occasionally co-reside at some point during their lives, the dominant pattern in the southwest of Finland was the "stem-family" (Moring 1994, 52–55; Nerdrum 1978). The situation in the northwest was not dissimilar: between 20 and 30 percent of the families consisted of two married couples, the majority of these were units of parents and one married child plus unmarried offspring (Luukko 1945, 67; Tegengren 1943, 62–64). But, in the 17th century, 30 percent of the northwestern households had several married siblings in addition to the parental generation, particularly in areas engaged in tar burning, multiple economy or colonising new areas. The frequency of stem families was often not calculated as they constituted the normal system (Matinolli 1969; Virrankoski 1961, 96–97, 1973, 131–132).

In the southern- and south-western parts of Finland, the population had filled most of the available "niches" by the 18th century. The fairly generous yields of a fertile soil had attracted a large population. Although the farms in the west did include woods and grazing land in addition to cultivated fields, the possibilities for expansion were virtually exhausted. The preservation of the family's wealth could occasionally be achieved even with land-division, but in many cases additional sources of income had to be found for younger children. The non-inheriting siblings had to choose between downward social mobility and migration, a situation common in many Nordic countries (Moring 2001). By the 19th century, the social composition of these regions was changing and the households had seemingly become smaller and less complex.

While the mean household size in western Finnish localities varied between 8 and 10 persons during the 17th and 18th centuries, the national population statistics in the 1860s show considerable regional variation. The national average in 1868 was 6.3 persons per household (Table 1), but in the south-west 5.3, in the south-east 7, in the far north 5.2, and in the north-central region no less than 9.4 persons. Although about 80 percent of the Finns were still primary producers, there were considerable differences in market orientation, urban connections and social stratification in the last decade of the 19th century. The densely populated areas in the south and west encompassed large numbers of small landless households or urban proletarian units while the sparsely populated regions in the northeast retained larger families of smallholders. Micro level studies for a number of localities in different parts of the Nordic countries show that social differences in household size and structure can be detected in the 18th as well as in the 19th century. Proletarians married later and resided in small nuclear families. The long-term changes in household size usually reflect proletarianisation, not a change of household system among farmers. This group retained the stem family, in many cases until the 20th century (Moring 2003, 90–100).

In pre-industrial Sweden, the patterns of retirement, co-habitation and co-operation between generations seem to vary with region and economic activity. In the north, the generations shared living space, work and child-care as long as the older generation was alive (sharing bread and bed). In the south, separate buildings can be found, that have accommodated the parents after retirement. The existence of a retirement contract might be a sign of a separated economy or it reflects the fear of the parents that their son might run into economic problems and be forced to sell the farm. The retirement contract was also a way of securing the farm for the heir when the holding was small: then the retirement payments constituted the total price for the farm and no claims could be made by sisters or brothers (Hellspong and Löfgren 1988, 242–243, 248–250; Högnäs 1941, 79; Löfgren 1974, 40–43).

During the 18th century, co-residence between generations is attested for 19 to 41 percent of the households, in eastern, northern and central Sweden. Elderly women were found in large numbers in the households of their married children. In central Sweden the influence of economic opportunities on household composition shows up in larger and more complex units in areas with multiple economic activity or demands on the work-force by landlords. In western Sweden where rates of proletarianisation were high the overall percentages of households containing old parents varied between 10 and 20 percent. However, if the households are distributed according to socio-economic criteria, the small proletarian unit can be distinguished from the larger landholding one (Table 1). The shift towards employment of married labourers, in 19th century eastern Sweden, promoted the increase of a mobile proletariat and affected the rates of small nuclear households (Eriksson and Rogers 1978, 163, 166; Egerbladh 1989; Gaunt 1978, 75–77, 80–82; Lundh 1995, 45, 55).

Table 1. Mean household size in Finland and Sweden, local and national figures (percentages)

	Finland		*Sweden*
Farmers (1770)	8.2	Farmers (1780)*	5.8
Crofters (1770)	3.5	Crofters (1780)	4.2
Farmers (1790)	7.0	Peasants (1790)**	5.1
Landless (1790)	3.0	Landless (1790)	3.3
Farmers (1859)	6.0	Farmers (1850)*	6.4
Crofters (1859)	3.2	Crofters (1850)	4.5
All (1868)***	6.3	All (1860)***	4.4
Farmers (1920)	4.7	Peasants (1890)**	5.0
Landless (1920)	2.5	Landless (1890)	3.4

Sources:
* Dala, Borgunda, Högstena (west Sweden).
** Tillinge, Svinnegarn etc (East central Sweden).
*** National figures: see Moring 2003, 94; Eriksson and Rogers 1978, 163.

Population and the Niche

The eastern part of Finland was always difficult to cultivate because its soil was poor. However, in the 16th and 17th century, the Crown's encouragement of colonisation of the eastern and the northern parts of the country, in combination with the right to stake out fields in the unclaimed woods, added to the attraction of this less fertile area (Jutikkala 1958;

Nikander 1958, 13, 19, 88–89). The cultivation of forest areas was based on the slash-and-burn technique. It gave good crops but required considerable labour input and access to large land resources. These particular features of the economy encouraged the establishment of large household groups with several married couples. The system has been described as a family business corporation (Hamynen 1993, 150–153). The late 16th century saw the spread of technology that enabled the utilisation of evergreen forests for slash-and-burn cultivation. Before this new "take off" in the colonisation process, the stem family seems to have been more common than the joint-family household. The need to keep the work-group together, and bring cultivation projects that lasted up to ten years to a conclusion, was reflected in inheritance rules and the system of contract based recruitment of families into the work unit instead of employing servants. In the late 16th century the majority of the households in some communities were work corporations functioning on a contractual basis. The strict interlinking of work-input, ownership and potential inheritance rights in the common law of eastern Finland reflected the economic realities of a particular stage in the development (Luukko 1957, 84–85; Saloheimo 1986, 7–22; Soininen 1954, 93–95, 146, 155; Soininen 1961, 170–179).

In 16th and 17th centuries northeast Finland, 25 to 40 percent of all households included at least two married couples, of which 15 percent were those of co-residing brothers. However, in some cases, the registered unit was not a residential unit but a work-group (Pirinen 1982; Soininen 1961; Soininen 1974, 93). In various localities of south eastern Finland, between one third and one half of the households housed several conjugal units, with 15–25 percent housing brothers. As formal retirement was not practiced, the registration also picked up the older generation more effectively than in the west, as may be seen in Virolahti parish (Table 2) (Immonen 1958, 88; Kähönen 1959, 729–732; Moring 1997; Voionmaa 1915, 390–393).

The phenomenon of maximising production by using extensive agriculture such as slash and burn in low density areas when population density increased has been described by Ester Boserup in her studies of the interactions between economy, demography and resources (Boserup 1965, 1981). The agricultural techniques however, were ecologically destructive.

Table 2. Household structure in Virolahti parish (south-eastern Finland), according to Laslett-Hammel classification (1818–1876) (percentages)

Year	*1*	*2*	*3*	*4*	*5*	*6*	*Total*
1818	1.9	1.9	32.8	11.9	48.5	2.6	100
1838	3.2	2.7	35.1	14.3	39.8	4.3	100
1851	4.0	2.3	38.7	13.1	36.3	4.8	100
1876	7.4	1.4	51.5	14.3	23.5	1.4	100

Sources: Taxation records, communion books.
Notes: Numbers of households are: 1818: 427; 1838: 490; 1851: 620; 1876: 921.
The classification is explained in Laslett 1972, pp. 29–31.
1: Solitary; 2: No family; 3: Simple family households; 4: extended family households; 5: multiple family households and 6: Indeterminate.

The ideal forests had to be at least 30 years old and with increasing population pressures, they became scarcer. To be able to maintain a continuous expansion, new agricultural units had to be established through division. While the taxation system and the population situation in Sweden-Finland were inimical to land division, the Russian individual-based taxes worked in the opposite direction. A study of 22 parishes in south eastern Finland, has demonstrated that between 1720 and 1818 (during the Russian annexation) hardly any restraint was put on the division of farms; in fact their number doubled. On the other hand, when the area was re-united with Finland, farm division was restricted. The multiplication of units virtually stopped and the field area grew by only 15 percent between 1830 and 1880, despite a considerable population growth (Kaukiainen 1987, 286–288). A shift towards greater cattle and butter production took place. The woods increased in value and wood products became a commodity for sale. Integration into the St Petersburg market opened up venues for economic activity other than work intensive cereal production. The household structures became smaller and less complex. The time of unending resources was over. Proletarianisation became a feature of this region, developing into a real problem by the early years of the 20th century; in 1912 one half of the population was landless (Kaukiainen 1987, 281; Moring 1998, 78–80; Moring 1999).

Economy and Marriage

The locality in southwest Finland used in this study, Korpo-Houtskär, had an economic structure based on a combination of arable farming, animal husbandry and fishing. The poly-cultural activity range had the consequence that labour was required for care of animals, fishing, milking, the spinning of wool for household consumption and sale, the manufacture of fishing tackle, the building and maintenance of boats, the production of household textiles, and the preserving of fish.

The control of the resources was tightly linked to land holding. Some of the villages experienced enclosure already in the 18th century, whereby access to formerly common land was restricted. In the 17th and early 18th centuries the socio-economic stratification had little impact on the social conditions as the underclass was very small and mostly consisted of so called "deserving poor" i.e. old widows and old incapacitated former farm servants or persons with physical disabilities. In the 19th century, however, the landless groups began to increase. The mix of economic activities was not an issue for this group. Whether employed by a farmer or holding a croft, they had no rights to the village common, woods or fishing-grounds and were dependent on a single source of income (Moring 1994, 56–57). In the 1850s new fishing techniques that made it possible to fish on the open sea and in areas that had not previously been exploited were introduced. The threshold of entry in the activity was low and little manpower was needed, with the result that it became possible to support a family solely on the proceeds of fishing and the selling of fish in the growing urban centres. This development removed the key economic constraints on the founding of new households and made possible a population explosion which culminated at the end of the nineteenth century. In the new households, the need for additional labour did not exist, neither the need nor even possibilities of creating strategies for continuation (Table 3) (Ahlbäck 1955, 84, 96, 129–132; Andersson 1945, 121–133; Forsberg 1895, 6–7; Nordberg 1924, 83–84, 55-56; Storå 1970, 23–29; Moring 1994, 57, 59, 65–69). In northern Sweden the social development was very similar to the one in western Finland. The rural society was dominated by the farming class in the 18th century. However, a population increase, caused by more favourable demographic development, effectively changed the balance between population and resources.

Table 3. Household structure in the parish of Korpo-Houtskär (western Finland) according to Laslett-Hammel classification (1770–1895) (percentages)

Year	*1*	*2*	*3*	*4*	*5*	*Total*
1770	5.0	1.8	51.3	19.2	22.7	100
1790	13.9	0.2	48.1	21.4	16.4	100
1809	9.4	3.6	55.3	18.7	13.0	100
1859	9.8	2.2	64.4	14.5	9.1	100
1895	15.9	0.6	62.0	13.7	6.9	100*

Sources: Tax registers, parish registers, communion books.
Notes: Number of households is: 1770: 339; 1790: 411; 1809: 470; 1859: 728; 1895: 1003. The classification is explained in Laslett 1972, pp. 29–31. 1: Solitary; 2: No family; 3: Simple family households; 4: extended family households; 5: multiple family households.
Servants in percentage of households: in 1770: 38.6 percent, in 1790: 37.7 percent, in 1809: 27.9 percent, in 1859: 23.2 percent, 1895: 12.4 percent.
*Including some households of unclear structure.

During a transitional period landholdings could be divided and land reworked, but in the long term young families were sliding into the landless class through the crofting system. The difference between being a crofter and a farmer on a small holding was not significant during a considerable part of the 19th century. These groups intermarried and individuals could move from one group to the other during a lifetime. Compared with southern Sweden, the social differences in the north were insignificant. By the last decades of the century, however, the pressure on the resources had increased and when the saw mill industry created a safety valve in the form of industrial employment, the landless flocked to the growing industrial centres (Brändström and Tedebrand 1993; Hellspong and Lofgren 1988, 76–77, 82–83).

While increasing economic opportunities might have made it possible to marry, living conditions for landholders and landless would not be similar. Many young people postponed their marriage either when saving some money or in the hope of the opportunity of marrying some time. The heir could marry any time and a girl who married an heir could look forward to a comfortable old age. As a result, a woman who married a farmer had both the safety of land and children to support her while the wife of a landless man could end up with neither as a result of a delayed marriage.[4]

The mean age at first marriage in the parish of Houtskär in the 18th century was quite similar to that in other Nordic countries; the overall figures were relatively high and the socio-economic differences considerable. In a cohort marrying between 1750 and 1790, the mean age was 26 years both for men and women (Table 4). On the other hand while children of farmers were 24–25 years when they married for the first time, the landless and their spouses had nearly reached the age of 29. By the 19th century the age at marriage had increased (Moring 1995, 249–259; Moring 1996, 97; Eriksson and Rogers 1979, 113; Sogner 1985, 102; Dyrvik *et al.* 1979, 128; Johansen 1997, 86–88; Winberg 1975, 177; Kaukiainen 1973, 116).

Even though land division which should have eased the establishment of siblings occurred in the parish in the 18th century, a study of birth order and marriage underlines the special position of the heir. In a cohort of young men and women married in Houtskär between 1740 and 1770, the eldest or only sons of farmers married at the age of 22.3, and their younger brothers had to wait until they were 26.

Table 4. Age at first marriage in the parish of Houtskär (western Finland) (1738–1825)* by gender and socio-economic status of parents

Marriage cohort	*Farmers Males*	*Farmers Females*	*Landless Males*	*Landless Females*	*All Males*	*All Females*
1738–1749	23.2	24.1	32.0	30.8	24.7	25.3
1750–1789	24.5	24.4	28.7	28.7	26.3	26.5
1790–1810	25.4	24.8	27.6	29.3	26.5	27.1
1817–1825*	26.8	26.2	27.5	28.0	27.3	27.0

Sources: Family reconstitution study, database of people born in Houtskär in the period 1817 to 1825: marriage records, baptismal records, communion books.
Notes: * year of marriage except for birth cohort 1817–1825, marked with a *, married in the 1840s and 1850s.
Age at departure of migrants in Houtskär, for birth cohort 1817–1825: men 23.4, women 25.0 years.

4 See: Gardberg 1948, Nygard 1989, Communion books of Korpo-Houtskär; Brändström and Tedebrand 1993, Sundsvall database.

The wives of these eldest sons and prospective heirs were 23 years old. Girls without brothers, who inherited the farm in their own right and brought their husband into the household married as early as 20. The daughters of farmers who married younger sons did so at the age of 24. Girls who married landless men did so at ages similar to the landless girls. The social destiny of these people seems to have been clear to them and they adapted their life accordingly (Table 5).

Table 5. Age at first marriage of farmers' children in Virolahti parish (eastern Finland) and Houtskär (western Finland), 18th and 19th centuries

	Virolahti	*Houtskär*
First son	26.6	22.3
Younger son	27.5	26.7
First daughter	23.1	
Younger daughter	24.2	
First daughter, head on home farm		20.0
Daughter, head on husband's farm		23.0
Daughter, wife of younger son		24.3

Sources: Communion books, tax registers, marriage registers beginning in 1738, Houtskär, western Finland; database of birth cohort 1790–1822, Virolahti, eastern Finland.
For 1850–1869, the age at marriage of landless women was 25 years.

In the northern Swedish communities of rural Sundsvall, age at marriage was somewhat higher but the cohort was born between 1815 and 1819 and did therefore not marry until the 1840s. The mean age at first marriage for women was 27 and for men 28 years old. Men ending their days as farmers married at 27, those who became labourers married at 28 and the crofters at 29 years old. Women who married farmers were on average 26 years old while women who married crofters were 27 and those who married labourers or farmhands were 28. Here, as in other parts of Sweden, women who married landless men married later than girls who became the wives of farmers. It might be of some interest to note that the daughters of farmers who experienced social decline seem to have married later, at 28, than girls who were the daughters of crofters. The data from western Finland, in Houtskär, indicates that a farmer's daughter who was the eldest child and married a farmer or brought her husband into the parental home tended to marry earlier than other women. These groups of women are always small and the results perhaps more indicative than anything else. It is however interesting to see that in northern Sweden these girls married at a mean age of 24.7. It seems that the girls who could count on a secure future gladly embarked on marriage earlier than the sisters in their birth cohort (Table 6).

Table 6. Age at first marriage in Houtskär (western Finland), the Sundsvall region (northern Sweden) and Virolahti (eastern Finland) by gender and socio-economic status of parents

Birth cohort	*Farmers Males*	*Farmers Females*	*Landless Males*	*Landless Females*	*All Males*	*All Females*
Houtskär						
1817–1825	26.8	26.2	27.5	28.0	27.3	27.0
Rural Sundsvall						
1815–1819	27.3	26.2	28.7	27.4	28.3	26.9
Virolahti						
1790–1825	27.0	23.6	28.5	24.5	27.0	24.0

Sources: Communion books, tax registers, marriage registers for 1738–1820, Houtskär (western Finland); database of birth cohort 1790–1822, Virolahti (eastern Finland); Database of women born in northern Sweden in the early 19th century.

It has sometimes been assumed that if a couple settled with the parents of either party, these parents were also active in the partner selection process. Orvar Lofgren, however, has established in his studies of night courting in the past that the degree of parental involvement depended largely on the social stratification of the local community. Ethnographical studies of premarital behaviour of young people in western Finland and in Sweden have also underlined the considerable autonomy of young people in rural society, sometimes emerging in stark contrast to the middle-class values of the observers. These observations can also find support in visitation protocols and other church records. In 18th and 19th century Finland, Sweden and Norway one in three brides was expecting a child when she married (Lofgren 1969, 37–38; Wikman 1937, 184–187; Moring 1994, 59–64).

Headship Transfer Prospects and Gender

In a society where a male heir was preferred to a female one, a girl with brothers looked sensibly for a partner elsewhere. A younger son on the other hand might wait and see if the older brother was healthy enough or otherwise capable of becoming a suitable head. The tendency of males to be less mobile than females can be seen in a cohort study of men and women marrying in Houtskär between 1776 and 1811. About 40 percent of the men ended their days on the farm where they were born while only about 10 percent of the women did so (Moring 1996, 104). A closer inspection of residence patterns and social mobility shows, however, that while the eldest or only sons ended their days as heads of the family farm this was not the case for their younger brothers. Those who married and remained on the parental land were often found in separate households of crofters. Whether the croft was registered as an administrative unit varies from case to case.

The prospects of the eldest son to end his life as the head of a farm were very good in western Finland. Out of 84 eldest sons born between 1780 and 1825, in the parish of Houtskär, followed throughout their life, 76 (90.5 percent) succeeded to headship on their parental farm, four (4.8 percent) married a girl without brothers and became head on her parental farm, two sons (2.3 percent) ended their life on their parental farm but under the headship of one of their siblings, and two sons (2.3 percent) experienced downward social mobility and died in the parish outside the farming class (Table 7). Although the farmers declined the option of giving the eldest son – or in the absence of sons the eldest daughter – legal guarantees to inherit the farm, in practice the eldest had a privileged position in relation to his siblings. When there were no sons the eldest daughter invariably came to head the household together with her husband, the only exceptions being when a brother and heir died after the eldest daughter had already married into another farm.

In the west, in cases when the head died young or even before he had become a head, the widow often remarried. The new husband then headed the farm until the eldest son of the first marriage became adult, married and was in the position to take over (Moring 1998, 70–71) (Table 8).

Table 7. Fate of two cohorts of sons in Houtskär parish, western Finland (percentages)

	Eldest son	*Younger son*
Head on farm of birth	90.5	3.8
Head on farm in home parish	4.8	25.9
Subordinate position on home farm	2.3	27.4
Landless in home parish	2.4	42.9
Total	100	100
Number under observation	84	77

Sources: Communion books and tax registers, registers of births, deaths and marriages, 18th and 19th centuries, for Houtskär parish (western) Finland.

Table 8. Headship transfers in 18th and 19th centuries, eastern and western Finland (Virolahti and Houtskär) (percentages)

	Virolahti (Eastern Finland)		Houtskär (Western Finland)	
Status of new head	*Short term* %	*Long term* %	*Status of new head*	*Short term* %
Eldest living son	48.6	85.7	Eldest living son	62.1
			Younger son	0.8
Son-in-law	2.7		Eldest daughter + son-in-law	15.2
Brother of head	10.8		Younger daughter	0.8
Widow	27.1	14.3	Widow (rem)	17.1
Other relative	8.1			
Stranger	2.7		To other relative	4.0
Total	100	100		100
Number under observation	37	35		123

Sources: Communion books, tax registers in Virolahti parish and Korpo-Houtskär parish.
Notes: Short term transfer = within five years of death of head; long term transfers = more than five years after the death of head; actually, some of the farms were divided during the period of observation. Heads of new residential units are not included in the calculation. Rem = remarriage, in the south west the widows heading farms generally remarried while those in the east did not.

Younger sons were however in more precarious positions. Sometimes infant and child mortality played into their hands and many a second son was heir by the time he reached adulthood. If the older brother survived and married, any hope of headship had better be forgotten. However, these sons were almost always the ones to marry a farmer's daughter without brothers or a farmer's widow because farms on crown land (the majority in the locality) could not be merged. If an eldest son wanted to marry an eldest daughter without brothers, either the one or the other had to give up their claims to the family land, a situation that did not occur very frequently. While it was very rare for a younger son to succeed to headship on his home farm, marrying into one was not unusual. Most of the younger sons however had to face the possibility of downward mobility (Table 7). Working on the family land when the brother had small children and the father was getting on in years was generally rewarded with a croft or upkeep for life. In these cases the younger brother sometimes brought his wife into the household for a year or two until the croft was set up.[5]

A study of the social and geographic mobility of young people in the early 19th century shows that about 50 percent of the farmers' sons did leave the parental household. The prospect of a subordinate position in their brothers' household or on the premises of their brothers' farm might not have been attractive. Half of the migrants from the parish were farmer's children and most of the men left before marriage at an average age of 23 years. Those who remained in the parish often left at marriage when they joined the household of their wife. Landless men went into service before marriage and moved between farms as farmhands after the age of confirmation.[6]

The social position of a woman in most cases depended on whom she married. For many eldest daughters, departure from home took place at marriage. This was not the case for all young women: landless girls in Finland and Sweden left the parental home for service before marriage and so did some younger daughters. About one third of the households and most farms employed male and female servants in the early 19th century. The chance of becoming the mistress of the household was quite good for firstborn daughters of farmers, 72 percent of the cohort in Houtskär did succeed to headship while only 51 percent of younger daughters did so. Partly the reasons were succession patterns in households without a male heir but also because eldest daughters married an heir more often than younger daughters.[7] The consequences in the long run of the male downward mobility were that an increasing number of women were mar-

5 For the life course study of Houtskär parish, see Moring 1996, 103–107.

6 Communion books, life course study Houtskär.

7 Communion books, life course study Houtskär.

ried to men who did not provide them with property and therefore security in old age.

Observations of a cohort of 89 sons of farmers, from northern Sweden, revealed similar patterns. Of the cohort, 31 percent experienced downward mobility. Of those dropping out of the farming class, 21 percent were eldest sons and 78 percent were younger sons. The sons who remained farmers remained on the parental land in the majority of cases. There were however examples of marriage with a girl who took over her parental farm. A total of 66 farmer's daughters were observed. Of these 43 percent married a farmer or brought a husband into their parental farm, 21 percent married crofters or became crofters, 6 percent married craftsmen and 7.5 percent married labourers. About 36 percent did not leave their home parish but stayed with their parents and in most cases had at least one stationary child of their own, and 9 percent became crofters in their home parish, mostly near their home of birth. But 83 percent of the daughters of farmers who died as farmers, lived with their adult children in old age, 48 percent with married sons, 23 percent with married daughters, the rest with unmarried children. The remaining 13 percent had no children or no children living in the parish.

Inequality between siblings was an established fact. To expect anything else would have been foolish. However, opportunities could arise for demographic reasons; marrying into a farm with only daughters, the death of the eldest brother or marriage with a widow. The other possibility was a croft or a cottage on the parental farm. The 18th century saw the rapid decline of infant mortality. The proletarianisation of rural western Finland and northern Sweden increased steadily over the 19th century until *fin-de-siècle* migration and 20th century urbanisation started drawing the population into expanding towns inside and outside the national boundaries. Young people stroved for an optimal use of existing opportunities while having a fairly realistic view of what was possible. Similarities in adaptation can be found elsewhere in Scandinavia and in central Europe (Eriksson and Rogers 1978, 141; Winberg 1977, 378–380; Schlumbohm 1991, 189–193; Segalen 1991, 74–77; Kertzer and Hogan 1991, 34–35; Moring 2003, 88–89).

Social changes created more opportunities to marry or earn a living in town for those without assets; as a result of migration of the children an increasing number of landless women were left without support in old age.

Family and Land

In Virolahti parish, on the present day Russian border, the division of farms had made possible a proportional increase of the number of landowners between 1755 and 1818. Although there was little increase in the number of holdings in the 1830s and 1840s, the farming population could take care of their growing numbers by enlarging the size of the households, which is reflected in an increased number of married brothers living together. However, during the second part of the 19th century when extensive farming was on the retreat and the field clearing period over, a shift in the household system can be detected. An analysis of households with two or more married couples reveals that after 1850, the co-residence of married brothers declined gradually. In 1851 more than half of the complex households were stem families and by 1876, 63 percent (Kaukiainen 1987; Moring 1999). A shift towards a different type of agriculture supplemented by other economic activities kept the farms viable but during the second part of the 19th century the families were faced with the problem of downward social mobility for some of the children.

Eastern Finland has been viewed as an area with low ages at marriage and large households, when looking at 17th and 18th centuries. The slash-and-burn agriculture is considered as one of the main reasons for these patterns, prevalent in regions with low population density and abundant accessible woodland areas (Voionmaa 1915, 390; Kahonen 1959, 729–732; Soininen 1974, 91–94; Immonen 1958, 88; Cistov 1976). However, the shift from an economy based on continuous expansion and periodic division of the units, to greater geographic stability and more intensive agriculture, had an impact on the number of extended families as well as on the ages at first marriage. Compared with western Finland, the households were still large and complex but the tendency to a decrease was already visible. The supplementation of labour through a contract had made marriage a possibility for those with little prospects. This type of recruitment was linked to slash-and-burn agriculture and disappeared with the changes in land use. During the second part of the 19th century, crofting increased in the east (Kaukiainen 1970, 413–415; Favorin 1992, 115–119; Soininen 1974, 382–385, 390–394; Gylling 1909, 177–180; Raussi 1966).

A sample of young people born between 1790 and 1824 in Virolahti parish in southeast Finland, shows a mean age at marriage of about 23 for women and 26 for men (the mean age at first marriage for women being as low as 21 in the region in the 1750s (Kaukiainen 1987, 271–277). While the eldest sons of farmers married at the age of 26.5, their younger brothers did so at the age of 27.5. Within the cohort studied for this project, 67 percent of farmer's sons were married by the time the youngest were 26 years old, only 4.6 percent left the parental household before marriage and the majority stayed on after the event.

While farmers' eldest daughters were approximately 23 years when they married, and their younger sisters 24, landless girls or the girls who married landless men were 24 years old. Of all women only 6 percent stayed in their own parental household after marriage (Table 6).[8]

Although there was a rise in age at marriage in the parish, the pressure on the resources could be discerned through a drop in marriages already between 1750 and 1818. The cohorts born in the early years of the 19th century were the ones faced with the realities of decreasing opportunities: 25 percent of the farmers' sons in the 1790–1825 cohorts had not married by the age of 50, and neither had 33 percent of the sons of the landless in the cohort. Actually 22 percent of the farmers' daughters and 38 percent of the landless girls were still unmarried at 50. The unmarried sisters and brothers could, to a large extent, be found on their parental farms while the unmarried landless hired themselves out as farmhands or maids.[9]

Sons and Mothers

While the old inheritance pattern favoured males staying in the parental household, the economic shift in the 19th century widened the birth-order and gap between siblings. The cohabitation of several married sons during their father's lifetime and sometimes of several married brothers after the death of their father in eastern Finland makes it necessary to note not only the birth order of individual children but that of their father as well. Even

8 Life course study Virolahti.

9 Communion books, database Virolahti.

though the farm property was held jointly by the present males, the most important decision maker was the head of the household and the tendency to favour the first born male child stands out clearly even though not as clearly in the east as in the west. Of 71 males dying as heads in Virolahti between 1825 and 1874, 43 were the oldest sons of farmers, 26 were second, third or fourth sons of farmers and 2 had risen from the landless group.

A comparison between two sets of headship transfers, one in a short and one in a long term perspective, shows that over time the eldest son had very good chances indeed to end up as head of the household (Table 8). In 21 out of 35 instances, the headship was transferred to an eldest son when the father died. In nine cases a younger son succeeded because the eldest was no longer alive. The succession could be affected by the tendency of widows to hang on to the headship and the system of separating headship authority from headship work. The better survival rates of women could also result in sons not surviving until their 40s or 50s having few chances of outliving their mothers.[10] In some cases the widow retained headship for life. The prospects of the children of younger sons depended on the sex of the head's offspring. The preference for vertical succession did in some cases result in headship descending to a grandson by a daughter rather than to a son of a younger brother. Only if the land was divided, would the younger branch have a chance at headship (Moring 1999).[11]

In the east, the widow of a farmer did not remarry very often, but relied on the work of her sons, brothers-in-law, sons-in law or other males within the household (sometimes farmhands in the 19th century). As a result, female headship seems to have been more common within farming families in eastern than in western Finland, even though, according to eastern customary law, women could not own farmland (Table 9). The widow of a younger brother stayed in the household if she did not remarry and pooled her work with her sister-in-law (Pylkkanen 1990, 318–320).

10 Communion books, tax registers, Virolahti.
11 Communion books, database Virolahti.

Table 9. Percentage of household headed by a widow, eastern and western Finland (percentages)

	Virolahti (Eastern Finland)				Houtskär (Western Finland)		
	Widow headed households	Widow headed farmers households	Widow headed landless households		Widow headed households	Widow headed farmers households	Widow headed landless households
1818	4.4	2.4	2	1790	12.6	3.9	8.7
1838	21.5	12	9.5	1809	11.1	1.2	9.6
1851	29	16	13	1859	14.4	6.8	7.6
1876	19.4	9.6	9.8	1895	13.2	4.2	9.0

Sources: Tax registers and communion books for Virolahti in eastern Finland (1818–1876) and Houtskär in western Finland (1790–1895).

Staying on the parental farm was a sensible option for younger sons who did not aspire to headship. A large proportion of the men that stayed in the parish were in fact younger sons (in the birth cohorts 1795–1824) with a mean age around 35 years. A number of these had participated in the taking up of permanent fields for cultivation. However, this process came to a halt in the 1830s and land division affected the size and the viability of the farm. This required farm households to secure non-agricultural sources of income (Kaukiainen 1970, 413–415; Favorin 1992, 115–119; Soininen 1974, 382–385, 390–394; Gylling 1909, 177–180). An analysis of the composition of the households shows that cohabitation between brothers was steadily decreasing from the 1830s. Consequently, farmers' younger sons were given crofts, and kept trickling down in the ranks of the landless (Moring 2000, 130–132).[12]

In a sample of 80 farmers' sons born between 1790 and 1825 who left their parental household, 33 percent moved in with their wives family, 35 percent remained in the parish but became landless; 21 percent left the parish and in 10 percent of the cases, the destination is unclear. Of these, only two were first sons of heads: one became head of his wife's home farm, the other left the parish as the tenant farm went out of the hands of the family; 39 were younger sons and 19 sons of younger sons. In Virolahti, the mean age at departure of these men was 27 years. One was

12 Virolahti Communion books, tax registers.

as old as 53, one was as young as 18, and the vast majority between 20 and 30 years.

As the custom of wives moving in with their husbands was common, the mean age of departure from home for women was the same as age at marriage i.e. 23–24 years. However, longitudinal studies reveal that men did move into the households of their wives if these had no brothers. Married daughters and even married sisters are found in their parental household in the 19th century. The reason for departure for farmers' daughters was generally marriage; however the situation for landless girls was different. They had to find work, preferably in the parish, and elsewhere if this was not possible. A handful of women left Virolahti, not to marry but to seek employment in St Petersburg and other urban centres (Moring 1998, 77).

Opportunities for landless men were more restricted than for farmers' sons: 40 percent of the landless men left their home at a mean age of 24 years. In some cases, they managed to become crofters in the parish or marry into the household of their wife. However seeking ones fortune in one of the nearby parishes or towns along the Baltic seems to have been fairly common among those with no prospects of access to land.

The prospects for farmers' children in eastern Finland changed radically in the 19th century. While in the past it had been possible to look forward to a safe future within the farming class it became increasingly necessary to look for opportunities elsewhere, as landless always had. The decline of labour intensive agriculture created a growing group of landless unwanted proletarians, who by 1900 encompassed such a large part of the population that they were conceived as a national problem. While proletarianisation reached the east later than the west, it also exacerbated the plight of the landless widow dependant of parish assistance (Moring 1998, 78–80).

Conclusion

Social obligations towards parents were similar in different parts of the country. In western Finland and northern Sweden, the eldest resided permanently with the parents; the co-residence of the younger siblings was usually more temporary and they had to find their own niche before marriage. In eastern Finland, all sons could co-reside and contribute to the maintenance of the parents as long as the slash and burn system prevailed. In western Finland and northern Sweden, formal or informal retirement did take place while in the east the older generation remained at the head of the household all their lives. Permanence and security was obtained through the presence of one or more presumptive heirs in the household. This was in accordance both with local custom and with the state's desire to preserve the number of taxable units. The problem caused by preference for eldest sons at the expense of other children was partly alleviated by land-division and the creation of crofts, but the downward social mobility of younger children was unavoidable in the long run. The prospect of change in social position was reflected in delayed marriage both of younger sons and their wives. After establishing themselves as householders, the farmers resorted to the stem-family system, something the landless were unable to do.

In eastern Finland, the economy and law made it possible to divide the land and co-reside at a comparatively late date. The positive prospects of farmers' sons were reflected in a lower age at marriage than among the landless. When ecological constraints stepped in, the system had to shift. All sons could not be retained, the proportion of joint-family households decreased while stem-families became more frequent among the landholders. The difference in age at marriage between brothers depending on birth order became a reality and younger brothers moved out of their parental household. The mean household size and structure was affected by an increasing number of small, simple landless households. Landless men usually worked until they died. Poor relief records show some examples of old disabled men but even in the late 19th century they are relatively few in numbers. The longer life span of women made it more likely that they would have to face the socio-economic changes in society.

The situation for women was to a large extent dependant on the social position of their husbands, with the exception of those who were heirs in their own right. The widow of a farmer was secure either as household head or as cared for by her children with or without a retirement contract. Even a crofter's widow retained the right to remain on the croft until she died and, particularly when living with an adult child, her situation could be quite acceptable. The increase in proletarianisation also increased mobility. With higher ages at marriage and children finding work outside the home parish the likelihood of old women having a fragmented support network became more of a reality.

Appendix

The Sources

The sources used for the study are person based taxation registers, communion books and parish registers of births, marriages and deaths. In the communion books individuals were registered in their household of residence over five or ten year periods, with information on changes in status like marriage, childbirth, and death. In case of migration the new place of residence was indicated. The registers had been created for the purpose of recording biblical knowledge, reading ability and church attendance of the parishioners. They are ideal for longitudinal studies because of their structure and the information on new whereabouts in cases of departure. The tax registers *(mantalslangder)* do not include children under the age of 15 for most of the 18th century but in the 19th century all household members, paying and non-paying, appear in the registers. In addition to this information about occupation, farm size etc. was generally included.

The households have been analysed for cross-sectional years in the 18th and 19th centuries: 2,458 households with 18,056 individuals from Virolahti in eastern Finland for 1818–1876, and 2,947 households with 13,100 individuals Korpo-Houtskär in western Finland for 1770–1895 have been studied. In addition an analysis of 1,400 households in 17th century Korpo-Houtskär has been undertaken. For the purpose of life course studies a database of 1,011 individuals born in Virolahti between 1790 and 1825 has been created. Each individual was provided with 29 identification and information points. For information on destinies in the west a life course database of 2,551 individuals born in Houtskär parish between 1742 and 1825 has been used. Some of these individuals also form a part of a family reconstitution study of 547 families married between 1738 and 1810 in the parish.

The sources for the information from eight parishes around the town of Sundsvall in northern Sweden is based on information extracted from parish registers of reading ability so called *husforhorslangder*. The extracted data has kindly been made available by the Umea Data Archive.

References

AARNIO, Aulis, 1991, "Perimysjärjestelyt maanomistusolojen kannalta", in Pia LETTO-VANAMO (ed.), *Suomen oikeushistorian pääpiirteet*, Helsinki, Gaudeamus, pp. 43–65.

AHLBÅCK, Ragna, 1955, *Kökar – Näringslivet och dess organisation i en utskärssocken*, Folklivsstudier IV, Helsingfors, Svenska litteratursällskapet i Finland.

ANDERSON, Michael, 1971, *Family Structure in Nineteenth-century Lancashire*, Cambridge, Cambridge University Press.

–, 1979, "Some problems in the use of census type material for the study of family and kinship systems", in Jan SUNDIN and Eric SODERLUND (eds), *Time, Space and Man. Essays in Microdemography*, Stockholm, Almqvist and Wiksell, pp. 69–80.

ANDESSON, Sven, 1945, *Åländskt skärgårdsliv*, Helsingfors.

ANKARLOO, Bengt, 1976, "Marriage and Family Formation", in Tamara HAREVEN (ed.), *Transitions, the Family and Life Course in Historical Perspective,* New York, Academic Press.

BERKNER, Lutz, 1972, "The Stem Family and the Developmental Cycle of the Peasant Household. An Eighteenth century Austrian Example", *The American Historical Review*, 77, 2, pp. 398–418.

–, 1975, "The Use and Misuse of Census Data for the Historical Analysis of the Family", *Journal of Interdisciplinary History,* 5, pp. 721–738.

BOSERUP, Ester, 1965, *The Economics of Agrarian Change under Population Pressure,* London, Allen and Unwin.

–, 1981, *Population and Technology*, Oxford, Blackwell.

BRÄNDSTRÖM, Anders and TEDEBRAND, Lars-Göran (eds), 1993, *Health and Social Change. Disease, Health and Public Care in the Sundsvall District 1750–1950,* Umeå, University of Umeå.

DYRVIK, Ståle, FOSSEN, Anders and GRONLIE, Tore, 1979, *Norges ekonomiske historie I*, Oslo.

EGERBLADH, Inez, 1989, "From Complex to Simple Family Households: Peasant Households in Northern Coastal Sweden, 1700–1900", *Journal of Family History*, 14, 3, pp. 241–264.

ELDER, Glen, 1978, "Family History and the Life course", in Tamara HAREVEN (ed.), *Transitions, the Family and Life Course in Historical Perspective,* New York, Academic Press, pp. 17–64.

ERIKSSON, Ingrid and ROGERS, John, 1978, *Rural Labor and Population Change*, Uppsala, Uppsala University.
FAVORIN, Matti, 1992, *Virolahden historia II*, Mikkeli, Virolahden kunta.
FRIBERG, Nils, 1954, *Dalarnas befolkning på 1600-talet*, Stockholm, Stockholms Universitet.
FRIBERG, Nils and FRIBERG, Inga, 1976, *Sveriges äldsta fullständiga husförhörslängd*, Stockholm, Stockholms Universitet, Kulturgeografiska institutionen.
FORSBERG, Anders, 1884–1885, "Ålands strömmingsfiske", *Fiskeritidskrift för Finland.*
GARDBERG, John, 1948, "Hushållning och byväsen kring norra delen av Skiftet", Skärgårdsboken, Helsingfors.
GAUNT, David, 1973, "Family Planning in the Pre-industrial Society", *Aristocrats, Farmers, Proletarians*, Uppsala, Uppsala University.
–, 1978, "Household Typology: Problems-Methods-Results", in Sune ÅKERMAN, Hans Christian JOHANSEN and David GAUNT (eds), *Chance and Change. Social and Economic Studies in Historical Demography in the Baltic area*, Odense, Odense University Press.
GUNNLAUGSSON, Gisli A., 1988, *Family and Household in Iceland 1801–1930*, Uppsala University, Uppsala.
GUNNLAUGSSON, Gisli A. and GARDARSDOTTIR, Olof, 1996, "A life course perspective on the household position of Icelandic widows", *Continuity and Change*, 11, 3, pp. 435–458.
GYLLING, Edvard, 1909, *Suomen torpparilaitoksen kehityksen pääpiirteet*, Helsinki.
HAJNAL, John, 1965, "European Marriage Patterns in Perspective", in David GLASS and David E. C. EVERSLEY, *Population in History*, London, Arnold, pp. 101–143.
–, 1983, "Two kinds of pre-industrial household formation system", in Richard WALL, Jean ROBIN and Peter LASLETT (eds), *Family Forms in Historic Europe*, Cambridge, Cambridge University Press.
HAREVEN, Tamara, 1978a (ed.), *Transitions, the Family and Life Course in Historical Perspective*, New York, Academic Press.
–, 1978b, "Family History at the Crossroads", *Journal of Family History*, 12, pp. 1–3.
–, 1994, "Recent Research on the History of the Family", in Michael DRAKE (ed.), *Time, Family and Community. Perspectives on Family and Community History*, London, Blackwell.
HELLSPONG, Mats and LÖFGREN, Orvar, 1988, *Land och stad. Svenska samhällstyper och livsformer från medeltid till nutid*, Lund, Liber.
IMMONEN, Toivo, 1958, *Kurkijoen kihlakunnan historia II*, Pieksämäki, Kukijoen historiatoimikunta Johansen.
JOHANSEN, Hans Christian, 1976, *Befolkningsudvikling og familiestruktur i det 18 århundrede*, Odense, Odense University Press.
–, 1988, "Folk og produktion pa fynske garde gennem to arhundreder", *Jyske Samlinger*, Ny Rekke, 17, 3, pp. 351–386.
JUTIKKALA, Eino, 1957, *Hämeen historia*, 2, 1, Hämeenlinna Karisto.
–, 1958, *Suomen talonpojan historia*, Turku, Suomalaisen Kirjallisuuden Seura.
KAUKIAINEN, Yrjö, 1970, *Virolahden historia I*, Lappeenranta, Virolahden kunta.
–, 1973, "Miksi kansa lisääntyi", *Historiallinen Aikakauskirja*, pp. 103–121.

–, 1987, "Population growth and land availability in south-east Finland 1750–1840", in Antoinette FAUVE-CHAMOUX (ed.), *Evolution agraire et croissance démographique,* Liege, Ordina Editions, pp. 263–290.

–, 1979, "Social structure and demographic development in a southern Finnish parish, Lohja, 1810–50", Helsinki, Suomalainen Tiedeakatemia.

KÄHÖNEN, Ester, 1959, *Vanha Äyräpää vuoteen 1700,* Helsinki.

KARSTE-LIIKKANEN, Greta, 1968, *Pietari suuntaus kannakselaisessa elämänkentässä 1800-luvun loppupuolelta vuoteen 1918,* Kansantieteellinen Arkisto 20, Helsinki.

KERTZER, David and HOGAN, Dennis, 1991, "Reflections on the European Marriage Pattern; Sharecropping and Proletarianisation in Casaleccio, Italy 1861–1921", *Journal of Family History,* 16, 1, pp. 31–45.

KORPIJAAKKO, Kaisa, 1985, "Maanomistusoikeuden kehityksestä ruotsalais-suomalaisen oikeusjärjestyksen mukaan", in Jukka KEKKONEN, Kaisa KORPILJAAKKO and Heikki YLIKANGAS (eds), *Oikeudellisen sääntelyn kehityslinjoja,* Helsinki, Gaudeamus.

LASLETT, Peter, 1972, "Introduction", in Peter LASLETT and Richard WALL (eds), 1972, *Household and Family in Past Time,* Cambridge, Cambridge University Press, pp. 1–89.

–, 1977, "Characteristics of the western family over time", in Peter LASLETT (ed.), *Family Life and Illicit Love in Earlier Generations,* Cambridge, Cambridge University Press.

LASLETT, Peter and WALL, Richard (eds), 1972, *Household and Family in Past Time,* Cambridge, Cambridge University Press.

LEVINE, David, 1977, *Family Formation in the Age of Nascent Capitalism,* London, Academic Press.

–, (ed.), 1984, *Proletarianization and Family History,* New York/London, Academic Press.

LUNDH, Christer, 1995, "Households and families in pre-industrial Sweden", *Continuity and Change,* 10, 1, pp. 33–68.

LUUKKO, Armas, 1957, *Suur-Lohtajan historia vuoteen 1809,* Kokkola, Suur-Lohtajan Kunta.

LOFGREN, Orvar, 1969, "Fran nattfrieri till tonarskultur", *Fataburen.*

–, 1972, "Family and Household among Scandinavian Peasants: An Exploratory Essay", *Ethnologica Scandinavica,* pp. 17–52.

–, 1976, "Peasant ecotypes: problems in the comparative study of ecological adaptation", *Ethnologica Scandinavica,* pp. 100–115.

–, 1978, "The Potato People", in Sune ÅKERMAN, Hans Christian JOHANSEN and David GAUNT (eds), *Chance and Change,* Odense, Odense University Press, pp. 95–108.

MATINOLLI, Eero, 1969, *Suur-Pyhäjoen historia vanhimmista ajoista 1860-luvulle,* Kokkola, Suur-Pyhajoen Kunta.

MITTERAUER, Michael, 1992, "Peasant and Non-peasant Family Forms in Relation to the Physical Environment and the Local Economy", *Journal of Family History,* 17, 2, pp. 139–159.

MORING, Beatrice, 1994, *Skärgårdsbor. Hushåll, familj och demografi i finländsk kustbygd på 1600-, 1700- och 1800-talen,* Helsingfors, Societas Scientiarum Fennicae.

–, 1996, "Marriage and social change in western Finland 1700–1870", *Continuity and Change,* 11, 1, pp. 91–113.
–, 1998, "Family Strategies, Inheritance Systems and the Care of the Elderly in Historical Perspective", *Historical Social Research*, 23, 1–2, pp. 67–82.
–, 1999, "Economic and ecological determinants of household organisation in the North-eastern Baltic Region", *Scandinavian Economic History Review*, 47, 3, pp. 48–68.
–, 2000, "Familjestrategier i det forindustriella Finland", *Keulakuvia ja peranpitajia*, Helsinki, Suomen Historiallinen Seura.
–, 2002, "Continuities and Discontinuities after the Death of the Household Head in Pre-Industrial Finland", in Renzo DEROSAS and Michel ORIS (eds), *When Dad Died. Individuals and Families Coping with Family Stress in Past Societies,* Bern, Peter Lang.
–, 2003, "Nordic Family Patterns and the North-West European Household System", *Continuity and Change,* 18, 1, pp. 77–103.
NALLIMAA-LUOTO, Terhi, 1990, *Hämeenkyrön historia 1722–1865*, Vammala, Hameenkyron Kunta.
NERDRUM, Monica, 1978, "Household structure in Finsröm parish", in Sune ÅKERMAN, Hans Christian JOHANSEN and David GAUNT (eds), *Chance and Change*, Odense, Odense University Press, pp. 136–142.
NIEMELÄ, J. H., 1889, *Asunnoista ja kansanelämästä Virolahdella*, SKS E 4.
NIKANDER, Gabriel, 1953, "Bebyggelsetyper och storfamiljsgardar i Savolax", *Finskt Museum,* 60, pp. 41–69.
NORDBERG, Karl, 1925, *En öst-åländsk skärgårdsby,* Åbo, Åbo tryckeri och tidnings.
NOTKOLA, Irma-Leena, 1989, *Luonnollisesta hedelmällisyydestä lapsirajoitukseen*, Helsinki, Suomen väestötieteen yhdistys.
NYGÅRD, Toivo, 1989, *Suomen palvelusväki 1600-luvulla*, Helsinki, Suomen Historiallinen Seura.
PALM ANDERSSON, Lennart, 2001, *Livet, kärleken och döden*, Goteborg, Goteborgs universitet.
PIRINEN, Kauko, 1982, *Savon historia,* II, 1, Pieksämäki, [Kuopio] Kustannuskiila.
PLAKANS, Andrejs, 1983, "The familial contexts of early childhood in Baltic serf society", in Richard WALL, Jean ROBIN and Peter LASLETT (eds), *Family Forms in Historic Europe*, Cambridge, Cambridge University Press, pp. 167–206.
–, 1987, "Interaction between the Household and the Kin Group in the Eastern European Past: Posing the Problem", *Journal of Family History,* 12, 1–3, pp. 163–175.
PYLKKÄNEN, Anu, 1990, *Puoli vuodetta, lukot ja avaimet*, Helsinki, Lakimiesliiton Kustannus.
RANTA, Raimo, 1985, *Vanhan Suomen talouselämä 1721–1743*, Helsinki, Suomen Historiallinen Seura.
RAUSSI, Eljas, 1966, *Virolahden kansanelämää 1840-luvulla*, Helsinki, Finnish Literature Society.
RUDOLPH, Richard, 1992, "The European family and economy: central themes and issues", *Journal of Family History*, 17, 2, pp. 119–138.
SALOHEIMO, Veijo, 1971, *Pohjois Karjalan asutusmuodot*, Joensuu.
–, 1986, "Savolaxarnas expansion pa 1500- och 1600-talen", in S. HUOVINEN (ed.), *Varmlandsfinnar,* Stockholm, Kulturfonden for Sverige och Finland, pp. 7–22.

SCHLUMBOHM, Jürgen, 1992, "From Peasant Society to Class Society", *Journal of Family History*, 17, 2, pp. 183–191.

SEGALEN, Martine, 1991, "Mean age at marriage and kinship networks in a town under influence of a metropolis: Nanterre 1800–1850", *Journal of Family History*, 16, 1, pp. 65–78.

SOGNER, Sølvi, 1979, *Folkevekst og flytting*, Oslo, Universitetsforlaget.

–, 1985, "Gifte kvinner i bondesamfunnet pa 1700-tallet", in Anna TRANBERG and Harald WINGE (ed.), *Kvinnekar i det gamle samfunn*, Oslo, Lokalhistorisk Institutt.

SOININEN, Arvo, 1954, *Rantasalmen historia*, Pieksamaki, Rantasalmen kunta.

–, 1961, *Pohjois-Savon asuttaminen keski ja uuden ajan vaihteessa*, Helsinki, Societas Historica Finlandiae.

–, 1974, *Vanha maataloutemme*, Helsinki, Societas Historica Finlandiae.

STORÅ, Nils, 1970, *Öståländskt krokskötsfiske. Folk-liv. Acta ethnologica europaea*, 1967–1968, 31–32, Stockholm.

TEGENGREN, Helmer, 1943, *Kronoby sockens historia*, Åbo, Kronoby kommun.

VIAZZO, Pier Paolo, 1989, *Upland Communities: Environment, Population and Social Structure in the Alps since the sixteenth Century*, Cambridge, Cambridge University Press.

VIAZZO, Pier Paolo and ALBERA, Dionigi, 1990, "The Peasant Family in Northern Italy 1750–1930", *Journal of Family History*, 15, 4, pp. 461–483.

VIRRANKOSKI, Pentti, 1961, *Kokkolan pitäjän yläosan historia*, Kokkola, Kokkolan Kunta.

–, 1973, *Pohjois – Pohjanmaan ja Lapin Historia*, III, Oulu, Pohjois-Pohjanmaan historia toimikunta.

VIRTANEN, E. A., 1934, "Kyläyhteiskunta ennen isoajakoa", *Suomen kulttuurihistoria II*, Helsinki.

VOIONMAA, Väinö, 1915, *Suomen karjalaisen heimon historia*, Helsinki.

WALL, Richard, ROBIN, Jean and LASLETT, Peter (eds), 1983, *Family Forms in Historic Europe*, Cambridge, Cambridge University Press.

WARIS, Elina, 2000, *Yksissa leivissa*, Helsinki, Suomen Historiallinen Seura.

WILLERT, Hanne, 1995, "Three-generational families in 19th century rural Denmark", *Scandinavian Population Studies*, 10, pp. 260–275.

WINBERG, Christer, 1977, *Folkökning och proletarisering*, Lund, Liber.

–, 1978, "Population growth and proletarianization", in Sune ÅKERMAN, Hans Christian JOHANSEN and David GAUNT (eds), *Chance and Change*, Odense, Odense University Press, pp. 170–184.

WRIGLEY, E. Anthony, 1983, "The Means to Marry; Population and Economy in Pre-industrial England", *Past and Present*, 98, pp. 121–150.

Achieving Well-Being in Spain through the Single Heir System (18th–19th Centuries)

Llorenç FERRER ALÒS

When families organize the social system, they think about how to transmit to their descendants both material resources (the land, the workshop, the capital, the rights on communities…) and non-material ones (position of power within the community, social prestige, etc.). In this way, the transmission of goods from one generation to the next occurs through a series of actions throughout the domestic cycle. Consequently, not only does the system of transmission determine the final destination of the goods, but family choices occur during the process. Then the system that is set up has to consider all the situations and give them a solution to achieve the greatest possible welfare for the members of the family. In this chapter we study how 18th and 19th century rural Spanish families achieved well-being, using the single heir transmission system.[1]

Broadly speaking, we could say that there are two major ways to transfer goods from one generation to the next: (1) the egalitarian system which treats all children (sons and daughters) equally – consequently, when the parents die, everything must be equally divided between children –; and (2) the single heir system in which only one child inherits family patrimony and the others receive some money to leave home and to get married (in the case of daughters) or to start another occupation (for sons). In both cases, families seek to maximize well-being for their members, and minimize uncertainty. This does not mean that contradictions do not exist, and to resolve them, they create specific – legal and/or customary – "institutions" to maximize individual well-being.

The single heir system rests on the idea that it is better for the patrimony to be kept in the hands of one person, without being divided, as it

1 About the single heir system (or "system of universal heir") in Europe, see Augustins 1989; Chiva et Goy 1981; Collomp 1983; Fauve Chamoux 1987; Le Roy Ladurie 1972; Zink 1993. About the Irish practices, see Arensberg and Kimball 1968. In Austria and Germany, see Berkner 1972; 1974. About Japan, where the model is very similar to Catalonia's, see Befu 1981; Kitaoji 1971.

guarantees the descendants' quality of life. That patrimony has to generate sufficient resources for the children who are not going to inherit. This kind of transmission system was widely used in Catalonia, the north of Aragon, the Basque Country, Navarra, Asturias, the Balearic Isles and some areas of Galicia[2] and we are going to refer to the practices of these variants.

In Spain, autonomous legislation areas in which customary laws prevailed coexisted with wide areas in which the 1505 *Laws of Toro* (Castilian legislation) prevailed until the 1889 Spanish *Civil Code* was enacted (Figure 1). It is a mistake to think that the single heir system prevailed in the autonomous areas, and equalitarian systems in the others. Equalitarian practices characterized autonomous areas like Navarra and Southern Catalonia, but not Guipuzcoa, Asturias or Galicia which were subjected to the Toro laws. The families were the ones who adapted the laws to their needs and conception of the world.

The main contradiction of the single heir system lies in the unequal treatment of the children. The family patrimony can only with difficulties generate enough resources generation after generation to ensure that the other children have the same quality of life as the heir. Consequently, the system is supposed to condemn the non-heir children to downward social mobility and is not capable of guaranteeing either the maintenance of their social status, or expected well-being.

2 For Catalonia, see Brocà Amell 1880; Faus Condomines 1902; Maspons Anglasell 1935; for the north of Aragon: Comas d'Argemir 1991; Costa 1981; Martin Ballesteros 1944; Moreno Almarcegui 1992; for the Basque Country: González Portilla and Urrutikoetchea 2003; Homobono 1991; Arrizabalaga 1997; 2002; Barrera 1991; Douglass 1988; Homobono 1991; Ibáñez Gomez *et al* 1994; Navajas Laporte 1975; Urrutikoetxea 1992; for Navarra: Mikelarena 1992; Moreno and Zabalza 1999; Ruiz *et al* 2002; Yaben 1916; Zabalza Seguin 1999; for Asturias: Gómez Pellón 1991; Pedregal 1981 (1902); for areas of Cantabria: Ceballos Cuerno 1999; Lanza García 1988; Saavedra 2002; for the Balearic Isles: Bestard 1986; Gomila Grau 2004; Morey Tous 1999 and for some areas of Galicia: Dubert 1992; Fernández Cortizo 1988; 2004; Lison Tolosana 1971; Pérez Garcia 2002; Saavedra 1988; 2002.

Figure 1. Spanish legislation areas: customary laws, Castilian laws of Toro and inegalitarian systems (mostly single heir regions) before the 1889 Spanish *Civil Code.*

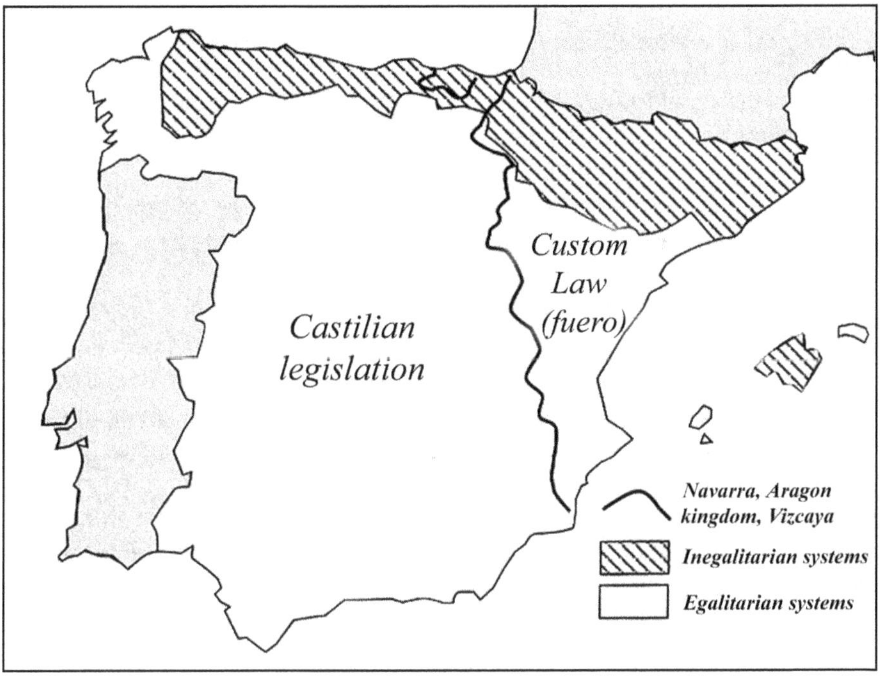

Source: Ferrer Alòs 2007a, p. 38.

The Ideology of the "House"

From the beginning, the system has been based on the unequal distribution of patrimonial goods: one of the children kept all the patrimony and all the social capital of the "house" and the other children were given money, and had to leave in search for another house and a job. To be accepted, this system requires that individuals be socialized to assume their roles and see advantages in it.

The heir or heiress received a house from his or her parents. This house provided the family with a name and with an identity that had to be preserved. It also generated resources necessary to preserve the family's social prestige, and family members had to work hard to increase its size (Faus Condominas 1902, 7–8; Yaben 1916, 169). Growing up in a specific house was also a source of pride. Thus all members assumed from the start that they had to improve the standing of the house, and had to ensure the decisions to reach that goal, as achieving it ensured the well-being and standard of living of its members.

Family members were aware that if each generation of their ancestors had divided their holding among their children, their own generation would have no "house" to share, and would consist of poor farmers on minuscule plots of land. They could receive large portions only because the family land holding had remained undivided, and perhaps even been enlarged by the sacrifices of previous members.

In this way, the house had always been a refuge. The younger son or daughter went to work elsewhere; he/she may have got married and settled out of the family home, but the "house" was the place where they could come back to when things did not work out well. Daughters who married but whose husbands died and who remained without any children were welcome if they came back home, as well as second sons whose plans did not work out. And if a child did not want to leave home because he thought he had no future away from it, then he could stay unmarried and work for the house.

All of these beliefs underpinned a powerful socialization process which ensured that everyone knew what role he or she had to play in order to achieve this general objective. We are aware that we are speaking in general terms. Obviously, the ideology of the house was more powerful in those families who had a considerable patrimony. The poorer families or those with fewer resources had to adapt the general rule to their own situation.[3]

3 See Gomila Grau 2004 on Majorca or Roigé 1994 on the Priorat county, in Catalonia.

The Choice of the Heir

Which son was chosen to inherit the patrimony and succeed his parents? There were different ways to proceed, all of them with advantages and disadvantages. Parents could choose the son best to serve the house and the family. This way parents could choose the son who was either better prepared, who would respond better to the situation or who was the most useful for a determined strategy. But: this created competition between the children and uncertainty about each one's future. That was the common practice of the Basque country and some areas of Navarra (Yaben 1916, 125–126), or Aragon (Costa 1981, 110). To minimise this uncertainty in parts of Vizcaya, Navarra or in the Ayala land of Alava, parents decided very soon who would be the heir, starting this way the necessary socialisation and apprenticeship process, while in other areas, the decision was delayed and could involve checking successor's competence (Homobono 1991, 104). In the Basque Country a great solidarity between brothers and sisters could also be noted:

> in the Basque society, the brothers and sisters are the most intimate friends from childhood and adolescence (Douglass 1973, 104–105).

This friendship might be a good antidote in front of the random choice of the heir.

Decisions could be based on birth order (and the sex of the children in some cases). The advantage was that nobody argued about who would be the future heir and all knew what role they would have to play and they could be educated to achieve it. However, the heir may not be the best prepared person, or the best qualified one, or the most convenient one at a given time. In Catalonia, for example, parents chose the first born male child as the future heir in nearly all the cases. In some areas of the Catalan Pyrenees, the first child who was born was chosen, whether it was a male or a female (Violant Simorra 1992). The saying "Qui primer neix, primer peix"[4] reflects that idea. When there was no male child, the first born daughter was given the name of *pubilla* (heiress). In some places, as in the well-off houses in Majorca, women did not inherit. In the absence of sons,

4 "To the first born, the first fish."

the first male child of a sister was chosen as heir (Gomila Grau 2004). But, in some areas of the Basque Country (Zuberoa and Lapurdi)[5] parents applied a strict primogeniture (or integral primogeniture): the first born is heir/heiress, male or female (Homobono 1991). We can understand the evolution towards the first born children to eliminate uncertainties, but, when this option is chosen, we should ask why the males were usually preferred to the females. In the Pyrenees in Navarra, for example, it is argued that it was to maintain the family name of the house, but eventually, it was said that it was

> because having a son suitable for the regime of the house, the parents show him more confidence when it comes to give the property than to a daughter, who finally has to follow the orders of her husband (Yaben 1916, 123–128).

Furthermore, males were fitter for farm work. Even when women inherited, it was because the males had emigrated to America or the daughter had been able to marry an "American" who came back a rich person and who moved into the house. The gender roles defined for men and women also conditioned those options. When the heir was clearly identified, the system tended to have much more structured rules.

Uniting two Houses through Marriage

The single heir system allowed the merging of two houses through marriage. If a family chose a male as heir and another family chose a female as heiress, then a wedding between the heir and the heiress was possible. When this happened, a "house" disappeared. In the Basque Country, this could be frequent as the heir could be either sex; in Catalonia, it was not so frequent because there were heiresses only when there were no males. This way, the system was unequal because it condemned a larger number of persons of one sex – females – to not being able to inherit. Anyway, even if heir-heiress marriage was legal and made those marginal houses possible, the customary practice was to avoid it. The resistance to the dis-

5 Soule and Labourd, Basque provinces, in France, Department of Pyrénées Atlantiques.

appearance of a "house", with all its history was an obstacle to this kind of marriage.[6] That does not mean that some families actually did not do it to improve their social situation.

Emergency Strategies to Restore a Hereditary Line

And what happened when the heir failed to reproduce, or his children died without descendants? In either case, the future of the house was in danger. Different ways to solve this problem and restore a hereditary line can be found in the sources.

The first strategy was to plan ahead, and entail the house, as in the way the English aristocracy did for its estates, to ensure it devolved to male family members. In Catalonia, for instance, families provided that when an heir died without descendants, the patrimony would go to his brother. If the brother had no descendants, it would go to a third brother. Daughters and their line could inherit only in the absence of direct male descendants. The disabled, members of the clergy, and those who had committed a crime were excluded from the line of succession. But as long as there were direct male descendants, the patrimony devolved to them. This arrangement prevented arguments and kept the peace.

The second way was *patull* marriage. The second son or a daughter married into the house, and promised to take care of the deceased heir's children and the surviving spouse. In return, the son (or a daughter) became heir (Violant Simorra 1992, 180).[7] Adoption or *afillament* was a third option, preferred by small holders with little patrimony and weaker

6 For the Catalan case, see Ferrer Alós (2005). Marriage was not sought, but there were situations which necessarily led to a patrimonial unification. The same opinion could be found in Barrera 1990, 199–202. In the French Basque Country, this type of marriage was not well thought of either (Arrizabalaga 1997). In Aragon that practice was named *juntar dos cosas* (join two things). J. Costa hardly devotes a couple of pages, which makes us think that it could exist, but few cases were found (Costa 1981, 261–265).

7 Below, we will mention "marriage on goods" *(casamiento sobre bienes)* practiced in Aragon and which is also called a *patull* in some areas. We will see that it had a wider intention.

or blurred family relationships. The child heir couple chose a nephew as their son and heir, who, in return for heirship, had to take care of them. Sometimes, the *afillat* was not a relative, but anyone who agreed to such a deal (Barrera 1990, 188; Faus Condomines 1902). In case the heir died, his widow could marry his brother (levirato) and continue the hereditary line again; in the same way, if the heir became a widower, he could marry his wife's sister *(sororato)* (Barrera 1990, 175).

In Vizcaya and Guipúzcoa, the death of a spouse without any descendants made the goods come back to the family line. Testamentary freedom existed but it had to be within the line (Ibánez Gómez *et al.* 1994, 39–41, Navajas Laporte 1975, 78–80). In this process of devolution of property in marriage, priority was given to the *troncalidad* or lineage.

Finally, there were no clear rules presiding over the choice of an heir among different children (regardless of sex and birth order) in regions where such a choice was possible. Things were made more difficult if the heir's parents had died. In these cases, a family council made up of members of the lineage and respectable people was set up. This council was responsible for assessing possible candidates and choosing the future heir who had to give continuity to the house. Its decisions were not challenged and that was the form used in the Basque Country or in Aragon to solve family crisis. Calling for a family council was another possible way to reduce tensions within the family when the expected plan failed.[8]

The Marriage, Key of the Single Heir System

The marriage of the heir is the key event in a single heir system, as it determines who the next link in the transmission chain will be. This is very different from the situation in equalitarian systems, where the post-

8 About the role of family council in Basque Country, see Navajas Laporte 1975, 84–86, 141–143. About family council in Aragon, see Costa 1981, 74–79. They existed in Catalonia but played minor roles as the hereditary circuits were more accurate (Faus Condomines 1902, 20–21). In Navarra, if a house remained heirless and without anybody who could name an heir, two relatives from each side would be designated and if they disagreed, they chose a third one (Yaben 1916, 128–129).

mortem distribution of the parent's property is the crucial moment (Ferrer Alòs 2007a).

Perpetuating the house implied that the children who were going to leave it would receive a sum of money. This amount defined their value on the marriage market, and determined which house they could enter, and which heir/heiress they could marry. Thus, in houses with several children, there were always brides or grooms leaving home and bringing to another house the dowry their parents had been able to spare. The dowry was normally commensurate with the wealth of the house they left, and the one they entered.

Precisely, because the future of a house is decided at the marriage of the heir, both families had to reach an agreement about all the situations that could occur, to give security to the ones who participated in the agreement. Clearly defining the rules of the game was one of the ways to assure well-being in all possible situations. The agreement was formalized in a document called *capitols matrimonials* or *capitulaciones matrimoniales* (marriage settlement).

Guarantee that the One who gets Married will be Heir

The first guarantee required by a person marrying an heir was that the parents would not change their mind in the future. Consequently, parents transferred their property to him or her in the marriage contract, to formalize his or her position.

However, the parents (the donors) could not make an unconditional transfer, which would leave them powerless, and at the mercy of being turned out of doors by the heir. Cultural norms and socialization process should have prevented this from happening. However, experience had probably shown this could happen and transfer deeds therefore used different forms depending on the nature of the problem to avoid. In many instances, solving one problem created another one, and, based on experience, families had to decide what the lesser evil was.

Two strategies prevailed in Catalonia. Either the parents gave all the goods to the heir, but kept a usufruct in them, and reserved a given amount of money for the establishment of their other children and for the burial. In this case the children were bound to maintain the parents in the house and to look after them when they were ill. That option could lead to a loss of authority on the part of the parents, to situations of disobedience on the part of the son who was already the owner and who could not be disinherited. But it also gave guarantees to the heir, who knew that he was working for something that was practically his property (Faus Condomines 1902, 21–22).[9]

But there were parents who wanted their child to be the heir but did not want to be tied up and, while alive, wanted to be able to do what they believed was appropriate for the patrimony *they* had received. So they developed the formula of *promesa de heredamiento* (the promise of inheritance) which consisted of not giving what one had but what one was going to have at the time of one's death. This way, the father could preserve his authority, his capacity of selling and disposing of the patrimony and the son had to wait for the father to die to come into the property. Logically, the parents committed themselves to support the younger couple, while they were working for the house. Obviously that system left the heir in a very weak situation, without decision making ability and without any possibility to accumulate his own capital. He had only a future promise. Some families, confronted with that problem, modified that model a little, and transferred some property, known as the *dote del heredero* (heir's dowry) to the child, while promising that he or she would become heir.

The objective was the reproduction of the house, so if the concluded marriage was childless, the son had no right to give the goods to whomever he wanted, on the contrary, they returned to those who had given them and in case these people had died, then to the new heir or to the family council who was to choose it. This way the rules of the games remained perfectly clear although sometimes reality strained the limit.

What happened when two couples – or the next generation – did not collaborate? The pact of food was the solution. The couple who did not

9 In the Spanish Basque Country, the parents gave all the patrimony to the new couple when they married, and they left the administration and management to the son. That was done with some kind of reservations and with the son's commitment to look after his parents (Douglass 1973, 116–123). In High Aragon, the passing of the inheritance did not take place until the parents' death (Costa 1981, 110). However, forming a family society protected all the members of the society much better.

own property (parents or heirs as the case may have been) was entitled to support as long as they worked for the house, and the agreement spelled out what the house should provide the couple, or the widow, if she preferred living elsewhere. In the case of a separation, the couple who kept the house was obliged to provide room and board elsewhere and some money.

Clarifying who the Fruit of the Marriage Belonged to

In Catalonia, the future heir received by contract a *promise to inherit* and worked exclusively for a house that was not his but would be. The *jove* (daughter-in-law), the woman who had married the heir, brought her dowry. If she left the house, she would be returned her dowry, but would not share in the gains the house had made thanks to her work.

The solution to that problem was the "conjugal society" which appeared in nearly all single heir areas, except Catalonia.[10] When cohabitation was impossible, the older couple agreed to pay for room and board elsewhere and provide some money to the younger one. In Catalonia, the lack of provisions to share the gains made after marriage left the woman unprotected; and with very little room for manoeuvre if she wanted to leave the house.

By contrast, in other single heir regions (Basque Country, Galicia, Asturias, Navarra), the families needed to clarify to whom the goods generated during the marriage belonged to and the solution found was setting up a "family society" between the two spouses at the moment of the marriage to define who will own the earnings and how. This was probably because the choice of the heir was here more open, and so the replacement

10 In Catalonia, the issue was solved through the *escreix*, discussed below. It was a fixed amount in lieu of payment for the woman's work during marriage (Faus Condominas 1902, 59). The non-existence of "conjugal societies" that protect all their members may be something recent. In reality, there are areas in Catalonia where they existed under the names of *"l'associació a compres i millores*" in Tarragona, *"l'agermanament"* in Tortosa or the *"convinença o mitja guadanyeria"* in the Aran Valley (Broca de Amell 1987, 833–844; Moragas 1934; Piñol Agulló 1946).

of the heir in case of death was far more possible. These family societies provided that the increases in patrimony were divided into two equal parts, one for each spouse. The societies received the name of *a mesa y mantel*, since they referred to the result of daily activities.[11] This "family conjugal society" recognized that the house was the result of the work of the parents, but also of the inheriting couple; it protected the widow in case of need and of unforeseen circumstances.

The Dowry, Spousal Contribution to the Marriage

Whoever entered into a house had to bring a dowry, as contribution to the well-being of the house. Dowries had to be commensurate with the wealth of the house, and consequently an individual was to marry at a given socioeconomic level.[12]

When a woman got married, she brought a dowry to the marriage. It did not have to be all her *legítima* (share of inheritance), but usually and to clarify the situation, when she received her dowry from her parents, she signed a document renouncing her inheritance rights, which in practice meant that the dowry was the *legítima*.[13] It was normally paid in cash (although it could also be land) and it could be complemented with money she had saved from her wages or paraphernalia goods (which did not come from the family).

11 For the Basque Country, see Navajas Laporte 1975, 81–82, 135–137; González Portilla 2003, 145–148; for Galicia, Rodríguez Ferreiro 1984, 453–458; for Asturias, Gómez Pellón 1991, 45–53. In Aragón, see the constitution of associations among brothers (Costa 1981, 224–237). In Navarra, spouses also shared out the *conquistas* (gains) done during marriage (Yaben 1916, 140).

12 Yaben (1916, 78) calculated the dowry to be a fifth part of the value of the house in which the spouse entered.

13 In the Catalan case, there still remained what was called *els drets de casa* (the rights of the house), which was a symbolic amount that was never received as payment, since it meant that the child, who had left, still had a relationship with the house and could come back if he/she wished. If they were paid, it meant breaking all kinds of relationships with the house of origin (Faus Condomines 1902, 33).

The Escreix *or* Esponsalici *as a Payment of the Dowry in Absence of Family Societies*

In Catalonia, when he entered the house the heir received the dowry brought by his bride. Outside Catalonia, dowries were contribution to the fund of family societies, when these were set up. At the death of either spouse, the gains made by the family society were divided equally between the survivor and the heirs of the predeceased.

In Catalonia, family societies did not exist. The heir took possession of his bride's dowry when she entered the house. But the husband had to pay an *escreix* or *esponsalici*, that is an amount proportional to the dowry (25 to 30 per cent). In some cases, the woman would receive the *escreix* in any circumstances, but restrictions were gradually introduced in the marriage contracts. First, the *escreix* went only to the children of the marriage, and subsequently, it was not paid at all if the woman became a childless widow (Maspons Anglasell 1935, 35). In some cases, the woman could receive the *escreix* in any circumstance, but little by little, the marriage contracts started to introduce limitations: first, the *escreix* always went in favour of the children of the marriage, so that if the woman ended up a childless widow, she was not paid. In real life then, the widow received no increases on her dowry as it had been the case in the past. In the 18th century, a widow in a well-off house had to think twice if she wanted to remarry into another house.

Reversion of Dowry

A dowry was free when the woman could do what she wanted with it. Provided for reversion, the dowries of childless women or of mothers of children too young to leave a will reverted to their house of origin at their death, less the cost of her burial. It was like a protection of the "house" of origin which yielded the daughter. If a woman was left a childless widow, the main objective of her marriage to give an heir to the house was not achieved, and the woman got then her dowry back so that she could remarry and start another life in another house. She was a widow, but in reality she was like a single woman for reproduction purposes.

Pious Causes to Marry Poor Maidens

Could a woman without a dowry get married? We have already said that the dowry was the value of the woman on the matrimonial market. Being without a dowry meant she was worthless and she could only aspire to a marginal marriage. One of the ways to help a woman was to improve her dowry. That is why some institutions founded "pious causes to marry poor maiden", which consisted of endowments, whose interests *(pensions)* collected every year, could provide dowries to poor maidens. One example is the foundation set up by Magí Oller from Manresa in the year 1805: he gave six thousand pounds that had to be invested in lands and loans, and from the money thus collected four dowries of 50, 80 or 100 pounds which had to be paid to four maidens from Manresa, always among the poorest girls or orphans (Sarret Arbós 1916, 63–66).[14] This kind of institution gave a chance to women who had difficulties on the matrimonial market, offering them some kind of value, so that they could improve their social position.

When the One who Entered the House was a Male

The single heir system always meant a spouse was brought into the house. In Catalonia, that spouse was usually a woman who brought a dowry with the reserves mentioned above. But when the heiress was a *pubilla* (the first-born daughter for lack of males), the one who entered the house was a male, a *pubill* according to the popular designation. Theoretically, that situation should not have caused problems, since there was a simple change of roles, but in real life, it was more complex.

When a male entered the house he increased its workforce and that had to be paid somehow. This is why the payment for the work he brought in,

14 Sant Benet de Bages, a monastery in inland Catalonia, reconverted in the year 1767 its alms in a "Causa Pía" (Pious Cause) to provide two poor maidens with money. The value of the dowries was 30 pounds (Book of the Council, Arxiu Monestir de Montserrat) and El Rdo. Anton Vila del Soler also founded a "Causa Pía" to marry poor maidens from the village of Artés (Ferrer Alòs 1991). For the medieval period, see Vinyoles 1980.

was done through the *soldada*, equivalent to ten years of wages (Faus Condomines 1902, 76–78).

Pre-determining the Heirs

Just a last problem was left to be clarified in order to perfectly strike up the hereditary scheme and for all its members to know what their role was. The marriage settlement also defined which was going to be the destiny of the patrimony. In Catalonia, the answer depended on the type of donation signed in the settlement. If the new heir was the owner, he could claim that he was going to name his first-born son as the heir and establish some replacements. That did not imply trust, because he was already the owner. On the other hand, if it was about a "promise of donation", the prediction of heir was done with a trust clause that could make him become a *hereu gravat*[15] if the father did not make a will at the moment of his death.

The fiancée had a special interest in entering into an agreement because the children of the first marriage would always be preferred to those of any other, and because the daughters would be preferred to the males of a second marriage. That option was not always made clear and it engendered a lot of problems when there were children of different marriages.

It was not solved this way everywhere. In Guipúzcoa, there was an agreement that if there were no descendants, the patrimonies of both partners came back to their respective origins, and if there were, it was the parents who would decide again which child was to inherit, since the priorities for the males and birthrights did not work. In these cases, the choice of who was going to be the new heir remained open and any son or daughter could be chosen according to each one's circumstances. Had the parents died, the family council or the testamentary executors were going to be very important in the cases when the "house" was left without a clear heir since it was that very institution which was going to name him/her.

15 A *hereu gravat* would succeed without risk of family conflict.

Measures Protecting Widows and Widowers

The single heir system could place the surviving spouse in a delicate situation. If widowhood occurred when there were no descendants, it was not a problem since one could easily come back to the primitive situation, as mentioned previously. If an heir died childless, his widow was given her dowry back so that she could leave the house and start her life again. If the partner who had entered the house died, the dowry was given back to the family of origin and the heir or heiress could marry again. In these circumstances, the *levirato* or *sororato* could be used to replicate the original alliance.

The problem arose if the partner became a widow or widower with children. If the widower was the heir, there was no problem with the properties since it had been promised to him in his marriage contract but his remarriage caused problem, as it brought a new wife in the house, who could try to have one of her children chosen as heir instead of one from the first marriage. To prevent this problem, marriage contracts identified the heir, but conflicts could not always be prevented (Yaben 1916, 45). So, one of the possible solutions to avoid this kind of conflict, was the "double marriages" as we shall see later.

A woman who had entered a house as a daughter-in-law had to give children to the house. Once she had given birth to at least an heir or heiress, she had no role left. If later she became a widow, she even ran the risk of being pitted against the heir who wanted to take the control of the house after his father's death. One solution to this problem was for the woman to take back her dowry, as well as her clothing and linen (trousseau), and seek to remarry with another heir. However, what did she do with the children she had from her first marriage? Did she take them with her? Did she leave them alone in the house looked after by some tutor? The solution was not an easy one.

Leaving the house created various problems. It weakened the house because it forced it to give back money that had been invested or spent from the dowry and betrothal good or trousseau, and the children who were to succeed in the house were left without a father and a mother. The situation was worse if the children were small and went along with the mother, since the house remained then without any protection. Sometimes, the dowry was not sufficient to allow the widow to start a new life, and consequently, this situation created a social problem: husbandless women. To alleviate this problem, single heir regions witnessed the emergence of the practice of usufruct.

In Navarra, for example, for a very long time, the widow collected the goods from the house in which she had entered, and made her life again somewhere else; she even could take her children with her.[16] In the same way, if the heir died, the goods went back to the one who had given them, and this person could even choose a new heir, leaving thus the widow completely unprotected. In this case, maintaining the house was more important than maintaining the widow, but that solution generated a lot of problems for the disinherited and widows who had very few resources. Different arrangements were used in Navarra to solve this problem: a) a "usufruct" for the widow or the widower, according to which the outside partner could stay in the house enjoying the usufruct of all the goods, provided he/she did not remarry; b) the reciprocal will in which each couple designated the other couple as their heir by intergenerational reciprocal wills, which created a "society" between old and young couples, and when one partner died, the other three partners shared the property equally; c) "marriage at home", according to which the widowed partner may marry someone of the family without losing the usufruct – it was especially useful when the children were small and the house needed labour force, and d) an arrangement according to which a "society" was formed between old and young couples and, when one partner died, the other three partners could equally share out the goods (Moreno and Zabalza 1999, 150).

Marriage at Home or Casamiento en Casa

"Marriage at home" *(casamiento en casa)* was a very interesting solution, which appeared in Navarra, in the High Aragon and in the Catalan Pyrenees. Joaquin Costa (1981) made a detailed analysis of its functions. According to this author, young widows or widowers hesitated remarrying or not, and when they did so, they did not know if they would lose their usu-

16 That clause was included in 36 to 44 percent of the contracts for the period 1540–1629 (Moreno and Zabalza 1999, 140–150).

fruct or not; on the other hand, if the widow left the house, she would leave her children alone and defenceless. We must add that with the death of a male heir, the house could be left short of male labour (assuming there were no second sons).

In this case, why not allow the widow or the widower to remarry in the very same house? This could be risky for the house; therefore, the family council had to approve the *casamiento en casa*. The main problem was that the new couple could have a lot of children and so jeopardize the rights of the late heir's children. For that reason, some conditions were set up: if the surviving spouse was a widow, she could marry the person she wanted (being rather old, she would have but few children), but if he was a widower, he would be allowed to marry only if the woman was above forty, which meant that, in practice, she would not be able to have children. This way, the widow or widower got married at home, the house had more labourers and the original problem was solved.

With time, the Catalans improved the protection of widows. First of all, the practice of *any de plor* (her first year of widowhood) appeared, which forbade the widow to ask for the return of dowry until a year after her husband's death (Brocà 1985, 862). The idea was to avoid a possible pregnancy before the husband's death that would generate inheritance problems. And second practice, the *tenuta* (Brocà 1985, 863) appeared, meaning that if she did not ask for the dowry, the widow had the right of usufruct of the husband's goods and she could enjoy the fruit produced in and by the house all her life.

The Destiny of Non Inheriting Sons and Daughters and their Quest for Well-Being

We already explained that the children who were not going to inherit received a *legítima*, usually money, as a help to maintain their social status. In practice, families could not spare such sums, because they could not raise them. Consequently the *legítima* did not allow younger sons to buy a *baserriak* (county house) or a *mas* (farmhouse) similar to the one of the heir (Ferrer Alòs 1993; 1998; 2004). This was the weakest point of this system. If the other children left the native house, they tried to buy a house and lands. A non inheriting son or daughter owned what he or she had received (the *legítima*) plus the dowry that his/her partner could bring in, unless he married an heiress (or unless she married an heir). Consequently, the standard of living of these non inheriting children would automatically be lower than the one of their parents. Various mechanisms were thus put in place to limit the downward mobility of non inheriting sons and daughters.

In Catalonia, where male primogeniture was the norm, different strategies were deployed for sons and daughters.[17] On the other hand, similar strategies were used irrespective of sex in regions where males were not preferred heirs.

Increasing the Incomes of the Younger Sons

One of the ways to improve the position of the younger sons on the marriage market was to ensure they accumulated assets above the *legítima*. In Catalonia, the families with little resources sent the younger sons, to work as farm boys or to graze the livestock, and let them keep their earnings toward their marriage. In country houses, the practice of *cabalejar* was very frequent: the second child received a piece of land and a few heads of livestock, and he kept the profits he could make from them for the moment when he wanted to leave the house.[18]

Daughters could increase their dowries by working as servants in country houses, spinning at home, or engaging in other activities, such as raising poultry, weaving, knitting, etc. Their activities were not the same as their brothers'. In addition, young women could receive funds from the "Pious Causes to marry maiden", discussed above. All this limited their downward mobility.[19] For a very long time, the destiny of the daughters was to get married and any other option was usually despised.

17 See the differential placement of the second children in Ferrer Alòs 1993.

18 About different ways to earn a little money while staying at home, for both males and females, see Santamaria Tous 1901, 30–35. This way, not only were the *legítimas* increased, but the houses could reduce their contribution. In Aragon, this money was called *cabal* (Costa 1981, 54).

19 See some examples of how it worked in Ferrer Alos 1991; 1993 and Marques 1998.

The Protection of the Second Children and Spare Heirs

In the single heir system, the heir and his spouse lived with his parents. The second child and his or her spouse were not allowed in the house, as this would cause conflicts. The second children, then, could stay in the house only while single.

The younger sons and daughters left the house, but they knew that they would always be welcome in that house. It was a bit like their insurance in case things did not go well. A daughter, for example, got married to the heir of another house. If she became a childless widow, then logically, she could ask for her dowry back and leave her husband's house. Her native house would warmly welcome her, arms open, until the moment when she would marry again. Younger sons on the other hand, were spare heirs. A second child could replace the heir though the *levirato* and the *sororato*. Santiago de Llobet explains that, in some houses, the youngest brother remained single until the heir had children (Llobet Masachs 1990, 76–77).

Family strategies to avoid downward social mobility of non inheriting children were multiple. Exchanging sons and daughters as marriage partners was one of them.

Exchanges of Children and Crossed Marriages of all Types

The simplest was for the heirs of two separate houses to marry a younger child from the other ones. This way, each house solved the problem of a second child. That scheme could get complicated with marriages between second children of different generations, which, eventually, had the same final result.[20]

When the problem of the widows was not yet entirely clarified (in 17th century Catalonia), the double marriages between the widowed father and a widowed woman on the one hand, and the future heir and the widow's daughter on the other hand were very frequent. That kind of marriage was especially useful to reduce the tensions that could occur if two women

20 In Catalonia, that practice was called *fer canvis* (making exchanges) and in Spain, we talked of *matrimonio a trueque* (barter marriage). In reality, it was much more frequent in zones like Galicia where the egalitarian system prevailed (Rey Castelao 1990).

from different families shared a house, one married to the widower and one to the heir. The mother and the daughter also brought a combined dowry and could go to a better house. On other occasions this kind of double marriage was meant to resolve a situation of emergency such as the case of the mother and daughter left alone with the patrimony. It was most probable that an heir and his son offered to solve the situation, since it implied patrimonial unification (Faus Condomines 1902; Ferrer Alòs 2005).

Definitive Celibacy

If the *legítima* was not enough to preserve one's social status and if the house needed additional workers, one possibility was to remain single in the house. This way, everybody won, the "house" did not have to pay the *legítima* and had enough workers, and the unmarried second son kept his social position. In return, the house would give him some kind of recognition, whether an affective one on the part of the nephews and nieces, or an active one as a councillor and authority in difficult situations. That role was surely more recognised with the males; the single women were reduced to a more domestic position.

Specific terms existed to refer to these unmarried individuals. In Aragon, for example, they were known as *tiones* (Navajas Laporte 1975, 240–244), in Catalonia, as *unclus*, *concos* or tietes (Barrera 1990; Faus Condomines 1902, 109) and in the Basque Country, as *mutilzarra* (old chap/old boy) or *neskazarra* (old girl) (Douglass 1973, 123). The *legítima* and some modest savings could accumulate during lifetime and were then used to improve the situations of married brothers or sisters or of nephews and nieces through gift while alive or legacies after death. Those also limited downward mobility of the recipient and increased his/her well-being.

Those who did not marry could enter Holy Orders. This was not an option open to everyone: priests had to have received a proper education, and convents asked for dowries. But it was a good option for those who could exercise it. Downward mobility did not occur. The Church was a prestigious institution, and its members had clearly recognised social roles. Young priests could also add to their *legítima* if they knew how to get ahead in the hierarchy. If a priest willed his estate to the heir of the house he had left, the latter benefited.[21]

Some priests used their ecclesiastic career to accumulate property. They had entered with a family contribution and left having multiplied it. These priests used to make a will in favour of the heir of the house from where they originated, but invested the accumulated capitals in the foundation of ecclesiastic benefices. The idea was very simple. The capital was invested in properties and in loans to little farmers and with the incomes, they financed an ecclesiastic benefice founded in some local chapel, whose patron or whoever named the priest who had to deal with it was the heir of the house. This way, some houses had benefices in which they placed a second child, and, with only one investment at the beginning, they could place a second child in each generation and likewise save themselves one *legítima*.

The Possibilities outside the House

The last possibility for second children was leaving the house. In the Basque Country, Navarra or Asturias, a second child could always aspire to marry an heiress and vice-versa, but the others either remained single or left the house. In Catalonia, where the eldest son was always the heir, the possibilities for a second child to marry a *pubilla* were rather remote (Ferrer Alòs 2005).

On leaving the house, the second child received his *legítima* to make his way in the world. If he used it to buy a farm, he did so in a different commune but this was viewed as downward mobility. Therefore he tried to become an artisan. In Catalonia, that was a frequent option and the itineraries of some younger sons showed that they were more successful than the heir.[22]

21 About the relationships between family and church from that perspective see Ferrer Alòs 1991; 2008. About the ecclesiastic benefices, see Ciuffreda 1992; Fatjó Gómez 1993 and Llobet 1993.

22 To give an example, Llogari Serra, a second child from the country house Serra de Calders was able to set up Pau Miralda's company with the help of partners, one of the most important ones dealing with America and the commerce of silk handkerchiefs (Vila Despujol 1988).

It was not always possible to learn a trade since it depended on the local economy. In some regions, emigration became a structural phenomenon, and *legítima* was used to finance it (Pedregal 1981 (1902), 115–121). Those younger sons who had gone away often helped their family of origin to improve their situation, if fortune had smiled upon them.

Women did not have such opportunities; their hope (besides *pubillas*) was to marry an heir and enter in another house. That differential role closed many doors to women, at least in those zones where the male primogeniture was absolute.

Emergency Strategies not Defined by Legal Institutions

The strategies described below are the result of the evolution of the single heir system over time, developed to respond to concrete problems. They were used to try to improve well-being through extra-legal practices (and were ignored by lawyers)

Delaying of the Heir's Marriage Age

Regardless of the strategies explained above, families could plan their fertility to reduce the problem of social downgrading. For example, if the birth rate went down, there were less second children, consequently, the *legítima* could be higher for each of them and provide a better establishment.[23] Did the birth rate fall in single heir regions? In Catalonia, it surely did not. The figures from the genealogies we managed to reconstruct give an average of 6.6 children born per generation and the spectacular demographic growth of the 18th century does not allow us to think family limi-

23 Yaben considers that when the heir had to provide more than three brothers and sisters with dowries, he would have reproduction problems, whereas less than three would be an ideal number (Yaben 1916, 77).

tation occurred (Ferrer Alòs 2003).[24] Obviously, if there was a reduction of the birth rate, there were two kinds of risk. On the one hand, it could produce a labor shortage on the farm and, on the other hand, in an environment of high death rate, people could end up without heir if the birth rate went down too much. We do not know if this fall occurred in other areas.

So, what the farmers who lived on a family patrimony did was delaying the chosen heir's marriage, or in other words, what was important was the time that passed from one transmission to the other, since it reduced the number of second children to place. Three generations in a century is not the same as four. The genealogies in Catalonia seem to confirm the existence of that strategy and in the Basque Country the age of marriage for the males was very high in the late 18th century.[25] There are extreme situations in which one has to look for imaginative solutions to continue maintaining the patrimony in the same house.

The donar-se *practice*

An elderly couple, a single man who remained without any relatives or a widowed woman could give himself/herself *(se dona)* or give themselves *(se donan)* to another family. In return for being looked after for the rest of their days, whoever gave himself/herself brought all his/her goods he/she had and offered himself/herself to work for the interest of the house and would be looked after by the host family.

24 The figures of demographic growth in Catalonia from 254 series of births which were supposed to account for 45.2 percent of the Catalan population, shows that the population doubled between 1700 and 1800 and this trend was only possible with high fertility rates (Ferrer Alòs 2007b).

25 The figures brought by Ibáñez Gómez *et al.* 1994, about rates of nuptiality, definitive celibacy rates for both males and females, and about the age at first marriage are conclusive for the areas of the Basque Country in which the country "house" system prevailed. In Catalonia, the figures available are more contradictory. The genealogies of well-off families (farmers and gentry) are overwhelming. Between a generation and the other, 30 years passed and most of the second sons remained unmarried in the house or entered in Church (Ferrer Alòs 2003). Unfortunately, the figures from 1787 Floridablanca census present a lot of deficiencies in the absolute figures (Simón Tarrés 1992).

It was a way to solve the problems of elderly people who remained alone and without anybody to look after them (Brocà 1985; Costa 1981, 267; Violant Simorra 1992, 159).

Fictitious Kinships and Communal Solidarity

We refer to the institution of the godfather and the godmother from baptism, which in some societies like the Basque Country's, generated a relationship of solidarity between godfather and godson. According to William Douglass:

> If the godfather needs help, the godson is obligated to support him. In this way the godson can contribute to the economic well-being of the godfather's house (Douglass 1973, 213).[26]

Likewise, the godfather is the one who will look after you and will help you if you have any problems.

Sometimes, beyond the family, we find communal institutions which also help to face problems which come up at certain concrete moments. The Basque *bazerriak* (country house) gather together in *auzoas*, a group of country houses in which a complex network of relationships are established, solving that way main difficulties due to a scattered habitat. In this environment, the *auzurrikourrena* appears. Each house has its own *auzurrikourrena*; that is to say that a house has the obligation to help another one in moments of difficulties (the death of a relative, to give a hand in the field, etc.). Each house is *auzurrikourrena* of another one, and it is not usually a reciprocal favour (Douglass 1973, 174).

In the Basque Country, when the owners of the house are ill and they cannot manage with work in the fields, the priest usually announces from the altar that a neighbour has a problem and the neighbours "worked out of charity". In Catalonia, there are also some similar practices, mainly when there is a widow with young children and without any labour force to work the land (Violant Simorra 1989, 332).

26 "Si el padrino necesita ayuda el ahijado se considera obligado a apoyarlo. En este sentido el ahijado puede contribuir al bienestar económico de la casa del padrino" (Douglass 1973, 213).

Conclusion

If we understand well-being as the satisfaction of material needs and of the individuals' personal growth, from what we have explained, we cannot doubt that a system of transmitting goods is a collection of rules, standards and practices which define the individuals' access to the family resources of their own family and of other families through marriage.

We focused on the analysis of the framework of the single heir which dominated northern Spain (from Galicia to Catalonia) (Figure 1) and which was based on the idea that a unique heir was given the family patrimony in return for looking after his/her parents and with the obligation of providing his brothers/sisters with the best things possible "according to the possibilities of the house" "and the possessions and power of the house". Those who practiced this system of family transmission believed that it assured much better the well-being of everybody than the equalitarian distribution[27] which divides the farms indefinitely.

This system tries to deal with a complex reality conditioned by biology, by social inequality, by political context, by economic development, etc. We have not considered how the well-being of a generation changes with economic or political changes, including taking into account social inequality. We have just limited ourselves in this chapter to raise the questions derived from the biological crisis and from the own logic of the system.

The single heir system had to solve the following questions: which child will be named heir? The first-born child regardless of his/her sex? The first male? According to the parents' will? And we have seen how each option presented its contradictions and how families tried to answer them. Property transmission systems had to solve the problem of how to guarantee the dowry of the in-coming partner. Parents had to decide whether they would donate all they had when the chosen heir married or release the patrimony at their death, because they might doubt whether the heir would fulfil his/her obligation to look after his/her parents. A problem also had to be solved: how to compensate the partner who came into the house for his work, at the time of the heir's death. Besides, the system had

27 It is obviously an ideological vision, since the equalitarian system would also have its mechanisms and its contradictions to try to provide its individuals with well-being.

its failure, for instance when death left a widow/widower without any children, sometimes with young children or with children already grown up. It had to decide what to do when the heir/heiress had no descendants and to determine how he/she would choose a new heir. It had to figure out how to place second children, and how to help them better their *legítima* so that they could be established in the best way possible outside the house.

There were no universal answers to these tensions. What is indeed certain is that "institutions", as the jurists say, were developed to solve difficulties that biology created, and perfectly conscious strategies were developed to reduce those contradictions and to achieve the best result possible for all house members.

Did the system provide all the individuals with well-being? Obviously, the well-being also depended on other parameters (the work opportunities in the area or outside of it, the level of development of other institutions, etc.) but it provided the individuals, males and females, with an important level of security and it made sense within the community in which he/she had to live. It also provided solutions for uncommon problems. The single heir system structured the individuals' life and gave them security. This way, specific practices developed which tried to solve all problems that could come up.

The price paid was a deep inequality between the status of sons and daughters, which derived from being at the service of the "house". The women did not leave the house to set up a business or be involved in any other activity, since their destiny was to get married. Working away from home was only a way to improve the dowry that had to be brought into the marriage.

This is the dilemma we are facing. The security system provided by the single heir system we described resulted in a marked inequality between the children and between the sexes. Socialization was a way to get each to accept his or her place, although some of them were worse than others. If that was accepted, it was because the children also believed in its advantages. Only when the economic contexts changed and economic opportunities increased, new solutions could be developed.

References

ARENSBERG, Conrad M. and KIMBALL, Solon T., 1968, *Family and Community in Ireland* Cambridge, Harvard University Press.

ARRIZABALAGA, Marie-Pierre, 1997, "The stem family in the French Basque Country: Sare in the nineteenth century", *Journal of Family History,* 22, 1, pp. 50–69.

–, 2002, "Female primogeniture in the French Basque Country", in Emiko OCHIAI (ed.), *The Logic of Female Succession: Rethinking Patriarchy and Patrilineality in Global and Historical Perspective*, Kyoto, International Research Center of Japanese Studies, pp. 31–52.

AUGUSTINS, George, 1989, *Comment se perpétuer? Devenir des lignées et destins des patrimoines dans les paysanneries européennes*, Nanterre, Société d'ethnologie.

AVENTIN, Mercè, 1996, "Estructures familiars i successió", in *La forja dels països catalans (segles XIII-XV). Història. Política, societat i cultura dels Països Catalans,* Barcelona, Fundació Enciclopèdia Catalana, pp. 140–159.

BARRERA, Andres, 1990, *Casa, herencia y familia en la Cataluña rural*, Madrid, Alianza Editorial.

–, 1991, "Sucesión unipersonal y familia troncal en Cataluña y el norte de la Península Ibérica (análisis comparativo)", *Revista de Antropología Social,* 0, pp. 179–204.

BEFU, Harumi, 1981, *Japan. An anthropological Introduction*, Tokyo, C. E. Tuttle.

BERKNER, Lutz, 1972, "The stem family and the development cycle of the household: an eighteen century Austrian example", *The American Historical Review,* 77, pp. 398–418.

–, 1977, "Peasant household organization and demographic change in Lower Saxony (1689–1766)", in Ronald D. LEE (ed.), *Population Patterns in the Past*, London/New York, Academic Press, pp. 53–69.

BESTARD, Joan, 1986, *Casa y familia. Parentesco y reproducción doméstica en Formentera*, Palma de Mallorca, Institut d'Estudis Baleàrics.

BROCÀ, Guillem Maria de Amell, 1980, *Instituciones del derecho civil catalán vigente*, Barcelona, Imprenta Barcelonesa.

–, 1987, *Historia del derecho de Cataluña especialemnte del civil y exposición de las instituciones del derecho civil del mismo territorio en relación con el código civil de España y la jurisprudencia*, Barcelona, Generalitat de Catalunya.

CEBALLOS CUERNO, Carmen, 1999, "Familia y alianzas matrimoniales en el valle de Guriezo (Cantabria). Estrategias de control en una sociedad del Antiguo Régimen", in Robert ROWLAND, and Angels TORRENTS (eds), *Matrimonio y nupcialidad: perspectivas interdisciplinares,* Logroño, Instituto de Estudios Riojanos, pp. 55–77.

CHIVA, Isac and GOY, Joseph (eds), 1981, *Les Baronnies des Pyrénées*, Paris, EHESS.

CIUFFREDA, Antonio, 1992, "Lo zio prete. Individui famiglie e parentela nella trasmissione dell'ufficio sacerdotale in una comunità pugliese in epoca moderna. Il clero di Manduria (XVI e XVIII secolo)", *Secondo Congresso Italo-iberico di demografia Storica*, Savona, ADEH, pp. 944–983.

COLLOMP, Alain, 1983, *La maison du père. Famille et village en haute Provence aux XVIIe et XVIIIe siècles*, Paris, PUF.

COMAS D'ARGEMIR, Dolors, 1991, "Casa y comunidad en el Alto Aragón, Ideales culturales y reproducción social", in Carmelo LISÓN TOLOSANA (ed.), *Antropología de los Pueblos del Norte de España,* Madrid, Universidad Complutense de Madrid / Universidad de Cantabria, pp. 131–150.

COSTA, Joaquin (ed.), 1981, *Derecho consuetudinario y economía popular de España,* Zaragoza, Guara Editorial.

DOUGLASS, William A., 1973, *Muerte en Murélaga. El contexto de la muerte en el País Vasco*, Barcelona, Barral Editores.

–, 1988, "The Basque stem-family household: myth or reality?", *Journal of Family History*, 13, 1, pp. 75–89.

DUBERT, Isidro, 1992, *Historia de la familia en Galicia durante la época moderna (1550–1830),* A Coruña, Edicios do Castro.

FATJÓ GÓMEZ, Pere, 1993, "El beneficio personado: un instrumento de promoción entre el clero secular (siglo XVII)", in *I Congrés d'Història de l'Església catalana,* Barcelona, pp. 325–342.

FAUS CONDOMINES, J., 1902, "Els capitols matrimonials a la comarca de Guissona (Catalunya Segriana)", *Revista Jurídica de Catalunya*, pp. 3–116.

FAUVE-CHAMOUX, Antoinette, 1987, "Le fonctionnement de la famille souche dans les Baronnies des Pyrénées du XVIIe siècle à la première guerre mondiale", *I Congreso Hispano Luso Italiano de Demografía Histórica*, Barcelona, ADEH, pp. 627–632.

FERNÁNDEZ CORTIZO, Camilo, 1988, "En casa y compañía: grupo doméstico y estrategias familiares en la Galicia occidental a mediados del siglo XVIII", in José Carlos BERMEJO BARRERA (ed.), *Parentesco, familia y matrimonio en la historia de Galicia,* Santiago de Compostela, Semata, Ciencias Sociais e humanidades, pp. 145–166.

–, 2004, "La tierra de Montes en el siglo XVIII: espacios matrimoniales y reproducción social", *Revista de Demografía Histórica,* 22, 1, pp. 43–76.

FERRER ALÒS, Llorenç, 1991, "Familia, iglesia y matrimonio en el campesinado acomodado catalán (s. XVIII-XIX)", *Boletín de la ADEH,* 9, 1, pp. 27–64.

–, 1993, "Fratelli al celibato, sorelle al matrimonio. La parte dei cadetti nella riproduzzione sociale dei gruppi agiati in Catalogna (secoli XVIII-XIX)", *Quaderni Storici,* 28, 83, pp. 527–554.

–, 1998, "The Use of the family: Property Devolution and Well-to-do Social Groups in Catalonia (Eighteenth and Nineteenth Centuries)", *The History of the Family. An International Quarterly,* 3, 2, pp. 247–265.

–, 2003, "Família i ciutadans honrats. Les estratègies d'adaptació de la petita noblesa catalana (segles XVIII-XIX)", *Estudis d'Història Agrària,* 16, pp. 169–215

–, 2004, "Kinship as a mechanism in the social structuring of Rural Catalonia (eighteenth and nineteenth centuries)", *Journal of Family History,* 29, 2, pp. 135–153.

–, 2005, "When there was no male heir. The transfer or wealth in Catalonia through women (the pubilla)", *Continuity and Change,* 20, 1, pp. 27–52.

–, 2007a, "Comment se perpétuer? Systèmes successoraux et transmission patrimoniale dans l'Espagne du XVIIIe siècle", *Histoire & sociétés rurales*, 27, pp. 37–70.

–, 2007b, "Una revisió del creixement demogràfic de Catalunya en el segle XVIII. Una revisió de les tesis de Vilar", *Estudis d'Història Agrària,* 20, pp. 17–68.

–, 2008, "Placing sons and daughters in the church: Strategies used by the gentry of Central Catalonia to maintain social status in the 17th and 18th centuries", *The History of the Family*, 13, 1, pp. 26–41.

GÓMEZ PELLÓN, Eloy, 1991, "Aproximación al estudio antropológico de Asturias", in Carmelo LISÓN TOLOSANA (ed.), *Antropología de los Pueblos del Norte de España,* Madrid, Universidad Complutense de Madrid/Universidad de Cantabria, pp. 31–62.

GOMILA GRAU, Antonia, 2004, *Família i herència a Mallorca*, Mallorca, Menjavents. Edicions Documenta Balear.

GONZÁLEZ PORTILLA, Manuel and URRUTIKOETCHEA, José G., 2003, *Vivir en familia, organizar la sociedad. Familia y modelos familiares: las provincias vascas a las puertas de la modernización (1860)*, Bilbao, Universidad del País Vasco.

HOMOBONO, José Ignacio, 1991, "Ambitos culturales, sociabilidad y grupo doméstico en el País Vasco", in Carmelo LISÓN TOLOSANA (ed.), *Antropología de los Pueblos del Norte de España,* Madrid, Universidad Complutense de Madrid/Universidad de Cantabria, pp. 83–114.

IBÁÑEZ GÓMEZ, Maite, ORTEGA, Arturo, SANTANA, Alberto, and ZABALA, Marta, 1994, *Casa, familia y trabajo en la historia de Bergara*, Bergara, Ayuntamiento de Bergara.

KITAOJI, Hironobu, 1971, "The structure of the Japanese family", *American Anthropologist,* 73, pp. 1036–1057.

LANZA GARCÍA, Ramon, 1988, *Población y familia campesina en el Antiguo Régimen. Liébana S. XVI-XIX*, Santander, Universidad de Santander.

LE ROY LADURIE, Emmanuel, 1972, "Système de la coutume. Structures familiales et coutumes d'héritage en France au XVIe siècle", *Annales (E.S.C.)*, 27, 4–5, pp. 825–846.

LISON TOLOSANA, Carmelo, 1971, *Antropología cultural de Galicia*, Madrid, Siglo XXI.

LLOBET MASACHS, Santiago, 1990, "El matrimoni i les cases pairals de la Selva a l'Antic Règim", *Quaderns de la Selva,* 3, pp. 69–102.

–, 1993, "La casa de pagès i la col.locació dels fills segons dins l'Església", *Quaderns de la Selva,* 6, pp. 79–106.

MARQUÉS, Josep, 1988, "Fundacions de Causes Pies al bisbat de Girona (segles XVI-XIX)", *Pedralbes,* 8, II, pp. 513–524.

MARTÍN BALLESTEROS, Luis, 1944, *La casa en el derecho aragonés*, Zaragoza, Estudios de derecho aragonés.

MASPONS ANGLASELL, Francesc, 1935, *La llei de la família catalana*, Barcelona, Ed. Popular Barcino.

MIKELARENA, Fernando, 1992, "Estructuras familiares y sistemas sucesorios en Navarra: una aproximación crítica desde las ciencias sociales a las perspectivas tradicionales", *Revista Jurídica de Navarra,* 14, pp. 119–145.

MORAGAS, Vicenç de, 1934, "Associació a compres i millores en el Camp de Tarragona", *Conferències sobre varietats comarcals de Dret Civil Català,* Barcelona, Academia de Jurisprudencia i legislació de Catalunya, pp. 193–219.

MORENO ALMARCEGUI, Antonio, 1992, "Pequeña nobleza rural, sistema de herencia y estructura de la propiedad de la tierra en Plasencia del Monte (Huesca), 1600–1855", in Rafael Benítez SÁNCHEZ-BLANCO, Francisco CHACÓN JIMÉNEZ, Juan HERNÁNDEZ FRANCO (eds), *Poder, familia y consanguinidad en la España del Antiguo Régimen,* Barcelona, Anthropos, pp. 71–106.

MORENO ALMARCEGUI, Antonio and ZABALZA, Ana, 1999, *El origen histórico de un sistema de heredero único. El prepirineo navarro (1540–1739),* Pamplona, Instituto de Ciencias para la Familia.

MOREY TOUS, Antonia, 1999, *Noblesa i desvinculació a Mallorca als segles XVIII i XIX. Les repercusions de la legislació desvinculadora sobre els patrimonis nobiliaris,* Barcelona, Publicacions de l'Abadia de Montserrat.

NAVAJAS LAPORTE, Alvaro, 1975, *La ordenación consuetudinaria del caserío en Guipuzcoa,* San Sebastián, Sociedad Guipuzcoana de Ediciones y Publicaciones S.A.

PEDREGAL, Manuel, 1981 (1902), "Asturias. Derecho de familia", in Joaquín COSTA (ed.), *Derecho consuetudinario y economía popular en España,* Zaragoza, Guara Editorial, pp. 113–120.

PÉREZ GARCIA, José Manuel, 2002, "Siete generaciones de gallegos (1650–1850): las claves de la reproducción social y demográfica en las Rías Bajas (Samieira)", *Cuadernos Feijonianos de Historia Moderna,* II, pp. 31–103.

PIÑOL AGULLÓ, Jose, 1946, "Asociación a compras y mejoras en el Campo de Tarragona", *La Notaria.*

REY CASTELAO, Ofelia, 1990, "Mecanismos reguladores de la nupcialidad en la Galicia Atlántica. El matrimonio a trueque", *Obradoiro de Historia Moderna,* Santiago de Compostela, pp. 247–268.

RODRÍGUEZ FERREIRO, H. M., 1984, "Estructura y comportamiento de la familia rural gallega: los campesinos del Morrazo en el siglo XVIII", in D.D.A.A (eds), *II Congreso de Metodologia Histórica Aplicada,* Santiago de Compostela, Universidad de Santiago de Compostela, pp. 439–458.

ROIGÉ, Xavier, 1994, "Herència i successió al Priorat. Entre la indivisió i la dispersió patrimonial", in Ponce SANTI and Llorenç FERRER (eds), *Família i canvi social a la Catalunya contemporània,* Vic, Eumo, pp. 73–94.

RUIZ, Cesar, MORENO, Antonio and CAYETANO, Fernández, 2002, *El mercado de la tierra y del trabajo en contextos sucesorios distintos. El caso de Navarra, 1530–1719,* Pamplona, Instituto de Ciencias para la familia.

SAAVEDRA, Pegerto, 1988, "Casa y comunidad en la Galicia interior (1750–1860)", in José Carlos Bermejo BARRERA (ed.), *Parentesco, familia y matrimonio en la historia de Galicia,* Santiago de Compostela, Semata, Ciencias Sociais e humanidades.

–, 2002, "Las lógicas de la organización familiar y reproducción social en la España cantábrica y noratlántica en el Antiguo Régimen", in D.D.A.A (eds), *Historia y perspectivas de investigación. Estudios en memoria del profesor Angel Rodríguez Sánchez,* Badajoz, Editora Regional Extremaña, pp. 141–149.

SANTAMARIA TOUS, Valentín, 1901, *Derecho consuetudinario y economía popular,* Madrid.

SARRET ARBÓS, Joaquim, 1916, *Reyal Confraria de la Puríssima Concepció. Els favets de Manresa,* Manresa.

SIMÓN TARRÉS, Antoni, 1992, "La població catalana a l'Epoca Moderna. Síntesi i actualització", *Manuscrits,* 10, pp. 217–258.

URRUTIKOETXEA, Jose, 1992, *"En una mesa y compañía". Caserío y familia campesina en la crisis de la sociedad tradicional. Irun, 1766–1845*, Donostia, Universidad de Deusto.

VILA DESPUJOL, Ramon, 1988, *Una família burgesa manresana en la Catalunya del segle XIX. Els germans Serra-Farreras (1797–1877)*, Manresa, Caixa d'Estalvis de Manresa.

VINYOLES, M. Teresa, 1980, "Ajudes a donzelles pobres a maridar", in Manuel RIU (ed.), *La pobreza y la asistencia a los pobres en la Cataluña medieval,* Barcelona, pp. 295–362.

VIOLANT SIMORRA, Ramon, 1989, *El Pirineo español. Vidas, usos, costumbres de una cultura milenaria que desaparece*, Barcelona, Altafulla.

–, 1992, *El cicle individual i familiar al Pallars*, Tremp, Garsineu.

YABEN, Hilario, 1916, *Los contratos matrimoniales en Navarra y su influencia en la estabilidad de la familia*, Madrid, Establecimiento tipográfico de Jaime Ratés.

ZABALZA SEGUIN, Ana, 1999, "El heredero ideal. Prácticas sucesorias en la Navarra pirenaica durante la Edad Moderna (1550–1725)", in Robert ROWLAND and Angels TORRENTS (eds), *Matrimonio y nupcialidad: perspectivas interdisciplinares,* Logroño, Instituto de Estudios Riojanos, pp. 239–251.

ZINK, Anne, 1993, *L'héritier de la maison. Géographie coutumière du sud-ouest de la France sous l'Ancien Régime*, Paris, EHESS.

Gender and the Intergenerational Transfer of Property and Social Position in the 18th and early 19th Century Northern Dutch Countryside

Richard PAPING

Myths on how in the past property and social position were transferred between generations are widespread. One of the strongest is the gendered norm of the (oldest, sometimes youngest) son following in the footsteps of his father (Hajnal 1965)[1] which can partly be related to customs of primogeniture in Great Britain, Catalonia, Scandinavia and Central Europe (Thirsk 1976). Daughters are supposed to have had chances to succeed only if there were no sons available. Their position must have depended heavily on the resources of the partner they married, which weakened their overall position in the household. In this case female upward and downward social mobility tends to be higher, as the social position of a couple is less related to the social background of the bride. Succession from one generation to the next is suggested to be the main way property (and social positions) was transferred.[2] In this way families usually lived in the same building for generations. In a society with a preference for nuclear family households, this continuity in (male) lineage logically resulted in late marriages, because couples first had to secure a livelihood (Fertig 2005). In this article I will use the case of the Groningen Ommelanden (hinterland) in the 18th and early 19th century to test this myth of continuity of (male) lineages for a very prosperous pre-industrial rural society. How large were the chances of intergenerational mobility for males and females and what does this mean for the position of women?

Though peripheral, the Dutch Ommelanden with its very fertile clay grounds and well developed money economy was a part of the extremely wealthy coastal Dutch region. It had about 50,000 inhabitants in the 18th century and was characterized by market-oriented farming (mostly me-

1 For examples see Ferrer Alos 2005; Dribe and Lundh 2005; Moring 2007; Pozsgai 2007.

2 See Sabean 1990 on Neckarhausen in Southern Germany and de Haan 1994 on farms in the eastern Netherlands.

dium sized farms of 10 to 50 hectares) and a wide range of non-agricultural activities for the local market, despite the vicinity of the large city of Groningen (23,000 inhabitants). Three important economic groups can be identified: (1) farmers, (2) landless labourers, (3) artisans, shop-keepers, schoolmasters and others working mainly outside agriculture (Paping 1995). The nobility, although financially quite influential until the beginning of the 19th century, was quantitatively negligible. Intergenerational occupational mobility after marriage was uncommon. Trades and handicrafts were nearly always jobs for life, and not an ordinary stage in the family life cycle as in the German village of Neckarhausen (Sabean 1990, 316–320). The Groningen clay area was a society with large economic differences within each village. However, social-cultural barriers between groups were not very high.

Most of the data presented relate to the Roman Catholic minority (some 6 percent of the population) for which a complete family reconstitution is available. The advantage of studying this group is that the researcher only loses track of children who migrate very far, as the region analysed comprises 1,000 square kilometres and includes 150 small and larger villages. For 18th century data, the quality and completeness of the database, which also includes information on occupations and land use, is very good. A disadvantage is that larger farmers and poor artisans (weavers and tailors often originated from the Catholic parts of nearby Westphalia) were slightly overrepresented in the Roman Catholic database, while farm workers were underrepresented (Paping and Collenteur 2004). In the 18th century, the demographic behaviour of the Groningen Roman Catholic minority (celibacy and age at marriage) does not seem to have differed a lot from that of the Protestant majority. Over time it was also in accordance with the general population development of the region.

At first, the problem of what social mobility can and can not show us about the gendered division of welfare and well-being in the past will be considered. Next, we will briefly go into the social structure scheme used. Then we switch to the importance of succession from father to son or daughter in the transfer of farms, but also of other positions. In the end the small role of family in these transfers will be related to the inheritance practices and the timing of the transfer of the inheritance.

Gender, Social Mobility, Welfare and Well-being

Pursuit of gender equality in the social-economic chances is one of the main drives of modern western society. The suggestion usually is that these chances differed enormously in the past. In a sense that is very true. Before 1900, the division of labour was nearly completely gendered in western societies and often (but not always) had more to do with customs than with sex related differences in capabilities. Some tasks were reserved for males and others for females, and there were just a few tasks that could be done by both sexes. This was both the case for household labour and for economically rewarded labour. Presumably, the division was more rigid in theory than in practice. A surplus of males or females in specific situations forced men and women to perform female and male tasks respectively for reasons of efficiency. For instance a widow with only daughters on a small farm would take over male tasks. Nevertheless, males and females had very different occupational prospects. A wide range of occupations were available for males, especially outside agriculture. The possibilities for females were far more limited, and these female occupations offered less economic rewards than comparable male occupations.

Gender differences resulted in a seemingly clear-cut division of male and female tasks after marriage. Males were the so-called providers, while females performed most of the "non-economic" (reproduction) and other non-market tasks within the household. It has to be taken into account that a lot of the non-market activities of females were not completely non-economic, as these activities in theory could also be performed by the market (cleaning, cooking, non-market production). The overwhelming prevalence of this family model is indeed suggested in a lot of census lists in which married males are stated to as having an occupation and most married females are reported as "without occupation". However, taking into account real life, these occupational references point more to prevailing ideology than they give a description of (economically rewarded) tasks performed, at least in the European countryside before 1900. Farmer and peasant wives had essential and specific tasks to perform. Labourers' wives did wage work in the summer half year and were in charge of small-scale gardening for self-provision; sometimes they did temporary proto-industrial activities such as spinning and knitting. Outside agriculture, it is a lot more difficult to generalise; the female share of economic activities seemed to have been smaller, except for proto-industry. Jobs generally called on specific capacities of the male provider (carpenter, schoolmaster) that females were not allowed to acquire. However, wives of small-scale industry and services self-employed males could for example be in charge of the shop or do supporting labour. Other possible economic activities of married females were again self-provisioning horticulture and proto-industrial activities. To conclude, before 1900 married females had a significant – though supposedly smaller – share in the economically rewarded activities of the household members. Their labour was usually closely related to the occupation of their husband.

Not only did married females participate in the economic work performed by the household, they also shared its rewards consisting in the availability of food, drinks, fuel, shelter, furniture, cloths and more luxury goods within the household. It was extremely difficult to prevent married women from taking advantage of some of those benefits (fuel, shelter, furniture). Presumably, they also received a part of the rest of the benefits, for instance as their "rightful" share, as the outcome of some kind of marital negotiations, or perhaps even for reasons of (male) social prestige (clothing).

One of the largest problems when studying the welfare of married women in the past is that it is nearly impossible to measure its level independent of that of their husbands. Occupational information on married females is extremely scarce, and if available, usually relates directly to the occupation of the husband. However, taking into account the previous discussion, this is not such a large problem. It is not necessary to measure the welfare level of married females independently of that of their husbands, because in practice these two were very closely related. The social-economic position of the husband can be considered a good proxy for the position of the wife, not only as an indicator of the kind of labour performed, but also of the social prestige and of the economic benefits accruing to married females.

The ability to consume – as measured by one's social economic position – is an indicator of material well-being. However, material well-being must not be confused with subjective notions of happiness or general well-being which are hard to measure objectively, even more so for the past. Well-being is a personal feeling inside an individual, which is nearly impossible to compare with the personal feelings of others. Economists consider (material) needs to be unlimited, and the more these needs are satisfied, the more utility accrues to an individual. However, this last statement is time and place bound as well as subjective. Rising consumption levels do not necessarily increase well-being, because of what Van Praag (2007) called the reference drift (the value attached to a specific consumption level falls if the consumption level of the reference group rises) and the preference drift (the value attached to a specific consumption level falls if one becomes used to it).

Nevertheless, other things being equal, one can assume (taking into account unlimited wants) that a higher material consumption level results in higher well-being than a lower one. Concluding, upward male and female social mobility then results in a higher well-being than downward mobility. This effect is even reinforced by the notion of the reference drift, which suggests that falling behind the reference group (the paternal social-economic position) as is usual in cases of downward social mobility causes a sharp fall in utility. Social mobility is also in a less material way connected to well-being, inasmuch as higher social mobility suggests more room for males and females to create a life of their own, independent of their social background. This sense of freedom can increase general well-being. A positive aspect is also that a higher social mobility will tend to redistribute people according to their capacities, which will also result in a general rise in well-being. However, it can also be argued that increasing (upward and downward) social mobility provokes a rising feeling of insecurity and a general fall in well-being.

Occupational information can be used to compare the position of different women, but it is of course not suitable for comparing gender-related differences between men's and women's socio-economic positions. In a gendered society perspectives and possibilities of males and females are usually based more on capabilities generally attributed to them than on personal qualities. Unfortunately, this gender-related discrepancy between capabilities and functionings (Robeyns 2007) is difficult to measure. We can observe a glimpse of the functioning of past people, but objectively we are barely aware of the relation of this functioning with specific capabilities and with personal intentions, which might have been even more important.

In every person's life, there are generally a few crucial "factors" which have a decisive impact on his or her fate. These factors include: (1) one's social background; (2) the kind of education one receives; (3) the marriage partner one chooses; (4) the start of one's professional career. Clearly, all of these factors are in someway or another interdependent and all greatly influence social position obtained later in life. Before the 20th century, the majority of people only received primary education or some even none at all. Much more important were the capabilities people developed during their teens and early twenties. Also the securing of a good position after marriage, when commonly couples started a consumption unit and a business of their own (a production unit) was of primary importance. To remain a live-in servant, a very usual phase in life for the poorer half of the juveniles in large parts of the countryside, was not an alternative (Schlumbohm 1994, 337–367; Paping 2005), while on the other hand the thought of settling down or staying in the parental home seemed to be very unattractive for most of the newly-wed, considering the number of nuclear households in Western Europe (Laslett 1972; Hajnal 1983; Verdon 1979).

The resources new couples used to obtain a position comprise: (1) savings of both bride and groom during their unmarried period; (2) parental inheritances and dowries of both bride and groom (and possible other inheritances); (3) working experiences of the groom and to a lesser extent of the bride; (4) financial credibility of the couple necessary to borrow funds for investment in house and firm. A newly-wed couple needed money to buy a house, workshop or farm, and the capabilities to successfully operate their farm, shop or business. If the female contribution to these resources is lower than the male's, there will be much more room for female than for male social mobility.

In theory, the new couple's household was a new independent economic unit. However, the example of the less "modern" village of Neckarhausen (Sabean 1990) shows that, even in such cases, the new couples could be tied to their still existing parental households, especially if most of their resources (land) originally belonged to these parental households, and their strategies were directed towards the succession of the next generation on the large family farm or towards slowly accumulating land during the family life cycle, as in the Kempen region in Belgium (Vanhaute 2004). Equal inheritances stimulated these kinds of strategies; however, they could be seriously hampered by the indivisibility of the larger farms, as for example in Belm in German Westphalia (Schlumbohm 1994, 54).

Social Structure and Social Mobility

The Groningen clay area in Northern Netherlands was characterised by a very specific social structure dating back to the 16th century. Due to specialisation some 40 percent of the rural inhabitants derived most of their revenues from non-agricultural activities. The agricultural sector consisted of landless labourers and of mostly quite wealthy farmers. Differences within the group of farmers were mostly due to the amount of land used. Only 10 percent of the land was owned by the users themselves; some 40 percent was in the hand of nobles, rich farmers and salesmen. Local and urban institutions, the provincial government, and patricians from the city of Groningen owned the other half. So 90 percent of the land was leased to the farmers, mostly on long terms according to a specific regional system called *beklemming*[3] which made it more difficult to evict farmers. Farmers were even allowed to sell their right to use the land; however they were prohibited to divide it. Population started to grow around 1750, and this growth accelerated after 1785. By 1830, more than half as much inhabitants were living in this region. Population growth was accompanied by a rapid increase in the proportion of farm worker families, while the number of farms remained quite stable. The share of the other groups remained constant (Paping 1995).

It is difficult to measure social status exactly with only information on occupations. Fortunately, we know the size of nearly all the farms, which allows us to breakdown this undifferentiated group of farmers into categories. About a quarter of the farms were between 5 and 15 hectares (category C), about a third between 15 and 30 hectares (category B), while some 40 percent were above 30 hectares (category A) (Paping 1995, 71). Because of the system of *beklemmingen* the right to use the land was priced in Groningen and also the larger the amount of land controlled the higher the necessary investments on livestock, equipment, buildings etc. Accordingly there was a strong relation between the amount of land used and the (gross) wealth of a household. Labourers can be split into two: a small group using 1 to 5 hectares (category D), and the majority having no significant amount of land at their disposal (category E). People whose primary occupation was not farming were also fitted into the classification

3 *Beklemmingen* refers to emphyteotic tenures.

presented in Table 1. This classification takes into account the necessary investments for specific jobs, using information from tax records and probate inventories.

Table 1. Social stratification of heads of households for the Groningen countryside (Ommelanden) in the 18th and first half of the 19th century

A	1. Large farmers (30 hectares and over), land owners, nobles. 2. Large merchants, higher officials, large factory owners; physicians, millers etc. controlling more than 5 hectares.
B	1. Medium-ranged farmers (15 to 30 hectares). 2. Medium-ranged merchants, large shopkeepers and inn-keepers, physicians, millers, small factory owners, medium-ranged officials, ship-captains; artisans and others controlling more than 3 hectares.
C	1. Small farmers (5 to 15 hectares). 2. Artisans with a workshop (bakers, smiths, cartwrights, glaziers, coppersmiths, shoemakers), small shopkeepers and inn-keepers, master of a barge, lower officials.
D	1. Crofters and farm labourers controlling 1 to 5 hectares, milkmen, gardeners. 2. Artisans without a real workshop (tailors, carpenters), weavers, peddlers, commission agents, carriers without land, police men.
E	1. Farm labourers. 2. Lower skilled subordinate workers in handicrafts and services; servants, paupers, soldiers.

Source: Groningen Roman Catholic Dataset. Social positions are measured about ten years after marriage.

Schluhmbohm (1994, 370–376) who used a four-class division found that in Belm in Westphalia, 76 percent of the females and 83 percent of the males marrying between 1771 and 1860 remained in the same class. Table 2 shows that, in 18th century Groningen Ommelanden, male and female Roman Catholics were much more mobile. If we do not take into account the 10 percent of people moving out of the research area, we have 1,660 cases left (males and females). 34 percent of these experienced downward social mobility (Table 3), while 20 percent managed to secure a higher position than their parents. This trend towards downward social mobility is not surprising, regarding the proletarianisation taking place from the middle of the 18th century onwards. The share of higher positions (A and B) connected with controlling large plots of land was falling, while the share of labourers (E) was increasing. The higher classes had more surviving children which reinforced this tendency towards downward mobility. Category A and B couples with offspring had an average of 2.9 children surviving till marriage or the age of 30. For groups D and E the average was 2.5.

Table 2. Social mobility of married Roman Catholics, males and females, born between 1721 and 1800 in the Groningen Ommelanden (percentages)

CHILDREN	PARENTS A Nobility, upper middle class and large farmers	 B Middle class and medium-ranged farmers	 C Lower middle class and small farmers	 D Poor artisans and crofters	 E Subordinate and unskilled labourers	 All
	%	%	%	%	%	%
A	53	16	3	2	1	15
B	23	24	12	3	3	13
C	10	28	33	19	12	21
D	3	14	20	45	24	22
E	4	11	17	20	54	20
Left the Ommelanden	6	7	15	12	6	10
Total (%)	20	18	23	24	16	100

Source: Groningen Roman Catholic Dataset. Social positions are measured about ten years after marriage.
Note: Number of males and females under observation: 1,838. Number of couples with off-spring: 771.

Continuity under the richest inhabitants was only limited. Nearly half of the people had to accept a lower position, mainly these were children of large farmers who themselves began a trade or managed only a mid-sized farm. The enormous fall from a large and wealthy farm or business to living on the edge of poverty (D and E) was experienced by 7 percent of their children. Poverty was not far away for anyone outside the noble class. However, it was not lack of chance which explained the high downward mobility of the children of the wealthy. Nearly a third of the people securing a position on the top, were of lower origin. Mainly these were children of medium-ranged farmers and better-off artisans and shop-keepers.

There were no large differences in social mobility between males and females in the Groningen Ommelanden. Females were only slightly more mobile, which tended to result in a marginally higher female risk of downward social mobility. The easiest ladder to upward mobility, namely marriages with partners from higher classes worked in nearly the same way for males and females. The occupations of a large part of the middle class outside agriculture were connected to skills of males (carpenters, smiths, weavers, tailors), and sons usually learned these skills as their father's apprentice. Consequently, sons were more likely to have the same occupation as their father, and were somewhat less mobile than females. However, even for males this was a very open society with more than half of them ending up in a different social position than their parents (Table 3).

Table 3. Rise in or fall in the number of social classes, Roman Catholic males and females born between 1721 and 1800 in the Groningen Ommelanden (percentages)

	+4	*+3*	*+2*	*+1*	*Equal*	*-1*	*-2*	*-3*	*-4*	*All*
Males	0	1	4	13	49	20	8	3	1	100
Females	0	1	3	16	43	22	11	2	1	100
Total	0	1	4	15	46	21	9	3	1	100

Source: Groningen Roman Catholic Dataset. Social positions are measured about ten years after marriage.
Note: Number of males and females under observation: 1,660.

Some simple correlations were made to explain the number of social levels in which individuals fell or rose. However, few meaningful relations were found. Change over time, gender and age at marriage proved not significant, as was the age at which the father or mother died. Only the number of surviving female children in the parental family had an impact on mobility, but only a very weak negative one (r=0.089; n=1,691), suggesting that having too many female children was somehow a burden for family perspectives, possibly because of lower female productive and income capacity.

Other factors than social background played an important role in the obtaining of social positions in the Groningen Ommelanden. Social positions were not at all secure from one generation to the next. It was possible to rise, but the risks of falling were much higher. Incompetence in this market-oriented society was heavily punished by a social fall. Under these circumstances the capabilities of both groom and bride were very important. Downward social mobility, as measured in this paper, can be blamed on the parents or on the children, because we measured the social position of each couple (parent or child) in the first ten years after marriage. Some of the downward mobility was a legacy of the parents' previous social fall; however, most of it was indeed the result of the inability of the sons and daughters to secure the same level as their father and mother. Of course, one must note that in the crucial years between the age of 12 and marriage, parental decisions, next to choices, behaviour and qualities of children played a mayor role in the acquiring of skills, funds, credibility and the social network, necessary to succeed in a market-oriented society.

One can argue that high social mobility based on personal achievements which leads individuals and couples to social positions better fitted for them, is beneficial for economic growth. It would go too far to say that in the Groningen clay area only capacities and skills counted; however, the region must have indeed benefited from certain tendencies towards a more efficient division of work between partners, taking into account not only inherited social resources, but also the personal qualities of both sexes.

Succession

In theory, most positions in the social hierarchy can be handed down to one's children, because farms, land, shops, workshops, ships and even subordinate positions can be passed on to them. Even a regular farm labour job could be handed over, and though this was presumably unusual, at least the labourer's house could be transferred. The large social mobility in the Groningen Ommelanden, however, does not point to an enormous preference for the transfer of property and position via succession from father to son (or even daughter). To illuminate this, Table 4 gives data on the transfer of farmsteads. There is not much difference between the figures for the Roman Catholics in the Groningen Ommelanden and for the parishes of Kloosterburen and Wierhuizen. Inasmuch as the Roman Catholics only formed one third of the population in these parishes, they indeed seem quite representative of the whole population.

Table 4. The transfer of farms in the Groningen Ommelanden and in the parishes of Kloosterburen and Wierhuizen, ca. 1710–ca. 1820 (percentages)

	Roman Catholic farmer couples marrying 1701–1780 (last farm only)	All transfers of farms in Kloosterburen and Wierhuizen 1721–1820
To daughter	13	13
To son	19	17
Widow remarrying	18	15
Widower remarrying	15	9
Inherited by other related persons	1	2
Sold	34	44
Total	100	100
Number under observation	340	184

Source: Groningen Roman Catholic Dataset; Database on the use of land in the eastern region, 1591–1830.

Goody (1973) calculated that about three quarter of the families with surviving children had sons who could succeed them. For instance, in 19th century Löhne in Westphalia two thirds of the successors were sons, and possibly even more important, inheritance was the usual way to transfer farmsteads (Fertig 2003). However, in the Groningen Ommelanden only a third of all the farms went to children, as much as 40 percent of these went to daughters, which made male succession less significant compared to elsewhere. Jan Benes and Aafke farmed 20 hectares of provincial land in Westerwijtwerd in Groningen in the beginning of the 18th century. Their children sold the farm and the lease in 1725 to their newly-wed sister Lutje Jans. She and her husband lived for a very long time, and in the end they were succeeded by their youngest daughter, who married afterwards in 1784 at the age of 35 with Hibbe Folkerts, originating from a farm of about the equal size. After her death in 1820, her son and daughter succeeded. The son was the only one to marry, in 1829, and he sold the family farm to strangers in 1847.

An interesting case is Wiske Aries, a 45-year-old single female, who was allowed to take over the large farm of Piloersema in 1778, a former small castle or *borg*, after the death of her mother, despite her having four older brothers, the eldest of whom was also unmarried. Only after Wiske's death, did her eldest brother buy the farm of 53 hectares from the other heirs. The others were not interested; because they had already acquired large farms, one by marrying an heiress, one by marrying a widow and one by buying a farm. Usually, however, daughters and sons were already married at the moment they took over the parental farm. About 9 percent of the males and 6 percent of the females reaching the age of 30 never married; however, in the three most wealthy social groups, female celibacy was lower (4 percent), suggesting these daughters were attractive partners, with a huge preference for marriage. Celibacy, however, did not play an important role in making it easier for a married brother to succeed than elsewhere. In some cases, an unmarried child like Wiske Aries took over the household while the married ones moved elsewhere.

Very important was that the surviving partner of a farmer couple very often remarried and stayed on the farm, just like in Belm in Germany (Schlumbohm 1994, 451–480). But, contrary to what occurred in Belm, Groningen Ommelanden children from a first marriage did not enjoy any special rights. The handing over of the farm to a new generation could in this way be delayed for decades. An extreme but illuminating example occurred in the village of Usquert. In 1732 Jacob Pieters Bos married Trinje Tewes, and they acquired the Papekop farm (41 hectares). He remarried Jakomina Klaasen in 1758. Jakomina remarried Jacob Jans Bos in 1766. Jacob remarried Trinje Willems in 1769. Trinje remarried Renje Berents Bos in 1786. Renje remarried Martha Freerks in 1798. In 1816 the Papekop farm was sold. Widows and widowers with a farm were, despite their age, attractive marriage partners in the Ommelanden. Table 4 suggests that widows were more inclined to remarry than widowers. However, this higher incidence has to be attributed to the higher number of widows (Table 5) caused by marital age differences, a lower mortality of women and a tendency to *post mortem* succession. There is absolutely no evidence that widows disposed rapidly of the farms after the death of their husband. On the contrary, they seemed to have been perfectly capable to run these – mostly large – farms using the labour of unmarried children or live-in servants, and they knew it.

Table 5. Civil status of heads of households of the 28 farms in Kloosterburen, 1800–1830 (percentages)

Couples	*Widows*	*Widowers*	*Unmarried*	*Total*
79	13	7	1	100

Source: Database on the use of land in the eastern region, 1591–1830.
Note: Number of years under observation: 760 years.

About a third of the farms were sold to non-relatives, mainly towards the end of the family life cycle. This was a very high proportion compared to Belm, where 38 percent of the farms went to males heirs, 13 percent to female heirs, 36 percent to remarrying widows and widowers, and only 13 percent to others between 1711 and 1860 (Schlumbohm 1994, 385). The same difference in the incidence of selling to non-relatives existed with Neckarhausen in Germany, where most of the plots of land were sold to relatives and not to strangers (Sabean 1990, 373–415). In their study of two parishes in southern Sweden between 1720 and 1840, Dribe and Lundh (2005) also find only a few non-relatives and a lot of sons and daughters succeeding after the death of a widow or widower. Succession practices in the Groningen Ommelanden seem to have been unusual for continental Europe; this has to be related to the region's very modern economy in the 18th century. Medieval law in rural Groningen strongly protected the continuity of land and the transfer of property through (male) lineages as we will see. Perhaps there were still cultural ideas about the necessity to hand over farms to the next male generation in the 18th century, but the practice had become completely different.

Several specific reasons can be discerned for selling farms. One is that the parents were old and wanted to retire. Derk Sjabbes (1697–1777) and Aaltje Klaasen (1708–1782) sold their 40 hectares farm in Zuidwolde to strangers in May 1770 for 4,000 guilders, despite the fact that they had three sons and two daughters. They bought a nice house in nearby Bedum. All their children had difficulties keeping the same social status as their parents. Some of them acquired smaller farms. One daughter married in February of the same year, and with her husband bought a 22 hectares farm in April 1770. Another reason to sell was that both parents died when the children were still too young to take over. However, when one of the marriage partners died young, the surviving partner usually remarried. More often, the farm was sold by the heirs after the death of the second parent, sometimes to one of the heirs, but also to strangers. In 1782, two married and three unmarried children of Freerk Jans and Martje Jacobs sold their parents' farm of 21 hectares in Westerklooster with 21 hectares to the unrelated and newly-wed Folkert Willems and Jeike Hindriks. In a lot of cases, no children at all survived to adulthood, sometimes relatives took over the farm, but most of the time the heirs sold it.

Folkert Willems is also a good illustration of another reason to sell a farm: debts. He had to sell his farm in 1807, having had serious money problems for some time. Possibly his inability to pay his children their maternal inheritance – which was compulsory at remarriage – had been the main reason why he had kept a concubine a few years before. Folkert ended his life as a farm labourer and seasonal butcher. Another important reason for selling farms was to get another one. Usually the new farm (bought or inherited) was bigger. There are also a few examples of farmers who sold their farm and bought a smaller one to escape bankruptcy.

Table 6 shows that, in all social groups, succession was not the prime way to obtain a social position. Not only the farms, but also shops, workshops and labourers houses were handed over to unrelated people. The reasons are the same as for farms. The parents were not ready to hand over their position when their children wanted to marry. Children were definitely not inclined to wait for it, and parents were not prepared to give up early. When the last of the parents died it was often too late for any of the children to return, inasmuch as that they already settled elsewhere in a definitive way.

Family successions, however, were more important than Table 6 seems to suggest. Just one of the two partners of a couple had to bring in a parental position. Nevertheless, nearly three quarters of the couples did not take over one of the parental households. Children's succession was most common among rich farmers (group A) and among poor weavers and tailors in group D. In the last category, it was mostly males who followed in the footsteps of their father, a consequence of gender norms precluding the transfer of handicraft skills to girls. In conclusion, 18 percent of the males, but only 9 percent of the females were able to take over the parental household, sometime before or after marriage. This difference more than explains the 6 percent difference in social mobility between males and females.

Table 6. Sons and daughters of Groningen Ommelanden Roman Catholics (born 1721–1800) taking over the household of parents or other relatives as heirs before or within ten years of marriage, according to social categories (percentages and numbers)

	Sons %	*N*	*Daughters* %	*N*
A. Nobility, upper middle class and large farmers	22	185	14	191
B. Middle middle class and medium-ranged farmers	14	157	8	171
C. Lower middle class and small farmers	17	168	4	238
D. Poor artisans and crofters	21	204	11	224
E. Subordinate and unskilled labourers	11	122	6	162
All	18	836	9	986

Source: Groningen Roman Catholic Dataset.
Note: Number of sons and daughters under observation: 1822.

Inheritances: Rules and Reality

Females were only slightly more socially mobile, which means that the social position of females from generation to generation was nearly as stable as that of males. Partly, these small differences can be explained by the legal customs of the Groningen clay area. In the Groningen countryside, the old medieval law still in force stated that a son ought to receive twice as much of the real estate as a daughter. However, the practice had become much different in the 17th and changed even more in the 18th century. A lot of marriage contracts were concluded between the more prosperous inhabitants of the Groningen Ommelanden. The bride and groom nearly always decided at marriage to give their future sons and daughters equal rights *(gelijke sibbe),*[4] which meant that each of them would inherit a share of real estate and movables. The same provision can be found in last wills. Even if there was not a marriage contract, the equal division of inheritances between sons and daughters (or more distant female and male relatives) was the ordinary practice. The value of the whole

4 *Gelijke sibbe* means "equal in all rights".

inheritance (farmstead, the right to lease the land, cattle, equipment, furniture and financial assets) was calculated. If one child took over the parental estate, he or she had to buy out the other siblings. Equal division between sons and daughters was also usual in the other parts of the wealthy Dutch coastal area (for instance Hoppenbrouwers 1992; Van Cruyningen 2000). Only some of the Groningen nobles persisted in the unequal division of inheritances, which seemed to have been a strategy to avoid impoverishment of the family in case of too many children. The system of equal inheritances combined with impartibility of the farmsteads can also be found in large parts of France, Spain, Italy and Belgium (Thirsk 1976). In the less modern eastern parts of the Netherlands the (usually male) successor was strongly favoured at the expense of other heirs (De Haan 1994).

Around the age of 25 (sometimes even at 20) orphaned boys and girls received *veniam aetatis*,[5] which meant that they could act independently. Unmarried females had just the same rights as males. However, if women married, they came under the guardianship of their husband. Married women were not deemed capable of alienating their own property without the consent of their husband. However, in practice the opposite was also the case. If married men transferred property or borrowed money, their wife was usually present, and if she was not, it was explicitly stated that he also acted on her behalf. Unless stated otherwise in a marriage contract, all possessions were co-owned by the bride and groom.

Widowed women and men could act nearly independently, because they were the guardians *(legitimi tutrix)* of their adolescent children. If sons and daughters were adult, they had (as heirs of their deceased father or mother) to consent to alienation of property. In case one of the parents remarried, three male guardians were legally appointed, ideally one from the paternal family, one from the maternal family and an external one (usually a neighbour). Unless otherwise stated in the marriage contract, the children received half the value of their parents' estates to be paid to them (or better their guardians) when they were 18 years old. At the age of 18 the children were usually – although not legally – seen as economically independent of their parents, which also meant that they were able to save money from their wages (Paping 2004). Usually the remaining parent

5 They received "rights of majority", or "emancipation".

borrowed the money of the inheritance from the guardians after the children had become 18.

If the surviving parent did not remarry, he or she usually had the usufruct of the heir's share. The couple's estate was divided only after the death of the second parent. If we take the ideal family for the transfer of property as consisting of one or two children, then 51 percent of the Roman Catholic families with off-spring in the Ommelanden (N=771) fit into this model. However, in 49 percent of the families, the inheritance had to be divided into at least three portions: 21 percent in three, 13 percent in four and the rest in even more parts. In one quarter of these cases there were only daughters, a figure which partly but not completely explains that a third of the succeeding children were daughters. We have already seen that even when sons were available, daughters could succeed. There are no reasons to believe that patterns differed for the Protestant majority.

From the point of view of the children, the extent of division of the inheritances was much more negative: 11 percent were the only surviving children, 17 percent had to divide the inheritance in two, 24 percent in three, 19 percent in four, 16 percent in five parts, and the remaining 13 percent in six or more parts. So, for the majority of the children the parental inheritance (if any) was too low to secure the same position as the parents had. We already mentioned that only the number of daughters had a small detrimental effect on the social mobility of the children in a family. For the rest, the number of siblings had no statistically significant effect on social mobility chances. This suggests that the actual size of the parental inheritance was not that important for social success or failure. Even for farmers the number of siblings – one, two, three or more – proved to be not important for the chances of social success, only the perspectives of the few farmer children without brothers and sisters were more positive. The insignificance of the size of the parental inheritance is remarkable, taking into account that large farms were bought and sold for huge amounts of money. Nevertheless, much effort was made to divide the inheritance as equally as possible. Possessions were inventoried and valued as, for example, in Neckarhausen (Sabean 1990, 193–198, 249–256).

Money was important. However, if one did not have it, one borrowed it. Nearly every new couple of farmers, merchants, or substantial artisans had to turn to this strategy to finance their farmstead, shop, business or house, which was made possible by a well functioning credit system. Of course the availability of own capital eased the obtaining of extra loans, but the social network, the accompanying financial credibility and personal capacities did too. The direct availability of inherited capital can not have been too important as two thirds of the Roman Catholics received their complete inheritance at the age of 30 year or even a lot older, while the median age at first marriage was about 28 for males and 25 for females. Most people had still one or even both parents at marriage.

It has been suggested that the high age at marriage in Western Europe has something to do with people waiting for an opening – the so-called niche-hypothesis – or having the possibility to create a new position (Hofstee 1954; Hajnal 1965; for critical notes: Van Poppel 1992; Fertig 2005; Zeitlhofer 2003). Clearly, in the Groningen Ommelanden couples usually did not wait for the death of their parents to marry and to be able to take over their position or to use the inheritance in cash to ease the obtaining of a position elsewhere. There was nearly no relation between marriage dates and the death of the last parent. It is thus not surprising that direct succession from one generation to the next was of limited importance. Parents were not prepared to give up their farm or shop if they were able to keep them, and until their seventies most of them were. Even if they lost capacities to work physically, they could hire unmarried servants to do the job, so retirement was unnecessary and unattractive. On the other hand, most married children were not inclined to stay for a long period in the parental household, waiting for an event (the death of the last parent) which still could take a long time. Only a minority remained at the parental home, to take it over in due time, so it is not appropriate to speak of a stem-family system as for instance in the highlands of South-East Norway or the Pyrenean valleys (Fauve-Chamoux 2006).

The result of the comparatively low incidence of succession was that the buying of an establishment (farm, workshop, house) became the most attractive solution for newly-weds in the Ommelanden. The availability of inheritances, dowries and parental loans to both bride and groom were important to establish such a good position. However, taking high social mobility into account, personal capabilities (skills, qualities and credibility) of the two marriage partners not directly related to social background were just as important, and a factor far more relevant than in less mobile societies.

Conclusion

In the Groningen Ommelanden equal inheritance practices were combined with the indivisibility of farm holdings, workshops and houses. In this modern market-oriented society, parental succession was remarkably unimportant. Succession by a child was just one of the options to transfer farms and other positions. Also, differences in the financial treatment of sons and daughters were comparatively small. However, about twice as many sons as daughters were able to succeed their parents, partly because of the gendered transfer of some specific job capabilities, but also because of a slight but by no way exclusive preference for a male successor. Low succession rates resulted in an open society with high intergenerational social mobility. This high mobility was partly triggered by the discrepancy between the moment of marrying and the moment children received the parental inheritance. As a result most newly-wed couples had to secure a position on their own as cohabitation with parents was generally not preferred. Both male and female resources must have been of great importance in this process of securing a position. Next to social background, the personal capabilities of both males and females were decisive in the quest for a good position as the near equality of male and female social mobility suggests. In this modern money economy, social background alone could not protect people from social failure due to their own incompetence. There was always the threat of downward social mobility.

The openness of society and the near equality of the sexes in the transfer of material resources (but still not of labour capabilities) was presumably closely related to the wealth and relatively modern economic and social structure of the Groningen Ommelanden, which can be seen as a good example of 18th and 19th century modern capitalistic European regions. However, the countryside of most of continental Europe had quite different characteristics. Further research is necessary to compare these results with more traditional regions. Questions to be addressed more extensively are: was social mobility indeed considerably lower in more traditional and less capitalistic parts of the countryside? Were succession and gender more important elsewhere, while personal qualities unrelated to social background were less? Furthermore, one can ask whether the disadvantage of the loss of security, because of the growing importance of market forces in the lives of people, is compensated by the growing chances people have, and by the resulting overall higher level of economic welfare. It can indeed be argued that a general movement in the direction of modern social-economic relations – as we already find in the Groningen clay area in the 18th century – in which not only social background and gender, but also other more personal capabilities explain social and economic chances, belongs to the core of the explanation of the economic success of Western society in the last centuries.

References

DE HAAN, Henk, 1994, *In the Shadow of the Tree. Kinship, Property and Inheritance among Farm Families*, Amsterdam, Het Spinhuis.

DRIBE, Martin and LUNDH, Christer, 2005, "Gender aspects of inheritance strategies and land transmission in rural Scania, Sweden, 1720–1840", *The History of the Family*, 10, 3, pp. 293–308.

FAUVE-CHAMOUX, Antoinette, 2006, "Family reproduction and stem-family system: From Pyrenean valleys to Norwegian farms", *The History of the Family*, 11, 3, pp. 171–184.

FERRER ALOS, Llorenç, 2005, "When there was no male heir: the transfer of wealth through women in Catalonia (the pubilla)", *Continuity and Change*, 20, 1, pp. 27–52.

FERTIG, Christine, 2003, "Hofübergabe im Westfalen des 19. Jahrhunderts: Wendepunkt des bäuerlichen Familienzyklus?", in Christophe DUHAMELLE and Jürgen SCHLUMBOHM (eds), *Eheschliessungen im Europa des 18. and 19. Jahrhunderts*, Göttingen, Vandenhoeck and Ruprecht, pp. 65–92.

FERTIG, George, 2005, "The Hajnal hypothesis before Hajnal", in Theo ENGELEN and Arthur P. WOLF (eds), *Marriage and the Family in Eurasia. Perspectives on the Hajnal Hypothesis*, Amsterdam, Aksant, pp. 37–48.

GOODY, Jack, 1973, "Strategies of Heirship", *Comparative Studies in Society and History*, 15, pp. 3–20.

HAJNAL, John, 1965, "European marriage in perspective", in David V. GLASS and David E. C. EVERSLEY (eds), *Population in History. Essays in Historical Demography*, London, Arnold, pp. 101–143.

–, 1983, "Two kinds of pre-industrial household formation system", in Richard WALL, Jean ROBIN and Peter LASLETT (eds), *Family Forms in Historic Europe*, Cambridge, Cambridge University Press, pp. 65–104.

HOFSTEE, Evert W., 1954, "Regionale verscheidenheid in de ontwikkeling van het aantal geboorten in Nederland in de tweede helft van de negentiende eeuw", *Akademiedagen*, 7, pp. 59–106.

HOPPENBROUWERS, Peter C.M., 1992, *Een Middeleeuwse samenleving. Het Land van Heusden (ca. 1360 – ca. 1515)*, Wageningen, A.A.G. Bijdragen 32.

LASLETT, Peter, 1972, "Introduction: the history of the family", in Peter LASLETT and Richard WALL (eds), *Household and Family in Past Time*, Cambridge, Cambridge University Press, pp. 1–89.

MORING, Beatrice, "The transmission of well-being, marriage and inheritance – Siblings and family property in 18th and 19th century Finland and Sweden", Paper presented in Minho, April 2007 (COST Action A34) [In the present volume].

PAPING, Richard, 1995, *"Voor een handvol stuivers". Werken, verdienen en besteden: de levensstandaard van boeren, arbeiders en middenstanders op de Groninger klei, 1770–1860*, Groningen, Regio Projekt/NAHI.

–, 2004, "Family strategies concerning migration and occupations in a market-oriented agricultural economy", *The History of the Family*, 9, 2, pp. 159–191.

–, 2005, "Oferta y demanda de criados rurales en Holanda, 1760–1920. El caso de Groningen", *Historia Agraria. Revista de agricultura e historia rural*, 35, pp. 115–142.

PAPING, Richard and COLLENTEUR, Geurt, 2004, "Population growth and social structure in a market-oriented agricultural economy in the Netherlands 1750–1820", *Obradoiro de Historia Moderna*, 13, pp. 75–99.

POZSGAI, Peter, "The transmission of land and marriage strategies in a Hungarian region (Torna county) in the 19th century", Paper presented in Minho, April 2007 (COST Action A34).

ROBEYNS, Ingrid, 2007, "When will society be gender just?", in Jude BROWN (ed.), *The future of Gender*, Cambridge, Cambridge University Press, pp. 54–74.

SABEAN, David W., 1990, *Property, Production, and Family in Neckarhausen, 1700–1870*, Cambridge, Cambridge University Press.

SCHLUMBOHM, Jürgen, 1994, *Lebensläufe, Familien, Höfe; Die Bauern und Heuerleute des Osnabrückischen Kirchspiels Belm in proto-industrieller Zeit, 1650–1860*, Göttingen, Vandenhoeck and Ruprecht.

THIRSK, Joan, 1976, "The European debate on customs of inheritance, 1500–1700", in Jack GOODY, Joan THIRSK and Edward P. THOMPSON (eds), *Family and Inheritance. Rural Society in Western Europe 1200–1800*, Cambridge, Cambridge University Press, pp. 177–191.

VAN CRUYNINGEN, Piet J., 2000, *Behoudend maar buigzaam. Boeren in West-Zeeuws-Vlaanderen 1650–1850*, Wageningen, A.A.G. Bijdragen 40.

VANHAUTE, Eric, 2004, "Structure and strategy. Two rural communities in the Kempen region of Belgium, 1850–1910", *The History of the Family. An International Quarterly*, 9, 2, pp. 193–220.

VAN POPPEL, Frans, 1992, *Trouwen in Nederland. Een historisch-demografische studie van de 19e en vroeg-20e eeuw*, Wageningen, A.A.G. Bijdragen 33.

VAN PRAAG, Bernard M. S., 2007, "Perspectives from the Happiness Literature and the Role of New Instruments for Policy Analysis", *CESifo Economic Studies*, 53, pp. 42-68.

VERDON, Michel, 1979, "The Stem Family: Toward a General Theory", *Journal of Interdisciplinary History*, 10, 1, pp. 87–105.

ZEITLHOFER, Hermann, 2003, "Die 'eisernen Ketten' der Heirat. Eine Diskussion des Modells der 'ökonomischen Nischen' am Beispiel der südböhmischen Pfarre Kaplicky, 1640–1840", in Christophe DUHAMELLE and Jürgen SCHLUMBOHM (eds), *Eheschliessungen im Europa des 18. and 19. Jahrhunderts*, Göttingen, Vandenhoeck and Ruprecht, pp. 35–63.

PART III

FEMALE LIFE COURSE AND WELL-BEING OUTSIDE MARRIAGE

Children Born out of Wedlock. Legal Rights and Social Reforms in Norway from the 17th Century to the Present

Kari TELSTE

The welfare of a child born out of wedlock is dependent on the ability and willingness of its mother, its father, and of the state to provide care and support. The bringing up of children has throughout Norwegian history been regarded as the responsibility of the parents. Until well into the 19th century, public authorities interfered in limited and special circumstances only. One particular circumstance that was continually discussed from the middle of the 18th century onwards was the maintenance of illegitimate children. It was taken for granted that unmarried mothers had to bear the economic – and social – burden of bringing up their children. The problem was, however, how to make the alleged fathers contribute to the subsistence of their children.

The purpose of this study is to outline the legal changes of the rights of children born out of wedlock from the 17th century to the present. The main focus will be on the relationship between these children and their fathers. I aim to show how social reforms over the centuries have affected the living conditions of such children, by outlining legislative changes such as the right to maintenance and inheritance from the alleged father and the introduction of social benefits. Social reforms may indicate how the obligations of parents and the state respectively are viewed culturally and how this has changed over the centuries.

A substantial amount of historical research on unmarried mothers and illegitimacy[1] has been conducted since the 1970s in both Scandinavia and internationally. Less attention has been given to the duties and responsibilities of alleged fathers. In this article, I therefore wish to trace the legal obligations of fathers as represented in sources such as laws and regulations, judicial statements and court cases. The behaviour and attitude of an

1 For an overview and discussion of historical research on illegitimacy, see Bull 2006.

ideal father will be compared with what these fathers actually did, as can be deduced from recorded maintenance payment conflicts.[2]

The Obligations of Fatherhood

Until the second half of the 18th century, fathers of illegitimate children had no legal duty to contribute to the subsistence of their children. Fathering a child out of wedlock still constituted certain obligations. For a start, the law would put considerable pressure on a man to marry the child's mother. An ordinance in 1617 introduced punishment for "loose living". Couples who had a child out of wedlock were heavily fined, but the fines were considerably reduced if they got married.[3] Moreover, the pregnant girl, her family and the neighbourhood would put pressure on the man to enter marriage. Thus, he was faced not only with legal consequences, but also with social and cultural expectations to marry.

My own studies, based on 17th and 18th century sources, indicate that unmarried couples fined for loose living often were in the process of marrying (Telste 1993a; 2000). When summoned to court, they would argue that they had planned to marry, but unfortunate circumstances had prevented their marriage. One circumstance often referred to was poverty; frequently it turned out that the man could not support a family. Some of these couples would postpone their wedding indefinitely, while others eventually would marry.

Another indication supporting the idea that pregnancy put pressure on the man to marry is the high rate of pregnant brides and the low rates of illegitimacy in the 17th and early 18th century. In several districts in Norway two thirds of the brides were pregnant or had already given birth to their first child (Sogner 1978; Telste 1993a, 72ff; Bull 2006, 12ff, 26).

2 The empirical basis of this article are sources studied in my doctoral thesis on breach of promise in the period 1700–1900 (Telste 2000), and my master thesis on control of sexuality in the 17th century (Telste 1993a). For developments from the end of the 19th century to the present, I have used other historical and sociological studies on the development of the welfare state and the conditions of unmarried mothers.

3 Ordinance on loose living of 12 October 1617.

An average illegitimacy rate of about 3 percent in the 17th century, rising to 6–9 percent in the second half of the 18th century, depending on regional variations, conforms to a more general European pattern (Sogner 2003a, 50; Bull 2006). Moreover, in contrast to the 19th century, most single mothers gave birth to one child only (Telste 2000, 345ff). Unless the girl had a reputation of being loose, an illegitimate child could be regarded as a lapse from virtue, the result of unfortunate circumstances or a breach of promise.

The legislation concerning breach of promise is particularly illuminative of the obligations facing a man who fathered a child out of wedlock. Since the Middle Ages Norwegian law had secured a well-reputed girl who had been seduced a right to claim marriage or reparation for the violation of her honour.[4] Cases that were tried locally or in the ecclesiastical courts in the 17th and the early 18th century indicate that pregnancy constituted a promise: a man had to honour his word (Telste 1993a; 2000; 2002). While poverty could explain why marriage had to be put off, the only other legitimate course of action to pursue if a man did not want to marry, was to question the paternity of the child. From the woman's point of view this was extremely offending, a violation of honour and an accusation of being morally loose. No man could be expected to honour a promise or pay reparation to a girl who had such a reputation. The woman therefore had no choice but to defend herself. As a rule, men failed to prove that they had reason to doubt the paternity and were generally sentenced to marry or to pay reparation.[5] This outcome confirms the cultural expectations at play. More importantly, as far as the child was concerned, paternity was acknowledged.

The majority of alleged fathers, however, did not question the paternity and they appear to have recognised their children.[6] But what did acknowl-

4 The right to claim damages was stated in King Christian 4's Norske Lovbog (Norwegian Law book) of 1604 that was mainly based on King Magnus Lagabøtes Law from 1276. King Frederik 2's ordinance on marriage given in 1589 and Norwegian Law of 1687, 6-13-4 and 4, contained similar provisions on the "violation of virgins". These provisions were modified by an ordinance in 1734, see note 13 below.

5 In the period 1731–1740, 66 cases of breach of promise were tried in the ecclesiastical court in Christiania. In one case only, the court found that the man had reason to dispute paternity (Telste 2000).

6 In the period 1652–1710, 502 couples were accused of loose living in two districts in eastern Norway. Only 32 alleged fathers – 6.4 per cent – questioned paternity (Telste 1993a).

edgement of paternity actually mean? There had until now been no legal duty to pay maintenance, but did that imply that these fathers had no duty to care for the upbringing of their illegitimate children?

What is in a Name?

"What's in a name?" asks Juliet in Shakespeare's tragedy *Romeo and Juliet*. The answer is that everything is in a name. The name is a sign of identity, of family background and social belonging. The christening was therefore a decisive moment of identification in the life of an infant. The vicar would duly record whether the child was legitimate or illegitimate and who its parents were. A child born out of wedlock faced the risk that its paternity would be denied, and its mother left to her own devices.

Until the middle of the 19th century most people in the Scandinavian countries were called by their first name and a patronymic e.g. Ole Pedersen or Mari Olsdatter. The patronymic confirmed that Ole was the son of Peder, and Mari the daughter of Ole, thus deciding the child's identity and place in the world. We know very little about the social and cultural standing of an illegitimate child whose paternity was uncertain or denied. As I will point to below, the right of an illegitimate child to assume the name of its father became a controversial issue at the end of the 19th century, at a time when the patronymic had lost ground to the surname.

Judging from church registers the name of the father was almost always registered. Court records give a slightly different picture. A handful of men would at any time dispute paternity. The question is whether men would bother to do this if they had no duties towards their children. But the question could also be posed the other way round: when most alleged fathers acknowledged paternity, could this be an indication that they did not care? Only a few traces remain as to the obligations of fatherhood prior to the introduction of maintenance payment.

One interesting question is whether the right of a seduced woman to claim reparation was thought to include maintenance for the child. The law makes no mention of the child, however, the reparation was meant to restore the honour of its mother. In one case only, I have found an explicit reference to maintenance. In 1716 a man was sentenced to pay the mother of his child a lump sum of money "in satisfaction for the violation of her honour and for the upbringing of the child they have begotten" (Telste 2002). This single example hardly proves that acknowledging paternity included the duty to support the child. There are indications, however, that unmarried mothers had certain expectations in this respect. When sentenced to pay fines for loose living in 1703, one girl remarked that she had sent a message to the father of her child: "If he would not help her and give her something for the child, she had let him know that she would leave it into his care" (cited in Telste 1993a, 107).

A Monsieur Christen Christensen Baare, apparently a man of high standing, made in 1727 a public statement that indicated a father's duties. Apparently he had seduced his mother's maid and he now wanted to acknowledge his child as legitimate. He declared that he had "brought up and provided for his son Anders Christensen, as is the duty of a father to his child and his son". Moreover, he had rented a place where the child's mother could give birth, had allowed her to stay in his house while breast-feeding the child, and finally had arranged for her marriage to a suitable man (Telste 2000, 164). His statement gives a unique glimpse into the ideals of fatherhood. A man had a duty to care for and secure the future of an illegitimate child and even for its mother.

There is evidence that a few men, like Monsieur Christen Christensen Baare, would eventually adopt their illegitimate children. Another way out that occasionally comes to light over the centuries was secretly paying another man to assume paternity and to marry the child's mother. This can be understood as a strategy to escape the obligations of paternity. On the other hand, the real father may not have wanted to give the child his name, but at least he wanted to secure his/her future.

To the child it was essential to be born in wedlock. The marriage of his/her mother, whether to his own father or to another man assuming paternity, had the power of transforming him/her from illegitimate to legitimate. This was also the case if the parents married some time after his birth. As the historian Sølvi Sogner has pointed out, when a legal provision regarding the legitimacy status of children was proclaimed in 1851, it led to a change in the behaviour of couples in the process of marrying. From then on, only children born after the marriage of their parents were seen as legitimate. In the 1850s the first born was increasingly born after the wedding and not before. The explanation could be that couples took into consideration the strictness of the new law:

> Couples who intended to marry anyway – and they were by far the most numerous – speeded up marriage celebrations. Bridal pregnancy may have been just as common as before, but pre-martial births became far rarer (Sogner 2003b, 218–219).

Why was it so important to be registered as legitimate? A legitimate child had, in contrast to an illegitimate child, the right to inherit both parents. With limited or no access to property and resources and in an inferior social position, a son or daughter of an unmarried mother could hardly expect to make an advantageous marriage (Bull 2006). Moreover, boys born out of wedlock found that certain occupations were closed to them. All over Europe, it was customary to exclude them from the trades. During the 17th century the king of Denmark-Norway repeatedly decreed that this exclusion was forbidden. Everyone was to have the opportunity to earn a living through honest work (Grevenor 1936, 42, 55, 59–60). Apparently, the king and the guilds differed over the understanding of honesty. Honesty was fundamental to artisans of all trades, and their opposition to the royal decrees may indicate a more general attitude towards illegitimate children as dishonest *per se*.

Men of means could easily arrange for the care of their children, either openly or in secret, and secure both their legitimacy and future prospects. The majority of fathers, however, were not in the same position. As we have seen, some men would be too poor to marry. How likely was it that they would be able to provide for their children, not to mention to find the means to secure the marriage of the mother? Also, as long as parents of illegitimate children were liable to pay fines, they risked that the bailiff would confiscate what small means they had. The fines due to the king were collected at the cost of maintaining the child.

Heartless Fathers? Making Fathers pay Maintenance

Men may ideally have had a duty to care for their illegitimate children, but there is little evidence to tell whether they actually did fulfil their obligations. What we do know is that most unmarried mothers lived in poverty, and that the responsibility for bringing up the child was generally left to them. In one bailiff's accounts at the end of the 17th century, he repeatedly noted that there were no fines to collect:

> she walks about with the infant in her arms begging for food (cited in Telste 1993a, 98ff).

The responsibility to support unwed mothers and their infants was thus left to the local community. Unmarried women mostly served as maids. A pregnant maid would immediately be turned out of service, thus losing her means of support. After the birth of her child, she might re-enter service, provided she could leave her child either with her own family or with strangers. Most probably unmarried mothers, if reduced to begging, were not popular in the local community. A system of poor relief was introduced in the 1730s, discriminating between the worthy and the unworthy poor. While the old, sick and disabled qualified for poor relief, the healthy and able-bodied were supposed to find work. Those who carried on a life of begging and vagrancy risked confinement in the work-house (Slyngstad 1994, 11ff). Since they were young and mostly fit to work, unmarried mothers were expected to make arrangements for the child in order to earn a living. Sometimes the problem was solved naturally. Infant mortality rates were generally high, especially for illegitimate children (Sogner 2003a, 58–59).

In the 18th century there was a growing awareness of the precarious situation of unmarried mothers and their children. Laws that imposed a duty on alleged fathers to pay maintenance were called for. In 1763, an ordinance on maintenance was proclaimed, stating that fathers should take care of the upbringing of their illegitimate children, and contribute with half the costs of their necessary maintenance until the child was ten years old (Sogner 2003a).[7] By this decree both parents were in principle made responsible for supporting their child. The idea was basically to prevent unmarried mothers and their children from becoming a burden on the poor relief authorities (Seip 1984, 52). This was also the case when punishment for loose living was finally abolished in 1812 (Telste 2000, 264–265). The king decreed that unwed parents would no longer be liable to pay fines, but in return had a duty "according to the law of Nature and the law of the

7 Ordinance on maintenance of 14 December 1763.

King" to care for their illegitimate children.[8] Finally, the "king" had understood that unmarried couples in poor conditions, who were forced to pay fines, were prevented from fulfilling their duty to maintain their children.

The enforcement of this duty was directed towards the father. In 1794, an ordinance once again emphasised the duty to pay maintenance. Apparently it was taken more or less for granted that the alleged fathers would try to escape this burden. The ordinance claimed that they were apt to shirk from the duty to care for their children and that such behaviour was in violation of Nature. These fathers were accused of acting in an ungodly and inhuman way, and of being so heartless that they would close "their ears to the voice of Nature", thus "escaping the just command of the law".[9] Fathers who failed to fulfil their duties were to be made to abide by it. They were to be imprisoned in order to earn the outstanding amounts by hard labour (Seip 1984, 189).

Did the representation of the heartless father have any root in reality? Conflicts over maintenance payment do indicate a reluctance of a few men to support their illegitimate children, but the general impression is that few conflicts ended in court.[10] This does not, however, prove that most fathers willingly contributed to the bringing up of their children.

The legal provisions for maintenance in 1763 and 1794, followed up by laws in 1821 and 1892, repeatedly stressed that the alleged father had a duty to contribute with half of the cost of bringing up the child. In 1821 the duty to pay maintenance was extended until the child was 15 years old (Seip 1984, 193, 188). These provisions also gave unmarried mothers a right to claim help from the public authorities to recover the maintenance payment, but the initiative was in reality left to them.[11] Countrywide studies made in the second half of the 19th century show that a minority –

8 Decree from the King's council on the abolishment of fines for fornication of 12 June 1812.

9 Ordinance on maintenance of 30 May 1794.

10 My qualitative study of court records from three Norwegian districts for two periods in the 19th century indicates that the number of paternity conflicts generally was low: in the period 1810–1819 a total of 29 cases were brought before the boards of arbitration, while 12 cases were tried in court in 1880–84 and 1890–94 (Telste 2000, 34). I do not, however, have the total number of illegitimate children born in these districts in these periods. Other sources may therefore give a more complete picture (Torstensen 1985).

11 In practice this meant that unmarried mothers had to sue the putative father in court, and from 1797 summon him to the newly established boards of arbitration.

only 34 percent of unmarried mothers – turned to the authorities for help. Only when a mother became a burden on the poor relief system, would the authorities take action against the father (Torstensen 1985, 83ff). Being dependent on poor relief meant existing on a minimum of subsistence, and was regarded as a shame. The result was that the majority of unmarried mothers laboured hard to support themselves and their children, taking on what casual work they could find.[12] They would pride themselves that they were able to earn a living by "their own hard work", and would often remark that they had to do without any support from the father whatsoever (Telste 1998).

Why did fathers so easily escape their duties? One possible explanation could be a change in the mentality regarding their sexual responsibilities. A seduction had led to legal, social and moral obligations, but in 1734 an ordinance modified the rules that had previously regulated breach of promise. The definition of a promise was changed from being the sexual act itself to become words uttered in public.[13] This change meant that it became impossible for most pregnant girls to prove a promise, as men from then on were expected to honour a promise made in public only (Telste 2000, 177ff; 1993b). A decent girl seduced by promises exchanged in secret, could no longer define herself as honourable. At a stroke she was turned into a woman of low moral, a woman of easy virtue who had forfeited her right to both marriage and reparation.

A change in mentality does not occur overnight, but is part of longer historical processes. The ordinance of 1617, introducing punishment for loose living, had expressively defined premarital sexual relationships as loose. Over the centuries, unmarried mothers that were fined accordingly were repeatedly characterised as "loose women". How did this definition of the mother affect the duties of fathers? There is no definite answer, but there is a possibility that men would be reluctant to assume responsibility for children that were the result of a relationship that they, with the help of the authorities, were able to define as loose.

Another possible explanation is more pragmatic. During the 19th century social and economic developments may have made it more difficult

12 Court records give an insight into the plight of unmarried mothers and how they earned a living, when they were accused of vagrancy. Single women were supposed to serve as maids, but in the 19th century, an increasing number of unmarried mothers had to find alternative sources of income.

13 Ordinance on "conception, and the resulting claim of marriage" of 5 March 1734.

to trace fathers of illegitimate children. As an industrialised society developed, men were constantly on the move in search of better paid work. Having sexual relations characterised by instability, many men may have regarded them as no more than a short adventure, while their girlfriends may have hoped for marriage. Many a girl would be left behind, while her boyfriend moved on to work in a new place, never to return to help her support their child (Telste 1998).

Call for Reforms

The lack of support either from the father or the poor law authorities had a price. In the second half of the 19th century there was a renewed concern for the plight of unmarried mothers and their children. With the exception of Denmark, the mortality rates for illegitimate children in Norway were higher than in any other European country (Seip 1984, 196). A statistical study published in 1907 proved that the risk of dying in infancy was twice as high for illegitimate as for legitimate children, and the risk increased in the period 1887–1907 (Sogner 2003a, 179–180).[14]

These mortality rates illustrate unmarried mothers' dilemma: the difficulty of combining wage labour with child care. Their time consuming struggle to earn a living left them with little or no alternative but to leave their children in the care of foster mothers (Sogner 2003a, 180). To a factory girl, the costs of care amounted to about 18–19 percent of her average annual income, while a maid would have to pay almost all her income (Torstensen 1985, 101). Foster mothers were popularly called "angel makers", referring to the high death rate of children in their care (Sogner 2003a, 180). According to one doctor's report, he had more than once found children suffering "a slow death of hunger and neglect" (cited in Seip 1984, 192). To keep costs down foster mothers would feed the children artificial nutrition, such as water mixed with sugar. Scandals disclosed that foster mothers deliberately turned children into "angels", in

14 In the period mortality rates for legitimate children were reduced from 12.8 to 11.1 percent, while mortality rates for illegitimate children increased from 21.6 to 27.2 percent.

order to get new ones, as younger children would give better profit (Seip 1984, 192, 193, 200).

In the 1880s better living conditions for unmarried mothers and their children became a feminist and a class issue. It was argued that existing laws exempted men from responsibility and allowed them to "carry on their licentiousness as if they were professional seducers" (Seip 1984, 191). At the time there was a growing interest in birth-rates and in motherhood and the importance of developing emotional bonds between mother and child. Better living conditions, health and nutrition were thought to secure the present and future existence of the nation. Thus, the welfare and protection of the child were placed at the centre of attention.

While most politicians agreed that reforms to secure unmarried mothers and their children better economic conditions were long overdue, other proposals were far more controversial. The liberals, supported by the labour movement and the movement for the emancipation of women, proposed that illegitimate children should have the same legal standing as legitimate children in respect of the right to inherit their father and to assume his name (Seip 1984, 190). The idea was to motivate fathers to take responsibility for their children beyond their economic duties. Thus the law would hopefully influence attitudes, so that the care of children would eventually be understood as an equal responsibility for both parents. The conservatives and parts of the feminist movement strongly opposed this proposal, arguing that the right to name and inheritance would place unmarried mothers on an equal basis with married women, thus weakening the institution of marriage (Blom 1984).

The proposal was in any case a radical break with earlier principles. So far the relationship between a father and his illegitimate child had been defined as purely economical. According to family law in the 19th century, an illegitimate child had, with some exceptions, a right to inherit his/her mother and her family, but could claim no inheritance from the father (Torstensen 1985, 75ff). A father was at liberty to decide that the child could inherit him, but the inheritance was limited by law to half of what legitimate children would receive. Legally, there existed no family ties between a father and his illegitimate child. If the father wanted to care for the child beyond the economic support, this was voluntarily and not obligatory.

The responsibility for the care and upbringing was firmly placed with the mother. The consequences for those children who were lucky enough to survive infancy would be growing up in poverty on a minimum of subsistence. Their mothers would have very little resources to leave to their children, and they could expect very little, if any help, not to mention inheritance, from their fathers. Most of them had to earn their own living from an early age, and contribute to the support of their mothers. In short, the future prospects of these children were far more limited than for legitimate children.

Securing the Rights of Children

A major social reform was finally passed in 1915 after a long and controversial struggle.[15] The principles were finally stated that both parents had equal responsibilities and duties, and that illegitimate children became judicially equal to legitimate children in respect of economic support, inheritance and the name of the father. Moreover, it was realised that the stipulated maintenance payment from the alleged father was insufficient, and that securing better living conditions for these children had to be made a public responsibility. The reform thus resulted in substantial improvements in the legal rights of illegitimate children and their mothers.

The reform made it easier to secure that alleged fathers fulfilled their duties. In principle every child had a right to know who his/her biological father was. The mother therefore had an obligation to name the father (Seip 1984, 197). Before 1915 the child had had no legal right to claim support from his father. Now the right to claim maintenance shifted from the mother to the public authorities. The registration of the birth of an illegitimate child would automatically trigger off a maintenance claim against the father. Thus the father, in the same way as the mother, had a duty to recognize his child biologically, morally, economically and socially.

For the first time in history, unmarried mothers were granted the right to claim social security benefits for six weeks before, and up to six months after the birth of the child, on condition that they breast-feed the baby and

15 The reform is known as the "Castbergske" children's laws, named after the liberal politician Johan Castberg.

were unable to support themselves (Seip 1984, 197–198). The aim was to secure the survival of the child, and it was stressed that these benefits were not to be seen as poor relief. A study of unmarried mothers in Bergen, however, indicates that before 1920 less than half the mothers claimed the new social security benefits (Blom 1984). The benefits may have been mixed up with poor relief in peoples' minds, and some of the unmarried mothers consequently preferred to support themselves. Others may have been unaware of their new rights. Gradually the number of unmarried mothers receiving benefits increased, and by 1940 every mother claimed the benefits due to her. It was taken for granted, however, that they would return to work, as soon as the contribution was stopped after six months. In the 1930s there was a growing tendency that unmarried mothers wanted to keep the child with them, and had to face the challenge of combining child care with work (Blom 1984).

The reforms of 1915 nevertheless represented a major shift in attitudes towards illegitimate children. Their maintenance was no longer seen as exclusively the responsibility of the parents. It was finally recognized that it was a public responsibility. Moreover, it was recognized that society had a duty to secure their health as well as a minimum of love and care from the time of their birth.

Epilogue – an Outline of Developments of the 20th Century

The reforms in 1915 laid the foundations of the Norwegian welfare state. During the 20th century welfare benefits for unmarried mothers have gradually increased, particularly in the second half of the century. Still, attitudes towards unmarried mothers living on public benefits have remained ambivalent. Their need to be loving mothers has been emphasized. At the same time they have been met with demands to find paid work. The superior aim has been, and is, to enable them to earn their own living (Blom 1984; Syltevik 1999).

The logic of welfare policies towards unmarried mothers has shifted as assumptions regarding women's role have shifted. The male-breadwinner-family, where men are assumed to provide income and women to provide care, has dominated for most of the century. Unmarried mothers were a social problem, because they lacked a male breadwinner and yet had children to support (Lewis 1997, 1–7). In 1964 social security benefits were considerably increased when unmarried mothers could claim benefits until the child was ten years old (Syltevik 1999). The idea was to enable them to fulfil their role as caring mothers, while at the same time being encouraged to support themselves. In a conflict between income and care, however, caring for the child was to have priority. Thus, the welfare state replaced the absent male breadwinner.

In the 1990s a change of attitude occurred. The emphasis in public debates turned from the importance of caring for children to the problem of the dependency of those single mothers who lived on social security benefits (Syltevik 1999). Statistics indicated that children of these mothers lacked the economic security of children growing up in two-parent families. This was probably due to the tendency that a majority of single mothers living on benefits gave birth at an earlier age and had little or no education and consequently fewer job opportunities than women who postponed having a family until finishing their degrees (Ugreninov 2003). Attention consequently turned to the need to enable unmarried mothers to earn their own living. In 1998 the right to receive social security benefits as single mothers was reduced from ten to three years, in order to encourage them to finish school or to find a job (Syltevik 1999).

This change of attitude may be seen as part of a general change of attitudes towards women and paid work. Norway, as the other Scandinavian countries, has moved away from the male-breadwinner-family model towards the assumption that all adults are breadwinners (Lewis 1997, 6). This shift occurred as a result of an increasing number of women entering the labour market from the 1970s onwards. Today, most mothers and women are wage earners. The focus in public debates has shifted from mothers as carers towards the public responsibility to provide day care institutions and the role of fathers as carers.

The ambition of the reforms in 1915 was to motivate fathers to take greater care of their children, but in practice their duties were limited to economical support (Blom 1984). This is logical considering that men for most of the 20th century were assumed to be breadwinners. When this assumption was replaced by the assumption that both parents should contribute to the family income, fathers were met with expectations to take more responsibility for the care of their children. Fathers have responded with a wish to develop closer emotional ties with their children, and appear to be transforming fatherhood (Sogner 2003a, 233ff).

In contemporary Norway, the role of the father in the family and the rights of divorced fathers have been placed on the political agenda. Still, fathers who have not been married to the child's mother find themselves in a weaker judicial position in respect of custody and regular contact with their children. This picture is complicated by the fact that half of all children are born out of wedlock, as an increasing number of couples prefer cohabitation to marriage. Several studies show that the mother is normally given the custody of the children when a cohabiting couple splits up (Jensen 1999). Moreover, fathers who have never lived with the child's mother generally have little or no contact with their children (Grødem and Hyggen 2002). These studies indicate that a child born out of wedlock, whether by a single mother or by cohabiting parents, does not have the same right as other children to develop a relationship with its father.

As a result, attention has turned to the problem of securing cohabiting fathers to assume parental responsibility. In spite of cohabitation being common, it is still treated as an exception and as a problem to be solved. In 2004 joint parental responsibility was introduced as a rule, provided that cohabiting parents sign an agreement at the time of the birth of their child. No plans exist to grant corresponding rights and responsibilities to fathers who have never lived with the child's mother.[16] This may suggest that these fathers cannot be trusted with the same responsibilities as divorced and previously cohabiting fathers. Consequently, the unmarried, non-cohabiting father may have contact with his child, if the mother agrees, but he has no formal obligations beyond economic support until the child is 18 years old. The single mother and her child are thought to form a unit, where the father is still excluded.

Family politics in contemporary Norway indicate that marriage still is seen to be the norm for parenthood. Historically, a family without a father has not been recognised as a "proper" family, and there has been a predominant attitude that motherhood belonged to marriage. This has also

16 See, among the official reports available on line on the Norwegian Government website, a text proposed to the Odelsting (the Lower House of the Norwegian Parliament) and published by the Ministry of Children and Equality entitled: "Om lov om endringer i barneloven (felles foreldreansvar for samboende foreldre)" [Changes in the child laws: joint parental responsibilities for cohabiting parents], *Ot. prp.* [Propositions of the Odelsting], nr. 82, 2003–2004. http://www.regjeringen.no.

affected the position of the alleged father, and has made it difficult to define exactly what his obligations and responsibilities should be. Throughout the centuries, the assumptions regarding these fathers have shifted from the honourable and caring father of the 17th century, to the careless and irresponsible father of the 18th century, and back to the responsible father as provider at the end of the 19th century. For the time being the unmarried father is construed as irresponsible, he is still associated with absence, and is reduced to economic support. Thus, the present ideal of the caring, responsible father does not include the unmarried father, and consequently places him in an uncertain position.

Historically, growing up with a single mother has influenced the well-being of children born out of wedlock, and for some children it does so even today. As we have seen, before the 20th century these children did not have the same rights as legitimate children to maintenance or inheritance. Not belonging to a family in the proper sense of the word has not only influenced their living conditions, but also their social status, and their future prospects of occupation and marriage. Often growing up in care under conditions of want and negligence, these children had little opportunity to form emotional ties with their mothers, not to mention their fathers. The absent father has thus influenced the economical, social and emotional well-being of children born out of wedlock for many centuries.

References

BLOM, Ida, 1984, "*Ingen mor maa til tidsfordriv sitte med sit barn paa fanget*. Konflikten mellom forsørgeransvar og omsorgsansvar blant ugifte mødre i Bergen 1916–1940", in Per FUGLUM and Jarle SIMENSEN (eds), *Historie nedenfra. Festskrift til Edvard Bull på 70-årsdagen*, Oslo, Bergen, Stavanger, Tromsø, Universitetsforlaget, pp. 25–44.

BULL, Hans Henrik, 2006, "The Rise and Fall of Illegitimacy in a Rural Society: The Case of Rendalen, Norway, 1750–1900", *Marriage decisions in a peasant society. The role of the family of origin with regard to adult children's choice of marriage partner and the timing of their marriage in Rendalen Norway, 1750–1900,* Faculty of Humanities, University of Oslo.

GREVENOR, Henrik, 1936, *Det norske håndverks historie, Bind II*, Oslo, Grøndahl and Søn.

GRØDEM, Anne Skevik and HYGGEN, Christer, 2002, *Samværsfedrenes situasjon, Rapport fra en spørreundersøkelse*, Oslo, Nova Rapport 15/2002.

JENSEN, An-Magritt, 1999, "Børn i den skandinaviske samboerfamilie", in Lars DENCIK and Per SCHULTZ JØRGENSEN (eds), *Børn og familie i det postmoderne samfund*, København, Hans Reitzel, pp. 342–364.

LEWIS, Jane (ed.), 1997, *Lone Mothers in European Welfare Regimes,* London and Philadelphia, Jessica Kingsley Publishers.

SEIP, Anne-Lise, 1984, *Sosialhjelpstaten blir til. Norsk sosialpolitikk 1740–1920,* Oslo, Gyldendal Norsk Forlag.

SLYNGSTAD, Marit, 1994, *Ulydighet og straff*, Oslo, Tingbokprosjektet.

SOGNER, Sølvi, 1978, "Illegitimacy in old Rural Society; Some Reflections on the Problem Arising from Two Norwegian Family-Reconstitution Studies", in Sune ÅKERMAN, Hans Christian JOHANSEN and David GAUNT (eds), *Chance and Change. Social and Economic Studies in Historical Demography in the Baltic Area,* Odense, Odense University Press, pp. 61–68.

–, (ed.), 2003a, *I gode og vonde dagar. Familieliv i Noreg frå reformasjonen til vår tid*, Oslo, Det Norske Samlaget.

–, 2003b, "Looking for the principles of marriage by looking at non-marital cohabitation. A Norwegian parish in the eighteenth and nineteenth centuries", in Christophe DUHAMELLE, Jürgen SCHUMBOHM and Pat HUDSON, *Eheschliessungen im Europa des 18. und 19. Jahrhunderts*, Vandenhoeck and Ruprecht, pp. 215–239.

SYLTEVIK, Liv Johanne, 1999, "Endret velferdspolitikk for alenemødre – Fra relasjonelt til individualisert moderskap", *Tidsskrift for Velferdsforskning,* 2, 2, pp. 85–101.

TELSTE, Kari, 1993a, *Mellom liv og lov. Kontroll av seksualitet i Ringerike og Hallingdal 1652–1710*, Oslo, Tingbokprosjektet, Universitetet i Oslo.

–, 1993b, "'Boys Should Ask and Girls Should Say No'. The Relation between Man and Woman in Ringerike and Hallingdal, 1652–1710", *Ethnologia Scandinavica. A Journal for Nordic Ethnology*, 23, pp. 36–44.

–, 1998, "Hoping for a Home of their Own? Expectations of Love and Marriage among Peasant and Working Class Women at the End of the Nineteenth Century", in Annebelle DESPARD (ed.), *A Woman's Place. Women, Domesticity and Private Life,* Kristiansand, Faculty of Arts, Høgskolen i Agder, pp. 76–88.

–, 2000, *Brutte løfter. En kulturhistorisk studie av kjønn og ære 1700–1900*, Oslo, Unipub forlag.

–, 2002, "Man of Honour. Representations of Gender in Norway in the 18th Century", *Ethnologia Europaea*, 32, 1, pp. 15–24.

TORSTENSEN, Heidi, 1985, *Ugifte mødre og barnefedre i Kristiania på 1800–tallet. Forskninger i forbindelse med fødsel, forpleining og forsørgelse av barn født på Fødselsstiftelsen,* Universitetet i Oslo, hovedoppgave i historie.

UGRENINOV, Elisabeth, 2003, "Hvorfor jobber så få alenemødre?", *Samfunnsspeilet,* 6, December (online article). http://www.ssb.no/ssp/utg/200306/06/

Illegitimate Children and Court Procedures for the Determination of Paternity in Portugal (1893–1966)

Gendered and Social Differences on Acceding to Inheritance

Helena Cristina F. MACHADO

Children born outside institutional marriage without a legal father, along with the uncertainty of biological paternity, have always posed complicated issues for legal systems, especially those that based ownership and inheritance of property on descent through the male line. Historically, paternity investigations have assumed great importance based on the dominant ideological conception of masculine authority as an economical and social status resource. Richard Collier puts it in these terms:

> Establishing an authoritative determination of paternity (proving the biological link) has historically posed considerable problems for legal systems. The importance of a man needing to be sure that a particular child is "his" has, not surprisingly, been accorded a central place within a legal system in which property rights based ownership and inheritance have traditionally passed through the male line. Within such a system of patrilinear, primogenital ordering, establishing with some degree of certainty a biological connection between a man and a child has assumed great importance (Collier 1995, 182).

In ancient societies, as well as in today's, the knowledge of ascendant's identity and the expected subsequent access to the intergenerational transference of material, symbolical and emotional resources provided by family could be considered vital elements for the individual's well-being. However, if nowadays the protection of rights of the children born outside the institutional marriage is consensual, in ancient societies there were several obstacles placed before the acknowledgement of the rights, namely, the access to inheritance, by the so-called "illegitimate children".[1]

Legal regulation of reproduction mainly reproduces patriarchal structures in society (Douglas 1991) and the importance of legal regulation of affiliation relationships seems to be emphasised by the phenomenon of children born outside legal marriage, who don't have a legal father, articulated with the uncertainty of biological paternity, often reinforced by assumptions about women's predilection for deception in reproductive matters (Diduck and Kaganas 1999, 130).

Accepting the currents of thought followed by cultural anthropology for quite a long time, since Lévi-Strauss's studies of kinship systems (Lévi-Strauss 1969), that the reproduction of human beings is also the reproduction of social relationships (Strathern 1992), this study, being rooted in a tradition of feminist legal studies, explores the social relationships which are reproduced by the courts of law and evoked in the context of paternity investigations – such as representations of paternity, maternity, family and femininity – that highlight the ideologically dominant gender relations, interpreted as means of reinforcing the socially subordinate position of women. This theoretical assumption will be used to explain how the Portuguese justice system, within court procedures for the determination of paternity (1893–1966), functioned as a mean of creating obstacles for illegitimate children to accede to inheritance. This happened because a woman had to prove in court to have good "sexual and moral manners" in order to improve the chances of getting legal acknowledgement of paternity of her illegitimate child. These legal cases also reinforced social differences on acceding to inheritance within the group of illegitimate children, namely, because only those people with some economic and cultural resources could actually engage in a judicial procedure to have their paternity recognized.

I will explore how the court's procedures in Portugal for the determination of paternity of children born outside legal wedlock and whose alleged father did not voluntarily recognize paternity can highlight the social and gendered processes that were vital in the past to be entitled to receive material and symbolic resources provided by the family, namely

1 In Portugal, since the Constitution of 1976, it is considered to be a discriminatory practice to use concepts such as "bastards" or "illegitimate" to name the individuals born outside legal wedlock. For the sake of clarity and considering the historical period under analysis, I will use the term "illegitimate" whenever justified.

the inheritance from the putative fathers. Which elements could favour, or otherwise be placed against, candidates to inheritance? In what terms was paternity defined and how were the "candidates" for recognition of extra-marital affiliation evaluated? I seek to answer these questions showing that paternity investigations reflect overall cultural stereotypes that penalize the woman who procreates outside legal wedlock and her descendants, who aspire to the material and symbolical resources of the putative father, within a society in which the dominant succession and inheritance practice is *post-mortem* and the favourites for inheritance are the firstborn male or female children (Durães 1988; 1995), it being an ordinary practice to ignore the illegitimate children in that process.[2]

Based on micro-analysis methods, this study analyses the sentencing of 1,327 legal cases of paternity investigation that took place between 1893 and 2000 in a court located in Northern Portugal. In addition, jurisprudence on the matter that is published during the considered period was also analysed and interviews of judges and Prosecutor Counsels were conducted, on a national level, over the years 2001 and 2002.

This research focused on the period between 1893 and 1966, trying to understand to what extent the courts acted as a mediator between individuals born outside legal wedlock who intended to have access to the inheritance of the putative father and the legitimate heirs. During the period under analysis, the paternity investigation was started by voluntary initiative[3] of the individuals (or their legal representatives) who wanted to have their father's identity recognised in court. This comes to illustrate the fact that only those individuals with some economic and cultural resources could actually try to have legal recognition of paternity, and that those who didn't possess enough resources were unable to have a "legal father" acknowledged, thus revealing how paternity actions themselves relate to social differences on acceding to inheritance.

2 The European concern with the defence of the rights of children born outside legal wedlock is only evident in the 1970s. Some paradigmatic examples come from the guidelines proposed by the European Convention of 15 October 1975, entitled *European Convention on the Legal Status of Children Born out of Wedlock*, which stipulated the need for the European Council member states to adopt common legal arrangements in this matter.

3 Only through the legal changes of the *Civil Code* in 1966, paternity investigations became mandatory in Portugal, under certain circumstances, and were no longer considered by individuals born outside institutional marriage as a strategy to accede to inheritance.

Regarding the studied court, a reduced number of paternity investigation cases are found between 1893 and 1966: only seventy cases against twelve hundred and fifty seven on the period between 1967 and 2000. This is partly due to a strangling imposed by the legal restrictions on the admissibility of paternity investigations which were made to protect the peace of the legitimate families' home (Pinto 1995), setting strong objections on the admissibility to file this kind of lawsuit as long as the putative father was still alive, specially if he was married, and stressing the legal imposition of official secrecy on the affiliation of adulterine children, which was enforced until 1966, at the time *Portuguese Civil Code* was revised.

Legal Framework of Paternity Investigations

It has not always been usual to establish the link between a child and his/her parents when the child is born to an unmarried woman. Ancient societies commonly denied family ties between such a child and his/her father and, therefore, access to familial transfer of material and symbolic resources. In ancient Roman law a child born outside of marriage was a *filius nullius*, i.e., it had no family ties with any of its parents (not even with its mother). It had not been self-evident that such a child should be entitled to financial support from his/her father or that he/she should have the right to inherit from him (and his relatives).

In fact, until the 1970s, affiliation laws in most western European countries protected the "legitimate family". There were very limited conditions for admissibility of a paternity investigation and it was almost impossible to have paternity recognized in the case of a married man. In fact, law almost appeared to have been designed to give the putative father a "sporting chance to get away with it" (Barton and Douglas 1995, 200).

Until the publication of the first *Portuguese Civil Code,* in 1867, the children born of unmarried parents that were not affiliated could freely investigate their paternity. Once the denominated *Seabra Code*[4] came into

4 Antonio Luis de Seabra, University of Coimbra, was in charge with the redaction of the Code.

force, it was established that paternity investigations could only take place by exception, under three very strict circumstances:

> 1) having a written statement from the father declaring his paternity; 2) being the son of daughter in possession of status, that is, reputed as such by the putative father and the community; 3) in the case of violent ravishment or abduction (Art. 130, *Civil Code* 1867, 25).

These conditions of juridical admissibility of paternity investigations were common to those established by the denominated *Napoleonic Code*, promulgated in France in 1804, whose fundamental legal principles were adopted by several countries such as Spain, Belgium, Luxemburg and Italy.

The *Portuguese Civil Code* of 1867 reflected much of the first French *Civil Code* (1804) impositions regarding Family Law and therefore established several restrictions on the investigation of paternity in order to protect the legitimate family. On the contrary, in ancient Nordic Law, the link between a child born to an unmarried woman and his/her father was acknowledged and it seems to be characteristic of Nordic countries that the task of establishing paternity of non-marital children (in Sweden since the late 1910s) has been considered society's responsibility. The legal situation in Nordic countries is not, however, in all respects identical. Let us consider as an example the question of how a refusal on the part of the mother to co-operate in the identification of the father is regarded (Eekelaar and Sarcevic 1993).

Despite some differences in family law systems, as far as affiliation laws are concerned, most Western European legal systems are historically interconnected and have some common legal dispositions, like the application of the Roman Law's rule of the presumption of paternity – *Pater est, quem nuptiae demonstrant*[5] – which legally ties men to any children born to their wives (Assier-Andrieu and Commaille 1995; Council of Europe 1999; Diduck and Kaganas 1999; Eekelaar and Sarcevic 1993; European Commission 1997; Forder 1993). As such, institutional marriage remains a privileged place as the preferred way of attributing paternity (Sheldon 2005, 541) and of transferring economic, emotional and symbolic resources. But the problem of paternity and access to resources

5 Means in Latin: "the father is the one attested by marriage".

like inheritance and property remains for what concerns children born outside legal marriage.

In Portugal, the judicial investigation of paternity, before becoming mandatory in 1966, had the main objective of enabling access to inheritance by illegitimate children who managed to have their paternity legally recognised. In fact, the *Civil Code* of 1867, in its 122d article, admitted the affiliation of all illegitimate[6] children, except those resulting from adulterous and/or incestuous relationships. Succession and inheritance rights were set in the 129th article which refers to the right to bear the parents' surnames, rights to support and alimony, as well as the right to succeed their parents and to take part in the inheritance.

In order to take part in the inheritance, the illegitimate children had to become legally affiliated (which could take place during the wedding registration), or have their paternity recognised in a judicial verdict, which in the latter case, would occur within an illegitimate paternity lawsuit, that I will analyze with further detail in this text.

If there were no other legitimate heirs, the legitimated children could inherit in full. However, if there were legitimate and legitimated[7] heirs taking part in the inheritance, the ones who were affiliated by voluntary recognition of paternity or by a judicial verdict, only had right to inherit the "legitime",[8] accordingly to what is stated the 1785th article of the 1867 *Civil Code*, the portion which rightfully belonged to the co-heirs, minus one third. Such disposition occurred if the affiliation happened at the time, or before, the matrimony that originated the legitimate heirs. If it happened otherwise, in the case of a post-matrimonial affiliation, the legitimated children's portion of the inheritance would be taken from the available third, that is, the remaining third of the inheritance that the deceased could dispose of freely, without exceeding the "legitime minus one third", thus not taking part in the legitimate heir's portion. And the 1992d article further adds that if there are many affiliated children in these conditions and the stipulated value of the "legitime minus one third" cannot be

6 It is important to stress that the concept of illegitimate would cover all children born outside legal wedlock, as well as in the 180 days after the ceremony and during the 300 days after a judicial decree of separation.

7 The "legitimated" heirs are all those who were at some point illegitimate and were later affiliated.

8 The "legitime" corresponded to the equally divided portion regarding two-thirds of the total inheritance.

achieved, then nothing more shall be due, the available third being divided among them.

According to Durães, based on studies of the testamental dispositions observed by families in the rural regions of Northern Portugal, during the 18th and 19th centuries, there was a major concern about two essential elements, namely, the indivisibility of the estate and the often landed property, as well as the egalitarian inheritance (Durães 1988; 1992; 1995; 2002). These concerns originated successional and inheritance practices that assumed several forms which were adapted according to the available land and wealth, thus creating, according to the author, four types of inheritance systems:

> System of egalitarian succession and inheritance; egalitarian succession system, favoured inheritance if the remaining third is used to benefit one of the legitimate heirs; single successional system and egalitarian inheritance; and finally, single successional system with favoured inheritance, being the favoured heir the successor or not (Durães 1992, 131).

Margarida Durães calls our attention to the fact that the systems of inheritance in the above-mentioned region were characterized by a

> hybrid and complex process, based upon an egalitarian division of patrimony that, nonetheless, one tries to keep undivided. An objective that is only possible with the conjugation of other behaviours (emigration, celibacy, postponed or late marriage), allowing the concentration of the land in the hands of the successor-heir. The latter will adopt, as far as possible, strategies towards the postponement of the division of shares and, when it becomes inevitable, the remaining co-heirs will be bought out of their share in order to consolidate the totality of the estate (Durães 1995, 75).

From the Seduced Woman to Recognized "Social Paternity"

In the *Civil Code* of 1867, the illegitimate paternity investigation lawsuit was forbidden, with the exception of the following cases: having a written statement from the father in which paternity was declared; being the son in "possession of status" (public recognition of the alleged paternity, designated by "social paternity"); and having occurred "violent ravishment or abduction, that coincided with the time of birth" (Pinto 1995, 138). The following example, taken from a sentence pronounced in 1935 in Vale Court[9], concerning an illegitimate paternity investigation lawsuit filed by a alleged son born in 1888, reveals a reasoning which is precisely based upon the existence of possession of status and in the occurrence of abduction, an event that presumes the use of violence, if not physical, then at least symbolical, emphasizing in a particularly ostentatious fashion the patriarchal conception of gender relations:

> In the year of 1887, after a short time of courtship, the late Visconde de Viamonte da Silveira, abducted the Petitioner's mother and took her to Quinta do Louro, his father's property, and there he took her virginity and began having sexual intercourse from which the P.[10] was born. Shortly after, he brought her to this city and rented and furnished a house for her on Rua de D. João I, in this city, where she gave birth. The birth of the P. coincided with the time of the abduction. Sexual intercourse of the late Visconde de Viamonte da Silveira with the P.'s mother continued after his birth until the above-named got married. When the P.'s mother became aware of the planned marriage, she sought to oppose it and, given her underage status, she took the necessary steps to file a lawsuit against the late Visconde de Viamonte da Silveira. Then, a relative of the late Visconde de Viamonte da Silveira, knowing of the fact, served as a mediator between him and the P.'s mother: in order to give up on the criminal lawsuit, the Visconde de Viamonte da Silveira gave her a small dowry. Since he began having sexual intercourse with the P.'s mother the Visconde de Viamonte da Silveira always took care and provided for her, paying the rent of the house he rented for her, providing for the childbirth expenses and all that she needed for her son. And even the Visconde de Viamonte da Silveira's own father, the P.'s grandfather, had delivered to the P.'s mother's house chickens, grain and wine, even after the marriage of that son of his. After the P.'s birth, the Visconde de Viamonte da Silveira, before and after the marriage, whilst his son was a child, would carry him on his lap, kiss him and gave him his hand for him to kiss, calling him son. After the P. grew up and reached school age, he gave him an allowance for school and dressing expenses. And when he was a grown boy he would many times give him money and always throughout his life he helped him. He employed him in the Castanheiro factory. Once the P. fulfilled his military duties he managed to find him a position in the public security police force. Whenever the P. met any trouble before the Public Office, or any other issue, immediately the deceased would spontaneously provide him with his services. Every dress-suit that the Visconde de Viamonte no longer wore, he would give to the P., and even after his departure, and by his recommendation, a suit was delivered to the P. […]. When the Visconde de Viamonte da Silveira was breathing his last, the family sent for the P., and the first died in the P.'s arms, which later helped in dressing the deceased (Records of "Illegitimate Paternity Investigation Lawsuits", Vale Court, 1932–1933).

9 Situated in the north-western region of Minho in Portugal.

10 "P." for "Petioner".

The high level of conditioning of illegitimate children affiliation was slightly changed by the "Law of Child Protection" of 25 December 1910,[11] which added a few more circumstances in which a paternity investigation was permitted, namely, in such cases as those of seduction of the mother by abuse of authority or confidence, or by promises of marriage, as well as in the case that the mother and supposed father notoriously lived as husband and wife during the legal period of conception (22d article of the Decree-Law nº 2 of 25 December 1910, cited by Pinto 1995, 270). With the reform of the *Civil Code* performed in 1910, the Portuguese judicial system then began to accept another situation in which an illegitimate paternity investigation lawsuit could be brought into action – the cases of "seduction performed with abuse of authority or trust, or by promise of marriage" (Pinto 1995, 138). This change in legislation caused the concept of seduction to be one of the most used terms in the judicial discourses about feminine sexual behaviour, substituting, by recurring use in the judge's discourses, the former arguments frequently used in the illegitimate paternity investigation lawsuits, which invoked the abducted woman's imagery as the last resort for the man who wanted to fulfil the desire to deflower a maiden.

The following extract, taken from a decision by the Portuguese Supreme Court of Justice on 26 May 1948, regarding a crime of ravishment by seduction is particularly illustrative of the concept of seduction that we repeatedly find in the illegitimate paternity investigation lawsuits records and, as such, profoundly revealing of the dominant patterns of social relations between men and women at that time:

> During courtship and by means of seduction with promises of marriage [the defendant] managed to engage in coitus with Armanda, who was a virgin and was 17 years and 5 months of age. It was also found proven that the offended lived with two, older, ill mannered, sisters to whose house often went, during night-time, boys from Macedo de Cavaleiros and other proveniences, staying there until early morning hours, dancing and such amusements [...] having the defendant seduced her, with courtship and promises of marriage, into having carnal union for the first time, thus managing to deflower her [...] the marriage promises, which the defendant denied, cannot be doubted in the

11 The Revolution of 5 October 1910 resulted in the proclamation of the First Republic, putting an end to monarchy in Portugal. The legislative changes put to effect by the above-mentioned "Law of Child Protection" of 25 December 1910, reflect the liberal tendencies which accompanied the doctrinarian and political actions that, since the creation of the Republican Party, in 1876, had been developed by this Party, whose primary objective was simply, since early on, to replace the regime.

> current state of the proceedings. And that these promises and courtship can be successfully used in these cases, in order to dominate and destroy the woman's moral resistance, to entrust herself into a man's hands, is common knowledge, as is current jurisprudence [...]. It stands from the instance's judgment that the minor did not behave like a corrupted or dissolute woman and that the defendant treated her as an honest girl; there was courtship and promises of marriage so that she would give in to his lustful desires. The licentious life led by her sisters [...] did not inhibit him to publicly promenade his sweetheart. Both were unmarried, without much difference in age and, as it would seem accordingly to their respective economic conditions, their social statuses were not very differentiated. The circumstances gave the marriage promises a ring of truth and seriousness, although, deep inside, they were complete bollocks (Portuguese Supreme Court of Justice 1948b, 133–135).

The concept of seduction associated to the illegitimate paternity investigation lawsuit assumes two distinct meanings: the seduction "with promises of marriage" and "seduction with abuse of authority". This distinction reveals the cultural conceptions of that time regarding the manner in which men and women should relate to each other, being that the seduction with promise of marriage could only be proven in court if the petitioner of the lawsuit could convince the judge that, at the time of conception of the alleged son or daughter, there was no impediment to marriage between the mother and the putative father.

If nowadays the impediments regarding marriage possess a strictly legal character (for at least one of the individuals is already married or because they relate to each other in the first degree), in earlier times those objections to marriage could have an exclusively social expression – for example, if both individuals in question were to belong to different social classes. The extract mentioned above also illustrates in what way social equality between lovers was considered by the judges to be a safe indication of the seriousness of the promises of marriage.

The following examples, taken from the records of an illegitimate paternity investigation lawsuit that took place in Vale Court in 1930 and from a sentence pronounced by the Portuguese Supreme Court of Justice in 1949, respectively, were selected in order to illustrate the dominant conception that the seriousness of the marriage promises could only be judicially proven in cases in which romantic engagement occurred between individuals who possessed similar social statuses:

> Olivia was a well-mannered, honest and virginal girl, living at the time, as she does nowadays, in her parent's house, aiding her mother with the house chores and also working as a seamstress, when R. began courting her. Their social status was, and still

> is, equal, for which the defendant's wedding promises were trustworthy, also given that the assiduity and continuity of a five year uninterrupted courtship constituted further elements that took the inquirer's mother to believe in the sincerity of the ongoing wedding promises that were even confirmed in letters. And, in spite of being obstinately besieged by R., Olivia managed to defend her virginity until R., by means of disloyal and treacherous promises of wedding which he swore to be firm, sincere and worthy, even speaking to his father, the A. about the wedding, and even proposing to her, managed to seduce her and deflower her (Records of "Illegitimate Paternity Investigation Lawsuits", Vale Court, 1930–1930).

Besides seduction with promises of marriage, there is another concept, the "seduction with abuse of authority" which is particularly illustrative of the patriarchal nature of gender relations. In cases where a position of social inequality between man and woman is found, the possibilities of seduction with promises of marriage fade away, and all is left is the alternative of seduction by abuse of authority, being that the notion of male authority may assume different expressions, sustained by the invocation of male superiority in terms of social standing, hierarchical relations or age. There are several examples found, but the phraseology that states such facts is almost identical, formulated in statements like the following, drawn from a judicial sentence pronounced in 1946:

> The mother of the petitioner was virgin and honest and reputed as such by everyone. In the beginnings of 1923, the investigated, abusing of his quality as master and his acquired confidence, he managed to convince the petitioner's mother to have sexual intercourse with him. And thus, on that February, he deflowered her, continuing after that to engage in sexual intercourse with her (Records of "Illegitimate Paternity Investigation Lawsuits", Vale Court, 1946–1946).

The woman's reputation within her own community is also an element to be considered by the judge upon the moment of making his decision, especially when it comes to the classification of the performed actions (the woman's consent in submitting to sexual intercourse) as a result, or not, of seduction. The importance assumed by the classifications of the woman's behaviour that emerge from the social background is rather explicit in the following excerpt from a Vale Court sentence:

> Reputation is a psychological or a conscience element that also pertains to law, and demeanour is a matter of fact, combining a whole, for that is the way the agent's state of mind is brought to surface [...] The public will also only deem the individual as the child of the investigated when his actions and the mother's convince them that she is his daughter. That was what happened in the present case. And so, it was proven that

> Rosa, the petitioner's mother, was a virgin when she engaged in sexual intercourse with the above-named Fernando for the first time, as she was also considered by the public (Records of "Illegitimate Paternity Investigation Lawsuits", Vale Court, 1946–1946).

And the judge proceeds in defining the concept of seduction, distinguishing the one which occurrence will carry penal consequences (in case the "offended woman" is a minor and a virgin), possibly being classified as crime of rape, from another type of seduction that may function, namely, as a pretext of admissibility for an illegitimate paternity investigation lawsuit in the case of absence of the elements of underage and virginity:

> There is only one kind of seduction, although it may have different consequences, depending on the seduced being under or over 18 years of age and on being, or not, a virgin. The petitioner, being under 18 years of age and a virgin, falls under the jurisdiction of the 392th article of the Penal Code, sanction avoided by the seducer if she is over 18 (Records of "Illegitimate Paternity Investigation Lawsuits", Vale Court, 1946–1946).

Public displays of courtship constitute another valued element by the Portuguese judges regarding illegitimate paternity investigation lawsuits. The recognition of the romantic affair by the community is fundamental, not only for the matter of judicial admissibility of the lawsuit, but also in an eventual judicial sentence favourable to the petitioner of the lawsuit in question. However, the fact which is most relevant in the argumentation presented by the judges in the considered period of time (1893–1966), at the moment of pronouncing a sentence, is the denominated possession of status or social paternity – when someone is reputed as being a son or a daughter by the supposed father and the community (article 130, *Civil Code* of 1867) – that is, the proof in court that the public considered the petitioner to be the son/daughter of the designated father. The elements that were used to sustain the argument of public visibility and social paternity were various, but generally pointed towards the economic function (of material support) which, socially, would be expected from a father.

The inquiries formulated by the judges – which illustrate the magisterial selection of the facts considered relevant to stand as evidence in court – of judicial sentences taken from the collection of files of illegitimate paternity investigation lawsuits found in Vale Court point, invariably, towards facts predominantly classifiable within the economic sphere. Let us consider the following example:

> When Eulália found herself pregnant, the investigated ordered part of the layette for the petitioner, which he later paid for? And the rest of the layette he bought in Porto was also paid for by the investigated? From Vizela, did Eulália go to Póvoa de Varzim with the investigated, always at his expenses? [...] When the petitioner was born, the investigated offered her all the affection, watching over so that she had no want or need? [...] Being one's daughter, he wanted her to be well dressed? And he always gave her money, clothes and other objects? And paid for her education in elementary school? And then he sent her to this city in order to graduate from the industrial school, paying for the expenses of such studies? And during the time of those studies the petitioner took lodging in D. Maria de Belém's house [...] at the expenses of the investigated that, as he paid for those expenses, always presented himself as the petitioner's father? The petitioner went on vacation to Póvoa de Varzim and the expenses were paid by the investigated? And for the purpose mentioned in the question above, the investigated provided clothes for the petitioner? For many years, the petitioner always spent her Sundays at the investigated's home, by his request, and there she had meals? [...] He gave her presents, among them, a pair of gold earrings? (Records of "Illegitimate Paternity Investigation Lawsuits", Vale Court, 1951–1951).

The manifestation of abuse of authority of a man over a woman appears taking the form of an exercise of power which is grounded on elements of hierarchical or economic nature, or on a conjunction of both. The typical example of such a form of exercise of power is the relationship established between the "master" and the "maid", which is a means of justifying the woman's persuasion to give up her "most precious gift", her moral arms – embodied in her virginity – and to "surrender" to the seducer. Let us examine the following illegitimate paternity investigation lawsuit that took place in Vale Court between 1964 and 1965, considered admissible by the judge and whose petitioner was a university student who alleged to be the illegitimate daughter of an already deceased professor that in 1943 had hired her mother as a handmaid, with him being 43 years of age and her mother 16. The judge pronounced the sentence as follows:

> The investigated, by his social position and difference in age, furthermore, by the fact that he was the master, enjoyed a great deal of influence over the petitioner's mother, a humble country servant (Records of "Illegitimate Paternity Investigation Lawsuits", Vale Court, 1964–1965).

The judges' mindsets, reflected upon the jurisprudence produced until mid-1960s, analyzed here, show clearly the social processes of configuration of the relations between men and women. Classificatory processes of feminine behaviour are undertaken, placing on opposite sides the "well behaved" women (virginal and resistant in face of men's advances, until they finally give in, vanquished by the exercise of the manly power of seduction) and the "misbehaved" (the frivolous and the seducers, who deviate from the dominant norms of feminine behaviour).

The theme of the virgin, innocent and seduced woman has occupied a great deal of jurisprudence and legal doctrine published in Portuguese juridical magazines, at least since the end of the 1960s until the mid–1970s. This does not mean that this imagery of femininity disappeared in later periods. On the contrary, it's still quite present in today's legislation (Beleza 1993).

The evaluation of a woman's sexual and moral behaviour that procreates outside wedlock has important impact on the production of sentences of paternity investigation lawsuits, which will be reflected on the possibilities to inherit from the putative fathers by children born of extra-conjugal relationships.

Children Born outside Legal Marriage and Obstacles in Accessing Inheritance

Up until legislative alterations created by the revised Portuguese *Civil Code* of 1966, which came to impose mandatory paternity investigation whenever a child is registered without the father's identification, it was the citizen, of full age, that would appeal to the court, trying to have his/her father's identity acknowledged. In the case of the under aged, the lawsuit was brought into action by the legal representative of the individual whose father's identity was unknown.[12]

In all of the paternity investigation lawsuits that took place between 1893 and 1966 in the Vale Court, the petitioners were: the children themselves – 38 cases (54.3 percent) –; a single case of a son's son – that is, an "alleged grandchild", corresponding only to 1.4 percent of the cases –; and, in situations in which the child is under age we find, as petitioners for

12 The current Portuguese law states that the paternity investigation may only be filed by voluntary request of the individual who seeks legal recognition of paternity, but only when the alleged son/daughter reaches full age. The mandatory paternity investigation is imposed only until the child reaches two years of age.

paternity investigations lawsuits, mostly their respective mothers – 26 cases (37.1 percent) – one case in which the petitioner was the grandfather on the mother's side (1.4 percent) and four cases in which the petitioner was the minor's legal guardian, without reference to a kinship degree, or any other form of affinity.

Considering the group of adult illegitimate children demanding for paternity recognition themselves, we came upon a total of thirty eight individuals – twenty two daughters and sixteen sons. Considering the civil status of the female children, fourteen of them were married (63.7 percent), one widow (4.5 percent), one divorced (4.5 percent) and six single daughters (27.3 percent). In the group of male children we found ten who were married (62.5 percent) and six who were single (37.5 percent).

The importance assumed by the mothers, on one hand, and within the ensemble of the illegitimate children, the number of female individuals registered as petitioners of "paternity investigation lawsuits" – 57.8 percent – on the other, some indications about feminine involvement in this kind of lawsuit are shown. In fact, according to research studies made in other countries, men generally appear in court more frequently than women, whether they appear as petitioners or defendants (Santos *et al* 1996). This fact comes to show that, namely, social inequality in access to justice is also laden with gender inequalities. Nevertheless, apparently, gender differentiation in access to justice seems to be strongly affected by the type of lawsuit in question, as women constitute the majority of petitioners in lawsuits related to family problems (nowadays, we must point out the importance of divorce suits) (Delgado 1996).

From the twenty two women that in the studied cases filed illegitimate paternity investigation lawsuits, 63.6 percent were married, which may indicate that the women's access to court has been quite dependant on the male protection provided by the respective husbands.[13] Furthermore, in all illegitimate paternity investigation lawsuits, which involved married women who wished to have their father's identity acknowledged in court, the petitioner side also included their respective husbands.

13 Up until the profound new reforms introduced in the *Civil Code* in 1977, the Portuguese law adopted the general principle inherited from Roman law, that the woman's situation within the family was under the rule of the *pater familias* who, not only had absolute authority over his descendants, but also over his wife. In this regard, when the woman married, she would stay under the strict dependence of the husband; while the unmarried and widowed women enjoyed a civil quality similar to men's (Sá 1996), as divorced women did from 1910 to 1940 and after 1977 revised *Civil Code*.

The decision to file an illegitimate paternity investigation lawsuit seems to be profoundly conditioned, not only by the possession of economic, cultural and social capital, suitable for an effective interaction with the judicial system, but also by a very harsh reality – the obituary situation of the alleged father. The weight of the legal framing which is reflected in a clear conditioning of the necessary requirements in order to file that sort of law case, is quite visible, insofar as in most of the analyzed lawsuits (52 cases, which amounts 74.3 percent of the sample), the alleged fathers were already deceased at the time the paternity recognition lawsuit was engaged. In other words, a possible legal acknowledgement of paternity could no longer pose a threat to the family constituted through institutional wedlock.

The obituary status of the putative father assumes great importance, as paternity recognition suits were started, in most cases, after the death of the presumed father, which may indicate that the ultimate goal of this kind of lawsuit was to attain legal acknowledgement of paternity in order to accede to inheritance. Thus, we find that the protection of family peace is a value of major importance for the judicial system because of the legal impediments that prevent public awareness of a possible voluntary affiliation of an adulterine son.[14] Notice that, in the single recorded case involving a living alleged father, the lawsuit ended up being considered inadmissible.

There are, however, other factors that explain the rare cases in which children born outside legal wedlock chose the judicial path in order to become candidates to inheritance. In this type of lawsuit, the petitioner is the citizen him/herself who deliberately chooses to file a lawsuit in order to have legal acknowledgement of the father's identity, which implies a series of resources – economical, social and cultural – which are necessary for an effective access to justice.

Besides, many individuals would drop an illegitimate paternity investigation lawsuit in exchange for certain parallel compensations, namely, material compensations by the defendants – heirs of the alleged father. As

14 The first Portuguese *Civil Code* (1867) under the influence of the *Napoleonic Code,* and similarly to affiliation laws common in European countries, prohibited the affiliation of adulterine children. With the "Law of Child Protection" coming into force in Portugal on 25 December 1910, affiliation became allowed, but would become subject to official secrecy. The latter imposition came to an end, in our country, with the coming into force of the 1966 *Civil Code.*

Carlos Silva (1998) states, the promulgation of the first *Civil Code* in 1867, by instituting successional and inheritance rights for illegitimate children, ended up in the creation of schemes used by the paternal progenitor in order to undo heirs, namely, by assuming themselves as the illegitimate children's godfather or by donating estates or money in order to keep inheritance claims away.

The young woman's image, innocent victim of the male's sexual advances, that has been recurrent in Portuguese law and jurisprudence (Beleza 1991) is found perfectly rendered in illegitimate paternity investigation lawsuits: mothers under the age of 24 lead with 70.3 percent (33.3 percent under 20 years and 37.0 percent from 20 to 24 years), bearing no reference to women over 35. The alleged father's age structure reveals, on the contrary, a more aged group, with dominance by individuals over 39 years old (34.2 percent). Nevertheless, we must point out a convergence of these individuals in the 20–29 age group (21.1 percent from 20 to 24 years and 26.3 percent from 25 to 29 years), in spite of the absence of individuals under the age of twenty.

The importance of the judicial protection of the legitimate family is clearly visible if we look into the mothers and alleged father's marital status at the time of the child's birth and at the time of the motion for lawsuit, respectively. Almost all mothers involved in these lawsuits were unmarried at the time of the child's birth (95.7 percent) and 92.8 percent were also at the time of the filing for lawsuit. In effect, mothers remain in the same marital status in both occasions, and there existed only two cases of unmarried mothers that were married at the time of the filing of the lawsuit; and only one case of a married mother at the time the minor was born and, by the time the lawsuit was filed, was already deceased.

The majority of the putative fathers were unmarried at the time of the minor's birth (67.1 percent) but, at the time of the motion for lawsuit, the situation changed a little – the 41.4 percent unmarried are opposed by 37.1 percent married men – which may indicate, on one hand, an easier access to the matrimonial market for men. On the other hand, this fact arouses the suspicion of the considerable impact that the single mother stigma had during the time considered, for which women in these circumstances saw their chances of access to institutional marriage considerably diminished.

In regard to the analyzed illegitimate paternity investigation lawsuits, a contrast is verified between the social standing of the putative father and the standing of the woman who gave birth outside of legal wedlock. On the woman's side concentration at the base of the social hierarchy is found: we have predominance of seamstresses (14 percent), housewives (22 percent) labourers (22 percent), and servants (25 percent). On the alleged fathers' side, there is dominance by proprietors with 42 percent. This gender bias in terms of social standing is articulated along with other modes of social subordination of the mother of the child born outside legal wedlock regarding the alleged father, it being common to have a relationship of economic domination over the mother, through the offering of gifts and money, eventually associated to an emotional and symbolical dependence.

Could it be that resorting to a court of law, trying to obtain legal acknowledgment of paternity, and therefore, having the chance to become a legitimate heir, was a strategy meant to be successful? According to the studied court, in 44.3 percent of cases, the court acknowledged that there was sufficient evidence of the alleged paternity and in 55.7 percent it deemed that there was not enough evidence of paternity.

Within all of the sets of lawsuits that were considered unfounded, one cannot help but notice that it was verified that in sixteen of such cases this result was not an immediate consequence of a judicial verdict, but an occurrence due to a voluntary nonsuit regarding the paternity investigation by the petitioner, as well as another case in which the petitioner failed to motion the lawsuit within the prescribed deadline.

The reading of the records of "illegitimate paternity investigation lawsuits" did not allow me to objectively understand the reasons which led the petitioners to give up the lawsuit. However, this fact may be a sign of the existence of a strong conditioning in acceding to the necessary cultural resources and skills for an adequate orientation within the judicial system by the petitioners. Therefore, I consider that the reasons that may have led some individuals to give up the lawsuit were mainly culture-related factors, namely, the absence of a truly secure and embodied perception of their rights and of acknowledgement of their issues as matters worthy to be solved through the formal devices of justice. Obviously, the individuals who chose to abandon the lawsuit may have done so in exchange for parallel compensations, namely, material compensations by the defendants of the "illegitimate paternity investigation lawsuit" in question – heirs of the supposed father. As Carlos Silva (1998) would say, in reference to a study about inheritance practices during the late 19th century and early decades of the 20th century in the north-western region of Minho in Portugal, one would, above all,

> ensure the (almost) full inheritance in benefit of the legitimate children [...] the biological parents and/or legitimate heirs, because of their supremacy regarding resources and the dependency of the "illegitimate" children and their mothers, they would concede to amicably grant the "illegitimate" co-heirs and their mothers with a parcel of land [...] or an "allowance" in cash, thus keeping them away from the inheritance" (Silva 1998, 260–261).

Other possible strategies in order to compensate the illegitimate child would be for the biological father to take on the illegitimate child in his house as his servant (Silva 1998, 262), or to conceal himself under the figure of a "godfather", or arranging one for his illegitimate child (Iturra 1986).

Conclusion

Although family law and civil proceedings concerning investigation of paternity of children born outside marriage may vary in the diverse national legal systems,[15] almost all societies now support efforts in order to establish parentage in these cases. However, in the past, the cultural and legal settings were quite different and several obstacles were posed to the legal recognition of paternity from the part of unmarried parents. This was justified on the traditional ground underlying the *Pater est* Roman rule itself, i.e., the consolidation of the family founded on marriage. Thus, the rule was seen as the necessary expression of the legal duty of fidelity (of the wife) which continued undiminished in all these situations (Senaeve 1993).

15 At the present day, several European countries, such as Scandinavian countries, Germany and Portugal have compulsory inquiries of paternity when the birth certificate of a child under two years old does not show the identity of the father. Other countries just give the court the power to investigate paternity in the course of existing civil proceedings regarding the child. That is the case in UK, where Family Law allows the Secretary of State, the alleged father or the person with custody to apply for a declaration of parentage of the child (Cretney 2003).

The legal acknowledge of one's paternity can permit access to economic, emotional and symbolical resources, that could otherwise be inaccessible, which may contribute in great measure for the individual's well-being. In fact, the acknowledgement of the ancestry has been seen, in occidental societies which tend to privilege biological links regarding issues of affiliation, not only as a means of acceding to economic resources and inheritance, but also as an important way of constructing an individual and social sense of identity. The importance of the establishment of parentage and the definition of its legal consequences, although controversial, might be central for the individual's emotional and economic resources, evoking a multidimensional concept of well-being that enables individuals, men and women, to live a "good" life and to compose their effective functioning, in the sense opened by authors like Amartya Sen (1985).

In past Portuguese society, the access to inheritance was particularly difficult to obtain for children born outside wedlock. As in many other societies, in the past and even today, institutional marriage remained a privileged place as the preferred way of attributing paternity (Sheldon 2005, 541) and of transferring economic, emotional and symbolical resources. But the problems of recognition of paternity and access to resources like inheritance and property have continued for children born outside legal marriage. From the moment that the Portuguese *Civil Code* of 1867 gives the illegitimate children succession and inheritance rights, although restricted, the biological father tends to conceal himself under the figure of a godfather or by arranging one for his illegitimate child (Silva 1998), which allowed the "bastards" access to a minimal spiritual and material legacy, at the same time it ensured almost integral transfer of the properties in favour of the legitimate descendants. The access to court, in order to try to have a legal recognition of paternity was one of the rare means that illegitimate children had, in the past Portuguese society, to struggle for access to the inheritance.

This study has examined the gendered and social differences on acceding to inheritance within the group of illegitimate children, which shows that the individuals that were most likely to obtain the legal recognition of paternity – and thus, the access to inheritance – were the children born of women considered to have a good sexual and moral profile, according to the cultural and patriarchal assumptions of that time, regarding the social roles of women and men. It is also rather visible that not all the population of illegitimate children had access to the legal mechanisms that could assure them the access to inheritance. On one hand, this sort of law case could not be admissible in court if the putative father was still alive, for the sake of protecting the legitimate family from "social scandal". On the other hand, the decision and the real capacity to file an investigation of paternity were profoundly conditioned by the possession of economic, cultural and social resources, which were most certainly not available to all.

References

ABBOTT, Pamela, WALLACE, Claire *et al.* (eds), 1991, *Gender, Power and Sexuality*, Basingstoke, Macmillan.

ASSIER-ANDRIEU, Louis and COMMAILLE, Jacques (eds), 1995, *Politique des lois en Europe: la filiation comme modèle de comparaison,* Paris, LGDJ.

BARTON, Chris and DOUGLAS, Gillian, 1995, *Law and Parenthood*, London, Butterworths.

BELEZA, Teresa Pizarro, 1991, "Legítima defesa e género feminino: paradoxos da feminist jurisprudence?", *Revista Crítica de Ciências Sociais,* 31, pp. 143–159.

–, 1993, *Mulheres, direito, crime ou a perplexidade de Cassandra*, PhD Dissertation, Lisboa, Faculdade de Direito.

BRIDGEMAN, Jo and MILLNS, Susan (eds), 1995, *Law and Body Politics: Regulating the female body*, Aldershot, Dartmouth Publishing Company.

CABRAL, João de Pina, 1989, *Filhos de Adão, filhas de Eva. A visão do mundo camponesa no Alto Minho,* Lisboa, Publicações Dom Quixote.

–, 1993, "A lei e a paternidade: as leis de filiação portuguesas vistas à luz da antropologia social", *Análise Social,* 28, 123/124, pp. 975–997.

CAPLOWITZ, David, 1963, *The Poor Pay More,* New York, Free Press.

COLLIER, Richard, 1995, *Masculinity, Law and the Family,* London and New York, Routledge.

COLLOQUY ON EUROPEAN LAW, 1999, *Legal problems relating to parentage: proceedings [of the] XXVIIth Colloquy on European Law*, Valletta (Malta), 15–17 September 1997, Strasbourg, Council of Europe Publishing.

COUNCIL OF EUROPE, 1999, *Legal problems relating to parentage*, Strasbourg, Council of Europe Publishing.

CRETNEY, Steve, 2003, *Family Law in the Twentieth Century: a History*, Oxford, Oxford University Press.

DELGADO, Pedro, 1996, *Divórcio e separação em Portugal. Análise social e demográfica, século XX,* Lisboa, Editorial Estampa.

DELUMEAU, Jean and ROCHE, Daniel, 2000, *Histoire des pères et de la paternité*, Paris, Larousse.

DIDUCK, Alison and KAGANAS, Felicity, 1999, *Family Law, Gender and the State. Text, Cases and Materials*, Oxford, Portland, Hart Publishing.

DOUGLAS, Gillian, 1991, *Law, Fertility and Reproduction*, London, Sweet and Maxwell.

DOUTHWAITE, Graham, 1979, *Unmarried Couples and the Law,* Indianapolis, The Allen Smith Company.

DURÃES, Margarida, 1988, "Herdeiros e não herdeiros: nupcialidade e celibato no contexto da propriedade enfiteuta", *Revista de História Económica e Social*, 21, pp. 47–56.

–, 1992, "No fim, não somos iguais: estratégias familiares na transmissão da propriedade", *Boletín de la Associación de Demografia Histórica*, 10, 3, pp. 125–141.

–, 1995, "Necessidades económicas e práticas jurídicas: problemas da transmissão das explorações agrícolas. Séculos XVIII–XX", *Ler História*, 29, pp. 67–88.

–, 2002, "Qualidade de vida e sobrevivência económica da família camponesa minhota: o papel das herdeiras (sécs. XVIII–XIX)", *Cadernos do Noroeste*, 17, 1–2, pp. 125–144.

ERICKSSON, Anders and SALDEEN, Ake, 1993, "Parenthood and science – establishing and contesting parentage", in John EEKELAAR and Petar SARCEVIC (eds), *Parenthood in Modern Society. Legal and Social Issues for the Twenty-first Century*, Dordrecht, Martinus Nijhoff, pp. 75–92.

EUROPEAN COMMISSION, 1997, *Directorate-General XII, Science, Research and Development Studies on the Socio-Economic Impact of Biotechnology: Genetic Fingerprints, Scientific Truth and Affiliation law*, Luxembourg, Office for Official Publications of the European Communities.

FORDER, Caroline, 1993, "Constitutional principle and the establishment of the legal relationship between the child and the non-marital father: a study of Germany, the Netherlands and England", *International Journal of Law and the Family*, 7, 1, pp. 40–107.

GARFINKEL, Irwin and KLAWITTER, Marieka, 1990, "The effect of routine income withholding of child support collections", *Journal of Policy Analysis and Management*, 9, 2, pp. 155–77.

GILBAR, Roy, 2005, *The Status of Family in Law and Bioethics: the Genetic Context*, Aldershot, Ashgate.

GREAT BRITAIN, Lord Chancellor's Department, 1998, *Court Procedures for the Determination of paternity. The Law on Parental Responsibility for Unmarried Fathers Consultation Paper*, London, Lord Chancellor's Dept.

GRUEN, Lori and PANICHAS, George, 1997, *Sex, Morality and the Law*, London, Routledge.

JACKSON, Stevi *et al.*, 1996, *Feminism and Sexuality: a Reader,* Edinburgh, Edinburgh University Press.

KAELBE, Hartmut, 1985, *Social Mobility in the 19th and 20th centuries: Europe and America in Comparative Perspective*, Leamington Spa, Berg.

LÉVI-STRAUSS, Claude, 1969, *The Elementary Structures of Kinship,* London, Eyre and Spottiswoode.

MATOESIAN, Gregory, 1992, *Reproducing Rape: Domination through Talk in the Courtroom*, Oxford, Polity Press.

MEULDERS, Marie-Thérèse, 1993, "Between nature and culture. The legal significance of parenthood in a changing world", in John EEKELAAR and Petar SARCEVIC (eds), *Parenthood in Modern Society. Legal and Social Issues for the Twenty-first Century*, Dordrecht, Martinus Nijhoff, pp. ix–xii.

PINEAU, Lois, 1997, "Date rape: a feminist analysis", in Lori GRUEN and George PANICHAS (eds), *Sex, Morality, and the Law*, New York, London, Routledge, pp. 428–443.

PINTO, Fernando Brandão, 1995, *Filiação natural*, Porto, ECLA Editora.

PIROG-GOOD, Maureen and GOOD, David, 1995, "Child support enforcement for teenage fathers: problems and prospects", *Journal of Policy Analysis and Management*, 14, 1, pp. 25–42.

POUZOL, Abel, 1902, *La recherche de la paternité: étude critique de sociologie et de législation comparée*, Paris, Giard et Brière.

RICHARDSON, Janice, 2005, "Feminist legal theory and practice: rethinking the relationship", *Feminist Legal Studies*, 13, 3, pp. 275–293.

SÁ, Isabel dos Guimarães, 1996, "Abandono de crianças, ilegitimidade e concepções pré-nupciais em Portugal: estudos recentes e perspectivas", in Vicente PEREZ-MOREDA (ed.), *Expostos e ilegítimos na realidade ibérica do século XVI ao presente. Actas do III Congresso da ADEH*, Porto, Afrontamento, pp. 37–58.

SANTOS, Boaventura de Sousa *et al.*, 1996, *Os tribunais nas sociedades contemporâneas. O caso português,* Porto, Afrontamento.

SCOTT, Ana Sílvia Volpi, 1999, *Famílias, formas de união e reprodução social no noroeste português (séculos XVIII e XIX),* Guimarães, NEPS, Universidade do Minho.

SEN, Amartya, 1985, *Commodities and Capabilities*, Amsterdam, North-Holland.

SENAEVE, Patrick, 1993, "The reform of affiliation law in France and the Benelux Countries", in John EEKELAAR and Petar SARCEVIC (eds), *Parenthood in Modern Society. Legal and Social Issues for the Twenty-first Century*, Dordrecht, Martinus Nijhoff, pp. 93–111.

SHELDON, Sally, 2005, "Reproductive technologies and the legal determination of fatherhood", *Feminist Legal Studies*, 13, 3, pp. 349–362.

SILVA, Manuel Carlos, 1998, *Resistir e adaptar-se. Constrangimentos e estratégias camponesas no Noroeste de Portugal,* Porto, Afrontamento.

SMART, Carol, 1987, "There is of course a distinction dictated by nature: law and the problem of paternity", in Michelle STANWORTH (ed.), *Reproductive Technologies*, Cambridge, Polity Press, pp. 99–117.

–, 1995, *Law, Crime and Sexuality: Essays in Feminism*, London, Sage.

SPAAS, Lieve and SELOUS, Trista (eds), 1998, *Paternity and Fatherhood: Myths and Realities*, London, Macmillan, New York, St. Martin's Press.

STRATHERN, Marilyn, 1992, *Reproducing the Future: Anthropology, Kinship and the New Reproductive Technologies*, London/New York, Routledge.

WALLBANK, Julie, 2004, "The role of rights and utility in instituting a child's right to know her genetic history", *Social and Legal Studies*, 13, 2, pp. 245–264.

Female Life Courses and Property Transmission in the Azorean Periphery (Portugal)

The Case of the Island of São Jorge in the 19th Century

Paulo Lopes MATOS

This study focuses on female life courses and family property transmissions during the 19th century in the island of São Jorge, a part of the Azores archipelago located some 1,400 kilometres west of continental Europe. The region, made up of nine islands, has always held a peripheral position within the Portuguese context. Furthermore, ever since the colonization of the archipelago – dating back to the 1440s – only the islands of São Miguel, Terceira and Faial have been beneficiaries of preferential development. The gradual development of trade and the geo-strategic nature of the functions performed by these islands, especially in connection with the Portuguese and Spanish Indias, gave rise to great dynamic building on the islands, with its truly pluri-continental geographic location right from the outset. Yet, away from the highly dynamic and cosmopolitan centres consisting of the main cities of Ponta Delgada (S. Miguel), Angra do Heroísmo (Terceira) and Horta (Faial), the Azores remained isolated and rural, and the other islands played only a peripheral role.

The island of São Jorge is truly rural. The terrain is hilly and only about 30 percent of its surface area is below 300 metres in altitude; the island's economy is based on cattle breeding. The island's natural environment is conditioned by its sharply undulating geography, and its population is correspondingly affected. There are two main groups: the first is concentrated to a great extent on the southerly side, with its more amenable climate, and the second is composed of a population dispersed throughout the central chain of mountains where pastureland is found. There indeed still exist various tiny hamlets dotted over the various *fajãs*, or small plains, sandwiched between sea and mountain. These small areas, where much of the demographic growth was concentrated in the 19th century, represent "proper communities, incompletely united [...] with a high degree of sociocentric conscience, heavy endogamy and a localist culture" (Sousa 1994, 74).

Our objective in this study is to understand many of the key mechanisms and norms of social reproduction in force in São Jorge, particularly family organization, the familial life cycle and the inheritance system prevalent during the 19th century. For this, we concentrate on the village of Ribeira Seca, under the jurisdiction of the council of Calheta[1] which, in terms of area and population, is the largest on São Jorge and one of the biggest in the Azores.

Figure 1. São Jorge and its major settlements

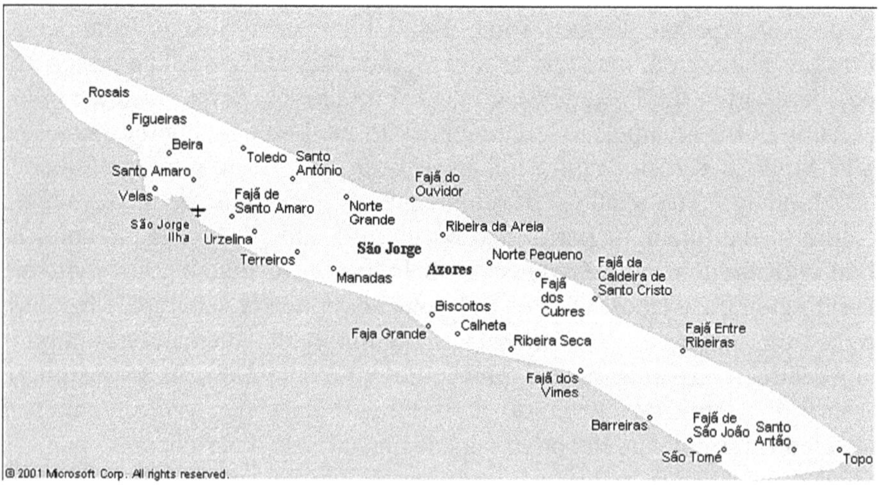

1 The village *(freguesia)* is the smallest civil entity in Portugal, and in this case corresponds to the parish *(paróquia)* of Ribeira Seca (a religious entity). A Portuguese council (*concelho* or *município*) is a larger territorial extent with civil purposes. Calheta Council includes the villages of Calheta, Ribeira Seca and Norte Pequeno. In 1855, Topo was also annexed by this council. In 1835, under Liberalism, districts were created. They corresponded to the widest civil area and included a variable number of councils. Both the councils of S. Jorge (Velas and Calheta) were part of the Angra do Heroismo district (Terceira Island) until 1975 when the Autonomous Region of Azores was founded.

The parish records available enable us to follow the life course of all residents between 1800 and 1910, while confession and communion lists *(libri status animarum)* depict household configurations. Hence, we can establish the family structure in both residential and biological terms and thereby gain a better understanding of the family life cycle.

The way in which patrimonial inheritance was handed down is detailed in inventories relating to orphans where the assets of the individual or couple were scrupulously enumerated in addition to the existence of dowry deeds, partitions made during one's life, and also last wills and testaments. To illustrate this, the sample taken is made up of about 120 Ribeira Seca disposable asset deeds with a further 90 from the other nine parishes of São Jorge Island. We do accept that the sample focuses overtly on one of the villages; however, this choice was intentional so as to enable the thorough study of one of the largest parishes in the Azores and hence understand the family cycle of life along with land ownership patterns.

The conclusions of this study would, in any case, have to be provisional. The absence of studies on the transmission of patrimonial inheritance on the archipelago (above all for the under privileged classes) qualify many of the hypotheses made herein. Furthermore, the sample is obviously insufficient for completely tracing the prevailing family cycle of reproduction on the island given all the complexities of patrimonial inheritance throughout the 19th century. Nevertheless, it remains highly relevant for discovering the main trends regarding the socio-economic organization of the family and its *modus operandi* when it came to social reproduction.

Families and Socio-Economic Status

Throughout the 19th century, intense population growth, demand for more productive land, and migration brought about direct consequences for this type of agricultural economy. It had turned to self-sufficiency as a consequence of the island experiencing difficulty in fully integrating the regional economic centres. The São Jorge market was restricted by the agricultural partitioning of its lands; however, this was not the only cause of economic stagnation, which was also due to the absence of any industry and or investment in agriculture (Sousa 2000, 129).

Geography was an obstacle to easy communication between the various population centres. In addition, it was difficult to balance the production of the various farm commodities: cereals, corn and wheat, various tubers – including the English potato and yams –, vineyards and cattle. In fact, the scarcity of land below 300 metres restricted the cultivation of corn or the setting up of vineyards, instead favouring wheat and tubers, the island's main produce. Cattle breeding dominated the island economy. Yet the breeding of cattle – mostly bovine – did not give rise to any parallel industry until the end of the 19th century when the first tentative steps in industrial dairy production were taken.

In 1875, Ribeira Seca had 3,198 inhabitants living in 742 households. The Church rolls indicate that about 80 percent of the population worked in the primary sector.[2] Countrymen (32 percent) – owners of small parcels of land but also working for farmers – constituted the single largest profession. They were followed by rural labourers (20 percent), many of whom were landless but working occasionally or for long periods of times for farmers or landowners.[3] At the other end of the hierarchy were the farmers (14 percent), who lived entirely off their land, and often close to the "self sufficiency house model",[4] and the landlords (11 percent). Most of them kept working the land, and consequently are included in the primary sector.

The secondary sector, which included artisans in this period, was very small (7 percent), and many secondary activities were agriculture related (Capela 1989, 26–40) confirming the predominantly rural nature of the parish. The most common craftsmen are the carpenters (3 percent), certainly employed in the maintenance of the 742 households recorded in 1875 and the makers of agricultural implements. In second place are the masons (one percent), who were also involved in the construction and maintenance of residential houses and public infrastructures.

2 The percentages are calculated on the total population.

3 Fishermen are very few (4 percent) in a village where there was no clearly identified fishing community as was the case of Velas and Calheta villages (council centres).

4 There is no full consensus around this concept. However, we here define it as a unit with the land and agricultural tools needed to achieve self-sufficiency in food terms. Normally, they are property holding families operating across distinctive ecological areas (wines, planted crops and pasture), using outside labour in times of greater agricultural hardship (Wall 1998, 101–112; Fonseca 1996, 711–748; Matos 2007, 77–84).

The "tertiary sector" included about 13 percent of the population and was constituted mostly of auxiliary personnel or "helpers" and servants, together representing about 76 percent of this labour sector. The remaining professions regrouped very few individuals (31), even if one included trade and public administration, further bringing to the fore the rural character of this village.

The testamentary deeds and the survey records demonstrate the existence of a class of landowners possessing very small but productive holdings, the exception being the various pastures belonging to large landowners. Thanks to the fiscal data provided by the *predial contribution* of 1881, we can link the principal activities and the annual collectable income (ACI) of each head of household.[5] This tax was levied on both farm land and urban estates. It is important to mention that the ACI corresponds to nearly 8 percent of total wealth. A rural worker declaring an ACI of 6,000 *réis* would have an estimated asset of 75,000 *réis* and his annual net income was about 3,750 *réis*.[6] The predial contribution was an individual tax payable on properties registered with the local treasury offices. Since inheritance occurred most of the time after death, the ACI normally coincided with the household income.[7] In 1881, 809 contributors were registered, 581 males and 228 females. However, there are several difficulties in identifying female owners due to a lack of information regarding civil status and age. Furthermore, married women are not always registered under their husband's surname. Female homonymy makes it impossible to calculate total household income. Thus, Table 1, which gives aggregate income by occupation at Ribeira Seca in 1881 (in *réis*), refers only to male heads of household. But 22.8 percent of heads were females, most of them with low taxable incomes (Matos 2007, 61).[8]

5 Main source: Biblioteca Pública e Arquivo Regional de Angra do Heroísmo (Public Archives of Angra do Heroísmo, henceforth BPARAH), Câmara da Calheta *(Calheta Council)*, Diversos (1720–1900), unclassified document.

6 This corresponded to nearly 5 percent of total assets but this value fluctuated across the regions of Portugal.

7 Regarding this issue and its methodological background see Rowland 1994; Brandão 1980, 173–207; Fonseca 1988, 63–106 and Rocha 1994.

8 Their total collectable income was 1,983,945 *réis* (15.2 percent of the total) with a maximum of 78,000 and a minimum of 400 *réis*. Mean and median were 8,701 and 4,300 *réis*, respectively. 61.7 percent of women had a collectable income below 5,000

Table 1. Collectable income by occupation at Ribeira Seca in 1881 (in *réis*), for male heads of household

Occupation	*Landlord*	*Farmer*	*Countryman*	*Rural worker*	*Fisherman*
Average	69,700	23,193	6,483	6,461	6,662
Median	25,250	21,050	5,200	4,400	5,300

Sources: Public Archives of Angra do Heroísmo, Câmara da Calheta *(Calheta Council)*, Diversos (1720–1900), unclassified document.
Notes: The total number of household heads in Ribeira Seca is 778 in 1881; 22.8 percent were females (Matos 2007, 61).

Rural workers with annual median income of around 4,400 *réis* are most representative of the village population. In various cases, these individuals owned the tiniest parcels of land, very small vineyards or arable fields, but in such a manner that many worked on the lands of larger landlords, and were frequently paid in kind, especially bread grains such as wheat. Close to these labourers were the countrymen whose taxable earnings averaged 5,200 *réis*. As they owned some land, they produced some farm commodities, but in most cases they would similarly have to work for the farmers or larger land owners on a weekly basis in order to support themselves and their families.

Farmers and landowners, whose annual taxable income ranged between 21,000 and 25,000 *réis* respectively were in a far better position. However, we must note that these two designations are often confused because landowners usually farmed their own land. Various researchers believe that the farmer was the one who possessed a pair of oxen and not just a plough, because the term's etymology implies one tills the land with one's own implements (O'Neill 1994, 100–104; Brandão 1994, 139–154; Wall 1998, 24–33; Capela 1989, 26–40). However, wills and deeds show that in many cases these farmers owned cattle, but no team of oxen. This also explains the importance of the breeding of both ovine (sheep) and bovine cattle to the local economy.[9] We therefore assume that the label "farmer" referred to one who owned land or cattle sufficient for his sustenance and was able to use hired hands if the need arose. It is only in rare

réis, 21.5 percent between 5,000 and 10,000 *réis*, and only 18.8 cent above 10,000 *réis*.

9 On the other hand, the *predial contribution* shows various farmers with annual incomes of about 20,000 *réis*, which in no way equates real wealth.

cases that we encounter someone who could really be self sufficient, given that just six of the 102 farmers listed in the *predial contribution* records exceed 50,000 *réis* annually. The landlord category covers a diversity of situations, highlighted by the disparity between the average (70,000 *réis*) and the median (25,000 *réis*) figures for earned income.

Male Emigration and Female Difficulty in Finding a Spouse

The island of São Jorge appears to have been scarcely populated in comparison to the rest of the archipelago; it had a population density somewhere between 54 and 75 inhabitants per km^2, in 1799 and 1878, respectively. Between 1800 and 1900, population grew by 0.19 percent annually, but during the last quarter of the 19th century the island lost a significant part of its population due to emigration to the United States (Matos 2007, 239–264; Silva 2004, 275–294; Amorim 2004, 65).[10] The demographic system prevalent on the island of São Jorge can be considered as "low pressure". Population stability was achieved by emigration. In the period under study, the average crude birth rate was around 27.0 per thousand while the mortality rate was just 19.8. This figure is uncommonly low for the period under consideration.[11]

Just as on the other islands of the Azores for which data is available – as in the case of Pico Island – emigration continued throughout the 19th century and assumed high proportions (Matos 2007, 243–252; Amorim 2004, 65). But by and large, it was young men who left – often before the age of 15 – creating a strong imbalance between the sexes. Between 1799 and 1900 the sex ratio of the 20–39 age groups oscillated between 38.1 and 78.1 percent in Ribeira Seca, which shows a clear imbalance in the marriage market (Table 2).[12]

10 Between 1875 and 1900, the annual growth rate was negative (-0.7 percent).

11 The life expectancy at the time of birth during this period was 51.1 years for the males and 55.4 years for females, which in part was due to the reduced infant mortality on this island (Matos 2007, 238).

12 The sex ratio is the number of males per hundred females. Figures for Ribeira Seca are based on the following sources: 1799 – BPARAH, *Capitania-geral*, box no. 6, "Mappa

Table 2. Sex ratio imbalance in Ribeira Seca (1799–1900)

Year	*1799*	*1832*	*1864*	*1875*	*1884*	*1900*
Sex ratio (global)	89.1	86.7	84.4	74.8	79.4	70,0
Sex ratio (20-39 years)	77.5	78.1	54.2	38.1	39.5	53.1

Sources: 1799: Statistic Map of the parish of Ribeira Seca; 1832: civil source based on Pascal lists; 1864: National Census; 1875, 1884 and 1900: Pascal confessional lists.
Note: Sex ratio is the number of males per hundred females.

The difficulty in finding a partner is demonstrated by the high average marriage age for both sexes: in the parish of Ribeira Seca, mean age at first marriage was never below 29.6 years for males and 27.8 years for females. All social groups showed a high average age, as can be seen in Table 3, but there were differences between the farmers (32.0), the peasants or countrymen (31.4) and rural workers (30.3). This situation was related to a major obstacle faced by would-be farming couples: access to land. This often did not happen until the death of their parents. On the contrary, rural workers, relying on their ability to work and therefore to earn, tended to get married slightly earlier.

Table 3. Mean ages at first marriage for males and females, in Ribeira Seca, according to occupation of the groom (1825–1910)

Period of	Farmers		Peasants		Rural workers	
marriage	*M*	*F*	*M*	*F*	*M*	*F*
1825–1849	29.7	27.3	28.7	24.9	27.3	25.6
1850–1874	33.3	28.6	27.9	28.6	31.8	29.8
1875–1899	33.0	27.8	31.9	30.1	32.6	29.8
1900–1910	32.2	25.7	34.3	28.6	31.3	28.6
Mean Age	32.0	27.5	31.3	28.8	30.3	28.1

Sources: Parish reconstruction database (1800–1910), by periods of marriage.
Note: Calculated on all celebrated marriages detailing both male and female ages. The total number is 1,333: 404 farmers, 342 peasants and 587 rural workers.

estatístico da freguezia da Ribeira Seca" (Statistic Map of the parish of Ribeira Seca)[…]; 1832 – BPARAH, *Governo Civil*, Prefeitura e Governo Civil de Angra do Heroísmo (1831-1835), "Relação de todos os indivíduos […]" (civil source based on Pascal lists); 1864 – *População. Censo no 1º de Janeiro de 1864, pp. 257-259* (National Census); 1875, 1884 and 1900 – Arquivo Paroquial da Igreja Matriz da Calheta (Parochial Archive of Calheta, henceforth APIMC), Pascal confessional lists of 1875, 1884 and 1900.

Table 4. Permanent celibacy for males and females in Ribeira Seca (1800–1910). Percentages, by cohort of birth

Period	*Male*	*Female*
1800–1825	9.2	19.4
1825–1850	20.0	17.6
1850–1875	15.5	27.8
1875–1900	13.1	22.7
1900–1910	15.8	28.2
1800–1910	14.8	23.2

Sources: Parish reconstruction database (1800–1910). Longitudinal analysis by cohort of birth.
Note: Celibacy is here the proportion of persons, in each sex, who reached age 50 having never married.

Permanent celibacy, especially among the female population, was also high, reflecting the shortage of men due to emigration. In the village of Ribeira Seca, 15 percent of men and 23 percent of women remained single in the 19th century.[13] During the second half of the 19th century, this percentage rose even higher on São Jorge attaining figures of 17 percent and 28 percent for men and women respectively (Matos 2007, 170) (Table 4).

The Incidence of Births out of Wedlock

One of the consequences of the obstacles to get married on São Jorge was the high incidence of illegitimacy, though this was also attributed to various other factors: namely strong endogamy and consanguinity, a *post-mortem* inheritance system and even some acceptance of birth outside of marriage among elites.[14] Illegitimacy was also a peculiar characteristic of Portugal, especially in the North. This phenomenon was by and large socially acceptable, and was not repressed by the authorities despite the large percentage of the municipal budget (20–40 percent) spent on found-

13 Celibacy is here the proportion of persons, in each sex, who reached age 50 having never married.
14 This issue was discussed extensively in Matos 2007.

lings (Goody 2000, 80–81; Sá 1996, 37–58; Amorim 1999, 32; Blaikie 1993, 12). Some anthropological studies based on the North of Portugal towards the end of the 19th century revealed that illegitimacy was related to inheritance restrictions and the need for a larger pool of labour as:

> for poorer women children are always an asset as their labour is highly valued. Better a bastard child than none at all (O'Neill 1983, 70–71).

But there is still a lack of studies on illegitimacy providing us with a proper and consistent interpretation of the phenomenon. Between 1800 and 1910, the average percentage of illegitimate children in the parish of Ribeira Seca was 19, while on the island of São Jorge, this oscillated between 13 and 24 percent between 1838 and 1900 (Table 5). Compared with the rest of the Azores, and even with the mainland, São Jorge therefore displays very high rates of illegitimacy in the last few decades of the 1800s. It is generally accepted that Portugal and Spain were one of the two countries of Europe with the highest percentage of illegitimate and abandoned children, a reality that strongly contrasted with the situation prevailing in Northern Europe (Laslett 1980; Hollingsworth 1981; Blaikie 1993).

Endogamy and consanguinity rates were higher on an island where marriage opportunities were already reduced, and where property was restricted to small areas of productive land. In the village of Ribeira Seca, the average figure for geographic endogamy was around 77 percent, while consanguinity reached 30 percent.[15] The longitudinal study of families in which one child needed a canonical dispensation for his/her wedding indicates that the workers and peasants managed to get just half of their children married, a figure that reached only 63 percent even in the case of the farmers.[16] Such a situation leads us to conclude that both wealthy and poor families displayed the same tendency to marry within their own group. In

15 We refer to ecclesiastical dispensations for consanguinity or affinity awarded by the bishop of Angra do Heroísmo e das Ilhas dos Azores (Diocesis of Angra and Azores islands).

16 A canonical dispensation requirement was compulsory whenever the future bride and groom were both kin and/or affine (that is related by marriage, until the 4th degree). In theory, only the Pope could authorize such impediments but by tradition Bishops could provide dispensation for poor persons *(in forma pauperum)* (Goody 2000, 27–31). A dispensation process for the poor cost on average 6,000 *réis*, but this amount oscillated greatly depending on the dioceses (Matos 2007, 191–203). A detailed view of this issue can be found in Monteiro 1890, 649–711.

addition, farmers, who were in a better economic position, were able to pay for more canonical dispensations (Matos 2007, 174–203).

Table 5. Percentage of illegitimate births in the Azores and Continental Portugal (1838–1900)

Islands	*Districts*	*1838–39*		*1873*		*1881*		*1886*		*1895*		*1900*
Sta Maria		11.3	10.7		6.6	12.5						
São Miguel	São Miguel	10.2				6.2	6.4		5.7		3.2	2.5
Terceira		15.6		12.8		9.1						
Graciosa	Angra do Heroísmo	16.7	15.2	20.5	15,8	20.0	13,1		11.1		8.3	6.6
S. Jorge		*13.1*		*23.2*		*23.9*		*11.6*		*15.2*		
Pico						8.3						
Faial	Horta					15.3	11.9		11.2		9.1	7.0
Flores						11.3						
Corvo						0						
Azores		11.9		10.9		9.1		8.1		5.6		4.3
Portugal								11.7		12.4		11.6

Sources: See Matos and Silva 2008, 43 (Table 7).

Household Composition and Dwelling Conditions for Single Mothers

We used the Laslett/Hammel household typology to analyse families on the island of São Jorge (Laslett and Wall 1972), although the principal objective of this proposal – the dichotomy between simple and complex families – ends up undervaluing/disfiguring some family forms on Ribeira Seca. In practice, Robert Rowland notes that this method is based "directly on the English experience, in which the common form of the domestic household is the simple family, and in which there are incomplete forms" (Rowland 1997, 52). Furthermore, Chácon Jiménez states that the merit of the Laslett method does not eliminate a critical and painstaking review of its results, for "its methods of work results prove sterile, in most cases, to explain the functioning mechanism of Southern European societies" (Chácon 1990, 20–21). Indeed, in most cases, such regional differentiations demand more sociological conceptualisation for, according to this author,

> the family is shown as a system of relations between the hereditary practice and the structure of relationships that transcends the actual familial unity (Chácon 1990, 23).

These criticisms however do not undermine the overall effectiveness of Laslett's classification, which is extremely important to generate a first insight into residential family composition (Wall 1983, 1–63). Table 6 shows the configuration of domestic groups in accordance with the Cambridge classification method.[17] Subsequently, we shall analyze the households displaying incidence of illegitimacy more closely in order to capture in the best possible manner the ways in which birth outside marriage had an impact on the family and single mothers' well-being.

What stands out in any of the three periods considered here is the fact the simple or nuclear type of family household accounts for around 56 percent of all cases, and neo-locality is the norm for new households.[18] In reality, longitudinal analysis of various households indicates that in a larger number of cases newly-married sons lived close to the parent's residence and in only rare situations would the parental dwelling be transferred to the son. Inversely, the "solitary household" (category 1) and "no family households" (category 2) – do not represent a large number of households, especially in 1839 and 1875. In 1839, the first category included around 5 percent of the total, although constituted of mostly unmarried people (category 1b). However, in 1900 "solitary" households had increased to 15.6 percent probably reflecting emigration to the United States.[19] The "no family" households represented about 11 percent of the

17 We used the Pascal lists of confession of 1839, 1875 and 1900. The 1839 list was chosen due to its coverage compared with the 1832 document (BPARAH, *Capitania-geral*, Mapas de População: 1808–1841, "Copia do rol da confissão dos freguezes [...]" (Copy of parish confessional role)). Sources for 1875 and 1900 are stated in Table 2. Unfortunately there are no lists between 1840 and 1874. Number of households in 1839 is: 580, in 1875: 742 and 839 in 1900.

18 The inclusion of fathers and single mothers, around 4.6 percent in the two years studied, ends up increasing the marriage ratios.

19 In the last quarter of the 19th century, emigration rose and female participation first began on a large scale. Parochial statistics for emigration (both legal and clandestine) reveal that, between 1872 and 1913, 2,309 inhabitants emigrated; 556 of them were

whole in the three observations especially the 2b, "Coresident relatives of other types".

Table 6. Household structure in the parish of Ribeira Seca in 1839, 1875 and 1900 following the Cambridge classification. Percentages

Category/class	*1839*		*1875*		*1900*	
1 - Solitary		4.8		6.3		15.6
1a - Widowed	2.1		2.6		6.2	
1b - Single or unknown marital status	2.8		3.8		9.4	
2 - No family		11.4		11.2		11.3
2a - Coresident siblings	4.1		3.0		3.5	
2b - Coresident relatives of other types	7.3		8.2		7.9	
3 - Simple family households		57.2		55.5		55.9
3a - Married couples alone	8.8		10.2		12.2	
3b - Married couples with child(ren)	41.0		37.5		34.7	
3c - Widowers with child(ren)	1.6		1.8		1.8	
3d - Widows with child(ren)	5.9		6.1		7.2	
4 - Extended family households		23.4		24.9		15.0
4a - Extended upwards	5.3		6.3		2.4	
4b - Extended downwards	12.4		15.1		9.3	
4c - Extended laterally	2.8		1.9		2.7	
4d - Combinations of 4a-4c	2.9		1.6		0.6	
5 - Multiple family households		1.6		1.3		1.3
5a - Secondary unit up	0		0.1		0.0	
5b (i) - Secondary unit down (male)	0		0.4		0.5	
5b (ii) - Secondary unit down (female)	0		0		0	
5c - Units all one level	0		0		0	
5d - *Frérèches*	0		0.1		0	
5e - Other combinations	0		0		0	
6 - Indeterminate	1.6		0.7		0.8	
TOTAL		100		100		100

Sources: Pascal lists of confession of 1839, 1875 and 1900.
Notes: For the Cambridge classification of household structures, see Laslett and Wall 1972.

women; 63 percent of emigrants (male and female) were between 15 and 50 years old. See APIMC, *Notas Estatísticas da Freguezia da Ribeira Seca (1872–1913).*

Table 7. Domestic household forms in some of the Azores Islands (1794–1879) according to Laslett/Hammel classification. Percentages

Island/Area	*Year*	*1*	*2*	*3*	*4*	*5*	*6*	*%*
São Jorge Island (urban)	1794–1839	7.6	15.2	55.5	15.0	0.0	6.7	100
São Jorge Island (rural)	1794–1839	5.7	11.1	62.9	16.9	0.7	2.7	100
Graciosa Island (urban)	1839	21.9	12.4	50.4	9.3	3.5	2.5	100
Graciosa Island (rural)	1839	14.6	11.9	59.5	11.4	1.3	1.3	100
Pico Island (rural)	1879	10.2	13.8	59.3	9.3	7.4	0.0	100

Sources: see Matos 2007, 374 with minor adaptations due to the integration of single mothers in category 2 ("No family").
Notes: Laslett classification categories are used here. 1: Solitary; 2: No family; 3: Simple family households; 4: extended family households; 5: multiple family households and 6: Indeterminate.
* Number of households under observation – São Jorge: 1730, Graciosa: 717, Pico: 333.

It is important to state that a large majority of 2b households were made of unmarried mothers with children or single fathers with sons. When dealing with this issue, Portuguese researchers normally classify unmarried mothers with offspring as "simple family households", as their family is deemed nuclear (for example, Wall 1998, 40; Pereira 1995, 98–99; Rowland 1984, 13–32; Brettell 1986, 170). However, this issue lies beyond the scope of this paper.[20] We seek here to classify Ribeira Seca's domestic structure following Laslett's model before setting out a specific proposal for this village (Table 9).

The most remarkable characteristic of Ribeira Seca's family organization was the important amount of extended households. Yet it is important to recall that the inclusion of the unusually large number of families with illegitimate offspring led to the rise of this category since all dwellings where "illegitimate grandchildren" resided were considered above as "extended" (Table 6). In fact, the proportion of those extended families

20 This issue is discussed extensively in Matos 2007, 367–428.

reaches 24 percent, almost a quarter of all the configurations of domestic households.

The distribution of households by type in the parish of Ribeira Seca is similar to the one in the remaining island of São Jorge as well as in a couple of the neighbouring islands, Graciosa and Pico. The prevalent domestic configuration was the simple family unit (category 3), whose percentage oscillated between 50 percent and 62 percent on the islands of Graciosa and São Jorge, respectively (Table 7).

Extended households were found in the urban and rural areas on the island of São Jorge. Part of the reason was the acceptance of illegitimate children by maternal grandparents, since most resided with their mothers and maternal grandparents.

The percentage of illegitimacy was also very high in Graciosa, but there, there were differences between the urban and rural areas. In the former, "solitary" and "no family" households were predominant, perhaps because families were less stable. Extended households were far fewer than in São Jorge as a large percentage of single mothers lived on their own in contrast to São Jorge (Matos 2000, 256–267).

Unwed Mothers and Marriage

To better understand the consequences of births out of wedlock for the mothers' life course and future well-being, we need to classify illegitimate offspring according to the marital status of their mothers when these women reached the end of their lives. It was therefore of interest to us to ascertain how many mothers of illegitimate children never married and how many of them married at a later age. For some, we lack this information but usually age at delivery is registered as well as identity, enabling us to reach the following conclusions in Table 8.

Table 8. Single mother future life courses, number of children born and eventual posterior marriage in the parish of Ribeira Seca (1800–1910). Percentages and mean age at first delivery

Type – situation	*%*	*Mean age at birth of first child*	*Number of children*
0 – Unwed at death	17	26.2	2.5
1 – Single mothers without further information about marriage or death	39	25.7	1.8
2 – Single mothers with subsequent marriage (father present at the baptism of the children)	26	26.2	1.8
3 – Single mothers with subsequent marriage (father absent at the baptism of the children)	18	24.4	2.1
Together	100	25.8	1.9

Sources: See Matos 2007.
Note: Number of cases/unwed mothers under observation: 911. Number of illegitimate children at birth: 1761.

Here, we distributed unwed mothers between those who later married and those who apparently did not.[21] The proportion of women who later married is rather high (44 percent). Out of those (26 percent) did not declare the name of the father at the baptism of the illegitimate children (type 2), and in the other 18 percent the father was present and accepted paternity of the child (type 3).

Family of Origin as a Refuge for Unwed Mothers

A new distribution of households based on this last information (Table 9) produces a view of family structures in Ribeira Seca closer to the past reality. It appears that unwed mothers usually stayed in their family of origin, living with their own parents. Consequently, "simple families"

21 We refer to single women who are not identified as having married at a later date in the parish (1800–1910), or on death (1800–1943).

(category 3) were less common than it seemed previously (62.9 percent) and corresponded only to 38 percent of the total in 1839, dropping to 32.5 percent in 1875. Inversely, the "extended households" (category 4) was more important as a consequence of "nuclear family" including illegitimate grandchildren: 54 percent in 1839 and 58 percent in 1875.

Table 9. Family and household configurations in situations of illegitimacy* and revised repartition of household structures in Ribeira Seca (1839, 1875, 1900)

Category/class	*1839*	*1875*	*1900*
A - Simple households	41.8	35.8	49.6
Aa – Single mothers	25.5	25.2	31.6
Ab - Single fathers	6.1	1.3	2.6
Ac - Consensual units	2.0	1.3	3.4
Ad - Siblings with downward extension	8.2	7.9	12.0
B - Extended households	58.2	64.2	50.4
Ba_1 - Complete extended family with descendents	23.5	26.5	23.9
Ba_2 - Incomplete extended family with descendents	28.6	30.5	15.4
Bb - Extended families (other combinations)	3.1	3.3	4.3
Bc - Grandmothers with children and grandchildren	3.1	4.0	6.8
Number of households in situation of illegitimacy	98	151	117

Sources: See Matos 2007, 398–428.
Notes: * "Family and household configurations in situations of illegitimacy", includes illegitimate children alive and under age 18.
Correspondence with Table 6 above concerning the classification of domestic households with incidents of illegitimacy and the regular Laslett classification is the following: Aa=3d, Ab=3e, Ac=2c, Ad=2b, Ba_1 and Ba_2=4b, Bb=4a-4c, Bc=4b.

This is evidence of the commonality of this behaviour. This reveals the non-stigmatisation of illegitimacy: a large number of single mothers remained enclosed in the bosom of their family of origin and enjoyed shelter there with their children, finding support and probably better everyday well-being than elsewhere. "Extended households" were undeniably common once we take the presence of illegitimate children into account in our revised distribution of household structures. In the first instance, the high incidence of extended households is possible thanks to high life expectancy at birth.

Table 10. Distribution of households including single mothers according to the "Family configurations in situations of illegitimacy" and current age in the parish of Ribeira Seca (1875)

Category/class	*Type 0*	*Ave-rage age*	*Type 1*	*Ave-rage age*	*Type 2*	*Ave-rage age*	*Type 3*	*Ave-rage age*	*Total*
A - SIMPLE HOUSEHOLDS	18		10		0		5		33
Aa - Single mothers	15	46.8	10	36.0	0		3	35.8	28
Ab - Consensual units	0	39.7	0		0		2		2
Ac - Siblings with downward extension	3		0		0		0		3
B - EXTENDED HOUSEHOLDS	25		13		12		7		57
Ba_1 - Complete extended family with descendents	13	31.7	8	29.7	5	29.8	4	31.0	30
Ba_2 - Incomplete extended family with descendents	8	34.1	3	33.3	6	30.1	3	32.5	20
Bb - Extended families (other combinations)	1	20.0	0		0		0		1
Bc - Grandmothers with children and grandchildren	3	34.0	2	31.5	1	33.0	0		6
Number of households in situation of illegitimacy	43		23		12		12		90

Sources: See Matos 2007, 398–428.

Indeed, when extended vertically, in a wider perspective and within the scope of the Laslett method, the "extended households" implies the coexistence of three generations. Out of the 185 (24.9 percent) extended families in 1875, 112 contained three generations (where the older generation retained headship). In summary, grandparents living with their grandchildren constituted 16 percent of Ribeira Seca families. In this sense, domestic configuration in the parish under study was undeniably complex.

Another observation has to be made concerning the "extended households" including illegitimate children alive and under age 18. As already explained, the sub-categories Ba_1 and Ba_2 come close to the category 4b in the Laslett/Hammel classification. Nevertheless, taking into consideration the presence or absence of both grandparents, we intend to separate the "complete family" (Ba_1) from the "incomplete family" (Ba_2).[22]

The last sub-category "single grandmothers with child(ren) and grandchild(ren)" (Bc) – which constitute a very specific sector kind of household with illegitimate children – is not frequent (around 4 percent) and includes the poorest families with illegitimate children (Table 10).[23]

Although it is very difficult to trace their precise life course due to migration, homonymy and domestic service positions, the majority of unwed mothers were living in extended households (57 cases) against 33 cases residing in simple households in 1875. But only mothers whose child was recognized by the father at baptism (category 2) were living with their parents, and the interval between conception and marriage was short. On the contrary, the other groups – especially never married women (category 0) – were more likely to be living on their own, on account of the mother's higher age. In the majority of these cases (76 percent), at least one of the woman's parents was dead and they had received an important share of the inheritance. To understand the process of transmission of assets in this society, we shall now study notarial records and how inhabitants of São Jorge Island used to hand their properties down to the next generation during the 19th century.

A Gender Approach to Inheritance Patterns in São Jorge

We are going to use a number of notarial and judicial instruments, with a preference for inventories in favour of orphans to uncover the main meth-

22 Ba_1 is a "Complete extended family with descendents" and Ba_2 an "Incomplete extended family with descendents" (the head is a widow or widower).

23 Or those clearly defined as "bastardy-prone sub-society" by Laslett" (1980, 219).

ods of asset transmission on the island of São Jorge. Out of 120 documents used – all public deeds of gift or will – 75 are from people living in the parish of Ribeira Seca, 15 in the town of Velas, 10 in the town of Calheta, 7 in the parish of Manadas and 13 in Norte Grande (Figure 1).[24]

Women are overrepresented in the sample of 104 deeds dealing with gifts/endowments during life or wills (69.2 percent). This is probably a consequence of higher female life expectancy and of the age difference at marriage. Two thirds of the widowed testators were females (Table 11).

Table 11. Testators by gender and civil status, on São Jorge (1800–1910). Percentages

Civil status of testator	*Male*	*Female*	*Total*
Married	52.0	28.1	34.3
Single	0	9.4	7.1
Widow(er)	48.0	62.5	58.6
TOTAL	100	100	100
Number of testators	32	72	104

Sources: Notarial and judicial inventories of São Jorge kept at the Regional Archives of Angra do Heroísmo.

This corpus shows that all testators, whether having heirs or otherwise, made use of legal provisions regarding the *terça*[25] and 17 percent divided it between several heirs. Besides the generalisation of this practice, which became institutionalised over generations, three conditions are frequent whenever a *terça* is bequeathed: the legatee's obligation to take care of the *legado pio,*[26] caring for and looking after the testator in old age – usually in the residence of the legatee – and, last but not least, the legatee would have the usufruct of the property but would only possess the land completely when both members of the couple had died.

24 Main sources are: BPARAH, *Cartórios Notariais*, Ilha de São Jorge; BPARAH, *Inventários Orfanológicos – Ilha de São Jorge* (Notarial and judicial inventories of São Jorge kept at the Regional Archives of Angra do Heroísmo).

25 Since the Portuguese Medieval Age the *terça* ("third part") corresponds to the patrimony that the couple could use freely in favour of anyone they wished. For more information on Portuguese legislation, see Durães's contribution to the present volume.

26 Normally a bequest to the local church, in the way of donations or masses, considered as a means of seeking salvation for the soul.

Table 12. Legado pio, assistance in old age and reserve of the usufruct of property. Number of occurrences and percentage according to the notarial deeds of São Jorge (1800–1910)

Number - %	*Legado pio*	*Assistance*	*Usufruct reserved*
N	61	22	53
% total	79.2	28.2	68.8
		Legado pio + assistance	
N		19	
% total		24.7	
		Legado pio + assistance + usufruct reserve	
N		11	
% total		14.3	

Sources: Notarial and judicial inventories of São Jorge kept at the Regional Archives of Angra do Heroísmo.

Table 12 reveals that a significant percentage of "third portion" legatees were burdened with *legado pio* for the salvation of the deceased's souls (79 percent). Similarly, a number of testators refused to transfer the usufruct of the properties (69 percent). In many cases, the future legatees could legally take possession of the land but could only enjoy its fruits after the death of the second parent. The appreciable percentage of testators who reserved the right of usufruct over their properties, favored a post-mortem system of property transmission, sparing the older couple the cost of dividing their assets and guaranteeing their control over property and goods until the death of the last spouse. Table 13 shows the length of time that elapsed between writing of the testament and the death of the testator.

A majority of males' and females' wills were written just prior to death (0 years) – 57 percent in the case of males and 46 percent in the case of females – but almost all men wrote their wills less than four years before their death.[27] These figures appear to confirm the delayed transfer of inheritance in which property ownership would, in 49 of the cases, be transferred soon after the death of the testators (less then a year), which in a manner displays the desire of the couple to possess absolute control over the inheritance even until the hour of death. The short time span between the writing of the will and death confirms that testators clung to their property as long as they could.

27 And, in several cases, just a few days before their death.

Table 13. Time gap between the making of the will and the death of testators on São Jorge (1800–1910). Percentages

Years	*Men*	*Women*
0	56.5	45.8
1	4.3	6.1
2	8.7	2.1
3	4.3	4.2
4	17.6	4.2
5	0	2.1
6	0	0
7	0	2.1
8	0	2.1
9	0	0
10	0	2.1
> 10	4.3	14.6
Unknown	4.3	14.6
%	100	100
Number of testators	32	72

Sources: Notarial and judicial inventories of São Jorge kept at the Regional Archives of Angra do Heroísmo.

Intergenerational Transmission Strategies within Families

The wish to preserve control over the estate is reflected in wills as well as in the deeds of gifts that are usually included in marriage contracts. In most of these documents the testator designated the beneficiary of the "third" free portion *(terça)* and included his/her eventual obligations, but the general strategy consisted of keeping the surviving spouse in legal possession of the estate. The data presented in Tables 12 and 13 confirms the tendency to maintain the family patrimony intact. This can be noted at two levels: in addition to the delays in the wills, couples avoided dividing property during their lifetime. Thus, deeds given in dowry are rare and, even here, in most cases, the testator only gives the usufruct of the land.[28]

28 In a sample of 137 pre-nuptial deeds dating from between 1800 and 1910, only 29 (21%) included gifts of property to children.

Moreover, in most wills the *terça* is given to an heir, but with serious restrictions. As a general rule, the legatee only takes possession of the land after both members of the couple had died. As if this were not enough, the legatee would also pay the funeral expenses, the *legado pio* and, frequently, assist the testators during their old age.

Let us examine some specific cases. This happened, for example, with Manuel Silveira Carvalho, a resident of Portal, who died prematurely in 1816, as a victim of an accident. He reserved the third part of his estate to be used for the salvation of his soul. The remainder was to be distributed to his three sons – who by law were the heirs of two thirds of the estate – but "with the condition that his wife would have the right of usufruct as long as she lived".[29] Similarly, Raulino Azevedo Machado, a rather large landowner, made his will in 1818 reserving the third for the usufruct of his wife, adding that from it would be taken thirty thousand *réis* reserved for her funeral and salvation of her soul". The remainder was to be divided equally among her sons and daughters with the condition that the said wife would enjoy, for as long as she lived, the right of usufruct.[30] Out of 30 married testators with legal heirs, 23 opted to give the free "third" portion to their children and they reserved the usufruct for their spouse in 72 percent of cases. Furthermore in general, when the testator allowed the heir(s) to use the land, he or she required assistance in time of sickness or difficulty until death, including for his/her surviving spouse.

Besides showing how generalized the use of the *terça* ("third") was, these notarial documents seem to indicate that the inheritance system was biased. In an overwhelming majority of wills, just one of the heirs, usually someone single, was designated to enjoy the usufruct of the share permitted by the law. But being a *terça*'s heir did not necessarily bring great advantages, because from its value he had to take care of the funeral expenses and Church bequests *(legado pio)*. Table 14 summarizes the notarial information detailing the situations of families and individuals, which shows the main trends in the inheritance of property.

29 BPARAH, Inventários Orfanológicos – Ilha de São Jorge, box 401, proc. 296, fl. 7.
30 Idem, box. 401, proc. 304, fl. 9.

Table 14. Property distribution forms on São Jorge (1800–1910) in wills. Percentages

Types of estate distribution	%
Equal division among the children	10.3
One or more unmarried children is advantaged	59.4
Advantages to the one(s) living nearby	19.9
Slight advantage to the first born male son	3.8
Unequal distribution	6.7
TOTAL	100
Number of testators	102

Sources: Notarial and judicial inventories of São Jorge kept at the Regional Archives of Angra do Heroísmo.

We were able to gauge the situation of the legatees and the respective operational philosophy in the transfer of property for 102 families where the documentation exists (85 percent of the total sample). In a majority of cases, unmarried children, irrespective of sex, were preferred (59 percent), They were almost always one of the youngest. In addition, daughters were more likely to be the recipient of the "third", again underlining the fact that daughters were less likely to emigrate and more likely to remain unmarried.

Compensations for Unmarried Younger Daughters Staying at Home

It was very common on São Jorge to choose the unmarried daughters to receive the *terça* – whether they bore illegitimate children or not –. This transfer of property was, in a certain sense, "corrective",[31] to the extent that parents attempted to do some justice to those that had remained unmarried. In the same way emigrant children "in parts uncertain" were also excluded. The single daughters' chances of marriage could increase,

31 From this the proverb common on São Jorge: "O mais novo casa para a casa" ("The youngest marries the house").

thanks to their getting the "third". But if marriage was no longer possible or was undesirable, then the "third" could function as a kind of compensation, guaranteeing the legatee a dignified means of subsistence.

However, on the exact opposite of this dominant pattern, one finds cases where a specific child, usually the first-born, is advantaged. These forms of property transmissions belong to the minority, and initially characterized "elite" landowners, before trickling down to smaller and medium land owners.

The 1839 will of D. Maria Teresa, daughter of Matias Teixeira Pacheco and of D. Maria Trindade Azevedo, shows how strategies in favour of a preferred heir played out. In this case, D. Maria Teresa, spinster and sister of António Vitorino Pacheco, sergeant major, agreed with the other testators to reduce the share of one of her nephews, the Counsellor of the Portuguese State and baccalaureate in philosophy, José Pereira da Cunha da Silveira e Sousa.

We know how D. Maria Teresa's property was transmitted, as well as what happened to the estate of her unmarried siblings António and Margarida. Only her sister, D. Joana Álvares Pacheco de Azevedo married captain José Pereira da Cunha. By some fortuitous circumstances, his brother, the eldest colonel João Pereira da Cunha, had accumulated a considerable fortune and, being unwed, intended to will it all to his nephew José Pereira da Cunha da Silveira e Sousa. D. Maria Teresa, well aware of the intentions of her brother-in-law, included António and José, in order to diminish the disproportion in the inheritance.

> To my nephew Joze Pereira da Cunha, son of my sister Dona Joanna Álvares and her husband Captain Joze Pereira da Cunha, I leave the best pair of bulls that may be mine on my death. I do not consider leaving him more estates, not because I do not love him, as also for his brothers, but because this nephew is going to be the lord of the entails of this house, and also of his uncle, the Illustrious Coronel João Pereira da Cunha; and because I know that more of his illustrious paternal uncles who have a love for him are planning to leave their estates, and because of this I intend to protect my other nephews so that all may live a most decent lifestyle. [...] That my brothers the sergeant major Antonio Victorino Pacheco and Dona Margarida Clara de Azevedo, will until they are alive enjoy the usufruct of the remainder of my wealth (April 1839).[32]

32 "Testamento com que falleceo a senhora D. Maria Thereza da Trindade [...] 6 de Abril de 1839". (Private archive of Silveira e Sousa's family. I wish to express my gratitude to Dr. Paulo Silveira e Sousa for allowing me to access this document).

Thanks to this parental inheritance José Pereira Cunha Silveira e Sousa became the largest landlord of all time on the island of São Jorge. Therefore, the lineage of this *house*, due to its wealth, is an exception in this otherwise rural and peripheral parish. This does not, naturally, signify the absence of similar forms of patrimonial transmission for the other families, only that they were more likely to characterize the wealthier ones.

Post-mortem Succession, Dowry, Donation and Care in Old Age

We must underline the fact that among less wealthy families *post-mortem* property transmission ensured that the testators supervised and administered their estates until their death. In this context, conventions such as dowry provisions in marriage contracts are less common. But even in these cases legatees should often assist their parents in sickness and pay for the *legado pio*.

In 19 (66 percent) out of 29 marriage contracts, the future spouses reserved for themselves the usufruct of the property left by the first deceased. This, in reality, is nothing but the promise of a donation, rather than a direct and automatic benefit, but one that would guarantee a future to prospective consorts.

For instance, when 19-year-old José Machado da Cunha and 32-year-old Rosa Luísa married, the father and stepmother of the bride gave her a dowry. The former gave her half the "third" but on the condition that she was to pay a *legado pio* of 10 thousand *reis*. The latter made a similar donation, but obliged the future bride to look after her "in her own house" and she would only receive full possession of this dowry after the death of her stepmother.[33] In another case, the mother of Isabel Eusébia gave her the "third", but stipulated that Isabel would have to set aside 20 thousand *réis* for her mother's *legado pio*. However, Isabel was only given the usu-

33 BPARAH, *Cartórios Notariais – Ilha de São Jorge*, Notas do tabelião Gregório António Carvalho de Albuquerque, book 9, fls. 19–21 (1839).

fruct of the lands and after the death of the donors the properties would have to be shared with the remaining heirs.[34]

The relative scarcity of documents providing for dowries, in conjunction with the keeping of the legal owns over the estate, shows the strong tendencies of couples to preserve their property intact, although usufruct could sometimes be allowed. High levels of migration were a result from this practice – wills and genealogical studies show that those who were absent did not share in inheritance. Emigration appears to have functioned as one of the primary mechanisms of alleviating "pressure on the house". Children – not being tacitly excluded by the parents – glimpsed better opportunities abroad. Yet, despite a high exodus of people, the ways estates were distributed after death gave a clear advantage to the younger individuals, usually the unwed daughters, or other descendents who, despite being married, resided close to the parents and thus could be of assistance to them.

The importance of assisting parents, whether by caring for them or by providing for them, is reflected in deeds where the bequeathers minutely laid down what they will give in exchange – usually the usufruct of the land. Sometimes, negligence on the part of the recipient led the donors to take the usufruct back and look for support elsewhere. For instance, in 1823, D. Maria Tomásia of the village of Calheta revoked the "third" left to her daughter Angélica, because the latter "instead of nursing her in her sickness till death [...] began to worry her with demands".[35]

A Transmission System Favouring Ultimogeniture

This study has led us to conclude that on this island, the practice of favouring one of the heirs was clearly prevalent. Yet, this system, despite being "imbalanced", should not be confused with the system where a couple associates one of the children in the running of the farm (privileged

34 BPARAH, *Cartórios Notariais – Ilha de São Jorge*, Notas do tabelião Augusto Butter Carvalhal de Lacerda, book 1, fls. 83–84 (1867).

35 BPARAH, *Inventários Orfanológicos – S. Jorge*, box 404, proc. 401 (Calheta, 1823).

heir/stem family system), usually at the time of the latter's marriage.[36] Indeed, as in a majority of the Azores islands, there does not appear to be any precise strategy of choosing an heir for the continuation of the family line. On the contrary, we came across an "assistance model", where parents gave some advantages to the younger unwed children in exchange of assistance during their old age. This is reflected in the distribution of household types, as extended family households[37] are more common than "multiple family households", which are the least common types.

As Andrés Barrera-Gonzáles stressed in a study on the transmission of property in Spain, the existence of the two main systems of property transmission (equalitarian and non-equalitarian models) does not preclude variations within each, for

> the variants of the equalitarian-nuclear family are also numerous, and are linked to a diversity of judicial and legal-customary traditions, both regional and local, and to the incidence of socio-economic factors (Barrera-Gonzáles 1998, 241–246).

Already in 1988, Francisco Chácon Jiménez had drawn attention to the existence of these two major systems, though

> the variety of the hereditary systems is such that a simple distinction between the divisible forms and indivisible forms constitutes a reductionism (Chácon 1990, 31–46).

In reality, the system in force on São Jorge appears to resemble practice similar to the Northeast regions of Spain (especially Galiza) where the legatee of *mejorado*, irrespective of the sex, received only an additional share, often in exchange for supporting the parents during certain periods in their life. Nevertheless, this additional share, about a fifth, would in no way give him the status of a "privileged heir" (Barrera-Gonzáles 1998, 230).

In a study on the ownership of land and inheritance in Minho (Northeast Portugal), Margarida Durães also argued that forms of property transmission were varied in this region. She concluded that the most common form of transmission of property occurred at one time only, when the couple willed the "third" to one of the children irrespective of their sex (Durães 2000, 353). This system, which is very similar to the one in São Jorge, protects the surviving spouse who keeps the estate in his or

36 For such inheritance methods, common to many regions of Trás-os-Montes or North East Portugal, see O'Neill 1994 and Brandão 1994.

37 Type 4 according to the Laslett/Hammel classification.

her possession. In this sense the "third" acts as an effective mechanism to guarantee the support of the survivor, and as a way to correct any eventual injustice among the heirs (Durães 2000, 561–563).

Conclusion

The marriage market, the family life cycle and the diverse methods of property transmission in the Azorean archipelago have not been subject to much research. Parish reconstitutions and longitudinal studies are slowly making possible a better understanding of family life conditions and reproduction systems, namely fertility, illegitimacy, together with forms and evolution of domestic household forms. Despite this effort, past Azorean families, especially those belonging to the underprivileged social strata, remain to be understood better.

This study took into consideration various trends in the marriage market and the inheritance system on the island of São Jorge. Marriage was not possible for all, given the scarcity of men, restrictions on cousin marriages and the *post-mortem* system of property transmission. Neo-locality was the norm, and parents delayed partitioning the estate until the death of the second spouse. The mean age at marriage was high, and so was the female celibacy rate, and male emigration rate. Given this situation, it is understandable that out of wedlock birth was common through the nineteenth century, sometimes occurring while waiting for the opportunity to marry.

References

AMORIM, Maria Norberta, 1992, *Evolução Demográfica de Três Paróquias do Sul do Pico (1680-1980)*, Braga, Instituto de Ciências Sociais/Universidade do Minho.

–, 1999, "O Minho: Comportamentos Demográficos através da Informação Paroquial", *Ler História*, 36, pp. 9–44.

–, 2001, "Família e Emigração: Um Estudo de Caso – S. João do Pico (Açores) nas duas Primeiras Décadas do Século XIX", in Maria Beatriz NIZZA DA SILVA (ed.), *Sexualidade, Família e Religião na Colonização do Brasil*, Lisboa, Horizonte, pp. 249–258

–, 2004, "Reprodução biológica e reprodução social: Comportamentos diferenciais oitocentistas nas Lages do Pico", *Revista de Demografía Histórica*, Asociación de Demografia Histórica, 22, 1, pp. 43–76.

BARRERA-GONZÁLES, Andrés, 1998, "Domestic succession, property transmission, and family systems in the agrarian societies of contemporary Spain", *The History of the Family*, 3, 2, pp. 241–246.

BLAIKIE, Andrew, 1993, *Illegitimacy, Sex and Society*, Oxford, Clarendon Press.

BRANDÃO, Fátima, 1994, *Terra, Herança e Família no Noroeste de Portugal. O caso de Mosteiro no século XIX*, Lisboa, Afrontamento.

BRANDÃO, Fátima and ROWLAND, Robert, 1980, "História da propriedade e comunidade rural: questões de método", *Análise Social*, 16, pp. 173–207.

BRETTELL, Caroline B., 1986, *Men Who Migrate, Women Who Wait: Population and History in a Portuguese Parish*, Princeton, Princeton University Press.

–, 1991, "Kinship and Contact: Property transmission and family relations in Northwestern Portugal", *Comparative Studies in Society and History*, 33, 3, pp. 443–465.

CABRAL, João Pina, 1986, *Sons of Adam, Daughters of Eve: The Peasant World View of the Alto Minho*, Oxford, Clarendon Press.

CAPELA, José Viriato, 1989, *A Câmara, a Nobreza e o Povo do Concelho de Barcelos. A Administração Municipal nos fins do Antigo Regime*, Braga, author's edition, pp. 26–40.

CHÁCON JIMÉNEZ, Francisco, 1990, "La Familia Española: Una Historia por Hacer", in Francisco CHACON JIMENEZ (ed.), *Historia Social de la Familia en España*, Alicante, Instituto de Cultura Juan Gil-Albert/Diputación de Alicante, pp. 7–32.

DURÃES, Margarida, 1995, "Necessidades Económicas e Práticas Jurídicas: Problemas da transmissão das explorações agrícolas. Séculos XVIII a XIX", *Ler História*, 29, pp. 67–88.

–, 2000, *Herança e Sucessão: Leis, Práticas e Costumes no Termo de Braga (Séculos XVIII-XIX)*, Braga, Universidade do Minho.

FONSECA, Hélder, 1988, "Sociedade e elites alentejanas no século XIX", *Economia e Sociologia*, 45/46, pp. 63–106.

–, 2000, *Herança e Sucessão. Leis, práticas e costumes no termo de Braga. Séculos XVIII–XIX*, 2 vols. Braga, Universidade do Minho.

GOODY, Jack, 2000, *The European Family. A Historico-Anthropological Essay,* Oxford, Blackwell.

HOLLINGSWORTH, Thomas H., 1981, "Illegitimate births and marriage rates in Great Britain 1841–1911", in Jacques DUPÂQUIER, Etienne HÉLIN, Peter LASLETT, Massimo LIVI-BACCI and Solvi SOGNER (eds), *Marriage and Remarriage in Populations of the Past*, London, Academic Press, pp. 437–452.

LASLETT, Peter, 1980, "The bastardy prone sub-society", in Peter LASLETT, Karla OOSTERVEEN and Richard M. SMITH (eds), *Bastardy and its Comparative History: Studies in the History of Illegitimacy and Marital Nonconformism in Britain, France, Germany, Sweden, North America, Jamaica and Japan*, Cambridge (Mass.), Harvard University Press, pp. 217–246.

LASLETT, Peter and WALL, Richard (eds), 1972, *Household and Family in Past Time*, Cambridge, Cambridge University Press.

MATOS, Paulo Lopes, 2000, "Santa Cruz da Ilha Graciosa (1799–1850). População, Grupos Familiares e Profissões", *Arquipélago-História. Revista da Universidade dos Açores*, 2ª série, 4, 2, special issue *In Memorium Ernesto do Canto*, Ponta Delgada, pp. 257–297.

–, 2006, "Endogamia e estratégias familiares campesinas numa freguesia da periferia açoriana. A Ribeira Seca da Ilha de São Jorge (1800–1910)", in Francisco CHÁCON and Xavier ROIGÉ (eds), *Familias y Poderes. Actas del VII Congreso Internacional de la ADEH. Granada, 1–3 Abril 2004*, Madrid, pp. 304–336.

–, 2007, *O Nascimento fora do Matrimónio na freguesia da Ribeira Seca da Ilha de São Jorge (Açores): 1800–1910*, Guimarães, Núcleo de Estudos da População e Sociedade.

MATOS, Paulo Lopes and SILVA, Susana Serpa, 2009, "Oscilações populacionais, grupos e comportamentos sociais (1835–1890)", in *História dos Açores, Do descobrimento ao século XX*, Instituto Açoriano de Cultura, Angra do Heroísmo, pp. 1–59.

MONTEIRO, António Xavier, 1890, *Manual de Direito Ecclesiastico Parochial [...]*, 3d ed., Coimbra, Imprensa da Universidade.

O'NEILL, Juan Brian, 1994, *Proprietários, Lavradores e Jornaleiras. Desigualdade Social numa Aldeia Transmontana, 1870–1978*, Lisboa, Dom Quixote.

–, 1987, *Social Inequality in a Portuguese Hamlet: Land, Late Marriage and Bastardy (1870–1970)*, Cambridge, Cambridge University Press [English version of previous book].

PEREIRA, Gaspar Martins, 1995, *Famílias Portuenses na Viragem do Século (1880–1910)*, Lisboa, Afrontamento.

ROCHA, Maria Manuela, 1994, *Propriedade e Níveis de Riqueza. Formas de Estruturação Social em Monsaraz na Primeira Metade do Século XIX*, Lisboa, Cosmos.

ROWLAND, Robert (1984), "Sistemas familiares e Padrões Demográficos em Portugal", *Ler História*, 3, pp. 13–32.

–, 1997, *População, Família, Sociedade. Portugal, Séculos XIX-XX*, Oeiras, Celta.

SÁ, Isabel dos Guimarães, 1996, "Abandono de Crianças, Ilegitimidade e Concepções Pré-Nupciais em Portugal. Estudos recentes e perspectivas", in Vicente PEREZ MOREDA (ed.), *Expostos e Ilegítimos na Realidade Ibérica do Século XVI ao Presente. Actas do III Congresso da ADEH*, vol. III, Lisboa, Afrontamento, pp. 37–58.

SILVA, Susana Serpa, 2004, "Emigração Clandestina nas Ilhas do Grupo Central em Meados do Século XIX", in *Actas do III Colóquio. O Faial e a Periferia Açoriana nos Séculos XV a XX*, Horta, Núcleo Cultural da Horta, pp. 275–294.

SOUSA, Paulo Silveira e, 1994, *Território, Poder, Propriedade, Elites Locais. A Ilha de São Jorge na segunda metade do século XIX*, Lisboa, Instituto Superior de Ciências do Trabalho e da Empresa.

–, 2000, "As Actividades Industriais no Distrito de Angra do Heroísmo: Um Mundo de Possibilidades Escassas", *Arquipélago-História. Revista da Universidade dos Açores*, 2ª série, 4, 2, pp. 127–186.

WALL, Karin, 1998, *Famílias no Campo. Passado e Presente em duas Freguesias do Baixo Minho*, Lisboa, Dom Quixote, pp. 24–33.

WALL, Richard *et al.* (eds), 1983, *Family Forms in Historic Europe*, Cambridge, Cambridge University Press.

Well-Being or Survival? Women's Future and Family Transmission Strategies in North-Western Rural Spain, 18th–19th Centuries

Ofelia REY CASTELAO

Following a time of strong growth in the seventeenth century, Galicia experienced economic stagnation caused by agricultural sclerosis and overpopulation in the 18th and 19th centuries. This led to high levels of emigration. There was no other solution in this territory characterized by the lack of modern, urban districts, and by the predominance of traditional agriculture, complemented by textile proto-industry and by fishing. Fields were divided between heirs at each generation which resulted in an extreme fragmentation of holdings, to the point that few farms were able to support a family without other incomes. Families managed to hold on but their activities were centered on survival; they either owned their land, or had long *usofructo* in them; they owned cattle, tools and equipment; and the rural communities controlled large acreages of land in common.

The communities survived thanks to family and collective strategies designed to preserve the patrimony in the families. Furthermore, the great homogeneity of these communities slowed down changes which could have benefited individuals at the expense of the group. And finally most enjoyed a modest standard of living, sufficient to satisfy basic food needs, avoid debt, enjoy other necessities and care for the aged, but they could not afford superfluous expenses.

Family strategies sought to ensure the existence of the domestic group even at the cost of sacrificing one or several of its members: the well-being of some and of others cannot be measured in the same terms as in other regions of the Iberian Peninsula which were characterized by different natural conditions. Property transmission systems were key to the long term survival of those communities. Castillan law (1505 *Laws of Toro*) applied in Galicia, and remained unchanged up to 1889 Spanish *Civil Code*: each child was entitled to a "legitimate" share irrespective of sex, but it was possible to advantage one child, and daughters could receive dowries. This frame allowed a wide range of practices. Galicians provided for their descendents, whether heirs or not, in two different ways.

Categories of Male and Female Heirs

Emigration created an imbalanced sex-ratio in Galicia. In 1787,[1] women outnumbered men in the group aged 16 to 50 years: 350,123 women were registered as opposed to 303,972 men. This imbalance was still noticeable in 1860, which influenced for a long time the gender division of work in the province. But in Galicia, gender was not a determining factor in the devolution of patrimony. The determining factors were the size of the family and the size of the estate to be divided. In turn, the size of the inheritance determined the heir's survival capacity. How was inheritance to be divided and among how many persons? These were the key questions. The 1753 *Catastro de Ensenada* allows us to find out the number and sex of potential heirs at the future opening of the family devolution processes in various rural regions of Galicia (Table 1).

We considered five different rural regions and noted the following characteristics: a) more than 13–15 percent of the farming families did not have children who could inherit and people would have had to select heirs from another branch of their family or find other solutions; b) between 23.2 and 30 percent of family households had only one child mentioned, a son or a daughter, and did not therefore have to select a heir; c) less than half of the families in the more populated regions and two thirds in the less populated had more than one potential heir; d) only one third of the families in the more populated regions, and 40 percent in the less populated ones had to choose between a man or a woman. Small family size and low rate of illegitimacy were the causes of this situation (aside from mortality). The result was that most children did not face any process of selection of heirs, but this did not mean that they would be privileged, nor did it guarantee wealth as it was most probable that they would only inherit all or part of a small holding (Table 2).

1 Sources for 1753: *El Catastro de Ensenada*, Provincial Historical Archives; for 1787: *Censo de Floridablanca*, Provincial Historical Archives; for 1860: Population Census.

Table 1. Categories of potential heirs, by sex, at the future opening of property devolution process, in various regions of Galicia, according to family households registered in the 1753 *Catastro.* Percentages

Family Households	Lugo	Costa Muerte	Bergondo	Cañiza	Ulla Valley
	%	%	%	%	%
Without children	14.5	27.8	13.3	24.7	15.0
One son	12.2	10.9	13.8	13.7	21.1
One daughter	11.1	13.0	9.6	13.9	9.5
Sons only	12.2	14.1	12.4	8.9	7.5
Daughters only	12.2	9.1	6.5	8.0	12.0
Sons and daughters	37.8	25.0	44.4	30.6	34.7
Total	100	100	100	100	100

Sources: For 1753: *El Catastro de Ensenada*, Provincial Historical Archives.
Notes: Number of family households considered: 172 for Lugo; 439 for Costa Muerte, 354 for Bergondo; 460 for Cañiza and 199 for Ulla Valley.

Table 2. Characteristics of agrarian holdings (land and cattle), population density and mean family size, in various regions of Galicia, according to the 1753 *Catastro* and 1787 census. Percentages

	Hectares	*Cows*	*Sheep*	*Persons per km2*	*Mean family size*
Galicia occidental					
Santiago	1.22	2.94	10.5	56.4	4.0
Tui	0.56	1.71	3.91	87.3	3.9
Coruña	1.70	4.39	15.32	64.6	4.0
Galicia cantábrica					
Betanzos	1.44	4.84	9.56	57.4	4.2
Mondoñedo	1.36	4.23	7.27	49.1	4.5
Galicia interior					
Ourense	1.85	2.67	8.55	28.3	4.5
Lugo	2.31	5.44	15.52	41.5	4.7

Sources: For 1753: *Catastro de Ensenada*; for 1787: *Censo de Floridablanca*, Provincial Historical Archives.

Poor rural families usually did not have enough land or livestock and needed a supplementary source of income, or went into debt. Poverty was also widespread; only a minority escaped it, and even they were not well off. The proportion of families belonging to the rural elite is difficult to estimate because fiscal sources are approximate and information on the size and characteristics of farms rather inadequate, as the following examples show.

In the Salnés region, in the rich and overpopulated western coast (100 inhabitants per square kilometre), well-off farmers made up only 11.3 percent of the total in 1753; they owned their livestock, their equipment, and approximately 3 to 5 hectares of land each; 22.8 percent of the land was owned outright and the rest was *enfiteusis* (perpetual leasehold); only 40 percent could be cultivated and was highly productive (Pérez Garcia 1979). Families were small (4 members) and there was a large number of single-person households (20 percent). In near-by less populated Covelo, (51.2 persons per square km), farm land was scarcer and less productive. There were few single-person households; on the contrary, there were many homes with 6 or more members (24.1 percent). The average family had 4.2 members: it disposed of 2.18 hectares of land and of 19.5 heads of livestock. This average hides the fact that only 15.8 percent of the total population reached that level. A family with 5 or more members possessed less than 1.3 hectares. Large families owned 40 percent less land than families with 4 members; and moreover, the larger the families were, the more children and elderly they included.

Mountain Commons Ensured Survival

These two very different districts – Salnés and Covelo – had access to mountain commons. The commons were not cultivated; they were a source of firewood and lumber, and were used to graze the livestock. Their resources did not compensate deficit production on the farms themselves, but they were available to all in the community and their use was not inheritable. The community therefore did not prevent new families from using them. In the mountainous northwest Galicia, where cultivated land made up from 14 to 21 percent of the surface area and the density of the population was only 14.2 persons per square km, the average size of holding was 1.22 hectares – 7.83 if one includes the mountain – but 86 percent of the holdings in Queixiero, 72.8 in Moeche or 58.5 percent in Cambas did not reach this size (Table 3). The minority of better off – but by no means wealthy – country people was very different: in Cambas, 14.6 percent possessed holdings of 53.5 hectares, controlled 53.8 percent of the land and 71 percent of the mountain. In other villages, they represented 10.4 percent of the population and owned an average of 11.8 hectares. However, only 6.2 percent of the land in those villages could be cultivated and the main crop was rye. This meant that subsistence depended to a large extent on the mountain, on which they grew grain every 15, 24, or 36 years, collected wood and combustible material and grazed the livestock, to the point that the commons contributed to a third of the families' income. There, the rights to use the mountain were reserved to family groups and these rights were inherited.

A typical family in this area had 4.6 members; there were few households of single persons (2 to 4 percent, except in Moeche which had 11.1 percent of them). But there were many farms with 6 or more members (30 percent). The size of the land holding and the number of heads of cattle available was greater among families housing many members. The best case scenario however was a family of 3 or 4 members, because larger households were burdened by unproductive children and elderly people, who contributed little to the family's income and well-being. The well-off minority was the one who controlled the greatest acreage of mountain suitable for grazing and occasional cultivation (Table 3).

Table 3. Size in hectares and other characteristics (cattle) of agrarian farms and mean family size, in mountainous northwest of Galicia, according to the 1753 *Catastro*. Percentages

Cambas	*–3 ha*	*De 3–5 ha*	*6–15 ha*	*16–31 ha*	*+ 32 ha*
% of farms	32.6	13.5	21.3	16.8	14.6
Mean family size	4.6	4.9	5.0	5.5	5.6
Land	1.9	4.3	15.9	24.2	53.8
Cattle	52.1	53.9	67.6	68.8	62.4
Queixeiro					
% of farms	37.4	19.1	20.0	33.0	10.4
Mean family size	3.7	3.9	4.5	5.5	5.3
Land	5.6	12.9	23.8	20.8	36.9
Cattle	8.3	17,0	17.9	22.0	35.0

Sources: For 1753: *Catastro de Ensenada,* Provincial Historical Archives.

For families of 3 or 4 members, anticipating family transmission did not create much problem. For mid-18th century Galicia, we consider that inheritance to be received was not a major strategic family question nor was the sex of the inheritor the most decisive element when selecting to whom or how much inheritance would be transmitted. The main decision was how and when. This was a decision that the parents made when they had all information available about their potential heirs. They then established some provisions, whether effective or not.

Gendered Trajectories According to Regional Family Models and Marital Status

The presence of a large number of individuals of the same age, in the same place and time was a determining factor for population reproduction; these people had entered the same marriage and labour markets in a non-elastic economy. The low birth rate in Galicia meant that many young males were either in a position of only child or already head of household: in the military levy of 1762, 27 percent of men aged 18 to 40 were only child, whether they were still unmarried and living with their parents (21.4 percent) or heads of households (5.6 percent).[2] Of course, their life could still change, but they did not have to compete with someone else. By contrast, the only son in this age group made up only 16 percent in interior Galicia, an area of large families where the competition for inheritance was much greater. This pattern reproduced the distribution of family models and enlightens the different transmission patterns, households being much larger and their structure more complex in interior Galicia than in the rest of the province (Figure 1).

2 Proportions were 38.2 percent in the southwest and 35.9 percent in Cantabria.

Figure 1. Mean household size in various regions of Galicia, according to the 1753 *Catastro de Ensenada*. Mean number of persons

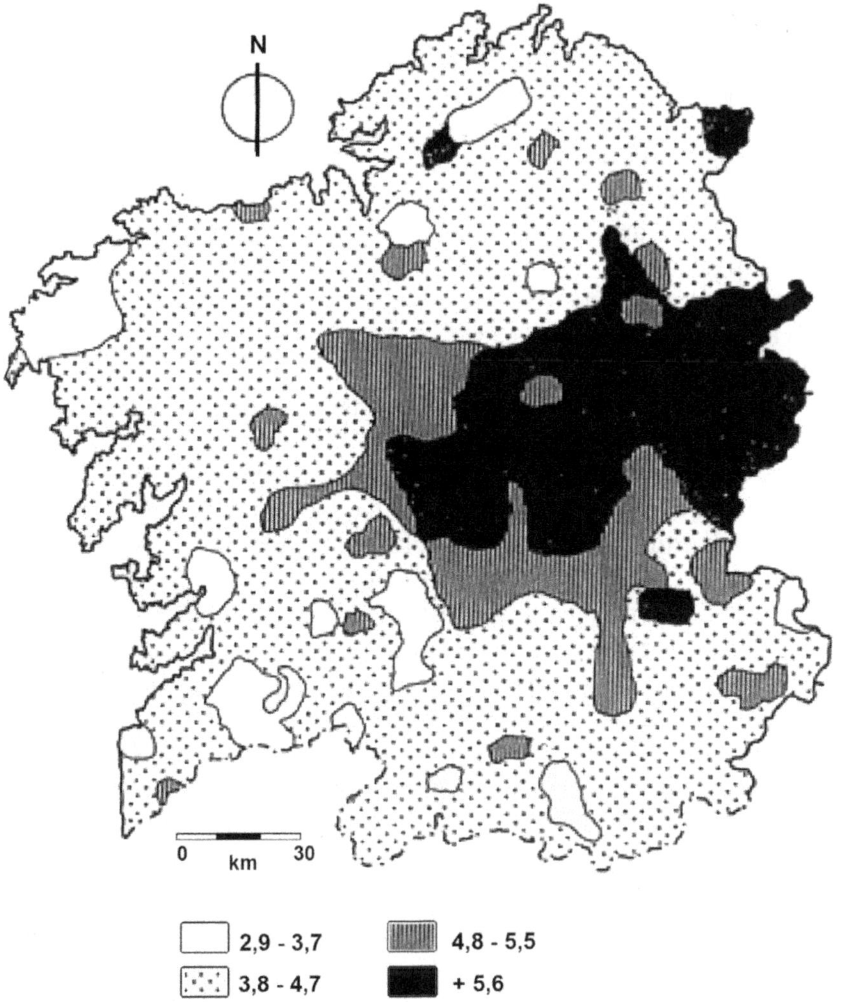

Sources: For 1753: *Catastro de Ensenada,* Provincial Historical Archives (Dubert 1992, p. 87).

Specific Family System of Interior Galicia

In interior Galicia, particularly when belonging to poor rural families, second children had few options to achieve a decent standard of living. This central region was less densely populated and residential units were large – averaging 5.3 persons in 1753 (according to the *Catastro de Ensenada,* appearing in dark grey and black on Figure 1) – and there were many extended households (31.1 percent) and some multiple families (7.2 percent). Farms were much larger than the provincial average; they were dedicated to rye, and later, to potato as well. Mountain plots were periodically cultivated after cutting and clearing to obtain more cereal. Local communities exercised a strong control over the use of these common lands and placed many obstacles to erect new houses.

In this poor economy, inheritance practice favoured the first-born male, who married in the house, following a stem-family rule (or *troncal* family, in Spanish). *Mejora* portion, like a *preciput*, was also used to advantage a child; a *mejora* was equivalent to an extra one-third share plus an additional one-fifth over and above the *legimate* portion of inheritance due to each child. According to Sobrado Correa, in Lugo region, most *mejora* (65.9 percent) went to one son (63.7 percent); some went to a daughter (13.7 percent) and the rest to various children or grandchildren. The *mejora* was given to the eldest son by the parents when he married; in return, he had to live with them and care for them; he had to run the farm, pay the debts and the taxes, support his unmarried siblings at home, provide them with their legitimate portion and his sisters with a dowry, while preserving the integrity of the family patrimony (Sobrado Correa 2001).

Younger males had few options there: some married heiresses in other families, others entered the clergy, and the majority remained single (definitive male celibacy was estimated at 18.2 percent in 1787, according to *Floridablanca Census*). Given that there were few jobs outside agriculture and farming, the only way to become independent was, in theory at least, to leave home. But men were needed to work on the family farm and for cutting and clearing, to the effect that they were retained as non-paid workers. Single-crop rye farming was seasonal and in the off-season young single people went to Castile or to Madrid to work. Single men did not marry in the places to which they travelled nor did they go to places very far away. Instead, they returned home to help their brothers who were heads of household, and who never migrated. Their single status and their dependency put these young men at risk of being conscripted in the military, but the number of those who left in order to avoid military service was small. Ecclesiastical careers were open to them as soon as they could achieve some education.

Successful Ecclesiastical Careers

In interior Galicia, better off rural families preferred that their non inheriting younger sons join the secular clergy rather than get married. Nothing limited the growth of the secular clergy: between 1591 and 1753, the number of priests grew enormously, and slowed down only afterwards.[3] In 1753 Galicia considered globally, there was one priest for every 40 families, and the number was even higher in interior Galicia (in Lugo region, there was even one priest for every 27 families). As there were only 3,500 parishes in the province, only a small proportion of the priests could be vicars of their church (36.6 percent in 1797 *Floridablanca Census*) and live from its income. Many priests benefited from an endowment or were chaplains, engaged in various civic activities and lived within their own family of origin. The geographic distribution of the clergy in Galicia reflects the socioeconomic characteristics of the different zones (Figure 2).

Clerics were numerous in interior Galicia, in part due to the abundance of noblemen *(hidalgos)* (16.6 percent) and above all because families were large in those districts, as mentioned above. Stem-family type inheritance practices favoured the eldest son, which in turn limited the younger children's possibility to inherit and to marry (18.5 percent permanent male

3 The number of priests grew 178 percent between 1591 and 1753. In 1753, 8,532 priests were registered in Galicia and in 1797 they were 9,121, according to *Censo de la Población de España de el año de 1797 executado de orden del Rey en el de 1801* (Madrid, Real Imprenta, 1801). This census is usually called *Censo de Godoy-Larruga.*
In western Galicia as in the interior region, the rate of entry into the clergy continued to grow until 1780; afterwards, it steadily decreased. The government as well as society at large felt there were more than enough priests, and various measures were taken to slow this growth. The government reduced the clergy's tax exemptions and required young priests to do military service. Creating endowment funds and chaplaincies became increasingly difficult. This, coupled with expanded professional opportunities, reduced the attractiveness of ecclesiastical careers.

celibacy). In consequence many women could not find a spouse, and stayed at home. Family holdings were much larger in this interior Galicia than in western Galicia and this made it possible for families to formally allocate some of their resources for the support of a priest. This took the form of endowments or chaplaincies. These incomes were tax exempt. The funds were managed by the family and, at the death of the beneficiary, were reintegrated into the family's assets.

Figure 2. Geographical distribution and density of the secular clergy in various regions of Galicia, according to the 1753 *Catastro de Ensenada*. Mean number of households for one priest

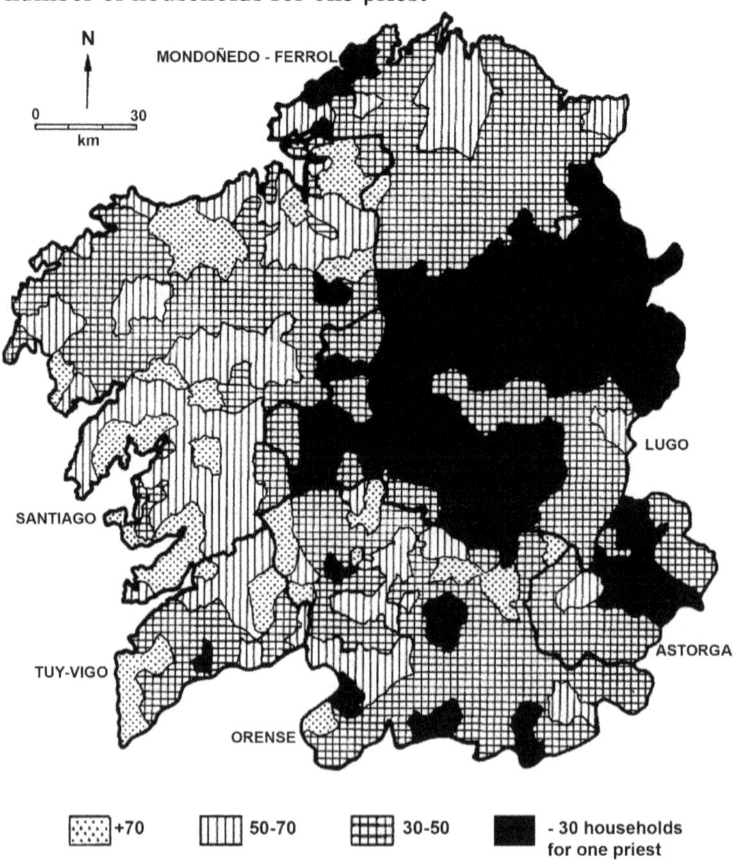

Sources: For 1753: *Catastro de Ensenada*, Provincial Historical Archives.

Thus, no property was alienated; a child was removed from the ranks of potential heirs although he could not marry; and in addition, social prestige was gained. By contrast, there were fewer priests in western Galicia than in the central region. In the coastal zones and in the valleys devoted to wine production, there were fewer noblemen (1.6 percent) and also small and nuclear families were the commonest.

Specificities Leading to Male Mobility

In 1787, contrasting with central Galicia, most of the population of north-western Spain (53 percent) lived in high density districts where most of the families were nuclear (86.7 percent) and of small size (3.9 persons), essentially because of low birth rates. People married late, male and female celibacy rates were high. Farms were small and produced mostly corn. Many rural couples had only one child alive, and when there was more than one, inheritances were not strongly unequal. Only a minority of young men became priests. Instead, many men emigrated, leaving women behind to run the family and household.[4] Being educated was a prerequisite to join the clergy, this requirement placed rural youth at a disadvantage. A study of the dioceses of Santiago provides us with the age, origins and qualification of male students. The majority had not attended university, and therefore they could only become priests, although an increasing number sought a civil service position. That way, they would secure a professional position, escape the countryside, and reduce the number of prospective heirs in their family and the likelihood of a prejudicial division of the parental estate. Whether living in the village or not, young priests of course were no longer prospective mates for the women of their generation.

4 For example, this was the case in the Lower Miño river region, an area with 111 inhabitants per square km in 1753 and a complex agrarian economy based on wine and corn. A study of 300 cases (Pérez García 1999) revealed that the average size of ecclesiastical endowment was 2.6 hectares between 1736 to 1774, 2.4 hectares during 1775 to 1799, 1.7 hectares during 1800 to 1824, and 1.6 during 1825 to 1859; as the average holding size in the area was less than a hectare, this shows their beneficiaries were the sons of the well-off peasants *(campesino fuerte)*.The 38 percent reduction between 1736 and 1859 provides information regarding the social descent of the new clergy.

Traditionally, estates were unequally divided, with one son or daughter getting a larger share. The other children who did not receive a *mejora* set up a new household and founded a family, using the legitimate portion of their parents' inheritance, as there were no limitations to the number of new households. But, given the small size of the majority of the agricultural land, it was necessary to look for other resources, working in complementary activities (which were easy to find) or to emigrate, or do both. This affected the younger children as well as the main inheritors or the husbands of female inheritors (sons-in-laws). Emigration entailed temporary and/or multi-annual stays in Castile, Andalusia, and Portugal, and permanent emigration to America particularly developed in Western Galicia (Rey Castelao 1994).

Absent Males and Working Females in Western Galicia

Families which resorted to off-farm labour and to emigration were always of larger size than the others. Temporary emigration was useful because the emigrant was supporting himself while away; if it was permanent, it eliminated a potential heir. Both sexes did not migrate at the same rate and neither did all men. For example, in 1719 Pontevedra, a coastal district with a high rate of emigration, emigrants were either young people under 24 (of pre-marriage age) or married men aged between 34 and 40 (Sanz Gonzáles 1994).

The circumstances of emigration were also different depending on the activities of the families. This is clearly shown by studying the 1753 *Catastro de Ensenada,* where households were listed with migrants mentioned as temporary absent family members. In farming families, single males made up 52.5 percent of the emigrants, others were married already; 52.7 percent of these absent single males were actually first-born; 30.1 percent were second-born, 12.9 percent were third-born. As for artisan family households, 58.9 percent of the emigrants were single, and among this category, 43.5 percent were second-born, 17.4 percent were third-born, and only 26 percent were first-born sons. Among day workers and seamen, only 19.2 percent of the emigrants were single, of which 80 percent were first-born and 10 percent second-born.

In this region of western Galicia, for rural families, most emigrants were married men – heads of household or not – but in other families with non farming activities, it was the young single men who emigrated. Different responsibilities of work *in situ* explain these two different patterns and choice of who should emigrate. By contrast with what was noted above for central Galicia, many of the singles who migrated from western Galicia opted to marry in their places of destination. Western Galicia however displayed a strong tendency to post-marital emigration: the young couple used their combined legitimate portions that they received from their respective family of origin, to finance their move away, and this practice was repeated with each generation.

For young males, the fear of military recruitment always acted as an important factor for emigration, especially after 1837, when military service became universal and compulsory. Twenty four percent of the young men absent from their home in 1719 documents and 31.2 percent in 1758–1759 could be found in the lists of the Marines. These numbers of absentees reveal that, contrary to single men in interior Galicia, military service was considered to be prejudicial to their future well-being as these young men had expected to be independent, thanks to their legitimate portion, which represented an extra income, compared to what they earned from various activities and from temporary emigration.

Since, in all western Galicia, married men used to migrate and were expected to return home with money, they did not emigrate to America. In districts where age at marriage was low, married men who emigrated were very young ones, and in the first stage of their family life course, but this situation was not the most habitual. For example, in 1719 Pontevedra, only 14.9 percent of men in age group 16 to 25 years old were married; the average age at marriage was over 25. Among farmers, 35.8 percent of emigrants were heads of household and another 11.5 percent were married but in a dependent position, that is, sons or sons-in-law of other heads of household. Among artisans, these two categories of married men emigrating amounted respectively to 35.8 percent and 5.1 percent. Among labourers and seamen they were still more numerous to leave: 75.9 percent and 4.8 percent. In consequence of these male strategies of temporary labour migration, women were left home with heavy responsibilities and work loads (Rey Castelao 2006; Rial Garcia 2001).

Family Strategies and Women: Late and Restricted Access to Marriage

Given imbalanced sex ratios, a consequence of high levels of emigration, as mentioned earlier, women made up the majority of the Galician working age population. As permitted by Castilian inheritance laws (the 1505 *Laws of Toro*), women received favourable treatment in the transmission of patrimony. They received a legitimate portion and a dowry, and also controlled their own property, were entitled to use their husband' estates *(usofructo)* and they tended to become heads of household and guardians of their children. In 1753, according to the *Catastro de Ensenada*, 19.2 percent of the households in Galicia were headed by a woman and, in many districts on the Atlantic coast the percentage climbed to 25 percent; this proportion decreased as one moved towards the interior as did the proportion of nuclear families (Dubert 1992).

The family exercised firm control over women's ability to marry. In an environment of tiny agrarian properties, celibacy and delayed age at marriage were a means to control biological reproduction and avoid the division of estates. According to the 1787 *Floridablanca Census*, the average female age at first marriage in Galicia was 25.7, and permanent celibacy was 17 percent; these figures are much higher than the ones for the whole of Spain (23.7 and 11 respectively) (Eiras Roel 1996). In many northwestern areas, the lack of young men to marry was mitigated by the presence of numerous widowers. Marriages with widowers were not frequent inland (5 to 7 percent of all marriages) but they made up more than 15 percent of marriages in western Galicia, and 20 percent in the Ulla Valley (Rey Castelao 1990). In the rich areas of western Galicia, where there were few possibilities to marry due to high emigration, the elevated proportion of single women was not an effect of exclusion from inheritance, but of the small value of their share.

So an important percentage of women lived alone on their legitimate inherited portion, and they dedicated themselves to agricultural work or to labour associated with fishing or with the textile industry. On the contrary, single women of central Galicia lived with their older brother who had benefited from main inheritance from their parents. The control of the village community on the resources and the limited possibilities within the agricultural system made the independent existence of women and of female heads of household difficult there. In large families living inland, the high number of single women and single men, who stayed in the family house, was part of a necessary strategy to sustain large properties which required abundant workers, as explained above.

The female celibate was poorly accommodated. There were only two types of labour available to accumulate a dowry: textile production (which was common in Galicia) and domestic service. For Galician women, this last activity did not correspond to a prenuptial occupation – *a life cycle service*[5] – because it was limited to the cities and towns of Galicia which were small and poor, or to the houses of the noblemen or ecclesiastics or rich rural farmers, although the necessity to work obliged many women, especially in inland Galicia, to leave their land to work as maids, especially in Madrid (Dubert 2006). The low levels of illegitimacy (1.8 to 5.5 percent of births on the Atlantic coast and 5.4 to 11.7 percent inland), and low level of premarital births (6 to 12 percent on the coast and 9 to 13 percent inland), indicate that the rigid control of matrimony was rarely transgressed (Dubert 1991).

The women that married did so by means of a very controlled system which set the age of marriage very late, and favoured blood marriages and exchange marriages *(matrimonio a trueque)*. These two types of marriages tried to avoid the dispersion of the family patrimony by uniting two families with similar or complementary properties, or inheritances that were balanced between the two partners. In overpopulated western Galicia, with high emigration, and a system in which there was little to share between the children, these two formulas were frequently practiced, combining them with an advanced female age of marriage (more than 26 years of age) and strong celibacy. In the Ulla Valley, exchange marriages were 22.3 to 29.8 percent of the total marriages in the first half of the 18th century, and 10 to 19.5 percent in the second half of the 18th century (Rey Castelao 1990).

Consanguineous marriages were more numerous in the mountain areas of the southwest, as in A Cañiza, on the border with Portugal (27.7 percent in the 18th century and 13.5 percent in the first half of the 19th cen-

5 The concept of *life-cycle service* was proposed by Peter Laslett and concerns the period of life spent by young people, males and females as servants before marriage (Laslett 1965).

tury).[6] The two formulas were combined in transition areas such as Tierra de Montes: 10 percent consanguineous marriages before 1740, 16 percent during the period 1740–1759, 20 percent in 1760 and onward, and 10 percent exchange marriages (Fernández Cortizo 2001). But these strategies were not usual in inland Galicia of large families, with a family system that favoured the first-born son. Not marrying was the way to control remaining women (Dubert 1989; Eiras 1990; Rey Castelao 1990).

Actually, consanguineous marriages and exchange marriages situated the women on equal footing with men, as they had the same exchange value for the family, and the dispersion of the family patrimony was thereby avoided. For this reason, these types of marriages did not make sense in areas that highly favored the first born. Exchange marriages also avoided favoring one inheritor over the others and celibacy for younger children remaining at home. For this reason, agreements were established between two houses with similar or equivalent patrimonies: the youth married among themselves and the families interchanged people more than goods and wealth. In this way, if a family had three or more children, it would retain at least two legitimate portions or one *mejora* and one legimate portion. In the case that only sons were married in both houses, the family retained the entire inheritance.

The simple formula of one brother and one sister marrying one sister and one brother of another family was common in regions where males were favoured upon the condition to marry and to head their native home. Female spouses changed houses without modifying their conditions of inheritance. The agreements between two brothers and two sisters were frequent (concerning even 42.8 percent of the couples in the overpopulated Ulla Valley in the 18th century) where the agreement between parents was made with a guarantee of the *legimate* portion in favour of the contracting parties. In these cases, a male abandoned the paternal house to become the consort of the heiress daughter who received the *mejora* of the other family, in such a way that second-born or older women and men received identical treatment.

6 See, in the present volume, chapter by Emília Lagido on consanguineous marriages as a strategy of well-being in Alto Minho.

Minimum Female Well-being, Privileges and Responsibilities

In so far as referring to the position of women and inheritance, what is certain is that the hereditary processes, within the two basic formulas that have been just discussed above – blood marriages and exchange marriages – reflected the necessity to adapt to the scarcity of adult men (Rey Castelao 2006). Except in inland areas, women were favoured more in Galicia than in other Spanish territories. Within Galicia, females were more favoured where the male multi-annual or permanent emigration was the highest practice: it was fundamental for parents to assure that someone would be responsible for their care in old age and would maintain the family property and family well-being. In the coastal areas, women had a notable independence thanks to complementary work (cottage industry or commercial activity), less constrictions within the village community and less presence of men – due in part to the high incidence of accidental death in fishing and in the Armada (the Navy). In districts such as the Morrazo peninsula (near Vigo), women received at least 80 percent of the dissimilar divisions made by the parents; 47 percent of the *mejoras* were conceded to daughters, especially those of minor age.

This extended formula shows the compatibility of the women with succession and inheritance, and recognizes their productive aptitude; their capacity as caregivers and the fact that they were grounded in the land and in the family (Rial García 2001). In the region of Santiago de Compostela, the wills of the parents designated their daughters as inheritors of the *mejora* in more than half of the cases (56.6 percent), especially when single women (57.8 percent of them) and youngest females in the family. However, if we refer to other notarial documents (donations, concessions, etc.), the preference was not so clear as it was in the western coastal region near Pontevedra and Vigo.

Closer inland, the daughters were treated less favourably; nevertheless, in Tierra de Montes (a transition zone), 39.4 percent of the *mejoras* went to a daughter, 31.8 percent went to a son, and 28.8 percent went to various sons and daughters. In the central region of Galicia, as said earlier, many females hardly benefited from inheritance and their destiny was then to stay single at home with their brothers, in the frame of stem families.

Conclusions

In summary, Galician women enjoyed a beneficial position with respect to inheritance, when compared with other Spanish models of family transmission. It is difficult to talk about differences according to levels of fortune because there were fewer options for women than there were for men. The daughters of rural families, even if wealthy, could not enter the convent. In 1800, in Galicia, there were only 25 convents with 585 nuns, and therefore it was not a solution for parents to send their daughters to religious institutions in order to assure them a safe, secure, comfortable life outside of matrimony.

As for the men in western Galicia – an area of nuclear families and of rather moderate unequal inheritance system –, to be a main inheritor did not make them wealthier nor did it assure their future. The small agrarian holding that they received obliged them to search for other activities or to emigrate. Children, males and females, received their legitimate share and, if they married, this was added to that of their spouses, by means of which, combined with emigration, they survived. Women could be rather independent but used to work hard, married or not.

By contrast, in central Galicia, where stem family system was the norm, particularly for noblemen *(hidalgos)*, the first born son used to receive, as main heir, the larger portion of the inheritance and a larger agrarian holding. He married to become head of household and took responsibility of continuity of the family house and all members. He never migrated, neither before nor after his wedding. But the family land he received was minimally productive. Inheriting first born sons had to take responsibility for the entire family, including brothers, sisters, uncles, aunts, etc. who had to contribute their work to the household economy and general well-being, including children and aging members. Of the single brothers who did not manage to wed with inheriting daughters of other families, the majority remained single, or frequently, became clerics, and most were obliged to emigrate sometimes in order to bring more resources home. It is impossible to know which of these situations yielded more well-being to family members.

The only thing that remains clear is that the Galician system of family transmission, with its overall two main specific different formulas (practiced within the same Castilian law), only intended to ensure survival to all children, males and females.

References

BARREIRO MALLON, Baudilio, 2004, "Estudiantes y curas de la diócesis de Santiago durante el siglo XVIII", in Maria de los Angeles SOBALER SECO and Maximo GARCIA FERNANDEZ (eds), *Estudios en Homenaje al profesor Teófanes Egido*, Valladolid, Junta de Castilla y León, pp. 103–130.

DUBERT, Isidro, 1989, "Estudio histórico del parentesco a través de las dispensas de matrimonio y los archivos parroquiales en la Galicia del Antiguo Régimen", in BERMEJO BARRERA, José Carlos (ed.), *Parentesco, familia y matrimonio en la Historia de Galicia*, Santiago, Tórculo Edicións pp. 167–192.

–, 1991, "Los comportamientos sexuales premaritales en la sociedad gallega del Antiguo Régimen", *Studia Historica*, 9, pp. 117–142.

–, 1992, *Historia de la Familia en Galicia durante la época moderna, 1550–1830*, La Corogne, Sada.

–, 2006, "Modernity without modernisation: the evolution of domestic service in North-West Spain, 1752–1900", *Gender and History*, 18, 2, pp. 199–210.

EIRAS ROEL, Antonio, 1990, "Mecanismos autorreguladores, evolución demográfica y diversificación intrarregional. El ejemplo de la población de Galicia a finales del s. XVIII", *Boletín de la Asociación de Demografía Histórica*, 2, pp. 51–72.

–, 1996, *La población de Galicia, 1700–1860*, Santiago, Fundacion Caixa Galicia.

FERNANDEZ CORTIZO, Camilo, 2001, *La Tierra de Montes en el s. XVIII. Estructura demográfica y sistema familiar en una sociedad rural*, Santiago, Universidad de Santiago.

GASALLA, Pedro and SAAVEDRA, Pegerto, 1998, "Alumnos, bachareis e catedráticos no século XVIII", in José R. BARREIRO (ed.), *Historia da Universidade de Santiago*, Santiago, Universidad de Santiago.

LASLETT, Peter, 1965, *The World We Have Lost*, London, Methuen.

PEREZ GARCIA, José Manuel, 1979, *Un modelo de sociedad rural de Antiguo Régimen en la Galicia costera: La Península del Salnés,* Santiago de Compostela, Universidad de Santiago.

–, 1999, "En los límites del virtuosismo agrario tradicional: la fertilidad de la comarca del Bajo Miño, 1730–1860", *Ler Historia*, 36, pp. 221– 245.

REY CASTELAO, Ofelia, 1990 "Mecanismos reguladores de la nupcialidad en la Galicia atlántica. El matrimonio a trueque", *Obradoiro de Historia Moderna*, pp. 247–268.

–, 1994, "Migraciones internas y medium-distance en Galicia, siglos XVI-XIX", in Antonio EIRAS ROEL and Ofelia REY CASTELAO (eds), *Migraciones internas y medium-distance en la Península Ibérica, 1500–1900*, 2, Santiago, Xunta de Galicia, pp. 85–130.

–, 1996, "Edad Moderna: Iglesia y religión", in Marco GARCIA QUINTELA (ed.), *Las religiones en la Historia de Galicia*, Universidad de Santiago, pp. 141–180.

–, 2006, "Les femmes seules du Nord-Ouest de l'Espagne: trajectoires féminines dans un territoire d'émigration, 1700–1860", *Annales de Démographie Historique*, 2, pp. 105–133.

RIAL GARCIA, Serrana, 2001, "Las mujeres y el patrimonio en dos comunidades costeras de las Rías Bajas", *Obradorio de Historia Moderna*, 10, p. 89–120.

SANZ GONZALEZ, Margarita, "Fases iniciales del fenómeno migratorio. Un ejemplo en la Galicia sudoccidental a comienzos del XVIII", in Antonio EIRAS ROEL and Ofelia REY CASTELAO (eds), *Migraciones internas y medium-distance en la Península Ibérica, 1500-1900*, 2, Santiago, Xunta de Galicia, pp. 517–522.

SOBRADO CORREA, Hortensio, 2001, *Las Tierras de Lugo en la Edad Moderna. Economía campesina, familia y herencia, 1550–1860,* A Coruña, Fundación Pedro Barrié de la Maza.

PART IV

FEMALE HEADSHIP, WIDOWHOOD AND OLD AGE

To Remarry or Not: Well-Being, Female Property and Widowhood in Early-Modern France

Antoinette FAUVE-CHAMOUX

Did matrimonial contracts and inheritance systems protect the widow or even, to some extent, did they favour her in early-modern France? So it may appear when considering many cases during the *Ancien Régime*. We may at least assert that laws or customs did not neglect the future of widows not only of course when they were in charge of young children, but also when left alone.

The extreme diversity of laws and Customs in the French Kingdom according to provinces as well as the discrepancies between legal provisions and their concrete enforcement (Le Roy Ladurie 1976; Béaur 2004) were such that any general assertion would be senseless. At least the notion of "human rights" which we may consider as a basis for the post-revolutionary legislation, was not a central preoccupation of these times. It would have been the only way to treat the case of widows as such, independently of other considerations. Of course the Christian tradition prevented ignoring their fate as human beings and inserted them in the larger frame of the family and the role they had to play for supporting family development and well-being of all members. For instance, especially in the South of France, perpetuation of the family estate was the main aim of regulation and only from that point of view could widows be favoured or not. The fate of widows was a direct consequence of the matrimonial customs or laws they were submitted to. Hence we need to outline these matrimonial dispositions.

Customs and Laws

From a legal point of view, and matrimonial law indeed, the French kingdom was divided into two parts. Firstly Northern France (that is most of the provinces with customary law)[1] was during the Middle Ages the seat for a slow elaboration of an original matrimonial system which was to persist, for instance, the *Coutume de Paris* (Bourdot de Richebourg 1724, vol. 3)[2] which is the one in effect in Quebec (Brun 2003). Its main characteristic was pooling movables and goods acquired. On the contrary, a second system prevailed in Southern France[3] (as well as in the province of Normandy, in the Northern part), where matrimonial joint estate was excluded.

There were however some attempts to unify such dispositions: according to secular law, widows had to comply with a minimum widowhood period (about one year) – *délai de viduité* – during which they could not remarry. This constraint actually intended to protect a possible posthumous child and was never dictated by Canon law, as one might have thought. Religious law allowed widows and widowers to remarry without any waiting period (Poumarède 1991). Let us note also, as an old tradition, the fact that all mourning expenses – ceremonies, clothing – were to be charged on the husband's succession, not on the widow's assets. Actually these expenses were substantial for notable women who, due to social pressure, had to wear costly clothes as a conspicuous sign of their widowhood, as they had to dress their servants, if any, accordingly.

As well as the "Written" law in the South (also called *Roman law*), the Northern customs did provide for the protection of widows at various levels. In practice, according to circumstances, notaries introduced detailed clauses in marriage contracts in order to increase or decrease the rights the widow would be entitled to.

1 See Annex 1 below on legislation.

2 The first printed edition of the *Coutume de Paris* is dated 1510 (Gouron and Terrin 1975, 199).

3 We cannot enter here into the details of the French Kingdom extension. Let us say that it covered most of the actual Northern France at the end of the Middle-Ages, as the South was directly submitted to the authority of the King, progressively, in the course of the sixteenth century.

Let us add that the kings legislated more than once on the widow's behaviour. In 1483, an *Edict of King René* penalized the widow remarrying in the course of the one-year mourning period: if she did, she could lose her dowry and the assets her husband could have given to her, and she lost guardianship on her children. However, after having contracted a new marriage, she could not give more than one third of her own assets to her new husband. Later, in 1560, King François II edicted an *Edict of second marriage (Edit des secondes noces),* with some still more restrictive dispositions about the assets a widow could donate to her new husband when her children by first marriage were still alive or even when she had grandchildren whose inheritance rights had to be preserved. In 1567, another edict, *Edit de Saint-Maur*, also called *Edit des mères*, prohibited a mother from inheriting her children's assets when they died. A last text, *Ordonnance de Blois* (1579), stated that any widow less than 25 years old would return back to the status of minor and be placed under the guardianship of her parents – including for permission to remarry – without free disposal of her own assets, nor the possibility to sign a contract nor to act judicially (Isambert *et al.* 1822–1833).

The aim of this royal legislation was of course to unify legal and customary practices in the kingdom (Annex 1). An effect of such disposition was to protect children by first marriage against the suspected consequences of their mother's remarriage, but, in any way, it did not modify the basic difference between North and South or provinces with Customs versus provinces with *Written law*. In the first set of provinces, the North, the widowed woman regained her own assets, and she was entitled to half the movables and assets of the conjugal community, as well as to a dower calculated on half the own assets of her deceased husband (sometimes only one third). In the second provinces, the South, the widow regained her dowry and received on her husband's assets an "increment" (the amount of which was related to the size of the dowry she brought at marriage). She also went on benefiting from miscellaneous assets ("out of the dowry") that she might have received through donations or successions (called *paraphernaux*), or from other personal assets resulting from her professional work. But, whatever the province, historians and jurists always observe a gap between law and practice.

Marriage contracts give, on the one hand, a fair picture of the way widows were treated. Wills, on the other hand, give global indications as to the different types of possible succession. And we ought to recall that poor couples seldom established marriage contracts. In absence of a notarized deed, local customs and practices were applied (Olivier-Martin 1922–1926).

Both systems, then, were shielding the assets and acquisitions of widowed women. We analyze first in detail the Northern matrimonial system involving joint estate between spouses – especially the Parisian case – and, second, the system, essentially in the South of France, with no conjugal joint estate, so as to assess what was at a widow's disposal to live or survive during the *Ancien Régime*.

Why few widows remarried in the past will be considered in light of what they could expect to get for maintaining or improving their well-being, including their independence and proper care for themselves and their children, after the difficult transition period of mourning.

The Northern France Conjugal Joint-Estate System: the Well-Being of the Parisian Widow

Detailed analyses of marriage contracts give a fairly good understanding of the property transmission patterns in Northern France, as Barbara Diefendorf showed when studying four neighbourhoods of Paris in the second half of the 16th century (Diefendorf 1983). A large set of 1289 Parisian marriage contracts were also analyzed by Roland Mousnier (Beauvalet-Boutouyrie 2001).[4] Apparently, in that last study, these contracts cover the entire social spectrum (Figure 1, below). Parisian parish registers as well as other nominative data disappeared when the Paris town hall burnt in 1871, hence the importance of notarial records for family historians of the capital city.

4 According to Beauvalet-Boutouyrie 2001, pp. 244–269, Roland Mousnier studied, in 19 notarial archives in Paris, 630 Parisian marriage contracts for the period 1660–1670 and 659 others for 1739–1749.

The Bride's Dowry as Part of Female Assets

During the *Ancien Régime* (before 1789), nearly all marriage contracts, which were notarized, mentioned the amount and composition of the bride's dowry. Most of the dowries in Paris were cash and movables (together 84 percent for the 17th century, 67 percent for the 18th century). As wording goes, "goods and rights of the bride consist all together of movables, clothes, linen, and money from her earnings and savings". But the dowry might also include some real estate – be it land, houses or annuities –, 16 percent in the 17th century, 33 percent in the 18th. So the proportion of "composite" or mixed dowries (with both personal and real estates) was increasing, to reach one third of all Parisian dowries in the 1740s. They included not only property given by the family, but also savings and earnings, often earned from domestic service.

Annuities (life- or perpetual annuities) constituted the major part of these mixed Parisian dowries, whose proportion and diversity grew with the 18th century. We note sometimes the presence of shares of the *Compagnie des Indes* or tickets of the *Royal Loterie.* Annuities were treated as real estate. When she became a widow, the woman was entitled to dispose of her annuities as she saw fit.

Creation of a Conjugal Joint Estate

After certifying the amount and composition of the dowry, the notary entered into the marriage contract the share of each spouse's assets to be included into the joint estate or community. The dowry – normally the assets the marrying woman's father gave her – was not her only contribution to the conjugal community: she might well have goods of her own. Each spouse's contribution to the community was of equal value and would bring the same value to the community, even if the amounts of their own original assets were different. Generally speaking, the smaller the dowry, the greater the portion of it that was turned over to the joint estate. In 18th century Paris, the personal assets of each spouse tended to be better protected, and indeed the bride's assets, since a smaller proportion of individual assets was then put in common (Table 1): more than 60 percent of the marriage contracts were concluded in the 1740s with only one third of the bride's personal assets contributing to the joint estate, against about one half in the 1660s. Goods acquired after the wedding became part of the community.

Table 1. Part of bride's dowry contributing to the conjugal joint estate. Parisian marriage contracts

	1660–1670 *% of contracts*	*1739–1749* *% of contracts*
1/4	2.7	2.8
1/3	39.6	60.8
1/2	44.0	32.3
2/3	10.8	4.1
the whole dowry	2.9	0
Total	100%	100%

Source: Roland Mousnier's Project, Parisian marriage contracts, cf. Beauvalet-Boutouyrie, 2001, p. 253.
Note: In this table are included only cases where the proportion of the dowry can be precisely calculated. For the first set of contracts, in the 1660s, 19.7% cases were unknown. For the 1740s, 7.3% of the contracts did not allow the evaluation and were excluded.

Marriage contracts planned post-mortem devolution of property. The joint-estate community was divided into two equal shares, one going to the surviving spouse, the other one to the heirs of the deceased. In addition, marriage contracts provided the widow with a dower – a claim on the husband's property if he died first. Such a marital system typical of Northern France was clearly linked, in my view, with a general neo-local marriage establishment. Besides, it also appears as particularly suitable for urban craftsmen's and merchants' families where the wife used to contribute daily to the life and prosperity of the family business.

Securing Well-Being: Dower, Preciput and Donations

While writing the marriage contract, after determining the composition of the conjugal joint estate, the notary, as mentioned above, recorded the *dower.*[5]

Jurists think that the dower was a substitute for the "morning gift" (the Burgond, Lombard or Frankish *Morgengabe*, given to wives or concubines), which the Church contested in its fight for monogamy and public marriage (Le Jan-Hennebicque 1993; Hughes 1978). We shall see below that anthropologists go on discussing the meanings of the benefits that the husband could also grant to his wife in Southern Written law areas (Testart 2001). At any rate, in Paris, the amount of the dower was actually related to the size and amount of the dowry. But, traditionally, the assets assigned to the dower were supposed to be linked to and produced by the real estate which the husband owned at the time of the wedding, together with properties that he could inherit later (therefore not depending at all on the bride's dowry). As a matter of fact, dower was a traditional and customary institution not necessitating any convention and precise mention of it was not needed in the marriage contract (Bart 1998, 308). This dower was secured and guaranteed by real estates such as groves or fish ponds, which were of course supposed to be well managed and allow regular revenue.

As we already noted above in 17th century Paris, a "prefix" dower was substituted more and more in place of this "customary" dower based on real estate: it was usually some money to be paid to the widow in one instalment. Some widows[6] had then the privilege to receive dowers made

5 This is the case in Paris, and in all Northern France customs, including the *Coutume de Normandie*. For more on the dower system, see for example Augustin 2003, Ourliac and Malafosse 1968, Ourliac and Gazzaniga 1985, Poumarède 1991.

6 For the purpose of the present paper, I reorganized the order of R. Mousnier's categories which were originally presented in the following order as:

1. Unskilled workers, small-timers, journeymen, shop boys, servants
2. Free craftsmen and guild masters
3. Merchants
4. Independent professional men and artists
5. Holders of finance or law offices
6. Senior civil servants, high grade clerks, secretaries, business managers and staff members
7. Career soldiers

up of life- or perpetuity annuities (Beauvalet-Boutouyrie 2001, 255)[7] (Figure 1); those were part of the elite. Occurrences of such dowers grew during the 18th century. We may analyze such a change as a concern to compensate for small dowries and to improve the protection of the widow.

Figure 1. Dower in the form of annuities according to socio-professional groups (Percent of brides concerned). Marriage contracts in Paris.

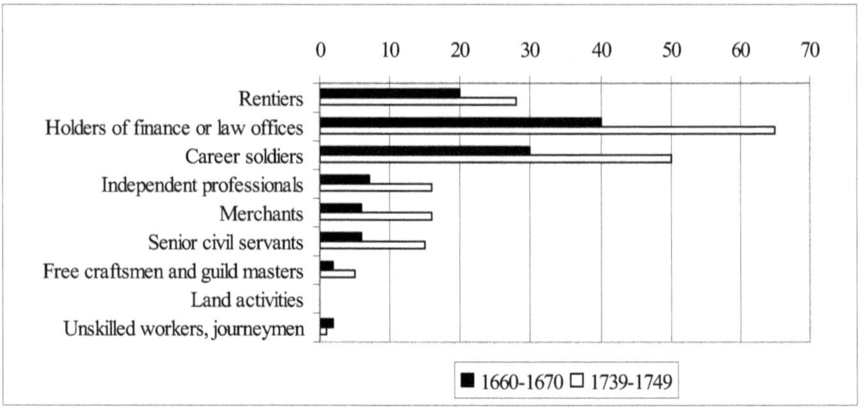

Source: Roland Mousnier's Project, Parisian marriage contracts, cf. Beauvalet-Boutouyrie, 2001, p. 255.

As poor socio-professional groups were more numerous on the whole, dowers in the form of annuities were the case for only 9 percent of widows during the first period (1660–1670); they numbered 18 percent between 1739 and 1749 and widows of all social strata were concerned in the end (Figure 1). But, as the graph shows, this practice was very frequent among the legal and financial professions, as well as for military. In that last case, we may think that grooms were conscious of their professional risks, although the main motive was obviously their recruitment then as *cadets*, i.e. younger sons of noble families, who did not inherit

8. Land activities
9. Persons of private means.
Unfortunately using "HISCO" system of classification was not possible since we had no access to the original data.

7 The team included Scarlett Beauvalet-Boutouyrie and Vincent Gourdon (University Paris IV, History).

landed property.[8] In more modest social classes, we may imagine an intention to compensate small dowries, so as to give the future widow some steady source of income.

When the dower allowed for large sums, as was the case for 10 percent of Parisian contracts, the parties could foresee their reduction when the couple had children. For instance a contract stipulated that the widow would receive an annuity of 6,000 pounds if childless at her husband's death, but only 4,000 if there were children alive.

A widow was in danger of losing her dower, in case of "misconduct", especially during the one-year mourning period. It is noticeable that female remarriage did not entail loss of the dower. As Molière's character Angélique says to her grasping stepmother Béline, second wife of her father Argan:

> There are other women who see marriage only as profit dealing, who marry only to gain dowers and to become rich when the ones they wed do die, who unscrupulously run from husband to husband to get their spoils. Such people indeed do it offhand and have little regard for the person (*Le Malade Imaginaire,* 1673, II, 6).

Let us add that the Parisian widow was entitled to receive one half of the goods acquired in common since marriage.

Another clause may be present in an early-modern Parisian marriage contract: a husband could assign a *preciput* in favor of his wife if she survived him – that is the right to withhold from his estate a previously fixed part before sharing out between heirs. Such a clause gave a real advantage to the surviving wife; and we observe, more and more, in the course of the 17th and 18th centuries, that husbands did grant financial advantages to their potential widows by marriage contract, especially when spouses belonged to the lower social groups. In the Anjou province, the surviving spouse got usufruct on the other half of the goods acquired since marriage, that is on the half belonging to the deceased.[9]

In Northern France, both husband's and wife's lineages shared net assets and liabilities of the conjugal joint estate. But the widow was never obliged to pay eventual debts if she decided to relinquish the conjugal community, but then she would lose her part of the movables and goods acquired. Clearly a Parisian widow could avoid paying the household's

8 Other opportunities than land rents were then available, such as investments in colonial business, of which returns were expected to be higher.

9 *Coutume d'Anjou*, first printed edition, 1509 (cf. Gouron and Terrin, 1975, p. 29).

debts. Practically all Parisian marriage contracts did secure a dower and a *preciput* for the wife in case of widowhood. Besides, some 10 percent – including the modest groups – provided for a gift, which was usually some usufruct drawn from the joint estate, under the condition that the couple remained childless. Other types of clauses could appear in the contract, for instance one which a bride specified in favor of her parents: if she happened to die before her husband, his obligation was to provide a life annuity to his mother-in-law (the bride's mother) as long as she lived.

Estimation of Paris Widow's Potential Assets

The average amount of assets a Parisian widow could expect to receive, according to her social status, after her husband's death, was estimated (Beauvalet-Boutouyrie 2001, 265).[10] Of course the table hereafter makes sense only when the conjugal joint estate had a positive value (see Figure 2 and corresponding Table 2).

According to Roland Mousnier's team, at the end of the Ancien Régime, a widow with children needed at least 500 pounds to live independently in Paris for about two or three years. After this period, she had to take a job, remarry or ask for assistance. This is the reason why widows were so fond of annuities with their regular falling dues and their 5 percent fixed rates or more – a good anti-inflation security. However we ought not to forget that marriage contracts were not usual in the poorest social groups, so that many widowed wives of unskilled workers or poor craftsmen became destitute, with an income under 200 pounds yearly.

10 We may note the discrepancies occurred in only 80 years concerning holders of offices and career soldiers, discrepancies which Beauvalet-Boutouyrie does not explain. We may understand such an evolution for finance office holders who then had indubitably access to privileged information. As for career soldiers, it remains to be explained why their financial means grew so much in this period.

Figure 2. Evaluation of widow's average potential assets (part of joint estate, dower and preciput cumulated), according to social status (in pounds – livres). Parisian marriage contracts

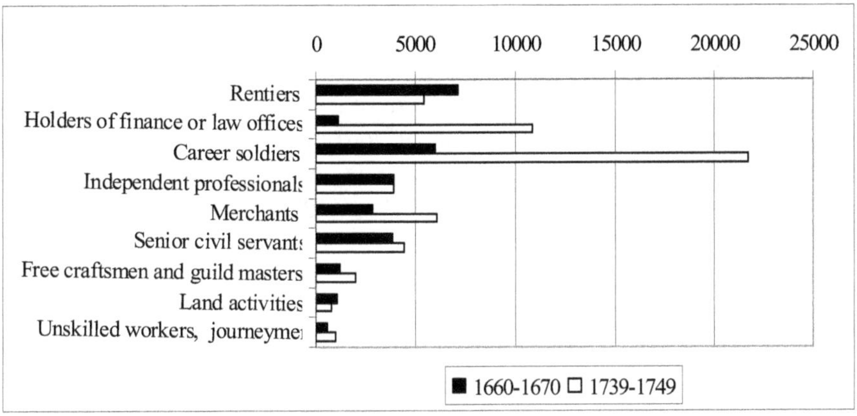

Table 2. Evaluation of widow's average potential assets (part of joint estate, dower and preciput cumulated), according to social status (in pounds – livres). Parisian marriage contracts

	1660–1670	*1739–1749*
Rentiers	7163	5455
Holders of finance or law offices	1143	10837
Career soldiers	6000	21737
Independent professionals	3913	3904
Merchants	2850	6047
Senior civil servants	3830	4464
Free craftsmen and guild masters	1239	1978
Land activities	1081	784
Unskilled workers, journeymen	553	967
Global mean assets:		
– part of joint estate included	3661	5440
– part of joint estate excluded	1373	2163

Sources: Enquête Mousnier, Parisian marriage contracts, cf. Beauvalet-Boutouyrie, 2001, p. 265.
Note: These data are included in Figure 2.

Marriage contracts might also include other clauses concerning the couple's parents, as we saw above, with a life annuity to the mother-in-law. In these parts of Northern France with egalitarian sharing of inherited assets, and general neo-local marriage settlement, the parents lived apart from their married children and had to clearly anticipate their future means and care in old days. As we shall see below, the "house-system", in Southern France, protected aged persons much more systematically, given the continuity of the family "house", which offered permanent shelter to ageing, disabled, sick or in need family members, be they single or widowed (Arrizabalaga 2003; Fauve-Chamoux 1998a; 2002b; 2005).

The Limits to Widow's Protection

All in all, under the terms of the Parisian customs, at her husband's death, a widow could in principle bank on what was left from her dowry, on her part in the joint estate, her dower, a *preciput* and some advantage her husband could have provided for. If the joint estate had taken on too many debts, she could wave her "waiver of right" *(droit de renonciation)*. The capacity for a widow to make use of that option appeared as soon as the Middle Ages in France, open at first for the nobility, then to commoners (Bart 1998, 311). But such a waiver of right was a case to be taken seriously, since it could also lead to loss of dower, as in Burgundy.

The matrimonial joint estate institution of Northern France was in no way like an ordinary business association or company. In practice, the bride's interests were more and more secured in the course of the Ancien Régime. Some jurists go as far as to interpret this growing protection of women, through marriage contract, as a sign of her being deemed a legally incompetent person, dependent first on her father and later, with marriage, on her husband who managed the community goods.

We may also say that the matrimonial customary system of joint conjugal community gave a fair protection, particularly to the Parisian widow, while the inheritance procedures did not advantage her as much. Gifts and presents between bride and groom were welcome, but such gifts between married persons was considered very suspect because of possible infringement on the couple's descendant's rights.[11] The Parisian custom – *Coutume de Paris* – indeed forbade direct or indirect advantages transmitted from one spouse to the other, be it a donation or the provision of a will. Nevertheless, there might have been a strictly regulated "mutual gift" of same value to the profit of the surviving spouse by mutual consent which had to be expressed in one registered and unique deed and was revocable. In that case, spouses were checked to be both in good mental and physical health! And in Paris, spouses could proceed to this mutual gift only if they had no child, a condition which was not always required elsewhere, as in Rheims.[12] Or they could at least decide mutual usufruct of some or all movables and acquisitions, so as to allow the surviving spouse to go on living in the conjugal premises. We understand therefore that a widow, who had enough for her living and who was experiencing at last as a widow what being an independent and responsible person meant, would not seek dependence and burdens in a risky remarriage, unless there was a good reason. In this light must be understood the case of a young, rich and amiable widow without children as depicted by Molière (*Le Misanthrope*, 1666) in the character of Célimène, who, aged 20, enjoys well-being and a happy independent everyday life as her own master in a nice Parisian house, and is reluctant to accept a new oppressive conjugal union with a jealous, antisocial and irritable Alceste, even if she loves him. She says:

> Moi, renoncer au monde avant que de vieillir,
> Et dans votre désert aller m'ensevelir!
> [...]
> La solitude effraie une âme de vingt ans;
> Je ne sens point la mienne assez grande, assez forte,
> Pour me résoudre à prendre un dessein de la sorte.
> (*Le Misanthrope*, 1666, Acte 5, last scene).

The Normandy province, in northwestern France, practiced by custom another system of marriage settlement and contract: no conjugal community of goods[13] and a dowry system,[14] arrangements close to those of

11 Roman law prohibits donations between living spouses. The *donatio propter nuptias* may be considered as a way to palliate such an interdiction (see below).

12 See *Coutume de Reims* in Bourdot de Richebourg, 1724.

13 First edition known of *Coutume de Normandie* is dated 1483 (Cf. Gouron and Terrin, 1975, p. 173).

14 Here *système dotal* is translated as "dowry system" or "settlement in trust".

Southern France. The Parliament in Rouen (the regional secular court) used to cancel all marriage contracts contrary to the Custom! No gift between spouses was allowed, so that "no good owned by a woman can get lost". At the husband's death, the widow got back all what she brought when marrying, i.e. usually a dowry. In the family of origin, male co-heirs had priority and already endowed girls had no access to any future family inheritance (Yver 1952, 1966; Musset 1997). But widowhood could improve female condition in a way: widows got a dower, which meant a life right on one third of their husband's own assets, which had been inalienable while they were married. Furthermore, widows inherited one third of their husband's movable goods if there were children, and one half when childless. Lastly, Norman widows received full property of half the movables and acquisitions (including real estate) and had usufruct on one third of the other acquisitions.

We shall now examine the widow's condition in Southern France where, on the basis of Roman law, there was usually no conjugal joint estate between spouses, but a general dowry system.

Southern France Matrimonial Systems without Conjugal Joint Estate: the Dowry and the House

The Settlement in Trust (Dowry System), the Donatio Propter Nuptias *and the* Augment *(Increment)*

In Southern France, where "Written law" still existed as a legacy of Roman law, the "pure" dowry system began to prevail in the 16th century. In the centuries before, according to pre-Justinian Roman law, characteristic of the treatment of assets at the disposal of the household was the contribution of the wife's family, called dowry, which became the husband's ownership (Bart 1998, 313), but he (or his family) had to repay back this dowry if marriage was dissolved. Wives might own other assets, called *paraphernalia* (meaning "off-dowry"), which they were entitled to dispose of as they saw fit. Besides, the wife was entitled to a gift of her husband, called *donatio propter nuptias* assessed at half the value of the dowry – a clause of the Justinian Code.[15] The interests of each spouse were thus treated independently. This settlement under which husband and wife administered their separate properties aimed at protecting the woman while safeguarding the interests of the family, especially of the children. When contracting marriage, the woman – or, better said, her parents – brought a dowry, usually some amount of money which could be converted into real estate, for a better protection, and also perhaps collect regular rent.

Of course enforcement of these principles was subjected to alterations in the course of European history. We already noticed, for countries with customary law in Northern France, that there was some concern for the widow's fate and that she got some privilege of usufruct concerning a part or even all of the joint estate (when childless).

According to law history for Southern France, the assets of the spouses were actually rather mixed until the 16th century, in a sense that the wife's assets were under the husband's administration. However marriage contracts and wills in this part of France often conceded to the widow (if she was not the heiress of her own natal house) some usufruct of a part of her husband's asset, usually half of it. But all goods acquired after marriage were deemed ownership of the husband, and this is quite easy to understand and logical when we only refer to the common "house" system (see below in details), where the wife was most of the time just in a position of daughter-in-law within her husband's house, without any real-estate property.

Anyway, the practice was complex. A widow with children usually went on living in her deceased husband's house and did not ask for restitution of her dowry, except when conflicting with her co-residents, husband's parents or siblings. Childless (and when not heiress to the house she lived in), she had to go back to her own family or tried to get residence in some kinship's house. Otherwise she settled by herself and lived alone, particularly in an urban surrounding. If a woman had to quit her husband's house when widowed, she then asked for her dowry back. This dowry may have increased. This "increment" *(augment)* secured her a

15 Justinien (482–565), a roman emperor, with residence in Byzance, was the initiator of considerable changes in Roman law, which was to become the basis of French civil law. Justinien transformed donation before marriage, "ante nuptias", into "donatio propter nuptias" (Code Justinien, 5,3,1).

legal mortgage on her husband's goods and in Written law areas was analogous to the dower in Customs areas. Its amount could correspond to half the value of the dowry – or even, in Bordeaux, it could be twice the value of the dowry. So local traditions were superimposed on Roman law, as Paul Ourliac, a specialist of this Roman law, said:

> Customs as those enforced in Northern France were never practiced in the South, so the customary geography there is much more confused. Enforcement of the Roman law in South-East France was quick, so that aboriginal eventual features disappeared. In South-West France on the contrary, customary features are still discernible in some areas; as well as North of the Loire river, provincial particularities are clearly perceptible; the local law in Toulouse or in Agen appears often as a middle course between various influences, as it is the case for the Parisian area; on the contrary, Pyrenean valleys preserve very original and probably very old customs (Ourliac and Gazzaniga 1985).

Paul Ourliac[16] published *the Coutumes de l'Agenais*, Customs of the Agen area (Ourliac et Gilles 1976, 1981), and he was particularly well aware of the way local South-Western France customs of inegalitarian transmission could survive with the advice of local lawyers. In the same line, Anne Zink described later those southern customs in her *Geography of South-West France customs.* And she noted accordingly: "local Parliaments did not object at all to enforcement of customs, although defining themselves as seats of written law" (Zink 1993, 483). From another point of view, in Alain Testart's recent study of dowries and other matrimonial transactions (*meta* in Lombardy, *donatio ante nuptias* or *donatio propter nuptias*, "morning gift", etc.), he happened to criticize Jack Goody's perspective by interpreting the "bride's price" – that the groom pays – as a horizontal transfer of belongings, and therefore a gift between partners or their representatives ("indirect dowry"). Considering Eurasian matrimonial systems, Testart showed on the contrary that dowry was a total inversion of the "bride price" transaction: the bride price is given most of the time directly by the groom to the bride's father, while the dowry is given by her father to the bride's groom (Testart 1996; 2001). The value of a dowry is considered to constitute the bride's inalienable and proper assets, even when the husband is entitled to be its financial administrator. At any rate, for Testart, the dowry system improved female potential autonomy, although

16 Paul Ourliac (1911–1998), used to live in Penne-d'Agenais, Lot-et-Garonne department.

the married woman remained globally in a state of dependence within the couple.[17] History of matrimonial transfers attracted much interest among anthropologists (Goody 1985, 243–264; Hughes 1978; Pellaton 1993) and such studies indeed would help historical demographers to interpret re-marriage frequencies, as seen in quantitative data, according to various cultures and socio-economic contexts.

Legal Dispositions in Favor of Widows According to Successoral Situations

In the southern system we just examined, goods acquired during marriage are supposed to be the husband's. At the widow's disposal are the dowry and her *paraphernalia* – these assets she got by succession, donation, or own occupation, as domestic service –, but it might well not be enough for a widow to live on. It is the reason why all Parliaments in the South granted the widowed person, when poor enough, some surviving layout called "quarte du conjoint pauvre" (a fourth for the poor spouse), already mentioned in the Justinian Code (Ourliac and Gazzaniga 1985, 108; Turlan 1966). Thus the surviving spouse, man or woman, could ask for a share of the pre-deceased's goods, one fourth as a usufruct (if no more than three living children); or, still in usufruct, an equivalent to one child share (when more than three living children); or one fourth in full property when childless.

But let us admit that sharing acquisitions was not handy in these French Southern areas with a "house-system", which supposed an heir or heiress marrying a non-heir or non-heiress and above all inviolability of each family patrimony (Fauve-Chamoux 2005). However, in South-West France where the house system was rather common, from the Bordeaux area to the Pyrenean mountains, some form of conjugal community appeared anyway with the 13th century, a kind of acquisition association or

17 Far from being a preponderant characteristic of marriage across the world, the dowry system is practiced in few societies. So it appears in the world map which Alain Testart established in revising the data of Murdock's *Ethnografic Atlas* (Murdock 1967; Testart *et al.* 2002, 176). Practice of dowry is only attested for Europe, for a part of India, in Tibet, Birmania and China. Everywhere else the common dominant institution is bride price.

company (Augustin 2003, 41; Lafon 1972; Zink 1993), defining a common pot in which spouses poured their gains. The marriage contract mentioned the dowry and the donations; it could also stipulate precisely how the spouses' parents would be helped when aging – usually the young couple being committed to maintain the old couple of the house in the common premises. And each spouse was allowed to make (revocable) donations to the other one during marriage.

Lastly, according to the "Written law", the husband might bequeath to his future widow a legacy – money or life annuity –, and his testament/will could also specify the conditions in which she would go on living in the house. He may also give to his future widow a usufruct on all his goods, and even, when childless, appoint her as "universal heiress". Therefore, the bride committed herself to take good care of all these assets before leaving them to her children after death, or, if childless, to her deceased husband's heirs.

So, in this case, the widow acquired the management of her husband's goods. Even though she did not gain ownership, she controlled a whole family patrimony, thus securing the household/house continuity. We may understand that a widow in such a position would be tempted not to remarry, so as not to lose these advantages. In this kind of contract, what was at stake was the survival of the house or of the family business. Many features of this "house" are similar to the Japanese "ie".[18] Intergenerational relations are specific, determining the relation between spouses and the future widow's condition. Frequently the widow herself would appoint a privileged heir by testament, if the house successor had not yet been designated.

The basic characteristics of the French southern "house system", and the South-Western model are summarized in Annex 2 below. We should stress that according to the local customs, the heir/heiress was not owner but the usufructuary and administrator of the family estate: as soon as he/she married and coresided with his/her parents, the heir/heiress knew that he/she would be responsible for the house and land, as well as for patrimonial transmission to the next generation. To sell any part of the "house" – land or building – presupposed the consent of a family council and a court ruling. Even when a sale was concluded, a family member could call the sale into question within one year and one day, exercising

18 See previous comparative studies between Pyrenees and Japan: Fauve-Chamoux and Ochiai 1998; Ochiai 2003; Fauve-Chamoux 2005; 2006.

his right of "lineage withdrawal" *(retrait lignager)* to recover the real estate for family use, which meant his own use (and not renting) (Derouet 2001).

Endowing girls was then practiced in both matrimonial systems, with or without conjugal joint estates, but, in the second one, in the South, it may have been considered as a first step towards a legitimate financial compensation due to non-heirs, males and females. To allocate a dowry to a girl when marrying (or taking her vows in a convent) was a sure way to exclude her from the family transmission to come, in whichever matrimonial system, while securing her future in a social milieu that her parents had chosen for her. This practice of exclusion after a dowry was given was common in all of South France with its non egalitarian Written law, but, as we saw above, it was also the case in some egalitarian law areas such as Normandy.

In addition, when it was common to allow the privilege of a *preciput* – an extra share – in favor of the chosen heir/heiress, giving a dowry to marrying out girls *(cadettes)* and to non-inheriting sons *(cadets)*, bore the same consequence: it excluded all non-inheriting siblings from real-estate transmission. Still the dowry allocated to a girl could possibly be recovered if, once widowed, she had to quit her spouse's house or if she died childless. But actually dowry restitution rarely occurred, all the more because this amount of money was very soon reinvested by the receiving family in a dowry for another child. Let us add that cross-marriages between two families were a way not to actually pay the dowries (they were fixed at the same amount and were fictitiously exchanged).

With the end of the *Ancien Régime*, in the South, marriages without conjugal joint estates were dominant, but protecting the personal patrimony of women was also somehow a matter of concern. For instance, when founding a new "house" by branching out, "cadets" (no-inheriting sons), from craftsman and small merchant's families, could well adopt a joint-estate settlement when marrying a girl without a dowry, so as to give her some kind of protection. This did occur with population growth in the pre-revolutionary period.

As strange as it may appear, "primogeniture", which helped so much to legitimate royal or feudal successions, that is the transmission of name and title, was very seldom expressed in the local laws of Southern France, except in some Customs of the Basque country – with "integral" primogeniture – and in Pyrenean valleys (Arrizabalaga 1998; 2005; Lacanette-

Pommel 1998; Zink 1993), concealing in fact another right, the right to choose the heir. This choice could be expressed through a donation or a will which was to specify how the family patrimony had to be transmitted, allocating a *preciput* to the chosen heir. But waiting practically until the family head's death to determine the conditions of inheritance was fairly rare. Who would be the heir/heiress of the house was decided long in advance and conditions of succession were usually settled when marriage contracts were negotiated with other families. We may note with interest that in Haute Provence (Verdon valley) practically all marriages were notarized at the end of the Ancien Régime. So the local historian may follow the history of all patrimonies, even the poorest (Collomp 1983). And we may understand some specificities of the female property right in light of this Provencal local law.

Female Property Rights

More than in the Pyrenean and South-Western countries, the local law in Provence strictly limited the rights of women to inherit. Alain Collomp analyzed the *Statuts de Provence*, already commented in the 18th century,[19] and pointed out a common feeling in that province (Collomp, 1983): the future of a family was considered as secured when it avoided as much as possible transmission in the female line.[20]

What happened then when the family head died "intestate" – without writing a will –, a case which one of the *Statuts de Provence* treats explicitly? In such a case, the sons divided up the patrimony, with a "legitimate share" reserved for the girls, the proportion of which depended on the number of living children. Sons received equal shares, whatever their birth rank. But the legitimate share for each girl was very modest: for two children, one boy and one girl, the boy got 5/6, the girl 1/6; for two boys and one girl, each boy got 4/9 and the girl 1/9. So we may easily conceive that

19 The first printed edition of *Statuts de Provence* is dated 1504 (Gouron and Terrin 1975, 230).

20 "Common wish by the fathers is to preserve the family name and dignity. And that can only be done through male children. Girls are the ultimate term and the end of the paternal family" (Jean-Joseph Julien, *Nouveau commentaire sur les statuts de Provence*, 1778, t. 1, p. 441).

the amount of dowries for females usually exceeded the "legitimate" share. Here we come into family strategies, where compensations to be given to each child were the effect of a subtle balance, a main preoccupation of a father who had no interest in stirring up conflicts.

Let us note again that these non-egalitarian practices were not exclusively practiced in the South. I mentioned elsewhere (Fauve-Chamoux 1998c) the possibility in Northern France to advantage such or such child. After Jean Yver (Yver 1953; 1954), we usually consider Picardy and Walloon countries, more or less from Amiens to Liege, as *preciput* areas (Fauve-Chamoux 2009).

Given the family "house" system where the sense of joint ownership was strong, it is a paradox that the matrimonial tradition of the South was essentially individualist. Roman law allows anyone, man or woman, to contract or make a will. Women experienced here a freedom that they did not enjoy in customs areas of the North. Noblewomen had all the property rights on their fiefs (see below the case of Esparros); heiresses gave their name to their husband, as in Bearn and Pyrenean valleys. Women acted as witnesses, managed their own goods and more often than not could sell them. Even the marriage settlement provides for equality between spouses (Ourliac and Gazzaniga 1985, 109). My monograph of Esparros (Fauve-Chamoux 1984; 1994; 1995; 1998; 2001), a very independent central Pyrenean village, illustrates these characteristics of the stem-family system of reproduction. Although implying exclusion of non-heirs/non-heiresses, this socio-economic system was surprisingly tolerant concerning the fringes of society. Bastards or unmarried mothers did not trouble peasant morals: sexual liberty was not prohibited for non-heirs; the Church became more lenient; the peasant community of the central Pyrenees was until 1840 one of the most illiterate in France, very different from literate Béarn. Culture in the Pyrenean Baronies was essentially oral. And the stem-family system of reproduction was the norm, even if families had to face and accept branching-out of new houses with demographic growth and expansion of cultivated land gained on communal property.

The Southern matrimonial system did protect wife's estates. They were also given some means of survival when widowed. At any rate, loneliness, for widows aged more than 65, was very rare during the Ancien Régime, as the case of Esparros (central Pyrenean area) clearly shows (Fauve-Chamoux 1996). Cases of loneliness grew, as well as in other stem-family areas, during the 19th century, due in part to the 1804 *Code civil*, but resulting above all from the increasing pauperization and rural exodus: young males and females left their villages, emigrating to towns or abroad, so the population was aging (Fauve-Chamoux 2002b, 107). Usually widowhood increased poverty in already economically unstable houses, especially since the poorest widows had married without a dowry and without a marriage contract (the case was different, in the Alpes de Hautes Provence where marriage contracts were commonly used at all social levels) (Collomp 1983). In Esparros in early modern time, before the French revolution of 1789, without notarial records on hand, it was difficult for me to evaluate precisely the type of personal assets women had at their disposal.[21] In addition to what was known through longitudinal reconstructed life histories, female heads of households could be traced through nominative listings and land registers. On the whole, widows could act with some authority in their house and were present in the local village and community of inhabitants.[22]

Early-modern documents – cadastres and tax lists – in Esparros gave an obvious proof that heading a farm was not only a male job. Women (12 percent of the occurrences), mostly widows, as well as men (88 percent), could head a farm house of medium or small size.

All of these features, especially sharing authority in the house or transmitting intact the whole house to the following generation, risked becoming obsolete with the new Napoleonian *Code Civil* adopted in 1804, which, taking account of violent revolutionary debates (Goy 1981; 1988), implied egalitarian sharing of inheritance, frequent matrimonial joint estate, only for goods acquired since marriage, and above all the wife's legal incompetence. What really happened?

21 A general family reconstitution was conducted with parish registers and civil registration sources from 1660 to 1914 (longitudinal individual and family studies). Nominative censuses were available every five years from 1846. Cadastres and tax lists gave further information on family belongings and economic status. For this Esparros monograph, no notarial records were collected. Other studies made an extensive use of them, so that the practice was rather well known for the Baronies (Augustins 1989; Bonnain 1986).

22 In many autonomous Pyrenean valleys, widows, when heads of "house", used to participate and vote in the democratic local *Assemblées des Habitants*, as can be seen in the Minutes of the village council.

The New National Law: Code Civil (1804) and Matrimonial Dispositions

Faithful to their egalitarian views, revolutionary lawmakers were the first to modify the rules for heritage. From 1789 and until 1795, they considered as their main objective the elimination of any legislation recalling feudal time – primogeniture and masculinity rights were suppressed, as well as some aspects of Roman law (to advantage a child by will was forbidden in 1793). Then a kind of simplified customary law was put in force, which only allowed for egalitarian sharing. The possibility to advantage a specific child with a part of inheritance was restated in 1801 and in 1803 the practice of *preciput* reappeared. Thus the *Code Civil*, adopted in 1804 after a long elaboration since 1800, was the result of a compromise between various customary laws or practices and ideological or revolutionary yearnings. It waves equality as the principle for successions, but allows advantaging one child – a girl as well as a boy –, the advantage "extra share", called *preciput,* being a third of the inherited assets when two children were concerned, a quarter when three children, etc. (Article 913, *Code civil,* 1841 edition). Also worthy of interest in its provisions is the recommendation – which may be read between the lines – to avoid as much as possible the dismantling of farms. This is the reason why the *Code Civil* did not bear consequences as disastrous as we could have expected for the traditional one-heir only succession, characteristic of Southern France. As Frédéric Le Play showed after visiting a Pyrenean valley – the Lavedan, in 1856 (Le Play 1875) – suitable strategies developed, coping with the new legal situation to save most of the tradition. Acting in collusion with lawyers and notaries, families were able to circumvent the egalitarian difficulty. How families elaborated new strategies was clearly shown for the Basque country (Arrizabalaga 1997; 2003; 2005; 2006). The main heir had to buy back, more or less fictitiously, his brothers' or sisters' shares; donations appeared suddenly just in time to vouch for the sharing balance, etc.

Concerning matrimonial dispositions, for all French couples not bound by a specific marriage contract, the *Code Civil* elected as a legal disposition the matrimonial status of joint estate for movables and acquisitions (article 1400, *Code civil,* 1841 edition): "The joint estate, which is coming into force with the simple declaration of choosing joint-estate marriage, or when there is no marriage contract, is bound by the rules expounded in the next six sections".

The husband was responsible for his wife's own assets – a wife deemed legally incompetent: "The husband administers all his wife's personal goods" (article 1428, *Code civil,* 1841 edition).

Customs were rescinded: "The spouses can no more stipulate generally that their association would obey to one of the customs, laws or local uses which previously were in force in the various parts of the French territory, and which the present Code rescinds" (art. 1390, *Code civil,* 1841 edition).

But the bride and groom might choose a settlement in a trust/dowry system (we ought not to forget that Napoleon was Corsican, thus originating from the authoritarian and anti-feminist area of the South-East we examined in the case of Provence): "They may however generally declare that they intend to marry under the regime or of joint estate or of settlement in trust. In the first case, the dispositions of chapter II will govern the rights of the spouses and heirs, in the second case, the dispositions of chapter III" (article 1391, *Code civil,* 1841 edition). The dowry system was to be rescinded in France only on 15 July, 1965.

Before the Revolution, as soon as he/she signed the marriage contract and married, a heir or heiress co-residing with his/her parents knew that sooner or later he/she would be responsible for the family house and its land, which he/she would hand down to the next generation (Zink 1993, 178–180). Widowhood was only a problem when happening before procreation. After 1804, the heir became legal owner with full capacity to exploit or alienate his goods, but only after the death of both parents, not just after marrying (and, with the Code, the heiress' husband got legal administration of the totality of his wife's goods – a great change as, until then, his status of son-in-law in the house was very mediocre: in the stem-family "house" system, the widowed childless son-in-law had to leave his defunct wife's house. According to the Barèges custom, he recovered only half of the dowry he brought along when marrying in.

The marriage contract was an expression of dispositions to come, and mentioning real ownership in a southern "house" made no sense as long as the parents were alive; the old generation kept the most authority on the house's management.

On the whole, in the stem-family system, non-inheriting girls practically owned only their dowry, when the heir or heiress enjoyed the whole real estate. It could happen that an unmarried woman had some piece of land or house, as an inherited share coming from some parents or relatives. If childless, she used to transmit it herself by will to the main heir of her native house – brother or nephew –, so that the real estate he managed would not be curtailed.

Conclusion

In *Ancien Régime* France, the role of women in transmission or devolution of assets as well as their responsibility in the management of their own household was far from homogeneous. Differences in inheritance systems were striking from one area to another, mostly between the North and the South (Augustins 1989; Béaur 2005), and we saw how there were also different for matrimonial conventions. Given regional regulations, difference could also be seen from one social group to another, as was shown above for Paris.

In early-modern France, life conditions for the female surviving spouse resulted both from types of matrimonial legal dispositions and transmission model – or, failing that, on local uses and customs. In Northern France, when married in joint estate, a widow could enjoy the prosperity of the family business, or be crippled with debts. She could expect a dower. When married in trust, with a dowry, as in Southern France, she could recover her dowry, once a widow, or mourn its disappearance due to the bad management of her husband.

All in all, we may think that the marriage financial arrangement in the Northern customary areas gave the widow a better protection. There she got her own goods back, and she was entitled to receive half of the movables and acquisitions which the spouses often accumulated after marrying. But, in case of debts, she had an explicit right to renounce the joint community and, with any under age children eventually alive, avoid liabilities.

In the Southern Written law areas, if the childless widow had to leave her husband's house, she got back her dowry and "paraphernalia", but these goods may not at all have been enough for her to live on or remarry, hence the "survival" clause of the *Roman law* called "the fourth of the poor spouse". In some parts of the South-West, there was also a specific marital arrangement, the "acquisition association", somehow an equivalent of the Northern conjugal joint estate.

In Customary areas, the widow may also receive a "dower", in Written law areas an "increment to the dowry". These survival life-gains both burdened the husband's belongings, but to different extents: the Northern dower affected half the husband's own goods, that is a good part of his wealth; on the contrary, Southern increment was a function of the dowry amount, and we know that dowries could be very modest.

But, there is still an open question: did the widows usually claim their rights? They probably did more in the North than in the South, given their living arrangements. Many women preferred to go on living and growing old in their defunct husband's house with one of their children or with an heir to the deceased husband, not demanding anything of their potential rights. In Southern France, the husband could also give some security to his widow by will. The low proportion of widows remarrying should be considered in light of legal and customary regional differences.

Acknowledgments

A very preliminary version of this essay was presented as a contribution to the 28th Social Science History Association (SSHA) meeting in Baltimore, 14 November, 2003, session on "Dowry, dower, wills and other economic transfers: family property and female economic subsistence in the past", Family/demography network. Another earlier version of this study was also discussed during the 14th International Economic History Congress, at Helsinki University, August 21–25, 2006, session on "The Economics of Widowhood" and later during the XIIIth International Conference of AEIHM, *La Historia de las Mujeres: Perspectivas actuales*, Barcelona, 19–21 October, 2006.

References

ARRIZABALAGA, Marie-Pierre, 1997, "The stem family in the French Basque country: Sare in the nineteenth century", *Journal of Family History*, 22, 1, pp. 50–69.

–, 2003, "Retirement strategies among women and men in farming households: the Basque Country in 19th century", Paper presented at SSHA, Baltimore.

–, 2005, "Succession strategies in the Pyrenees in the 19th century. The Basque case", in Marie-Pierre ARRIZABALAGA and Antoinette FAUVE-CHAMOUX (eds), *The History of the Family: an International Quarterly*, 10, 3, pp. 271–292.

–, 2006, "Pyrenean marriage strategies in the nineteenth century: the French Basque case", in Marco H. D. VAN LEEUWEN, Ineke MAAS and Andrew MILES (eds), *International Review of Social History*, 50, Supplement 13, pp. 93–122.

AUGUSTIN, Jean-Marie, 2003, "La protection juridique de la veuve sous l'Ancien régime", in Colette H. WINN and Nicole PELLEGRIN (eds), *Veufs, veuves et veuvage dans la France d'Ancien Régime*, Paris, Honoré Champion, pp. 25–88.

AUGUSTINS, Georges, 1989, *Comment se perpétuer? Devenir des lignées et destins des patrimoines dans les paysanneries européennes*, Nanterre, Société d'ethnologie française/Université de Paris X.

BART, Jean, 1998, *Histoire du droit privé de la chute de l'Empire romain au XIXe siècle*, Paris, Montchrétien.

BEAUR, Gérard, 2004, "Land transmission and inheritance practice in France during the *Ancien Régime*: Differences of degree or kind?", in David GREEN and Alastair OWENS (eds), *Family Welfare. Gender, Property and Inheritance since the Seventeenth Century*, Westport, Praeger.

BEAUVALET-BOUTOUYRIE, Scarlett, 2001, *Etre veuve sous l'Ancien Régime*, Paris, Belin.

BONNAIN, Rolande, 1986, "Droit écrit, coutume pyrénéenne et pratique successorale dans les Baronnies, 1769–1836", in Isaac CHIVA and Joseph GOY (eds), *Les Baronnies des Pyrénées*, vol. 2, Paris, EHESS, pp. 157–177.

BOURDIEU, Pierre, 1962, "Célibat et condition paysanne", *Etudes rurales*, V–VI, pp. 32–135.

–, 1972, "Les stratégies matrimoniales dans le système de reproduction", *Annales E.S.C.*, 27, 4–5, pp. 1105–1127.

BOURDOT DE RICHEBOURG, Charles Antoine, 1724, *Nouveau coutumier général ou Corps des coutumes générales et particulières de France et des provinces connues sous le nom de Gaules... avec les notes de MM. Toussaint Chauvelin, Julien Brodeau et Jean-Marie Ricard,... jointes aux annotations de MM. Charles Du Molin, ... François Ragueau et Gabriel-Michel de La Rochemaillet, mis en ordre... et enrichi de nouvelles notes*, Paris, Michel Brunet, 4 vol.

BRUN, Josette, 2003, "Le veuvage en Nouvelle-France au 18e siècle. De la Coutume de Paris aux contrats de mariage de Louisbourg", in Colette H. WINN and Nicole PELLEGRIN (eds), *Veufs, veuves et veuvage dans la France d'Ancien Régime*, Paris, Honoré Champion, pp. 71–88.

CAVALLO, Sandra and WARNER, Lyndan (eds), 1999, *Widowhood in Medieval and Early Modern Europe,* Singapore, Longman.
"Code civil", 1841, in *Les Trente codes des Français*, Paris, Martial Ardant frères, pp. 11–245.
COLLOMP, Alain, 1983, *La maison du père, famille et village en Haute Provence aux XVIIe et XVIIIe siècles*, Paris, PUF.
DEROUET, Bernard, 2001, "Parenté et marché foncier à l'époque moderne: une réinterprétation", *Annales (HSS)*, 56, 2, pp. 337–368.
DIEFENDORF, Barbara, 1982, "Widowhood and remarriage in 16th century Paris", *Journal of Family History*, 7, 4, pp. 379–395.
FAUVE-CHAMOUX, Antoinette, 1984, "Les structures familiales au royaume des familles-souche: Esparros", *Annales E.S.C.,* 39, 3, pp. 513–528.
–, 1993, "Household forms and living standards in preindustrial France: from models to realities", *Journal of Family History,* 18, 2, pp. 135–156.
–, 1994, "Mariages-sauvages contre mariages-souches", in Martine SEGALEN et Georges RAVIS-GIORDANI (eds), *Les Cadets,* CNRS, Paris, pp. 181–194.
–, 1995, "The Stem family, demography and inheritance: the social frontiers of autoregulation", in Richard L. RUDOLF (ed.), *The European Peasant Family and Society,* Liverpool, Liverpool University Press, pp. 86–113.
–, 1996, "Aging in a never empty nest: the elasticity of the stem family", in Tamara HAREVEN (ed.), *Aging and Generational Relations over the Life Course*, Berlin, Walter de Gruyter, pp. 75–99.
–, 1998a, "Vedove di citta e vedove di campagna nella Francia preindustriale: aggregato domestico, trasmissione e strategie familiari di supravvivenza", *Quaderni storici,* 2, pp. 301–332.
–, 1998b, "La reproduction familiale en milieu paysan: le destin des exclus", in Gérard BOUCHARD, John A. DICKINSON and Joseph GOY (eds), *Les exclus de la terre en France et au Québec, XVIIe–XXe siècles*, Septentrion, Québec, pp. 73–94.
–, 1998c, "The stem-family and the preciput: the Picardy-Wallonia model", in Antoinette FAUVE-CHAMOUX and Emiko OCHIAI (eds), *House and the Stem Family in EurAsian Perspective / Maison et famille-souche: perspectives eurasiennes*, Kyoto, International Research Center for Japanese studies, pp. 138–167.
–, 2000, "Veuvages et remariage en France pré-industrielle", in Anne-Lise HEAD-KÖNIG and Liliane MOTTU-WEBER (eds), *Les femmes dans la société européenne,* Genève, Société d'histoire et d'archéologie, pp. 281–302.
–, 2001, "La transmission des biens par les femmes: les héritières dans une perspective comparative (XVIIIe–XXe siècles)", *Obradoiro de Historia Moderna*, 10, pp. 29–54.
–, 2002a, "Strategies of household continuity in a stem-family society: from heirship to headship", in Renzo DEROSAS and Michel ORIS (eds), *When Dad Died. Individuals and Families Coping with Distress in Past Societies,* Peter Lang, Bern, pp. 121–140.
–, 2002b, "Widows and their living arrangements in preindustrial France", *The History of the Family, an International Quarterly*, 7, 1, pp. 101–116.
–, 2003a, "Female transmission in comparative perspective", in Emiko Ochiai (ed.), *The Logic of Female Succession: Rethinking Patriarchy and Patrilinearity in Global and Historical Perspective*, Kyoto, International Research Center for Japanese Studies, pp. 11–29.

–, 2003b, "Le rôle des femmes dans la transmission des biens en France: 18e–19e siècles", in Christian DESSUREAULT, John A. DICKINSON and Joseph GOY (eds), *Famille et marché, 16e–20e siècles,* Montréal, Le Septentrion, pp. 245–260.

–, 2003c, "Démographie et stratégies de continuité familiale au sein de la famille-souche des Pyrénées", *Balance de la historiografia modernista. Mélanges offerts à Antonio Eiras-Roel,* Santiago de Compostela, pp. 147–164.

–, 2003d, "Patterns of leaving 'house' in a 19th c. stem-family society", in Frans VAN POPPEL, Michel ORIS and James LEE (eds), *Leaving Home in Western and Eastern societies, 16th–20th,* Peter Lang, Bern, pp. 200–220.

–, 2003e, "Besitzweitergabe, familiäre Machtverhältnisse und die Rolle der Frauen im Frankreich des 18. und 19. Jahrhunderts", in Reiner PRASS, Jürgen SCHLUMBOHM, Gérard BEAUR and Christophe DUHAMELLE (eds), *Ländliche Gesellschaften in Deutschland und Frankreich, 18–19. Jahrhundert,* Göttingen, Vandenhoeck and Ruprecht, pp. 167–185.

–, 2004a, "Transmission des biens, pouvoirs familiaux et rôle des femmes en France: 18e–19e siècles", in Gérard BEAUR, Christophe DUHAMELLE, Reiner PRASS and Jürgen SCHLUMBOHM (eds), *Les sociétés rurales en Allemagne et en France (XVIIIe–XIXe siècles),* Rennes, Histoire des sociétés rurales, pp. 141–156.

–, 2004b, "Stratégies intergénérationnelles à Esparros. Des logiques de reproduction à court ou à long terme (XVIIe–XXe siècles)", in Gérard BEAUR, Christian DESSUREAULT and Joseph GOY (eds), *Familles, Terre, Marché, logiques économiques et stratégies dans les milieux ruraux (XVIIe–XXe siècles),* Presses Universitaires de Rennes, Rennes, pp. 91–104.

–, 2005, "A comparative study of family transmission systems in the Central Pyrenees and northeastern Japan", in Antoinette FAUVE-CHAMOUX and Marie-Pierre ARRIZABALAGA (eds), "Family transmission in Eurasian perspective", *The History of the Family: an International Quarterly,* Special issue, 10, 3, pp. 231–292.

–, 2009, "The stem family and the Picardy-Wallonia model", in Antoinette FAUVE-CHAMOUX and Emiko OCHIAI (eds), *The Stem Family in Eurasian Perspective. Revisiting House Societies, 17th–20th centuries*, Bern, Peter Lang, pp. 203–252.

GOODY, Jack, 1985, *L'évolution de la famille et du mariage en Europe*, Paris, Armand Colin. [Translation of *The Development of Family and Marriage in Europe,* Cambridge, Cambridge University Press, 1983].

GOURON, André and TERRIN, Odile, 1975, *Bibliographie des coutumes de France, éditions antérieures à la Révolution*, Genève, Droz.

GOY, Joseph, 1981, "Normes et pratiques successorales dans la France paysanne des 18e et 19e siècles. Propositions pour une enquête", in Joseph GOY, and Jean-Pierre WALLOT (eds), *Société rurale dans la France de l'Ouest et au Québec, 17e–20e siècles*, Paris, EHESS, pp. 71–90.

–, 1988, "Code civil", in François FURET and Mona OZOUF (eds), *Dictionnaire critique de la Révolution française,* Paris, Flammarion, pp. 508–519.

HILAIRE, Jean, 1994, *La vie du droit*, Paris, PUF.

HUFTON, Olwen, 1984, "Women without men. Widows and spinsters in Britain and France in the eighteenth century", *Journal of Family History,* 9, 4, pp. 355–376.

–, 1995, "Women without men. Widows and spinsters in Britain and France in the eighteenth century", in Jan BREMMER Jan and Lourens VAN DEN BOSCH (eds), *Between Poverty and the Pyre. Moments in the History of Widowhood*, London, Routledge

HUGHES, Dian Owen, 1978, "From brideprice to dowry in Mediterranean Europe", *Journal of Family History*, 3, 3, pp. 262–296.

ISAMBERT, François André *et al.*, 1822–1833, *Recueil général des anciennes lois françaises, depuis l'an 420 jusqu'à la Révolution de 1789*, Paris, Belin-Leprieur, vol. XIV.

LACANETTE-POMMEL, Christine, 2003, *La famille dans les Pyrénées de la coutume au code Napoléon*, Estadens, Pyrégraph.

LAFON, Jean, 1972, *Régimes matrimoniaux et mutations sociales. Les époux bordelais 1450–1550*, Paris, Sevpen.

LAFOURCADE, Maïté, 1989, *Mariages en Labourd sous l'Ancien Régime. Les contrats de mariage du Pays de Labourd sous le règne de Louis XVI. Etude juridique et sociologique*, Bilbao, Université du Pays basque.

–, 1992, "Droit successoral et droit matrimonial en Pays Basque sous l'Ancien Régime", in Roland GANGHOFER (ed.), *Le droit de la famille en Europe, son évolution de l'Antiquité à nos jours*, Strasbourg, Maison des Sciences de l'Homme, pp. 517–529.

LE JAN-HENNEBICQUE, Régine, 1993, "Aux origines du douaire médiéval (6e–10e siècles)", in Michel PARISSE (ed.), *Veuves et veuvage dans le haut moyen âge*, Paris, Picard, pp. 107–121.

LE PLAY, Frédéric, 1875, *L'organisation de la famille selon le vrai modèle signalé par l'histoire de toutes les races et de tous les temps*, Tours, Mame.

LE ROY LADURIE, Emmanuel, 1976, "Family structures and inheritance customs in sixteenth century France", in Jack GOODY, Joan THIRSK and Edward Palmer THOMSON (eds), *Family and Inheritance. Rural society in Western Europe 1200–1800*, Cambridge, CUP, pp. 37–70 [English translation of "Système de la coutume. Structures familiales et coutume d'héritage en France au XVIe siècle", *Annales E.S.C.*, 1972, 27, 4–5, pp. 825–846].

LEVI-STRAUSS, Claude, 1983, "Histoire et ethnologie", *Annales E.S.C.*, 38, 6, pp. 1217–1231.

MURDOCK, George Peter, 1967, *The ethnographic Atlas*, Pittsburg, University of Pittsburgh.

MUSSET, Jacqueline, 1997, *Le régime des biens entre époux en droit normand du 16e siècle à la Révolution française*, Caen, Presses de l'Université de Caen.

OCHIAI, Emiko (ed.), 2003, *The Logic of Female Succession: Rethinking Patriarchy and Patrilinearity in Global and Historical Perspective*, Kyoto, International Research Center for Japanese Studies.

OLIVIER-MARTIN, François, 1922–1926, *Histoire de la Coutume de la prévôté et de la vicomté de Paris*, Paris, Ernest Leroux.

OURLIAC, Paul and GAZZANIGA, Jean-Louis, 1985, *Histoire du droit privé français: de l'an mil au Code Civil,* Paris, Albin Michel.

OURLIAC, Paul and GILLES, Monique, 1976, *Les coutumes de l'Agenais.* Tome 1. *Les coutumes du groupe de Marmande*, Paris, Picard.

–, 1981, *Les coutumes de l'Agenais*. Tome 2. *Bouglon, Montpezat, Montréal, Outre-Garonne et Bruilhois*, Paris, Picard.

OURLIAC, Paul and MALAFOSSE, Jehan de, 1968, "Le droit familial", *Histoire du droit privé*, vol. III, Paris, PUF.
PARISSE, Michel (ed.), 1993, *Veuves et veuvage dans le haut moyen âge,* Paris, Picard.
PELLATON, Frantz, 1993, "La veuve et ses droits de la Basse-Antiquité au haut Moyen Age", in Michel PARISSE (ed.), *Veuves et veuvage dans le haut moyen âge,* Paris, Picard, pp. 51–97.
POUMAREDE, Jacques, 1991, "Le droit des veuves sous l'Ancien Régime (17e–18e siècles) ou comment gagner son douaire", in Danielle HAASE-DUBOSC and Eliane VIENNOT (eds), *Femmes et pouvoirs sous l'Ancien Régime*, Paris, Rivages, pp. 64–76.
TESTART, Alain, 1996, "Pourquoi ici la dot et là son contraire? Exercice de sociologie comparative des institutions", *Droit et Cultures*, 32, 2, pp. 7–35 (première partie).
–, 2001, "Nouvelles hypothèses sur la dot", *Droit et Cultures*, 42, pp. 183–210.
TESTART, Alain, GOVOROFF, Nicolas and LECRIVAIN, Valérie, 2002, "Les prestations matrimoniales", *L'homme*, 161, pp. 165–196.
THIBORD, Fernand, 1996, *Les familles-souches de la vallée de la Colpach, 1766–1890*, Luxembourg, Imprimerie centrale.
YVER, Jean, 1952, "Les caractères originaux de la coutume de Normandie", *Mémoires de l'Académie des Sciences, Arts et Belles-Lettres de Caen*, t. XII, pp. 307–356.
–, 1953, "Les deux groupes de coutumes du Nord: le groupe picard-wallon", *Revue du Nord*, pp. 197–220.
–, 1954, "Les deux groupes de coutumes du Nord: le groupe flamingant", *Revue du Nord*, pp. 5–36.
–, 1966, *Egalité entre héritiers et exclusion des enfants dotés. Essai de géographie coutumière*, Paris, Sirey.
ZINK, Anne, 1993, *L'héritier de la maison: géographie coutumière du Sud-Ouest de la France sous l'Ancien Régime*, Paris, EHESS.

Annex 1: On French *Ancien Régime* Legislations

Customs – *Les Coutumes* – are a set of traditional practices becoming judiciary law with the time for a given territory endowed with a court of justice or "Parliament". Valid for each territory or province situated mostly in Northern France, these customs were all published in French during the 16th century (Gouron and Terrin 1975; Ourliac and Gazzaniga 1985, 108).

Together with these customs, Written Law (also called "Roman Law" – *Droit romain* –), which was ruling the Southern part of France, constituted secular laws *(droit laïc)*, against Canon law: this last law regulated of course the ecclesiastical world, notwithstanding its implications concerning the practices which where required from all believers (mostly the whole population). Ecclesiastical courts had to enforce this type of law, ahead of the secular courts to which sometimes they asked to enforce their sentences – a process which was not without clashes. Let us add that in the 13th c. Universities (Paris, Bologna, Oxford) these two types of law were taught in two different Faculties: Theology and Law.

The King of France, since the Middle Ages, also had the possibility to act judicially and above all to edict some regulations which in principle were valid for the whole kingdom, but these royal "edits" were specifying some particular points more than constituting a general law.

Annex 2: The "House System" in Early-modern France, Regulating Marriage and Inheritance

"Integral" transmission of real estate was a long tradition for the "Occitan"[23] peasants in South-western France, and above all in the Pyrenean "Baronnies". The ways these customs remained in force are now well known, as this theme was of concern together for jurists, ethnologists and historians as well.[24] The "house" (*maysou, domus, ostal* or *etche* in the Basque country) was to be transmitted, in continuity, to a privileged heir/heiress, who, once married, stayed in the natal house in common everyday life with his/her parents. This "identical" reproduction system imposed permanent intergenerational cohabitation; it also supposed constraining local wedding practices: a privileged child – be it the first born

23 "Occitan" southern population spoke "oc" language, while northern population spoke "oil" language. P. Ourliac stressed the many connections between linguistic and customary characteristics (Ourliac and Gazzaniga 1985).

24 Cf. notes above and reference list. Claude Lévi-Strauss (1983), as an ethnologist, pointed out the major role of family strategies and their importance to preserve the "House", Pierre Bourdieu (1962, 1972) as a sociologist gave new views about family life from examples in Béarn – all achievements of great interest for historians who, studying matrimonial practices (or celibacy) in association with ethnologists, tried then to understand how real or symbolic family assets happened to be inter-generationally shared out since the modern ages.

or not, be it a male or female heir – married and kept living in the house, another child married another neighbouring heir. Let us note that this non-egalitarian patrimony transmission was a usual practice in all European aristocratic societies, be it an effect of the *droit d'aînesse* as in France, or of a "majorat" as in Spain. We ought to acknowledge the pioneer work of Frédéric Le Play who was the first one to describe this family system, calling it "stem-family".[25]

"House", in Bearn, as the Basque country and in all the Pyrenean mountains, meant:

a) the whole of the family-owned real estate, and means of production
b) the rights going with this entity,
c) the family home and the family group living in it. Indissociability of house, patrimony, family lineage and name of the house was the rule.

These "family assets", also called "avitins" (from the latin "avus", grandfather), defined as those which at least three persons of the same lineage owned in successive generations (according to the *For de Bearn*, dated 1551)[26] were inalienable (Lacanette-Pommel 2003, 12).

According to the Bearnese Custom, these *avitins* assets fell to the eldest son, his brothers and sisters being deprived of any right of succession. Besides, the share of inheritance they might receive in compensation was not a matter of right. It was customary and its value was left to the father's decision, as was the girl's dowry. But we must recall that a non-heir son marrying an heiress also had to be endowed: an heiress does not bring any dowry at marriage, her husband – as son-in-law – brings one as he enters his bride's house, whose name he takes.

25 Le Play 1875.
26 A *For* is a southern Custom.

Female Headship, Household Position, and Gendered Well-Being in Peasant Societies

Evidence from the Territories of the Historical Kingdom of Poland (18th century)

Mikołaj SZOŁTYSEK

Measuring the quality of life[1] in preindustrial peasant societies – for either women or men – is a challenging task. Firstly, there may only be a dearth of precise information regarding gender differences in incomes and other aspects of standards of living, and well-being in general. Secondly, the usual speechlessness of historical peasants presents another obstacle: in most instances all we know about rural society comes from narrative or statistical descriptions drawn up by representatives of different social classes who looked at peasants' lives through the lens of their own presumptions, prejudices and all other aspects of their *habitus.*[2]

When it comes to the investigation of the quality of life in Eastern European peasant societies, however, another discouragement appears. From I. Wallerstein (Wallerstein 1974), F. Braudel (Braudel 1985), and R. Brenner (Brenner 1989), to East European historians such as I. Berend

1 There does not appear to be a single, generally accepted definition of quality of life (QOL) in the extensive literature generated on this subject over the past thirty years. Although there may be various ways of defining QOL ("well-being", and the "standard of living" are most often treated as its equivalents), the concept usually refers either to the degree of need satisfaction within the areas of physical, psychological, social, activity, material and structural needs, or to goal-achievement, or to social utility (Hørnquist 1989; Felce and Perry 1995; Cummins 2005). For the purpose of the present study it is enough for the quality of life to be meant as a descriptive term referring to people's emotional, social and physical well-being, and their ability to function in the ordinary tasks of living.

2 Obviously, many universal standards of measurement of well-being are contestable from the perspective of "cultural relativism" which is akin to anthropological thinking; see the discussion of that issue in Wilk 2005.

(Berend and Ránki 1982), J. Topolski (Topolski 1974a; 1974b) and W. Kula (Kula 1976), the early modern Eastern European social and economic environment has often been pictured as quite unfavourable for the existence of peasant families (Wyczański 1978; Cerman 2008). As early as the sixteenth century, Eastern Europe became the first periphery of the capitalist world-system, with its rural classes being increasingly subjected to exploitation by local landowners, who – in turn – became suppliers of grains and other primary products for western core territories. Eastern Europe retained its position as a region of traditional socioeconomic structures well into the early nineteenth century, while at the same time Eastern European societies – and this applies to both the landowning elite and the peasant strata – are supposed to have lacked capitalist principles of calculation by comparison to the more individualistic and rational cultures of Northwestern Europe.

In most historians' accounts of the European past, the peasant economy in Europe under the rules of the "second serfdom" was regarded as a sort of a completely separate world.[3] Not infrequently, the picture of the socioeconomic setting in Central and Eastern Europe is pervaded by references to a distinct and changeless peasant economic mentality that reified self-subsistence, retreated from the market, rejected cost calculations, and made decisions that were "irrational" or "uneconomic" from the point of view of profitability. In this sense, communalism, egalitarianism and traditionalism would be the prime characteristics of peasant societies east of the Elbe River (Ogilvie 2001, 430–434). In addition, semi-ethnographic accounts of eighteenth-century travelers, as well as reports of foreign bureaucrats and officials regarding standards of living in the historical Polish territories, can easily discourage one from taking an optimistic view of the chances for creating, or even sustaining, individual and social well-being in this area. Foreign travelers entering the historical Polish lands wrote not only about "arid sands and vast forests," but also of "a poor and enslaved population, dirty villages, and cottages little different from the savage hunts" (Wolff 1994, 19). Prussian bureaucrats and officials reiterated this

3 The term "second serfdom" is often used in the English-language literature as shorthand to refer to the massive growth in landlord powers over the rural population during the early modern period, essentially in Central and Eastern Europe. This institutional context refers to the institution of *Gutsherrschaft* (manorial lordship) or *system folwarczno-pańszczyźniany* (system of manorialism with compulsory labour) – as it has been called in the Polish historiography. See more in Cerman 1999; Hagen 1998; Melton 1998; Ogilvie 2001; Topolski 1974b.

"dark" picture by referring to the peasantry's inclination toward drunkenness and laziness, describing the miserable conditions of their premises, and pointing out peasants' supposedly inherent propensity towards dirtiness and exposure to the most dangerous and humiliating diseases (Łukasiewicz 1995, 56–74, 75–76).

Most of all, however, when it comes to peasants' social and economic activities and their family behaviour under the second serfdom, most of the research studies (including the Polish historiography) seem to offer ready-made answers. The majority of studies dealing with the above-mentioned issues have taken for granted that East and Central European peasant communities corresponded very well with the prime characteristics of serf dependence typical of that part of Europe during the early and late modern period – namely, juridical subjection; migration regulations; legal attachment to a particular social status; subjection to communal payments and duties (including the most harsh compulsory labour); limited right to private property; limited choice of occupation; and unprotected personal dignity (Mironov 1996, 323; Plakans 1975; Kula 1976; Woźniak 1987; Orzechowski 1959). In other words, peasants' choices and actions have usually been presented as severely constrained by landlords, who attempted to interfere in almost every aspect of their subjects' everyday lives: from marriage contracting, through residential arrangements, to the regulation of labour markets and dues. Consequently, one may say, in the world of Eastern European peasants, a substantive individual freedom to lead the life one had a reason to value was severely restricted (Sen 1999, 14).[4]

Such unfavourable conditions for the development of familial or individual well-being applied in particular to the female rural population. Although it has been suggested that the distinctive feature of the Polish inheritance pattern from the Middle Ages onwards was equality between brothers and sisters (Guzowski 2007), at the same time there were countervailing forces at work disempowering rural women during certain stages of their life-cycles. Firstly, although eligible to inherit immovable

4 For a more nuanced view on this topic see: Wyczański 1978; Woźniak 1987. Sosnowska (2004, pp. 276-282) gives a good summary of this still unresolved debate among Polish economic historians. More recent research offers somewhat different portrayal of the Eastern European setting in this regard, undermining a traditional image of rigid landlord structures and weak peasant property rights in this area (see Cerman 2008). Similarly, but from a different angle: Seppel 2004; Szołtysek & Rzemieniecki 2005.

property both from a father and from a deceased spouse, women's capabilities with regard to management and usufruct of real property could be quite constrained under the rules of the "second serfdom". This is illustrated by some of the landowners' regulations cited in W. Kula's well-known *Annales* article. Thus, for instance, one regulation stated that:

> Widows of deceased plowmen must remain in possession of all the deceased's property under surveillance of the members of the village council and also of two plowmen [...] who are guardians... It is ordered that the guardians ensure that the widow remarries within a year, and she must be warned that if during that period she does not remarry, then at the end of the year, counting from the day of her husband's death, everything will be sold at auction (Kula 1976, 195).

Another landlord regulation ordered that:

> Aged widows who can no longer marry as a consequence of their age must, at the very beginning of their widowhood, be removed from their farms, with the exception of those who have an adult son or daughter who is able to marry shortly after the father's death. In such a case, it is advised that the marriage be hastened; when it has been contracted, the entire family may remain on the farm (Kula 1976, 196).

So, could Eastern European peasants (and, more specifically, women in those peasant societies) have created a space for individual well-being under such material and institutional conditions? My essay attempts to offer a partial answer to this question. Here, the main characteristics of female-headed households and women's household position on the historical Polish territories will be suggested as offering the preliminary clue to understanding female options in serf society more generally.

What, then, are the implications of the analysis of historical household data for understanding human well-being? For most preindustrial populations it was the family and the household that most profoundly determined the living standards of family groups and individuals. Household systems, it is often assumed, not only determined who people would live with, who they would live for, and which networks of cooperation they would make use of; the household system, through these pathways, also influenced many fundamental aspects of social organization and behaviour, which in turn influenced demographic outcomes, health, and welfare (Das Gupta 1999; Green and Owens 2004). Households not only provided the basic context for production and consumption, but also engaged in complex tasks relating to social reproduction, as well as influencing power relationships (Wilk and Netting 1984; also Verdon 1998, 34–37). In addition, households often influenced group strategies of resource management, migration, and ways of exploiting commercial opportunities (Arrizabalaga 2007). In other words: family or household organization extensively affected, shaped, and often determined the well-being of individuals, families, and communities. Consequently, understanding different household systems in terms of the ways in which they affected family and individual well-being remains an important research agenda.

When it comes to the measurement of women's opportunities, female headship (the incidence of households headed by women) is widely regarded as a key element of social structure. It can be interpreted as a positive indicator of the extent to which women were able and willing to manage an independent household. Thus, female headship can tell us a lot about options available to women generally (Wall 1981; Ogilvie and Edwards 2000, 966). This holds true especially for the period before the advent of modern statistical records, during which women's economic position was only rarely documented in a manner amenable to quantification.[5] In spite of that, this chapter will not focus exclusively on this single important measure of female well-being in past societies (even if that measure is inarguably a highly important one), and an attempt will also be made to broaden the perspective by taking into account wider issues of the female household position and its life-cycle changes.

However, the actual quality of life is even more multidimensional (e.g. Felce and Perry 1995; Sen 1999; Robeyns 2003), and thus, there will obviously be several other components of well-being lost sight of in this analysis. Approaching a more complete picture of the female life quality would require – at least from the historical-demographic perspective – elaborating on several additional issues, to name a few: women's exposure to excess mortality (McNay *et al* 2004; Alter *et al.* 2004), the availability of kin outside the household (Kertzer *et al.* 1992), characteristics of the marriage market, demographic constraints on the individual life-cycle (Laslett 1988), power relations within the family (Sabean 1990; Beck 2001; Seccombe 1990), and many others.[6] There are, however, inherent difficulties in pursuing such a holistic approach to historical communities

5 There is an extensive historical-demographic literature focused on different socio-structural aspects of women's position and opportunities in pre-industrial societies (Fauve-Chamoux 1983; 2002; Moring 2002; Wall 1981; 2002; Ochiai 2002).

6 Compare the recent review of existing "lists of functionings and capabilities" in Robeyns 2003.

– especially when investigation is being carried out in large numbers at an aggregated level, and that concerns particularly the research presented in this essay. Therefore, to infer the quality of life dimensions from demographic data on household status and life-course contexts often remains the only practical, even if not an ideal, solution.

The structure of this essay is as follows. First, a general overview of the research project on which it is based and the database that will be utilized is provided. In a second step, I focus on female headship rates and on selected characteristics of female-headed households. I then attempt to investigate several aspects of the female life course. Regarding all these issues, in the course of the demographic description I also attempt to infer their implications for well-being. Before the concluding remarks, the results of the preceded statistical-structural analysis are confronted with the insights into a micro-study of one of the communities from the larger quantitative sample.

Data and Sample

The data used in this essay come from a much larger project whose aim is to re-assess the geography of family forms in historic Europe. The original purpose of the project was to collect as much individual household-level data as possible, for parishes located on both sides of the transitional zone that was supposed to run through the historic Polish territories demarcating different family and household formation systems (Hajnal 1982; Mitterauer 1999; Kaser 2002; Laslett 1983). With the use of such historical sources, the aim was to investigate whether there was a borderline distinguishing Central European family patterns and marriage behaviours from those widely considered as "unique" to North-western Europe, and if so, to identify where exactly this frontier was located, what its distinguishing features were, and which factors were responsible for its existence (Szołtysek 2008).

The database developed for this purpose is one of the most extensive collections of household lists for a group of preindustrial European communities (*CEURFAMFORM Database*). At present, it contains entries for almost 11,061 households from 84 parishes, which cover a total population of 62,732 people.[7] The majority of the parish household data comes either from the so-called *Libri Status Animarum* (the lists of parishioners created by priests for the purpose of church registration), or from their equivalent in the form of the Polish civil-military registration of inhabitants (1790–1792),[8] and dates from the period 1766–1799. All of these censuses precede the abolition of serfdom in the territories in question. The character of the censuses – the fact that they mostly do not contain any information related to economic status of the families, nor to the social living conditions of individuals they encompassed – posed, however, certain limits on the extent to which particular aspects of gendered well-being could have been directly analyzed.

The parishes selected for the present analysis formed a long belt extending from the western fringes of the historical Kingdom of Poland (regions 3 and 4, encompassing 35 parishes) towards the southern borders of the province of Great Poland (regions 1 and 2, encompassing 20 parishes) (Figure 1). From that area the data coverage extends southwest into the ethnically and religiously mixed territories of Prussian Silesia (region 8, encompassing 14 parishes), and well into the most north-western parts of the Lesser Poland province of the historical Polish Commonwealth (region 7, encompassing 13 parishes). Two additional parishes give a northern and north-eastern extension to the marked territories. The regional division was proposed mainly on the basis of administrative or geographical factors.

7 These numbers represent respectively 2.5 percent of total households and almost 3 percent of the population (noble families and clergy excluded) in the western provinces of Poland in 1789 (estimates based on the returns of the first Polish census from 1789; source: Gieysztorowa 1976, 114).

8 For less than a tenth of all households in the sample, the data were derived from different types of local tax records. All of these household lists registered groups of people as residential units (Hammel and Laslett 1974, 86–90), in clearly marked, separate blocks. The residential unit comprised not only the core family of the head, but also his immediate and more distant relatives, as well as coresident servants and "inmates" or "lodgers".

Figure 1 Polish-Lithuanian Commonwealth before 1772 and its administrative divisions into voivodships.

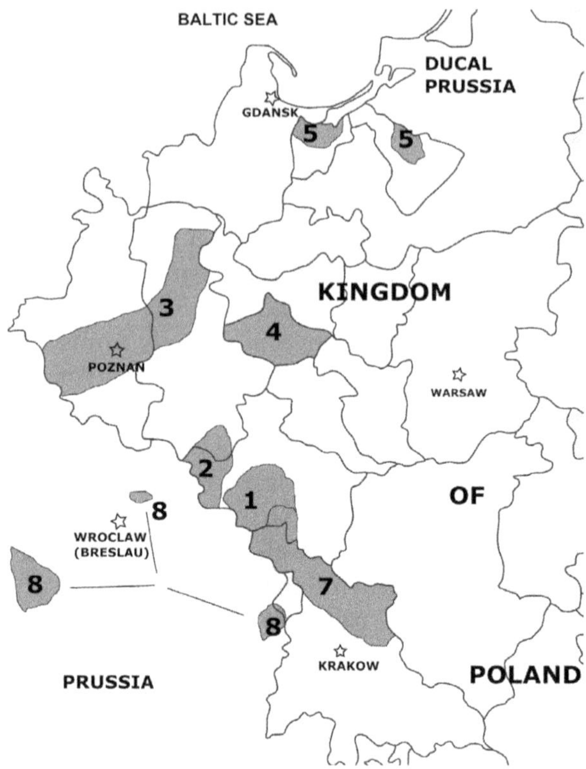

Notes: Map design: M. Szołtysek and J. Newman.
Reference is made to historic boundaries of the western part of the Polish-Lithuanian Commonwealth before 1772 and its administrative divisions into voivodships.

Each region represents some kind of unit within the administrative structure of the Polish Republic or the Prussian Kingdom, be it a voivodship, a "land", or a district. Most of the parishes included in the database shared a common framework, as they were all located in the part of Europe where marriage and household formation were, at least from the normative point of view, under strict manorial control owing to the system of the second serfdom. However, some local and regional variations persisted.[9]

9 The inhabitants of two parishes in the north (region 5), and also a minority of peasant householders from regions 3 and 4, were free peasants paying money rents for their

Female Headship in the Family System of the Historical Polish Territories

There is no definite agreement as to what should be considered as the main constitutive components of a family system (Wall 1991, 623). In most accounts, however, a small set of inter-related variables such as household size, household composition, and household structure, are commonly treated as the primary, even if not the sole, indicators of the prevailing pattern of family and household organization in a given area (Laslett 1983; Czap 1983, 145). The family system on the territories I am concerned with was primarily based on houseful *(dym)* that were mostly moderate in size (mean houseful size of 5.8 persons per unit)[10] and simple in structure. The distribution of household structures according to the canonical classification scheme (Hammel and Laslett 1974) demonstrates an overwhelming domination of nuclear households (77.7 percent of all households), with the proportion of complex family units not exceeding 9 percent of all units registered. Living in domestic groups containing more than 6 persons and at least two conjugal units was experienced by, respectively, one quarter and slightly above one tenth of the total population. Coresidence with non-nuclear-family kin in the household was a relatively rare phenomenon in the parishes investigated. On the other hand, high proportions of servants were discernible, with a clear life-cycle pattern in their age distribution. Although there was no absolute relationship between entry into marriage and entry into household headship among males in the localities studied, for most male progeny formation of family and attaining headship were not clearly separate events in the life-cycle (Szołtysek 2008). In terms both of household structure and of the incidence of servants, the Polish data discussed here appeared much more

long-term land tenures. A mixture of labour obligations *(corvées)* and money rents also prevailed in region 7. The eastern part of region 8 was essentially characterized by the system of manorialism with compulsory labour dues, while in the western part of it money rents prevailed again, and peasants combined small agriculture with proto-industrial activities. The latter played an important role also among the population of region 5 (Szołtysek 2008).

10 Mean size of residential group drops to 5.2 persons if coresiding non-related inmates are excluded from the calculations. The Polish census returns of 1789 reported a mean houseful size of 5.3 persons (Gieysztorowa 1976, 114).

akin to the northwest European family pattern and household formation rules, than had previously been expected (Hajnal 1982).[11]

Table 1. Regional distribution of female-headed households, historical Kingdom of Poland (18th century)

Region	No. of parishes	Households (N)	Female-headed households (N)	Female-headed households (%)
Region 1	11	1,568	48	3.1
Region 2	9	1,317	48	3.6
Region 3	9	846	39	4.6
Region 4	26	2,063	105	5.1
Region 5	2	545	59	10.8
Region 7	13	2,511	64	2.5
Region 8	14	2,211	100	4.5
All regions	84	11,061	463	4.2

Source: Szołtysek and Pasieka, *CEURFAMFORM Database*.
Note: In this and all following tabulations, female heads are represented by those who were widowed, or deserted by their husbands.

More importantly, the family system discussed here diverges significantly from household systems which are more prone to strengthen the agnatic core of the family and to develop patriarchal structures (Kaser 2002). These features of the prevailing family system created the general structural framework which conditioned women's opportunities and capabilities in the populations analyzed. The basic questions addressed in this essay can be initially approached by investigating the proportions of female-headed households, keeping in mind that the incidence of domestic units headed by women was a positive indicator of their economic and social position (Ogilvie and Edwards 2000, 964) (Table 1).

If we break down the whole sample into regions, it is clear that the most striking feature of the findings for these seven regions is that female headship was, on average, quite rare. What is more, if we exclude region 5 as departing from the rest of the sample in its socioeconomic structure, we are likely to end up with the conclusion that female headship did not vary significantly across the rest of the rural population. Although some indi-

11 Another crucial variable – proportions ever married – is discussed in the following paragraphs.

vidual parishes might have had female headship rates close to ten per cent or even higher,[12] the regional averages were always much lower, and at the same time, one out of ten parishes in the dataset contained no female heads at all.

These figures prompt us to ask two interrelated questions. First, do these low rates reflect a small number of long-lasting female-headed households, or alternatively a larger number of shorter duration? If a modelled functioning system of peasant serfdom communities is taken for granted (Kula 1976), the first alternative would have to be rejected. Actually, however, this reasoning cannot be demonstrated statistically as the data we have used so far is invariably cross-sectional. A scanty set of longitudinal evidence, restricted to the Prussian province of Silesia (region 8), is rather ambiguous. For the small Lower Silesian parish of Döberle (County of Oels), five female-headed households were detected in the 1747 listing (their existence could possibly have preceded that date) and then followed through the successive enumerations of 1749 and 1755.[13] Four of these women retained the headship at least until 1749 (one woman died before or during that year). In 1755, however, none of these women were heading their households anymore (two of them had to pass down the headship either to coresident relatives or to non-related persons; the other two presumably died, leaving their households to sons).

12 Standard deviation: 3.7 percent. The highest incidence of households headed by women was 24 percent (in the parish of Bronisław, region 4). Median value for the whole dataset equals 3.7 percent.

13 State Archive in Wrocław: Składnica Ewangelickich Ksiąg Metrykalnych we Wrocławiu, "Seelen Register Döberle Carlsburg, Jenckwitz und Gutwohn," sygn. 27, 29, 37 (microfilmed). Author's calculations.

Table 2. Proportions of female-headed households – the Polish rural sample in comparison with other data concerning urban Poland and rural Bohemia (18th century)

Region	Number of parishes	Total households (N)	Female-headed households (N)	Female-headed households (%)
Polish rural sample	84	11,061	463	4.2
Frýdlant estate (Bohemia), 1722	NA	NA	37	2.2
Liberec estate (Bohemia), 1722	NA	NA	27	4.4
Praszka town, 1791 (southern Poland)	1	161	NA	4.3
Radziejów town, 1792 (north-central Poland)	1	124	NA	13.7
Wieluń town, 1791 (western Poland)	1	261	NA	19.0
Kraków town, 1791 (southern Poland)	NA	1,159	NA	22.7
Warszawa town, 1791 (central Poland)	1	4,122	NA	24.8

Sources: for "Polish rural sample", Szołtysek and Pasieka, *CEURFAMFORM Database*; for two Bohemian estates, Ogilvie and Edwards 2000, 969; for Polish towns 1791–1792, Kuklo 1998, 97.
Notes: "NA" means data non available.

However, serial household listings for another Silesian locality (Bujakow parish, 1766–1803), embedded presumably in an institutional context not very different from the one discussed above, brought evidence of the system's flexibilities and, in particular, of a considerable degree of autonomy of peasant women regarding heading a household (Szołtysek 2007). The implications of this study for understanding female well-being in serf societies will be discussed further in subsequent sections.

More importantly, however, we are tempted to ask the second question – namely, what the figures presented in Table 1 actually tell us about the scale of female independence and autonomy. In isolation, such low percentages may seem 'normal' considering the functioning of rural communities under the rules of serfdom. In such a context, a farm not headed by a married couple was often considered unviable. It was mostly married couples and not solitary persons who were entitled to manage a farmstead and to perform duties for the landowners (Kula 1976, 195; Woźniak 1987,

108). Some comparisons may be helpful for a better understanding of the figures presented so far (Table 2).

When compared with the data for two eighteenth-century Bohemian serf estates, the Polish figures reveal very similar phenomena. It seems justified to assume that such low figures of female headship in Polish areas were rather typical of rural conditions in Eastern Central Europe, even if some departures from this overall pattern were discernible on some German, Austrian and Hungarian territories (see Ogilvie and Edwards 2000, 971). Even more illuminating is the comparison with the estimations made for some late-eighteenth-century Polish towns (Kuklo 1998). A huge discrepancy shows up between the rural conditions we analyze and between what is supposed to be an urban experience on the same territories and roughly under the same historical circumstances. If we exclude the rather exceptional case of the small town of Praszka, rural female headship rates were 3 to 6 times smaller in rural areas than in towns. We may summarize this part of the investigation by saying that in the preindustrial rural communities of historical Poland, female-headed households constituted only a marginal phenomenon in socioeconomic and family life. If we agree that a much higher incidence of households headed by women in the towns in Polish territories was caused by a weakened feudal regulation of these urban communities (e.g implying higher territorial and social mobility, as well as a more extended labour market than in the countryside),[14] then the strong manorial institutions of the second serfdom must be described as adversely affecting women's economic positions in rural areas, and consequently, reducing female well-being.[15]

14 Kuklo 1998, 65–69. However, during the sixteenth and seventeenth centuries, women's juridical status remained handicapped in Polish towns as well, constraining female chances of economic success in financial and trade sectors (Bogucka 1990, 185).

15 This observation seems to be supported by slightly higher female headship rates in regions with higher incidence either of personally free peasants or a property usufruct based on money rents (regions 3, 4, and part of region 8).

Table 3. Number of males per 100 females of specified relationship to household head, historical Kingdom of Poland (18th century)

Region	No. of parishes	Lone household heads	Off-spring	Relatives	Servants	Other unrelated	Sex ratio
Region 1	9	113	111	67	140	65	106
Region 2	9	83	104	56	163	59	96
Region 3	7	51	105	80	164	50	98
Region 4	22	73	110	68	157	79	107
Region 5	2	54	104	65	119	56	100
Region 7	11	80	104	71	151	60	98
Region 8	5	79	108	59	134	61	99
Total	65	76	107	67	151	65	101

Sources: Szołtysek and Pasieka, *CEURFAMFORM Database*. Calculations based on data for 65 parishes (19 excluded as containing less reliable data).
Sex ratio: Number of males for 100 females in total.

In order to approach women's position within households more directly, sex ratios of particular categories of people within domestic groups such as lone household heads, offspring, relatives, servants and also coresiding inmates, have been tabulated (Table 3).

As might be expected, since women were generally younger than their spouses, and would generally outlive them, most of the lone household heads were women.[16] Although this tendency was a prevalent one, the data from region 1 provides exceptions to that rule, indicating a possible further deterioration of female autonomy there. When it comes to offspring, however, some regional data reveals sex ratios visibly above a hundred. There can be two possible explanations to that pattern: either it resulted from sex differentials in mortality, or it indicated females' earlier exit from the parental home. As we will see later, the second explanation seems more plausible, which means that, at least in part of the population under study, females were less desirable as members of the family labour force in farming and therefore had to leave the parental home earlier than their male siblings. This will evidently have had implications for their well-being.

16 In the category of lone household heads, all non-married household heads have been included, that is never-married as well as ever-married but widowed, males and females together.

Also already evident is that a majority of the young rural labour force recruited in the form of life-cycle servants were male, and the surplus of male servants shows up strongly across the whole sample.[17] It also emerges very clearly from Table 3 that the two most feminized household positions were those of non-nuclear-family relatives and unrelated inmates coresiding in households. Whether that is also an indication of females' less advantageous socioeconomic opportunities and a deterioration of their quality of life remains an open question. Whereas Hartmann has argued for the prime importance of female life-cycle service seen in terms of the historical development of female autonomy in Western Europe (Hartmann 2004, 40, 192), other scholars have been much less optimistic regarding the general well-being implications of the institution of domestic service (Laslett 2000 [1965]; Schulte 1984). The very exploitative character of service was also the *leitmotif* of the predominantly Marxist Polish economic historiography well into the 1980s (Leszczyński 1956; Baranowski 1986).

More recent approaches have revealed, however, a more nuanced picture of service in the historical Polish territories by pointing out its general resemblance to the north-western European model (Kopczyński 1995; Kamler 2005), as well as its positive life-cycle implications for household formation, at least for males.[18] When it comes to inmates (*komornicy* in Polish; *Hausleute*, *Kammerleute* or *Inwohnern* in German), on the other hand, the specialised literature on the Eastern Central European inmate population stresses a probable non-homogeneous character of this group.

17 The sixteenth-century inventories of villages in Lesser Poland also bring plentiful evidence of servants with a strong life-cycle profile (see Kamler 2005, 42–45).

18 In the previous micro-study of one Upper Silesian community it has been suggested that for disinherited male offspring the time spent in service or lodging (as inmates) in households of non-kin could have possibly played a role on a way towards the formation of a family (Szołtysek 2007, 33–34).

Table 4 : **Summary characteristics of male-headed households, Polish rural sample**

Region	Mean household size (inmates excl.)	Mean household size (inmates incl.)	Conjugal family units per household (mean)	Mean no.of offspring per hous.	% hous.with coresident kin	Mean no.of kin per hous.	% hous.with servants	Mean no.of servants per hous.	% hous.with inmates	Mean no.of inmates per hous.
REG 1	4.9	5.2	1.1	2.11	17.9	0.23	38.2	0.60	13.1	0.28
REG 2	5.6	6.4	1.1	2.70	21.6	0.24	38.1	0.64	30.4	0.79
REG 3	6.0	7.0	1.2	2.32	26.5	0.38	53.8	1.28	34.9	0.87
REG 4	5.5	6.4	1.2	2.30	17.7	0.22	48.4	0.99	32.8	0.99
REG 5	4.9	4.9	1.0	2.14	10.9	0.14	29.2	0.65	2.7	0.05
REG 7	5.4	6.2	1.1	2.24	23.2	0.35	33	0.73	25.6	0.70
REG 8	4.8	5.1	1.2	2.24	28.1	0.48	28.7	0.49	20.9	0.51
Altogether	5.3	5.9	1.1	2.30	22	0.32	39.2	0.77	24.4	0.65

Source : **Szołtysek & Pasieka**, *CEURFAMFORM Database* . Calculations for columns: (1-2, 4) based on the sample of 70 parishes (14 excluded as unreliable); (3, 5-6) based on all parishes; (7-8) based on data for 75 parishes (9 excluded as unreliable); (9-10) based on data for 81 parishes (3 excluded as unreliable).

***Conjugal family unit (CFU)** is defined as consisting of one of the following groups of people: married couple, married couple with child(ren), widowed or solitary person with child(ren).

Table 5: Summary characteristics of female-headed households, Polish rural sample

Region	Mean household size (inmates excl.)	Mean household size (inmates incl.)	Conjugal family units per household (mean)	Mean no.of offspring per hous.	% hous.with coresident kin	Mean no.of kin per hous.	% hous.with servants	Mean no.of servants per hous.	% hous.with inmates	Mean no.of inmates per hous.
REG 1	3.8	4.2	1.0	2.24	18.8	0.25	22.9	0.33	18.80	0.42
REG 2	3.5	4.3	0.9	2.15	6.3	0.08	20.8	0.29	33.30	0.79
REG 3	2.9	4.1	0.9	1.59	20.5	0.18	15.4	0.21	35.90	1.08
REG 4	3.9	4.9	1.1	2.25	11.4	0.07	30.5	0.59	30.50	0.94
REG 5	2.6	2.6	0.8	0.98	3.4	0.03	13.6	0.59	1.70	0.02
REG 7	3.9	4.3	1.1	2.38	18.8	0.20	14.0	0.28	19.30	0.39
REG 8	3.8	4.2	1.1	2.42	20.0	0.29	25.0	0.33	22.00	0.52
Altogether	3.6	4.2	1.0	2.05	14.4	0.16	21.5	0.41	23.00	0.60

Source : **Szołtysek & Pasieka**, *CEURFAMFORM Database* . Calculations for columns as in table 4.

The inmates might constitute the most socially inferior rural strata, but also those most prone to rely on the "economy of makeshifts" and on various proto-industrial activities (Ogilvie and Cerman 1995; on Poland: Obraniak 1968; Orzechowski 1956, 156; Szołtysek 2003, 36–239).[19] That living as an inmate in a household headed by non-relatives might not have automatically implied poverty, inferiority and severe capability deprivations is also suggested by the age profile of the adult female population of inmates (age 15 and above), 80.1 percent of which was in productive age at the time of census takings (age between 15 and 54). Such a picture is, however, somewhat altered by the fact that 55 percent of the adult women were either lone mothers with children or solitary persons with no relatives in the households they lived in.[20]

However, to reveal the gender dimension of the issues discussed, a comparison of male- and female-headed households must be pursued.[21] Their main characteristics are summarized in Tables 4 and 5.

First, not surprisingly, it appears that female-headed households were significantly smaller than male-headed ones (columns 1 and 2). This difference was larger than a single person on average, indicating that the crucial difference was not only due to the loss of a spouse. On the other hand, the difference between male- and female-headed households (on the regional level) in the mean number of coresiding offspring (column 4) does not seem to be critical. This means that having the same childbearing burden as households headed by married couples, female-headed households could have been less successful in acquiring the labour force necessary to sustain their economic well-being. In the first instance, this seems to be corroborated by the almost twice as small incidence of servants among female-headed households when compared to male-headed ones (column 7). In addition to that (column 8), female heads had significantly

19 Apart from widows and widowers (and also some soldiers), this group comprised some village artisans and workers of the manor (both married and unmarried) who, having no access to landholdings nor possessing separate houses, rented parts of the peasant premises (usually a room) from the landowner in exchange for cash quitrent or some labour duties. No direct information on the social and economic living conditions of the inmate population investigated here, their household functions and work, was given in the censuses.

20 Both estimations based on data for 2,309 individuals from 62 parishes (22 parishes excluded as unreliable).

21 Inmate households are not included in the analysis, and are considered only as a part of main household units.

fewer servants on average (0.41 per one household compared to the male heads: 0.77). That seems to be an indication that female-headed households were less economically viable and therefore more exposed to threats to the well-being of their members.[22] Moreover, it appears that female heads could hardly compensate their labour needs by means of other household members. First, female-headed households had kin less frequently attached to them (14.4 percent compared to 22 percent), and they contained a significantly smaller number of coresiding relatives on average (0.2 per one household compared to 0.32).

Figure 2. Household and family dependency ratios* by age of household head: male- and female-headed households, Polish rural sample, historical Kingdom of Poland (18th century)

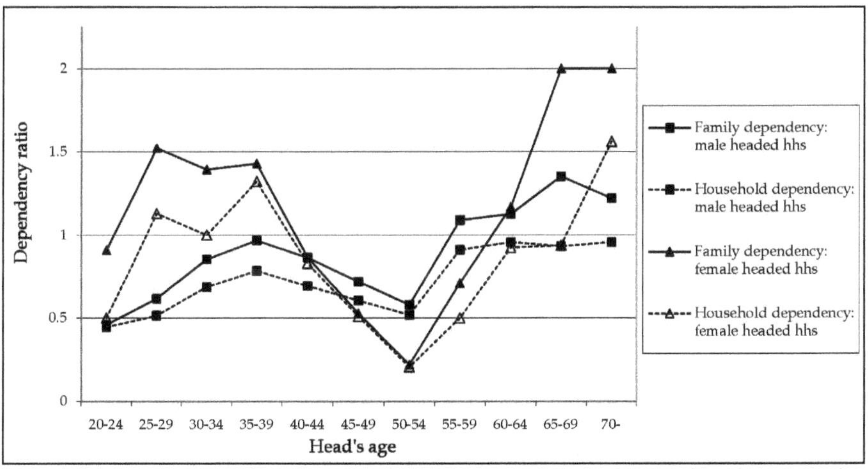

Sources: Szołtysek and Pasieka, *CEURFAMFORM Database*. Calculations based on data for 62 parishes (22 excluded as unreliable): 7,386 male-, and 351 female-headed households.

Notes: **Family dependency* is defined as the number of people in the family aged 0–13 and 55 and older ("consumers") to the number aged 14–54. *Household dependency* refers to the corresponding ratio for the household (that is, including servants, but not inmates).

22 However, since some of those female households could potentially get some income from other activities than farming, this does not automatically mean they were poorer than male ones.

Second, although there were almost no differences between male- and female-headed households in terms of the presence of inmates, we must presume that the latter category could hardly satisfy female heads' labour requirements. It is an established fact that in most cases, inmates, although inhabiting the same premises as the head's family, constituted separate production and consumption units (Orzechowski 1959).

A more insightful approach to these issues comes from the application of the concept of family and household dependency ratios (Dribe 2000, 71–79). Although, family and household dependency ratios were almost the same for male- and female-headed households at the aggregate level (respectively: 0.82 and 0.68 compared to 0.81 and 0.70), these measures had an important life-cycle character (Figure 2). While male-headed households were able to avoid the most unfavourable dependency situation for the larger part of their development, and were trapped in it only once their heads had passed the age of 55, female-headed households seem to have been more negatively affected by the proportions of "consumers" to "producers" over the family and the household life-cycles. In particular, there appear to have existed two highly inconvenient stages of family development for households headed by women.

One occurred before a female household head attained the age of 40 (which was the case for almost 30 per cent of all female-headed households), which presumably implied living with a large number of dependent children below working age. The second took place during the later stages of the family life-cycle with households headed by elderly women above 60 years old (15 percent of all households headed by women), and might have been the outcome of the working of "nuclear hardship", when most of the adult children had already left the parental home. In both cases, the family dependency ratios reached levels suggesting a serious possible threat to the family's standard of living. Surprisingly, however, female-headed households were relatively successful in offsetting unfavourable changes in family dependency comparing to male-headed ones. During both aforementioned stages of the life-cycle, the differences between family and household dependency ratios are clearly marked, accounting for a significant effect of substitution of family labour for hired servants. Still, more than the half of all female-headed households in Figure 2, those with heads aged 40–59 years, were able to keep household dependency at reasonably low levels, even compared to households headed by males. Interestingly, that happened almost exclusively through the utilization of an excess supply of family labour. This inevitably tells us a great deal about women's efficiency in household-labour strategies.[23]

We can summarize by saying that there were several structural characteristics of female-headed households in historical Polish territories which could have actually made them less advantaged in satisfying their labour needs and possibly their well-being. These were a similar childbearing burden but smaller available labour power; a lower incidence of servants among female headed households; less frequent attachment of kin to households as well as a lower average number of kin. Again, this seems to corroborate the idea that there was a negative relationship between the quality of life and various characteristics of female-headed households under the rules of the "second serfdom". This picture, however, must be adjusted considering the relative efficiency of female-headed households in coping with unfavourable family dependency ratios. Female-headed households appear to have been quite capable of sustaining their subsistence level by using various labour strategies.

The subsistence level, however, was not the only thing female heads had to worry about. The well-being of households headed by women should be more properly viewed in terms of their labour capacity in relation to the amount of arable land they possessed and, most of all, with regard to the whole variety of feudal obligations imposed on the household unit. Village court rolls from early modern Poland provide accounts of cases of widows who were unable in the long run to render the required labour duties and pay the household's tax burden, and therefore decided to resign the headship and to sell off the land.[24] We may hypothesize, then, that although female-headed households could be quite effective in their struggle to survive (that is, in keeping the household's subsistence at a reasonable level), they were more vulnerable in their attempts to retain their social position within the structure of village society.

23 But does not neccessarily suggest an overall positive effect on female-headed households' well-being. See more in the following paragraph.

24 See, for example: Vetulani 1957 (entries no. 106, 182, 224, 234). That was, however, by no means exclusively the experience of female-headed households (see *ibid.*, entry no. 173).

Gendered Well-Being through Time: Life-Course Perspectives

Well-being was not a constant attribute of individuals; rather, it was liable to change over the course of time. This could happen either because a family to which one belonged went through different phases of its developmental cycle (Chayanov 1966; Rowntree 2000 [1901]), or because the individual himself or herself passed through various "statuses" of the life-cycle (Hareven 1978). The almost exclusively cross-sectional character of the sample investigated here offers only very limited means of dealing with the development of the structure of domestic groups over the family life-cycle, not to mention with individuals' life transitions. However, a synthetic cohort approach, introduced to historical studies of family composition by Berkner (Berkner 1972) and subsequently popularized by a number of Cambridge-based scholars (Wall 1987) provides a possible, if partial, solution to these limitations. Equipped with this tool, we may ask how women's position in the household changed over the life-course, and we can hypothesize some general implications of these changes for their well-being.

In Figure 3, sex differentials in the person's household position are given according to the individual's relationship to the household head. They are, however, restricted to categories of coresident inmates and non-nuclear kin alone. The rationale behind this is the idea that changes in proportions for these two categories across the life-span say something crucial about the capability sets of alternatives which males and females enjoyed under the second serfdom.[25] This analysis is undertaken under the assumption that proportions for the first category mentioned above (inmates) may be indicative of a somewhat weakened social position for an individual, whereas membership changes in the second (non-nuclear kin) may define one's position with respect to the feasibility of family welfare (Laslett 1988; Oris and Ochiai 2002).[26]

25 "Capability set of alternatives" is defined as an individual's freedom to achieve alternative functioning combinations (see Sen 1999, 74-75).

26 This seems to be in accordance with peasants' own perception of the status of "inmates" *(komornicy)*. At least on some occasions, peasants did their best not to have their immediate kin 'fall into maltreatement in the nooks of somebody else's houses' (see Płaza 1969, entry no. 708). Sometimes, living as an inmate (in *komorne*) was a

Figure 3. Sex differentials in the position in the household by relationship to household head, Polish rural sample, historical Kingdom of Poland (18th century)

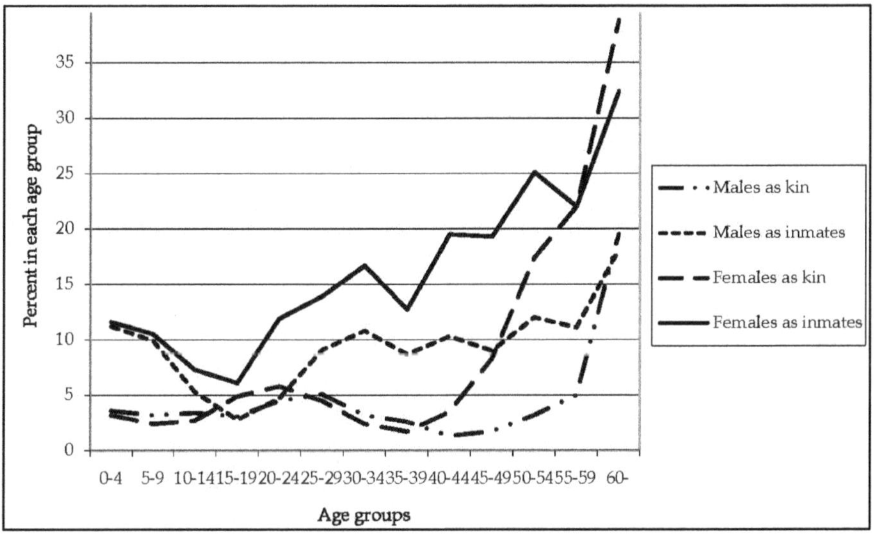

Sources: Szołtysek and Pasieka, *CEURFAMFORM Database*. Calculations based on data for 62 parishes (22 excluded as unreliable): 3,089 males, and 4,644 females.

Figure 3 reveals fairly clearly three critical points of difference in the male and female life-courses. Until the late teens the differences are hardly visible, with roughly the same proportions of men and women having the position of inmates and kin. Then, around the age of 20, the female life-course pattern starts to diverge from the male one. At the same age as a large proportion of men went into service (see next paragraph), a significant proportion of females aged 20–35 became inmates. This proportion had a tendency to increase steadily after the age of 39. In a way, this figure provides evidence of a world of unequal socioeconomic and institutional opportunities for the sexes. From the age of 40 onwards, another discrepancy between men and women appears, as it was mostly females who predominated among kin coresiding in the households of relatives

last resort for solitary women. Those not fortunate enough to afford it were sometimes exposed to the most humiliating living conditions (see Vetulani 1957, entry no. 214). However, one must keep in mind the remarks made above regarding the diverse characteristics of the inmate population.

during later stages of life. This feature may have certain implications for understanding the extent to which the "nuclear hardship" mechanism suggested by Peter Laslett operated in these communities (Laslett 1988).

Figure 4: Offspring living with parents in households by sex and age, Polish rural sample, historical Kingdom of Poland (18th century)

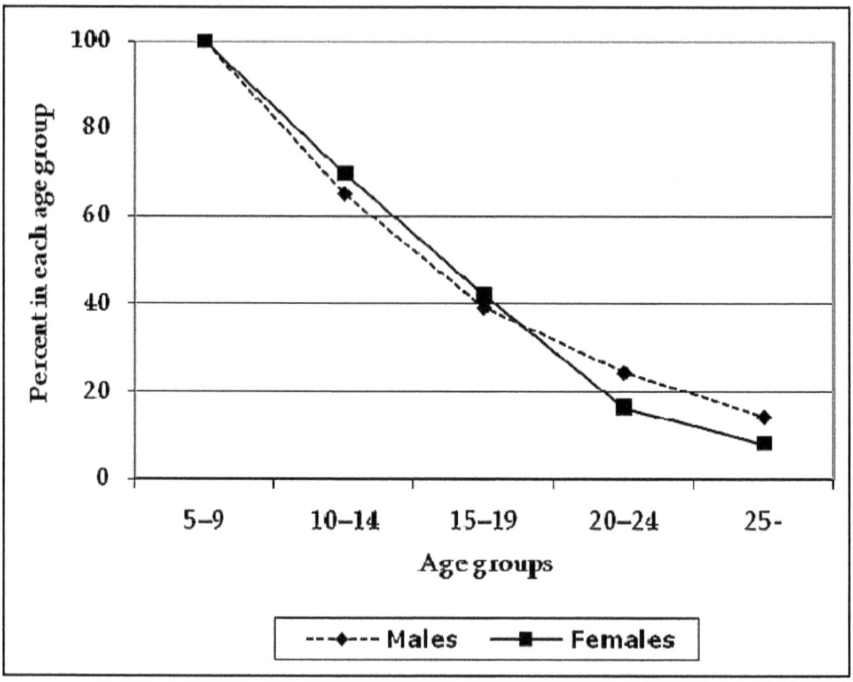

Sources: Szołtysek and Pasieka, *CEURFAMFORM Database*. Offspring of living-in inmates included. Calculations based on data for 54 parishes (30 excluded as less reliable): 7,057 males, and 6,506 females.

The timing of the departure of young adults from the parental home as well as the routes they took out of the home in the transition to adulthood are another two issues potentially informative about the framework within which individual well-being was determined. In a first step, a very simple measure of the speed of exit from the parental home is provided; by counting the number offspring aged 10–14, 15–19 and so on, relative to the number aged 5–9. Although this method can tell us nothing about the precise age of leaving the parental home and should obviously be adjusted by making allowance for deaths occurring during the teens (Wall 1987, 91), it is helpful in discerning general patterns in the population.

As Figure 4 indicates, depletion of the offspring group occurred at almost the same pace for males and females until the late teens. During that part of the life-cycle the whole process was rather abrupt for male and female offspring alike, and there can be little doubt that adolescence was characterised by a large-scale movement away from parental home quite independently of gender. Again, at some point around the age of 20, male and female life-courses began to diverge, increasing the pace at which young women found themselves on the road to independence.

This process can also be investigated on the basis of regionally aggregated data. First, there seems to have existed non-negligible differences in patterns of life-course transitions between regions, with different implications for individual life-choices and life-chances.[27] However, the one thing that almost all regions had in common was a significant difference between male and female exit rates. In 4 out of 7 regions analyzed, it was the female exit rate from the parental home that was significantly higher. For every hundred offspring aged 10-14 resident with parents, there were fewer than 50 still present aged 15-19. This seems to support the hypothesis already advanced: as far as rural conditions from the historical Polish territories of the late serfdom period are concerned, it appears that daughters and not sons were the first to leave the parental home.[28]

What routes did males and females take out of home in the transition to adulthood? Obviously, many females left the parental home to exercise the responsibilities associated with the running of a husband's household. Women came to exercise these house holding responsibilities much earlier than men (Figure 5), and for approximately 5 percent of the female population it already took place within a few years after the age of puberty. During the life stages which, from the point of view of household formation, were most formative, that is 20–24 and 25–29, there were respectively four and almost two times more household heads among women than men.

27 Exit rates (number of offspring aged 15–19 as a percentage of number of offspring aged 10–14) ranged from 48.9 to 85.4 percent for males, and from 50 to 76.6 percent for females (source of calculations the same as in fig. 3). On the method, see Wall 1987, 90–91.

28 Regional differences in this regard may arise either from different inheritance patterns, or – more probably – from specifities of local ecotypes (Mitterauer 1992).

Figure 5. Headship rates by sex and age-group, Polish rural sample, historical Kingdom of Poland (18th century)

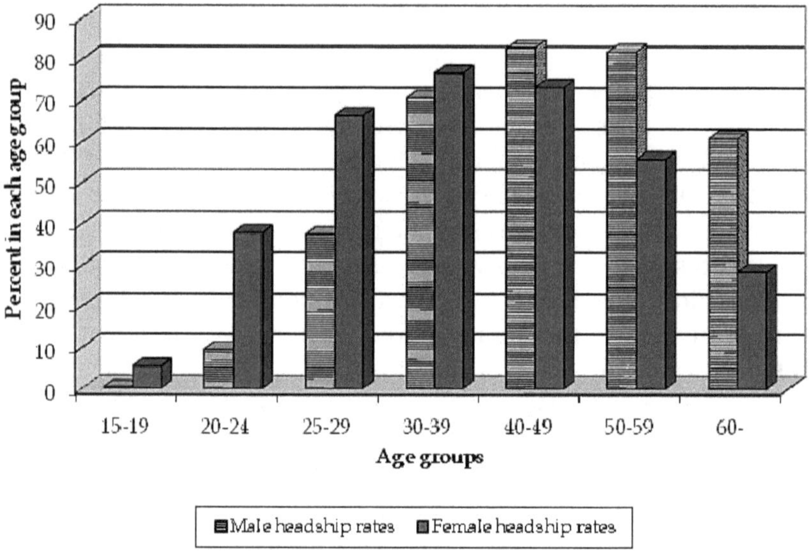

Sources: Szołtysek and Pasieka, *CEURFAMFORM Database*. Calculations based on data for 69 parishes (15 excluded as less reliable): 14,989 males, and 14,879 females. Headship rates defined as percentage of population of each sex heading a household or married to household head.

To the extent that headship, defined in this way, does measure the achievement of adult status, women entered earlier into "full adulthood" than did men in all regions. Whether this can be taken as an indicator of women's early attainment of high levels of well-being, however, is disputable. Leaving apart many other issues, we may point out that early entry into headship position might have constrained female opportunities for pre-marital accumulation of goods, and therefore might have substantially weakened their bargaining power in gender relations within family after marriage (Hartman 2004).[29]

Other noteworthy points include trends in headship over the later stages of the life-cycle (Wall 1987). In this regard, a great discrepancy in

29 There is also a close connection between women's well-being and the adverse effects of high birth-rates (Sen 1999, p. 198). The populations investigated here were traditionally considered as following the pattern of "natural" – or unrestricted – fertility well into the beginning of the twentieth century. See Gieysztorowa 1976, p. 133.

male and female living conditions shows up: while among males high headship rates were retained well into the 60s, female headship started to decline significantly from the age of 40 onwards. Among the elderly of 60 and above, headship was less than half as frequent among women as among men. The declining headship rates in the female population in the later stages of their life are probably indicative of women's increasing dependency in old age. This obviously had certain implications for women's well-being and suggests a possible narrowing of the capability set of opportunities to enhance the quality of life in old age.[30]

However, in all age-groups in the sample there were some men and women who were neither household heads nor spouses of the head, indicative of other options available for them besides family roles. Female marriage patterns are very telling in this regard, as they clearly reveal that the pressure toward early marriage was not pronounced in any region of the sample: only 6.7 percent of the total female population aged 15–19 was already married, and even in the group aged 20–24 almost 57 per cent of females remained unmarried (Szołtysek 2008).

So, what were these other options outside the family? Did men and women take advantage of them to the same extent? These questions lead us back inevitably to the issue of service. First, there is a clear life-cycle pattern in the age distribution of servants, among both the male and the female sub-population (Figure 6). This indicates that for men and women alike, being a servant was not a life-long condition, but rather a contractual, life-cycle experience. It started quite early in one's life course, for roughly one fifth of the male and female population between the ages of 10 and 14.

30 Declining headship rates among females would have inevitably worked in that direction unless the standard of living of women giving up headship was safeguarded by detailed retirement contracts. Village court rolls from southern Poland provide a wealth of material indicating quite extensive welfare provision for retiring household heads, including widows.

Figure 6. Proportions of servants by age and sex, Polish rural sample, historical Kingdom of Poland (18th century)

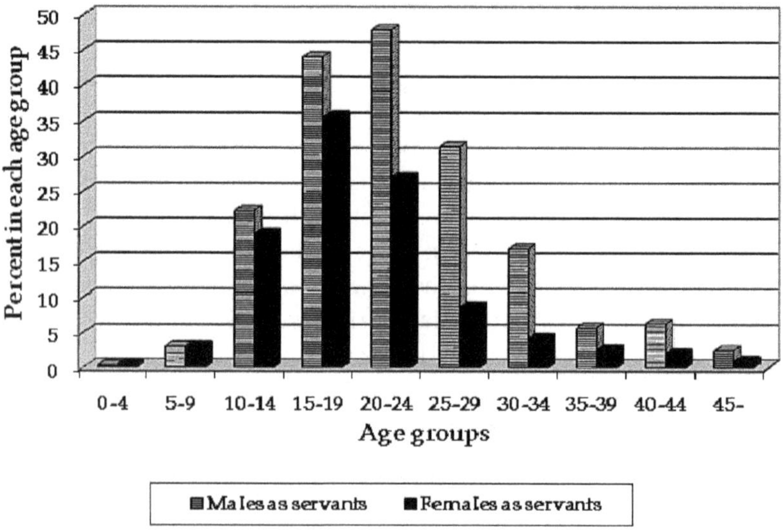

Sources: Szołtysek and Pasieka, *CEURFAMFORM Database*. Calculations based on data for 62 (22 excluded as less reliable): 23,484 males and 23,252 females.

For both sexes, the proportion of servants increased up to the late teens, but after that, they began to drop significantly for females. During the late 20s and early 30s, when a non-negligible proportion of males could still be found in service, there were only one-tenth to one-twentieth as many women active on the labour market. To some extent, this was probably compensated for by the proportions of women active as inmates, but this does not change the overall picture of rather constrained earning and labour capabilities for women outside the parental or conjugal family when compared to men.

A final exercise may shed some more light on the picture of women's residential and socioeconomic opportunities (Figure 7). In this case, all individuals listed in households were classified according to whether they were or were not members of a core family group, defined as including unmarried children resident with at least one parent, married couples, and lone parents.

Figure 7. Relationships within households, females, Polish rural sample, historical Kingdom of Poland (18th century)

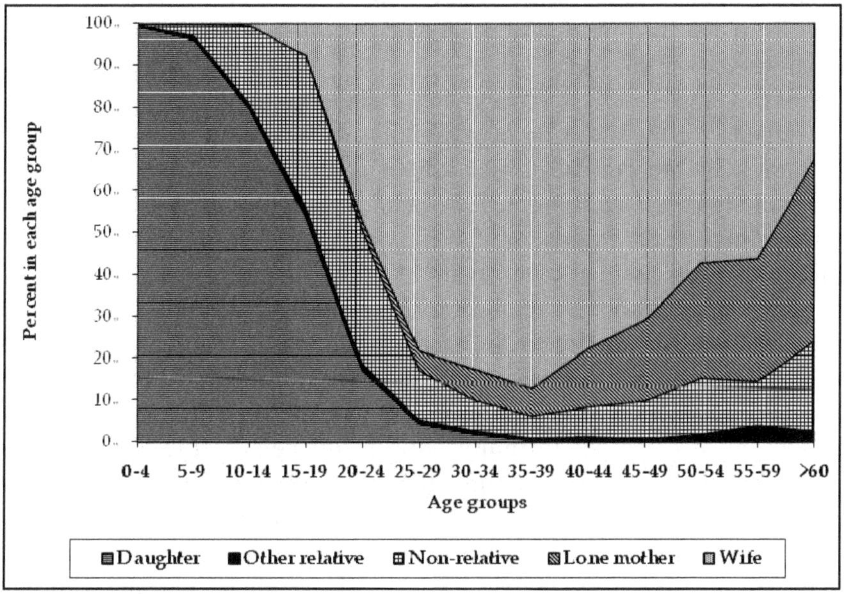

Sources: Szołtysek and Pasieka, *CEURFAMFORM Database*. Calculations based on data for 68 parishes (16 excluded as less reliable): 22,623 females.

All persons who were not members of core families were classified according to whether they lived with relatives, with non-relatives only, or alone (the focus is on the female population only) (Figure 7).[31]

The most distinctive features of the pattern revealed can be briefly summarized as follows: (1) there was a very marked gradual departure of female offspring from the parental home – almost completed before the age of 25; (2) female coresidence with non-relatives occurred during almost all stages of the individual life course, but with a slightly higher prevalence during the late teens and early adulthood, and then again after completion of reproductive activity; (3) living with relatives in the absence of other close family ties was spread across a number of different stages of the female life-cycle, but was restricted to a minority of women

31 Contrary to the previous exercises, in this case the relatives have been identified not by their relationship to the household head but by their relationship with *any* household member (including inmates) in the absence of closer family ties (Wall 1998).

in particular age-groups; it slightly grew in importance among some elderly women; (4) a relatively short period of functioning in family roles within complete families (between the age of 25 and 54 mainly), was almost from the beginning accompanied by the steady increase in lone motherhood over the years.

Points 1 and 2 indicate two counterbalancing processes with differing significance for the question of individual well-being. Leaving the parental home and entering the households of others (very often non-relatives) may well signal losing a "protective belt" in the form of welfare functions as performed by the immediate family, and may therefore pose a threat to different aspects of one's well-being. On the other hand, the freedom of unmarried women to seek employment outside the family by entering the labour market (those appearing as non-relatives in Figure 7) cannot be understated, as it put young females at the centre of contractual relationships and transactions, and enhanced their position in the intra household distribution of resources in future families of their own (Sen 1999, 115–116).[32] Points 2, 3 and 4 in conjunction make strong argument for certain hardships (possibly emotional and psychological rather than purely economic) to which female individuals were exposed while coping alone with their everyday lives. As women advanced in years, a large proportion of them (at least 40 percent of those aged 50 and above) had neither spouses nor kin or children as sources of support in old age.[33] Generally speaking, what the structural patterns in Figure 7 may suggest is a clear life-cycle effect on female well-being.

32 However, some other scholars (Izydorczyk-Kamler and Wyczański 1990, 278–281) revealed the very competitive nature of a market for hired labour, in which female servants were usually less successful than male ones in meeting their goals when it came to the wages they received (on the basis of data for southwestern Poland, 1530–1636).

33 Because of a clear life-cycle pattern in the age distribution of servants discussed above, it is assumed that coresidence with non-relatives at later stages of one's life was almost exclusively related with possessing the status of an inmate *(komornik)*.

Gendered Well-Being through Time: the Results of a Micro-Study

As we reach the limits of socio-structural analysis based on a cross-sectional approach, I would like in this final section to come back to the issue of the benefits of analyzing female headship in a more dynamic way. The data presented in the following paragraphs comes from a micro-investigation of one Polish-speaking community in Prussian Upper Silesia at the end of the eighteenth century (Szołtysek 2003; 2004; 2007). Its significance for the subject of this essay is twofold: first, the study focuses on a population which existed under strict manorial control typical of the second serfdom; second, households and individuals could be followed through fifteen sequential census-type "communion books", allowing more dynamic aspects of female headship to be revealed.

There were 25 widows registered as household heads in the parish during the period of study (1766–1803). The average duration of their remaining in charge of the headship was slightly less than two and a half years, which still seems high if we take into consideration that under the prevailing normative rules, widowed women were supposed to head households only very temporarily (Orzechowski 1959). Moreover, the duration of female headship ranged from one and a half months to as much as eight years (changes in position of the women include remarriage, retirement, translocation, or death). Roughly speaking, more than one third of these women were in charge of households for longer than two years. Those retaining the headship for even longer were older than those who held that position for a shorter period of time. This is surprising, for one would expect precisely the former category to show evidence of manorial intervention into their household choices (Kula 1976). One can observe, however, that widows keeping the headship for longer than one year appeared much more seldom in the case of large farmers than in the case of smallholders. Remarriages of widows accompanied by a transfer of headship to their husbands usually occurred before one and a half years had elapsed. In most but not all cases this transpired if there was no adult son or daughter's husband in the household (Szołtysek 2004).

Moreover, a widow's decision to hand over the farm did not necessarily imply relinquishing any future matrimonial plans. This was the case for Sophia Swoboda, widow of a smallholder and weaver, who held the household headship for two and a half years after her husband's death. In 1797, the son took over the farm just after his marriage, but in the next year the widow also remarried, staying in the household as *Auszüglerin* (retired household head).

In addition to that, some family stories discernible from household lists and parish registers suggest a further significance of female agency and women's empowerment despite the normative structures of the 'second serfdom'. Because of the limited space available, only one case must suffice to shed light on these issues.

The family in question held a large farmstead in the village of Paniowki, in which the widow ruled for at least seven years after her husband's death in 1759 (Szołtysek 2003, 289–290). Left with two pre-adolescent children (a daughter of 10 years and an 8-year-old son), the female-headed household presumably had a high demand for the labour power needed for cultivation of the land and rendering the compulsory labour dues. In response to that demand, a servant was hired by the widow, a male who within the year became the husband of the now 17-year-old daughter of the widow. Through the coresidence of the two conjugal family units under one roof (widow and her son, plus daughter with son-in-law), this household governed by a widowed woman was able not only to increase its labour capacity, but also to reduce its expenditures (through inclusion of the male servant in the family labour group). Notwithstanding that, a year later, the widow herself brought her second husband into the household and the couple together ruled over the farmstead for the next five years. The original female head gave up the headship to her son-in-law only after her second husband's death.

The extent to which the landlord could have actually interfered in the strategic actions taken by the female-headed household described above is not stated in the sources. Nor is the potentially important role of other kin, neighbours, and the local bailiff.[34] However, it is hard to believe that such a successful managing of the large farm by a woman would be possible in a community environment lacking in any recognition and acknowledgement (even if partial and conditional) of the importance of female

34 On the key role of the village headman (German *Scholtz*; Polish *sołtys*) among Bohemian serf communities, see Ogilvie 2005.

agency.[35] Allowing women to act as responsible and reliable persons meant giving them the chance to choose a life style they had reason to value.[36]

Conclusion

The population we have investigated in this essay came from a region traditionally considered as unfavourable for the development of women's independence and for the enhancement of their capability set. To a large extent, the analysis carried out here has brought to light a mixture of pros and cons with regard to that picture.

First, it has been revealed that female headship was, on average, rare across almost all investigated regions in this large sample. With a great degree of certainty it may be stated that in the pre-industrial rural communities of historical Poland female-headed households constituted only very marginal phenomena in socioeconomic and family life in most of the populations in question.

The analysis of sex ratios in specific categories of household members revealed females' earlier exit from parental home. This in turn produced a two-fold result. On the one hand, young women were expelled earlier and

35 That is also reflected in the extent to which widows' welfare in old age was protected by means of retirement contracts – widespread among rural families of Upper Silesia well into the 1920s (see County Court Archive in Żory, *Grundacten von Klein Paniow*).

36 Kula's normative model of relationships between the landlords and peasant families – and women governing households in particular (Kula 1976), appears too mechanistic when the evidence revealing actual practices of rural classes is scrutinized. Widows resigning the headship can actually be found in existing village court rolls from southern Poland. However, the circumstances surrounding these events run counter the usual assumptions about the nature of landlord-peasant interactions. Not only were female widowed heads buying and selling land, but also their decision to give up the headship seemed to be dictated by purely economic concerns, rather than having resulted from the landlord's interventionist policy (see for example: Płaza 1969, 59, 587, 589, 675, 688, 695, 698, 721, 755). However, only partial observations are offered here, and they cannot be taken as fully supporting a theory of "communal autonomy" of serf communities; see the discussion of the issue in Ogilvie 2001; 2005.

at a faster pace from the provision of family welfare than men. On the other, leaving the parental home earlier and more abruptly opened up prospects for entering the market for hired labour and for getting acquainted with contractual labour relationships to a much greater extent. Female chances on the labour market still may not have been equal to male, however. It has been shown that the majority of the young rural labour forces recruited in the form of life-cycle servants in this society was male, and the surplus of male over female servants shows up strongly across the whole sample. The extent to which women's chances for well-being might have actually been compensated for by living in kin-related households or by engaging in various coping strategies subsumed under the "economy of makeshifts" is not unambiguously clear.

The comparison of male- with female-headed households reveals that the latter were generally smaller and, more importantly, less economically viable. As a consequence, they were more exposed to various threats against the well-being of their members. However, scanty evidence we have at our disposal seems to suggest that the cross-sectional character of the data can actually mask some important time-variant changes which may have helped to sustain and even to extend the well-being of female-headed households. That women as household heads were not solely the victims of economic and demographic constraints imposed on them is also revealed by the fact that female-headed households were more successful in offsetting unfavourable changes in family dependency compared to male-headed ones. Local variations would be of prime importance in determining the sustainability of households headed by women over time.

Time, again, would be an important factor determining women's well-being for other reasons as well. The evidence presented, both aggregated and localized, suggests a significant life-cycle effect on female well-being: the older the women were, the more exposed they found themselves to forces endangering the stability of their residential patterns, and the more threatened their well-being appeared to be.

To sum up: if we do not want to restrict ourselves to advocating further and more comprehensive research on the subject, then what is already known suggests that women's economic position in the rural areas of historical Poland was affected adversely rather than favorably by the manorial institutions of the second serfdom. Consequently, these institutions must be regarded as having a negative influence on female well-being.[37] However, the most serious limitation of the approach presented here is inherent in the very nature of historical accounts of the subjective experiences of individuals in the past. As many standard measures of well-being were developed on the basis of observation of Western (post-) industrialized societies (Robeyns 2003), they may not be fully applicable to understand historical agents. If "capability" is taken to represent the alternative combinations of things a person (a woman particularly, in this context) is able to do or be – the various "functionings" he or she can achieve (Sen 1993, 30) – then a careful and constant effort is required on the part of the researcher in order not to impose our own value systems on historical agents. Although it would be hard to dismiss all universalist accounts of central human functions and capabilities (e.g. such as the ability to live to old age in dignity) (Nussbaum 2000, 5; Robeyns 2003, 74, 76–77), people of the past were mostly silent about their subjective preferences.

After all, the past is a foreign country.

References

ALTER, George, MANFREDINI, Mateo and NYSTEDT, Paul, 2004, "Gender Differences in Mortality", in Tommy BENGTSSON, Cameron CAMPBELL and James LEE (eds), *Life Under Pressure: Mortality and Living Standards in Europe and Asia, 1700–1900,* Cambridge (Mass.), MIT University Press, pp. 173–208.

ARRIZABALAGA, Marie-Pierre, 2007, "Household organization as an indicator of individual well-being from a gender perspective in the Western Pyrénées", Paper presented at the COST ACTION A34 First Symposium, "Well-being as a Social Gendered Process", Modena, Italy, 26–28 June, 2006.

BARANOWSKI, Bogdan, 1986, "*Ludzie gościńca w XVII–XVII w.*", Łódź, Wydawnictwo Łódzkie.

BECK, Rainer, 2001, "Traces of emotion? Marital discord in early modern Bavaria", in Richard WALL, Tamara K. HAREVEN and Josef EHMER (eds), *Family History Revisited. Comparative Perspectives*, Newark, University of Delaware, pp. 135–160.

37 Time, however, may verify that picture as more comprehensive investigation of existing qualitative evidence from the historical Poland will eventually advance in the future.

BEREND, Ivan T. and RÁNKI, György, 1982, *The European Periphery and Industrialisation, 1780–1914*, Cambridge, Cambridge University Press.

BERKNER, Lutz K., 1972, "The stem family and the developmental cycle of the peasant household: an eighteenth-century Austrian example", *The American Historical Review*, 77, 2, pp. 398–418.

BOGUCKA, Maria, 1990, "Women and economic life in the Polish cities during the 16th–17th centuries", in Simonetta CAVACIOCCHI (ed.), *La donna nell'economia secc. XIII–XVIII*, Prato, Istituto Internazionale di storia economica Francesco Datini, pp. 185–194.

BRAUDEL, Fernand, 1985, *Civilization and Capitalism 15th–18th Century*; vol. 3, *The Perspective of the World*, translated from the French by S. Reynolds, Berkeley, University of California Press.

BRENNER, Robert, 1989, "Economic Backwardness in Eastern Europe in Light of Developments in the West", in Daniel CHIROT (ed.), *The Origins of Backwardness in Eastern Europe,* Berkeley, University of California Press, pp. 15–52.

CERMAN, Marcus, 1999, "Serfdom and family". Paper presented to the Conference "Household and family in past time", Palma de Mallorca, 9–11 September, 1999.

–, 2008, "Social structure and land markets in late medieval central and east-central Europe", *Continuity and Change*, 23, 1, pp. 55–100.

CHAYANOV, Alexander V., 1966, *The Theory of Peasant Economy*, Homewood, Irwin.

CUMMINS, Robert A., 2005, "Moving from the quality of life concept to a theory", *Journal of Intellectual Disability Research*, 49, 10, pp. 699–706.

CZAP, Peter, 1983, "A large family: The peasant's greatest wealth: Serf households in Mishino, Russia, 1814–1858", in Richard WALL, Jean ROBIN, and Peter LASLETT (eds), *Family Forms in Historic Europe,* Cambridge, Cambridge University Press, pp. 105–151.

DAS GUPTA, Monica, 1999, "Lifeboat versus corporate ethic: social and demographic implications of stem and joint families", *Social Science and Medicine,* 49, 2, pp. 173–84.

DRIBE, Martin, 2000, *Leaving Home in a Peasant Society. Economic Fluctuations, Household Dynamics and Youth Migration in Southern Sweden, 1829–1866*, Lund, Lund Studies in Economic History.

FAUVE-CHAMOUX, Antoinette, 1983, "The importance of women in an urban environment: the example of the Rheims household at the beginning of the Industrial Revolution", in Richard WALL, Jean ROBIN, and Peter LASLETT (eds), *Family Forms in Historic Europe,* Cambridge, Cambridge University Press, pp. 475–492.

–, 2002, "Widows and their living arrangements in preindustrial France", *History of the Family*, 7, 1, pp. 101–116.

FELCE, David and PERRY, Jonathan, 1995, "Quality of Life: Its Definition and Measurement", *Research in Developmental Disabilities*, 16, 1, pp. 51–74.

GIEYSZTOROWA, Irena, 1976, *Wstęp do demografii staropolskiej*, Warszawa, PWN.

GREEN, David R. and OWENS, Alastair (eds), 2004, *Gender, Property and Inheritance since the Seventeenth Century*, Westport, Praeger.

GUZOWSKI, Piotr, 2007, "Marriage strategies and inheritance system in Polish peasant families in the 15th–17th centuries". Paper presented at the COST ACTION A34 Second Symposium "The Transmission of Well-Being: Marriage Strategies and Inheritance Systems in Europe (17th–20th Centuries)", University of Minho, Guimarães, Portugal, 25–28 April, 2007.

HAGEN, William W., 1998, "Village Life in East-Elbian Germany and Poland, 1400–1800", in Tom SCOTT (ed.), *The Peasantries of Europe: From the Fourteenth to the Eighteenth Century* London, Longman, pp. 145–190.

HAJNAL, John, 1982, "Two kinds of preindustrial household formation system", *Population and Development Review,* 8, 3, pp. 449–494.

HAMMEL, Eugene A. and LASLETT, Peter, 1974, "Comparing household structure over time and between cultures", *Comparative Studies in Society and History*, 16, 1, pp. 73–109.

HAREVEN, Tamara K., 1978, "Family history and the life-course", in Tamara K. Hareven (ed.), *Transitions: the Family and the Life-Course in Historical Perspective*, New York, Academic Press, pp. 17–64.

HARTMANN, Mary S., 2004, *The Household and the Making of History. A Subversive View of the Western Past*, Cambridge, Cambridge University Press.

HØRNQUIST, Jan Olof, 1989, "Quality of life: concept and assessment", *Scandinavian Journal of Social Medicine*, 18, 1, pp. 69–79.

IZYDORCZYK-KAMLER, Anna and WYCZANSKI, Andrzej, 1990, "La femme et l'économie rurale en Pologne aux XVIe et XVIIe siècles", in Simonetta CAVACIOCCHI (ed.), *La donna nell'economia secc. XIII–XVIII*, Prato, Istituto Internazionale di storia economica Francesco Datini, pp. 275–282.

KAMLER, Anna, 2005, *Chłopi jako pracownicy najemni na wsi małopolskiej w XVI i w pierwszej połowie XVII wieku*, Warszawa, Jacek i Krzysztof Olesiuk.

KASER, Karl, 2002, "Power and inheritance: male domination, property and family in Eastern Europe, 1500–1900", *History of the Family*, 7, 3, pp. 375–395.

KERTZER, David I., HOGAN, Dennis P., and KARWEIT, Nancy, 1992, "Kinship beyond the household in a nineteenth-century Italian town", *Continuity and Change*, 7, 1, pp. 103–121.

KOPCZYŃSKI, Michał, 1995, "Służba na wsi kujawskiej u schyłku XVIII wieku", in Anna ŻARNOWSKA (ed.), *Pamiętnik XV Powszechnego Zjazdu Historyków Polskich, vol. 2*, Gdańsk-Toruń, pp. 67–77.

KUKLO, Cezary, 1998, *Kobieta samotna w społeczeństwie miejskim u schyłku Rzeczypospolitej szlacheckiej. Studium demograficzno-społeczne*, Białystok, Wydawnictwo Uniwersytetu w Białymstoku.

KULA, Witold, 1976, "The Seigneury and the Peasant Family in Eighteenth-Century Poland", in Robert FOSTER and Orest RANUM (eds), *Family and Society. Selection from the "Annales. Economies, Societes, Civilisations"*, Baltimore, Johns Hopkins University Press, pp. 192–203.

LASLETT, Peter, 1983, "Family and household as work group and kin group: areas of traditional Europe compared", in Richard WALL, Jean ROBIN and Peter LASLETT (eds), *Family Forms in Historic Europe*, Cambridge, Cambridge University Press, pp. 513–563.

–, 1988, "Family, kinship and collectivity as systems of support in preindustrial Europe: a consideration of the 'nuclear-hardship hypothesis'", *Continuity and Change,* 3, 2, pp. 152–175.

–, 2000 [1965], *The World We Have Lost Further Explored*, London, Methuen.

LASLETT, Peter, WACHTER, Kenneth W., and LASLETT, Robert, 1978, "The English evidence on household structure compared with the outcomes of microsimulation", in Kenneth W. WACHTER, Eugene A. HAMMEL and Peter LASLETT (eds), *Statistical Studies of Historical Social Structure*, New York, Academic Press, pp. 65–87.

LESZCZYŃSKI, J., 1956, "Ludzie luźni i czeladź najemna na Śląsku w pierwszym dziesięcioleciu po wojnie trzydziestoletniej", *Sobótka*, 11, 4, 513–580.

ŁUKASIEWICZ, Dariusz, 1995, *Czarna legenda Polski: obraz Polski i Polaków w Prusach 1772–1815*, Poznań, PTPN.

MCNAY, Kirsty, HUMPHRIES, Jane and KLASEN, Stephan, 2005, "Excess female mortality in nineteenth-century England and Wales", *Social Science History*, 29, 4, pp. 649–681.

MELTON, Edgar, 1998, "Population structure, the market economy, and the transformation of Gutsherrschaft in East Central Europe, 1650–1800: the cases of Brandemburg and Bohemia", *German History*, 16, 3, pp. 297–327.

MIRONOV, Boris N., 1996, "When and why was the Russian peasantry emancipated?", in Michael L. BUSH (ed.), *Serfdom and Slavery: Studies in Legal Bondage*, New York, Longman, pp. 323–347.

MITTERAUER, Michael, 1999, "Ostkolonisation und Familienverfassung. Zur Diskussion um die Hajnal-Linie", in Vincenc RAJŠP and Ernst BRUCKMÜLLER (eds), *Vilfanov zbornik. Pravo-zgodovina-narod. In memoriam Sergij Vilfan*, Ljubljana, ZRC, pp. 203–221.

–, 1992, "Peasant and non-peasant family forms in relation to the physical environment and the local economy", *Journal of Family History*, 17, 2, pp. 139–159.

MORING, Beatrice, 2002, "Widowhood options and strategies in preindustrial northern Europe. Socioeconomic differences in household position of the widowed in 18th and 19th century Finland", *History of the Family*, 7, 1, pp. 79–99.

NUSSBAUM, Martha C., 2000, *Women and Human Development. The Capabilities Approach*, Cambridge, Cambridge University Press.

OBRANIAK, W., 1968, "Sytuacja demograficzna komorników i czeladzi chłopskiej w wieluńskiem w końcu XVIII wieku", *Przeszłość Demograficzna Polski*, 2, pp. 109–117.

OCHIAI, Emiko (ed.), 2002, *The Logic of Female Succession: Rethinking Patriarchy and Patrilineality in Global and Historical Perspective*, Kyoto, International Research for Japanese Studies.

OGILVIE, Sheilagh, 2001, "The Economic World of the Bohemian Serf: Economic Concepts, Preferences and Constraints on the Estate of Friedland, 1583–1692", *Economic History Review*, 54, 3, pp. 430–453.

–, 2005, "Village community and village headmen in Early Modern Bohemia", *Zeitschrift für Geschichte und Kultur der böhmischen Länder*, 46, 2, pp. 402–451.

OGILVIE, Sheilagh and EDWARDS, Jeremy, 2000, "Women and the 'second serfdom': evidence from Early Modern Bohemia", *The Journal of Economic History*, 60, 4, pp. 961–994.

OGILVIE, Sheilagh and CERMAN, Markus, 1995, "The Bohemian Census of 1651 and the Position of Inmates", *Social History/Histoire Sociale*, 28, pp. 333–346.

ORIS, Michel and OCHIAI, Emiko, 2002, "Family crisis in the context of different family systems: frameworks and evidence on 'When dad died'", in Renzo DEROSAS and Michel ORIS (eds), *When Dad Died: Individuals and Families Coping with Family Stress in Past Societies* Bern, Peter Lang, pp. 17–81.

ORZECHOWSKI, Kazimierz, 1956, "Uwagi o komornikach na Górnym Śląsku u schyłku epoki feudalnej", *Zeszyty Naukowe Uniwersytetu Wrocławskiego*, 6, Seria A, pp. 119–160.

–, 1959, *Chłopskie posiadanie na Górnym Śląsku u schyłku epoki feudalnej, Studium historyczno-prawne*, Wrocław, Zakład Narodowy im. Ossolińskich.

PLAKANS, Andrzej, 1975, "Seigneurial authority and peasant family life: the Baltic area in the eighteenth century", *Journal of Interdisciplinary History*, 5, 4, pp. 629–654.

PŁAZA, Stanisław (ed.), 1969, *Księga sądowa wsi Iwkowej, 1581–1809*, Wrocław, Ossolineum.

ROBEYNS, Ingrid, 2003, "Sen's capability approach and gender inequality: selecting relevant capabilities", *Feminist Economics*, 9, 2–3, pp. 61–92.

ROWNTREE, Benjamin Seebohm, 2000 [1901], *Poverty. A Study of Town Life*, Bristol, Policy Press/Joseph Rowntree Charitable Trust.

SABEAN, David W., 1990, *Property, Production, and Family in Neckerhausen, 1700–1870*, Cambridge, Cambridge University Press.

SCHULTE, Renate, 1984, "Infanticide in rural Bavaria in the nineteenth century", in Hans MEDICK and David W. SABEAN (eds), *Interest and Emotion. Essays on the Study of Family and Kinship,* Cambridge, Cambridge University Press, pp. 77–102.

SECCOMBE, Wally, 1990, "Starting to stop: working class fertility decline in Britain", *Past and Present*, 126, 1, pp. 151–188.

SEN, Amartia K., 1993, "Capability and well-being", in Martha C. NUSSBAUM and Amartia K. SEN (eds), *The Quality of Life*, Oxford, Oxford University Press, pp. 30–53.

–, 1999, *Development as Freedom*, New York, Anchor Books.

SEPPEL, Marten , 2004, "The Assistance of Manors to Peasants in Cases of Subsistence Crisis in Seventeenth-Century Livonia", *Acta Historica Tallinnensia*, 8, pp. 3–19.

SOSNOWSKA, Anna, 2004, *Zrozumieć zacofanie. Spory historyków o Europę Wschodnią (1947–1994),* Warszawa, Trio.

SZOŁTYSEK, Mikołaj, 2003, *The population of the parish of Bujakow in 18th and 19th century. Between "the unique" household formation system and peculiarity of borderland*, Unpublished PhD dissertation, University of Wroclaw, Poland.

–, 2004, "Astride the Hajnal line – household and family in the Upper Silesian parish of Bujakow, 1766–1803", *Polish Population Review*, 11, pp. 59–93.

–, 2007, "Central European household and family systems, and the 'Hajnal-Mitterauer' line: the parish of Bujakow (18th–19th centuries)", *The History of the Family*, 12, 1, pp. 19–42.

–, 2008, "Rethinking Eastern Europe: household formation patterns in the Polish-Lithuanian Commonwealth and European family systems", *Continuity and Change*, 23, 3, pp. 389-427.

SZOŁTYSEK, Mikołaj and RZEMIENIECKI, Konrad, 2005, "Between 'traditional' collectivity and 'modern' individuality: An atomistic perspective on family and household astride the Hajnal's line (Upper Silesia and Great Poland at the end of the 18th century)", *Historical Social Research*, 30, 3, pp. 130–170.

TOPOLSKI, Jerzy, 1974a, "Economic decline in Poland from the Sixteenth to the Eighteenth centuries", in Peter EARLE (ed.), *Essays in European Economic History, 1500–1800,* Oxford, Oxford University Press, pp. 127–142.

–, 1974b, "The manorial-serf economy in Central and Eastern Europe in the 16th and 17th centuries", *Agricultural History*, 48, 3, pp. 341–352.

VERDON, Michel, 1998, *Rethinking Households: an Atomistic Perspective on European Living Arrangements*, London, Routledge.

VETULANI, Adam, 1957, (ed.), *Księga sądowa Uszwi dla wsi Zawady, 1619–1788*, Wrocław, Ossolineum.

WALL, Richard, 1981, "Women alone in English society", *Annales de démographie historique*, pp. 303–317.

–, 1987, "Leaving home and the process of household formation in pre-industrial England", *Continuity and Change*, 2, 1, pp. 77–101.

–, 1991, "European family and household systems", in *Historiens et populations. Liber Amicorum Etienne Helin,* Louvain-la-Neuve, Academia, pp. 617–636.

–, 1998, "Characteristics of European family and household systems", *Historical Social Research,* 23, 1–2, pp. 44–66.

–, 2002, "Elderly widows and widowers and their coresidents in late 19th- and early 20th-century England and Wales", *History of the Family,* 7, 1, pp. 139–155.

WALLERSTEIN, Immanuel, 1974, *The Modern World-System: Capitalist Agriculture and the Origins of the European World-Economy in the Sixteenth Century*, New York, Academic Press.

WILK, Richard, 2005, "Quality of life and the anthropological perspective", *Feminist Economics*, 5, 2, pp. 91– 93.

WILK, Richard R. and NETTING, Robert Mc, 1984, "Households: Changing forms and functions", in Robert Mc. NETTING, Richard R. WILK, and Eric J. ARNOULD (eds), *Households: Comparative and Historical Studies of the Domestic Group,* Berkeley, California, University of California Press, pp. 1–28.

WOLFF, Larry, 1994, *Inventing Eastern Europe: The Map of Civilization on the Mind of the Enlightenment*, Stanford, Stanford University Press.

WOŹNIAK, Andrzej, 1987, *Kultura mazowieckiej wsi pańszczyźnianej XVIII i początku XIX wiek (Wybrane zagadnienia)*, Wrocław, Ossolineum.

WYCZAŃSKI, Andrzej, 1978, "Czy chłopu było źle w Polsce XVI wieku?", *Kwartalnik Historyczny,* 85, 3, pp. 627–641.

Gender, Well-Being, and Old Age for Persons without a Life-Companion

A Rural Case Study around the Turn of the Century 1900. Rendalen, Norway

Sølvi SOGNER

Security in old age for the needy has been a perennial problem at the intersection between private and public responsibility. The modern welfare-state is only a recent post-second world-war phenomenon. Historically, according to Norwegian law, parents and children and married couples have had reciprocal obligations of economic support. Individuals without these close family relations would thus be especially vulnerable in old age. In this paper, we shall look at the situation of the unmarried a century ago in the context of a rural Norwegian parish, Rendalen.[1] The discussion is based on the census of 1910.[2] We have fairly good information about the parish back into the 18th century (Bull 2006, 25–28).[3]

The focus is on the well-being of elderly unmarried people, compared with widowed and divorced men in old age from a gender perspective. Only people aged 60 and more will be investigated. This cut-off line is chosen because around age 60 farmers used to step down and transfer the

1 Rendalen is a vast, sparsely populated parish (c. 4,000 km^2) in south eastern Norway, close to the Swedish border, had a population of 1,685 in 1801 and 4,255 in 1910. Main industries were agriculture, animal husbandry, and forestry. The parish is situated in a highland area, with farms located at 250–540 meters above sea level, and summer pastures up to 940 meters.

2 Censuses are not accessible until after a hundred years. However, The Norwegian Historical Data Centre in Tromsø has computerized the census in anticipation of opening up for general availability in 2010. I am grateful to be an early user.

3 Parish registers are available for 1733–1900. For 1762 there is a nominative listing of households and household members aged 12 and above, and nominative censuses exist for 1801, 1865, 1875, 1890, 1900, and 1910. Families are linked in a database. However, time constraints have prohibited here full use of the available data.

farm to the next generation (Homlong 1995). Also generally speaking people above 60 years of age are past marriage age. Death and out-migration had taken their toll, and influenced the outcome. How old people, still alive and present in the community, fare in the last stages of life represents to the spectator – at the time as well as for posterity – an idea of life in old age, dependent upon gender and civil status.

Were the "over 60s" able to support and take care of themselves? If they were not, what was their situation? Did single men and women experience old age differently?

To understand the situation of individuals within the traditional, pre-industrial household economy, what I would call a "household context approach" has been chosen. We will look at the household position of single and widowed men and women from the farmer and the cottar-worker class respectively. The following positions are relevant: a) Head of household, b) Resident kin, c) Unrelated lodger, d) Servant, e) Pauper.

Well-being will be assessed according to how well they succeeded in old age. Success will be estimated according to the household position achieved. Hypothetically, those who became heads of household were the most successful – and paupers and servants, the least. Intermediate positions are less clear cut and more difficult to assess, and will be evaluated in relation to access to resources – such as a pension, capital, property, kin support, working capacity.

The Norwegian collective term to describe the position of a person coping alone without a life-companion is *enslig*; it applies to those permanently single, widowed or divorced. The English term "solitary" comes closest to the Norwegian term, and will be used in the chapter. However, it is not be confused with the use made in Peter Laslett's household typology where "solitary" is reserved for the household head (Laslett 1972, 31).

The data presented are: (1) "Solitary" people in general, (2) Single people, (3) Widowed people. A general discussion and conclusion follow.

Senior "Solitary" People in Rendalen in 1910

A sample of the 1910 census, consisting of the first 200 people with year of birth 1850 and before has been extracted for further analysis (Appendix, Table 3). They constitute 46 percent of this age group.[4] The sample is representative of the socio-economic composition of the population. People are sorted into the traditional two main social groups – farmers and cottars.[5] Some farmers combine farming with ownership of forests or sawmills, some are full time farmers, but most farmers combine farming with some subsidiary activity. The farmer group was also replenished from below as many of the oldest cottages were sold and turned into small farms in the 19th century. Cottars, workers, lodgers also combine more than one activity, but will here be amalgamated with the cottar group, their living conditions being very similar. New activities associated with ongoing modernization do not seem to have affected the occupational structure of the senior segment of the population to any noticeable degree, the new activities were combined with the ones of the farmers or cottars in the traditional combinatory way.

Figure 1 shows the household position held by 98 "solitary people", the term used here for the single, widowed and divorced men and women without a life-companion. All not currently married people over age 60, whether cottars or farmers, are grouped together in this figure, which aims at providing the full picture for the two genders.

4 Actually the first 217 persons aged 60 and over in the census are taken into account here. In 1880 the parish was split in two, the old main parish Øvre Rendalen and the subsidiary parish, Ytre Rendalen. The paper is based on Øvre Rendal which is entered first in the census.

5 Figures concerning socio-differentiation (farmers and cottars) are not provided in this essay: they may be found in detailed previous studies on Rendalen (Sogner 1976; Bull 2000; 2006).

Figure 1. Household position of old age persons (aged 60 and over), without a life-companion ("solitary"), by gender. Rendalen, 1910

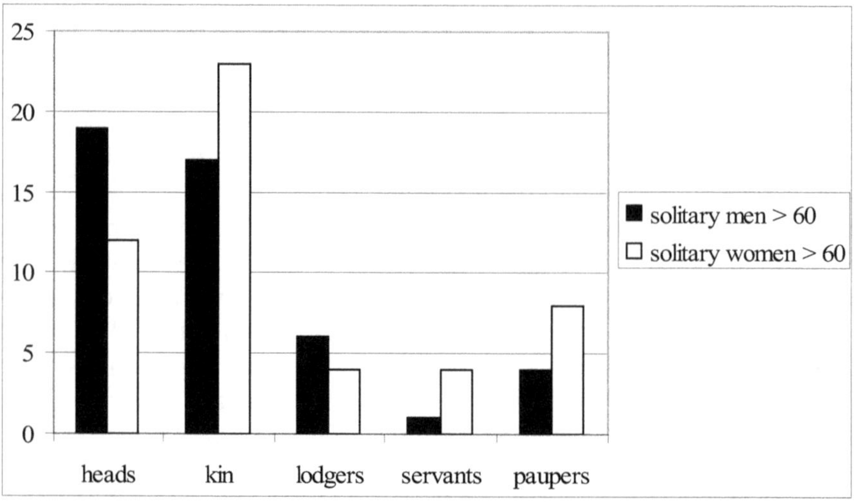

Source: 1910 census, 46% sample. See Appendix, Table 4 for figures.
Notes: "Solitary" means living without a life-companion. "Paupers" receive poor relief. Currently married men and women are excluded. Single, widowed and divorced persons are included. Divorced persons are: one man among paupers, one woman among resident kin, and one woman among servants.

There is approximately the same number of solitary men as solitary women in 1910: 47 men and 51 women. The comparison is made on the basis of the actual number of persons, not on percentage, as the numbers are so similar. The figures are small, admittedly, but significant, as they are drawn from 46 percent of the population.

Men top the list for household heads and for lodgers with no stated family ties to the household they are living in. Women on the other hand are mostly resident kin, servants and paupers. In what follows supplementary information from the census will be presented to give substance and context to these figures.

Single Men and Women above 60 Years of Age

The household position of single men aged 60 and over compared to the household position of single women is shown in Figure 2. Senior men, whether farmers or cottars, were most likely to be household heads (Sogner 1976).

Figure 2. Household position of single men and women aged 60 and over. Rendalen, 1910

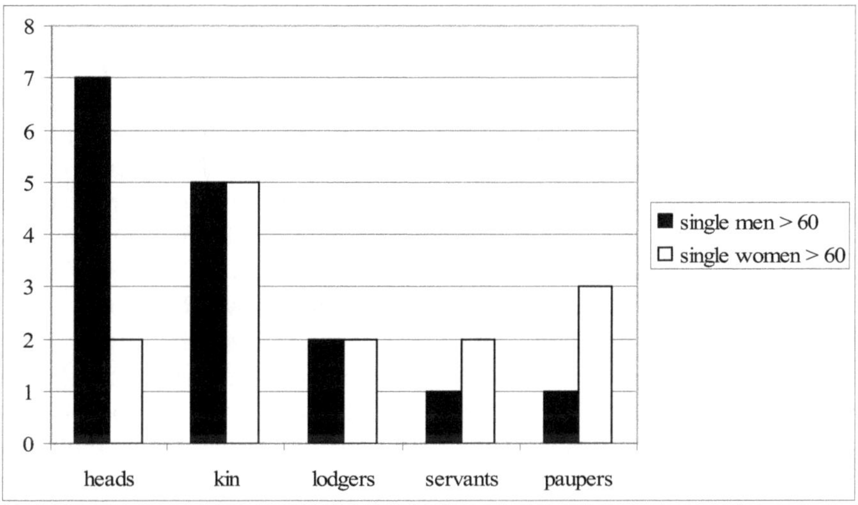

Source: 1910 census, 46% sample. See Appendix, Table 4 for figures.
Note: "Paupers" receive poor relief.

Almost half of all single men over 60 headed their own household – four farmers and three cottars. The farmers were on the young side; their mean age is 61. The cottars were clearly older – mean age 72. The bachelor farmers' households had a mean size of 7.2 persons, and were packed with servants and lodgers. One household headed by a single man had 12 members – head + 9 servants (a couple among them), one lodging day labourer (woman), and one lodger (carpenter) –. Another household had 8 persons (head + 5 servants, one lodger with servant). Another had 7 members (head + one man servant, a widowed housekeeper with three small children, and one widow, unrelated, on retirement *contract*). The mean household size (MHS) would in fact had been 9, but for one household of only 2 persons (a 60-year-old farmer and his 33-year-old servant girl from outside of the parish); we do not know whether this situation was a *concubinage* set-up or a prospective married household.

For cottars, mean household size (MHS) seems almost an irrelevant term: one household had four members, while the other two were one-person households! Only one of three was a proper cottar, one was a "user of a cottage"; one was a house owner and lumberjack. Their common denominator was having a house at their disposal, an asset which could be used to advantage. Thus the 77-year-old "user of a cottage" had three lodgers in his household, an unmarried lumberjack and a married day labourer couple.

The two single senior female household heads represented the two social extremes: one, an 83-year-old woman was the owner and the head of an 8-persons farm-household; she lived in a separate retirement building on the farm and had some means at her disposal. The bewildered census registrator, who evidently had little experience with spinster heads of large households, even noted her down as both *husfar* (housefather) and *husmor* (housemother), the usual terms for the married heads of household. The other female head, a 75-year-old woman, owned her own house, lived by herself all alone, and did spinning for a living.

Concerning resident kin, old single men and women were most commonly found as members of others' households, as resident kin or unrelated lodgers. Family ties were regularly stated in the census. Family relationship was far more usual than unrelated lodger status. Five men and five women had family ties to the household heads, whereas two men and two women were unrelated lodgers. All these households were very populous.

A gender difference meets the eye: the position in the household of three single men was based on retirement contracts (more will be found about such contracts below); this concerns two fathers of the present farmer,[6] and one uncle. Two men did not have contract, but were named as *rentiers* in the census, and thus contributed towards their own support. One of them was a 66-year-old man, whose 76-year-old sister was widowed and retired with contract. He was the only man explicitly mentioned

6 Those two fathers are registered as bachelors: their sons were probably born out of wedlock but recognized.

as giving a hand in the work needed for running the household: he chopped wood.

The five single women, on the other hand, who were resident kin without retirement contracts contributed with their work. The exception was an aunt, 68, with some means of her own. The other four women were active: A sister of the head, 66, did housework; three with unspecified family ties supported themselves – one (75) by knitting and spinning, one (67) as a milkmaid, and for the third (79) information is lacking, but she was staying in a family with three little daughters below age 13, so she may have had an opportunity of making herself useful.

Two old bachelors were unrelated lodgers. One, a worker (76), engaged in fowling and fishing, was lodging with a shoemaker and his small family, a wife and a 14-year-old son. The other, an 80-year-old man with retirement contract, was lodging with two bachelor brothers in their late 30s; the household also included the brothers' unmarried sister with her one-year-old son (the heads' foster son), and a 12-year-old foster daughter, an unspecified relative,

One of the two women lodgers (64) was staying in a farmer/lumberjack's household. She had some means, and was lodged in a separate building, in a household of 10. It sounds good. However, in the census she is named *innerst*, which is the traditional neutral term for lodger, but a term which by 1910 was becoming obsolete and increasingly used to designate a really poor person. Also, the house in which she was staying was *drengestua*, the lodgings of the male servants. The other female lodger, an 83-year-old *føderådspike* – i.e. a spinster with a retirement contract – supplemented her income by doing housework in a household of 14.

Women outnumber men as servants and paupers. One man (67) was a servant, doing farm- and forestry work. Two women were servants: One, 68, was a housekeeper in a 3-persons household, consisting of a widower-farmer household head (79) and an unmarried female head of household (58), who was the house owner and had some means. The other (66) was the senior female servant in a household of 14.

Finally there was an 81-year-old male pauper and three female paupers aged respectively 75, 82 and 84, all living in the Poorhouse of the village, founded in 1901.

Widowed Men and Women above 60 Years of Age

Widowed are not single in the usual sense of the term. However they cope alone and it is of interest to compare their situation to that of the single men and women. Does having been married have an influence, positive or negative, on their living conditions in old age? How do widowed people cope, from the perspective of gender and well-being?

There were 30 widowers and 35 widows over 60 years of age in 1910. Figure 3 presents the household position distribution of widowers and widows. Again we use the actual numbers, not the percentages.

Figure 3. Household position of widowers and widows aged 60 and over, Rendalen, 1910

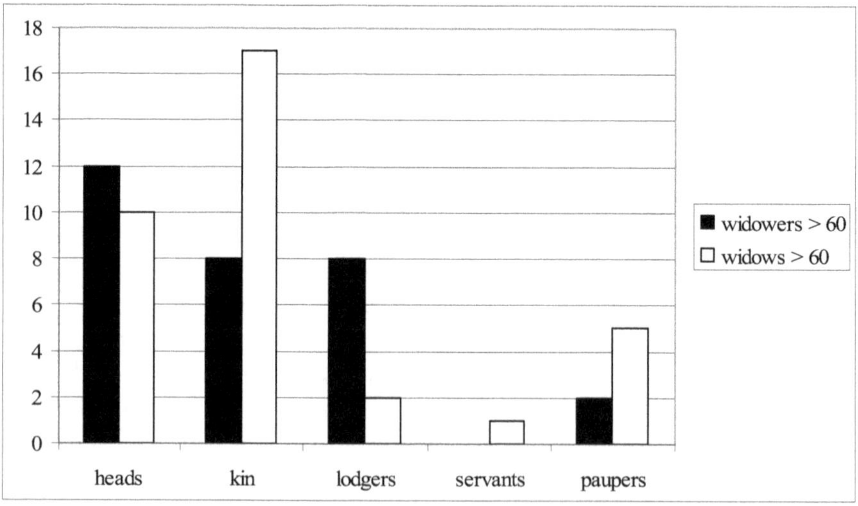

Source: 1910 census, 46% sample. See Appendix, Table 4 for figures.
Note: "Paupers" receive poor relief.

Twelve widowers aged 60 and over were heads of household – four cottars (mean age 68), four farmers (mean age 77.5), and four farmers with retirement contracts (mean age 83). Farmer household heads, whether retired or not, had larger households (mean household size of 7.8 persons as against 4.3 for cottars) and continued as heads further into old age than cottars do.

Whereas senior single women hardly ever headed households, we find ten heads of household among the widows[7] – four farmer widows, four cottar widows, as well as two widows, heads of household but in a retirement position, with retirement contract. A widow was legally of age and could head a household by herself, if she so wished. Or, she could retire if she preferred, and it was doable. Her choice would depend on age, status and inclination.

Fourteen widowers and fifteen widows were listed in the census as respectively *føderådsmann* and *føderådskone* – terms referring to their retired condition as explain below – but some of them were not actually head of household. If the couple retired together, they might after retirement refrain from joining their successors' household as simple members, and instead choose to form a separate household and thus instead acquire headship of a – usually – simpler and reduced household. The husband would certainly be the formal head as long as he was alive. But as his widow the former wife would now be in a position to act as head of household. In so far as the household usually would be simpler and less demanding to run, it may have been easier for her to retain the head position, in spite of advanced age.[8] These reflections are relevant for the six farmer widows, and they choose differently – four continued, two retired but stayed on as household head.

What about the four cottar widows? A 76-year-old worker, living alone, knitted for a living. A 66-year-old cottar's widow had a 15-year-old son, who worked as a farmhand, and was also renting lodging to a vagrant hairdresser from Bergen. A 77-year-old worker, was living with her unmarried daughter and the latter's four children, aged 0 to 17; the daughter was doing housework, washing and baking for a living, and the oldest son, 17, was doing paid farm and forestry work. An 86-year-old cottar's widow was disabled, but her spinster daughter is in charge; two foster daughters also contributed to the household: the 23-year-old one did needlework, while the 7-year-old girl was paid for by the Poverty Commission in charge with poor relief (see below).

7 In general, however, it can be claimed that there is great similarity in age and household composition for widowed heads, no matter of which gender. Farmers' widows aged 60 and over have a mean age of 73.5 and a mean household size of 5.5, while cottar widows have a mean age of 76.3 and a mean household size of 3.5.

8 When, in the 1910 census, a widow is listed as a *føderådskone* as well as *husmor* (female head of household) I have registered her as head of household.

Concerning resident kin, five widowers were fathers of household heads (mean age 78), three with retirement contracts. The oldest father, 87, was being provided for by his son, the household head, although he has a retirement contract.

An additional seven widowed men were registered by me as resident kin. Of these, five were called *føderådsmann* and appear clearly as the retired farmer, maybe even the father of the present farmer, but the relationship is not explicitly stated in the census – maybe because it is too obvious. The other two are explicitly mentioned as related.

There were seven widowed mothers of heads of household. Six were mothers of *husfar* and had retirement contracts, and in the census they are called *føderådskone*. The seventh was mother of *husmor,* 94 years, without a contract, and was not called *føderådskone*.

In addition there were three plain "mothers" (mean age 69). All three were listed as working for their living, two as milkmaids and one doing housework. Only the one doing housework was called *føderådskone*. She was 74, living in a 3-persons household with her unmarried son and daughter, both in their late 30s. The son was a farmer and at the same time telephone operator (we are in 1910), the daughter was a servant, taking care of the cattle. The widowed mothers, doing dairy work (mean age 66.5) were attached to modest households, one headed by a farm worker, the other by a farmer-lumberjack. Otherwise, the general tendency was for the father's mother and not the mother's mother to stay on as household member, a response to the equally general rule that it was a son, and not a daughter, who succeeded to the farm, and therefore the paternal grandmother possessed symbolic and real capital, based on formal and informal rights and insight accumulated over the years, and may with greater equanimity face old age. Finally there were seven widows, all named *føderådskone*, but not as *husmor*. Family relation was not mentioned, with one exception, a lodger. However, they were all enumerated as resident kin, as the men were, for the same reason as for the men.

Four widowers were unrelated lodgers: a *rentier*, a contract holder, and two still working: a 68-year-old carpenter (butcher at the same time), and a 71-year-old lumberjack. Two widows were lodgers – one did handwork like spinning (64), the other (69) did washing as well as taking part in seasonal work *(onnearbeid)*.

No widower was a servant, but one widow (70) was, in a 17 person household. Two widowers (mean age 88) and five widows (mean age 80) were paupers and inmates in the Poorhouse, which had been created in 1901.

Some marriages did not end in widowhood, but in divorce. One man and two women were divorced. The man was an 81-year-old pauper in the Poorhouse. The woman (65) – registered as a mother – was a housekeeper for a young widowed lumberjack and his baby son. The other divorced woman (74) was also a mother; she was provided for by her unmarried daughter, a 42-year-old unmarried seamstress and head of household

Gender and Well-Being in Old Age for Persons without a Life-Companion

Formal and Informal Norms

Who were responsible for the old when they could no longer provide for themselves, economically and physically? In medieval law, paupers had the right to be supported by those next of kin who should have inherited them in case they had died in wealth instead of in poverty. Negligence might be fined.

We find two main types of socially functioning families in the traditional peasant society – farmers and cottars.[9] The former comprises the more affluent households, based upon ownership or rental of a farm. The latter is clearly made of under-privileged cottars living at the discretion of the farmer on whose land the cottage was situated, and for whom the cottar might also have work obligations. The cottar family might easily ex-

9 The settlement pattern in Rendalen is characterized by separate farmsteads. The majority of the farmers were freeholders. As population increased, farms were divided up and new settlements sprang up in outlying areas. The number of farms nearly tripled from 112 in 1762 to 300 in 1900. In the eighteenth-century there was a rise of a semi-landless group called *husmenn* (cottars), renting a small piece of land on the premises of a farm. The lease period was usually for life and as part of the payment of the lease the cottar and his family might often work on the farm.

perience drastic downward social mobility and become beggars, drop-outs, regular paupers.[10]

Farmers as well as cottars regularly combined farm work with other activities, like crafts or trade. In the case of Rendalen forestry was important, and in the course of the 19th century previously non profitable forests were commercialized, strengthening social inequality in an otherwise fairly homogenous society. This comes out clearly in the 1910 census, where the clerk distinguishes between "farmer and forest owners", plain "farmers" and "farmer and lumberjack".

Farmers were in general in a position enabling them to take care of others in need of care. A system for this developed over time: *føderåd*. This is a retirement contract dating back to the Middle Ages. These contracts were oral for a long time. Eventually, however, written contracts became the rule. Such contracts were not legally compulsory, but people must have seen it to be in their own interest to formalize the agreement, and a lot of these contracts survive (Bull 2000, 92).[11] To possess rights that could be asserted and upheld in court was increasingly important as time passed, family ties weakened, and farms increasingly passed out of stable family ownership and became a commodity in the market. Also relatives further removed, or outright non-related persons, were free to make use of such contracts, and indeed might be more inclined to do so, as in their case no norms might serve them to be taken care of in old age.

The principle behind a retirement contract is the transfer of rights in exchange for certain specified goods and services. The retiring head yields headship to the successor, in exchange for provision in old age. Retirement contracts are thus intimately connected with the farm. Frequently the retirement process, however, will have been gradual – from active participation to care.

A retirement contract did not obligate the holder to live on the farm. The goods and services were in principle transferable, and if we meet with a contract holder, living in a cottar family, it may be that the old person has a retirement contract with a farm, but has moved, for whatever reason, maybe to stay with a more congenial son or daughter.

We do not know if the use of the term *føderåd* in the census actually refers to specifically termed contracts, authorized in court, or refer to the

10 60 percent of the "poorest poor" in one parish were of cottar stock in the 18th century, according to Per Assev (1990).

11 41 registered deeds from the period 1835–1865.

generalized habit in Rendalen of including old parents in the family household for life (Bull 2000).[12] People would act according to local custom, and the practice in Rendalen was to use the term *føderåd* for this practice, and the terms "føderådsmann og føderådskone"[13] for the old man and woman enjoying the contract.

Such contracts could be drawn up for other relatives as well (Bull 2000, 65). Parents would do it for handicapped children at the time of their own retirement. The new farmer, the eldest son with the birthright to take over – often not yet married at the take-over – might do it for celibate siblings who contributed substantially to the operation of the farm, such as a spinster sister who had managed the household over long time, maybe also cared for the old parents, or bachelor brothers who combined informal assistance on the farm in the busy seasons with farm and forestry work. The farm, if viable, thus served as a collective means of subsistence. This was not always possible – or desirable.

If private support was unavailable, the local community was responsible and the pauper would receive help according to a rotation system, called *legd,* already practiced in medieval time, but formally organized for the countryside only in the course of the 18th century, region by region, starting in 1741 (Dørum 1995). Poor people were passed around the parish and given the basic necessity to keep them alive, spending some two weeks on each farm belonging to that particular rotation circle. In each parish a "Poverty commission", consisting of the local vicar and some farmers, administered the poor relief. The commission had at its disposal, on the one hand a small fund based on a tiny annual tax – 8 shillings for men, 4 shillings for women – levied on the group of potentially needy, i.e. cottars, servants and farmers' children. The fund made possible to extend a small monetary contribution to poor people in their own home. Some correction houses were set up in towns, to deal with the "undeserving poor", the vagrants, supposedly unwilling to work. The "deserving poor", on the other hand, should be taken care of, each in his or her parish.

12 Separate dwelling quarters may even have been erected because this was an area with abundant building material and plenty of space.

13 This means in English, "føderådsmann" and "føderådskone".

A Comparison of the Situation in 1910 with the Earlier Period

We shall look briefly at the situation in Rendalen in 1801,[14] in order to get a backdrop against which to see the situation in 1910. What was the situation for the really destitute in Rendalen in 1801?[15] We find seven *old paupers* being passed around from farm to farm, "on the parish" as the expression goes. They were all women, aged 65 to 87. For one of them information is lacking, but three are widowed, three are single. In addition, three households and three individual persons receive public poor relief in their homes – they are all widowed or handicapped, above 60 and of cottar stock.[16]

Actually, public support was not provided until family support had been exhausted. What then about family and kin support? In almost half of all farmer households, we find kin present, but only in 12 percent of cottar households.

At age 60 and above, 18 farmers were still active, whereas 23 had retired. Cottars above age 60, however, still clung to their old living: 25 cottars above age 60 were still active, only two had retired. In all of these cases (but one), the cottar's wife was younger or of the same age as her husband.[17] Having a spouse able to work was necessary to keep the household going. In addition, in five of these cases an adult son or daughter was also present in the household. The future prospect of taking over the lease for the cottage may be an attraction for the adult children to stay with the parents.

No widower headed a cottar household, but six widows did – three were in their 50s, three were aged 60 and above. And in all cases but one – the youngest widow, aged 53 – adult children were present in the household, ready to take over. In some cases the take-over had already taken place. One grand-parent couple, one grandfather as well as eight grand-

14 For 1801, we use the entire census and not sample figures.

15 In Rendalen, in the 1801 census, 29 children are registered as foster children – these are not necessarily poor but may be orphans, in need of care and without family and kin to help.

16 In one case, the husband, aged 44, is probably not mentally fit; his wife is registered in the census as head of household and "widow" for lack of a better term for something so extraordinary!

17 Of the 11 cases of husband aged 60–69, 8 of the wives are under 60; in the 6 cases where the husband is 70–79, the same is true in 5 cases.

mothers (all but one aged above 60) were staying in their adult child's cottar household.[18]

The old contributed towards their support. All but one of twelve relatives present in cottar households were aged above 60. Five of eight grandmothers staying with their adult children in the latter's cottar households had a retirement contract *(føderåd)*, two did handiwork for a living. They all had a place to live, but they made a personal contribution towards their support.

The situation around 1865 has also been looked into (Bull 2000, 90–95). In 1865 the majority of parents with adult children was either on contract or worked for their living. In some cases the children were unable – or unwilling – to help. One blind old man lived with his son, a cottar, and received support from the Poverty commission. The wife was on the rotation system, as described above. She might have stayed with another son, who had a small farm, but an old uncle was already on contract there. At one farm, they took care of their uncle, but his wife was on rotation. An old widow on retirement contract remarried: she took her meals as before together with the household heads, but her new spouse had to make do for himself, and what he could scrape together.

If the situation in 1910 has a lot in common with the past, changes did take place. In Norway, the old rotation system was abolished by the Poor Law of 1900, and, in Rendalen, a regular Poor House was set up in 1901 to accommodate the most miserable of the old people.

In 1910, roughly 11 percent of the population was above the age of 60, the same as in 1801.[19] The distribution between the different civil statuses changed, however, in the course of the century – only slightly for women, more markedly for men (Table 1).

18 One elderly couple (he aged 64-she aged 62), related to the household heads, had a private pension.

19 In 1801, 183 individuals were aged 60 and over out of 1,685 (10.8%). In 1910, 476 individuals were aged 60 and over out of 4,255 (11.1%). The sex ratio, however, was higher for the aged 60 and over in 1910, 113 men per 100 women as against 89 men per 100 women in 1801.

Table 1. Marital status of men and women aged 60 and over in Rendalen, 1801 and 1910. Percentages

	MEN				*WOMEN*			
	Single	Married	Widowers	Total	Single	Married	Widows	Total
1801	22	69	9	100	12	46	41	100
1910	14	59	27	100	14	50	36	100

Source: 1801 census; 1910 census, 46% sample.
Note: One divorced man and two divorced women are included among the widowed in 1910. For figures, see Appendix, Table 3 below.

The most striking difference is the relative rise in the proportion of widowers. The most probable explanation for this change is the decrease in remarriage. Widowers aged 60 and over counted for only 9 per cent in 1801. In 1910 they had tripled their share. The census 1910 does not, as does the census 1801, give information of the "serial number" of the marriage. In the earlier period (1733–1828) we find that for all age groups every third widower remarried, whereas only one in ten widows did. Even after age 60, 12 percent of widowers remarried, but no widow did (Sogner 1976, 339). Thus widowers re-entered the group of married men, most probably with a younger wife and an increased chance of keeping a living wife well into old age. It is a fair assumption that, for men, having a living spouse in good shape must have been one of the most influential factors for securing well-being in old age.

The Advantage of Ever-married Seniors over Never-married

The data presented in this chapter conveys the overall impression that the single men and women aged 60 and over were not doing as well as widowers and widows (Table 2). The widowed have by definition been married. This indicates a more favourable start in adult life for this group than for of the permanently single. To succeed in the marriage market they had to have had a comparative advantage of sorts – material wealth, good physical condition, work capacity, etc. In addition, while married they had years to accumulate rights, assets, own children and affines – all of which were presumably advantageous in later life. The problematic situation of the divorced – a special case of singleness – accentuates this reasoning.

Table 2. Household position and marital status of men and women aged 60 and over, without a life-companion, in Rendalen, 1910. Percentages.

	MEN				*WOMEN*			
Household position	Single	Widowed	Divorced	Total	Single	Widowed	Divorced	Total
Head	43.7	40		40.5	14.3	28.5		23.6
Resident kin	31.3	40		36.2	35.7	48.5	50	45
Lodger	12.6	14.4		12.7	14.3	5.8		7.8
Servant	6.2	0		2.1	14.3	3	50	7.8
Pauper*	6.2	6.6	100	8.5	21.4	14.2		15.8
Total	100	100	100	100	100	100	100	100

Source: 1910 census, 46% sample.
Note: For figures, see Appendix, Table 4 below. Individual registered as "paupers" received poor relief from the parish.

It matters little for men without a life-companion whether they were widowed or single to achieve a position of headship of household in old age. Widowed or single, men held a favoured position as household head – only a slight downward tendency is discernible, from 44 percent to 40 percent. For women, however, matrimonial status was far more important. As widowed they were heads of household twice as frequently as when single. In either case they attained this top position much less frequently than men – 14.3 percent as single, 28.5 percent as widows. However, the households that women headed were often quite miserable, seriously casting doubt on the choice of this variable as a significant sign of well-being. "Household head" appears to need some qualification if it is to serve as an indicator for well-being, materially speaking. All three one-person households found in the Rendalen sample, irrespective of the gender of the head, belonged to the unprivileged.

At the other extreme– the positions of servant and "pauper" representing failure in old age – widowed men were only slightly better off than bachelors – 6.6 percent as against 12.4 percent. This variable, however, had the clearest implications for single women. While widows stood for 17.2 percent, single women counted for 35.7 percent. From a gender perspective women were clearly disadvantaged.

The proportions of men and women aged 60 and over who lived in households headed by others were very even: only 10.2 percent are unrelated lodgers (12.7 percent for males, 7.8 percent for females). More women than men, whether single or widowed stayed as resident kin in the household, but staying with kin was the norm, for men as well as for women: approximately one third of all single men and women are resident kin. In fact, if we look at the position as head of household combined with that of resident kin, we find that 50 percent of all single women over 60 were either household head or resident kin; for single men the figure is 75 percent. Family norms in Rendalen changed slowly, probably more slowly than in many other local societies. The old practice of cross-generational cohabitation continued in Rendalen well into the 1950s (Bull 2006, 92)! So much for our findings concerning household position of senior individuals by gender.

Gender and Well-Being when Facing Old Age

Two general observations may be added to our previous conclusions concerning well-being of males and women aged 60 and over living without a life-companion. First, women more often than men tend to be listed as workers. Both men and women contributed towards their own support, either through their own labour, or by means of other assets – retirement contracts dominated in this respect, but also through "own means", or renting living quarters to lodgers. However, in the census this information tends to concern specified work more frequently for women than for men. This is the case, even though women tended to be older. Mean age for single women aged 60 and over was 73.9, while for single men it was only 70.7. The same discrepancy is found for the widowed: mean age for widows was 79.1, while 76 for widowers.

Our second remark is that old people, in 1910 Rendalen, found themselves in populous households and were not isolated. Both genders stayed in households with many people – mean household size for single women was 7.8, for widows 6.6, while similarly for men it reached only 6.3 and 7.2.

These are interesting observations when looked at from today's perspective – when a meaningful life so often is seen as dependent upon work identity and unhappiness is associated with loneliness. In rural Norway, at the turn of the century 1900, senior men and women were rarely living alone. Women who were without a life-companion earned often their living or could benefit from family help, if possible in the frame of a retirement contract arranged with a younger family member. If very poor, seniors, men and women, received some poor relief.

References

ASSEV, Per, 1990, *Rangspersoner, bønder og husmenn. Befolkningsutvikling i Luster på 1700–tallet.* Dissertation in history, University of Oslo.

BULL, Hans Henrik, 2000, *Hushold og generasjonsskifter i Rendalen 1762–1900.* Dissertation in history, University of Oslo.

–, 2006, "Marriage decisions in a peasant society. The role of the family of origin with regard to adult children's choice of marriage partner and the timing of their marriage in Rendalen, Norway, 1750–1900", *Acta Humaniora,* Dissertation Nr. 268, University of Oslo.

DØRUM, Knut, 1995, "Fattigdommen på landsbygda på 1700–tallet", *Heimen,* 32, pp. 73–83.

HOMLONG, Beate, 1995, *"...i vores eiende lemstue...". Kårskipnaden i Etne 1716–1901.* Dissertation in history, University of Bergen.

LASLETT, Peter, 1972, "Introduction", in Peter LASLETT and Richard WALL (eds), *Household and Family in Past Time,* Cambridge, Cambridge University Press, pp. 1–90.

SOGNER, Sølvi, 1976, *Folkevekst og flytting. En historisk-demografisk studie av 1700–årenes Øst-Norge,* Oslo, Universitetsforlaget.

Appendix

Table 3. Marital status of men and women aged 60 and over in Rendalen, 1801 and 1910. Numbers

	MEN				WOMEN			
N	Single	Married	Widowers	Total	Single	Married	Widows	Total
1801	19	59	8	86	12	45	40	97
1910	16	68	31	115	14	51	37	102

Source: 1801 census; 1910 census, 46% sample.
Note: One divorced man and two divorced women are included among the widowed in 1910

Table 4. Household position and marital status of men and women aged 60 and over, without a life-companion, in Rendalen, 1910. Numbers

	MEN				WOMEN			
	Single	Widowed	Divorced	Total	Single	Widowed	Divorced	Total
Heads	7	12		19	2	10		12
Resident kin	5	12		17	5	17	1	23
Lodgers	2	4		6	2	2		4
Servants	1	-		1	2	1	1	4
Paupers*	1	2	1	4	3	5		8
Total	16	30	1	47	14	35	2	51

Source: 1910 census, 46% sample.
Note: Individual registered as "paupers" received poor relief from the parish.

Provisions for Care and Neighborhood Funds in Early Modern Kyoto

Mary Louise NAGATA

This study addresses the resources and assistance available to residents of Kyoto under the Tokugawa regime in the first half of the nineteenth century. A previous study addressed the emergency assistance provided by the state and city governments in times of famine, flood, fire or other disaster that would cause the price of rice to suddenly jump (Nagata and Hamano 2006). This study addresses assistance at a more local, less drastic every day level provided by neighborhood funds and other provisions made for care.

In the European context, studies of public assistance usually focus on larger administrative units such as the Poor Laws of various nations like Great Britain and how they were administered at the local level, or the later system of welfare that replaced the Poor Law as regular assistance provided by the state. Charitable institutions established by or through religious institutions such as orphanages, and established by various voluntary organizations also provided assistance for targeted groups in need such as unmarried mothers, abandoned children, or the widows of guild members.

In Japan, the state provided assistance in case of major emergency in the form of one time distributions of rice and cash, leaving regular assistance to local organizations. Kyoto neighborhood funds are one example of resources collected and provided by the local community. Buddhist temples also provided assistance as did trade associations. The *Shingaku* movement, popular among large merchant houses, also provided public assistance in times of emergency, but these other resources will not be the focus of this study for reasons of time and space.

The first part of this investigation addresses the neighborhood funds and requests for assistance from them. This part addresses the source of these neighborhood funds, their administration, what kinds of assistance they were used for, and who received the assistance under what conditions.

Early modern Japan was a stem-family society and certainly the family was the first resource for assistance. Most households in Kyoto, however, were nuclear households and the temporary nature of most residences in this highly mobile population meant that multi-generation households may have been difficult to form or maintain. The second step in this investigation, therefore, will be analysis of co-residence, especially of the elderly, and the provisions for care by family and kin. Widows are of particular concern for this analysis.

Kyoto Neighborhoods: Administration, Mediation and Assistance

Kyoto was the political capital of Japan at the beginning of the Tokugawa period (1600–1868). When Tokugawa Ieyasu established his government in Edo, Kyoto continued to be the political center for western Japan and the potential focal point for rebellion because the emperor and the old court nobility continued to live there. For this reason, the Tokugawa regime established two offices, the Kyoto deputy *(Kyoto shoshidai)* and the castellan of Nijo castle *(Nijō jōban)* to represent the shogun's government in western Japan and keep watch over the imperial court. Two city magistrates, the *higashi bugyō* in the east and the *nishi bugyō* in the west, were entrusted with the administrative control of the city's other political and legal affairs with a third magistrate, the *kura bugyō*, in charge of the treasury and financial affairs (Kamada 2000, 343, 353).

The details of city administration, however, were controlled by Kyoto neighborhoods. Kyoto neighborhoods had already established an autonomous identity and administration before the mid sixteenth century when Japan's process of reunification began, resulting in the Pax Tokugawa under the Tokugawa regime. The unifiers and the new regime respected this autonomy. Each autonomous neighborhood had its own administrative officials and laws called *machi bure* or *shikimoku* although the neighborhoods varied when they compiled their own laws and how they chose their officials (Kyoto City Library for Historical Documents 1999).

Kyoto neighborhoods were each about one city block in size with all of the residents that lived on either side of the street in that block included in the neighborhood. The administration consisted of an "elder" called the *machi toshiyori* and three representatives called *gonin gumi*.[1]

These officials compiled the annual population registers and other various registers required by the state. In the process, they also kept track of births, deaths, marriages, divorces, adoptions, leases of land or housing, wills, debts and other contracts, the travels of other household heads in the neighborhood, and various moves into and out of the neighborhood. According to the laws of many neighborhoods, these officials also mediated civil disputes of various kinds and were available to consult for advice (Kyoto City Library for Historical Documents 1999).[2] When public assistance was distributed, these officials calculated how much to apply for and how to distribute the assistance.

The neighborhoods also formed tight communities that were the basis for civil society and various activities. Neighborhood residents paid regular dues amounting to residential taxes to the neighborhood administration; a portion of these funds were remitted to the city government and a portion was kept for neighborhood use. The neighborhood administration also collected fees paid on the occasions of weddings, adoptions, headship succession and retirement and for various activities. They organized excursions to local festivals and hosted parties for various celebrations. Although there is little information or research yet detailing the exact process of determining how the monies were used, the officials in the neighborhood administration were likely responsible for this task, although decisions may also have been made in councils of heads of house-

1 The representatives were technically the heads of five-household responsibility groups from the system of shared responsibility the Tokugawa regime adapted from Ming dynasty China's *li jia* system. Kyoto neighborhoods, however, often had forty or more households. The population registers of Seidō neighborhood, for example, record twenty-three official residences and around thirty households per year while Sujikaibashi neighborhood registers record fifty-two official residences and more than seventy households per year. Nevertheless, both neighborhoods had three officials called *gonin gumi*. Obviously, the *gonin gumi* represented many more than five households each, even in a small neighborhood like Seidō. Although there were differences by neighborhood as to how these officials were chosen for office, the positions were often rotated among male heads of household in the neighborhood. The rotation could include all male heads of household or be limited to households that owned their residences or various other criteria determined by the neighborhood.

2 The laws of Takoyakushi neighborhood are explicit about these duties.

hold. The fees and dues collected from neighborhood residents formed a fund that residents borrowed from in need and repaid with interest. Money from this fund also provided dowries for foundlings to be adopted by households in other parts of the city or outside the city and could provide some funds for rebuilding or other assistance (Nagata 2003a). The main focus of this investigation is the assistance provided from this fund to neighborhood residents and outsiders who had claim on the neighborhood community.

Adoption and Provisions for the Care of Children

Adoption in early modern Japan was usually a transaction in which a member of one family – often a son, daughter or sibling of the head of household – became a member of another family, normally as a son or daughter of the adoptive household. The transaction included a dowry that accompanied the adopted child and was typically paid in two installments, possibly to allow a transition period and oversight regarding the care of the child in the adoptive household. If the adoption did not work out for some reason, the dowry would be returned with the child.

Adoption was a common feature of the early modern Japanese family system and an integral part of the process of headship succession and inheritance. Recruiting a capable heir appears to have been the main function of adoption in rural villages (Kurosu and Ochiai 1995; Kurosu 1998). In Kyoto, too, many adoption contracts included the stipulation that the adopted child would be the heir of the adoptive household and succeed to headship, even when the child was a girl or adopted as an infant. Kyoto residents, however, also used adoption as a way to provide care for otherwise unwanted or inconvenient children (Nagata 2003a). This section will focus on the role of neighborhood communities in using adoption to provide care for foundlings and the neighborhood fund to provide dowry and other necessary funding for their care.

The following documents detail the discovery and subsequent provisions for care of a foundling child who had been abandoned and found in Taishiyama neighborhood in the commercial center of Kyoto city. Not only did the neighborhood find a couple to adopt the child, hiding the fact that the child was a foundling, but the neighborhood paid a substantial amount of money to the couple for their trouble.

> A baby boy (the document names him Isaburō) was discovered in Taishiyama neighborhood in the fifth evening hour (7–9 pm) on the twenty-fifth day of the eleventh month of 1806.[3] He was found abandoned on the west side of Aburanokoji Street in the middle of the block on the north side of the shop Ibarakiya Heishichi was renting from Tsukokuya Jinbei. The neighborhood immediately undertook his care and reported their find the next morning of the twenty-sixth to the office of the magistrate of the month. The West magistrate ordered that the neighborhood should care for the child and ask around for someone to receive him. Upon asking around, the neighborhood found a decent couple and, knowing they (the wife) still had milk, reported this to the magistrate. After discussion on the last day of the month, (the neighborhood) decided on the first (of the next month) to write up a contract, omitting that the child was a foundling, and added some money. The neighborhood community asked Ioriya Sōbei (a resident of the neighborhood) to act as the child's parent and arranged for Wakasaya Isuke and his wife Tomi to adopt the child.[4]

The money allocated for this transaction is itemized at the end of this document as: brush and ink: 100 *mon*[5] and 200 *mon* respectively, fees paid to the neighborhood agents: 1 *monme* to Takeuchi and 1 *monme* to Fujii, plus five *mai* of white silver and 100 *hiki* of copper to the caretaker sent by Zenbei, and 13 *monme* for one cotton cloth, possibly swaddling for the baby. The above document was attached to the adoption contract which acknowledged the receipt of five *mai* of white silver.

The adoptive parents agreed that they would take very good care of this newborn ("born this year") baby boy named Isaburō and promised that they would not later send him into service in a distant province or any shady occupation such as in a tea house or as an actor. Moreover, they

3 Japan was following the lunar calendar, so this date is not precisely the same as November 25, 1806. The exact date, however, is not important to the argument.

4 This document was attached as an addendum to the neighborhood's copy of the adoption contract, Adoptive father Wakasaya Isuke, wife Tomi, guarantor Hiranoya Rokubei [to Ioriya Sōbei], "Yōshi issatsu no koto," Adoption contract, 12/1/1806, Taishiyama neighborhood collection B9, Kyoto City Library for Historical Documents.

5 A *mon* is the basic coin for copper close to the value of 180cc (two bowls) of rice. One *monme* is 3.75 grams usually used as the basic valuation for silver money; 100 *monme* equals one *mai* or 375 grams. One *hiki* is 25 *mon* or approximately equal to 25 dollars.

promised to pay the money back if the adoption did not work out and the guarantor promised to mediate and settle any problems that should occur.[6]

When a child was discovered abandoned in a Kyoto neighborhood, the child was temporarily given into the care of the neighborhood gatekeeper or treasurer, an employed position in the neighborhood administration, who cared for the child while neighborhood residents searched for a couple willing to adopt the child. They typically looked for a couple who had recently lost a child so the adoptive mother still had milk. Hiding the fact that the child was a foundling was also important because foundling children could be subject to discrimination and poor treatment from the assumption that only women of suspicious origins would abandon their children (Sugawara 1994). Appointing a neighborhood resident, usually the gatekeeper or treasurer employed by the neighborhood, to represent himself as the natural parent of the child was necessary for hiding the fact that the child was a foundling. The contract stipulation that the adoptive parents would not send the child to work in a "shady occupation such as in a tea house or as an actor" was also partly a recognition of the potential discrimination against foundling children together with the possibility that the adoptive parents might plan to profit by selling the child into prostitution. Actors and employees in tea houses were known for their connections to prostitution as a profession.

Taishiyama neighborhood residents may have believed that Isaburō was now taken care of and they could forget about him now that the formal requirements of a contract were fulfilled. However, the adoptive parents Wakasaya Isuke and his wife Tomi returned two years later in the sixth month of 1808 claiming that his care had caused unexpected hardship for Tomi, who had been ill. After some discussion, the neighborhood paid an additional five *kan* in copper coins and Isuke promised not to bother them again.[7]

Isaburō was not the first foundling that Taishiyama neighborhood took care of. Another document in the collection dated 1800 records how the neighborhood provided for the care of a lost child found in the neighbor-

6 Adoptive parent Wakasaya Isuke, wife Tomi, guarantor Hiranoya Rokubei [to Ioriya Sōbei], "Yōshi issatsu no koto," Adoption contract, 12/1/1806, Taishiyama neighborhood collection B9-10, Kyoto City Library for Historical Documents.

7 1 *kan* equals 1,000 *mon*. Adoptive parent Wakasaya Isuke, wife Tomi, guarantor Nataneya Zenbei [to Ioriya Sōbei and the neighborhood association], "Issatsu", Receipt of assistance money, 6/1808, Taishiyama neighborhood collection B11, Kyoto City Library for Historical Documents.

hood on the twenty-second day of the New Year and arranged for a farmer to adopt the child with a dowry of 100 *ryō* (1875 grams) of silver.

Providing for the care of foundling children apparently could be an expensive undertaking, yet the neighborhood community was able to provide funding for this charitable activity. Moreover, they were expected to do so. The money came from the neighborhood fund of dues and various fees collected from households residing in the neighborhood. A document from Taishiyama neighborhood dated 1722 (Kyōhō 7) details the dues each household should pay into the fund. These dues formed a kind of residential tax with renters paying less than owners.[8] From this money, 600 *mon* was paid each month to the gatekeeper for the neighborhood and the remainder saved for other costs or needs (Hayashiya 1981, 83).

Adoption was clearly considered the best way to provide for foundling children. Other research has shown that unwanted children in other situations were also provided for through adoption (Nagata 2003a). The family of the child usually provided the funds for the adoption and thereby for the basic care for the child. Foundling children, however, had no family to provide either care or dowry. The willingness and even public expectation that the neighborhood community would do the same for the child of a stranger highlights that the neighborhood community was the basis for civil society and charitable activity. The neighborhoods pooled their resources to maximize their own survival, but also to assist in the survival of others.

In summary, Kyoto neighborhoods used the funds they regularly collected from their resident members through dues and other fees to provide assistance as necessary. Neighborhood communities went to some effort to provide care for foundlings abandoned in their neighborhoods and used money from the neighborhood fund to provide the adoption dowries for these children, both male and female. Moreover, this mechanism was the preferred method for providing care for such children and expected by the state. The neighborhood responsibility toward the foundlings, however, did not end with the adoption contract as the adoptive parents could still

8 In 1722 there were 46 residences owned by their residents. Forty-five owners paid 39 *mon* each and one household was exempt from dues for the year, acting in the administrative capacity as the neighborhood elder instead. In addition, these 45 households paid 2 *kan* 812 *mon* each month for a total of 33 *kan* 748 *mon* per year. Renters were divided between those who had residences facing the street and those who rented housing behind the other residences. Frontside renters paid 12 *mon* each and backside renters paid 8 *mon* each.

claim assistance from the neighborhood based on the fiction that a neighborhood resident was the natural parent of the child.

The neighborhood community was also the basis for local civil society and used their funds to go on excursions, attend festivals and other social activities. Examination of the social activities is outside the scope of this study. However, the fund also provided a kind of safety net that neighborhood residents could borrow from in times of need as explained in the next section.

Retirement, Succession and Provisions for Elderly Care

One of the general perspectives on elderly care in stem-family societies is the implication that one child is "persuaded" to stay home and take care of the old parents in exchange for inheriting all or a larger portion of the family assets. However, families in early modern Japan had a slightly different perspective on this issue.

First, headship succession was not inheritance of the family assets, but succession to the responsibility to manage those assets. Adopted heirs recruited from outside the family, could not decide to pass the assets out of the family or divide the assets without the agreement of the larger kinship group (Katakura 1986). In other words, headship succession did not mean transfer of ownership rights, but of management responsibilities. This was even more an issue when the family was a business or branch of a business that was in debt. This section addresses the relation between headship succession and provisions for care in three respects. First is the retirement and continued co-residence of the former head. This would seem to follow the exchange of position and control of assets for care thesis. The second addresses provisions for care that were made without co-residence in a major succession dispute. The third and main focus will be requests for loans from the neighborhood fund based on claims of "hardship" with relation to inherited property or businesses.

Analysis of retirement and co-residence in this study begins with the population registers of nine Kyoto neighborhoods compiled annually, between 1842 and 1868. The Kyoto religious and population investigation registers called *Shūmon ninbetsu aratame chō* provide excellent demographic data for this quantitative part of the analysis. The registers were compiled in the ninth month of each lunar year and list each resident according to religious sect and household residence. Each listing records basic demographic information for men and women such as name, age and relation to head of household as well as the birth province of each person listed and this information is the basis for analysis of co-residence. There are population registers compiled before 1843 for many of the neighborhoods in the data sample, but the Kyoto registers do not record age before 1843, so these earlier registers will not be used for this analysis. The neighborhoods providing this data represent a broad cross-section of the common population of Kyoto. Members of the nobility, clergy or warrior classes, however, were not included in the registration.

Sujikaibashi and Hanaguruma neighborhoods are both located in the Nishijin silk textile district of the city and their residents were heavily involved in the production of silk textiles. Shijō Nakanomachi, Takoyakushi, Seidō, Taishiyama and Sannō neighborhoods are all located in or near the commercial center of the city and their residents include many enterprises of varying sizes with many employees. Shimizu neighborhood in the south edge of the city was a suburban neighborhood containing a few farmers and many peddlers. Finally, located near the imperial palace and one of the main highways into town, Matsu'ue neighborhood was home to several restaurants, tea houses and inns.

The data analysis is based on person years rather than individuals. Ten person years could be ten individuals observed once each, two individuals observed five times each or many other combinations. The total person years observed in the combined data set are 14,437, but differential coverage means that any given year there are 100–1200 people observed. See Annex 1 for observations, per neighborhood, per year.

The analysis begins with examination of the members of each household for co-residence, by gender, from the perspective of each individual with servants, parents, spouse, children, siblings, other stem kin such as grandparents or grandchildren, non-stem kin such as aunts or nephews, and other non-kin who are not servants such as boarders listed within the household. I include fictive kin such as in-laws together with the real kin groups. The information on co-residence was used to calculate the proportion of person years spent living with each type of co-resident by five-year age groups and sex including those recorded as living alone. The result is the probability of co-residence with various kin or non-kin.

Examination of the co-residence of elderly men and women, defined as sixty years and older, in these population registers reveals some interesting perspectives on headship succession. Table 1 examines, for elderly men and women, co-residence with spouse, co-residence with both spouse and child, co-residence with child, but not spouse, and co-residence with spouse, but not child. The third category should be mostly widows, but some spouses may have been absent for reasons other than mortality. The fourth category would suggest couples that may have chosen to live independently.

Table 1. Elderly coresidence with/without spouse and children, aged 60 and over, by gender, in person years and probability, nine Kyoto neighborhoods (1842–1868)

Co-residence	*Women*	*Men*	*Total*
Spouse	89	295	384
Spouse and child	49	211	260
Child, not spouse	356	77	433
Spouse, not child	40	84	124
Total person years*	522	418	940
Probabilities of co-residence			
With spouse	0,170	0,706	0,409
Spouse and child	0,094	0,505	0,277
Child, not spouse	0,682	0,184	0,461
Spouse, not child	0,077	0,201	0,132

Sources: Population registers *(Shūmon ninbetsu aratame chō)* for Sujikaibashi, Hanaguruma, Shijō Nakanomachi, Takoyakushi, Seidō, Taishiyama, Sannō, Shimizu and Matsu'ue neighborhoods.
Note: * Categories of coresidence are overlapping.

Table 2 examines elderly men and women who have been listed as "parent" of the head of household for co-residence with and without spouses and co-residence with grandchildren (or great-grandchildren). This analysis focuses on couples and widows/widowers who have retired from headship and continue to co-reside with the new head couple.

Men had a 25 percent probability of retiring, passing headship to their heirs and continuing to live with them after retirement. By retiring, these men could better control the succession process ensuring that headship indeed went to the heir of choice. They could also continue to advise the new head, providing for a smooth transition process. Most were still living with their wives and the majority had co-resident grandchildren. We can picture them enjoying an easy, but active life in retirement.

Table 2. Retired elderly, aged 60 and over, by gender, coresidence with/without spouse and grandchildren, in person years and probability, nine Kyoto neighborhoods (1842–1868)

Co-residence	*Women*	*Men*	*Total*
with spouse	22	72	94
without spouse	311	29	340
with grandchildren	195	70	265
Total person years*	333	101	434
Probabilities			
with spouse	0,066	0,713	0,217
without spouse	0,934	0,287	0,783
with grandchildren	0,586	0,693	0,611
Probability of retirement	0,638	0,242	0,462

Sources: Population registers *(Shūmon ninbetsu aratame chō)* for Sujikaibashi, Hanaguruma, Shijō Nakanomachi, Takoyakushi, Seidō, Taishiyama, Sannō, Shimizu and Matsu'ue neighborhoods.
Note: * Categories of coresidence are overlapping.

Men were far more likely than women not to retire, but keep headship until their death, even though co-resident with their likely adult children. These men remained active and enjoyed the continued care of their wives as well as the assistance of their children. Upon their deaths, their widows continued to live with their adult children and grandchildren. So, the stem-family system did appear to provide for the care of the old couple, especially if they had children who were willing to prepare for the responsibility of headship as well as taking ownership. At the same time, while some elderly couples did not live with children, this situation was much less common. Elderly couples did not commonly choose to live alone as shown in Table 1.

A complicated inheritance and succession dispute in the Fukui family in the period 1820–1834 shows that retired couples sometimes did move out and live separate from the new head. Fukui Sōuemon adopted an heir in 1819 and the new Fukui Sakuzaemon succeeded to headship in 1823, at which time Sōuemon moved out to live with his mistress in a separate household. In this case, the adopted head Sakuzaemon disowned his adoptive father Sōuemon, but also paid him 600 *ryō* of gold to provide Sōuemon's living expenses for the rest of his life (Nagata 2003b).[9] A later aspect of the dispute after Sōuemon's death in 1831 was Sakuzaemon's responsibilities to care for Sōuemon's daughters by his mistress Iwa. When Iwa provided proof that Sōuemon had acknowledged the three girls as his daughters, the legal settlement required Sakuzaemon to provide for their care as part of his duties as head of the Fukui family and business (Nagata 2003b). When Iwa died in 1836, Sakuzaemon provided for their care through adoption with another large monetary settlement of 5 *kan* (or 100 *ryō*) (Nagata 2003a). Here again we can see the use of adoption to provide care for unwanted children, as discussed in the previous section above.

The analyses at this point suggest that the head of the family in the larger sense, not just of the household, was expected to provide care and support for all family members, male and female, as part of the duties of headship. The best way for a person to ensure he or she would be cared for in old age was to marry, have children and have an organization to pass on to one of them, or to adopt an heir who would take on the responsibility of care together with management of the family assets and family business. What happened, however, when that business was in debt? That was the case for Fukui Sōuemon that led him to adopt Sakuzaemon as his heir in the first place, but most families would not be so fortunate to find such a solution to the problem.

The neighborhood funds provided another resource that young men who had just succeeded to headship could draw on in need. Since these funds were formed from money that each resident household paid to the neighborhood community administration, they could be regarded as a financial resource pool. Two brief case studies provide information on the level of assistance that could be had from this source.

In the first case study, Omiya Genbei inherited the house, property and name of Omiya Genbei in 1817 as he succeeded to headship. At the end of

9 This is a very large sum approximately equal to 3600 grams of silver. One *ryō* of gold was the value of 18 liters of rice thought to be enough to feed one adult man for one year and approximately a modern value of $1,000 USD. Fukui Souemon, Bigoya Nofu, Hishiya Tomi and Sayo [to Fukui Sakuzaemon and Tambaya Gensuke], "Issatsu", Notice of single payment to Souemon of living expenses for the remainder of his life, 7/1823, Fukui Sakuzaemon Masu Za collection.

1822, Genbei had some unspecified financial trouble and borrowed 50 *ryō* from the neighborhood promising to repay it as soon as possible. This history is reviewed in a document written in 1827 when Genbei requested and received a further delay in payment of this debt claiming that he now owed his clients as well.[10] There is no further information available regarding this case.

In the second case study, Fujiya Gisuke inherited a branch of a larger business upon the death of his father Gihei, in 1862. Taking his father's name, he promised to take care of the business and give it over to his mother Naka if there should be any trouble.[11] He was later asked to sell the house and property to help the main house pay some debts. They had already received a down payment of 250 *monme* of silver on that sale. Gihei borrowed money from the neighborhood to return the down payment and separate his branch from the main business. In the sixth month of 1864 Gihei had been slowly repaying the money owed the neighborhood and now paid off the debt including any late fees he had accrued claiming that the business had been unexpectedly profitable.[12]

The documents for these cases do not fully explain the circumstances behind the hardship they claimed for borrowing money from these neighborhoods. Nevertheless, both cases were related to the headship succession process and both heirs borrowed money from their neighborhoods to invest in their businesses and, in the case of Gihei, continue providing care for his mother Naka.

In summary, the head of a family had the responsibility for managing the assets of that family and providing support and care for its members. Although many men seemed to prefer to retain headship until death, others chose to retire and pass the responsibilities of headship on to the next generation knowing that the next head was also obligated to support them. Usually the parents or widowed mother of the new head received this support through co-residence. However, the new head was expected to

10 (Omiya Genbei), "Issatsu no koto," Agreement, 3/1827, Hakurakuten neighborhood collection B3, Kyoto City Library of Historical Documents.

11 Main house Fujiya Yasubei, deceased Gihei's wife Naka, his son Gisuke [to the elders Sumiya Jizaemon and the neighborhood association], "Issatsu", Succession agreement, 3/1862, Shiogama neighborhood collection, Kyoto City Library of Historical Documents.

12 Fujiya Gihei and mother Naka [to the elders and Shiogama neighborhood association], "On negai mōsu kōjō sho," Request, 6/1864, Shiogama neighborhood collection B20, Kyoto City Library for Historical Documents.

provide support even when other members of the family lived separately. This support was not only provided to the former head couple, but also to other members of the family including the acknowledged children of a mistress. One way to provide this support was co-residence, but other arrangements such as adoption could also be found. If there were serious financial difficulties in providing care, a Kyoto resident could appeal to the neighborhood he or she lived in and borrow money from the neighborhood funds.

Gender Differences in Co-residence, Life Course Transitions and Provisions for Care

The patterns of co-residence shown reveal certain gender differences in co-residence and the success, or not, of provisions for care of the elderly. These patterns also reveal the gendered pattern of the life course as children were born, sometimes into three-generation households; they left home to enter domestic service, but with multiple departures and returns, until they finally left home to marry or bring a spouse home to co-reside with the parents. Then children were born to them, the old parents died, a spouse might die, children began to leave home, but one of them remained home bringing in a spouse, and grandchildren were born as the cycle repeated itself in the next generation.

There were a number of definite transitions in this life course, with the ages and even the content of these transitions varying by gender. I call a "transition age" the age when co-residence with a certain category that had been extremely common, such as living with parents from birth until leaving home, falls below fifty percent, and these ages often represent the median age for a life course transition (Hareven 2000). Transition in the reverse direction occurred when co-residence with a certain category that had been rare rose above fifty percent. In our Kyoto sample, the transition age for leaving home to enter service was twelve for boys and sixteen for girls (Nagata 2008). The transition ages varied by gender, but also varied whether servants were included or excluded from the calculation. The transition age for beginning co-residence with a spouse, for example, is 29 for men and 25 for women when servants are included, but 28 for men and 23 for women when servants are excluded.

The transition age analyses are shown in Table 3.[13] The key transition ages for understanding elderly co-residence are the beginning of co-residence with spouse, the end of co-residence with parents, whether because the child moved to a separate household or the parents died, and the end of co-residence with spouse. The transition ages for beginning co-residence with spouse are close to the end of co-residence with siblings highlighting both that married siblings did not co-reside and unmarried siblings tended to leave the household when one sibling married. The end of co-residence with parents is a few years after the beginning of co-residence with spouse suggesting that newlywed couples were likely to spend a few years co-resident with the parents of one or the other spouse. On the other hand, there is no transition agc for the end of co-residence with children suggesting that the end of co-residence with parents was the combined result of the stem-family mechanism with mortality. Only one child couple co-resided with a parent couple while the others lived separately and most people not only had children, but continued to live with at least one child until death. Moreover, elderly residents had a good chance of living with their grandchildren if they lived long enough as shown by the transition age for beginning of co-residence with stem kin (Table 3).

A final aspect of the transition age analyses shows that women ended co-residence with their spouses at fifty-five, but that men had no such transition. This difference could be the consequence of several factors. Men tended to be older than their wives and elderly male mortality was likely higher than elderly female mortality. Moreover, men may have been quicker and more likely to remarry than women when they lost their wives. In any case, the data shows a much higher probability of women, rather than men, living as widows with their children or other relatives.

13 Servants were not included in this analysis since most were not at risk for marriage while in service and following servants after their service period is nearly impossible with the Kyoto registers.

Table 3. Transition age for beginning or ending co-residence with some kin, by gender, nine Kyoto neighborhoods (1842–1868)

	Male	*Female*	*Both sexes*
Parent end	32	25	27
Siblings end	27	23	23
Spouse begin	28	23	24
Child begin	31	25	29
Other stem kin begin	66	63	66
Spouse end	*	55	63

Sources: Population registers *(Shūmon ninbetsu aratame chō)* for Sujikaibashi, Hanaguruma, Shijō Nakanomachi, Takoyakushi, Seidō, Taishiyama, Sannō, Shimizu and Matsu'ue neighborhoods.
Note: * Such transition did not exist for men.

The easiest, but most intimate way to provide assistance was co-residence. The analyses show a clear preference for co-residence with stem kin, but also some reluctance for co-residence with non-stem kin and non-kin. There were, however, gender differences in this pattern. Men living with non-stem kin were more likely to do so when they were young than after age forty-five when they became more likely to live alone or with their siblings. In other words, young men were more likely to use the resources of non-stem kin such as uncles or cousins than older men who were more likely to go it alone. Women, however, were more likely to live with non-stem kin until they were over sixty. This suggests that even non-stem kin were willing to provide assistance in need, but men, at least, preferred independence if they could manage it. But women may have found survival more difficult living alone and so relied on any kin relations willing and able to provide assistance. Close examination of the registers reveals some evidence that even in-laws could be relied on for care since some of the siblings and non-stem kin listed in the register were relatives of the wife of the head of household where the head was not an adopted (in-marrying) son-in-law. The co-residence of these in-laws, however, tended to be very temporary and only a small proportion of the whole.

In summary, Kyoto residents in the middle of the nineteenth century preferred to live with their stem kin. Most were married and had children and co-residence with children continued without a transition to an empty nest in older ages. Alternatives were living with siblings, with other non-stem kin including in-laws and living alone. People of both genders preferred to live alone rather than live with non-kin and older men preferred to live alone than with non-stem kin. Solitary households were most likely to be elderly residents of sixty year or older, but elderly residents were far more likely to live with their children and grandchildren than to live alone or live with anyone else. Elderly women were far more likely to be widowed than elderly men, likely the result of differential mortality and age at marriage.

Conclusions

Families were certainly the main source of support in early modern Kyoto. Adult children worked with their parents until succeeding to headship of the family business and taking over the responsibility to manage the family assets and provide for the family in general. This succession could wait for the father's death or could occur with the father's retirement.

The easiest way to provide this support and care was through co-residence. Few older couples or individuals lived independently, but they received family support even when they did. At the same time, elderly kin could rely on a broad kin network including nieces, nephews and in-laws for care, although support through co-residence with stem kin relations was most common.

Adoption was another way to provide care and family for infants or small children who had none to provide for them. Money was usually provided in adoptions as some small recompense for the care given to the adopted child and here is where local public assistance from neighborhood community funds played a role. Records regarding the care provided for abandoned children are most often found in affluent neighborhoods. The neighborhood community would take immediate action to find a couple that had recently lost a child so the mother still had milk and arrange for the couple to adopt the foundling child paying the couple a dowry from the neighborhood fund. This sometimes gave the adoptive parents the right to claim further assistance from the neighborhood in case of need.

Neighborhood communities had funds formed from the regular dues collected each month from neighborhood residents. This money was a community financial pool that could be used for a variety of activities, but residents also used these funds as a resource when money was short. Thus neighborhoods acted as the basis for mutual funding activities and insurance.

References

HAREVEN, Tamara K., 2000, *Families, History, and Social Change: Life Course and Cross-Cultural Perspectives*, Boulder, Westview Press.

HAYASHIYA, Tatsusaburō *et al.* (eds), 1981, *Shiryō Kyōto no rekishi 12: Shimogyō ku* [Documentary history of Kyoto, v. 12: Shimogyō ward], Tokyo, Heibonsha, p. 83.

KAMADA, Michitaka, 2000, *Kinsei Kyōto no toshi to minshū* [The city and people of early modern Kyoto], Kyoto, Shibunkaku Shuppan, pp. 343–353.

KATAKURA, Hisako, 1986, "Edo machikata ni okeru sōzoku" [Inheritance among Edo townsmen], in Reiko HAYASHI *et al.*, Kinsei Josei Shi Kenkyukai (eds), *Ronshū kinsei josei shi* [Collection of essays on the history of early modern women], Tokyo, Yoshikawa Kobunkan, pp. 177–218.

KUROSU, Satomi, 1998, "Long Way to Heirship, Short Way to Retirement: Adopted Sons in a Northeastern Village in Pre-Industrial Japan", *History of the Family: An International Quarterly*, 3, 4, pp. 393–410.

KUROSU, Satomi and OCHIAI, Emiko, 1995, "Adoption as an Heirship Strategy under Demographic Constraints: A Case from 19th Century Japan", *Journal of Family History*, 20, 3, pp. 261–287.

Kyoto City Library for Historical Documents (ed.), 1999, *Kyōto machi shikimoku shūsei* [Collection of Kyoto city neighborhood laws], Kyoto City Library for Historical Documents.

NAGATA, Mary Louise, 2003a, "L'adoption à Kyôto aux XVIIe et XIXe siècles", *Ebisu*, 31, Maison Franco-Japonaise, Tôkyô, pp. 59–83.

–, 2003b, "Mistress or Wife: Fukui Sakuzaemon vs. Iwa, 1819–1833", *Continuity and Change*, 18, 2, pp. 1–23.

–, 2008, "Migrations et entreprise à Kyoto au début de l'époque moderne", in Corine MAITE and Manuela MARTINI (eds), *Entreprises en mouvement: Migrants, pratiques entrepreneuriales et diversités culturelles dans le monde, XVe-XXe siècles*, Valenciennes, Presses Universitaires de Valenciennes, pp. 149–166.

NAGATA, Mary Louise and HAMANO, Kiyoshi, 2006, "Households in Need of Assistance: Welfare in Early Modern Kyoto", presented at Social Science History Association meeting, Minneapolis, November.

SUGAWARA, Keiji, 1995, "Kyoto no machi to sutego: yōiku shi tachō e yōshi ni" [Kyoto and abandoned children: care for them and adopt them out to other neighborhoods], in Tadakuma IWAI *et al.* (eds), *Machi to kurashi no Kyoto shi* [The Kyoto history of urban life], Kyoto, Bunrikaku 1994, 2d ed., pp. 192–195.

Annexe

Annex 1. Population per neighborhood per year, nine Kyoto neighborhoods (1842–1868)

YEAR	*Hana-guru-ma*	*Sujikai-ba-shi*	*San-no*	*Shijo Naka-nomachi*	*Shimi-zu*	*Mat-su'ue*	*Sei-do*	*Tai-shiy-ama*	*Takoy-akushi*	*Total*
1842					48					48
1843		275	61				117		311	764
1844	227	273					110		315	925
1845	240	284		325			94		284	1227
1846	251	2					105	292	305	955
1847					56		111	299	309	775
1848	241	252			49		99	16	315	972
1849		267			46		114		321	748
1850	256	269			42	38	100		314	1019
1851		260			41		100		308	709
1852					45	48	100		310	503
1853							90		317	407
1854						43	100			143
1855					57	7	112			176
1856		286			52		103			441
1857	245	272					109			626
1858	254						117			371
1859	222						114			336
1860	202	234					119			555
1861	176			261	44		121			602
1862	179	222					120			521
1863				280			116			396
1864	192						62			254
1865	195						105			300
1866	201						114			315
1868	193				54		102			349
total	3274	2896	61	866	534	136	2654	607	3409	14437
Ave-rage*	218	263	61	289	49	45	106	304	310	577

Sources: Population registers *(Shūmon ninbetsu aratame chō)* for Sujikaibashi, Hanaguruma, Shijō Nakanomachi, Takoyakushi, Seidō, Taishiyama, Sannō, Shimizu and Matsu'ue neighborhoods.
Note: Average persons by year.

Lightning Source UK Ltd.
Milton Keynes UK
UKHW021317120922
408730UK00025B/457

9 783034 300568